P.O.W.

A Definitive History of
the American Prisoner-of-War Experience
in Vietnam, 1964–1973

John G. Hubbell

in association with Andrew Jones and Kenneth Y. Tomlinson

READER'S DIGEST PRESS
Distributed by
Thomas Y. Crowell Company—New York—1976

For Ron Storz, Norm Schmidt,
Ed Atterberry,
J. J. Connell, "Freddy" Frederick,
Ken Cameron, "The Faker," Betty Ann Olsen,
Hank Blood, "Roberts," "Top Benson,"
and all the others, North and South,
who didn't make it back.
I hope I have told it the way it happened
J. G. H.

Line drawings from *Prisoner of war,* by John McGrath, Copyright © 1975 by U.S. Naval Institute, Annapolis, Md.

Manufactured in the United States of America

Library of Congress Cataloguing in Publication Data

Hubbell, John G
  P.O.W̄.: a definitive history of the American
prisoner-of-war experience in Vietnam, 1964–1973.

    1. Vietnamese Conflict, 1961–1975—Prisoners
and prisons. 2. Prisoners of war, American.
I. Jones, Andrew, 1921–
II. Tomlinson, Kenneth Y.
III. Title.
DS559.4.H8   959.704'37   75-45125

ISBN 0-88349-091-9

1 2 3 4 5 6 7 8 9 10

Acknowledgments

When the editors of *Reader's Digest* decided to proceed with the work, Board Chairman Hobart Lewis made emphatically clear that the *Digest* would accept none of the profits, if any, which might accrue to it from the book; any and all such profits were somehow to be distributed to the returned POWs and/or as they saw fit. At the same time, the *Digest,* anxious that the work be as complete as possible, literally handed me a blank check. Two valued staff members, Senior Editor Andrew Jones and Associate Editor Kenneth Y. Tomlinson, both of them journalistic veterans of the Vietnam War, were detached from all other tasks and assigned full-time to the project, to assist for as long as they were needed. Additionally, all of the *Digest*'s editorial offices, staff, and research facilities were made available. The *Digest*'s concern was to make a significant contribution to the body of American history, to do something of singular value for its country, which had come upon parlous times in Vietnam. If such a contribution were to reap profit, it was to be up to those who had lived and made the history to dispose of it.

Surely publishing annals will record no worthier venture. Yet, in my own twenty-four-year association with the *Digest,* I have found such generosity to be typical, even traditional—it is like Lila and DeWitt Wallace, the founders of the organization, and their professional heirs to do such a thing.

Insofar as the work itself was concerned, Jones and Tomlinson were absolutely indispensable. To make the point as emphatically as it should be made, it is necessary to risk the appearance of immodesty: I do not believe that a more complete history of a prisoner of war experience is likely to be produced. I am satisfied that the kind of deep perspective that was hoped for has been achieved. Without the often heroic efforts of Jones and Tomlinson, it simply would not have been possible. Together and singly, we traveled to all corners of the United States to interview returnees. There were nearly two hundred interviews, ranging in length up to thirty-odd hours. There came a time when, if the book was ever to be written, I had to retreat to seclusion, to organize a growing mountain of research, to develop narrative insights and tell the story. Jones and Tomlinson stayed afield for most of two years, traveling, digging, continuing to build the mountain. In short, they were invaluable, and I certainly do not know what I would have done without them.

Or others. *Reader's Digest* Managing Editor Kenneth O. Gilmore, then head of the magazine's Washington bureau, proposed the book to me. Together, we outlined our hopes to Adm. Thomas H. Moorer, then Chairman of the Joint Chiefs of Staff, asking for his guidance and support. Moorer had been impressed with a series of *Digest* articles that had played a powerful role in helping to make the nation POW-conscious. He was enthusiastic at the idea of such a history, and support and guidance were forthcoming in unstinting measure.

Moorer's brilliant aide, Navy Capt. John C. Mackercher, an associate on many journalistic adventures, was by now an old friend, one whose presence on any assignment involving the military ensured integrity. He arranged for background briefings and access to vital informational materials and generally saw to all kinds of progress.

The then Assistant Secretary of Defense for Public Affairs, Jerry Friedheim, put his office at my disposal. His Deputy Assistant, Air Force Gen. Daniel "Chappie" James, was energetic in arranging introductions to and interviews with many POWs. Working under James, Army Maj. Marvin Braman was tireless in tracking down others and putting me in touch with them.

In fact, the military public affairs officers and enlisted men who are entitled to my gratitude are too numerous to mention—but some were so helpful that they must be mentioned: Air Force Maj. Michael Burch, Air Force Lt. Col. Ernest Moore, Navy Comdr. Clark Gammel, Navy Comdr. Robert Lewis, Navy Lt. Comdr. Owen Resweber, Navy Comdr. Thomas Coldwell.

Robert M. Hoerner, Director of the Staff of the House Internal Security Committee (now defunct), was generous with his time and provided much important background information.

Ross Perot, the Dallas computer magnate, had long been known for his active interest in POW affairs. Likewise, he took an interest in this project, arranging a meeting with retired Army Col. Arthur "Bull" Simon, who planned and led the Sontay raid. Simon gave me the first really detailed account of the action, from its conception and the call for Green Beret volunteers to the withdrawal from the empty prison camp. Many, myself included, had thought the raid a failure, for no prisoners were found at Sontay; it seemed an indication of a poor intelligence operation. But as the narrative reveals, Simon, who was perhaps more vitally interested in the intelligence on the place than anyone else in the world, remains satisfied with the information he had; and insofar as the POWs were concerned, the raid was a huge success.

A major problem was to be comprehensive without being repetitious. This involved a good deal of painful editing. The absorbingly interesting stories of many are not told simply because the similar experiences of others are offered at dramatic high points of the story. Not included are the stories of some who contributed most generously to the development of the manuscript, not only their own experiences but overall background knowledge. A notable example is Navy Capt. Edward H. Martin, one of the most stalwart Americans to reach Hanoi. Another is Army Green Beret Col. Raymond C. Schrump, who never reached Hanoi—he spent nearly five years in chains in various jungle camps in South Vietnam, resisting his captors' blandishments. Martin and Schrump belong in America's pantheon of heroes.

This book owes much to many such men: Navy Capt. Allan C. Brady, Air Force Col. Frederick A. Crowe, Jr., Air Force Maj. John Borling, Air Force Capt. Ralph T. Browning, Marine Pfc. William A. Baird, Marine Capt. James V. DiBernardo, and Army Sgt. Donald Rander, to name but a few.

I am indebted to many of my *Reader's Digest* colleagues for all manner of professional support and assistance: Roving Editor David Reed; Washington Editor William Schulz; Alicia Boyd; Katherine Clark; Virginia Lawton; Patricia Lawson. Senior Editor Michael Blow, who worked on the manuscript, certainly is one of the most thoughtful and skilled editors I have ever known.

My typists, Marge Erler and Helen Pappas, transcribed verbatim hundreds upon hundreds of hours of tape-recorded interviews, then patiently typed and retyped a manuscript that in its original form achieved encyclopedic proportions.

Gratitude is an entirely inadequate word for what is owed some. My editor on the project was *Reader's Digest* Editor-in-Chief Edward T. Thompson, who has been my good friend for many years. I have never known him so well or appreciated him so much. His closely reasoned judgments and critiques served constantly to improve the narrative. His unwavering faith in the work remained a much-needed source of reassurance, and his patience with the author was nothing short of unbelievable. Throughout, he kept an excellent good humor, and seemed always to know when a word of encouragement was needed. I could not have done better for an editor; by any standard of personal or professional measurement, he is one of the best of men.

My wife, Katherine Hartigan Hubbell, was in every sense a full partner. She read every word dozens of times, analyzed every thought and criticism, and offered countless thoughts of her own that helped shape the telling of the story. She has my thanks and, as always, my deepest love.

JGH

Contents

Illustrations follow page 320

Foreword

Like millions of other Americans who in February, 1973, watched on television the dramatic homecoming of the POWs, I found myself absorbed in the event, and full of wonderment at the men. Suspicions of a harsh confinement notwithstanding, most who were returning after years of imprisonment seemed to be healthy, both physically and spiritually. Certainly, most still knew how to smile, and to speak with what seemed an almost old-fashioned enthusiasm for their America, a country long and tragically riven with dissension over the war.

Suddenly, one was intensely aware that these men really existed. True, for a long time they had been an emotional rallying point for the country; most of the most ardent protagonists on both sides of the war issue had at least been united in a common concern for the welfare of the POWs. Still, for many Americans the POWs had until now remained pretty much a nameless, faceless group, a vague entity. No longer. Now, suddenly, they were living, breathing, walking, talking, smiling young men, husbands, sons, brothers, fathers, friends from whom we all had been separated for a very long time and who at last were coming home. It had been such a long war and, for so many of them, such a long captivity that they seemed almost to be returning from the dead.

Most Americans, even if they did not understand the war, knew all too well what had happened during the war years, in South Vietnam and in the United States. What no one knew was how America had done in the Communist prisons of Vietnam. Exactly what had happened to these men, who had been gone so long and who now were returning in apparent fine fettle? American military men are taught that the prisoner of war camp is but an extension of the battlefield, and that if captured they are to continue the fight, to keep as many as possible of the enemy tied down. Thus, in this longest of American wars, some of these returnees had remained in combat longer than any other Americans in our history. What had it been like? What had been the nature of their battle? What of their captors' strategy and tactics, and how had the POWs countered them? How had they been treated? How had they acquitted themselves? How had they endured?

Such thoughts were also in the minds of editors of *Reader's Digest*. For years, I had been writing on national defense and related matters for the *Digest*. Now, I was queried as to whether I might be interested in exploring the possibility of writing a narrative history of the POW experience in Vietnam. Explorations were conducted. So rich were the earliest assays that the *Digest* quickly committed itself to the work.

The dimensions of the evolving narrative were frightening, as I had known they would be. To weave together the strands of hundreds of lives over a nine-year period was to find a collective experience that seemed so much larger than life that the writer of fiction surely would hesitate to submit it for publication—it might have been too much to believe, except that there it was, a history that contemporary Americans actually had lived, and many had lived to recount: tales of unrestrained savagery are matched and overmatched by tales of towering courage, self-sacrifice and endurance. There was gripping high adventure, inspirational patriotism, the meanest treason, great, belly-laugh humor, tragedy, death, enormous sadness. The toughest, most pragmatic men tell of the power of prayer, are convinced they are the beneficiaries of miracles, and are convincing about it.

Onstage, too, came supporting and bit players, including "Fidel," a brutal Latin torturemaster whom the prisoners believe to be Cuban; a visiting American professor who insisted to one POW: "No son of a bitch like [then Secretary of State] Dean Rusk can tell me where to go!"; three American women, members of a visiting peace delegation, who described an Air Force pilot to his captors as "wayward," for which he was beaten and cruelly tortured; another, well-meaning lady, a famous American novelist who was permitted a visit with the famous Air Force ace, Col. Robinson Risner and unwittingly caused Risner hours of difficulty; Wilfred Burchett—"Wellfed Bullshit," the POWs called him—the Australian journalist who reports communist wars from the communist side. And others.

And much more. The hellish jungle prison camps of South Vietnam and Cambodia, where living conditions always were worse and the treatment as bad as and worse than in Hanoi. In these camps, too, injuries and disease often went untreated, there was deliberate starvation, torture, murder, and again humor and survival. Americans ought to know how their fellow Americans endured in these camps, how they lived and died in them.

That is why the work was done. The American POW experience in Vietnam is part of our heritage, and Americans ought to know about it.

I had anticipated that at times the work would become profoundly depressing. After sitting through many long interviews in which some of the best and toughest men I have ever known cried as they remembered, I expected that the writing would involve some especially long and lonely hours. But, oddly perhaps, depression never came. I looked forward every day to getting back at it. Nor was there any hangover depression when it was finished. I think this may have been due to the fact that essentially it is such a positive story, above all else a story of a great American performance at a time, on her 200th birthday, when America needs badly to know how great she still can be.

JGH

PART I

1

The Old Timer

He was the first to launch from the aircraft carrier USS *Constellation,* at precisely 2:30 PM. The ship sent ten A4 Skyhawks streaking up the Gulf of Tonkin through bright, crystal-clear skies, toward the torpedo boat base at Hon Gay, northeast of Haiphong. Suddenly, for the first time, the full realization of what was happening shocked him. *My God,* he thought, *this is war! We're going into battle! This could be the start of something big!* He was not frightened; rather, he was suffused with the same feeling he used to have before high school athletic events—butterflies, and a tingling, jumping sensation in his legs; an infusion of adrenalin.

They found four torpedo boats and a coastal patrol vessel at Hon Gay and obliterated them. He had walked his .20-mm cannon fire straight up the side of the coastal patrol ship and had held it on the bridge, watching pieces breaking away and flying in the air. He had been aware of tracer fire and flak bursting all around him, but had not broken off until his guns were empty. Then, as he had pulled up and away, a violence of yellow had exploded nearby. His engine had begun clanking and rattling, and the aircraft had begun shaking as though to tear itself apart. Fire warning lights gleamed; other lights indicated that his hydraulic and utility systems were gone; smoke poured into the cockpit and the stick froze. He fought with it, trying for altitude that would carry him farther out to sea. It was no use; he was on fire and out of control. His last words to his squadronmates were "I'm getting out. I'll see you guys later."

Thus on August 5, 1964, did Hanoi acquire its first American shootdown. He was Navy Lt. (j.g.) Everett Alvarez, Jr., twenty-six, of San Jose, California, and he probably was as ready as anyone could have been for the adversity that came upon him.

———

He had been born in Salinas in December, 1937, a winter child of the Great Depression, to poor Mexican-American parents. They had not had much schooling and were determined that their children, Everett and his two sisters, should be educated. His father, a welder, had not been able to earn much money, so his mother had gone to work, too, in a cannery's packing sheds. Each day for years on end she had gone off to work at 6 AM, returning home in the evenings to clean house, wash clothes, make dinner. He recalled that she had done this cheerfully, that he had never heard her utter a serious or really angry word about her lot.

Devout Catholics, the parents had sent the children to Catholic schools, had seen to it that they were imbued with the tenets of the faith. At home and in school Ev also had been taught to revere his country and to be willing to fight for it. When he had been thirteen and had first gone to work in the bean and tomato fields around San Jose, his parents had made him understand that he must apply himself, must provide his employer with an honest day's work for the pay he received—and be thankful that he lived in a land where a man who wanted to get ahead had every chance to do so.

He had embraced his parents' ideas and values, and they had encouraged him in all he had done. Like many youngsters, he had grown up dreaming that he would become a football star, but he had been too small and slight at first even to make his high school varsity squad. He had been relegated to the lightweight reserves.

"Keep your chin up," his dad had kept telling him.

"Don't be discouraged," his mother had said, "just do the best you can."

He had kept on working out and practicing, day after day, rain and shine, all through the year. He had not put on much size or weight, but eventually he had made the squad, then had become an all-league end.

He had entered the University of Santa Clara, working during summers at a cannery. No brilliant student, he had studied hard and done well, and by 1960 had earned his degree in electrical engineering. The same year, he had entered the Navy's flying training program. After earning his commission and wings, he had been assigned to Attack Squadron 144. He took pride in what he had accomplished, and in the knowledge that his Navy superiors and contemporaries rated him highly.

His achievements each had required long and intensive effort, and there had been periods of deep discouragement. But he had always been able to find the strength he had needed to keep pressing ahead. That strength was rooted in good memories, and in the sounds of well-loved voices saying, "Don't be discouraged . . . keep your chin up . . . do the best you can." In Hanoi that strength was to serve him well for many long years.

––––––

Attack Squadron 144 had boarded the *Constellation* in the spring. Alvarez, whose friends called him Ev or Alvy, enjoyed flying and being in the Navy. Normally, he would have enjoyed the cruise that peacetime summer. There was fun in Hawaii, Japan, and Hong Kong, and a lot of flying. But he had been married in February and was anxious to return to his bride, Tangee. Prior to *Constellation's* departure on May 5 from San Diego, he had noticed that things were happening in Southeast Asia that might prolong the cruise. Still, Vietnam was an Army show; in fact, Air Force and Navy aircraft were prohibited from overflying even South Vietnam. The situation did not seem likely to change drastically. Ev told Tangee, "Don't worry. I may not come home right away, but I'm coming home."

On August 2, *Constellation,* in Hong Kong, had been alerted that North Vietnamese torpedo boats had attacked the American destroyer *Maddox* in international waters of the South China Sea. By the night of August 4, *Constellation* was plowing toward the South China Sea when word came that *Maddox* and another destroyer, the *Turner Joy,* were under attack. Ev, conscientious and full of professional pride, was pleased to be one of a handful of *Constellation* pilots selected to provide the destroyers with air cover. Reaching the scene after about a seventy-minute flight, the *Constellation* aircraft switched to the destroyers' radio frequency—bedlam! No one seemed to know what was happening, yet everyone seemed to be talking at once. A babble of voices kept reporting "sonar contact" and "surface contact"; one kept insisting that a torpedo was headed its way; another kept demanding a turn to starboard, while still another kept advising urgently, "Turning to port! Turning to port!"

Alvarez was appalled. But before the confusion on the surface had been able to infect those in the air, a single voice, calm and authoritative, took charge, established a discipline that seemed to have a settling effect. This was Comdr. James Bond Stockdale, forty, a squadron commander who was leading an air contingent from the carrier USS *Ticonderoga*. Ascertaining that Alvarez was carrying flares, Stockdale directed him in the lighting of the sea area. Ev had seen three sets of what appeared to be U-shaped wakes, such as could have been made by high-speed boats approaching the destroyers, then turning away from them; he saw no torpedo boats, however. Then, low on fuel, he was forced to return to *Constellation*.

By the time Alvarez awakened next morning, President Lyndon Johnson, satisfied that North Vietnamese torpedo boats had attacked American ships in international waters for the second time in three days, had ordered punitive air strikes against all five of North Vietnam's torpedo boat bases and two supporting oil storage depots.

Again, Ev was pleased to be one of those chosen to make the strike. The flight deck crew around his plane was all enthusiasm and encouragement. Smiling broadly, the enlisted men shook his hand, patted his shoulder, waved thumbs-up signals at him.

"Go get 'em, Mr. Alvarez!" someone said.

"Sir, it's about time!" said someone else. "It's about goddamn time!"

"Good luck, sir. Good luck!"

———

But his luck had not been good. After shootdown, he had parachuted into the water. He remembered having been warned not to wear his wedding ring into combat, that if he ever fell into the Communists' hands they would use the fact that he was married. He stripped off a glove, removed the ring, held it for a long moment, looking at it, then let it go, watching it sink out of sight.

There was a high-pitched whine, and something clipped his flight suit at the elbow. He looked behind him, and on came a small boat, straight toward him. There were five smoking rifle barrels pointed in his direction. Behind the crouched riflemen stood a man with a handgun, who appeared to be in charge, and another poised to heave a hand grenade.

The boat approached to within twenty yards, then turned and began making a wide circle around Alvarez. The riflemen fired a salvo, and the bullets splattered the water all around him. There was no doubt in his mind that they could have hit him; obviously, they wanted to take him prisoner, and he seemed to be out of options. He waved a hand in the air, indicating his willingness to be taken. The man with the handgun motioned to him to raise both hands, high. He did so, and the boat moved in close. For the first American shot down in North Vietnam, the longest war has just begun.

———

Alvarez was frightened. He had been completely wrapped up in rope, like a top. His captors squatted around him on the deck, talking to each other, and occasionally one of them would scream at him and kick him. He was certain that he was about to be hanged by his ankles, skinned, relieved of his testicles and finally his head. He said the Lord's Prayer and gave himself over to Divine Will.

He was transferred to a torpedo boat, where a non-English-speaking Vietnamese in civilian clothes struggled to ascertain his nationality. He kept saying something that sounded like "Me? Me?"

For some reason, Alvarez answered in Spanish, "Que? No entiendo." ("What? I don't understand.")

The man pointed at Alvarez and asked, "U.S.A.?"

Alvarez nodded and said, "Unhuh."

The man's jaw dropped, and for a long moment he stared at the prisoner, his eyes widening. He turned to an officer, muttering "My, My." The word spread, and soon everyone on the boat was looking around and peering into the sky. These people, Ev realized, had not had the slightest idea who had bombed their naval base.

———

He was not treated badly. He was taken to a room in a building at the naval base, and throughout the afternoon photographers kept coming in and taking pictures of him. No English was spoken, but the photographers labored manfully through sign language to make him understand that he was to bow his head and look as though he felt guilty for what he had done, to appear to be submissive to his captors. He made no effort to do so. Finally, the photographers climbed up on the table and took pictures of the Caucasian looking up at them from an inferior position. Late in the day an older man in civilian clothes came in and spoke to Alvarez in English.

"I want you to answer some questions," he said. "What is your name, and where are you from?"

Alvarez gave his name and rank, and said he was from the United States Navy. When the interrogator wanted to know his squadron and ship, he refused to answer. He was chagrined to note that part of the wreckage of his aircraft lay in a corner of the room, broadly stenciled with the advice that it had been an A4C aircraft belonging to Attack Squadron 144, operating off *Constellation.*

"You have participated in a hostile action against the Vietnamese people," the interrogator said. "I am a representative of the Vietnamese people. It would be better for you if you would answer my questions."

Again, Alvarez refused to identify his squadron and ship. At last, the interrogator asked, "Are you hungry?"

He was famished. It occurred to him that he had not eaten since breakfast. "Yes," he said, "I am hungry."

"Would you like some food? Nice, hot food?"

He had visions of steaming dishes of hot rice, sweet and sour pork, chow mein, chop suey.

He was served a plate of moldy, malodorous meat, which he was unable to eat. Later, he was taken to a jail, where his flight suit and underwear were taken from him, and he was given a pair of light cotton, blue and white striped pajamas.

Then he was placed in a cell with two Vietnamese prisoners, one of whom spoke such excellent English that Alvarez suspected he was a plant. His cellmates were friendly and helpful—one of them even insisted on giving him a pillow he had made. Alvarez was grateful and cordial in return, but would discuss nothing of consequence with them. He stayed in the Hon Gay jail for two days, during which time he was interrogated by English-speaking officers. He gave them no conversation until he was asked, "Why did you come here to bomb us?"

"Because your torpedo boats attacked our destroyers," he answered.

The interrogator looked at his companion. The two spoke to each other in Vietnamese. They put down their pencils and closed their notebooks. "Look," the interrogator said, "you have been used as a tool. It is a lie, a fabrication. There were no torpedo boats out there. Your government did criminal actions against our country, and your government has deceived you."

He was sent back to his cell. There were more interrogations. He refused to say whether or not he was married and had children. "I gave you my name and rank, and I am not obligated to answer any other questions," he said. They did not press him.

After his two days in the Hon Gay jail, he was put in a Russian-made jeep and driven in a southeasterly direction toward Haiphong. Somewhere in the hills inland, his guards put him in a sizable brick farmhouse, where he remained for four days. He had a bedroom, was well fed, and was allowed to bathe and to shave. Several times daily he was interrogated by an officer who resembled an owl—indeed, American POWs later would refer to this man as Owl. His small nose was hooked, like an owl's beak, his hair stood straight up, and he had big, wide eyes.

One midnight, Owl awakened him, saying he had to return to Hanoi and needed information about Alvarez's mission. When Alvarez said he could supply none, Owl said, "We know you are married, that your wife's name is Tangee, and that you have no children. Your father's name is Everett, and he lives in San Jose, California, with your mother, whose name is Soledad. You were a member of Attack Squadron 144 aboard the USS *Constellation,* and your wing commander's name is Donald B. Edge. Do you think you can hide anything from us?"

Alvarez was startled at the extent of the information Owl had. Then he realized that it was rudimentary, the sort of thing the North Vietnamese could have gleaned from the American press after news of his shootdown had been released. Nevertheless, it was difficult to deny undeniable facts about himself. He decided to give Owl some misinformation.

He told him that he had not been piloting an attack aircraft, but a search plane, and that he had carried no weapons. His mission, he said, had been to look for torpedo boats off the coast of Vietnam and to call back to the ship if he found any.

"Show me your route," said Owl, producing a map.

Alvarez drew a wavy line from Hon Gay out into the Gulf of Tonkin.

"Where did you take off from?" Owl wanted to know.

"Somewhere in here," said Alvarez, drawing a circle with approximately a two-hundred mile diameter in the Gulf, hundreds of miles from *Constellation*'s position.

Happily, Owl gathered up his papers and departed. Ev wondered if it mattered to these people what kinds of answers one gave them; he surmised that anything would do, so long as an interrogator had something to show his superiors.

Alvarez left the farmhouse early on the morning of August 11, for Hanoi. It was a long, hot, uncomfortable jeep ride. By early afternoon he had reached Hoa Lo prison, in Hanoi, a place of dark renown that was to become known to the world as the "Hanoi Hilton."

––––––––

Hoa Lo prison is North Vietnam's main penitentiary, and the Administrative headquarters for the country's entire prison system. It occupies the whole of a large, not quite square city block in the middle of the city of Hanoi. The south side of the Hoa Lo block angles northwesterly, from the southeastern to the southwestern corner; thus, the western leg is not so long as the eastern leg. The prison grounds are surrounded by a massive concrete wall; it is approximately sixteen feet high, and estimates of its thickness range up to six feet. Shards of curved and jagged glass, the remnants of French champagne bottles, protrude by the thousands from the top of the wall. Many of the shards are at least six inches high; most are an iridescent greenish-blue, but here and there an odd piece is seen to glow red. The effect is pleasingly decorative—unless, of course, one is an escape-minded prisoner. For there would be no vaulting this high, wide wall. On reaching the top, one would first somehow have to make his way across the several feet of sharp jagged glass protrusions; then find his way through three strands of barbed wire which tilt outward, toward the street. Two of the barbed wire strands are stretched so low as to preclude the possibility of crawling under them, and an electrified strand is set just high enough so that one would have trouble going under it or over it. In short, it would be no simple matter to cross the wall and slide down to the street. To cap matters, guard towers are mounted atop the walls at the prison's four corners.

Entry into Hoa Lo is from Hoa Lo Street, only a block long, on the eastern side of the prison. Massive iron gates toward the lower end of the street give into a cobblestone alleyway about fifteen feet wide that

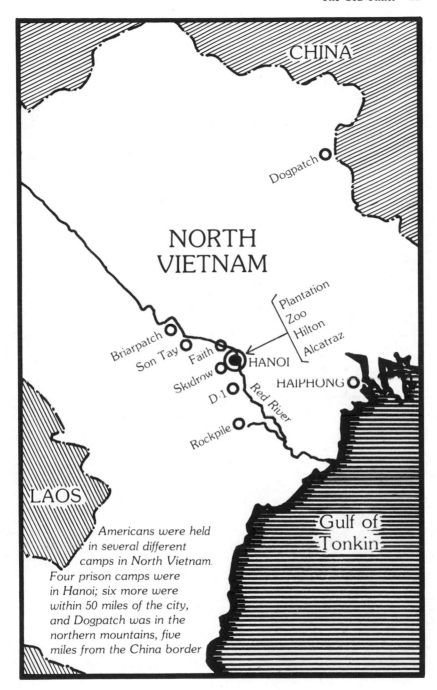

CHINA

Dogpatch

NORTH
VIETNAM

Plantation
Zoo
Hilton
Alcatraz

Briarpatch
Son Tay
Faith
Skidrow
D-1
Red River
HANOI
HAIPHONG

Rockpile

LAOS

Gulf of
Tonkin

Americans were held
in several different
camps in North Vietnam.
Four prison camps were
in Hanoi; six more were
within 50 miles of the city,
and Dogpatch was in the
northern mountains, five
miles from the China border

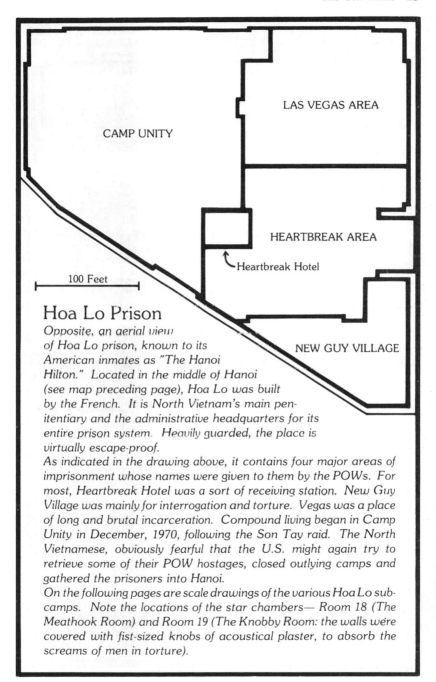

CAMP UNITY

LAS VEGAS AREA

HEARTBREAK AREA

Heartbreak Hotel

100 Feet

NEW GUY VILLAGE

Hoa Lo Prison

Opposite, an aerial view of Hoa Lo prison, known to its American inmates as "The Hanoi Hilton." Located in the middle of Hanoi (see map preceding page), Hoa Lo was built by the French. It is North Vietnam's main penitentiary and the administrative headquarters for its entire prison system. Heavily guarded, the place is virtually escape-proof.

As indicated in the drawing above, it contains four major areas of imprisonment whose names were given to them by the POWs. For most, Heartbreak Hotel was a sort of receiving station. New Guy Village was mainly for interrogation and torture. Vegas was a place of long and brutal incarceration. Compound living began in Camp Unity in December, 1970, following the Son Tay raid. The North Vietnamese, obviously fearful that the U.S. might again try to retrieve some of their POW hostages, closed outlying camps and gathered the prisoners into Hanoi.

On the following pages are scale drawings of the various Hoa Lo subcamps. Note the locations of the star chambers— Room 18 (The Meathook Room) and Room 19 (The Knobby Room: the walls were covered with fist-sized knobs of acoustical plaster, to absorb the screams of men in torture).

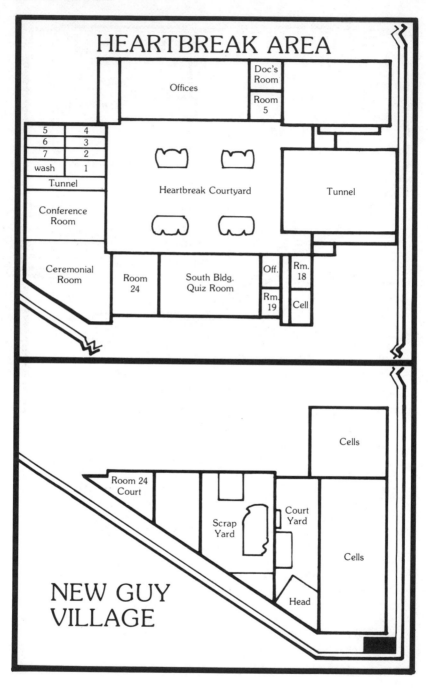

HEARTBREAK AREA

Offices

Doc's Room

Room 5

5	4
6	3
7	2
wash	1

Tunnel

Conference Room

Heartbreak Courtyard

Tunnel

Ceremonial Room

Room 24

South Bldg. Quiz Room

Off.

Rm. 18

Rm. 19

Cell

NEW GUY VILLAGE

Cells

Room 24 Court

Scrap Yard

Court Yard

Cells

Head

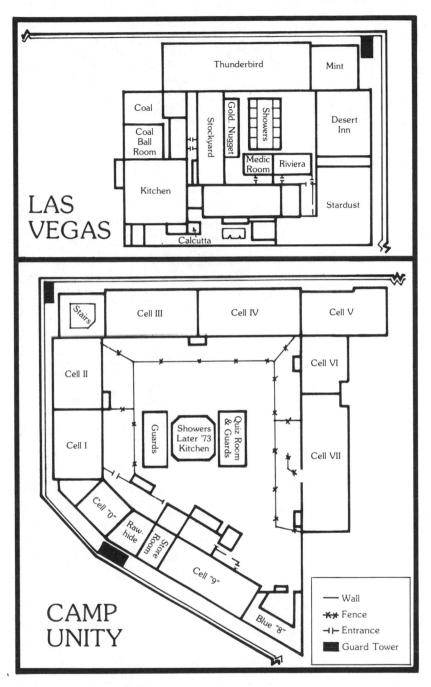

LAS
VEGAS

Thunderbird

Mint

Coal

Coal
Ball
Room

Stockyard

Gold. Nugget

Showers

Desert
Inn

Medic
Room

Riviera

Kitchen

Stardust

Calcutta

CAMP
UNITY

Stairs

Cell III

Cell IV

Cell V

Cell II

Cell VI

Cell I

Guards

Showers
Later '73
Kitchen

Quiz Room
& Guards

Cell VII

Cell "0"

Raw-
hide

Store
Room

Cell "9"

Blue "8"

—— Wall
✷✷ Fence
⊣⊢ Entrance
■ Guard Tower

THE ALPHABET - ONE HAND P.O.W. MUTE CODE

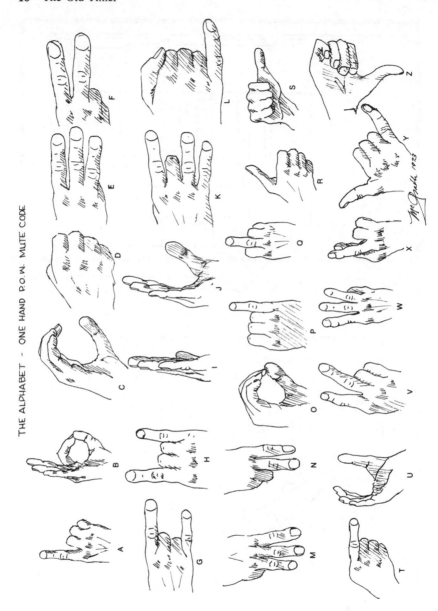

encircles the prison like a dry moat. Across the alleyway, more massive gates open into a tunnellike underpass beneath a building. At the opposite end of the underpass are yet a third set of heavy iron gates. As the captive moves through, each set of gates is slammed shut behind him before the next is opened. The trip from Hoa Lo Street through the three gates is seventy feet long. The sights and sounds of entry are impressive, deeply dispiriting—there's a finality to the heavy, metallic clanging shut of the gates, and in the dark tunnel the hollow, echoing resonance of voices and footsteps induces a terrible sadness, an utter loneliness. It is almost a relief to get through the last set of doors and out into a reasonably presentable courtyard.

The courtyard is one hundred feet long, sixty-five feet wide. It is flanked by two-story, grimy-white stucco buildings—once, long ago, the buildings were a bright, clean white. Behind, above and to the sides of the underpass entryway, are similar buildings. The cobblestone driveway proceeds straight through the courtyard to another gate at the far end, which opens through another underpass, a roof between two one-story buildings. The building on the right contained eight cells, and would become known to American prisoners as Heartbreak Hotel. In the courtyard, alongside the driveway, stand four sizable flower beds, two on each side. Each is twenty-two feet long, fifteen feet wide. These gardens are well tended, and plantings are planned so that floral arrays bloom in color sequences that complement one another. Here and there in the flower beds stands a low tree. The landscaping helps to offset the dinginess of the place, not for the benefit of the prisoners but because the courtyard area contains the administrative offices for the prison system—this section of Hoa Lo is essentially a government headquarters, a place where officials work and visitors are received. Prisoners were rarely to gaze upon the relatively pleasant courtyard.

———

Alvarez was given two blue shirts, two pairs of khaki trousers, two pairs of athletic shorts, two sets of underwear, and a belt. He was assigned to Room 24, on Hoa Lo's main courtyard. A large room, it was about eighteen feet long and fifteen feet wide. It contained a metal frame bed, a table, and two chairs. An interpreter explained to him that the courtyard would be available to him from 7 AM until 10 AM, that it would be closed during siesta period and then opened to him again from 2 PM until 5 PM. He was told that if he needed anything, he had only to ask the guard, who was to be summoned with the words "Bao Cao" (pronounced Bow Cow).

He could not believe anyone expected him to eat the food he was served, much less live on it. Typically, he would uncover a bowl to find a chicken head floating in grease. There would be small pieces of carrot and kohlrabi, and occasionally the hoof of a cow, mule, or pig. There would also be nails, fingernail clippings, strands of coarse animal hair, and shrimp—unshelled, uncleaned, and staring at him through eyes that had not been removed. Once, he was served a blackbird complete with feathers, lying on its back with its feet sticking up—but with its eyes closed.

Alvarez could not understand how even the rats could eat the stuff. He encountered his first rat early on. It awakened him one night rattling the dishes containing his untouched dinner. It was the size of a large cat. He started up in his bed, and the rat ran out through a drainhole. He got up and looked outside, to see where the rat had gone. As his eyes became accustomed to the darkness, he perceived that the bushes and trees were alive with rats, hundreds of them. His skin crawled.

Before long he realized that he was in a survival situation. If he were to stay alive, he had to eat the repulsive food. As quickly as he began eating, he was afflicted with severe intestinal disorders. A virulent dysentery seized him. He would vomit the meals up, then force himself to eat them again, even though they were full of blood. An uncontrollable diarrhea dehydrated him and weakened him, and his stool, too, was full of blood. He ran a high fever, and his weight fell off alarmingly. Soon he could fit his hand around his thighbone; he had weighed 155 pounds when he was shot down, and within a few weeks he was skin and bones. When his captors realized how ill he was, he was put on a diet of unseasoned rice soup containing small pieces of chicken. Soon he felt better.

———

A shadow on the wall next to him brought him leaping from his bed. It was a lizard, a small gecko. Suddenly he realized the things were all over the place, and he ran about the room frantically trying to kill them. A guard educated him to the fact that geckos are harmless to men, and are efficient mosquito catchers. After that he was to spend countless hours watching geckos play with each other.

Boredom consumed him. He asked his interpreter for something to read. He was given an open letter to President Kennedy that had appeared in the New York *Times*. Headlined "We Protest," it opposed American involvement in Vietnam and was signed by fifty clergymen, scientists, and others.

"Is this all you have?" Alvarez asked disgustedly.

"We are very poor," the interpreter said. "We do not have many things in English in our library. We are a poor country, but we are independent now."

"Well," said Alvarez, "that's just fine."

In the days that followed, the interpreter returned often, trying to "educate" him. He sought to establish the extent of Alverez's knowledge of the National Liberation Front (the Viet Cong) in South Vietnam. "Do you know what the NFL is, have you ever heard of it?"

"Yeah," he answered, "the National Football League."

One day the interpreter said, "Your wife is very beautiful. I have seen a picture of her that came over the teletype."

Alvarez's heart leaped. "Can I see this picture?"

The interpreter brought it the next day. It was a news service wirephoto. Tangee sat in a white chair. She looked beautiful. She held a handkerchief in one hand and obviously had been crying. Clearly, the photograph had been taken just after she had received word that her husband had been shot down. His heart went out to her; he wanted to cry with her.

"Do you have any children?" the interpreter asked.

"No."

"I saw a picture where she is with a little boy."

He brought this picture the next day. It was Ev's cousin's three-year-old daughter, his own goddaughter, sitting on Tangee's lap. He was allowed to keep these pictures, and he managed to keep them through all the years that followed.

From a Vietnam News Agency bulletin he was given he learned that no one had seen his parachute open and that the U.S. Navy assumed him lost at sea. How to get word out that he was alive?

Three young Vietnamese men and a girl introduced themselves to him as representing the "Voice of Vietnam" radio program. They proceeded to interview him.

"How do you feel?" he was asked.

"I think I'm okay," he answered.

"What do you think of the Vietnamese people?"

"Gee, I don't know."

It went on in that vein; inane questions, noncommittal answers. Then he was asked if he would like to broadcast a message home over the "Voice of Vietnam." He knew his government frowned on a POW's broadcasting, making tapes, writing; to do so was to play into the hands of enemy propagandists. Still, there was a time for the exercise of initiative, and his situation was unusual—his government did not know he was alive. It seemed essential to try to get word out that he was a prisoner. He took advantage of the broadcast offer. He taped, "I am Lt. (j.g.) Everett Alvarez, Jr., United States Navy, 664124. I want to tell my wife and my folks and friends at home that I am alive and well, and that I have been treated well so far."

The four visitors stared at him. "Is that all?" someone finally asked.

"Yes," he answered. He had no intention of stating more than the simple truth. And eventually that was what got out.

"What do you think of your situation?" his interpreter asked.

"Well," he said, "I'm a prisoner of war." It seemed enough to say; by definiton it was a terrible situation to be in.

"There is no war here," the interpreter replied.

"Has there been any more action against this country by our military?" Alvarez asked.

"No," said the interpreter. "You will have to stand trial for your action."

"I'm in the military," Alvarez explained, "and that was a military action."

"You will have to stand trial," the interpreter insisted.

The threat worried him. The United States and North Vietnam had no diplomatic relations. How could his government, then, ever arrange for his release? Through a third-party government? Indeed, would Hanoi release him, or would they keep him and "make an example" of him? Anxiety mounted, and a terrible depression deepened.

He found Vietnamese names and dates scratched onto the walls in the courtyard; the latest date he could find was 1960. People had lived here before, and he wondered how long they had lasted. He wondered how long he would last. He did not believe he could last long without help. He began to pray. He had practiced his Catholic faith, attending mass regularly and receiving the sacraments. But he had never really worked at prayer. He did so now. He developed a prayer sequence and concentrated on it when he was locked alone in his cell, during mornings, afternoons, and evenings: the Lord's Prayer; the Hail Mary, the Apostles' Creed—"I believe . . ."

He had been an altar boy and found that he was able to re-create the entire mass. He used a nail to carve an altar onto a wall in a small courtyard behind his cell, and a crucifix above. Below the altar he engraved the words "In God We Trust." Off to one side, on a stone pillar, he inscribed, "Lt. (j.g.) Everett Alvarez, Jr., United States Navy—Shot Down and Captured 5 August 1964—Arrived Hanoi 11 August 1964."

He was careful with the carving; he did it as well as he could. It took a lot of time, occupied his mind, and gave him something to do with his hands. He went to mass before the altar every morning. He would awaken and decide that he was back aboard *Constellation* and attending mass with his shipmates; or participating in the celebration of the mass in the Mission, back at Santa Clara; or dressed up and going to a Sunday mass with his family back in Salinas, where he grew up.

He declined a chance to write a letter home, then thought better of it; a prisoner of war without a war, he was confused at his situation. He decided he had best try to communicate along every avenue that was offered to him, in hopes something would get out and people would know he was alive. In letters to his wife and parents he included the information that he was to be tried for crimes.

The interpreter returned with the letters, saying, "You do not have to tell your people about your trial."

He scratched out the words, and the letters were sent.

He began to exercise in his cell. He did chin-ups at the door and calisthenics. He worked hard at keeping the cell clean, in an effort to make it less attractive to the rats. He talked a guard into giving him a rag and some water, and he scrubbed the floor often. He began carrying on long, loud conversations with himself; he would choose friends with whom he wanted to discuss various subjects and would imitate their voices, even to their inflections. Occasionally he would stop and reflect that anyone who heard him would think him crazy, would not understand that this mental-vocal exercise was helping him to retain his sanity.

He learned that dysentery telegraphed its punch. The day before it would strike, he would awaken dizzy and mildly nauseous. He learned enough Vietnamese from his interpreter to warn the guard, "Hey, dow dow, toy chom bak." ("I'm dizzy. I'm weak.") This guard, an impassive creature, looked like the central character in the comic strip "Alley Oop"—he was out of the Stone Age; in fact, the POWs eventually would identify him as Stoneface. Usually, he paid no heed to the prisoner's pleas, and Ev would lie on his bed awaiting the sickness.

But one day after he had warned Stoneface, the guard disappeared and returned later with a tray of food. Curious, Ev uncovered a dish and there lay an omelet—as beautifully golden as any he had ever seen. Under another cover lay a dish of home-fried potatoes, looking exactly as though they had been served up in any first-class American restaurant. On another dish lay a slice of white bread, and on another a tomato. Suddenly the nausea was gone and he was eating, the first food he had enjoyed since arriving in Hanoi. He became aware that tears were streaming down his face, and then he lost control and was crying like a baby. The good meal triggered an emotional release, and he felt better when he had finished crying.

One evening he was taken to an exhibition in downtown Hanoi. He was told that he would learn that the DRV (Democratic Republic of Vietnam) had shot down eight American aircraft on his last mission. The wreckage of four of these aircraft has been assembled, so that Alvarez could see for himself.

Floodlights in an open yard illuminated billboards showing an AD Skyraider and an A4, both of them diving in attack. Around the yard lay piles of wreckage.

"Here is your airplane," an escort told him. And there it was, a piece with "411" painted on it. It had been pulled out of the shallow water where it had gone in. He looked it over, carefully, then followed the escort to several other piles, each of which was presented to him as a different victim of the DRV's deadly antiaircraft gunners. In one pile he found a vertical stabilizer, part of the tail assembly, with "411" stamped on it. In another pile he found part of a wing he was able to identify as his own, and in still another a droppable fuel tank from 411.

His hosts were smug, gloating, as they ushered him through this exhibition. He was able easily to ascertain that the piles contained the wreckage of not more than two aircraft. He could not believe that they actually expected him to believe what they wanted him to believe, that there were four aircraft here. He decided he could not let them think they had deceived him.

"Look," he said, "these are not the pieces of four aircraft. You did not shoot down four aircraft, much less eight." He began leading his dismayed captors about the piles, showing them how everything fit together.

"It is not true," someone protested weakly. "These are four."

"Baloney," he said.

He was returned, in an angry silence, to his cell.

———

Early on Monday, September 21, he was taken into the room next door to his cell. There, behind a table, sat a Vietnamese he had not seen before. This man was well dressed in civilian clothes. His demeanor and bearing, however, were distinctly military, and he wore military boots that were polished to a high luster. He was flanked by two officers, who deferred to him in the most obsequious fashion. One of these was Owl, the English-speaking Vietnamese Alvarez had met in the Hon Gay jail, and the other was one whom he thought of as Chihuahua, because of his striking resemblance to that breed of canine.

"I have been sent here to interrogate you," the man in civilian clothes said. He spoke impeccable English.

"You are a lieutenant junior grade and you are young. You don't know much, but we want to know what you do know. Let me make it clear to you right now that there is no way that anyone can help you here. Your government can't help you. There is no war. You could be tried. It all depends on you, on your attitude and how you conduct yourself."

Then began a period of six consecutive six-day weeks of interrogation. Each session began at 7 AM and lasted until 5:30 PM, with time out for lunch and siesta. Alvarez was surprised and puzzled at the way it began. First, the interrogator ascertained that the prisoner was a football fan, and launched on a description of how soccer is played.

"No, no," Alvarez interrupted. He explained how American football is played. The interrogator listened, apparently with great interest.

Ev pondered this development as he lunched alone in his cell that day. Then it occurred to him that the interrogator had chosen the subject, football, as a device to get him talking, a prelude to plying him for military information. He had no important military information to give, but if he resisted, refused to supply any information, they might torture him. How might he react to torture? Would he say things he should not say?

There was nothing to do but to play it by ear; he might have to take torture, but he would start out by pleading ignorance, lying, getting away with as much as he could.

The interrogator began the second day by telling him again, "Everything that happens here will depend on you. How is your health?"

"I feel good now," Ev replied.

"The food is much better now? It is more to your liking?"

"Yes."

"You know, it could get worse again. And you have a nice room. That could get worse, too."

He nodded. He understood the threat.

"The newspaper says your father works with FMC," the interrogator said. "What is FMC?"

"That is Food Machinery Corporation," Alvarez explained.

"That's what?"

"Food Machinery Corporation."

"Ah, Foot Machinery Corporation."

"Yes."

"And what does he do with this Foot Machinery Corporation?"

"You know, they make machines for feet."

The interrogator and his two assistants traded glances. "Machines for feet?" he asked.

"Yeah, you know, machines that make shoes and stuff like that."

It went on like that, day after day. Often, the chief interrogator would come alone, and Ev would stall for time by interrogating him. "Tell me," he would say, "in the war with the French, how did you manage to communicate between different areas?"

"Ah, it was very difficult," the interrogator would say. He would put his notebook aside, lean back, and talk for hours. He would explain how French patrols had seemed to be everywhere, all the time, and how it had been necessary to develop and use trails in the remotest parts of the mountains and jungles; how volumes of food were carried—meat packed inside of rice balls—what kinds of equipment were carried, and how the villagers helped.

Sometimes Ev would get him going on the history of Vietnam, or on the country's economy, subjects which proved to be of consuming interest to the interrogator. Such sessions would last for entire days. The interrogator would end them reluctantly, saying, "You know, we must get back to work and answer questions."

Eventually the questions turned to military subjects. "How do you land on a carrier? How fast does it go? How do you stop? Does the deck expand, to make it bigger? Does it unfold?"

Ev had dreaded the military interrogation. Now, he thought he was being put on, then was flabbergasted to realize that these questions, posed by professional military men, were serious.

"Gee," he said, "you know, I have no idea how fast the ship goes. I was never told."

An officer was brought in who was purported to be an aviation expert. He wanted to talk about the catapults on carrier flight decks. "We have seen pictures of you taking off and landing," he said, "and you use this thing that sticks down that is part of the catapult."

"What thing?" Ev asked.

The interrogator drew a rough sketch, and Ev realized that he meant the tail hook a carrier aircraft drops when landing to catch the arresting wire on the flight deck.

"Airplanes don't use that on takeoff," he said. "They use it when they land."

"Well," someone said, "how many aircraft can you take off? How many can you watch?"

"Oh, gee, I don't know," Ev said. "Gosh, I don't have the vaguest idea."

"Do you have a swimming pool?"

"Oh yeah, we have a nice swimming pool."

"What do you like best about the ship?"

"The popcorn machine."

"Popcorn? What is popcorn?"

He spent half an hour describing it, then held his captors rapt with long descriptions of ice cream sundaes and cheeseburgers.

For some reason, they seemed anxious that he not know he was in Hanoi and went out of their way to try to make him believe otherwise.

"Do you know where you are?" he would be asked, out of a clear sky.

"I think I am somewhere near Hanoi," he would say.

"Hmmm. Yes, well, Hanoi is very, very far away. We have to get up very early, so that our driver can bring us here to work with you."

"I see," said Alvarez, who watched them park their bicycles in the prison yard building each day.

Once Owl was looking at his watch and telling the chief interrogator that it was time to return to "Hanoi, over here," and pointing off in one direction. The chief interrogator was talking to Alverez, paying no attention to his comrade, and did not see him pointing.

Alvarez asked, "Hanoi where?"

"Over here," said the chief, raising his arm, crossing it over Owl's outstretched arm and pointing in the opposite direction. For a long moment the two Vietnamese sat looking at each other, their arms crossed. Then the chief interrogator pointed in the direction in which Owl was pointing—just as Owl decided it would be best to point in the direction his chief had chosen. The chief reached over, pulled Owl's arm down, and began pointing vigorously and saying, "Over here, over here. In Hanoi. We must go!"

Alvarez could not resist telling the suddenly disconsolate twosome, "Hell, I know where Hanoi is. It's all around me."

———

He wanted out of Vietnam; he wanted to go home. But after two months his release did not seem to be in the offing. No one mentioned that any sort of negotiation was under way for him, nor, he was told, had there been any more military action against the DRV by the United States. "The United States can do nothing for you here," the chief interrogator said. "You won't go home until you learn the truth." The truth, he was given to understand, was to be found in stacks of propaganda he was given concerning the war against the French, the peoples' struggle against the Saigon regime and its "odious" American allies.

He grew anxious, fearful that he would be here for a long time. He began pacing his cell at night, wondering what he could do to spring himself. He decided he had to seize some opportunity to put on a real act, convince the Vietnamese he was "sincere"—their favorite word for people who saw things their way. The chance came when they caught him in a lie.

"We have found some rounds in your guns," his interrogator said. "They were jammed. You told us that you were not armed, that you were only a search airplane."

He wondered how to make the situation work for himself. Before he could devise a way, he was ordered to return to his cell and "think about it."

The next morning he told the chief interrogator, "I have to admit something to you." He kept his voice low, penitent, even managed to squeeze some tears up into his eyes.

"Yes? Yes?" the interrogator said excitedly. "Go ahead! Yes?"

"I didn't tell you the truth about what I was carrying in my aircraft."

"Yes? Yes?"

"I was carrying twenty millimeter guns with rounds in them. I fired at your boats. I lied to you about that."

"Yes! And you had rockets and bombs?"

"No, no rockets and bombs."

"Why did you lie?"

"Because I thought if I told you the truth you would kill me."

"Oh, no no! Don't think that. We are not going to kill you." For the first time, Ev knew that this was true, that they were probably not going to do anything at all to him. Throughout the weeks of interrogation, they had referred constantly to world opinion, and now, suddenly, he understood how important it was to them. They wanted desperately for the world to think highly of them, and knew they could not earn approval by murdering their only American captive.

———

On October 2, he was given a short letter from his wife. Tangee wrote, "I'm so happy to hear that you are alive and well and being well taken care of. Don't worry about me. I'm fine. Tell me, now that I'm going to have to be making the car payments, what day are they due?"

Tangee had been making the monthly installment payments on the new Buick Skylark from the beginning. Her question was a signal that no one at home was certain he was alive. He was given writing materials and told he could send mail to his wife and parents as often as he wished. He began writing twice weekly and received mail regularly. Tangee vowed that she would wait for him forever, and said, "Don't worry, our government is doing everything it can for you." This bolstered his morale, even when his interrogators, who read all his letters from home before giving them to him, chided him about it.

"Your wife says your government is trying to help you. Do you believe that? That your government can help you?"

"Of course."

"Oh, if you believe that there is no hope for you. No hope at all."

His parents assured him that he was never out of their minds, that they prayed for him constantly, and that he must "keep your chin up."

———

His interrogation period ended with the chief interrogator adjuring him to "show a good attitude and good behavior, and you will be released and go home. You'll see."

He understood by now that "good attitude" and "good behavior" meant that he must change his ideas, make himself useful to his captors for propaganda purposes. He vowed to himself that that would not happen. When he went home, he would go with his head high. He would be able to face his wife, his parents, his friends in the Navy, and to walk in his home country knowing he had done his best, that he had nothing to apologize for.

He was left alone for long periods. On the pillar where he had inscribed his name and shootdown and arrival dates he carved "October 12, 1964—Columbus Day." Over the altar on the wall he engraved the legend "Lord, I am not worthy that Thou should enter under my roof, but say the word and my soul shall be healed."

He made a chess set out of paper and played against himself. He drew plans for houses, then furniture to put in them.

Chihuahua came to his cell each week to urge him to write to Ho Chi Minh pleading for amnesty. "Ask for your release. He's a good man. You'll see." Ev refused to do so.

It grew cold, far colder than he thought it could in the tropics. Temperatures dropped into the thirties, humidity stayed high, and winds seemed constantly to whip through the open windows, down the hallways, and under the doors of the unheated building. He was chilled to the bone all the time. He kept asking for the underwear he had been wearing when he was captured, and finally it was returned to him, along with a black knit seaman's watch cap he had forgotten packing in his survival vest years earlier.

The food worsened again, but he forced himself to keep eating. Mail reached him regularly. He knew that his wife and parents were thinking of him and praying for him, and it helped. He "attended mass" at his altar regularly. Sometimes he would look up at the sky and think, *Well, God, it's getting to be a long time. How is she taking it? Is she okay?*

———

He had called Tangee one weekend during his senior year in college when he had needed a date. He had never seen her, but a cousin who had married her sister had insisted she was a "knockout," and Ev had found this to be an understatement. They had dated steadily for a long time. They were in love. Then he had entered the Navy and there had come a time when the young man had wanted not to be tied down, when he had to be free, so they had broken off. But it had not taken him long to realize that she was everything he wanted, and when he had gone back she had been waiting for him.

After that they had been so close, so much a part of each other, that it had never been necessary for him to propose marriage. It had never been a question of whether to get married, only when. He had not planned on making a career of the Navy, but a substantial portion of his obligation had remained to be served, and he had not been certain of the wisdom of tying her down to a marriage until his duty tour was completed.

"If you want me to wait," Tangee had said, "I'll wait. I'll wait as long as it takes."

But she had not wanted to wait, and neither had he, and so they had gotten married. It had been the best thing that had ever happened in his life, coming home to her and having her with him.

It was the best thing in his life now, the knowledge that she was waiting, and that she would wait as long as it took.

On the pillar, beneath the Columbus Day inscription, he carved "November 25, 1964—Thanksgiving."

———

On December 14, Chihuahua told him of a conference under way in Hanoi of "The Vietnamese Peoples and Peoples of the World Against U.S. Imperialism and Aggression in Indochina," and that American delegates wanted to see him. Curious as to the kind of Americans who would come to Hanoi, he agreed to a meeting. He was taken to an old French colonial residence on a street near the Lake of the Restored Sword. Here he was introduced to an American Negro couple, Mr. and Mrs. Robert Williams. Williams was tall, weighed perhaps 250 pounds, and wore a goatee. Shaking hands with Alvarez, he said, "I come from the United States. They call it the land of the free, but, man, there ain't no freedom there." He then launched into a lengthy monologue dealing with racism in America.

Oh, hell, Ev thought, *a nut.*

The table at which they sat was laden with fruit and cookies. Feigning interest so as to keep Williams talking, he set about devouring as much as he could. Williams went on and on, confiding his life story. He advised Alvarez that he had "got into trouble with the law," in his native North Carolina and had gone into exile in Cuba. From Havana, he said, he broadcast a radio program entitled "The Voice of Free Dixie" into the southern United States. He said that he and his wife had just visited Communist China, were now returning to Havana, and wanted to offer Alvarez the opportunity to tape-record a message for his family for delivery over "The Voice of Free Dixie." Ev kept gorging himself with bananas, oranges, apples, and cookies. He stopped eating momentarily, to assure Williams that he had no wish to tape any messages. Then he continued his assault on the goodie bowls.

Williams assured Alvarez that the Vietnamese are nice people and that it was cruel of the United States to bomb the country. He said he thought Alvarez was being used, and that he might be able to get him released. "I know Ho Chi Minh," he said. "Ho Chi Minh is nice people. I can talk to Ho Chi Minh. Would you like me to talk to him?"

"Go ahead," Alvarez said agreeably. "Talk to him."

"Well, wait a minute, now, you gotta do somethin' yourself, too. You gotta write him, ask him for your release."

"Forget it," Ev said. "I'm not going to write anything." Alvarez finished the last of the fruit and cookies. Then he stood, saying, "Well, it's time for me to go home. It's getting late." He walked out. That night he went to sleep fully confident that Williams was one of the most ignorant people he had ever met.

———

On the pillar below the Thanksgiving Day inscription, he carved "December 25, 1964—Christmas Day."

It was his first Christmas away from home. Even in the Navy, he had always managed a Christmas leave, for it had been a special time in his family. On Christmas Eve all the cousins and uncles and aunts came for a tamale dinner, then exchanged gifts under the tree and went together to midnight mass. He prayed his own midnight mass. He had been alone for nearly five months now; until that night he had thought he was getting used to the loneliness.

A week later he carved on the pillar "January 1, 1965—New Year's Day." He wondered what kind of year it would be.

Chihuahua became increasingly adamant that he write a letter to Ho Chi Minh, asking for amnesty. He thought that now might be the time to accede to the demand. He decided to write a letter, but to stick to his initial game plan of appearing to give more than he was giving:

> To Whom It May Concern:
> I am Everett Alvarez, Jr., lieutenant (junior grade), United States Navy, service number 664124. I was captured August 5, 1964, at Hon Gay. I feel that during my internment I have shown good attitude and good behavior, and feel you should review my case for release.
> Thank you.
>
> /s/Lt.(j.g.) Everett Alvarez, Jr.

A few days later Chihuahua returned with the paper, waving it and sputtering, "What is this? What is this? You write, 'To Whom It May Concern.' You must write to Honorable President Ho Chi Minh! Apparently you have not understood anything I have told you. You say nothing about your good treatment. You say nothing about the aggressive war in South Vietnam. You say nothing about how the United States violated the agreements on Vietnam."

"Well," Alvarez said, "I am not going to say all that."

"Then it is hopeless for you," Chihuahua said. "It is hopeless."

At 9 PM on February 9, four Vietnamese in civilian clothes entered his cell. They walked about the place, examining it and looking carefully at him. Finally one of them said, "Today, United States has bombed Vietnam."

"Where?" asked Alvarez. "In South Vietnam?"

"South-central Vietnam."

The visitors left. Ev pondered the news. If the United States was getting into the war in a serious way, it couldn't last long. He was full of a strange mixture of apprehension and optimism.

Two days later he was given a Vietnam News Agency release which advised that American planes had bombed North Vietnam. Then the turnkey delivered him a note asking him to explain a list of abbreviations of American military ranks. *The war's on,* he thought to himself. *The hell with them. No explanations. No more conversation. No more writing. Nothing.*

The next day he was taken to an office where Owl was waiting for him. Ev had not seen Owl for months. He looked troubled. "We need your help," Owl said, holding up a handful of kneeboard cards Navy pilots carry.

Oh, God! Alvarez thought. These cards were full of all kinds of classified information—fuel specifics, ordnance loads, dive angles, settings for different bombs. He was amazed that they had them, and guessed they had retrieved them from a downed aircraft. "I have never seen cards like that," he said. "I don't know what they are all about."

He was taken back to his cell. *Well,* he thought, *the war is on. It's really on.*

A Vietnam News Agency release advised on the February 11 shootdown and capture of U.S. Navy Lt. Comdr. Robert H. Shumaker. According to the report, Shumaker, whom Alvarez did not know, had been selected to be an astronaut.

Ev was again taken to interrogation. *Screw it,* he thought, *Now we play the game the way it's played in wartime.*

He refused even to say "Good morning." He sat mute all day long, as over and over again three new interrogators kept after him for information: "Who gives the political lectures on the ship?" "What about the chaplain? Isn't he the one who gives the political lectures?" "Where do you learn about your politics?" "What kind of airplane were you flying?"

Frustrated and angry, his interrogators sent him back to his cell in the late afternoon.

Among the new interrogators was one in his late teens who, because of his sizable ears, would become known to the POWs as Rabbit. His English was poor, but he seemed determined to make a mark for himself. One day he came to Ev's cell, sat down, and began lecturing him on Vietnamese history and on the purity of the Communist cause.

"Look, you are wasting your time," Ev interrupted. "I have heard all this many times. I don't believe it. You are not going to convince me."

A quick rage seized Rabbit. He shouted, "You think I am wasting my time! You think I am not doing good! You have heard this many times! Get up!"

Ev stared at the young man, wondering if he was unbalanced.

"Get up!" Rabbit screamed.

He stood, facing the interrogator.

"Go over there," Rabbit instructed loudly, "and stand in the corner."

Ev walked to the corner of the cell. *Oh hell,* he thought unbelievingly, *he's making me stand in the corner. Like a little kid!*

When he was facing into the corner to Rabbit's satisfaction, the interrogator stalked out. Presumably, the chastened prisoner was to remain in the corner and meditate indefinitely upon his bad attitude. Ev sat down, trying to make himself believe that what had happened had actually happened.

Near the end of February he saw a car pull into the compound. It disappeared behind a high wall, into the extreme southeast corner of the prison. He guessed that the sedan might be carrying Bob Shumaker, the second living American shootdown in the north. He walked out into his courtyard to the wall separating him from the adjoining area and yelled several times, "Hey, Shumaker!" There was no response, but somehow Ev knew that he had guessed right, that Shumaker was there; that either he could not hear his call, or circumstances prevented him from answering.

He sighed and turned back to his cell. At last, he thought, *I'm not alone anymore.*

Since the fall of the Diem regime in November, 1963, South Vietnam had remained in political chaos. The country's numerous anti-Communist factions had been unable to unite, and in a dizzying succession of coups and countercoups, the government had changed hands nine times. Meanwhile, the Communists by early 1965 were moving close to victory, a situation the Johnson Administration found intolerable. Thus began the Americanization of the war.

In February, when Communist attacks against bases in South Vietnam resulted in the deaths of more than thirty Americans, Presi-

dent Johnson ordered retaliatory air strikes against military barracks and staging areas at Dong Hoi, North Vietnam. The raids prompted Moscow to warn that such American behavior might require the Soviet Union to take "further measures" on behalf of North Vietnam. At home, Johnson had bipartisan support, but there were some expressions of concern over the situation.

On March 7, the first American combat troops reached South Vietnam, 3,500 Marines charged with the defense of the big airbase at Da Nang. By the end of June they were to be in the field, not in support of South Vietnamese forces, but engaging the enemy on their own.

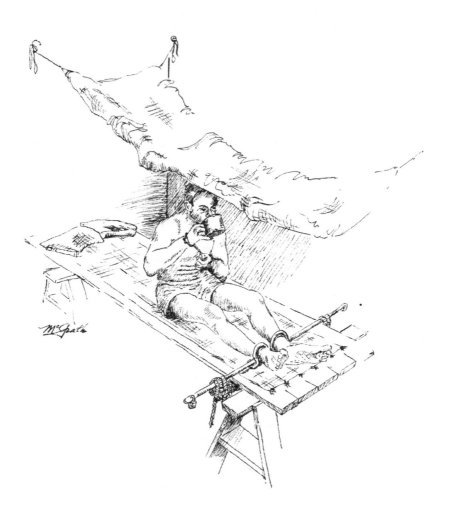

2

Finding Friends and Making Codes

Several times that winter and early spring of 1965, Bob Shumaker asked his interrogators, "What happened to Alvarez? What have you done with him?"

The reply was always the same: "He is in a far-distant camp."

Actually, the two Navy pilots were not more than a shout apart. Alvarez was in Room 24 on the south side of the main Hoa Lo courtyard. Shumaker was in a cell in a building in the southeast corner of the compound, an area future prisoners would name New Guy Village.

Immediately on reaching Hoa Lo, Bob learned that his captors knew a great deal about him. As the second American pilot shot down in North Vietnam—and the first in six months—he was the subject of much attention in the American press. Thus, it was known that in 1951 he had been valedictorian of his New Wilmington, Pennsylvania, high school class; that he had graduated eighth in the 1956 U.S. Naval Academy Class of 686; that he had been selected for the astronaut program but had been disqualified by a minor physical problem; that he had come to Vietnam on the aircraft carrier USS *Coral Sea* as a member of Fighter Squadron 154, and that his commanding officer was Comdr. William Donnelly. They knew that Bob and his wife, Lorraine, had a son, Grant, who was only three months old, and that Bob's father, Alvah, was an attorney. They also knew that his mother, Eleanor, had never wanted him to fly. Bob's interrogators castigated him for hours for being such an evil son as to go against his mother's wishes.

To Bob's horror, his captors produced a map they had obtained from his crashed aircraft showing targets, alternate targets, and ingress and egress routes. They would not let him see the map, and he could not clearly remember much of what was on it, so was unable to construct any plausible lies. He was frantic—he felt that, without saying a word, he had given away vital future target information. Still, these were maps pilots had to carry. So far as he knew, no thought had ever been given to the matter of destroying them, probably because it was not expected that maps would survive in aircraft brought down in combat.

Knowing all that they knew, Bob's interrogators were free to bear down on other questions:

"When your ship is anchored out there, in which direction is it pointed?"

"How many windows do you have in your stateroom?"

"How many chickens does your father have?"

Bob stuck to name, rank, service number, and date of birth. He was amazed at the apparent stupidity of his interrogators, most of whom had introduced themselves to him as army majors. The questioning went on, day after day. Sitting through the interrogations involved a real physical agony. The pain issued from what Bob would learn many years later was a compression fracture of the lower vertebra—a broken back. He had ejected from his crippled F8E Crusader jet on the morning of February 11 just in time to deploy his parachute; it had popped open perhaps two seconds before he hit the ground. He had landed in a sitting position, and his back had taken the impact. Notwithstanding all that he had to live for and wanted to live for, the pain was such that the idea of death seemed not altogether unattractive.

During the thirty-six-hour trip to Hanoi after capture, he had been paraded before a number of hate rallies, where he had believed he might be executed: at one point, he had thought he was to be beheaded; at another, a crowd of about three thousand seemed intent on stoning him to death; and at another, he stood for ten minutes before a firing squad. These had all been efforts to wring confessions of heinous crimes from him; of having participated in unprovoked air raids that had resulted in the deaths of Vietnamese babies. Bob had refused to admit to such crimes. Each time he had been certain that death was imminent. But each time the bluff had collapsed. He was glad still to be alive, and the certainty grew in him that the enemy had no intention of killing him. What he was not certain of was whether the pain was going to cost him his mental faculties. He began complaining and pleading incessantly for medical attention. These requests were ignored, and the interrogations continued.

After many day-long interrogations, he decided that he had to let them think they were getting something; otherwise, they would never stop, would never provide him with medical attention, and he really feared the pain would drive him insane. To establish his credibility, he told them his father's true age. Then he said that his father earned $5,000 per year, and that he had fifteen chickens. He told them that he had no idea how much money he earned himself, because he turned all of it over to his wife.

Even though he had given them nothing but meaningless or untrue information, he suffered a terrible remorse. He felt that somehow he had betrayed his family and country and wondered, desperately, how to retrieve the situation. Months later, he would learn that higher military authority advocated exactly the course he had followed: to resist to the point where loss of sanity seems imminent, then to give in with simple, plausible lies that were easy to remember, in case the same questions were asked again.

Shumaker's interrogators now felt they were getting somewhere with him. In his cell it was explained to him that although he was not a prisoner of war but a "creemenal"—the Vietnamese pronounced their *i*'s like *e*'s—and therefore not entitled to the treatment guaranteed by the Geneva Convention, he was to be accorded medical attention. His flight suit and boots were returned to him—he had been wearing light, cotton pajamas—and he put them on for a trip to a hospital. He was taken a short distance from the prison in a Russian-made jeep, then ordered to debark and to walk to a building, said to be a hospital, a half-block distant. The reason for the walk was immediately apparent: both sides of the street were lined with scores of photographers. Bob imagined that soon the world would be treated to scenes of himself, an injured American "air pirate" (a favorite term of his captors), obviously in pain and in need of help, walking freely into a hospital in lenient and humane North Vietnam.

Reaching a large room in the hospital, he found two Vietnamese, a man and a woman, in white smocks, awaiting him at an examining table. Bob assumed the man to be a doctor and the woman a nurse. Both kept smiling enthusiastically at a crowd of thirty-odd photographers who had stationed themselves around the room. In later years, when Bob came to understand the power of propaganda and Hanoi's reliance on it as a primary weapon, he would remember this day and rail at himself for not having walked out of the room.

As directed, he sat on a stool beside the examining table, and the nurse began asking questions: "What are your father's political beliefs?" she wanted to know, beaming at the cameramen.

"I am not going to tell you that," Bob answered. "The question is out of bounds and has nothing to do with what is happening here."

The nurse smiled down upon him, nodding as though he had just explained all of his physical woes to her, and that she understood. She looked up and smiled and nodded at the doctor, who stood on the other side of the examining table, and he smiled and nodded back, as though he understood, too.

"What is your father's state of health?" she asked. It was as though she had not heard his answer, and again she was favoring the cameramen with a glorious smile. The cameras were clicking and whirring and flashing.

"I refuse to answer," Bob said angrily. The nurse gazed upon him compassionately, then again traded nods and smiles with the doctor.

"What are your political leanings?" She grinned brightly.

There was no stopping the charade; it was going to be played out no matter what Bob answered, or whether he answered. He went mute, waited for the farce to end, assuming the doctor would then get on with the examination.

At last, the doctor, suddenly serious, came around the table, stood behind Bob, leaned down, placed the fingers of both hands lightly on the patient's back, looked at the nurse, muttered to her in Vietnamese, smiled down at Bob, then abruptly left the room. The nurse advised, "The doctor said that you will be feeling better soon." Then she, too, departed. The examination was over. He was returned to his cell without so much as an aspirin. In the eight years he was to spend as a prisoner of North Vietnam, that was as much medical attention as he was ever to receive for his broken back.

In the weeks that followed, Bob's interrogators devoted themselves to his education. They delivered what seemed to him to be a day-by-day account of four thousand years of Vietnamese history and described glorious and victorious struggles against the Mongols, the Chinese, and the French, and the justness of the Vietnamese people's cause against the illegal, repressive Saigon regime and against American imperialism. Each day there were two and often three lectures, each of which lasted approximately three hours. By the end of March, Bob estimated that he had sat through 250 hours of this. "They must have cast-iron bottoms," he marveled to himself. "They *must* have.'

———

Alone much of the time, he could reflect on how it was that one who, as a youngster, had wanted to be a veterinarian, had come to such captivity. Once, during high school, he had read an article in *Boys' Life* magazine about the Naval Academy, and his interests had changed. His father had taken him to visit both the Naval Academy and the Military Academy at West Point, and he had made up his mind. His mother, who had lost a brother in World War II, had not been enthusiastic at the prospect of a military career for her son, but she had wanted him to have the kind of life he desired. His captors had ranted at him for going against his mother's wishes; Bob was certain that, in newspaper interviews, Eleanor Shumaker had been quoted as saying the kinds of things any distraught mother might say on learning that her only son had been shot down and captured.

Bob had graduated from the Naval Academy a company commander. Then had come flying training, two duty tours in the Mediterranean, and the Navy's postgraduate school at Monterey, California. He now held advanced degrees in aeronautical engineering and aeronautical electronics; he was a long way from veterinary medicine—a long way from anywhere!

He was glad he had treated himself to one extravagance. Lorraine had borne him their son, Grant, in November, 1964, just prior to his departure to the Western Pacific. There had been a twelve-day stopover in Hawaii, and he had insisted that Lorraine and Grant fly out to be with him. It had all but exhausted their finances, but they had had grand fun together. As the years passed, he would come to regard their Hawaiian idyl as the best investment he had ever made.

———

He longed for friendly, American company.

Twice each day a guard escorted him to a bath and latrine area in New Guy Village. In mid-March he became aware that a few minutes after he was locked back into his cell, someone else was being walked through the courtyard outside, toward the bath-latrine. Laboriously, he would struggle down to the foot of his cell door, to peer through a nearly two-inch crack near the bottom, hoping that he would see another American. One day he saw a tall, thin, young American, so in need of a shave and haircut that he appeared to have stepped straight out of the previous century. He seemed to be uninjured and in good health, and wore the same kind of light cotton pajamas with vertical blue and white stripes that Shumaker was wearing. *You poor son of a gun,* Bob thought, *am I glad to see you!* He began wracking his brain for ways to communicate with him.

The new arrival was Air Force 1st Lt. Hayden J. Lockhart, Jr., twenty-seven, of Springfield, Ohio, a 1961 graduate of the Air Force Academy. An F-100 pilot, he had been downed on March 2, north of the Demilitarized Zone (DMZ). A few minutes after he had reached the ground, he had suffered the supreme frustration of seeing a rescue helicopter come in and hover directly above him while its crew had remained oblivious to his frantic waving and had looked *around* the area for him, and not *down.* After a reasonable time under heavy fire, the helicopter had pulled up and gone to look for him elsewhere—at one point a crewman had dropped a ladder and climbed to the ground, shouting Lockhart's name and looking for him until he was forced to withdraw with a leg wound. Lockhart had engaged in a short gun battle with some North Vietnamese militia, then had escaped to the jungle and evaded the enemy for seven days before being captured.

Shumaker devised a way to communicate with the new prisoner. Both men dumped and cleaned their waste buckets, small, tar-lined pails, in the same latrine. The place was filthy, full of cobwebs, enormous spiders—some measured nine inches across their backs!—cockroaches, rats, and an overpowering stench. The guard rarely entered the place; he usually locked Bob in alone. Bob found a small piece of loose cement that had oozed between a couple of bricks, lifted it, found a cavity large enough to hold a note he had written, in brick dust on a small piece of coarse toilet paper: "If you get this signal, scratch your balls as you walk out of the bath." He reasoned that such a message should convince an American that another American was trying to make contact with him, and that he would respond. He deposited the note, replaced the loose cement, then, with a chunk of red brick, scrawled another message in letters eighteen inches high on the plaster wall, directing Lockhart to the lengthier note. He was gambling that the guard would not enter the latrine area.

For days Bob watched and waited. Lockhart never signaled in the prescribed fashion. Angrily, Bob wondered if the man was blind. The answer was, nearly. Lockhard had poor eyesight, but by sheer strength of desire and academic performance at the Air Force Academy had gotten himself waived into flying training. He had lost his glasses during ejection or evasion and simply could not see Shumaker's foot-and-a-half-high message.

One day, after Lockhart had washed his extra set of pajamas in the bath area, Bob watched him hang them on a line in the courtyard. Later, he washed his own extra pajamas, hung them on the line next to Lockhart's, and slipped a note into a pocket of Lockhart's pajamas.

For four days he watched through the crack in his door, but Lockhart never went near the laundry. Bob was nearly beside himself! He wished he could get close to the Air Force pilot not so much to talk to him as to kick him for not gathering his laundry.

Finally, Lockhart approached the clothesline. A guard with him reached up to see if the pajamas were dry, felt the pocket, found Shumaker's note. An English-speaking officer was summoned to read it. Bob watched through his crack as the officer and guard looked toward his cell. It was clear Lockhart did not know what they were talking about. He was allowed to take his laundry, was returned to his cell, and the next day was removed to the Heartbreak Hotel cellblock, approximately in the center of the Hoa Lo prison compound. Shumaker was not to see him again for a long time. Within a few days Bob was taken before his interrogator and warned against violating camp regulations by communicating.

"Nech time," he was told, "we shall have to punish you. Nech time, we shall have to tie you up, and maybe put you in leg irons. Nech time, it will be very bad for you." Bob did not have the slightest idea what leg irons were; in the months and years ahead he would learn all too well. But, at the moment, he was bemused at the trouble the Vietnamese have saying ''next.''

During March and April a Vietnamese attired in sport clothes, including a jaunty hat, visited Bob in his cell each day for about an hour. The man spoke English, not well but understandably, and his sole purpose seemed to be to ingratiate himself with the prisoner. Once the visitor confided that he was going to see an American movie entitled *Blow*. This turned out to be *Gone With the Wind*. The man himself was soon gone—his efforts apparently were unproductive.

Bob wasn't saying much the Vietnamese could use, but from their standpoint—as he would later come to understand—they were making progress. At least he was talking, and handled properly he might eventually say something of value. They decided to expend some lenient and humane treatment on him.

On April 21, seventy days after his capture, he was given a letter from his wife. It was double-sealed in a Red Cross envelope and had come through International Red Cross headquarters in Switzerland. It was a short, bland note that did not address itself to the subjects closest to his heart—her own welfare and that of their infant son, Grant. At the suggestion of well-meaning Department of Defense advisors, Lorraine had avoided saying anything Bob's captors might conceivably use against him. Now he yearned for home with an emotion unlike anything he had ever known. He wondered if he would ever see his family again. During April and May his interrogators badgered him to write Ho Chi Minh, requesting amnesty and asking for release; perhaps Ho would grant the request and Shumaker would soon be with his wife and son again. Bob refused to consider the suggestion.

He worried. When his interrogators were not rambling on with their endless history course, they were telling him how American military forces rapidly were being cut to pieces in South Vietnam. Early on, he had been told that on the air strike on which he had been bagged, a big one involving seventy-five Navy planes, twenty-two aircraft had been shot down. Bob knew that this was preposterous. In his cell afterward, he found himself laughing. *By golly, they sure can tell lies. Twenty-two airplanes!*

But as the Communists well knew, isolation distorts reality. A few days later Bob was wondering, *Is it possible that they shot down twenty-two airplanes on that strike?*

Soon, he was telling himself, grimly, *I suppose it's possible. I sure don't think so, but they could have done it.*

Finally, after a time, he lay in his bunk feeling sorry for the wives and widows of the other twenty-one pilots.*

Each day he spent long hours keeping watch through the crack near the bottom of his cell door, wondering if he would ever again see another American walk by, planning how he would contact him. He found dried ink spots in the drawer of a desk in his cell. He rejuvenated the ink with drops of water and matchsticks. Using the matchsticks as pens, he put a message on a piece of toilet paper. The note asked the recipient's name. It told of a couple of places in the latrine area where cement or bricks were loose, and notes could be hidden. All he needed was someone to send this message to.

Finally, someone arrived. He was tall, good-looking with wavy blond hair, husky—perhaps 175 pounds. Clearly apparent in his whole demeanor was that he was unafraid, alert, tough, the best kind of company in a combat situation. Bob rolled up his message until it was no larger than an ordinary pencil eraser and tied it with some threads from his pajamas. On his next visit to the latrine he placed it beneath one of the loose pieces of cement, leaving lengths of thread hanging out. He placed a large piece of toilet paper scrawled with the words "Take Me" next to the privy hole where the new prisoner would dump his waste bucket. Then, impatiently, he waited. It was May 15, more than three months since he had communicated with another American, and he could hardly contain himself.

On his next visit to the latrine Bob found his notes missing. In place of the one he had hidden beneath the loose cement he found another, scratched onto a piece of toilet paper with the charcoaled end of a matchstick. It said simply, "Storz, Capt., USAF."

Ron Storz had been one of the first pilots to qualify for a new, vitally important, terribly dangerous Air Force job. He was a forward air controller, . . . FAC. The mission was to fly alone, low and slow in a light plane, to find and fix an elusive jungle enemy, to call in and direct air strikes, then to perform postattack reconnaissance. Storz had been shot down on April 28 and had reached Hanoi in early May. He was to become one of the great heroes of the American prison experience in Vietnam. To Shumaker, drowning in silence, his cryptic message was a lifeline. Bob could not recall ever having been so elated.

Other young Americans began arriving: Air Force Captains Herschel "Scotty" Morgan, of Asheville, North Carolina, and Car-

---

*Only three aircraft, Shumaker's included, were shot down.

lyle Smith "Smitty" Harris, of Preston, Maryland; and Navy Lieutenants Phillip N. Butler, of Tulsa, Oklahoma, and Raymond A. Vohden, of Springfield, New Jersey. The prisoners began scratching their names onto the insides of the flat metal handles on their meal pails, and as the pails circulated a limited communications system began developing between New Guy Village and Heartbreak Hotel.

On June 1, Shumaker scratched a greeting he hoped would reach a new arrival, Air Force 1st Lt. Robert D. "Bob" Peel, captured on May 31, 1965, to let him know he was not alone and, hopefully, to give him a laugh. The message did reach Peel. It read, "Welcome to the Hanoi Hilton." To Shumaker's vast chagrin, the appellation would leak out into the world and would stick, though many would never understand the sarcasm that had been intended; the name would conjure visions of comfort, if not luxury, and not of the filthy, vermin-infested place Hoa Lo prison actually is.

A population explosion was under way in New Guy Village. The Vietnamese complained that things were getting crowded. On June 25, Shumaker's cell door opened and in walked Harris, Butler, and Peel. The four were to be cellmates. Shumaker could scarcely believe his good fortune—it had been 133 days since he had spoken face to face with another American. The guards warned them that there was to be no loud conversation, laughing, or noises, then left them alone. Nearly two days passed before the excited prisoners were able to stop talking to each other, even to rest. After they had finally settled down, it was determined that Shumaker was the senior ranking officer (SRO); the Navy had advanced him early to the rank of lieutenant commander. The mantle of leadership, therefore, fell upon him. By now Bob knew how vital communications were in this kind of situation to morale, spirit, even sanity. It was possible this group would be split up again, and the Vietnamese showed no inclination to let them communicate with other Americans. So the first order of business, Shumaker decided, was to devise some efficient communications systems, ways of sending notes, signaling, and so on.

Smitty Harris recalled something he had learned while attending survival school at Stead Air Force Base, Nevada. An instructor had explained how some American POWs during the Korean War had communicated by tapping a code on pipes or walls. The sergeant had called it the "A F L Q V" code, for the letters which were at the heads of five alphabetical groups in a twenty-five-letter square:

A B C D E
F G H I J
L M N O P
Q R S T U
V W X Y Z

Wherever necessary, the letter C substitutes for the letter K, which is dropped because it is not needed as often as C, and the even twenty-five-letter square is necessary for speedy transmission of messages. The code is much easier to learn and use in a prison situation than the Morse Code because only dots are used, no dashes. The first signal refers to the number of the row, reading across; thus, one tap means the letter to be sent is in the A B C D E row. The second signal refers to the column, reading down; thus, one tap followed by one tap would mean the letter is A. Five taps followed by five taps would mean the letter is Z. "Tap Code" spelled out is: ....(T). .(A) ... .(P) . ...(C) ... .(O) . ....(D) . .....(E).

To speed transmissions, all kinds of abbreviations were to be used: the letter Z alone meant "says." ZED meant "said." The letter T alone meant "tea." The letter W alone meant "wide." GBU meant "God bless you." HBH meant "Heartbreak Hotel." NGV meant "New Guy Village."

Given time, a prisoner who wanted no misunderstanding about what he was saying would spell out every word carefully. For example, there was no mistaking the contemptuous statement a captured Marine tapped out with a broom he was wielding in a cellblock hallway one day—it came right after the prisoners had been treated to a song by an American antiwar activist who had visited Hanoi. The message was "JOAN BAEZ SUCCS." Years later, Air Force Capt. Jon Reynolds, who was living in the cellblock at the time, would recall, laughing, "It brightened my whole day."

The tap code was to become the primary means of POW communication. It got an early test when guards found a note in the bath area at New Guy Village from the Shumaker group meant for Air Force Maj. Lawrence N. Guarino, a June 14 shootdown who was in solitary. The group was split up on July 5. Phil Butler was left solo in the New Guy Village cell, and Shumaker, Harris, and Peel were taken to solitary cells in Heartbreak Hotel. As soon as the guards departed the Heartbreak cellblock, Shumaker began whistling the Navy song "Anchors Aweigh."

Back came the opening bars of George M. Cohan's melody "It's a

Grand Old Flag.'' Then a stage whisper: "It's clear.'' The new arrivals were instructed to identify themselves, then to climb up to the transoms over their cell doors and pull back or remove the cheap, orange-crate-like wood covers that had been put in the transoms to block communication. Ron Storz was now in Heartbreak, in a cell so positioned that he could see, under the gap at the bottom of his cell door or through his transom, the only access door into the cellblock. It was he who whistled signals. Heartbreak Hotel's special "It's a Grand Old Flag" was the all clear; danger was "Pop Goes the Weasel."

Other Heartbreak inmates were Scotty Morgan and Air Force Capt. Paul A. Kari, a June 20 shootdown. Shumaker, Harris, and Peel taught the others the tap code, and all practiced it assiduously. There were many interruptions. Guards passing by made a practice— indeed, seemed to make a ritual—of stepping into the Heartbreak cellblock to relieve themselves; most would stand in the corridor and urinate onto the floor of a cell that had been made into a bath area for the prisoners.

At first the prisoners had trouble remembering the tap code characters long enough to put them together and form words; then to remember words long enough to form sentences. Soon, though, concentration and proficiency began to improve. These July, 1965, Heartbreak Hotel inmates were the apostles of the communications system that became the blood of POW life. They established it and taught it to each other. Then, as they were separated, each man taught others, who taught still others. In time the tap code was to become nearly second nature to most prisoners; sending and receiving were scarcely more difficult than speaking or listening to someone else speak.

Eventually, sophisticated offshoots of the tap code were developed. A man walking through a courtyard to a bath area could send a short message as clearly as a third-base coach. For example, a man under heavy pressure to make an antiwar statement would know that as he passed through an empty courtyard, many pairs of American eyes would be fastened on him, looking for a message, and he might want his compatriots to know that so far he had been able to hold out. So he would scratch his head, which meant Row One, then his shoulder, which meant Column Three, and the letter would be C; scratch his shoulder, which meant Row Three, and his elbow, which meant Column Four, and the letter O; scratch his shoulder, Row Three, and touch his toe, Column Five, and the letter P; and so on until he had silently spelled out the word c-o-p-i-n-g.

In the vermin-infested prison the guards saw nothing at all unusual in all this scratching; in fact, they were constantly picking and scratching at their own problems. They also coughed, cleared their throats, and spit a great deal, and had no idea that when their prisoners did the same thing they usually were talking to each other. One cough was equivalent to one tap; two coughs to two taps; clearing the throat to three taps; a cough and a spit to four taps; clearing the throat and spitting to five taps. Sometimes, especially when a prisoner was being taken to or from an interrogation and the others wanted to buck him up—"Hang tough, ol' buddy, our prayers are with you!"—or wanted information—"Are you okay?" "Any torture?"—the amount of coughing, throat clearing, and spitting that went on seemed too much even for the rheumiest guards, and they could not get out of the cellblock fast enough.

On July 16, Shumaker, Harris, and Peel were taken from their Heartbreak Hotel cells and reunited with Phil Butler, in New Guy Village. The punishment for having tried to contact Larry Guarino—eleven days in solitary confinement—was over. The guards warned the excited men to keep their voices down, but it was difficult.

And alone, in a cell not far away, Maj. Guarino wondered, bitterly, who those Americans were who seemed to be getting along so well with the enemy.

Guarino, Junior Birdmen, and a Tough Guy from Canoe U.

As for himself, Guarino had not been getting along at all well with the enemy. Debarking from an armored personnel carrier into the main courtyard of Hoa Lo prison, he had been met by Rabbit, shouting, "You dirty, rotten criminal! Why did you come here to murder my people? Now you are going to pay for your crimes!"

"Who do you think you're talking to?" Guarino demanded. "What are you, a corporal or something? I am a major in the United States Air Force. I demand some respect and proper treatment. I demand to see the camp commander."

"You are no major here!" Rabbit shrieked. "You are nothing here but a criminal!"

"I demand my rights under Geneva!"

"Rights? You have no rights! You are a criminal! We are going to hang you!"

"Horsecrap!"

Guarino was locked into Cell #1 in New Guy Village. It was dank and dirty, perhaps sixteen feet long, seven feet wide. It contained a metal frame cot, and in back, in the corners below a barred window, stood two cement bunks. At the ends of these were ancient, rust-covered stocks, secured with large padlocks. It was obvious the stocks had not been opened in many years—probably not in modern times. Larry was glad that at least he had not been born into an era where such things had been used.

His flight suit was taken from him, and he was given a pair of blue and white striped pajamas. A guard indicated that a small can, about the size of a fruit can, was to be used as a toilet. Alone, Larry prayed for strength and guidance, pondered the strange, indeed mystical things that had been happening, and wondered why such things should be happening to him. True, he had been born into and raised in a devoutly religious (Catholic) family, but so had millions of others, and his own family's devotion to its faith had not been so constricting as to preclude certain of its male members from having bootlegging connections during the prohibition era. Larry had all his life been a regular Sunday and Holy Day of Obligation mass attender, but had pretty much taken religion for granted. Essentially, he had been a man of this world and was not yet anywhere near the stage of life where he was giving undue thought to the next. Still, things had been happening:

He had been flying F-105 strikes out of Korat, Thailand, since December, 1964. All the while, a sense of dark foreboding had been building in him. By the morning of June 14, 1965, he knew that his number was up. He had not liked anything about the day. The weather was marginal, and the mission and briefing had struck him as overly long and complicated. Prior to takeoff he had offered a gloved hand to his squadron commander, Bill Craig, and said so long.

"What do you mean, 'so long'?" Craig had demanded. "I'll see you in about an hour and a half."

"Sure," said Larry, heading for his aircraft. But he had known he was not coming back.

He was shot down somewhere in the countryside. He was captured by militia, wielding rifles and two-handed swords. His wrists had been bound behind him, and he had been marched through many villages, where crowds were summoned to jeer him, stone him, pull his hair, kick him, and knock him to the ground. He was bruised and bloodied, he was threatened, and he was frightened; at the same time, he knew with absolute certainty that he would be all right, that he would survive. But he was relieved when at last he was turned over to the Army.

Once, during the long, steaming hot trip to Hanoi, there had been a rest stop for the troops aboard the personnel carrier. To ensure that the prisoner would remain one, his legs and feet had been tied together, and he was wrapped in blankets that completely covered his head and face. He was left alone in the enclosed back of the vehicle. Sweat poured off him and soaked into the blankets. He fought for air, could get none, felt himself beginning to suffocate. He thought, desperately, of the certainty he had had since the moment of capture that he would survive; somehow, the certainty was still there, yet he was dying, smothering under a covering of smelly, sweat-soaked rags at the side of a road far, far from home. He prayed. He sweated, he struggled for breath and life, he waited for death, and he prayed. He could not get clear of the smothering blankets, and no one came to assist. But suddenly there were breezes, cool, sweet, refreshing, swirling gently all about him. He breathed deeply, easily, gratefully. He had never been more comfortable in an air-conditioned room, on a beach, anywhere. He kept on praying, in thanksgiving. When the troops returned and unwrapped him, he felt cool and relaxed. Outside there seemed not a breath of air in the whole world.

He reflected that he had been to Hanoi before, in late 1944. Flying a P-51 out of Chungking, China, he had helped escort a flight of B-24 Liberator bombers whose mission was to knock out a bridge in the city, which was then held by the Japanese. Larry had not lingered long in the area that time. With 135 combat missions behind him in the European theater, where he had shot down three Messerschmitts, he had flown only twenty-one more in the Pacific war before going home. With his wife, Evelyn, his childhood sweetheart, he had settled down in Newark, New Jersey; had gone to work as a toolmaker for the Lionel Corp.; and had joined the Air National Guard, so that he could keep his hand in flying, which he loved. He was recalled during the Korean War, and by the time that duty tour ended he had decided to make a career of the Air Force. Things had gone well until now.

Guards came and took him to a room where he met Owl. Interrogation began. Frightened though he was, Larry knew that he dared not show it; military interrogators would know how to exploit fear. He refused to supply more than name, rank, and serial number.

"We know that you took off from Korat," he was told. This information had been on his parachute pack and in his flight suit.

"I did like hell!" Larry answered.

"We know you did!"

"No," he said. He decided to try to confuse his captors with misinformation. "I took off from Da Nang."

Indeed, Owl was thoroughly confused, and the interrogation ended. The next day it began again. "You say you took off from Da Nang..."

Larry interrupted to deny having said this.

"But you said yesterday..."

"I don't know what I said yesterday. I was tired, or sick. I didn't take off from Da Nang."

"From where did you take off?"

"I didn't say."

Frustrated, Owl began lecturing him on the justness of the DRV's cause and on how Guarino had been misled by his political leaders. Larry interrupted to ask, "Who do you think you are talking to, a five-year-old kid? With a line of crap like that?"

Owl glared at him. "You are very *im*polite," he said. "Very *im*polite."

"Crap!"

The session ended.

———

After dark, alone in his cell, he heard a door slam and then someone whistling the tune "Up in the air, Junior Birdmen..." He jumped up on a bunk and looked out a barred window. All he could see was a high, thick wall with jagged glass implanted along the top and laced with electrical wires. He could not see the ground below but knew from the whistling that an American was there.

"Yank!" he whispered loudly.

"Yeah!"

"Who is it?"

"Bob Peel."

"Bob! This is Larry Guarino!"

"Larry! What a place to meet you again!"

Guarino and Peel had known each other at Clark Air Force Base in the Philippines before either had come to Vietnam. Larry had read about Bob's being shot down on May 31.

"How are you?" Bob asked.

"Okay," Larry answered.

"What happened to you?"

"The same thing that happened to you, Bob. Listen, your name has been released as definitely captured."

"Oh, God, that's a relief. I was so worried about my parents!"

"Well, no sweat. Your name is out, and they say you're okay. Are you okay?"

"Yeah, I'm fine. Shh! Someone's coming."

Larry jumped down off the bunk. He heard Bob move away.

———

"Do you know that your people have bombed our country with B-52s?" The interrogator was a man of about forty-three, Larry's own age. He kept chain-smoking and running his hands through bushy, graying hair. The prisoners would come to identify this man as Colonel Nam, or the Eagle—he wanted the POWs to think he was a Mig pilot but kept saying things that showed he knew nothing at all about flying.

"On what date did the B-52s come?"

"June sixteenth."

"Where did they bomb?"

"Very close to here. Why do you think your side did that?"

"It's very simple: retribution."

"For what?"

"You shot me down. They are not going to let you get away with that."

Eagle, in a sudden paroxysm of rage, came snarling around his table to the stool where Larry sat and landed a roundhouse open-palm slap on the American's face that knocked him from his stool, sending him sprawling across the floor.

Back in his cell, Larry wondered whether the blow was in punishment for his sarcasm or whether the interrogator actually believed the B-52s had struck in retaliation for Guarino's shootdown—it would not have surprised him.* He was certain only that this interrogator was not going to put up with any more nonsense.

He stared at the wall, not seeing it, absorbed in his thoughts about

---

*B-52s did not bomb anywhere near Hanoi until December, 1972.

the situation. Then, suddenly, three English words scratched onto the wall swam into focus: "Look under bench."

His heart was pounding! What bench? He looked frantically about the cell. In a corner stood a tiny wooden stool. Stuck into a crack on the underside was a small piece of folded paper. "Hi, Yank," the message said, "this is the interrogation center. You will be here four to six weeks. No torture yet. Pray, trust in God." It was signed "Yank."

Larry was elated at hearing from another American. He moved about the cell excitedly, searching the walls for more messages. He found a calendar scratched onto the wall near the cell door. The days were marked off one by one, starting with April 28—about six weeks earlier. And etched into the black paint on the cell door was the name Storz. He did not know Storz but was grateful to him. He looked forward to meeting him, so that he could tell him how much his message had meant to him.

––––––

For two days the meals served to Larry were excellent, so delicious that he thought he might have trouble keeping his weight down. Even the first night, after he had traded shouts and insults with Rabbit, there had been a savory soup, an entree of three slices of well-prepared pork, a serving of green beans, and two kinds of bread.

Things changed abruptly after he had maintained his defiant posture for a second day. A turnkey opened his cell door and indicated that Guarino should stand at attention when he entered. Larry remained seated on his bunk and invited the guard to go to hell, observing that U.S. Air Force majors did not stand for North Vietnamese corporals. Finally, the hungry prisoner was persuaded to go out into the corridor and pick up his dinner, which had been rolled in on a cart. It was in two bowls. One contained a mixture masquerading as a soup—some water and what appeared to be swamp grass; there was an odor of steel about it. The other bowl contained a serving of rice—old, stale, hard, and liberally sprinkled with dirt.

Larry returned the meal untouched. Immediately he was taken to an interrogation with Owl.

"Why have you not eaten your food?" Owl asked.

"I have no intention of eating such filthy stuff as was served to me tonight," he answered.

"You are being punished!" Owl shouted. "All the others, all of your friends cooperate with us. Only you do not cooperate."

Larry recognized this as the military interrogator's ruse; it was so transparent. He did not believe other American prisoners were cooperating. His overriding concern was to abide by the Code of Conduct, to be a good officer, to do an honorable job as an American prisoner of war.

"Well," said Larry, "I ain't gonna cooperate! I gave you my name, rank, and horsepower, and that's all you're gonna get! Now, I wanna eat, and I'm not gonna eat that crap you sent me!"

But the slop kept coming; every meal, every day. Larry refused even to try to eat it. He would take only water.

The ropes that had bound him during the trip to Hanoi had opened numerous small cuts, and these became infected. His captors would do nothing about the festering sores. Larry bit them open, sucked out the pus and spit it on the floor of his cell. The infections did not alarm him; he had always had strong recuperative powers.

What did begin to bother him was the hunger. The pangs were severe. He had had an ulcer operation a few years earlier, and he worried that there might be a recurrence.

The interrogations continued. One day Owl was joined by a senior officer whom he treated with great deference. This man, whom the POWs would identify as Dog, remained utterly impassive. He was handsome, obviously intelligent, and, although he did not utter a sound, Larry felt certain that he understood every word that was spoken. The next day the interrogation was conducted by Dog alone.

"You must understand," he told Larry, "that your position here is and will always be that of a criminal. You are not now or ever going to be treated in accordance with the Geneva agreements, because this is an undeclared war. You have criminally attacked our people, and it has been decided that you are always to be treated as a criminal. You must cooperate and show repentance for your crimes to earn good treatment. Sooner or later, you are going to show repentance. You are going to admit you are a criminal. You are going to denounce your government. You are going to beg our people for forgiveness."

Thus, by mid-June, 1965, Hanoi had determined to treat its American prisoners as common criminals.

The food did not improve, and Larry continued to fast.

There were interrogations by a number of different interrogators. Eagle, the interrogator who tried to suggest that he was a Mig pilot, wanted to know, "How do you bomb in an F-105?"

"Oh, about the same way you do in a Mig," Larry said.

"Yes?"

"Yeah. You know, just kind of point the airplane down and then pull up and let the bomb go. Just kind of by guess and by God."

"From how high do you bomb?"

"Depends on the weather. Just kind of pick out your own altitude and go ahead and let 'er fly."

"How do you navigate the F-105?"

"Oh, we do the same thing you do in a Mig."

"What do you mean?"

"You know, just DR [Dead Reckoning]. Just time and distance, the same way you do."

"Yes." Eagle nodded his head knowingly. Larry was convinced the man had never seen the inside of an airplane. The session ended.

There was another session with Dog, who seemed terribly nervous; he was actually trembling and kept glancing toward the door. "Sit down," he told Larry. "Now, I am going to ask you some things, and I want you to answer loudly and clearly, do you understand? Loudly and clearly!"

From Dog's manner, Larry decided that the meeting probably was being tape-recorded, and that the interrogator's health and welfare depended upon a productive session.

"Now," said Dog, "loudly and clearly, give me your name, rank, and serial number."

Larry gave these.

"Now, tell me, how were you shot down?"

"Okay," said Larry. "I took off from Da Nang. I flew up here, and when I got close to the target I think my engine crapped out."

"Say that again!" Dog shouted. "Say that again!"

"I think my engine just kind of crapped out over the target," Larry said, "and I bailed out."

Dog's nervousness became even more pronounced. He did not understand what Guarino was saying. What did he mean "crapped out"?

"Augured in," Larry explained. "It bought the farm."

Dog fidgeted anxiously. He was pale. He muttered to himself. "Tell me how you were shot down?" he pleaded.

"Well, my engine crapped out. . . . ."

The session ended. But for Larry the propaganda war had just begun.

———

Soon another American arrived and was installed in Cell #3, two beyond Guarino. This was Navy Lieut. J. B. (for John Bryan) McKamey, twenty-nine, of Fillmore, Indiana. Piloting an A4 Skyhawk off the carrier *Midway,* he had been shot down and captured near Vinh on June 2. It had taken him nearly three weeks to reach Hanoi. When guards were not about, Guarino and McKamey were able to talk to each other out of the barred windows at the backs of their cells, through the moatlike alley between the cell block and the outer wall of the prison. McKamey, who had been bagged two weeks earlier than Larry, was unable to tell him of any progress in the war. He did supply the startling and erroneous information that Alvarez, the Navy pilot who had been shot down and captured nearly a year earlier, had reportedly been executed by a North Vietnamese firing squad.

When McKamey was fed, the fasting Guarino could smell it, and whatever the Vietnamese were serving the new man, no food had ever emitted more tantalizing aromas. His imagination came to the enemy's aid; even when McKamey was not eating, the smell of Larry's favorite dessert filled his world: toasted pound cake with vanilla ice cream and peach preserves—Evelyn had made it for him often. Evelyn! He prayed she was all right.

He became alarmed. Except for the awful hunger, he had not noticed any change in himself during the first week of his fast. He had weighed 162 when he was shot down and judged that he had remained close to that weight; apparently the natural fat one stores up had been sufficient to keep things stabilized for a short time. But by the end of the second week he seemed to be disappearing before his own eyes. Suddenly, he could count his bones and fit a hand around the middle of his thigh. He knew that he had to eat, that if he did not do so he would die, or become so weak that he would not be able to take advantage of any escape opportunity that came. He began trying to take some rice. He complained to Dog about the dirt on it.

"The cook puts it there to show you how much he hates you," Dog confided.

"Well, tell the cook I'm impressed," Larry said, "and how about keeping the dirt off the food. When am I going to get something to eat? I can't keep going like this. I have a bad stomach."

Dog was unsympathetic. "You can't have good treatment unless you show that you are sorry for your crimes," he said.

———

One night Larry was awakened by the sound of his cell door opening. A guard approached his cot, trying to walk softly; obviously he did not know he had awakened the prisoner and did not want to disturb him. Larry lay still, pretending to be asleep, wondering what the guard was up to, not knowing whether to be frightened or not. He opened his eyes as much as he dared, not enough so that the guard could see that they were open. To Larry's amazement, the guard was gazing down at him with one of the saddest, most sympathetic expressions he had ever seen on anyone; the man's face was a map of kindness. He was holding a blanket. Larry had not been issued a blanket. The guard came close, slowly lifted Larry's head, put the blanket beneath it, smoothed it, then laid his head back down on the blanket, so gently that he was hardly aware that it happened. Then the guard turned away and tiptoed out of the cell, closing and locking the door as quietly as he could.

———

On July 1, Larry was taken to an interrogation with six Vietnamese. A civilian presided. He wore glasses, and a white shirt and black trousers. He did not speak English, but Larry could tell that his loud opening remarks were distinctly unfriendly. Nervously, a young interpreter told the prisoner, "You came here to murder us. You are a criminal. You do not deserve good treatment. Now you must tell us all about your aircrafts." He held up crudely made models of an F-105 and an F-104.

"I'm not gonna do that," said Larry quietly.

After the translation the interpreter turned back to Larry and said, "You are going to be severely punished. Are you going to tell us about your aircrafts?"

"No," said Larry.

The civilian left, angrily. So did the others. Finally, the interpreter left, too. Larry was alone. He thought about what had just happened. *They bring you in front of a crowd of people to impress you, to scare the hell out of you. They give you a choice, then threaten you if you don't make the right choice. Then they leave you alone to think about it and get scared. Well, it worked. I'm scared!*

Larry was returned to his cell. He waited, frightened. At 9 PM a group of guards came in with hammers. They knocked his metal frame cot apart, piece by piece, and carried the pieces from the cell. A guard ordered him to put his mosquito net up over one of the cement bunks at the back of the cell and to put his toilet can on the opposite bunk, within reaching distance. The guard used a large key to open the padlock on the stocks at the foot of Larry's new bunk and lifted the hinged top. The stocks had not been used in so long that the hinges creaked and squealed. The heavy metal bar that formed the top of the assembly was about three-quarters of an inch thick and three inches wide, and was shaped for the ankles. The thing was so rusty as to virtually guarantee infection to anyone who was locked into it.

Larry could not make himself believe that he was actually going to be put in the stocks. People simply did not treat prisoners of war this way in this day and age—that was what the Geneva Convention was all about, and North Vietnam was a signatory. He was scared but still in possession of his wits and certain that this was merely a scare tactic.

The guard ordered him onto the bunk. He was made to put his right leg into the stocks; he was allowed to keep his left leg out. The stocks were locked together, and the guards left.

––––––––––

The food did not improve. The rice stayed stale and dirty, but once he managed to get half a bowl of the stuff into himself. Occasionally, he would find some small pieces of pigfat in it and was able to chew the rinds off them. A thick pumpkin soup was substituted for the swamp grass soup. Once the soup bowl contained the skull of what probably had been a dog; there was no meat on it.

Larry felt himself becoming very weak, to the point where it took a huge effort just to sit up. About July 12 he became aware that J. B. McKamey was gone. It had been a quick, quiet, middle-of-the-night move, and now there was no one to talk to. He certainly had no intention of talking to those other Americans (Shumaker, Harris, Butler, and Peel). The four were living together in some sort of large room, nearby. He could hear them talking and giggling together. He could smell their food. He assumed that they had sold out, that they were cooperating with the enemy. He did not know Navy men Shumaker and Butler, but he had known Peel, and Harris had been a squadronmate and friend. He was surprised, saddened, angered at them all. He would have nothing to do with them.

Once each day he was taken out of his stocks for ten minutes and was allowed to empty and clean his waste bucket in a latrine in the New Guy Village courtyard. On these trips he would hear the other four call his name but would not acknowledge. In the latrine area he would find notes to him in which they identified themselves and asked him where he was being kept. He would not respond.

On July 20 Larry heard someone close by whistle the opening bars of "Anchors Aweigh." He responded with a few following bars, then whispered loudly toward his cell window, "Yank?"

"Yeah." The answering whisper was strong.

"What's your name?"

"Jerry Denton. Commander, United States Navy." The voice was firm, authoritative. "Who are you?"

"My name is Larry Guarino. I used to be a major in the Air Force before I got smoked."

"Guarino!" Denton exclaimed. "I've heard of you!"

"No kidding? How'd you hear of me?"

"Your name has been released by the gooks as captured."

"Oh boy, that's great!" Larry said. His spirits were rising. He was relieved, almost euphoric to know that Evelyn and the government knew him to be alive and a prisoner, and thus that Hanoi would be held accountable for him. And there was a strength and confidence in Denton's tone that was reassuring. The man obviously was a leader. Larry was anxious to keep the conversation going. "What kind of airplane were you flying?" he asked.

"Ha, ha, ha," Denton answered mockingly. "That's what *they'd* like to know."

Wow, Larry thought happily, *this guy is tough! Just what I need, someone to bolster up my courage.*

"Hey," he said to Denton, "I'll bet you're from Canoe U." ("Canoe U." is what military men often call the Naval Academy.)

"That's right," Denton said. "Tell me, how are they treating you here?"

Larry looked down at the stocks locking his right foot and at his skinny body. He did not want to say anything that would worry Denton or adversely affect his morale. If he was going to stay tough, he needed Denton to stay tough.

"Oh, they're not treating me too badly," he said.

"Well, don't worry," Denton said, "we'll hack 'er."

"Yes, sir!" Larry said, "We'll sure hack 'er!"

On June 18, B-52s based on Guam had carried out the first heavy bombardment raids against Communist positions in South Vietnam.

An American policy of "gradualism" was now in effect, a steady, step-by-step increase in military pressure which, it was hoped, would not trigger Soviet or Communist Chinese intervention, but would induce Hanoi to negotiate.

On June 19, a military junta led by Air Vice Marshal Nguyen Cao Ky had taken firm control of the Saigon government.

By July, there were 75,000 U.S. combat troops in South Vietnam, and Defense Secretary Robert McNamara was observing that since Diem's fall the military situation had worsened. On July 28, President Johnson increased American troop strength to 125,000 and said more were available if needed.

Friends, Nightmares, and the Briarpatch

Some would say that a war was no place for the likes of Comdr. Jeremiah A. Denton, Jr., who, after all, was the father of a happy family of seven children. Others would argue that such a background was good preparation for command responsibility and warfare. In any case, the 1946 Naval Academy graduate had approached his career with verve, imagination, and the enthusiastic support of his family. He was shot down on Sunday, July 18, 1965, while leading a twenty-eight-plane strike from the carrier *Independence* against the heavily defended port facility at Thanh Hoa. He was strongly optimistic by nature, not given to melancholy or self-pity.

Denton had been scheduled formally to assume command of Attack Squadron 75 on Tuesday, the twentieth. In fact, squadron members already were calling him Skipper and laughing hard at his jokes—for example, before the strike that Sunday he had told his pilots that they probably could expect lighter than usual antiaircraft opposition. He pointed out that the place had been raided so many times in recent days that the North Vietnamese with their limited supply of trucks were bound to have trouble keeping the AA batteries supplied with ammunition. He had not meant this in jest, but the pilots, who were accustomed to storms of AA fire over Thanh Hoa, had taken it that way. As it turned out, Denton had been right. There was only light flak at Thanh Hoa that day, but he was downed. He and his bombardier-navigator, Lt. (j.g.) William M. "Bill" Tschudy, sitting alongside him in their A6 jet Intruder, had parachuted into captivity. They had been taken separately to Hanoi.

Denton had reached Hoa Lo prison as dawn was breaking on July 19, and was taken immediately into interrogation. In Navy survival training he had been instructed that officers who had had advanced schooling in international relations who became prisoners of war could feel free to defend their government's policies. He had only recently completed such advanced training, at the Naval War College in Newport, Rhode Island, and he launched upon a vigorous defense of the American effort in Vietnam.

His interrogators listened avidly, occasionally interrupting to assure him, "Ah, you talk like a bandit! You talk like Chonson! You talk like Rusk! You talk like Mocknomora!"

He did not understand, at this point, that his captors were delighted with his loquacity; that they could not care less what he said so long as he talked. There would be time enough to persuade him to say the things they wanted the world to hear from him.

The session ended, and he was stashed in New Guy Village Cell #4. Denton whistled loudly, he sang songs, he kept himself and Guarino entertained. The guards kept admonishing him to be silent, kept warning him and Guarino to stop communicating. The two prisoners paid little heed.

Denton was taken to interrogation each day. He was surprised at the kind of rudimentary military information the enemy sought: the number of catapults on his ship, the number of aircraft the ship carried—none of this could be classified top secret. But he would give them nothing. He was worried. He was aware that he was the first A6 pilot to fall into the enemy's hands and feared the Vietnamese might be working their way up to interrogating him on the new aircraft. It occurred to him that his captors might apply more torture than he could take and extract information about the A6. He made up his mind that if this seemed to be happening, he would kill himself. Like Guarino, Denton was a devout Catholic, and the option of suicide was not open to him. However, his position, which he was prepared to defend before the throne of Heaven, was that he would not have committed suicide, but fallen on the field of battle in defense of his country. He found some shards of glass in the New Guy Village courtyard and secreted them in the latrine area. If need be, he would use them to slash his wrists.

————

Unable to elicit any response from Guarino, the Shumaker-Harris-Butler-Peel group turned its attentions to Denton. He found notes to him in the latrine area, asking him to identify and locate himself for them. He discussed it with Guarino. Larry explained that he was highly suspicious of the four, that the fact that they were living together and obviously enjoying life, talking, laughing, and in possession of writing materials seemed ample evidence that they had sold out. "Better not have anything to do with them," he warned Denton.

"Larry," Jerry replied, "I think the V may be pulling something on us, trying to divide us. I'm gonna give it a try." Notes were exchanged, and it was immediately clear that Denton had judged correctly. Guarino was chagrined to learn that the four had each already done a stretch of solitary confinement for their efforts to contact him and was greatly relieved that his judgment had been erroneous.

"Don't worry," the group messaged Denton, "only threats so far. No torture."

Smitty Harris, who was desperate for some important news from home, scrawled a large note to Guarino and left it in the latrine: "For God's Sake, Larry, will you please answer?"

Larry used a burnt matchstick to write a reply: "Smitty, your wife's okay, and the baby boy was born."

Harris was ecstatic.

————

Denton, the senior ranking officer (SRO) in New Guy Village, took command. "Follow the Code of Conduct," he ordered. "Think about escape. I want a note about it every day, and I want a map of this camp." He became obsessed with the idea of getting out of the place. At this point Guarino finally told Denton that he was locked in stocks.

"Oh, Lord!" Denton said. "Do you mean it? You're in stocks?"

"Yeah," said Larry. He was sorry he had told him. Denton was devastated; Larry could almost hear Jerry's morale sinking into the floor.

Denton began working on the metal bar that formed the top of the stocks on his own bed—it was not padlocked. After six days he succeeded in breaking it off. He found a place in the rear wall of his cell, just below the steel frame of the barred window, where he could insert one end of the bar. For days he dug and pried at the window frame. He was just about to tear the whole window assembly out of the wall when he was caught.

Had Denton succeeded, he would have been able to climb through the hole in his wall into the moatlike alley outside. To escape the prison, he would still have had to scale a high wall and cross its wide top, full of imbedded glass and covered with electrical wiring. Had he made it over this wall, he would have found himself in the middle of Hanoi. From here he would somehow have had to make his way across many miles of hostile, densely populated country-side, a Caucasian among millions of Asians, to the sea and the U.S. Seventh Fleet, or to some safe place in neutral Laos. He had no plans for doing any of these things; his plan did not extend beyond tearing a hole in the cell wall; it had not been entirely rational.

Jerry admitted this to himself as he lay with his right leg locked in stocks in Cell #3—the damage he had done to the wall in Cell #4 had made it necessary to move him one cell closer to Guarino. But despite his own failure, he wanted everyone to keep thinking and planning on escape. Right now, he had other problems.

"Larry," Jerry asked, "how do you take a crap in those stocks?"

Guarino, who did not know Jerry was now in Cell #3 and in stocks, did not want to sound as though he were feeling sorry for himself. "Ah, heck, that's a long story, Jerry," he said. "You don't want to hear that."

"Yeah, I'm interested," Denton said. "I've been trying to figure it out for three days. How the hell do you do it?"

Guarino went through a laborious explanation of how he had found that with one leg in the stocks he could roll over, get up on his knees, and get his waste bucket under himself. In fact, he had evacuated only once, after he had been in the stocks sixteen days—and only twice since his capture.

Finishing what he felt to be the somewhat degrading explanation, he demanded half-angrily, ''What the hell do you want to know that for?''

''Because,'' Denton admitted, ''I've been in these stocks for three days, and I couldn't figure it out.''

Guarino laughed. He had not complained, because he had not wanted Denton to think him a weak sister; and Denton, anxious that Guarino not think him weak, had not wanted to tell him he was in stocks.

Larry grew desperate. Twice a day, when the turnkey brought him a meal, he would point at the scar on his stomach, made when his ulcers had been operated on, and explain that he needed clean, nourishing food. Nothing was done about it. He continued to starve. He prayed. He said countless rosaries, using the bars on the cell window to count off the prayers.

Still, he grew weaker. After forty-seven days of starvation, he could not lift his head from his rack. Then Rabbit was talking to him, asking him about his stomach, showing surprise and great sympathy and insisting that Guarino would not have been punished this way had he only explained about his ulcers. He was brought a soup full of pieces of celery and chicken, and a half-loaf of bread.

In starvation, memory had embellished the first meals he had been served in this prison; he recalled them as among the most delicious he had ever eaten. But the celery-chicken soup and bread were better. He practically inhaled the meal.

During July and August the Vietnamese also began serving their American prisoners reading material. There was a virulent anti-American tract which had been written by Lord Bertrand Russell, the English philosopher. Larry could not understand the man's passionate hatred for the United States.

Some of the other stuff was actually amusing. One pamphlet dealt with the defeat of the French at Dienbienphu. It was full of admiring statements allegedly made by unnamed French officers: ''No,'' the Vietnamese conquerors were told, ''you did not kill only 150 of our people at that time. In fact, you killed over 600 of our officers.'' Also, ''You killed 900 instead of only 200. Oh, yes, your claims were far below normal.'' The American captives soon realized that they were being conditioned—at least, Hanoi thought they were—to accept all Hanoi's claims as overly conservative understatements.

———

By the end of August, 1965, more than a score of Americans had reached Hoa Lo prison, and on the night of August 31, many of the earliest American settlers in New Guy Village were dispersed to make room for newcomers. Guarino was blindfolded and taken to a cell in a small building in the north central area of the compound.

This cell was seven feet long and seven feet wide. There were cement bunks along both side walls, and the bunks had stocks at the ends. There was a two-foot-wide aisle between the bunks, where the prisoner could walk if he was not locked in the stocks. The cell had a high ceiling, and at the top of the rear wall, about sixteen feet up, were two small windows. There was heavy wire screening on the insides of the windows and, beyond the screening, heavy steel bars. These small windows admitted the cell's only light, except at night when a low-wattage light bulb was turned on and left on, so that guards could check the prisoner through a peephole in the door.

The cell was grossly filthy. It seemed to be a gathering place for all the mosquitoes in the world. And the rats! Some were in the cell or running through it all the time. Others were different—a kind of whitish-gray, with webbed feet, and so big they could not squeeze through the wide gap at the bottom of the cell door. They would stick their heads down into the gap and look up at Larry. They had great white teeth. Sometimes, when they were staring at him, their tails, half as big around as a man's wrist, would curl under the door. When Larry was taken to empty his waste bucket in the latrine in this area, he would see the gigantic rats loping away from stools as large as those produced by big dogs.

There was an abundance of scorpions, too, large, greenish things that came up out of the toilet area and under the gap of the cell door, looking for food. They looked like fiddler crabs, with huge claws swinging on their big tails.

And there were armies of big, fast ants. When Larry's food was brought in, he had to race to get it eaten before the ants overran it.

It was a place of horror. Outside, somewhere nearby, there was constantly the sound of running water. Also, there were the sounds of hogs, snorting, slurping at slops, their stomachs roaring. And loud in the background there was a tearing, screeching, grinding sound of metal against metal. This was the prison's sheet metal shop. Work here began at dawn each day and lasted until dark, and Larry felt sure that the noises issuing from the place finally would rip him loose from his sanity.

But worst of all in this grimy, reeking place was the utter loneliness. There was no one near with whom he could communicate. He had never known such misery, such soul-shattering despondency. He was living a nightmare, and he dreamed one. On the third morning he was in this cell he awakened himself with his own screaming. He had seen Evelyn crying for him, as though her heart would break. She was not the type to cry, but the sight was as real as any he had ever seen, and it panicked him. He could not stand the thought of Evelyn sitting alone and crying, with no one to comfort her, on the far side of the world. He screamed her name and cried for her. He was chilled, shaking with cold, yet sweating profusely. The wall on the opposite side of the room seemed to be moving toward him, intent on crushing the life out of him. He screamed more loudly, tore away his mosquito net, swung his legs over the side of his bunk, and braced his feet against the cement bunk opposite him, to hold off the advancing wall.

He cried and whimpered for hours. At length he was consoled. The guard came who had shown him sympathy and kindness one long-ago night in New Guy Village. His face was full of an immense sadness and there were tears in his eyes. He held out his hand and indicated that Larry should take it. He did so, and the two men's fingers intertwined for a long time. The touch of another human being seemed essential to life, and Larry was desolate, almost frantic again when the kind guard left.

Larry was anxious that other Americans know that he was alive, and his location. He began scratching messages onto the insides of the metal handles on the mess pails: "G. near to God. Alone in the Pigsty." "Bad place. Bad. Bad. Bad." "Panic in the Stockyard."

"Stockyard" seemed an apt description of the place, what with the noisy hogs, the gigantic rats, and the other livestock. The pails circulated. Other Americans saw the messages, sensed the lonely panic that had inspired them, and wondered what they could do about it.

———

Guarino had no way of knowing that he was not alone in the Stockyard. Ev Alvarez had resided there since June 21, in an equally dismal cell only a few doors from Larry's. He had clammed up completely in February, and the Vietnamese had stashed him here, convinced that he did not mean to speak to them anymore.

Outside the cellblock a tiny courtyard was divided by a wall, so that neither American prisoner could see the other when he visited the bath area. One morning Larry was washing at the trough when he noticed soapy water spilling down through the gutter below, and then came a distinctly American voice singing, "Oh, what a beautiful morning . . ."

"Oh, my God!" Larry cried. It was almost too good to be true, the sound of the voice, the song! Was he really hearing it? Or was it a dream?

The singing stopped. "A Yank," Alvarez said matter-of-factly. "What's your name?"

"Guarino!" Larry shouted.

A thrill shot through Ev. He thought Larry had said "Geronimo!"—the name paratroopers shout when jumping, to expel air from their lungs. *The paratroopers are here!* he thought excitedly.

"Who are you?" Larry asked.

"Al," Ev answered. He could hear the turnkeys returning and did not want them to hear him shouting his name.

Both returned to their cells full of confused excitement.

After the comparative opulence of Room 24, the tiny, filthy, Stockyard cell had been a shock to Alvarez, too. His rations had been cut in half, and now, instead of having access to the outdoors during most of the mornings and afternoons, he had but ten minutes per day to empty and clean his waste bucket and to wash his clothes and person. In addition to the noises that tortured Guarino's ears, Ev could hear one other—the sounds of Vietnamese guards flogging indigenous women prisoners. It was done at night, near his cell. He would hear the lash of the whip through the air, and then hear it crack against flesh. The women would groan, and then begin to cry and scream, and the flogging would go on and on.

To escape such noises—to escape the totality of his misery—Ev stuffed little rags into his ears. He took to lying on his bunk all day long, daydreaming. He dreamed of Tangee, of all the things they had ever done together and the things they wanted to do; of every job he had ever had or had wanted to have; of every friend he had had, and of the things they had done together; of everything he had done in school, of every football game he had ever played, of everything he had done in the Navy. In effect, he re-created his life as he had lived it, then thought through all the possibilities that had existed. Then he allowed his imagination to make the most of each possibility. He lived many lives in that cell.

But always in the back of his mind was the life-sustaining certainty that liberation was not far off, that soon—surely within a few months—American bombers would come to Hanoi and tear the place apart. When the prison was hit, he would find a way out, steal a bicycle, make for the coast. His physical characteristics, he thought, should not attract much attention. His complexion, inherited from his Mexican ancestors, was not noticeably different from the Vietnamese. He was not much taller than the average Vietnamese, and by now was certainly no heavier, weighing about a hundred pounds.

One day, while eating his half-ration of mashed pumpkin, Ev discovered a message penciled onto the wooden bottom of his bowl: "Is there a wop in Hanoi?" It was signed "Percy." Percy was Air Force Capt. Robert B. Purcell, thirty-four, of Louisville, Kentucky. Flying an F-105 out of Korat, he had been downed on July 27, and the "wop" he was in hopes of finding was his old pal, Larry Guarino. At the time, Alvarez had no idea who either of the principals were who were referred to in this message. He knew only that it was the kind of message Americans would send each other, and the thought he was not alone in this place, that more and more Americans were joining him, shook him free of the lethargy his daydreams had induced. Bob Purcell's search for his "wop" friend brought Alvarez alive.

Ev came off his bunk and began exercising. He did push-ups and sit-ups and walked long distances in his tiny cell—he would take three steps from the front wall to the rear wall, then turn around and take three steps back. Almost immediately, he began to feel better. He jogged in place. He carefully examined the bottom of every dish that came into his cell. On one he found several names: Shumaker. Storz. Morgan. Harris. Vohden. *Holy smokes! Is that Ray Vohden? I know him!* He added his own name, and two days later he found a message on the bottom of a dish: "Hi, EA, the score is Navy 7 and Air Force 7. We're doing good work in the south, hitting bridges, roads, communications lines. Don't worry. Won't be long now." It was signed "Storz."

They know I'm here! It won't be long!

He found another message, this one on the handle of a mess pail: "G. near to God. Alone in the Pigsty." Who was "G"? What did it mean? Was he nearby? To be sure, there were a lot of piglike noises coming from somewhere close.

Indigenous male prisoners occupied several of the cells between Alvarez and Guarino. When one of these, a little man with a round face, would take his daily turn at the water trough, he would wait until the guard had departed, then shout "Yoo hoo!" toward Ev's cell, and whistle the opening stanza of either "Cherry Blossom Pink and Apple Blossom White" or the Marine Corps Hymn. Ev could see the man through a crack in his door and would respond with the second stanza of whichever melody the man chose. Then, instead of attempting to communicate, the man usually would explode in maniacal laughter or embark on a wild whistling binge. Ev decided he was crazy and thought of him as the Crazy Guy.

One day, the Crazy Guy did communicate. In sign language he advised that another American was in a cell beyond the wall. He used a rag to pantomime wiping tears from his eyes—the American had been crying and he made motions toward his head—the American was out of his wits. It all seemed to tie together—the note from "G," who was "near to God," and the Yank who thought he was Geronimo.

Ev felt concerned for the distressed fellow American and wondered how he could help. He took a towel from a Red Cross package that had reached him months earlier and handed it to the turnkey, making it clear he wanted it delivered to the other American. The turnkey indicated that he understood, but the towel never reached Larry.

———

On the evening of September 13, guards entered Larry's cell and ordered him to roll up his blanket and mosquito net. He was blindfolded, led out of his cell, and taken on a circuitous walk through the prison grounds. He was frightened; his heart was pounding so that he could almost hear it.

"Do not be afraid. You will not be harmed. You go to a new place." He recognized Eagle's voice.

"Will there be anybody else there?" Larry asked.

"Mmmmmm," answered Eagle.

Others climbed into the vehicle. The prisoners were required to keep their blindfolds on. Someone sat down alongside Larry. Larry nudged him. "Who are you?" he asked.

"Al," came the answer.

"Al who?"

"Alvarez."

"Oh, God! God! Where you been? You been here all the time?"

"Yeah."

Guards interrupted to order Alvarez to move across to a seat facing Guarino. Two more prisoners climbed aboard. "Who are you?" Ev whispered to the one who sat next to him.

"Butler, Phil Butler. Who are you?"

"Alvarez."

"*Alvarez!*" Butler almost jumped out of his skin. He was talking to a legend, one year, one month, and eight days after the long-missing Alvarez had flown to oblivion.

Butler, who, along with Bob Shumaker, Smitty Harris, and Bob Peel, had done some time in solitary for an early-summer attempt to contact Guarino, had not yet met Larry. But he had heard so much about him from Smitty Harris that he felt he knew him, and he had been deeply worried about him when he had seen those frightened messages from the Stockyard. He wondered what the Vietnamese had done to create such panic in so good and strong a man. Now he learned Guarino was sitting opposite him. He had to let Larry know that he was not alone anymore, that he was among good friends. He reached across to the opposite seat, found one of Larry's hands, took it in his own, squeezed it reassuringly, and held it for a long time. He did not say a word, but somehow he was able to transmit warmth and friendship and sympathy. It was one of the nicest things Larry could remember ever happening to him.

————

The four prisoners—Hayden Lockhart had also climbed aboard—were taken to a camp thirty-five miles northwest of Hanoi, on the Red River. The Vietnamese name for the place was Xom Ap Lo; the Americans called it the Farm at first, but soon rechristened it Briarpatch.

It was a grim prison. An aerial view would have shown it to resemble a large tic-tac-toe grid. The compound was approximately 250 feet long on each side. High walls divided it into nine different yards, each of them about 80 feet by 80 feet. In the center of each

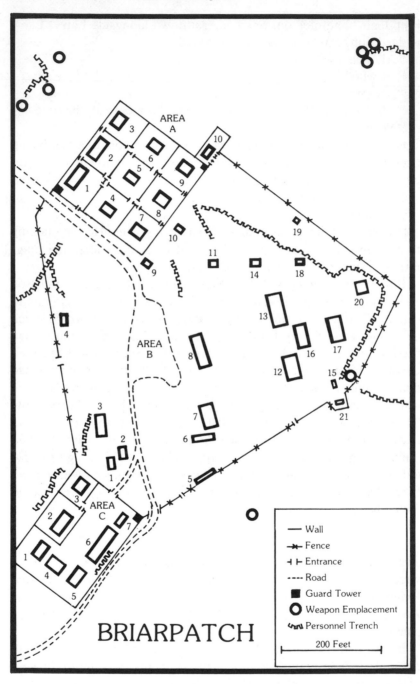

BRIARPATCH

— Wall
✳ Fence
⊣ ⊢ Entrance
---- Road
■ Guard Tower
◯ Weapon Emplacement
〰 Personnel Trench

200 Feet

yard was a small cellblock. Each cellblock contained four cells, one on each side of the building. These cells were perhaps seven feet wide and ten feet long. Alongside each wall was a bed of thick, hard wooden planking. Only inches separated the beds; there was no walking room between them—the only place where a prisoner might exercise was in a three by seven foot area at the ends of the beds. There were no lights.

But on that night of September 13, there was a brief happiness. It had been more than a year since Ev Alvarez had been face to face with another American. Now, at last, he had an American cellmate, and he was nearly bursting with excitement. He was trying to organize his thoughts. He did not know what to say; his heart was in his throat, and he was not sure he could say anything. His cellmate was Larry Guarino, who, after his long, hot summer of solitary confinement and physical and psychological abuse, was also full of excitement. They shook hands, they talked, they laughed. They stumbled about in the small, dark cell, and discovered that it was as filthy as the cells they had come from.

"How do you turn the lights on in this place?" Larry asked.

"Do not talk!" ordered Rabbit from the window. "Absolute silence!"

Alvarez pointed at the glowering official. "Hey, Larry," he said, "see that guy there? I hate that son of a gun. I *hate* him. He's a *prick!*"

Within a few minutes Ev was marched out of the cell and into another, of his own.

Fall 1965— A Long Time of Testing Begins

Navy Comdr. James Stockdale reached the Hanoi Hilton on Sunday morning, September 12. He was carried in on a stretcher, taken to the far end of the building on the south side of the courtyard, and ensconced in Room 24, where Alvarez had spent the previous fall, winter, and spring. Eagle, Owl, and Dog came into the room behind him. Dog introduced himself as "commander in charge" of the prison camp system, and asked Stockdale for confirmation that he was Commander of Carrier Air Group 16, operating off the carrier *Oriskany*. Jim gave his name, rank, and number.

Dog now delivered a short tirade on American perfidy, denounced the Tonkin Gulf raids of August, 1964, condemned violations of the DRV's sovereignty and confided that his wife had a formal education and was a medical doctor serving in the field, in South Vietnam. The session ended after about fifteen minutes, and Jim was left alone with his thoughts.

Stockdale was indeed CAG 16. He had been shot down three days earlier, on September 9, between Vinh and Thanh Hoa. On ejecting, he had suffered a broken bone in his back, and upon capture had been beaten savagely by a gang of raging civilians. During the melee, his lower left leg had been bent sideways from the knee at a nearly 90-degree angle and was badly broken. He had been rescued by North Vietnamese Army personnel, who took him to a hut and held him under guard.

The next day a doctor had examined Jim's leg, then produced a surgical saw and surgical knife. Jim had implored the man not to amputate. The Vietnamese did not understand English, but seemed to comprehend Jim's pleas and was sympathetic. He brought out a large hypodermic and injected Jim with a colorless fluid. Almost instantly, the patient lost consciousness. He awoke late that day to find his broken leg in a cast; a second cast had been placed on his broken left shoulder.

In this crippled condition he had reached Hanoi. He was depressed, worried, frightened. Foremost in his mind were studies he had made years earlier, while working toward his master's degree in international relations at Stanford University, of how American POWs during the Korean War had been brainwashed, had been made submissive enough to make treasonous statements against their government. How smart, how tough would one have to be to withstand brainwashing?

Also, he was upset that he had been recognized as one in authority. There was no question in his mind that the military professionals among his captors were well aware of the kinds of military secrets an Air Wing Commander had to know—information their Chinese and Russian allies would like to have. To what lengths would they go to extract it? Torture? Drugs?

And what of vengeance? A year earlier, as a squadron commander, Stockdale has received attention from the American press for having led the three principal actions on the Tonkin Gulf raids. The North Vietnamese were hardly likely to feel kindly toward him.

Stockdale prayed, and thought hard. He was convinced that this was going to be a long war. Somehow, he had to buy himself some time and plot a proper course. There could be no leaks, no surrender of precious information.

———

At the Briarpatch the rule of silence was not yet being strictly enforced. Shortly after dawn on Tuesday, September 14, his first morning there, Alvarez was allowed outside his cell to empty his waste bucket and wash his dish. Locked up again, he went to his window and asked the guard for a cigarette. The guard opened the window, gave him one, and stood smoking with him. Along came another prisoner, back from emptying his bucket in the camp latrine. He wore a blue shirt and ragged blue shorts, stood well over six feet tall, was muscular and handsome, with wavy blond hair. There was no fear in this man. He was tough and sure of himself, and it showed in his eyes and in the way he walked. Nodding at Alvarez, he asked the guard, "Is he a captain or a major?"

The guard, who knew no English, did not answer. Nor did Alvarez, who was momentarily awestruck. The prisoner walked on, around the corner of the building. Moments later Ev heard him at his basin, washing.

Ev suddenly realized that the man thought him to be a Vietnamese. His coloring was much the same and, slight to begin with, he had lost much weight. He had to identify himself for his fellow American. He shouted, "How about a lieutenant jaygee?"

The sound of washing stopped. "That sounds like a Yank talking over there," the voice said.

"It is," Ev answered.

"What's his name?"

"Alvarez."

The blond head popped around the corner. "Where the hell have you been?"

Ev observed that he had been around.

The guard displayed little interest in this exchange. When he had finished his cigarette, he departed. Ev learned that his impressive-looking new friend was Ron Storz. He had come to this place two weeks earlier, on the night of August 31, along with Bob Shumaker, Smitty Harris, Scotty Morgan, Bob Purcell, and Bill Tschudy. He was anxious to know where Alvarez had been kept for the past year and how he had been treated. Ev briefed him. Soon the two were aware of a lot of chatter between their own building and another on the other side of a wall. They heard Guarino, in another cell in their building, ask, "Hey, who's over there?"

"Bob Shumaker."

"Shumaker? Hey, you got television? There's an antenna on your roof!" Larry laughed. The "antenna" was a lightning rod.

"When did you come up and who came with you?" Shumaker wanted to know.

"Last night," Larry answered, "with Butler, Lockhart, and Alvarez."

"Where is Alvarez?"

"I don't know. He was in here for about five minutes last night, then we were talking so much they ran him out of here."

Storz, in the cell directly behind Guarino, could not make himself heard by Larry. He yelled to Alvarez, "Ev, tell Larry who is in this building."

Alvarez did so, and now found himself being grilled; the others had to know that he wasn't a plant. He was asked which squadron he had been in aboard *Constellation;* and whether he knew various people on the ship whom he should have known.

"What do your friends call you?" someone asked.

"Ev."

"Wasn't there another name?"

"Yeah, Alvy."

"Yeah, that's it," someone finally said. "That's him."

"Hey, Ev," Smitty Harris yelled, "how does it feel? This must seem like Coney Island to you, being with other Americans."

Alvarez tried to explain to his fellow jailbirds that he felt as though he had been liberated, but words seemed inadequate. He was having difficulty understanding that it was really true, that after all these months he was with a lot of other Americans and was actually able to talk to them.

Grim as the Briarpatch was, the company was good and so was the entertainment—the daily American air strikes against the military installations around the nearby Sui Hai Dam. The POWs watched, enviously, exultantly, as the fighter-bombers rolled in, delivered their lethal payloads, then pulled up and away. In a sense, it was a wrenching experience to see the attacking aircraft streak off after expending their ordnance; the POWs could not help thinking that in a little while these pilots would be back at their bases, reading letters from home, drinking beer, eating well, showering, walking about freely. Still, it was grand to watch them in action, especially since enemy aircraft gunners seemed unable to down any of them. On Wednesday, September 15, Lt. Col. Robinson Risner, commanding the 67th Tactical Fighter Squadron, got his canopy knocked off, but this merely made things uncomfortable. His wingman, Ray Merritt, closed up on him, and Risner led his flight home to Korat.

Far below, from his cell window, Larry Guarino watched them go. Suddenly, he was full of a dreadful premonition. He called to Smitty

Harris, on the other side of a wall, "Hey, I got some real funny feelings about Risner. Real strong feelings about Risner and his assistant ops officer, what's his name? Ray something . . . Ray . . ."

"Ray Merritt," Harris answered. Smitty had been a member of Risner's squadron.

"That's right," Larry answered. "Gee, I've got the strangest feelings about those two guys." He worried about them all the rest of that day and through much of the night. He had known Robbie Risner for a long time; the two had been close friends. He recalled that *Time* magazine had featured Robbie on its cover earlier in the year, describing the Korean War ace (eight Migs destroyed) as the classic example of the kind of dedicated, military professional who was leading the American effort in Vietnam. *Boy,* Larry thought, *if the gooks ever get ahold of him, they'll skin him alive!*

The next day, Thursday, September 16, Risner and Merritt both entered Hanoi's prison system.

———

Risner was shot down and captured approximately ninety miles south of Hanoi. He reached Hoa Lo at midmorning on September 18 and was installed in Room 18, off the main courtyard, just to the left of the entrance to the prison. Room 18 was also to be known as "The Meathook Room," for a hook that extended down from the ceiling—some uncooperative Americans were to be trussed up and hung from this hook, upside down and rightside up. Entry into Room 18 was from a hallway through French doors with opaque windows. It was a large room, perhaps 30 feet by 20 feet. High on the wall, looking down on the hallway, was a window which had been boarded over. For interrogations, the room usually was set up with chairs behind a conference table covered with a blue drape. The prisoner was made to sit on a low stool before the table. During punishment or torture sessions, the place was emptied of everything but a waste bucket, which was usually left full of the previous interrogatee's leavings. Room 18 was a dirty, sinister-looking place. Here and there, patches of dried blood fastened clutches of hair to the grimy walls.

Rabbit joined him, and interrogations began immediately. As quickly as Risner established that he would answer no questions beyond those sanctioned by the Geneva Convention, he was made aware that the Vietnamese knew a good deal more about him than name, rank, and serial number. The *Time* article was quoted to him; so were other articles that had appeared in American newspapers the previous spring, after Risner had been awarded the Air Force Cross for leading a maximum-effort air strike in which three important North Vietnamese bridges had been destroyed.

"Do you want to see your wife and family again?" he was asked.

"Yes," he answered, "I expect to."

"Only if you talk and answer the questions we ask will you see them."

The full, soul-shattering impact of being separated indefinitely from his wife and family reached him on his second day in Hoa Lo, as he was served his morning meal, a miserable, weedy gruel. Robbie's existence centered on his wife, Kathleen, and their five sons who ranged in age from 16 to 3½. Mealtimes had been especially precious, a time of joy, where all had shared in the small and large triumphs, problems, and plans of each. By now, word of Robbie's shootdown would have reached his family. He could see Kathleen, her eyes abrim with tears as she served the boys, who would be casting covert glances at their father's empty chair and thinking private thoughts.

No one had ever gone to war better prepared than Robinson Risner. Deeply religious, he was at peace with God, and engaged in activity he knew to be absolutely right. He had no regrets over anything he had ever done and he was not afraid to die. But he could not ward off a deep sadness at the prospect of long separation from his family.

Over the next two weeks more than a dozen interrogators had at Risner. He would not cooperate. He was assured that he was a war criminal. There was much talk of turning him over to the people, who would tear him apart. He was told that he would be burned at the stake. These threats were lost on him; he simply was not able to believe them. In any case, he was as ready to die as he ever would be.

Soon he was installed in a Heartbreak Hotel dungeon. Sensing that there were other Americans in nearby cells, he waited until he thought the guards were out of earshot, then sang, softly and to the tune of "McNamara's Band":

Oh, my name is Robbie Risner,
I'm the leader of the group.
Listen to my story,
And I'll give you all the poop.

Up from several cells came greetings from three members of his own squadron: his wingman, Maj. Ray Merritt; one of his flight commanders, Maj. Ronald E. Byrne; and Capt. Wesley Schierman. Another Heartbreak resident was Navy Comdr. Wendell Rivers, an A4 pilot off the carrier *Coral Sea*. Rivers, who had flown nearly one hundred missions, had made a ritual before each mission of running into his room, which was on the route between the ready room and the flight deck, and kissing a lipstick impression his wife had made on a water pipe, then kissing a picture of his wife and children. On September 10, a second mission had come up, and it had been necessary to brief and launch on a crash basis, and there had been no time for the ritual. Shortly, Wendy had found himself parachuting into North Vietnam and grousing to himself, "Shit! Shit! Shit! Here goes the next two years of my life!"

All wanted to know how long Risner estimated the war would last. Reporting that Defense Secretary Robert McNamara had indicated it would be over by next June, he affected a cheerful optimism. He deemed it his duty as senior officer to try to keep up the others' morale. "Don't sweat it, guys," he said. "We can stand on our heads 'til June."

He hoped it made them feel better. Privately, he found the thought of imprisonment in this place for another ten months intolerable.

Early on Ev Alvarez's first Sunday morning at the Briarpatch, there was a religious service. There had not yet been any breakfast. The prisoners had last eaten at about 4 PM the day before, and were hungry. The window shutters had not yet been opened, and the tropical sun poured a searing heat onto the roofs of the cellblocks. In their dark cubicles the prisoners swam in their own sweat. During the week, Storz had briefed Alvarez on the Sunday service, and now someone yelled to him that it was time to begin. He knelt on both knees and began saying the Lord's Prayer. He could hear the muffled voices of the others praying with him, in his own building and in the other buildings. Their captors had warned them to maintain absolute silence, but they prayed anyway, as loudly as they could. As Ev prayed, he thought about the others—like him, they were hungry, unshaven, stinking dirty, and locked up in hot, reeking cells a half-world away from the country and people they loved. But none was feeling sorry for himself. In the best sense, they were behaving as American military men should. They were organized, together in prayer, asking for guidance and strength.

Now, the prayer finished, Ev stood and faced the east, toward the

United States. He put his right hand over his heart, and with the others recited, "I pledge allegiance to the flag of the United States of America, and to the Republic for which it stands . . ."

Finally, all voices raised in song, and Ev thought he had never heard the "Star-Spangled Banner" sung more strongly or with such feeling.

By the time the short service ended, there were tears streaming down his face. He wept unashamedly, but not in sadness. He was nearly bursting with pride at being part of such a company of men.

On the evening of Sunday, September 20, the Briarpatch prisoners were blindfolded, handcuffed, and put aboard trucks. On the trucks their feet were tied together. They began coughing out their names to each other: "Storz." "Morgan." "Alvarez." "Guarino." Then Rabbit was shrieking at them, demanding silence. The trucks began moving.

Their new home was to be the "Zoo," a compound on the southwestern edge of Hanoi. All the Briarpatch prisoners made the move. The POWs surmised that the Vietnamese did not want to chance losing their hostages in the heavy air attacks on the military sites around the Briarpatch.

The Vietnamese name for the Zoo was Cu Loc. The POWs called it the Zoo because most agreed that it was an inside-out place, where the animals looked at the people.

The complex was not built to house prisoners. Apparently it had been a film studio. Approximately 100 yards square, the compound contained fourteen single-story buildings of various sizes. In the center was a large swimming-pool area. There was nothing inviting about the pool; it was full of filthy water, dirt, garbage, and small fish that the Vietnamese guards raised for food. It stank. Large, black film canisters and 35-mm filmstrips lay scattered on the grounds. The buildings were in disrepair, with most of their windows boarded up and their interiors full of dirt, dust, broken glass, and all manner of insects and rodents. It had been many years since there had been any human life in the Zoo.

The POWs were scattered into the different buildings, locked in rooms behind louvered French doors. When the guards were not at hand, these doors could be pushed outward an inch or two, and the men could see and speak to each other.

But there wasn't much chance for conversation. There were more

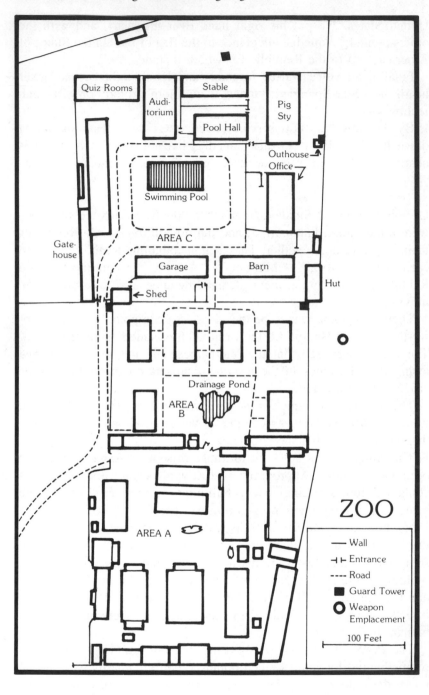

guards now, roaming the compound, warning the prisoners on the rule of silence, and leaving the impression that they hoped they would catch them breaking the rule.

Larry Guarino was in an end room in a building the prisoners called the Pigsty, near the southeastern corner of the compound. He scratched a cross onto a wall and spent much time kneeling before it, praying for strength and help. He could not get Robbie Risner out of his mind. He had lost much sleep worrying about his old friend since that day at the Briarpatch, when those ominous feelings had engulfed him while watching the air strikes. He prayed hard that Robbie would be spared capture.

On September 30, Larry completed an intensive prayer session, then rose to push open his louvered door to see a prisoner being ushered into a cell. He was thunderstruck; it was Risner! Again, Larry knelt before his cross, this time to raise unshirted hell with the Lord!

Since his shootdown on August 26, Navy Lt. (j.g.) Edward Anthony Davis had been keeping impressive company. He would have much preferred the company of his bride, Lois, whom he had married only two weeks before leaving for the war, but since that was not possible, he was not doing badly at all; indeed, there had been moments that he had actually enjoyed. Like the morning he entered Hoa Lo prison. Blindfolded and with his hands bound behind him, the young 1962 Naval Academy graduate first had heard the whistled strains of the Air Force song, then "Anchors Aweigh." At the latter, he straightened, adjusted his step, and began marching in rhythmic cadence across the big prison courtyard. Then many people were whistling, much louder, setting a smart pace for him. His guards had to hustle to keep up. Ed marched in time to the tune all the way across the courtyard to Heartbreak Hotel. Not in the most stirring full-dress parade at the Naval Academy had he ever been so proud of being a member of the United States Navy.

His blindfold was removed in a Heartbreak Hotel dungeon and his soaring spirits were dashed. The place was an insult to the senses, the sight and stench of it; it reeked of misery. Seconds after his heavy cell door was slammed shut, however, his morale was restored. In answer to several calls, he got up into his transom, pulled away the flimsy wooden cover, and met the high-spirited inmates who, through cracks and pinholes in their boarded-up windows, had whistled him across the grounds. There were three Navy men: Comdr. Bill Franke, who had been commanding officer of Fighter Squadron 21, operating off the carrier *Midway*. He had been shot down on August 24. In another cell was Franke's radar intercept operator, Lt. Robert B. Doremus. In another, Lt. (j.g.) Richard M. "Skip" Brunhaver, wearing a smile as big as the sun. There were also two Air Force pilots: Ron Byrne and Wes Schierman. All expressed delight at having Ed with them. The gloom of the dungeon notwithstanding, the place was aglow with lighthearted banter.

He remained in Heartbreak a day and a half. Then he was moved to New Guy Village, two cells from Jerry Denton. He stayed there a week and got to know Denton well. Ed felt a boundless admiration for this tough, sharp senior officer. Denton had lots of conversation about his children—food for depressing thought; yet he remained cheerful and kept his attentions focused on the present situation, made it clear he meant to provide strong leadership to any who were junior to him. He remained unfailingly and infectiously optimistic. He always believed release was imminent, always was thinking about escape, and always believed that the next meal would be better than the last. The only thing that worried Denton was that he thought he had blood poisoning. In July he had spent ten days in rusty stocks, and one of his feet had been cut on the sharp edges and had become infected.

"I'm getting red streaks up my leg," he told Davis.

"Are the glands in your groin swollen?" Ed asked.

"Yes," said Denton, "they are."

"Good. That's fine. I'm glad to hear that."

"Why? What does that mean?"

"That means the glands are cleansing the infection," Ed assured him. "It means your body is fighting the infection, and you're on the topside of this thing."

Ed did not know any such thing, but didn't want Denton worrying over something he could do nothing about. Equipped with his reassurances, Denton, the chronic optimist, did not become overly concerned as the infection worsened. The leg swelled and he ran a high fever for days. The Vietnamese finally treated the cuts with sulfa and warned him to keep them dry. This proved impossible, since he had no shoes or sandals, and had to walk to the latrine area, awash in slimy water, in his bare feet. At length, he was issued a pair of sandals. As he began to recover, he and Ed Davis were moved to the Zoo.

There, Davis was locked in a room in the Garage, a building facing the west side of the swimming-pool area, next to a similar building a few yards to the south called the Barn. One morning, one of the inmates in the Barn was let out for air and exercise. Ed watched through his louvered door as the prisoner came toward his door. He recognized the man but couldn't attach a name to him. The man dropped to the ground in front of Ed's door, began doing push-ups and speaking, in low tones—but the voice was smooth, confident, reassuring.

"Good morning, Ed. I am Colonel Robinson Risner. Call me 'Robbie.' I'm senior officer in the camp. We've got things going for us. We've got pretty good communications established. I've heard some good things about you, and it's awfully nice to have you with us."

Robbie Risner! Ed thought. *Of course I've seen him before, on the cover of* Time! *He was an ace in Korea, he's the Air Force's best, and he thinks it's nice to have me with him!*

Risner kept on talking. He told Ed who the POWs were in the other rooms in the Garage and the Barn. He briefed him on the camp routine and verbally supplied a lengthy operational order, which was a plan to live by. All this time, to Ed's amazement, the senior officer kept pumping push-ups at a pace that did not slacken; he must have done a hundred or more, talking all the while, and was not even breathing hard by the time he finished passing on his lengthy instruction. He jumped to his feet and walked away.

Good company, indeed!

———

Risner had reached his dark cell in the Barn in early October. He had knelt at the back wall and stage-whispered his name down into the open drain-air vent that ran beneath it, hoping Americans on one side or the other would hear him.

"Percy, Colonel!" came the answer. "Bob Purcell here!"

Purcell! Robbie was delighted. Percy's flight leader and wingman both had reported that he had been hit at an altitude of two hundred feet and had gone down in flames; neither had seen a parachute. Risner had assumed that he was dead.

Ascertaining that he was SRO in the Zoo, Robbie sought a meeting with Dog, the camp commander. At length, he was taken before Dog's assistant, an officer the POWs had named Spot, for a golf-ball-sized area on his right cheek that had no pigmentation. Risner complained that the cells were filthy and insisted that each should be supplied with a broom so that the prisoners could sweep out. He also demanded that prisoners should not be required to sleep on the cold, dirty floors, that they must have beds. He demanded, too, that lights be installed in the cells, so that prisoners could at least see what they were eating. He complained that the prisoners needed to wash more than once every fourth day and that they needed daily exercise. "We don't even treat pigs this badly in our country," he said.

"You are a liar," Spot snarled. "Get out!"

Back in his cell, Robbie called to Purcell, "Bob, I want the word spread around the camp: everyone is to pray for brooms, lights, outside exercise, and beds." This order was greeted with what Risner perceived to be a stunned silence. "Did you get that?" he asked.

"Yes," said Percy, a Catholic. "I am just trying to remember how to pray in Latin for a broom."

The SRO was quite serious. In Risner's judgment, the POWs had a few weapons available to them, and far from the least of these was prayer. They had no choice, he thought, but to make the most of it.

The next day wooden sleeping pallets were delivered to each cell. Shortly, the POWs were taken separately from their cells daily for fifteen minutes of air and exercise. A few days later Robbie heard some scrambling about on the roof over his cell, and then Percy, next door, sonorously intoning, "And he said, 'Let there be light,' and there *was* light . . ." Suddenly, a tile in the roof opened, and a naked light bulb snaked down into Risner's cell and went on!

———

Strong leadership was vital if men were to survive and resist effectively. Risner made policy and offered behavior guidelines. His orders and thoughts were tapped and talked through walls, men with pencils copied them onto lengths of toilet paper, memorized them, passed them along, read them aloud to others when it was safe to do so. Risner wanted all the information that could be gathered concerning the camp layout, the guards' quarters, individual guards' habits, and the surrounding countryside. The POWs were to study everything about the place with an eye toward resistance and escape, were to learn to pick locks and to neutralize the electrical system. They were to save all wire, string, nails, pieces of metal, wood, and soap—anything that might conceivably prove of value to communications or to an escape effort. ''Be good Americans,'' the men were told. ''Live by the Code of Conduct. Pray together at one PM each day for unification of effort.''

Finally, Risner urged that POWs who had been behaving insolently toward the guards stop doing so; satisfying though such conduct might be, it was worse than fruitless, for it resulted in the withholding of food. ''Don't cooperate with the enemy,'' the SRO said, ''but remember that you catch more flies with honey than with vinegar.''

Risner was now transferred to a cell in the Barn, the building just to the south of the Garage. The Barn was full of Americans who were being subjected to prolonged interrogation—Ed Davis, Wes Schierman, Bob Shumaker and others whom the Vietnamese apparently deemed especially bad attitude cases. Risner's cell was between Davis' and Shumaker's. Then, suddenly, Shumaker was gone, replaced by Ron Storz. Risner yearned for the sight and sound of other Americans. He had found and secreted a two-foot length of reinforcing rod, about as big around as his little finger. He sharpened one end of it and began digging a small hole through the cement wall that separated him from Storz. The wall was about two feet thick. In the middle of it were two rows of bricks laid end to end against each other. These bricks had holes through the lengths of them, but Risner had difficulty finding them. He struggled for days, digging small holes through the cement, then running up against solid brick and starting over. The wall took on the aspect of Swiss cheese.

After about a week, Ron Storz learned what Risner was doing. The SRO advised Storz as to how to acquire a digging tool of his own. He knelt at the back of his cell, reached down into the drain, below floor level, then brought his hand up into the inside of the wall, got a grip on a reinforcing rod and pulled and twisted at it until he had broken off a length. Storz began digging and pounding with an enthusiasm that carried him through to Risner's cell the same night. Spurred on by such success, Risner finished his own observation ports by the following morning. The prisoners would take turns standing back from these observation holes, so that their neighbors could savor the sight of another American. Then they would come together and visit, talking for hours about their families, school years, careers, hopes, and dreams.

''Visiting'' proved a tonic to the spirit. The word spread around the camp and holes began filling the walls in the other buildings. To conceal them, pieces of soap were molded into easily removable plugs.

The Vietnamese kept taking prisoners to interrogation, trying for professional and personal information, anything they could get. Men were roused in the smallest hours, taken to quiz rooms at 2 AM and 3 AM, when physical resistance was at its lowest, grilled, forced to sit on a small stool for six to seven hours before returning to their cells. But there was nothing Risner regarded as real punishment. Nor, he thought, was there to be any. He was wrong.

Knutson—A Pretty Tough Nugget

The long horror began sometime after dawn on Tuesday, October 19, 1965.

"Knutson, Rodney Allen. Lieutenant, junior grade, United States Navy. Service Number: 667751. Date of Birth: 29 September 1938."

Having provided his captors with all the information that is required of prisoners of war by the Geneva Convention, to which both the United States and the Democratic Republic of Vietnam (DRV) are signatories, he would provide no more. Yet the guard remained in the cell, thrusting a sheet of paper and a fountain pen at him and demanding additional, military information. The paper, handwritten in English, required him to identify his aircraft carrier, squadron, the type of aircraft he had been flying, the kind of ordnance he had been carrying, his target, and more. Rod shook his head emphatically. He refused to accept paper or pen. He turned away from the guard, walked to the pallet that was his bed, sat down on it, crossed his arms and legs, and leaned back against the wall.

The guard followed him, scolding him in Vietnamese. He grabbed Knutson's hand and put the paper in it; he grabbed the other hand and put the pen in it. The anger was rising in the young American; he was appalled that the enemy would so grossly violate the rules of warfare, and that apparently he was expected to casually betray his oath as an American military officer and the American fighting man's Code of Conduct. Slowly, deliberately, Rod held the paper up in front of the guard's face, stabbed the pen through it, then contemptuously tossed the pen and paper on the bed pallet.

The guard stood rooted, a look of disbelief on his face. Then he ran from the cell. In his haste he forgot to lock the cell door. Quickly, he turned back, locked it, then scurried away.

Rod did not have to wonder long what would happen. Within a few minutes the cell door opened again and an officer and five guards entered.

"How are you?" the officer asked in English.

"Okay," Rod answered.

"How did you like your evening meal last night?"

"Okay." Actually, Rod had barely sampled it. It had consisted of a small bowl of "soup"—really lukewarm water with a few pieces of leafy matter, some bitter-tasting kohlrabi, and a moldy chunk of bread full of weevils and hair. Rod had not been hungry, and the appearance and odor of the food had done nothing to awaken his appetite. Even so, he had taken a few bites; it was his duty now to keep up his strength. But he had deposited most of the meal in his waste bucket.

Now the officer walked to the bucket, reached down, lifted the lid, gazed at the food scraps, then at his prisoner. He said, "You insult the Vietnamese people."

———

Small wonder after the events of the past two days that Rod had little stomach for food. He was a radar intercept operator (RIO). At about 11 AM on Sunday, October 17, he and his pilot, Ens. Ralph Gaither, had been blown out of their F4B (Phantom II) fighter approximately thirty-five miles northeast of Hanoi. Both had parachuted safely onto a countryside that seemed to be crawling with militia. Descending, Rod had heard bullets ripping the air around him and had seen bullet holes appear in his parachute canopy.

The two Americans landed two hills apart and Knutson lost sight of

Gaither. Then he saw a lot of Vietnamese rushing toward him, some of them already within 150 yards, shouting, screaming, and shooting at him. He hit the quick-release device that freed him of his chute, threw his hardhat and oxygen mask aside, and began running, faster and harder than he had ever run before in his life.

He found a depression in the earth, tried to hide himself with a few branches and leaves, but was quickly discovered. He decided against trying to fight his way out of the country with a .38 pistol. But when he tried to surrender, an apparent madman armed with an AK-47, a Russian-made automatic rifle, tried to kill him, firing several rounds at him but missing the mark. In desperation Rod had fired back—his had been a tracer round, one that could be seen from the air by rescue units, and he had seen it enter the Vietnamese's head, just below the right eye. The man collapsed onto his face.

In the same instant Rod sensed a presence behind his right shoulder, whirled, and saw a rifle muzzle only inches away aimed at his head. He fired his .38 straight into whoever was holding the rifle. There was a blinding flash, an explosion—then oblivion.

By nightfall he was in a village jail. The right side of his flight suit was soaked with blood. There were pockmarkings all over the right side of his forehead and face, probably powder burns. A slight crease extended from the right eyebrow down across the side of the nose, through the lips, and down over the chin. There was a small cut on the eyebrow, and from this a thin trickle of blood oozed down along the side of the nose. There was nothing to account for the large amount of blood that soaked the flight suit. Rod deduced that it had belonged to the rifleman he had shot.

He wondered what had become of Ralph Gaither. He had seen the pilot briefly after capture, as both were being marched to this village, but not since. Ralph had been wearing a large bandage on his neck. Rod wished he were here, so that together they could formulate some sort of escape plan. But the two friends were not to meet again for many years.

Knutson had been in the jail less than an hour when a small Army contingent had collected him and taken him to Hanoi. It had been a slow trip with many stops. At every village and hamlet, an officer with a bullhorn would summon all the locals to look upon the captive. As they looked, the officer would harangue them; Rod had no idea what the man said, but knew it was no tribute to his character, for within moments the people always would begin to mutter angrily, then shriek and shake their fists. They would come close to punch him, twist his nose, pull his hair and ears, and spit on him, and when the guards pushed them away they threw rocks at him. He had acquired some bumps and bruises during the trip, but the most serious damage had been to his feelings. He was angry, astonished at military men who would expose a captured military man to the populace and behave in such fashion.

He had reached Hoa Lo at dawn. He had been taken to a room and seated on a low stool facing a table covered with a blue cloth. There were two empty chairs behind the table. A small, thin Vietnamese entered. He had a long nose and two long front teeth, and the effect was a mouselike appearance. He wore green trousers and a green shirt with the sleeves rolled up—both fit him like large bags. He seated himself behind the table and half smiled at Rod. "How are you?" he asked.

"I'm okay," Rod answered.

"The bandage on your head—are you injured?" His English was better than passable.

Rod did not answer; he was tired and simply did not feel like talking to the enemy other than to provide the information required of him by the Geneva Convention. The man seemed not to notice that he had received no answer.

"You are limping very badly," he continued. "Is your leg injured?"

Rod remained silent. The man wrote in silence for a few minutes, then asked for Rod's name, rank, serial number, and date of birth. Rod gave the answers. Then the man asked, "What kind of aircraft were you flying?" Rod refused to answer, citing the Geneva Convention. The man continued with a series of questions:

"What ship are you from?

"What was your mission?

"What was your target?"

Rod declined to answer each question. In a firm but not unfriendly manner the man said, "You must answer all of the questions. It is for your own health. Your fate is in our hands." Then he started all over again, with the same questions, and got the same responses from Rod. Finally, the interrogator gathered up his papers and left, saying, "Sit and think carefully."

As soon as the cell door had been locked behind the interrogator, Rod rose, walked to the door, pulled the curtains aside from the barred windows, and looked outside. It was getting light—just twenty-four hours ago, he had been breakfasting on his ship, the aircraft carrier USS *Independence,* with his squadronmates. Now he was a prisoner in an alien land.

He did not know what now lay before him. The life behind him had been a good one. The oldest of three children, he had been born and raised in Billings, Montana. He had enjoyed the outdoors, hunting, fishing, and skiing. He had been a typical teenager, graduating from high school eager for independence and adventure. His parents had wanted him to go on to college, but tired of school, he had joined the Marine Corps. He had been a boot camp honor graduate and had thoroughly enjoyed his entire hitch. Returning home, he had been ready for more school. Enrolling in Billings's Eastern Montana College, he had helped pay his way by driving a school bus and, during summers, an oil tanker. He had enjoyed college. He had earned good grades and by the time he was a senior was vice-president of the student body, president of his fraternity, and was listed in *Who's Who in American Universities and Colleges.*

During college Rod had settled on a career; it was the military life for him—he wanted to fly. Taking his bachelor's degree in 1962, he had joined the Navy Air Corps, and again he had done well, graduating from cadet training at Pensacola as a regimental commander. But he had suffered the bitterest frustration of his life when he had failed the demanding eye examinations of his final physical prior to advancing to flying training. It had disqualified him for pilot training, but he gladly had settled for the so-called Back Seater Program, and had become a RIO, an essential nonpilot flight officer. Thus had he come to North Vietnam.

He was a military professional by now, and still had a war to fight for his country. The Code of Conduct for Members of the United States Armed Forces specifically called on him as a POW to "... *continue to resist by all means available"; to "... make every effort to escape and to aid others to escape"; to "... keep faith with my fellow prisoners"; to "... give no information or take part in any action which might be harmful to my comrades"; to "take command ... if I am senior,"* otherwise, to "... *obey the lawful orders of those appointed over me and* [to] *back them up in every way"; to "... give only name, rank, service number and date of birth, and* [to] *evade answering further questions to the utmost of my ability. I will make no oral or written statements disloyal to my country and its allies or harmful to their cause. I will never forget that I am an American fighting man, responsible for my actions, and dedicated to the principles which made my country free. I will trust in my God and in the United States of America.*''

The Code. Those were his orders now. He would live by them and, if necessary, die by them.

Rod could see no one out the windows. He shouted, "Hello, are there any Americans around?"

No answer. Rod called out several more times, but still no answer. It occurred to him that if there were other Americans within earshot they might think this an enemy trick, an attempt to get them to say something they shouldn't say. Perhaps if he did something genuinely American, an American might answer. He whistled several bars of the Marine Corps Hymn.

"Are you a Marine?" someone yelled. The voice, distinctly American, came from somewhere off in the west.

"No, I'm Navy," Rod yelled back.

"When were you shot down?" the voice asked.

"Yesterday morning."

"What is your name?"

"Knutson. Rodney Allen Knutson."

"My name is Peel. Bob Peel. Air Force. First lieutenant. Are you injured?" It was important that as many POWs as possible know the names and conditions of the Americans who entered the enemy prison system. The more who could account for one another, the more likely it seemed that the enemy would see to it that men survived.

Rod answered, "I have a swollen knee and a cut on my face . . ."

Before he could finish, a guard came running and shouting to his cell. He banged his fists on the cell door, screamed at Rod, reached through the bars, and grabbed him by the throat. Rod stepped back, out of reach, wondering at the man's behavior.

"Is there a guard out there?" Peel yelled.

"Yes," Rod answered, "but it's okay, he can't get to me."

Peel did not reply. Rod asked, "Are you still there?" No answer. "Are you still there, Peel?" Rod yelled. Still no answer. The guard kept shouting and hammering on the cell door. "Bob Peel, are you there?" Rod shouted. No answer. The guard turned and ran, still shouting. Several more times, Rod shouted for Peel, but there was no reply. Soon the guard returned with a half-dozen angry officers, including one who had interrogated him earlier.

"You must not talk to anyone else," the interrogator shouted. "It is not allowed! You must do nothing but what we tell you to do! You must sit on the stool!" He picked up the stool, placed it in a corner of the room, and ordered Rod to sit on it, facing the corner. Then he and the others left the cell, slamming and locking the door.

Rod prowled the room. He found a notebook in a table drawer; in it were a number of names: Jeremiah Denton, Everett Alvarez, Robert Shumaker, Herschel Morgan, Robert Peel, Hayden Lockhart, Raymond Vohden. He recognized two of them besides Peel: Alvarez, the first American shootdown; and Comdr. Jeremiah A. Denton, Jr., who was from Rod's own ship, *Independence*.

Rod felt duty-bound to do something about the book. All instinct insisted it would be wrong to leave undisturbed an enemy list of American names. He ripped out every page bearing an American name, tore each page into small pieces, then looked for a place to dispose of the pieces. There was none—no wastebasket, no toilet, no open window. He scattered the pieces back into the table drawer and urinated on them, hoping the urine would cause the ink to blur so that it would not be apparent as to why he had torn those particular pages out of the book.

Shortly, his interrogator returned. He seemed angry, determined to get some answers. He ordered Rod onto the stool and began asking the same questions he had asked earlier. Rod sat mute. The interrogator slammed both hands down on the table, got up, walked around the table, leaned close to Rod, and shouted that he was a "piratical air pirate," a "malicious murderer," an "imperialist aggressor." He advised, "If you don't answer the questions, you will be severely punished. You must be sincere. What kind of aircraft were you flying?"

"Lieutenant jaygee," Rod replied.

"What is your squadron?" The interrogator's voice was rising.

"Service Number: 667751."

"What was your mission?" He was nearly screaming.

"Date of birth: 29 September 1938."

"What was your target?" he shrieked.

"Knutson, Rodney Allen."

"Pick up the stool and get back in the corner! Sit and think carefully!" The interrogator stormed out of the cell.

There were two more sessions that day. In late afternoon Rod was finally taken from the cell, marched into a small courtyard and around a corner into another cell in New Guy Village. This cell was dank, perhaps eight feet wide and twelve feet long. It was lit by a dim naked light bulb which was to remain lit day and night. There was a barred window in back, about eight feet above the floor. There were two concrete bed pallets. At the foot of each was a set of built-in ankle stocks.

A small open drainage hole in the rear floor of the cell angled through a two-foot-thick wall to the outside of the building. The door to the cell was of heavy planking. There was a small hatch in the door which opened from the outside, enabling guards to look in on prisoners whenever they wished.

As Rod entered, he was given a porcelain cup, a mosquito net, and a thin straw mat, like a beach mat, to use as a mattress on the concrete bunk. Left alone, he pondered an etching—probably made with a nail—on one wall of the cell. It was an Air Force F-4, scratched into a circle perhaps five feet in diameter. He wondered who his predecessor in the cell had been. He also wondered about the prospects for escaping. He climbed onto a bunk, jumped, and got a grip on the sill of the barred window and looked outside. There was the high, thick wall, its top embedded with the shards of jagged glass, and the barbed and electrified wire. The prospects were not promising.

Then a guard came with food—that vile food. After a feeble effort to eat, Rod placed it on the opposite bunk and set about trying to figure out how to get his mosquito net up—there was no string, no nails in the wall to hang it on, and the guard outside the door ignored his pleas for help. Mosquitoes were swarming into the cell through the window, the drainage hole, a crack under the door. Finally, desperate to get away from the mosquitoes, Rod climbed under the net, propping it as best he could with his arms and knees. He was very tired—it had been about forty hours since he had risen from his comfortable bunk on *Independence*. He lay quiet, and sleep was almost upon him when the rats arrived.

They came through the drainage hole. The first one he saw was a huge, repulsive-looking animal about the size of a jackrabbit. Rod lay still, watching the thing, wondering if it was going to attack and wondering what to do if it did. The rat came close to the bunk, jumped up on it, came within inches of Rod's face. As quickly as Rod bolted upright to defend himself, the rat was gone, out the drainage hole. As quickly as he lay still again, the rat was back, and had company, a few rats no bigger than mice and a few as large as small dogs, perhaps two feet long from nose to tail tips. These were the filthiest-looking creatures Rod had ever seen, and he guessed they were disease-ridden. He had had all his shots, including plague shots, before reaching this part of the world; even so, a bite from one of them might cause much misery, even death. Had he survived thus far to succumb to a rat?

The exhaustion that was upon Rod now was such that he was willing, even eager, to take his chances sleeping with the rats in the cell. He hoped that if they made contact with him he would awaken in time to drive them off before any could bite him. He tried to sleep. The sound of the rats rattling his dishes went on and on. Finally, he crawled out from under his mosquito net. The rats raced from the room, down the drainage hole. He picked up the dishes, climbed up on his bunk, and stretching, managed to get them onto the windowsill. He climbed back under his mosquito net, confident that he had put an end to the noise.

As soon as he was still, the rats came back in. Almost immediately, the first rat leaped up the wall to the windowsill and got into the dishes, to resume its dinner. Again Rod climbed out from under his net, and the rats scampered down through the hole. He got the dishes off the windowsill, lifted the board covering his waste bucket, and dumped what was left of his dinner into it. He put the lid back on the bucket, then placed the bucket in the drainage hole, at the wall, so that the rats couldn't get through. He got back under his net and soon noted that smaller rats were getting through the two-inch opening at the bottom of his cell door. It didn't matter—he could live with them.

He would learn to live with the big ones, too, but he didn't know it yet.

———

Life in Hoa Lo was lived by the gong, a piece of resonant metal hanging from a tree and struck—many times to signal each event—with a metal rod. There was a get-up gong, about 6 AM; a chow gong, for breakfast, about 10 AM; a siesta gong, about 11 AM; a get-up gong, about 2 PM; a chow gong, for dinner, about 4 PM; and a go-to-bed gong, at about 9 PM. It had been shortly after the get-up gong on the morning of October 19 that Rod so contemptuously rebuffed the guard's attempt to have him supply military information. Now this officer, whom he had never seen before, and these five guards had entered his cell; he had immediately been asked how he had eaten his meal the previous evening, and had been proved a liar.

"For insulting the Vietnamese people," the officer said, "you must be punished."

Mentally, Rod steeled himself. He was made to lie flat on his stomach. A guard slipped a loop of clotheslinelike rope around one arm, just above the elbow, stood on the arm and pulled and cinched the rope until it could not have been made any tighter. In this manner, several such loops were tightened around each arm. With the circulation thus cut off, Rod almost immediately lost all feeling below both elbows; he could not feel or move his hands and fingers.

Then one guard stood in the middle of his back while others began drawing his elbows together behind his back—the elbows do not easily come together behind the back, so this took some work.

When the elbows were tied tightly together, he was made to sit up in his bunk and his ankles were locked into the stocks at the foot of the bunk. The officer delivered a brief lecture about throwing away good food and demanded that Rod apologize to the Vietnamese people.

"Do you apologize to the Vietnamese people?" he asked.

Rod sat silent, stared straight ahead. The anger was mounting again, that these people would treat a prisoner of war in such fashion, but now he was apprehensive too—how far would they go? He was convinced that what was happening had nothing to do with his having thrown away food, or stabbed a pen through a piece of paper, or anything else he had done to show displeasure at their behavior. These "offenses" were to be used to extract something far more important from him than a mere apology. But what?

He recalled from his survival training that, generally, captors who punish and torture prisoners of war eventually give up on men who refuse to break, but continue so long as they believe there is a chance that a man might yield. Rod was determined to impress upon them that time spent with him would be wasted.

The officer barked instructions to one of the guards, who stepped in close to the bunk and slapped Rod, hard, with an open palm to the side of the face.

"Do you apologize to the Vietnamese people?" the officer repeated.

Rod remained mute. Another hard slap, from another guard, on the other side of his face.

"Apologize!" the officer demanded. Rod kept his silence, staring ahead. Another slap. Another demand for an apology. No acknowledgment. The tempo and strength of the blows increased. Soon the two guards were curling their fingers inside the palms of their hands. In addition to hitting him on his face, they were hitting him on his head and on his ears, and they were ramming the heels of their hands under his jawbone and chin. Rod, who had done some college boxing, rolled with these punches as best he could, tried to protect his ears by holding them down against his shoulders, and concentrated on keeping his face devoid of expression.

The session had lasted for some minutes when the officer directing it stopped it, leaned close, and said, "You insult the Vietnamese people. I spit on you!" He spit in Rod's face—and, at last, the anger boiled over.

Rod spit a full measure of bloody saliva back into the officer's face. The officer backed off, wiping his face and speaking angrily to the guards. Rod knew things were about to get worse, but he was satisfied that he was giving them no reason to think him an easy mark.

The guards swarmed in around him. Three held onto him at the shoulders and arms. The other two stood in front and took turns smashing their fists into his face as hard as they could. They broke his nose* and several teeth—the sides of the front teeth were in slivers, and once, when his jaw was slammed upward and sideways, he felt the side of a molar break off. After Rod had been hit perhaps forty times, the officer called off the guards.

The ankle stocks were opened and Rod was turned over on his stomach. Then his ankles were locked back in the stocks. He lay with his face turned toward the officer. He saw a guard enter the cell with a bamboo club about three feet long and two and a half inches in diameter.

"Are you going to apologize to the Vietnamese people and admit to your mistake?" the officer asked shrilly.

Rod lay silent. The officer signaled and the guard with the bamboo club brought it down hard across his buttocks.

"Apologize!"

No answer. Another blow.

---

*More than seven years later, X rays at Oak Knoll Naval Hospital, Oakland, California, confirmed that Knutson's nose had been broken. It had healed itself.

"Apologize!"

No answer. Another blow.

The demands for an apology became louder, and came closer and closer together. The guard kept laying it on with the bamboo club, and the awful pain seemed to double with each blow. Rod was having trouble keeping his composure now—the spirit did not want his tormentors to have the satisfaction of seeing him cry out in agony, but the flesh was weakening. The beating went on and on, and the officer leaned close. "You must cry out in pain, to show your suffering," he hissed.

Rod had taken about twenty blows by the time he knew he could no longer keep the pain from showing. He lifted his head and turned it toward the wall, so that the officer could not see him grimacing and crying. The guard kept on beating him, and Rod could see the blood spattering onto the wall—the seat of the heavy flight suit had not even been torn, yet so much blood had welled up on his shredded buttocks that it was coming through the suit. He was frightened now; he had never known such pain in his life. The beating continued, and he wondered desperately what he could do to get them to stop.

At last, he screamed a long, loud scream. Immediately, the officer halted the beating, ordered the guards from the room, and followed them out. Rod was left alone, lying on his stomach, locked in the ankle stocks and tied in the ropes.

He lay quiet for several minutes, trying to catch his breath and gather his wits, trying to comprehend the brutalities that were being visited upon him. He had never even dreamed of such pain as he had suffered, and it would not recede, he could not get rid of it. But suddenly he realized that the pain he was feeling was not in his buttocks, but in his arms, shoulders, and chest cavity; it was being inflicted by the ropes that had been tightened around his upper arms and then used to tie his elbows together behind his back. He tried to roll onto one shoulder, to put pressure on it and ease the tension of the ropes. He was able to stay that way only very briefly—the pain was so intense that he could not bear to stay in one position for more than a few seconds.

No one came to the door to look in on him, and the dreadful certainty grew that they meant to leave him like this. He fought silently with the terrible pain as long as he could. Then, when he was sure he could no longer retain his sanity without doing so, he began screaming. He cried and pleaded for help. He shrieked obscenities at his captors. He prayed and counted and screamed and cried until his voice was gone. Then he lay silent again, writhing in an agony he would never have believed men could inflict on other men.

After about two hours a guard came into the cell, unlocked the stocks, and made Rod turn around and sit up, on the bloody pulp of his buttocks. The pain was excruciating, but nothing compared to the horror of pain that still tore at his chest and shoulders. The guard got behind him and let out the ropes binding his elbows together until the elbows were about two inches apart—but he did not loosen the ropes that had been tightened as nearly as possible to the bones of the upper arms. As soon as he left the cell, Rod lay back and rolled to one shoulder—the loosening of the bindings around his elbows had relieved the pain slightly, and he hoped he could work the ropes still looser. Suddenly, the guard charged back into the room, angrily pulled Rod upright, and several times hit him in the face. He indicated that Rod was not to lie down and not to sleep.

Rod's eyes were swelling shut, and he could feel a rawness and swelling over his whole face. His tongue was split and bleeding, but with it he could feel his shattered teeth and split lips—the lips were caked with blood. So were the nostrils. He tried to get his hands in position to work at the bindings at the elbows, but to no avail. Even if he could have reached the bindings, he could not have done anything with them, for his hands were useless—neither hands nor fingers gave the slightest response to commands from the brain. They were bloated, had turned coal black, and hung useless—it was as though these parts of him were dead.

And so he sat up, enduring his bloody agony. Late that morning a tray of food and a jug of water were brought in and placed on the opposite bunk out of his reach. The food didn't interest him, but he had never known such a thirst. He would have given much for the water—but not what this enemy wanted. A few hours later the food and water were taken away. Occasionally he would try to lie back on one shoulder and rest, but each time he did so a guard would rush in, pull him upright, and smash him in the face two or three times. He sat up all day and all night. He was determined not to yield and to survive. But it occurred to him that the status of some who had been shot down was unknown, and that if his captors killed him, either accidentally or intentionally, no one would ever know whether he had died in an aircraft or a prison camp.

He no longer had the use of his mosquito net, and the mosquitoes that swarmed in at dusk added to the intensity of his misery. He worried about the rats that came in again during the night—would they smell the blood and come after him? He worried about infection. At times he became so frightened that he found himself trembling. Then he would compose himself and concentrate on the business at hand—surviving, keeping his sanity, not breaking. He had to keep his bloodied head moving against his shoulders constantly, to wipe away the feasting mosquitoes. He felt the rats when they jumped up on his bunk, brushed against him, ran across his legs—he kept trying to make sudden movements to drive them away, but as strength ebbed it became more and more difficult to do so.

The next morning his ankles were removed from the stocks, and a guard indicated that he was to get off his bunk and follow him. Blind, Rod could not see to follow. For several minutes the guard tried to force his swollen eyelids open with his fingers. Finally, he locked Rod's ankles back in the stocks and left him. He sat alone all that day. Occasionally, he tried to lie back and rest, but each time a guard would come up and jerk him upright and slap him or punch him in the face. A few times a guard came in and took out his water jug, emptying it just outside his cell, where he could hear the water splashing to the floor. Then he would noisily refill the jug from some nearby tank and return it to the cell.

By the next morning, October 21, the swelling around the eyes had diminished enough so that Rod could see out of his left eye. A guard took him out of the stocks, loosened his ropes, and ordered him to follow. Painfully, he climbed down off his bunk and found that he could not straighten up. For two days and nights he had been sitting upon the torn mass of his buttocks, and a huge scab had congealed itself into the flight suit. At best, he could not raise himself out of a severe stoop. Also, the forty-eight hours in the ankle stocks, which were built a few inches up from the level of the bunk, had kept a back pressure on his knees, and they were swollen and did not bend easily. So walking was precarious. He could not support himself with his arms and hands—these were still loosely tied, and he had no control over them anyway; they flopped about uselessly, like alien members of his body. Within a few minutes he began to wish they did not belong to him, for as the blood began to force its way back through his forearms and hands, he learned a throbbing new agony, similar to but far more intense than the pain that comes of blood recirculating through a frostbitten member.

He was taken to an interrogation in the first cell he had been in. The mousy-looking interrogator was sitting behind the table. Rod refused to answer all the same questions that had been put to him before. He was taken back to his cell and again locked into the ankle stocks, his arms tied as tightly as possible behind him. Soon he was screaming again against the pain in his chest cavity and shoulders. After about two hours the bonds were loosened slightly and he was left alone for another two hours. Late in the afternoon he was taken to another interrogation. Again he refused to answer any questions.

"You will be punished until you apologize to the Vietnamese people," the mousy-looking one told him, "and until you cooperate and show your sincerity." He was put back into the stocks and ropes.

On the morning of October 22, he was again brought to interrogation and warned that he would be punished more severely if he continued to refuse to answer questions.

"I am not going to answer your questions," Rod said. "I am not required to, by international law. You are abusing me. You are violating every international precept concerning the treatment of prisoners of war."

"You are *not* a prisoner of war, you are a war criminal!" the mousy one shouted. "Your fate is in the hands of the Vietnamese people! Get out!"

As Rod turned to leave the room, the interrogator called the guard back to say something to him. Rod shuffled away hurriedly to a water tank across the hallway from his cell. He had not had any water in nearly four days and nights; his mouth and throat were parched, his beaten lips scabby and swollen. He found a half coconut shell floating in the tank. He reached for it, but his swollen, black hands and fingers would not function. The guard was running after him, and he was frantic somehow to get some water up to his lips. Finally, he got the coconut shell between the heels of his hands and scooped up some water. The guard was nearly upon him, and there was no time to drink—he threw the water up to his face. He caught some in his mouth, but most of it splashed over his face—it had just been boiled, to make it drinkable, and was still hot enough to burn. Now the guard was pounding him in the middle of his back; then, as Rod turned, he smashed him in his face. He locked him back in the stocks and tied him into the ropes for two more hours. Then another interrogation.

It went on like that for endless days and nights. Once Bob Peel came to the water tank outside Rod's cell. In a loud voice he told

Rod, "I am pretending to talk to the guard. Do not talk to me, but if the answer is yes, cough twice. If the answer is no, cough once. Are you okay?"

Rod took this as an inquiry as to whether he was dying; he did not think he was dying, so he coughed twice.

"Okay," said Peel. "I have left a note for you under the stool in the bath. Pick it up the next time you go to bathe."

Although he was not able to tell Peel he was in no position to go anywhere, Rod wanted him to know that he had the message. He coughed twice.

At some point in the kaleidoscoping days and nights of interrogation and pain, Peel was back, his voice full of consternation. "I see you have not found the note," he said to Rod. "Did you look for it?"

Rod coughed once—no, he had not looked for it.

Peel, who had no idea of Rod's situation, was confused. "It is under the stool," he snapped. "Look for it!"

During this time a fear unlike any he had ever imagined began growing in Rod. This fear was not of death, but of life—he actually became afraid that his torturers would not kill him, but would keep him alive and keep torturing him. He felt himself weakening, wondering what meaningless thing he could say or do to get them to stop the torture. Then, each time they locked him in the stocks and tied the pain back into his chest and shoulders, he would tell himself that he could hang on at least until the next interrogation. Then, at that next interrogation, the sight of the hate-ridden little mouse of an interrogator would bolster his determination to keep going, to take their worst through one more torture session.

On the morning of October 25, the interrogator told Rod that he could waste no more time with him, and that the high command had given him permission to take whatever measures were necessary to secure his cooperation. "Will you cooperate?" he asked.

"I have already told you everything I can," Rod replied. "I have nothing more to say."

There was a long coil of rope on the interrogation table. The mousy one handed this coil to the guard and gave him some instructions in Vietnamese. The guard took him back to his cell, made him lie face down on the bunk, locked his ankles into the stocks, and bound him tightly again at the elbows. The long tail of the rope that was binding the elbows was then passed over a chain hook embedded in the ceiling, then pulled around one of the bars in the window. The guard then began hoisting Rod toward the ceiling. He lifted him until his knees could only brush the bunk, and he could barely touch it with his forehead or the tip of his nose. It was not possible for him to relieve any weight.

Rod could not believe this new pain—shrieking through every fiber, penetrating and clinging from the top of his head to the tips of his toes. There was no getting used to it. It got worse with every passing second. Rod was certain that his shoulders were being torn from their sockets. This time he was able to hold his silence for only a few seconds. He began screaming and crying. After a few minutes a guard walked in, looked at him, turned and walked out again, and Rod went on screaming and crying until he had no voice left and until the tears would not come anymore; then, noiselessly and tearlessly, he went on screaming and crying.

After a while a guard took him down, untied him, took him out of the ankle stocks and to another interrogation. He was so full of pain and the memory of it that he was quivering and shaking, so hoarse from screaming and crying that he had difficulty speaking. He managed to convey to the mousy one that he was ready to talk, but that first he needed food and water. A guard brought a banana and a half cup of water. He ate and drank slowly, giving his ravaged body a long time to absorb the intake, and giving himself time to collect his wits. The interrogator and an older, more dignified-looking Vietnamese waited. Then the mousy one asked, "What kind of aircraft were you flying?"

"I'm not going to answer that question," Rod said.

"You said you would talk."

"I'm not going to talk."

The interrogator spoke to the guard, who picked up the coil of rope and began escorting Rod out of the room again. But he had reached his limit; at this point he could accept no more torture. He needed time, and at this moment his body could buy him no more time. He had to change his tactics, talk, tell lies. He knew that if he were found out he would be tortured again, but he needed time. "Wait a minute," he said. "I'll talk to you."

"What kind of aircraft were you flying?"

"An F4H." The fact that his aircraft had been an F4B had been stenciled on all the flight and survival gear they had confiscated;

moreover, the H model had been discontinued years earlier. But his interrogator accepted the answer happily.

"Who was with you in the airplane?"

"You have already captured him. You know the answer to that question. I don't have to give it to you."

"But what is his name? I must know that you are being sincere."

"But you already know the answer to that question; I don't think it's necessary that I answer."

"What was your job in the aircraft?"

"I was an observer."

The interrogator began writing industriously. "What does an observer do?"

"First of all, I am not a regular crewman. I am a recreation officer. The man who was supposed to fly in that airplane was sick, so I took his place."

"What did you do?"

"Looked for other airplanes, and looked to see if any bullets went by. Things like that."

The interrogator wrote all of this down. He translated everything into Vietnamese for the older man at the table, who listened intently and nodded. "What does a recreation officer do?" he wanted to know.

"On the aircraft carrier," Rod explained, "there is a very large swimming pool. It is my responsibility to keep the swimming pool full of water and to make sure the water is the proper temperature so that people don't get cold. And I play records, music, over the loudspeaker."

The interrogator accepted these preposterous answers without batting an eye. "Records?" he said wonderingly. "Why do you not use tapes?"

"Tapes?" Rod said, feigning surprise. "No one on an aircraft carrier has ever heard of tapes." The interrogator seemed delighted at the superiority of Vietnamese technology. Rod thought he had an accurate measure of his interrogator's ignorance now. He relaxed, and his spirits began to rise.

"You are from Montana," the interrogator said. "Tell me, what does your father do there? Is he a peasant? Is he a farmer?"

Rod was surprised that the enemy knew he was from Montana; he had no idea how they had acquired this information, or how extensive their knowledge was of his personal life. He decided to find out. His family—father, mother, brother, and sister—lived in Billings, and his father was a traveling salesman. He decided to lie about it. He confided that his father was a chicken farmer, and that his family lived in a village called Farm District Number One.

These answers pleased the interrogator and affected his attitude toward Rod. It was obvious that he felt he had accomplished a great deal by finally getting the stubborn Montanan to talk, and that he wanted to keep him talking; he was handling him with kid gloves now, smiling pleasantly and letting the conversation flow. "Tell me about yourself," he said. "Did you have a job while you were going to school?"

"Yes," Rod replied, "I was a truck driver."

"Oh, a truck driver! Did you drive an Army truck?"

"No, I drove a peanut truck."

"What did you do with the peanuts?"

"I sold the peanuts to basketball players."

"Who were your friends while you were growing up?"

"I didn't have any friends. I lived out in the country, in Farm District Number One, where there were no other children."

"Who did you play with?"

"I played with myself. And when I got tired of playing with myself, I played with my dog."

After about two hours the interrogation ended. The mousy one said, "I must check all of your answers. If you have not been sincere, you will be punished again."

This frightened Rod. He had given so many ridiculous answers that would be easy to prove were lies.

He was returned to his cell, where a meal and a jug of water were waiting for him.

That afternoon he was taken to the bath area. He was given a small bar of lye soap which, he was told, was for washing his clothes, his dishes, and his body, and which was to last him for a month; a tube of toothpaste three inches long and three-quarters of an inch in diameter, which had to last him a month; a cheap toothbrush that had to last a year; a towel fourteen inches long and ten inches wide; and a pair of blue and white striped pajamas.

The bathhouse had been ambitiously named. There was no tub or shower, only a cold water faucet and a pan on the floor. Rod could not get his flight suit off. It had welded into the enormous scab on his buttocks. The guard yanked at it, tried to tear it off, but stopped when he saw the agonizing pain this was causing. He left, returned with a large dishpan of warm water, got Rod to sit in it, and as the water cooled he kept replacing it with warm water. Rod sat in the warm water for about two hours before he could get the flight suit off. Then the guard swabbed Rod's haunches with a red liquid disinfectant and applied a gauze bandage, and Rod put on his pajamas.

While he was alone in the bathhouse, Rod sneaked over to four privy holes, reached down through them with his bloated, numb hands, and felt around for Peel's note. He could not find it.

That afternoon he went through another two-hour interogation. The mousy one was gone—Rod would never see him again. His interrogator now was the distinguished-looking older man who had earlier sat in as an observer, for whom the mousy one had translated everything into Vietnamese. Rod had assumed the man knew no English, but he was far better with the language than the mousy one had been. And he was very friendly. He advised Rod that he had checked out the answers he had given that morning and that some of them were not correct. "You have lied," he said.

Rod felt a thrill of fear. He was not ready for more torture; not yet. The interrogator asked many of the same questions that had been asked earlier, and Rod gave the same answers. The interrogator did not press him on any of them. Relieved, Rod went on in the same vein, remembering what he had learned in survival training, to keep his untrue stories simple and easy to remember as the interrogator continued to press him for military and biographical information.

That night Rod was given a blanket and means for rigging up his mosquito net. He crawled under it eagerly; this was to be the first night he had been allowed any sleep in more than a week. But he lay awake for hours, almost in tears—he had never been so disappointed in himself. They had broken him, made him talk! He knew he had given them absolutely nothing of value; yet he could not dissuade himself that he had let his country down.

He was interrogated sixteen times during the remaining days of October. Every other day he was allowed to go to the bath area. On his second trip he found Bob Peel's note. The first sentence gave him the first laugh he had had in a long time. "The treatment here is pretty good," Peel had written. "They don't mistreat you too awfully much. . . ."

Rod decided that Peel and his companions must be some pretty tough nuggets if they thought this kind of treatment was pretty good.

———

It seems clear that when Hanoi began collecting American prisoners of war, it did not know what to do with them or about them. The Communists were a long time coming to a decision. Fourteen months elapsed between the capture of Ev Alvarez and the brutalization of Rod Knutson, the first POW to undergo severe torture. Thereafter, many times over a period of many years, many prisoners were told by their interrogators that Hanoi was well aware that it could never defeat the United States on the battlefield, but that it fully expected to win the war—it would win decisively on the propaganda front. It would bring a weight of world and American opinion against the American war effort in Vietnam, and in time that weight of opinion would prove to be irresistible. So it was that at this point Hanoi set out to enlist the aid of its American prisoners on what it deemed to be the war's most important front.

7

Hanging In There

One day in October, Robbie Risner's cell door opened to admit Dog, the camp commander, and a stout, bull-necked, scowling civilian. The civilian strode about the cell, looking it and the prisoner over. Finally, he stood before Robbie and snarled, "So—you are also Korean hero!"

"I cannot answer that question," Robbie said, "that's military information."

The civilian's neck swelled and his face reddened. He shouted, "We are preparing for your kind! You will soon see that you will answer our questions!" He turned and left the cell, Dog at his heels.

Toward the end of the month Ron Storz returned from interrogation to urgently warn Risner, "They've found everything! If you've got anything you don't want them to have, get rid of it. Pass the word."

Robbie had no time to do anything but fill his communications holes with rocks, soap, and pieces of bone he had salvaged from meals and to wonder frantically what had happened.

In a surprise inspection the Vietnamese had discovered the communications holes between Storz's cell and the one beyond it. Ron had managed to eat several Risner policy papers, but the inspectors had found one in the next cell. Using it as a search checklist, they were combing every cell in the Zoo for the materials the SRO had directed his men to seek and save. The POWs lost everything they had collected, every piece of wood, wire, metal, soap, string, every nail. Communications holes were being found everywhere.

Ron Storz had been missing for three days by the time he got back and warned Risner. He had been taken into a bare, lonely cell somewhere which seemed to be inhabited by every mosquito in Southeast Asia. He had been stripped down to his shorts and made to sit on a stool, and it had been demanded of him that he betray Risner as the organizer and leader of prisoner resistance. He had refused to do so, and now, as Robbie filled up their communications holes, Ron tapped a question: "Have you confessed?"

"Never!" Risner replied.

"Neither will I" tapped Storz. "G B U." ("God Bless You.")

"G B U," Robbie answered. Then guards arrived and took him from his cell. He was brought to a room in the Barn away from the others. He was seated on a stool before a table. On the table were pencil and paper. Storz, he was advised, had told all, and now it was required that Risner confirm what Storz had admitted—that Risner was the instigator of prisoner resistance, that he had set himself up as the camp commander, that he was organizing a revolt by the prisoners, and that he had been sent to this place by the American government to do these things.

He was left alone to write this confession. Each hour, guards entered to see if he had done so. When after twenty-four hours Robbie had not lifted pencil to paper, he was taken to the camp commander's office in the headquarters building, called Gook House by the POWs, at the northeast corner of the camp. The camp commander was now a man the prisoners named Fox; he had superseded Dog, who was still on hand as deputy. Fox was middle-fortyish, perhaps five feet seven inches tall, weighed about 160 pounds, and kept his thick, black hair combed straight back. "You will be severely punished," he told Risner, "unless you admit to all of your mistakes. Here is a pencil and paper. Write!"

"I will not write," Robbie said.

"You know you were breaking the camp regulations. You were communicating, and telling others to resist." He waved the length of toilet paper containing Robbie's policy. "From now on, you will not make a sound. You will not communicate. You will not talk. You will not look at others. Do you understand?"

"Yes," said Robbie, "I understand. I understand that I am to be silent, like an animal, and that you are going to treat us like animals! Don't forget, someday we will tell our story to the world, and the world will know what you Vietnamese really are!"

Fox was beside himself with rage. He shouted in Vietnamese to the attending guards. He waved the SRO's policy paper at them, pointed to Risner's admonition to the POWs that one catches more flies with honey than with vinegar, and told them, "He calls you flies! *Flies!*" Then several of them came at Robbie, grabbed him, pinned his arms behind his back, held his head up.

"Open mouth!" someone ordered.

He refused to do so. Thumbs were pressed hard against his cheeks until his mouth was forced open. Then balls of crumpled newspaper were shoved into his mouth. A stick was used to shove them over his tongue and deep into his throat. Robbie felt himself gagging and panicking. He had a cold and had been having trouble breathing through his nose, and now he was unable to breathe through his mouth. More newspaper balls were pressed in, until his throat and mouth were full. He could not salivate. He was suffocating, and he was scared—the idea of dying in combat, or even of being deliberately tortured to death had never really frightened him; but somehow, the idea of dying like this, for no reason, did frighten him. He was determined not to accept such a death. He concentrated, subdued panic. By immense effort of will, he kept thrusting air from his lungs up to his throat and forced himself to take air through his swollen nasal passages, breathing slowly, carefully, evenly.

He was blindfolded, his wrists were tied tightly behind him, his ankles were bound, and he was thrown into the back of a truck. He was taken from the Zoo to Hoa Lo. There, his bindings, blindfold, and gag were removed, and he was taken into Cell #1 in New Guy Village. The stocks at the end of a cement bunk were unlocked and opened. Robbie was ordered onto the bunk, his ankles were locked into the stocks, and he was left alone. His morale had never been lower. The Zoo was no bargain, to be sure, but this lonely place was the end of the world.

———

Shortly after Risner was put in stocks, written "Camp Regulations" were posted on the inside of the door of every POW cell. According to these regulations:

> *U.S. aggressors caught red-handed in their piratical attacks against the DRV are criminals. While detained in this camp, you will strictly obey the following:*
> *1. All criminals will bow to all officers, guards and Vietnamese in the camp.*
> *2. All criminals must show polite attitude at all times to officers and guards in the camp, or they will be severely punished.*
> *3. All criminals will truthfully answer, orally or in writing, any question, or do anything directed by camp authority.*
> *4. Criminals are forbidden to attempt to communicate with each other in any way, such as signals and tapping on the walls.*
> *5. Any criminal who attempts to escape or help others to do so will be severely punished.*
> *6. Criminals who follow these camp regulations and show a good attitude by concrete acts and report all those who want to make trouble will be rewarded, and shown a humane treatment.*

There were twenty such regulations. There was no way that an American POW could adhere to them and at the same time abide by his own Code of Conduct. The regulations demanded that the prisoners commit treason, against each other and against their country. As it turned out, the Vietnamese, in promulgating these impossible regulations, were merely establishing the launching platform for a grim program; they were providing themselves with an excuse for punishing and torturing their American prisoners. Starting now—Rod Knutson was just coming out of the torture wringer at Hoa Lo—the Vietnamese were to apply as much punishment and torture as required to extract an apology from an American POW for having broken any of the regulations. After apologizing, the transgressor was to be afforded an opportunity to demonstrate his "sincerity" by offering something in atonement: military information; information about other POWs; written or tape-recorded statements that might persuade other POWs to cooperate, or be used in the DRV's propaganda program, or held and used later, to blackmail the prisoner for something more valuable.

Thus, by the end of October, 1965, the battle was joined in the prison camps of North Vietnam.

————

With Risner at Hoa Lo, his deputy at the Zoo, Jerry Denton, assumed command. Denton, who had been in a cell in the "Office," a sizable building facing in the south side of the swimming-pool area, was moved into the cell in the Barn that Risner had vacated. He passed the word out that Risner's policies remained in effect.

It was a time for strong leadership—and strong stomachs. The diet, a small bowl of cabbage soup twice daily, had hardly been adequate to begin with, but at least it had been hot and contained a reasonably good ratio of cabbage to liquid. But one day in late October the bowls were placed on the ground in front of the cellblocks and allowed to stand while the fall breezes cooled the soup and carried dust and grit into the bowls. When they were finally delivered, the famished prisoners found only a few scattered pieces of cabbage leaf floating in the water, and these had not been cleansed of the human excrement the Vietnamese use for fertilizer.

"That's shit!" the POWs assured each other. "They want us to eat shit!"

"Better eat it. It's all there is. We've got to keep up our strength. Maybe it's got protein."

But the foul diet was not the uppermost of SRO Denton's worries. Rough stuff was happening.

————

On November 2, Ed Davis said a prayer to his long-deceased grandmother. It was All Souls' Day, and he asked her to look after him. Just as he finished the prayer, his cell door swung open, and armed guards took him out to an interrogation. Leaving his cell, he cast a baleful glance heavenward, wondering at his ancestor's competence.

The interrogator was Rabbit. He wanted Davis's biography, first the military aspects: the ship he was from; the squadron he had been in.

"Name, rank, number, and birthdate," Ed said. "That's all you get."

"You do not have to write anything down," he was told. "Just tell us."

Ed sat mute. Rabbit kept at him for a while, then sent him back to his cell. He was put on short rations—half a cup of water and a small piece of bread. After two days there were more long hours of interrogation, this time with an officer called Frenchy, because he spoke English with a French accent. The man was intense, perhaps a bit demented. He asked the same questions Rabbit had asked, and again Ed refused to answer.

"You must answer!" Frenchy shouted. "We will make you answer!"

"Can't answer," Ed said.

He was returned to his cell, kept on starvation rations. The hunger became a torture. The aromas even from the filthy meals being served to the others had him salivating.

Two more days and Ed went back to interrogation. The same questions were asked, and again he refused to answer them. He was made to stand facing against a wall, with his hands raised as high as he could get them. After a while, his arms felt as though they were crushing down into their own sockets. Armed guards kept watch, urged him to keep them high He "held up the wall" all that night. *I'm a test case,* he thought. *They want information from us that they are not entitled to, and they picked me to see how much they have to do to a man to get what they want. I've got to hold on! I've got to convince them it takes too much, that it isn't worth it!*

Sometime after dawn he was returned to his cell and his wrists were cuffed together in front of him. Except for the few minutes each day that it took him to eat his sparse rations, Ed wore these cuffs day and night. He was exhausted, starving. He wondered how long the Vietnamese meant to go on with him.

———

Hard times caught up with Bob Shumaker, too. One day in early November he was pressing against his cell door, in the Barn, trying to identify passing POWs, when the rickety door gave way. He was accused of trying to escape and thrust into the blackest darkness he had ever known. The room was in a theater the prisoners called the Auditorium, facing the northeast side of the swimming-pool area. Quite literally, Bob could not see his hand in front of his face. He waited for his eyes to accustom themselves to the pitch darkness; but after a while he realized that his eyes were not going to penetrate this blackness. Slowly, cautiously, he moved along a wall, feeling ahead of himself with his hands. The stench of urine and excrement was nearly overpowering, and as he moved he felt webs wrapping themselves about him, and had to keep brushing crawling things off himself. There were larger things, too, that ran and scurried.

The room was large, perhaps fifteen feet square. Aside from a small waste bucket, there was nothing in it. No bunk, no pallet, no mat to sleep on. Only himself, the bucket, and the vermin.

He was not allowed out of this place, not to bathe or to clean his bucket. Guards emptied the bucket once each day but did not clean it.

The pitch blackness soon induced vertigo. He was unable to see anything of the world around him, but he seemed constantly to be spinning and falling through it. The intensity of the vertigo varied, and at its worst brought on a violent nausea. He vomited up the rotten meals that were served to him, and added much bile and blood. He tried to vomit into the bucket, but there was not much room, for now a terrible dysentery took hold, and the once-per-day emptying of the bucket was not enough. Urine, watery excrement, and vomit splashed about on the floor. Often, he did not know whether it would be best to squat over the bucket, for the dysentery, or to hunch over it, for the vomiting. Once, squatting, he became so dizzy that he fell away from the bucket and onto the floor, knocking himself out.

The Vietnamese made no attempt to clean the stinking room nor to help Bob clean it. He crawled along the edges of the room, finding pieces of straw. These he fashioned into a fragile broom and kept trying to sweep his own filth into a corner, away from himself.

He lost track of time. He lay on the floor for long periods, drifting in and out of sleep, unable to think of anything beyond the misery that claimed him. Then, after a very long time, someone came and gave him some pills. Whether or not they helped, the dysentery ran its course. He felt better. He was able to contemplate his empty, black world, and to wonder if he would ever leave this place.

———

At Hoa Lo, Rod Knutson's wounds were healing rapidly. This surprised him, because of the severity of the beatings and torture that had been administered to him and the fact that he had received no medical attention. Scabs had formed around his upper arms, where the ropes had been, even though the sleeves of his flight suit had been down during the rope torture. His buttocks, where he had been beaten so mercilessly with the bamboo club, were covered with a huge scab.

In the middle of the night on October 29, the guards entered his cell, awakened him, ordered him to roll up his gear in his blanket—his cup, toothbrush, toothpaste, towel, and mosquito net. He was blindfolded and marched to a cell in Heartbreak Hotel. The next morning he awakened to the sound of a cell door opening and feet shuffling. He got down on his hands and knees, looked under a gap at the bottom of his own cell door, and saw a set of crutches emerge from the cell directly across the corridor. Then came one foot and the other, the latter with a cast on it. He could not see who the injured man was. It was Jim Stockdale; he was being taken to the bath area. Rod did not know Stockdale, and he had no way of identifying the owners of the several other pairs of feet that were escorted past his door after Stockdale had been locked up again.

Other eyes watched as Rod was taken last to the bath area. There he found a faucet, a pipe with a shower head on it, and nearly zero water pressure. Locked in his cell again, he heard the guard depart. Then someone whistled "Mary Had a Little Lamb . . ."

"Roger," said an American voice, "it's clear."

Americans! Rod had to see them. He looked around his cell, spotted the makeshift wooden cover over the transom, climbed up on the end of his bunk, clawed at it, finally ripped it off. There, grinning at him from a transom diagonally across the corridor, was Lt. (j.g.) Porter Halyburton, a squadronmate and friend. Unbeknown to Knutson, Halyburton had been shot down on the same mission. Except for Stockdale, with his broken leg and shoulder, the others were up in their transoms, too: Lt. (j.g.) Duffy Hutton, also off Rod's ship, and Air Force Capt. Tom Collins. Rod learned that his pilot, Ralph Gaither, had been in this cellblock but had been taken elsewhere.

"You look a little beat up," Halyburton observed.

Rod described what had happened to him since he had arrived in this prison. The others listened in appalled silence. Some of them had been locked in stocks for brief periods after having been caught communicating, but none had imagined the kind of bestiality Knutson was describing. When he finished his tale of horror, they were silent for a while. Then they began discussing it. To Rod's amazement, a consensus began to develop that he had brought the unspeakable treatment upon himself, that his attitude toward his captors had been more belligerent, more aggressive than necessary.

Rod was deeply hurt. He believed—*knew*—that he had done a good job, had performed as American military men are expected to perform. The enemy had resorted to barbarism to extract information, violating not only the Geneva Convention, but every rule of civilized behavior.

Rod was proud of his performance, but at length he turned for an opinion to SRO Stockdale, who had listened carefully to the exchanges. "I think you did a fine job, Rod," Stockdale said. "I think you took the right approach. Give them nothing; make them take it from you, and make sure they take nothing of value. You did just fine. Hang in there."

Until he heard these encouraging words, Rod had not realized how much he needed them.

Jim Stockdale had a feeling there was a lot more "hanging in there" that would have to be done. He had reached Heartbreak Hotel on October 25 after having spent a month in a hospital. The hospital had been full of medical amateurs who did not seem to know how to give injections without inflicting pain on the patient. The place had also been filthy. Once Jim felt constrained to ask the doctors if the rats that freely roamed the premises might be rabid. He was assured matter-of-factly that rabies occurred only in European rats.

The doctors proved incompetent to build him the new left knee he required. His unrepaired leg was encasted, he was issued a pair of ill-fitting crutches, and was returned to the prison system.

The depression induced by the sight of the Heartbreak dungeon dissipated immediately at the sound of the first American voice Jim had heard since his capture. "Goddamn this hard bed!" called out Porter Halyburton. Stockdale could have kissed him. Gloomy as the setting was, it was good to be back among Americans. Communications were easy, and Jim found that most of the POWs had been interrogated a number of times. These quizzes by their captors had been concerned mainly with biographical trivia; at the time, no one in Heartbreak had been seriously mistreated.

Jim studied the preposterous Vietnamese regulations that had been affixed to the inside of his cell door and pondered the options short of treason available to a POW. There really were none, he concluded. Stockdale believed in the Code of Conduct; he believed it unreasonable for a military officer to avoid his responsibilities to others, and the worst imaginable reason for doing so would be to minimize the risk of harm to oneself. Leadership and communications were the blood and sinew of survival and resistance. Now, having heard Knutson's frightening story, he knew that the Americans in captivity and the Code of Conduct were in for a long time of testing.

The POWs were not issued special clothing for the winter of 1965–1966. They continued to wear light cotton pajamas, and most stayed huddled day and night under light cotton blankets. Only a few had been allowed to keep their socks, and only about half had been issued sandals. The November chill penetrated to the marrow, and at the Zoo blood ran even colder as new arrivals from Hoa Lo spread word of the torture that had been inflicted on Rod Knutson.

Zoo SRO Jerry Denton had known Knutson back at the Oceana, Virginia, Naval Air Station, and aboard *Independence*. He felt sick at what he had heard. His concern intensified for young Ed Davis, in the next cell. Davis continued to give the enemy nothing, and the Vietnamese kept increasing the pressure on him. He was kept on starvation rations. Once, Denton caught a glimpse of him and was shocked; everyone was losing a lot of weight, but Davis looked like his own skeleton. In this condition he was being denied sleep. A number of times he had been taken to interrogation and had been made to "hold up the wall" throughout the night. Now Ed's wrists had been locked tightly behind his back in torture cuffs, a devilish, pain-producing device that could be ratcheted through skin and sinew down to bone. With these "hell cuffs" on he could not lie back and go to sleep. In addition, his ankles were shackled together in "traveling irons"—the name was ironic—a very heavy iron bar ran through brackets at the backs of the U-shaped shackles and the sharp edge of the bar rested atop the heels. It was agonizing to try to walk in this rig, and agony was the goal.

Yet Ed's spirits remained high. At interrogations Rabbit and Frenchy would ask, "Is your mind corrected?"

"Nope," he would answer, "not if that means, am I going to answer your questions."

The torture cuffs hurt. They were not ratcheted down to the point where they caused the hands to go numb; only to the point where they caused great pain. Denton, whose admiration for the younger man kept mounting by the day, kept tapping to him, keeping him company, encouraging him, praying with him, telling him jokes and stories he hoped would get his mind off his suffering. He would end sessions by tapping, ". . . brought to you by the makers of Denton's Odorless Honeybuckets, the Honeybucket with a lid . . ."

As the mistreatment continued, Denton, worried for Davis's survival, suggested, "Maybe you should consider giving them some kind of answer, something that doesn't mean anything but will satisfy them."

Davis would have none of this and replied hotly, "I don't think that way, sir, and I can't believe anyone else would, either."

Denton said, "I just want you to consider the idea. We have to find the best way to get you out of this situation."

Chagrined at his outburst, Davis decided to try Denton's suggestion. He told his interrogators he would answer one of their questions. They waited expectantly. "I started school," he confessed, "when I was six years old."

The interrogators were delighted with this intelligence. It was clear they felt they had achieved significant progress with Davis, that now that he had talked, he could be persuaded to keep talking. They fired more questions.

"You bastards," Ed said, "I told you I would answer one question. That's all."

Later he reported to Denton, "I answered a question, and it didn't stop anything. It was like, 'Now we've started and we can go from here.' Sir, it doesn't work!"

Ed found a nail and was able to manipulate it with his fingers into the lock of the cuffs behind him. He tapped to Denton, "A miracle!" He had been saying a rosary, and on the last "amen" the nail had found the lock release and the cuffs had broken open. He locked them back on, then snapped them open again, several times, assuring himself that he could get in and out of the cuffs at will. Now, able to relieve his wrists of pain and to get back into the cuffs whenever he heard guards approach, he could lie back, rest, resist indefinitely.

Denton worried, too, about Ens. Ralph Gaither, Rod Knutson's pilot. Every few days there were POW reports of guards marching Gaither through the yard, blindfolded and with his hands cuffed behind him. No one in the Barn knew what they were doing with him. Denton surmised that he was getting the same treatment Ed Davis was getting. He wondered why the V were concentrating on the young men; Gaither was the most junior officer at the Zoo and Davis was senior only to Gaither. Perhaps they thought the young men would be the easiest to break; or that the seniors would cave in more easily after their younger, stronger juniors were tamed. Jerry felt helpless about Gaither. There was no way to offer him moral support. He prayed for him.

An observation hole Ralph Gaither had cut into his cell had been discovered. He had been before Rabbit, who offered to let him atone by supplying biographical information. Ralph declined. At a signal from Rabbit, a guard standing behind the stool on which Ralph was seated delivered a roundhouse open-palm slap to the right ear. The blow sent him sprawling, stunned him. Slow getting up, he was yanked back onto the stool and asked the same questions, again and again. Each time he refused to answer, he received a stinging, open-palm blow over an ear. He knew that they were trying to break his eardrums, and the slaps were so hard that he could not understand why they did not break. But there was no blood; the eardrums remained intact. His ears rang and his head ached. The slapping went on and on.

He was brought back many times for more of the same. Often, Rabbit made him kneel on the floor for hours at a time, with his wrists manacled painfully behind him in torture cuffs. He answered no questions. Once, Rabbit screamed that Gaither had to die—that it made no difference to the DRV; that Hanoi would simply explain that he had died of illness in captivity, and that no one would ever be the wiser. Then he had a guard hold a rifle barrel to Ralph's temple and squeeze the trigger. It clicked against an empty chamber.

Finally, Rabbit seemed to give up on Gaither. His hands were cuffed behind him and he was left alone in his cell.

All the while, the Vietnamese were transforming the Zoo into a prison camp. In all the buildings brick walls were built in the large rooms, dividing them into numerous small cells. Windows were bricked up. Louvered French doors were replaced with doors of heavy wooden planking that bolted closed and were fitted with peepholes so that guards could look at will into any cell. The only daylight or air in these cells was the little that filtered through cracks and gaps in doors and through a single, brick-sized air vent high on outside walls. In each cell a single, naked, low-wattage light bulb hung from the ceiling and stayed lit day and night. Each cell was fitted with a small blue box containing a radio speaker. For hours each day the POWs were treated to an endless stream of propaganda.

Outside, separate toilet facilities were erected for each building. Walls went up between cellblocks and toilet areas, so that prisoners could not see each other to communicate. A wall went up around the perimeter of the camp, and sentry towers were installed. The place took on a depressing aspect of permanence.

Still, optimism kept flaring. Navy Lieut. James F. Bell (captured Oct. 16, 1965) reached the Zoo with word that spokesmen for the involved governments were talking seriously about getting the war ended. This news so excited many POWs that they made out long shopping lists of items to buy in post exchanges on the way home and traded information as to the locations of various shops in Hong Kong and Honolulu.

––––––

One morning at the Zoo the guards collected the Pigsty POWs' waste buckets and carried them behind the stable. This was unusual. Normally, one or two prisoners were made to collect the buckets and empty them in a cesspool behind the Pigsty. Guarino and Bill Franke, in the next cell, speculated that higher authority had arrived and was conducting a surprise inspection of the buckets, examining them for messages to be passed by the collecting prisoners. They were right.

Unable to find any messages in the buckets, the inspector, a short, stout party in civilian clothes and sunglasses, made straight for Guarino's cell. He was accompanied by numerous armed guards and by Dog, who ordered Larry, "Get up against the wall!"

Larry was intrigued by Dog's obsequiousness toward the civilian. He was obviously important. He strode arrogantly about the cell, staring at the walls where Larry had scratched out a cross, the Ten Commandments, and a calendar. Then, standing in front of Guarino, he shouted fiercely, "Do you know what you have done? Do you know what you have done?"

"Me?" said Larry. "I haven't done anything. I've been locked up here for five and a half months."

"You! You! You!" the man screamed. "Paahtically you! Paahtically you!"

"What are you talking about?" Larry demanded. Dog, he noted, was standing at the far wall, quivering with fright.

"You have come and murdered our children," the civilian

shouted. "Our wives. Our families. You have come to kill the Vietnamese people!" The man was beside himself, raging, and now Dog joined him and raged along with him, shouting through the spittle that formed on his lips. They railed on, threatening punishment, death. Then, suddenly, came an uproar from a cell several doors distant, a prisoner shouting, "Bo! Bo! Bo!" He wanted his waste bucket back, fast!

Larry's visitors stormed from his cell, heading for the noisy one. They flung the door open and stopped, aghast. In the middle of the floor lay a large stool. The prisoner shrugged. "I told you I needed the bo. I told you."

Speechless, the Vietnamese stalked away, their noses high in the air. Guarino wondered if it had been a diversionary action, to get them off his back? Or an act of defiance? Or simply a natural function that would not be denied? Whatever, it had certainly sent them into retreat! The phonies. They could torture men, make them live in dirt and filth, make them eat food painted with dung, let wounds fester with infection, yet this had thrown them! Guarino found himself giggling.

Within minutes, the joyous message was tapping through walls and flashing from building to building: "He shit on the floor . . . made them look at a turd . . ."

———

At Hoa Lo, Robbie Risner lived in a greater misery than he could ever have imagined for himself. An active man, the great fighter pilot had once been a rodeo rider, and was an avid outdoorsman, hunter, fisherman, golfer. He had never been comfortable sitting still long. It was bad enough to be locked in a small, dark cell, but to have both legs locked immobile, in stocks, was intolerable. He did not know how people could long retain their sanity in this situation. Claustrophobic feelings threatened; he fought off panic, reminded himself that the previous summer Larry Guarino had spent twenty-odd days in stocks and had come through it all right. There was no alternative.

So Risner would do it, too, and knew how he would do it. There was a great deal of important mental work to be done, vital personal tasks that would keep him too busy to remember that he was locked in stocks. Someday, he would have to sit down with each of his sons and help them plan their college years. There was no better time than now to get started with his share of the thinking. The first night in stocks he made plans: next morning, he would start with his oldest son, Rob, Jr., who wanted to study veterinary medicine at Oklahoma State University. Robbie, who knew something about animals, would try to help his son plan his college life. Should he live in a dormitory or a fraternity house? How much should be budgeted for food, clothing, and social activities? Should he plan to attend school during the summer months or take a break, get a job, do some traveling?

Next, he would plan schooling for each of the four younger boys. He had always hoped that some of his sons might want to go to the Air Force Academy. Perhaps it would work out that way.

The project never had a chance. It was unbearable for Robbie to dwell on thoughts of home and family. He quickly realized that he dared not do so. But how to occupy his mind, keep himself from becoming obsessed with this vile confinement?

Robbie lost himself in prayer. He blocked out large portions of his days and prayed, for his family; for other POWs; their Vietnamese captors; and finally, for strength and wisdom for himself. He did not pray for release from captivity or from the conditions of his own confinement—these matters, it seemed to him, were to be accepted and endured, and would be resolved in God's own time.

During his first three days in stocks he received no food or water. Thereafter he was favored intermittently with a small portion of bread and a cup of water—sometimes twice in a day, sometimes once, sometimes not at all. Occasionally, the guard who brought these servings would make him eat the bread first, then place the water on the opposite bunk, out of Robbie's reach, and leave it there. The parched prisoner would have to sit and look at it all day and night.

Completing his prayer schedule, Robbie would reconstruct his previous interrogation by Dog, who came from the Zoo each night to quiz him. He would try to anticipate the questions Dog would ask at the next quiz. These interrogations took place in Room 18, a few yards around a corner from his cell, and afforded brief relief from the stocks. No guards were present at these sessions, and Dog invariably opened the proceedings by assuring Risner, "You must confess to what you did in the other camp."

"I have nothing to confess," Robbie would say.

"You taught others to resist! You tried to take over the camp! You must tell us: What kind of aircraft were you flying? Where did you fly from? What targets will the Americans bomb?"

"I have nothing to say to you," Robbie would answer.

It was cold. Robbie kept a cotton blanket wrapped around himself all the time but was never able to stop shaking. He spent all his days sitting up in the bunk, from the get-up gong, at about dawn, until the go-to-sleep gong, at 9:30 or 10 PM, hoping that the effort it took to remain upright would tire him to the extent that he would be able to sleep through the night. But when he finally drifted into sleep, a violent shivering always awakened him.

He remained in the stocks and on the starvation diet. Very occasionally, he was let out for five minutes to clean his waste bucket and to wash himself. He became ill, lost control of his body functions. His pleas were ignored, and he lay in his own filth for days.

A camp radio speaker was installed next to his cell window, and the volume was turned up so as to enable people in distant places to hear it. Starting with the get-up gong, it spewed forth an unbroken stream of noise until the go-to-sleep gong. The noise came in Vietnamese and English—Communist propaganda. Also, there were long stretches of discordant Oriental music. After one day of this incessant clamor Robbie feared, seriously, for his sanity. It was worse than anything that had happened to him, even the stocks. When the thing came on again on the second morning, he went immediately, almost angrily, into prayer: *God, you are going to have to help me! You have just got to get that thing turned off. . . .*

As he continued the prayer, he became aware that the noise had stopped, that the speaker had gone silent. He kept on praying, hard, even fiercely, certain the thing would come on again momentarily, and trying to make God understand that it was crucial to His servant, Risner, that some sort of lasting, Almighty damage be done to the accursed speaker. Shortly, a group of chattering guards arrived to examine the thing, to poke and punch and fiddle with it. Robbie prayed with an intensity that almost had him sweating. At last, the guards walked away. The speaker never came on again.

It Could Never Happen to Me

November 13, 1965, was Navy Comdr. Howard E. Rutledge's thirty-seventh birthday. He was executive officer of Fighter Squadron 191, operating off the aircraft carrier USS *Bon Homme Richard*—the *Bonnie Dick*. Howie Rutledge spent part of that birthday evening reading message traffic and musing to himself over the fate of Navy Comdr. Harry T. Jenkins, skipper of Attack Squadron 163, operating off the carrier *Oriskany,* and the only American pilot downed in North Vietnam that day. He did not know Jenkins, but hoped he was okay, and felt secure in the knowledge that such a thing could never happen to him—he was too old, too experienced, too battlewise a hand for the Communist gunners.

Rutledge had good reason to feel confident. From the beginning of his career he had been on the first team. A member of the first Navy jet squadron ever committed to combat, flying F9F Panther fighters off the carrier *Valley Forge* at the outbreak of the Korean War, he had flown two complete tours without ever having been downed. The fighter pilot's feeling of invincibility, of almost contemptuous disdain for enemy antiaircraft gunners, had grown in him.

He had reached the *Bonnie Dick* on June 25, had flown more than seventy missions, and his confidence had grown. But he felt bad about Harry Jenkins, the fifty-fifth American shootdown, and he prayed God to bless him and see him through.

————

Harry Jenkins was downed on his 133rd mission. He was shot down because he, too, felt invincible. He had pitted himself so often and so successfully against enemy gunners that he had grown complacent, even careless. He was on road reconnaissance, looking for military vehicles between Dong Hoi, North Vietnam's southernmost major city, and the Demilitarized Zone (DMZ). Armed with two 1,000-pound bombs and two 500-pounders, Harry took his A4E Skyhawk down low and flew slowly, looking for traffic along a tree-covered road next to a river. Suddenly he heard a .37-mm antiaircraft gun begin firing. Looking down, he saw tracers streaming past, close on his left side.

He poured on the throttle and climbed for an overcast, at four thousand feet. The aircraft did not respond as rapidly as he would have liked, but he was not worried about it and did not bother to "jink," to keep constantly changing his heading during the climb-out. A few seconds later he was hanging in his parachute and watching his aircraft, blown into two large pieces, burning fiercely on the ground below.

Coming down, Jenkins castigated himself bitterly for his carelessness. He worried about his wife, Marjorie, in San Diego, and their three kids. There was no time to dwell on such thoughts, however; he was about to become a prisoner of war. He would just have to make the best of it.

He landed on a small rise where there was no place to hide. Within a few minutes he was captured by armed militia. He spent the next three hours under guard in a trench, watching SAR (search and rescue) aircraft from his ship roar up and down the area looking for him, old A-1 propeller aircraft that can fly low and slow. Some of these were practically driving along the roads, at altitudes of ten to fifteen feet. The enemy shredded them with defensive fire, but none were shot down.

For three nights the militia moved him from village to village, standing him in the centers of crowds and exhorting the crowds into frenzies of hatred. There was always much screaming and fist shaking, and occasionally some rock throwing, and once an old man had to be stopped from pile-driving a bamboo pole into Harry's head. He was never hurt, however, and never became terribly concerned over the hate rallies; he thought this sort of thing probably was to be expected when shot down among an undereducated, overpropagandized people.

He was delivered to the Army at Vinh. An English-speaking officer interrogated him. "Your name?"

"Jenkins, Harry T."

The officer looked up at him appraisingly. "You have escaped us many times," he said. As a squadron commander who at this early stage of the war already had flown well over a hundred missions, Harry had received some attention in the American press. His name was known to the enemy.

It took ten days to reach Hanoi. Bound and blindfolded in the backs of trucks, he had time to reflect: Harry was paying part of the price of a boyhood dream. Growing up in Suitland, Maryland, a Washington, D.C., suburb, he had worshipped naval aviators, never wanted to be anything else. The best Sunday afternoons of his boyhood had been spent with his father at Hoover Field, where the Pentagon now stands, watching airplanes take off and land. When it had rained, they had gone to the Smithsonian Institution to look at the famous airplanes there. Harry had filled his bedroom with model airplanes. On graduating from high school in 1945, he had won entry into the Navy's flying training program, had been sent off to college, and had received his wings and commission in 1948. So he had lived his dream, loving every minute of it. Even with what was happening to him now, Harry had no regrets. How many men ever got to live their dreams? It was worth it.

Jenkins reached Hoa Lo at dawn on November 23 and was taken to Room 18, the Meathook Room. He was seated on a low stool before a table, behind which sat an English-speaking Vietnamese officer whom Harry judged to be perhaps forty-five years old. This man kept chain-smoking and running his hands through bushy, graying hair. Later he learned this was Colonel Nam—Eagle. Harry made it clear he would answer no more questions. In a confident, dispassionate tone, the officer said, "We have ways to make you talk."

Harry thought he was bluffing. He took it for granted that there existed a bond of respect between professional military men of opposing forces.

Three guards took Harry to a cell. There he was made to sit on the floor. Tight-fitting, U-shaped manacles were clamped onto his ankles, from rear to front, and a long, heavy steel bar was run through brackets in front, locking them in place. The bar lay heavily, sharply atop the ankles, and now pieces of heavy lumber were tied to it, increasing the weight. Next, Harry's wrists were tied tightly behind him, and his upper arms were laced tightly together from elbows to shoulders. That done, he was left alone. Jenkins was the first senior officer to be thrust into torture immediately on arriving in Hanoi.

Harry was astounded. He could not believe the pain, or that the human body could be wrenched into such a position—he was certain the bone in the middle of his chest was going to burst straight up through the skin. He could not believe human beings could do this to other human beings. He was suffused with a cold anger, but this soon was lost in a preoccupation with pain. Harry kept rolling from shoulder to shoulder, trying to relieve the pressure. Once he looked down past a bent shoulder and saw his right hand, full of frightening reddish, whitish, purplish color. There was no feeling in it, and the fingers did not respond when he concentrated on trying to move them. He was sure the hand was lost to him, that if he survived this torture it would have to be amputated.

Sweat soon soaked through his heavy flight suit; it was as though he had been swimming. He began to dehydrate. A thirst more appalling than the pain developed, and it was this thirst that finally, after about three hours, caused him to cry out. A guard came, the most vacant-eyed individual Harry had ever seen. Utterly devoid of expression, he walked slowly around the agonized prisoner, gazing down at him. This guard, who would become known to the POWs as Pigeye or Straps and Bars (his favorite instruments of torture), was a professional torturer and would inflict more pain on more Americans than any other member of Hanoi's prison system. Harry pleaded for water, got no response.

Twenty minutes later, when Harry knew he could last no longer, that his mind or body or both were at the breaking point, his interrogator asked him if he were ready to give the answers he had been asked for.

"Yes," Harry whispered.

He was left in the torture rig as the interrogation began, until he had given a number of facts that indicated to his captors that he was now willing to talk; he identified his ship, his squadron, and the type of aircraft he had been flying—nonclassified things his captors already knew, as it turned out. His credibility established, Harry was taken out of torture and back to the interrogation room.

For the first time, he was really scared. He had learned that the enemy was not bluffing. And he was brokenhearted at his own inability to accept more torture; it had never occurred to him that he could be broken, and the knowledge shattered him. He assumed that his compatriots who had been captured ahead of him had been subjected to the same sort of mistreatment, and that they had not broken, as he had. He was desolate, certain that for a few hours of pain he had sold out on all that was dear to him, that he had betrayed his country. He wanted to die, and in the days ahead would pray to die; but he sensed that this option would be denied him.

The interrogating went on for days. The military information sought was always rudimentary: what targets were to be hit, when missions would be flown, and what kinds of bombs would be used. Harry knew the answers to none of these questions, but knew that a plea of ignorance would not be accepted. To his disgust, he found himself naming targets that were already under frequent attack; explaining that missions in the future were to be flown at dawn, during mornings and afternoons, at dusk, and probably at night; and that high-explosive bombs were to be used. This was accepted.

When asked his opinion on the war, Harry asserted his conviction that it need never have happened had the United States in the late 1940s taken proper steps to prevent the Communist takeover of China.

"You don't understand," he was told. "You are nearly forty years old, and your social and political loyalties have been formed. We do not expect to make a Communist of you, but you will see the truth."

On November 29, Jenkins' interrogation period ended. He was moved from New Guy Village to Heartbreak Hotel, and locked in Cell #7. His captors needed the New Guy Village interrogation room to work on the fifty-sixth American shootdown, Navy Comdr. Howard E. Rutledge. The physical torture and the anguish that went with being broken apparently exacted a toll on Jenkins's faculties. Out in the hallway, he thought, an American pilot lay dying on a stretcher, and someone kept asking him, "What's your name? Are you Charlie Wack? Are you Hank Bolling?"

Charlie Wack was Harry's squadron maintenance officer; Hank Bolling was his operations officer. Whoever it was on the stretcher, he wasn't answering. Then a sharp object, probably a rock, struck

Harry's cell door. Harry stayed quiet, listening to the attempt to extract information from the injured pilot before he died. Actually, there was no pilot dying in the hallway. The voice was Jim Stockdale's; he was trying to contact Jenkins. Not realizing that, Harry remained silent.

Heartbreak Hotel was not fully booked that day. In Cell #1 was Air Force Capt. George McKnight, who had been downed on a search and rescue mission on November 6; Cell #2 was empty; in Cell #3 was Stockdale, the senior ranking officer in the building; in Cell #4 was Navy Lt. Comdr. Duffy Hutton, downed on October 16; in Cell #5 was Marine Capt. Harley Chapman, shot down on November 5; in Cell #6 was Air Force 1st Lt. Jerry Singleton, a helicopter copilot, downed on November 6; Jenkins was in Cell #7, and Cell #8 was the bath area.

The next day guards came into Jenkins's cell, gave him a haircut, and handed him a bamboo broom to sweep out the cuttings. Through cracks in their cell doors the other prisoners watched. When Harry was locked in again and the guards had departed, he heard, "Harry Jenkins! Jim Stockdale!"

"CAG," Harry said, pressing himself to his door, "where the hell are you?"

Stockdale told him to get up on the end of his bunk and open his transom. He explained that McKnight, in Cell #1, was "clearing" for them, that by getting down low and looking through the gap at the bottom of his cell door he could see the shadows of approaching guards and would whistle the danger signal, the opening bars of the cigarette commercial "Winston Tastes Good . . ." At that sound all transoms were to be closed and communications to cease.

Jenkins told the others of the abuses he had been subjected to and confessed that he had not been able to hold the line at name, rank, number, and birthdate. He told this compulsively, like a repentant sinner seeking forgiveness. The others heard him out and made no comment. This reinforced Harry's assumption that all had been tortured as he had, had suffered it without breaking, and were displeased with his poor performance. He was crushed.

In fact, Rod Knutson was the only POW known to have been tortured, and there had been some feeling that Rod had needlessly made things rough on himself with an overly belligerent attitude. But Harry was a good deal older than Rod, a seasoned combat commander. By no stretch of the imagination could his behavior after capture be described as anything but entirely proper. Yet he had been tortured past his breaking point. His report suggested that their North Vietnamese captors were starting an organized torture program. And so, in the silence that Harry mistook for censure, each of his fellow inmates was actually wondering how long before he would be tortured and how he would perform.

———

Howie Rutledge's feelings of invincibility and his F8E Crusader jet were blasted to smithereens on November 28. He parachuted into a small village which seemed overpopulated with exceptionally hostile people. The crowd was full of murderous intent, and Howie had tried to run from them. But one howling, machete-waving pursuer had nearly caught up with him, and Howie had been left no choice but to shoot the young man dead with his .38 revolver. At length, Howie was surrounded, captured, and beaten to limp insensibility. By the time it was over, five of his front teeth had been jarred loose, his left leg would not support him, and his right wrist was swollen to about three times its normal size—he assumed it was broken.

He was seated on a retaining wall in the village square. A small man in an undershirt and short pants arrived. From a black bag he took disinfectants and cleaned and dressed wounds on Howie's head and face, then bandaged them. That was the last act of compassion Rutledge would know from the Vietnamese for more than seven years.

An Army contingent collected him, and he reached Hoa Lo prison at about 7 AM on November 29. He was interrogated immediately by Eagle, who warned him that he would be punished if he did not answer all questions put to him. Howie spent the day insisting on his rights under international law. That evening, he was taken to Room 18 and handed over to Pigeye.

Rutledge reached Cell #2 in Heartbreak Hotel on December 2. For three days he had been locked in ankle manacles, beaten with bamboo clubs, and rope-tortured until his arms were a deep, deep blue and, he was sure, lost to him forever. Then guards had "walked" a three-quarter-inch pipe up and down his shinbones. At last, he had agreed to answer questions. The interrogator wanted to know such things as Rutledge's squadron, ship, air wing, the names of other pilots. Howie had provided a lot of erroneous information, which was eagerly accepted. He was devastated at having given more than the Code of Conduct allowed. Then an American voice was saying, "New Guy in Cell 2, what's your name?"

Howie did not know he was in Cell #2, but knew he was a new guy. Briefly, he wondered if this were an enemy ruse to trap him into a communication attempt as an excuse to torture him for more information. He decided he had to chance it. There was nothing he now needed so much as to talk to another American. He got onto his bunk, got the wood pulled back from the transom, and introduced himself to Jim Stockdale, next door in Cell #3. Howie told of his tortures and confessed that he had given more than the Code of Conduct allows. He was nearly in tears by the time he finished. "I feel like a traitor," he said.

"Welcome to the club," said Harry Jenkins from the transom in Cell #7, directly across the hallway.

"Don't feel like the Lone Ranger," said Stockdale reassuringly. "You did your best."

Then, from Cell #1, George McKnight whistled the new danger signal, "Pop Goes the Weasle," and communications shut down. But now, Howie Rutledge and Harry Jenkins, the two Heartbreak residents who had plumbed the low points of their lives, felt much better about themselves.

––––––

On November 28, Robbie Risner lost control of his body functions for the third time. He was served a bowl of soup with some sort of weedlike greens in it. Presumably, this was supposed to cure him. The soup was served in a porcelain bowl, and he was given an aluminum scoop to eat with. This scoop, he found, marked well on the porcelain, and he was able to satisfy a compulsion that had been gnawing at him for weeks. At the bottom of the dish he wrote, "Over." On the outside bottom he wrote, "Risner stocks 28 days. Okay." He felt sure that some American was washing the dishes he used, and would see this and pass the word. No matter what happened now, Americans would know that Risner had been alive as of this date and something of what he had endured.

That day, however, the guard who served Robbie his meals and who never had shown the slightest interest in his dish, picked it up, turned it over, and looked at the bottom side. The guard did not speak or read English; he knew only that the words should not be there. He left. Robbie received no food at all for two days.

When he awakened early on December 2, he found himself praying, "I'm miserable. I'm cold. I'm hungry. I would like to get out of these stocks. I would like some warm clothing, and another blanket and some food."

That night, after thirty-two days, Robbie was released from the stocks. An interrogator the prisoners called Mickey Mouse entered the cell with two guards. First, dramatically, Mickey Mouse intoned, "You have opposed our government. You have killed our people. You have tried to communicate with others. Now you will be severely punished."

Risner's arms were pulled behind him, and his wrists were tied tightly together. Patches of coarse, horsehairlike material were pushed into his eyes, then bound against them, so tightly that Robbie thought his eyeballs might be punched back into his head. Now, he swung around on the bunk and got up, onto the floor on his bare feet. He shivered in the cold. A rope was affixed around his neck, and he was taken outside.

For a long time—Robbie estimated it at between one and two hours—Mickey Mouse and the two guards led the barefooted prisoner on the leash through drainage ditches full of freezing, filthy water, into hedges, up against trees, across stretches of ground covered with nuts that had fallen from the trees, into buildings, up and down steep stairways. Again and again, he was crashed into trees and bushes, allowed to walk into walls. He would fall, then be yanked roughly to his feet and pulled onward. On and on it went, around and around the prison grounds. Weak, starved, cold, hurting, Risner was near exhaustion.

At last, he was taken into a room and thrown down on the floor. The tight blindfold remained on. The guards tied Robbie into torture ropes. Tight half-hitches were applied to one arm, from the wrist to the shoulder. As each loop was strung, a guard stood on the arm and pulled the rope as tightly as he could. Then he took the rope a few inches up the arm and tied a new half-hitch. Every few loops, he stopped and slapped the tied arm, as though it were a package of meat that had to be secured as tightly as possible. The same thing was done with the other arm. Then the arms were pulled behind his back and tied together from the elbows to the shoulders.

Robbie felt his right shoulder pull out of its socket, and he could feel the left shoulder trying to pull out. Pain seemed to be exploding all through him, but its vortex was the chestbone, which strained tightly against the skin; he was sure that momentarily it would burst out of his body.

Now his legs were tied in tight half-hitches from the ankles to just below the knees. The ankles were bound together and a long rope from the ankles was pulled behind Robbie, looped around his neck, and pulled until his body formed an arch. To forestall choking, Robbie had to force his back into a tighter arch. The intensity of the pain stunned him. He could not believe the agony that was in him, a living evil, writhing into every nerve ending. There was no part of him that was not suffering; he was soaking in a pain that far exceeded anything he had ever imagined.

After a time Mickey Mouse came down close to Risner, snarling, "Shut up!" Only then did Robbie realize that he was groaning, that the noise was being squeezed out of him involuntarily. He could not stop. Mickey Mouse snapped orders at the guards, and one of them repeatedly smashed his fist into Robbie's face. Robbie hardly felt these blows; the pain from the bindings was so great that it overwhelmed all other feeling. He did not believe it would kill him, but he was *certain,* he *knew* that it would soon render him unconscious. He waited for this blessed oblivion.

But oblivion did not come. Instead, incredibly, he remained conscious and the pain kept intensifying. In prayer, he pleaded for strength, for unconsciousness—he still was confident that God would let him die before He would allow his country's enemy to extract more from him than he was allowed to give. But where was death? Where was oblivion? Where was anything but the pain that kept mounting toward a crescendo and never reached it? *God, I read where Your grace is sufficient . . .*

Someone in another room was screaming now; they were torturing another American. For a moment Robbie lost himself in compassion for his countryman. Then a guard was down on the floor with him again, punching his face, angrily demanding silence, and Robbie understood that the screams he heard were not someone else's, but his own.

Suddenly, he discovered a way out of it all. By relaxing the arch in his back he could choke himself. He let it happen, let the rope from the ankles to the neck begin to strangle him. He felt fine about it, even blissful as the blackness approached. He was escaping; he was going to make it!

The guards got to him before he could die. The noose was taken from around his neck. He was not to be allowed to strangle himself. He was frantic. There had to be a way to die; there *had* to be!

He waited for the guards to become preoccupied in conversation. Then, with the ankle-to-neck rope gone, he was able to get up onto his knees and throw himself forward and downward on the cement floor, onto his head and face, trying desperately to knock himself out—if he were lucky, he might be able to knock himself dead. He could feel the wounds tear open on his forehead and face, could feel the bone structure in his nose give way; it was nothing. He got back onto his knees and managed a second good heave before the guards could get to him. For several minutes they pounded their fists into his face and body. Then they tied him to a post so that he could not punch himself against the floor.

There was no losing consciousness, there was no death. There was only the pain. He stayed with it as long as he could. Then, his mind, his will, his body refused to accept any more.

"I'll talk," he breathed.

But they wouldn't let him talk, not yet; Risner had to be broken completely, once and for all. Later, he would understand why. He would be told, "Every Vietnamese knows who you are. Your picture has been in our newspaper. There is nobody we would rather have captured except Johnson, Rusk, and McNamara." Risner's captors assumed that the American people would pay close attention to what this military leader had to say about the war; and that the other American prisoners would take their lead from Risner, would accept his wisdom and parrot it to the benefit of the Democratic Republic of Vietnam.

But the first step was to force Risner's complete, unconditional surrender; to let him thoroughly explore fields of pain he did not know existed; to make him understand that there was nothing, *nothing* that was worth such suffering. And so they kept him there, in the agony, and he could not help weeping and screaming at it.

Sometime before dawn the ropes on his arms were eased to the point where the pain ebbed slightly. Mickey Mouse said, "Now you must sign a statement of apology to the Vietnamese people, and answer our questions."

Robbie's blindfold was removed. He was given pen and paper. He sat up on the floor, next to a stool with a candle on it. His hands and arms were useless. One of the guards folded the prisoner's hand around the pen, then made it form the letters and words as Mickey Mouse dictated: "I was made to violate the sovereign air space of the Democratic Republic of Vietnam, and to commit crimes against the Vietnamese people." It was a short statement. The guard helped Robbie sign it; no one would ever have recognized the childish scrawl as his handwriting, and there was no way anyone could know the price he had paid for that unrecognizable scrawl.

He was returned to his cell in New Guy Village. Blood had caked in the wounds on his head and face and on his arms, which were deep blue. He got onto his bunk, pulled his single blanket over himself, got over on one side and pulled his knees up underneath his chin. It was the first time in thirty-three days that he had been able to do this, and his memory could find nothing that had ever felt so good. He lay like this, savoring the comfort of the position, for perhaps ten minutes. Then, at the first note of the get up gong, he scrambled off the bunk onto the floor and began exercising. He could not do anything that involved the arms and hands, but he could jog in place and do bending and twisting exercises—he could move! It had been a long time since he had been able to move.

During the two weeks following his torture Risner was interrogated intermittently. At these sessions, with the memory of horrendous torture still vivid, he sparred as best he could. Once he met with an officer the prisoners called Cat, who would later be identified as Major Bai. This officer was the commander in chief of Hanoi's prison system and one of the chief architects of the program to terrorize, torture, and subjugate the American POWs. He appeared to be slightly older than Risner, and somewhat better educated than most Vietnamese the prisoner had seen. And he was vain—he liked to talk of having come from a wealthy family, of having attended Hanoi University. He tried to establish a rapport with the well-known American. "We are bitter enemies," he said, "but we can still respect each other as officers. What are your political beliefs?"

Robbie refused to answer.

"You are widening the gap of hatred between us," he was told.

"Are you prepared to make restitution to the Vietnamese people for your crimes?"

He was not taken back into torture. Instead, on December 18, he was installed in a cell at Heartbreak Hotel. Immediately, as the guards departed, he sought contact with other Americans. Asked to identify himself, he said, "It's Risner."

"Is that you, Robbie?" a voice asked eagerly. This was Air Force Capt. Jon Reynolds, who had been downed a few weeks earlier. He had never even seen Risner, but he knew the name and the legend, and his use of the nickname was by no means a disrespect for rank, merely a glad impulse. Risner knew it.

"That's right," he said. "It's me."

"Sir, did you know you had made full colonel?"

"No, that's wonderful news!"

Reynolds, Risner learned, was in bad shape. On ejecting from his crippled F-105, his limbs had flailed violently, and both arms had been broken about an inch below the shoulders. He also had suffered a broken jaw and had a badly wrenched right leg, and was unable to walk. His captors had made not the slightest pretense of attending to his injuries. Instead, he had been interrogated and, when he had refused to yield more than name, rank, and number, had—despite his broken arms—been rope-tortured until eventually he had provided a lot of fictitious information.

Robbie also heard of the tortures to Jenkins and Rutledge, then told of his own. He wanted the others to know that he had resisted to the best of his ability, but that he had been broken, that statements had been extracted from him that he did not believe. He wanted them to remember this if and when they heard his voice delivering enemy propaganda over the camp radio.

Risner was senior to Jim Stockdale, who immediately deferred to him as SRO. Robbie told the others of the prison he had come from, the Zoo, and that Denton, Shumaker, Storz, Alvarez, Guarino, and others were there.

He suffered a private anguish, more grievous than the tortures he had known. He despised himself for having broken. But as a military officer to whom others looked for leadership, he could not afford to show his misery. Men needed strength and encouragement, and it was incumbent on him to try to provide it. A deeply religious man, a lay preacher in the Baptist Church, he sought strength in prayer and urged the others to pray, for themselves and each other, for those at home who waited for them, for their country, even for their captors: "Remember that the Vietnamese are God's children, too. He loves them as much as He loves you and your children. What is happening is all in His plan. Have faith. God loves you. He won't forget you. Everything will work out as He wills it."

―――――

Through December the Zoo population continued to burgeon, and the Vietnamese began assigning cellmates, even for such "murderous air pirates" as Guarino and Alvarez. Maj. Ronald E. Byrne, Jr., a member of Risner's squadron, joined Larry on November 17. The next day, Air Force Lt. Thomas J. Barrett, twenty-six, was stashed with Alvarez; except for five September minutes with Guarino at the Briarpatch, Barrett was the first American Ev had been with since his shootdown. He could not believe his good fortune; he didn't know what to say. "God," he said, "you look heavy."

"Yeah," said Barrett, "new shootdown. How long you been here?"

"Fifteen and a half months."

Barrett's jaw dropped. He started over, as though there had been a misunderstanding. "How long you been here?"

"I'm Alvarez. Alvarez."

Barrett stared at him. At last, in a faraway voice he said, "Yeah. I remember now."

They talked for hours. Ev drained Barrett of news of the world outside. "How long do you think we'll be here?" he wanted to know.

"Not more than a couple of months," Barrett said.

As the days passed, Alvarez watched Barrett try to cope with a classic case of "newguyitis." Young, healthy, active, and extremely intelligent, it was difficult for him to accustom himself to close confinement, to being denied access to sunlight and fresh air. He strode about the small cell, tore down his mosquito net, put it up again, threw things around, pounded on the wall. "Ev," he asked, "how will we know when they are going to release us?"

"The first thing that will happen," Alvarez answered, "is that they will come and give us shaves, haircuts, and clean clothes. They they'll put us on a bus and we'll go to the airport to Hanoi, or to Haiphong, where we'll get on a ship. But first, they'll come and give us shaves and haircuts. That's how we'll know."

They shivered in winter cold awaiting the telltale shaves and haircuts. They entertained each other with improbable tales of high school and college years. They laughed a lot. When guards heard them, they would kick at their cell door and shout, "Eeeh! Keep silent!" And Ev would kick at the inside of the door and shout, "Keep silent!" back at the guard. At this, both prisoners would break up in laughter, certain that it was the funniest thing that had ever happened. The guards were not yet entering the Zoo's cells to enforce regulations.

———

Ed Davis decided that it was his own fault that the enemy finally broke him; after twenty-seven days in interrogation he had given way to anger and had indulged in foolish bravado that had led to his undoing. He was certain he had betrayed his country and his fellow POWs. He was inconsolable, full of a great, bitter anger at himself.

The interrogators had been double-teaming him, keeping at him around the clock. Sometimes, at the interrogators' direction, eager guards slapped and punched him about. He was made to kneel for hours on end before the interrogators' desk, and to "hold up the wall" for consecutive days and nights. When interrogations were not in session, he was kept in his cell in the leg irons, his wrists locked behind him in hell cuffs. Guards were instructed to see that he did not sleep. For Ed, the whole business was uncomfortable, but by no means unendurable. He was winning his battle, but he wondered how long it would be before the enemy would credit him with victory and give up on him.

Then, late on the night of November 29, after he had been locked into rear cuffs, a guard ordered him to lie on his stomach on the floor and began lacing his arms together with rope. Ed did not know what the guard was trying to do, but did not like the idea of being tied with ropes. He climbed to his feet. The guard began knocking Ed about the cell. He forced him down onto his stomach again, sat on him, and again began applying the ropes. Ed's temper snapped. He dumped the guard from his back and he rose toward him menacingly. The guard scrambled to his feet, obviously frightened, and backed away, raising his fist as though to defend himself, even though the prisoner resembled a live skeleton and his hands were locked behind him.

Near-exhaustion had robbed Ed of his good judgment. The attempt to tie him infuriated him, and the fury gave him the strength he needed to frighten the guard, to make the bully back off and cower.

But Ed's new strength left quickly, and he had no option but to submit. The humiliated guard angrily cinched the ropes tightly around the prisoner's upper arms, then left him alone.

Ed was aware that his arms and hands were numbing, then the pain of the ropes superseded the numbness. He pressed his back against a corner of the concrete wall near the cell door and began sliding up and down, trying to saw through the ropes. The sawing put additional pressure on the ropes, intensifying the pain; and it wasn't working. The pain was all through him now, like something alive, trying to get out and engulf him.

By the reckoning of Jerry Denton, in the next cell, it was approximately forty-five minutes after the guard left Davis's cell that Ed began screaming. Instantly, Storz, Schierman, Denton, Vohden, and others in the Barn began kicking and banging against the insides of their cell doors, roaring, ''Bao Cao! Bao Cao! Bao Cao!'' They had no idea what torture was now being inflicted on Ed, but wanted a Vietnamese officer, wanted the torment stopped. It was intolerable!

It was the interrogator Frenchy who entered this din. He toyed with Ed, but did not order the ropes loosened. Instead, he talked to the suffering prisoner. ''You are going to answer the questions?'' he asked.

''Yes!'' Ed screamed. ''Yes!''

Still, Frenchy would not order the ropes removed, or even loosened. Over and over again he squeezed Davis for guarantees of cooperation. Ed kept screaming, crying, whimpering, begging.

Finally, after perhaps twenty minutes, Frenchy ordered a guard to loosen the ropes slightly. Ed was left in the ropes for the remainder of the night. The next morning they were removed, and he was taken to interrogation. There he gave up the biographical information the enemy wanted. Innocuous stuff about his birthplace, schools, places he had lived, parents' occupations, jobs he had held. He lied about everything.

It was a short session, nothing like the round-the-clock affairs that had become routine in recent weeks. It was held in a room in the Auditorium. As Ed left the place, the room next door suddenly erupted in greeting: ''How ya doin', Ed, y'ol sonofagun! This is Percy—Bob Purcell.''

Startled, Ed stopped to listen. Guards were running to Purcell's door, kicking at it, shouting angrily at him, demanding silence. The tough, gregarious Purcell went on as though the guards weren't there.

He had been isolated and put on short rations in this place weeks earlier. Many times, through a gap in his door, he had seen Ed trudge to and from his month of interrogation, and he had heard much of what happened through the thin wall separating the rooms. Today he had heard the climax and knew that Ed needed some bucking up. He kept on shouting, over the kicking and screaming of the guards. "You finally beat 'em, Ed! Thank God it's over for you! Hang in there, buddy, we're goin' home soon!"

Ed had never heard of Bob Purcell, but he knew in that moment that he loved the man. He was thrilled by Purcell's courage, and encouraged by his words. It meant everything to know that someone like this had been watching, had somehow known or guessed at what was happening, and thought enough of his performance to cheer him on at high risk to himself. Percy. Bob Purcell. He wouldn't forget the name. It belonged to someone worth knowing.

Back in his room, Davis could not live with himself for having broken. Even though he had given his interrogators nothing but lies, he had *broken!* Tearfully, he tapped to Denton that he thought he might have held out longer than he did. This self-judgment reduced Denton to tears. He tapped back, "For God's sake, Ed, you did your best. You have nothing to be ashamed of. We are all proud of you. When they get around to the rest of us, I hope and pray we will do as well as you have."

Unexpectedly, the Christmas spirit was upon the Zoo. In late November a group of civilian authorities had inspected the camp and the leader, in fluent English, had asked SRO Jerry Denton, "Do you want to continue eating shit?"

"No, of course not," said Denton.

"Then," he was told, "you must condemn the policies of your government. Until you do that, you will continue to eat shit."

The POWs opted for a continuation of the predigested food. But on December 1, the meals came hot, clean, and far more substantial, steaming bowls full of cabbage. Jerry Denton could scarcely credit his senses. He tasted the stuff, tentatively, then began eating it in great hungry gulps. As he ate, he became aware that tears were streaming down his face. He could not control himself. For the first time since early childhood, he was blubbering like a baby. He went to the wall to tap to Ed Davis, to see that he also had received a hot meal and that the SRO was not accepting a special favor. Davis interrupted to tap, "Sir, I am crying like a baby."

Jerry went to the opposite wall to find that Ron Storz, too, was trying to retrieve control of his emotions. So it was throughout the Zoo; men were crying their eyes out over their first relatively decent meal in more than a month.

The hot meals continued, and the POWs were issued sweatshirts, which helped against the raw, winter cold.

On December 15, Larry Guarino was given a letter from his wife, Evelyn, and allowed to write a letter home. His letter never reached Evelyn, but he was allowed to keep hers. He read it a thousand times, and shared it as often with Ron Byrne, his cellmate—no letter ever received by any POW ever could be his alone; these were to be shared, read and reread by all.

On Christmas Eve a pause in the American bombing began. Larry, Ron Byrne, and Air Force M. Sgt. Arthur Cormier, also Catholic, were blindfolded and taken from the Zoo back to Hoa Lo. Cormier, a helicopter crewman, had been downed on a search and rescue mission on November 6. The three had accepted an offer to see a Catholic priest, to make Christmas confessions and receive Holy Communion. The event took place in Room 24, off the main Hoa Lo courtyard, where their blindfolds were removed. An elderly priest was on hand, and so were numerous armed guards and Rabbit. The POWs were given some pieces of candy. They ate these, wondering what arrangements had been made to ensure the privacy of their confessions. To their amazement, they discovered there was to be nothing private about them at all.

"Get on your knees, Guarino," snarled Rabbit. "Now, confess your crimes to the priest. Tell him how many times you have come up here, how many missions you have flown. And you also, Byrne."

The priest did not involve himself in the farce. He administered absolution and distributed Communion to the three Americans, and they were returned to their cells in the Zoo.

At the Zoo that day Dog told Alvarez, "Today you are allowed to write a letter home. First you can read your letter." He handed Ev a letter from Tangee.

It had been written in September. She told him no one knew whether he was alive, and that she had been advised to stop writing. But she had decided to write him now in hopes he was alive, and that the letter would find him.

In reply, Alvarez wrote that he had a roommate (he had been warned not to mention Barrett's name, and understood that the letter would not be sent if he did so). He and his roommate, he said, talked a lot about sports and said the rosary together every day. He ended by saying, "I hope my little girlfriends, Kathy and Mona and Marcia, are all right." He explained to Dog that these were his wife's little nieces, and that he always called them "my little girlfriends." This was true of Kathy and Mona. Marcia was Tom Barrett's fiancée. This letter was received by Tangee, and analysts in Washington soon deduced that Tom Barrett was alive and rooming with Ev Alvarez in Hanoi.

Returning to his cell after writing the letter, Ev found a guard giving Tom a haircut and a shave. Barrett could hardly contain himself. "Aren't you excited?" he demanded. "We're going home!"

Ev shook his head; he could not work up any enthusiasm. "Tom," he said, "it's just Christmas Eve. That's all."

———

Christmas dinner: potato soup full of chunks of real potatoes, hot turkey, vegetables, salad, bread. Alvarez and Barrett could smell it coming. A guard put the dishes on the ground, outside, in front of their cell door. The two prisoners got down onto their knees, gazed hungrily at the food from the gap at the bottom of the door.

"Tom," said Ev, "when we get that food, don't spill it! Don't spill a drop of that juice!"

"Yeah, yeah!" Barrett replied, impatiently. In less than three months, a large part of his two hundred pounds had evaporated. Like Alvarez, he was now a gaunt, starved shadow of himself.

The two salivated, worried that the rats that roamed the yard would get at their dinner, that birds would foul it. They blew mightly through the gap, trying to dislodge the ants that swarmed over the food. Now came another guard who opened the door, and behind him stood Frenchy, motioning expansively at the food. "Merry Christmas," said he.

The POWs snatched up the precious fare, carried it inside, seated themselves before it, savored every mouthful—they did not bother to clean off all the ants; it was just too bad about any that went down. After the meal they were served coffee and a half-bottle of Hanoi beer. They toasted each other and the folks at home. The small portion of beer made them slightly giggly.

All the POWs received the Christmas turkey dinner. Larry Guarino, who had spent many wartime Christmases away from his family, spent the day absorbed in thoughts of them, his face awash in tears. He was vaguely aware of holy music, coming over the loudspeaker in his cell.

As the calendar worked its way toward New Year's Eve, there were sixty-four Americans in Hanoi and its environs who had reason to feel that 1965 had not been a very good year.

As 1965 ended, Americans at home had much to contemplate. In the fall, Peking had described its support of the Viet Cong as the focal point of a strategy by which the Communists of the world's "rural areas," Asia, Africa, and Latin America, would encircle and over-come the "cities" of the Free World, North America and Western Europe. For the moment, at least, the strategy appeared to be work-ing; greatly intensified American military efforts seemed unable to stem the flow of arms and men from North Vietnam into the south. But President Johnson insisted the United States must persevere, that to do otherwise would be to ensure Communist domination of all Southeast Asia and would undermine American credibility throughout the world.

At the same time, Johnson kept repeating his willingness to negotiate, to go anywhere and meet with anyone at any time to put an end to the war. On Christmas Eve, he halted the bombing of North Vietnam and launched a "peace offensive." American emissaries in many world capitals sought through the good offices of others to arrange for negotiations with Hanoi. All efforts proved fruitless. The air campaign against North Vietnam was resumed on January 31, after a thirty-seven-day hiatus.

Things Get Rough All Over

The new year did not seem promising.

With the pause in the bombing for Christmas and the Vietnamese Tet Lunar New Year, the influx of POWs slowed. The Communists worked with the material on hand. By January 8, the crippled Jim Stockdale had been broken in the ropes.

CAG had known it was coming. Since his release from the hospital, in late October, he had been interrogated several times and had heard other Heartbreak residents describe their sessions. What impressed him most of all about the questioning was the enemy's lack of interest in meaningful military information. The questioning continued to focus on trivia.

This had caused a deepening unease in Stockdale. He could understand a straightforward attempt to extort military information from a POW. But no case could be made for what the Vietnamese were doing with their American prisoners—terrorizing them, breaking them to Hanoi's will, tenderizing them, like so many pieces of meat, for inclusion in a propaganda stew.

On December 30, Major Bai, the prison system commander whom

the POWs called Cat, got the excuse he needed to move against Stockdale. That day, Stockdale, a cigarette smoker, used up his ration early. He tapped his plight to Robbie Risner, a nonsmoker, who accepted his cigarette rations and saved them for other Americans in just such situations. Using thread from his clothing, he tied a small bundle of smokes together and tried to pass it to Stockdale, but the cigarettes spilled into the corridor, and a guard caught Stockdale trying to retrieve them. Late that night Stockdale found himself in a cell in New Guy Village, where he was told that he had violated camp regulations by communicating with others; it would now be necessary to punish him.

He spent nine days locked in stocks in the windy, bitter cold cell. On the tenth day he was taken to Room 18, where Rabbit, Cat's sullen interrogator, ordered him to "write a letter to the U.S. Foreign Secretary of State and explain the true story of the war and the determination of the Vietnamese people to fight on." Jim refused to do so. Rabbit barked an order, and Pigeye threw the prisoner down onto the floor and hustled him into the ropes.

Long after the incredible pain had receded to the dim reaches of memory, Stockdale would remember clearly the utter dispassion with which Pigeye approached his work. His eyes were entirely empty of expression. The man was medieval; a professional torturer, one who actually made a life's work of inflicting intolerable pain on other people. There was no humanity to see anywhere in his face, nor in the efficient way he went about his grisly work.

Stockdale swam in the pain Pigeye gave him. He was sure he would drown in it, pass out or die, but Pigeye would not let him do either of these things. Finally, when he could stand it no longer, he heard himself say the words that the hovering Rabbit demanded he say: "I submit."

Instead of writing to the "Foreign Secretary of State," Jim persuaded Rabbit to let him write to the Office of the Chief of Naval Operations, where good friends would see the letter for what it was, a product of duress. The Vietnamese did not like the letter, and it was never sent. In the days that followed they extracted what they deemed far more valuable material from Stockdale. He filled out a questionnaire concerning activities and lectures given by chaplains aboard U.S. Navy vessels—for the Vietnamese knew the chaplains to be "political officers"; he also wrote a long, worthless tract on the subject of "Command and Control."

Like others, he had given the enemy little or nothing; and like others, he was near despair for having broken at all. He resolved to pull himself together, to hang tough. He prayed for recovery from his leg and arm injuries, for the physical strength that would enable him to conduct himself as he had always hoped and even assumed he would in such a situation.

Young Ralph Gaither also was under intensive pressure that January. Along with eleven other POWs, he had been moved from the Zoo to the Briarpatch in early December. Two weeks before Christmas, Ralph was summoned to interrogation and asked for an oral biography. He refused to speak—like many POWs, he suspected that his parents, in Miami, Florida, might be worked for money and antiwar statements. He was locked in handcuffs and put on half-rations. Meals had become skimpy, and he had begun to wonder how long his strength and will to resist could last. Wes Schierman, in the adjacent cell, tapped through the wall: "Why not give them a bunch of lies?"

At a quiz a few days later, Ralph advised his interrogators that his father worked for the B. S. (Baker Sierra) Railroad in Birmingham, Alabama, and was a member of a union, the Fraternal Order of Railroad Drivers—the interrogators were most approving of this membership. They remained noncommittal, though, when Ralph went on that his male parent was a devoutly religious Big Foot Indian, who regularly attended the Footwashing Baptist Church of America. His grandfather, Ralph said, had been an Indian chief, Chief Crockagator, and had lived in the Happy Hunting Grounds, where he had spent his entire life hunting alligators and mudfish.

Moving on into his military career, Ralph let it be known that his wingman had been Dave Brubeck and that he had had an excellent briefing officer named Walter Winchell.

The interrogators wrote furiously, straining to keep up with the rush of information the young American gave them. They listened carefully, nodding, only occasionally interposing a brief question. Now that the criminal was talking, they took no chances that they might stem the flow.

Finally, it was done. The interrogators were happy, entirely satisfied. Ralph found a full meal awaiting him in his cell. The next night he was brought back to interrogation to clear up some points on which his captors were confused. "Everything I told you was a lie," Ralph said.

"Why did you lie? Now you must tell us the truth!"

"I'm not going to tell you the truth."

The interrogators were becoming enraged. "What do you mean? You *must* tell us the truth! The camp commander will punish you!"

"If you want another biography, I'll give you one. But I will never tell you the truth."

The interrogation ended in confusion. Gaither had thrown his inquisitors so far off pace that they did not know what to do about it—or, at the moment, with him. He was returned to his cell. His hard times were not over by any means, but so far he was outscoring his enemy.

———

As the American bombing pause continued into February, Hanoi apparently reckoned that Washington was about to come to terms and that it was time to get the hostages in proper shape for their return to the United States. Great concern was evinced over the POWs' physical condition. At the Zoo every prisoner received a thorough medical examination. Weights, hearts, and blood pressures were checked; eyes, ears, noses, and throats were explored. Urine specimens were collected, and a new officer came on the scene, knocking at each cell door, holding open the peephole, displaying a small jar and saying, "You must make stool. In this bottle. You undahstan?" Then he would place the bottle down, before the cell door. A turnkey would open the door, and the officer would stand back, gloatingly, as the American had to bend down before him—to bow—to pick up the bottle. There was something hilarious about it, this pompous little man striding about, making people bow and promise to provide him with samples of their feces.

"Whatta we gonna call him?"

"The way he struts around he looks like he thinks he's Jesus Christ. How about 'J. C.'?"

With many, the name J. C. was to stick. Others felt it a blasphemy and insisted on some other identification.

"He's dumb, and looks dumb. How about 'Dum Dum'?"

Thus, to many, J. C. was Dum Dum, or "Dum Dum, the shit collector." As time passed, the POWs would learn that there was not much about him that was funny.

———

The bombing pause ended, and so did the examinations. On February 3, Navy Lieut. Gerald Coffee, flying armed reconnaissance off the carrier *Kitty Hawk,* became the first American shootdown of 1966. It took him about three weeks to reach Heartbreak Hotel. He was nearly in despair. His right arm had been broken during ejection. Instead of attending to the injury, his captors had interrogated him, and when he refused to talk, he was bound, gagged, beaten with rifle butts, kicked in the groin, and tortured in ropes. He was paraded through villages as a "demon from the South China Sea." He was shown the identification card of his bombardier-navigator, Lt. (j.g.) Robert Hanson, who had ejected with him, and was told that Hanson had been shot—Hanson was never seen again.

Coffee anguished over his wife, Bea, back in California, pregnant with their fourth child; and for Bob Hanson and his wife, Pat. His eyes roamed his Heartbreak cell. Inscribed deeply into one wall was the legend "God will find strength. Robinson Risner, September 18, 1965." It reminded Coffee of something he needed to remember.

"New man in Cell 1, who are you?" It was Risner's voice. Coffee got up onto his transom and met him and two other new entries: Navy Lieut. Render Crayton, an A4 pilot off the carrier *Ticonderoga;* and Lt. (j.g.) Larry Spencer, an F-4 radar intercept officer off the carrier *Enterprise.* Crayton had been downed on February 7; Spencer on February 18. Neither had yet been tortured.

Coffee told of his experience. Then SRO Risner described his month of agony. The younger men listened, horrified, as Risner, who wanted the younger officers prepared for the worst, described the bending that had ripped a shoulder from its socket and separated his ribs, and of how he had been starved. He could not rid himself of a terrible pain that had lodged in his ribs and chest, and could not get over the hunger. He gave them the names of every prisoner he knew had been at Hoa Lo and the Zoo and ordered them committed to memory; when the war ended, he explained, the Vietnamese would have to account for every man. He taught them the tap code; and he told them: "Remember, we are only going to be here a short time. Do the very best you can. Go home proud. The Lord will never ask you to endure more than you are able. Remember to pray for the Vietnamese."

———

Now a season of torture got under way at the Zoo.

"Skip" Brunhaver was first. The Vietnamese wanted his personal history. He refused, and was cuffed, tied at the ankles, rope-tortured, thrown onto the floor in one of the stinking bath areas. Days passed; he was served no food and only a minimal ration of water. When fellow POWs came to adjacent rooms in the bath area, he managed to tap out his plight and ask for advice. Bob Shumaker tapped back: "Hold out as long as you can. Meanwhile, think of some good lies you can give them."

Skip held out for a week.

On February 7, it was Jerry Denton's turn. He was taken to the room in the Auditorium, where Bob Shumaker had spent six wretched, pitch-black weeks in November and December. Denton's arms were pulled behind him and torture cuffs were ratcheted onto his wrists, down to the bone. His ankles were shackled into traveling irons, with the iron bar resting heavily, sharply, across the tops of his heels, so that when he was forced to walk the bar cut deeply into his heels. A guard began punching him in the face, knocking him sprawling, then yanking him up and hitting him again. Jerry, who had done some boxing at the Naval Academy, kept bobbing and weaving, trying to roll with the punches.

The beating lasted for about twenty minutes. Then the light was turned off and he was left sprawled on the floor, alone, in black darkness. After perhaps ten minutes, the light came on, the door opened, and in came the guards. Denton failed to show proper respect, failed to rise to his feet quickly enough; this called for another beating.

This scene was repeated many times: cuffed and shackled, Denton could not possibly rise quickly enough to satisfy the guards. Finally, he was able to find his way through the blackness into a corner. He kept his shoulders braced against the corner, and when he heard the guards' keys rattling in the cell door lock, he would begin walking his shoulders up the walls so that he would be on his feet by the time they entered. But only rarely was he able to rise quickly enough to avoid another lesson in manners.

Denton was not allowed out of the room to empty his waste bucket; it remained full. Whenever the guards left the room, they moved the bucket; if the cuffed, shackled prisoner had to use it, he would first have to find it. Denton crawled about the darkness, feeling with his head for the bucket. When he found it, he would have to push it to a wall in order to laboriously get himself into position to use it. This pushing procedure would cause the bucket to spill a portion of its contents, and the prisoner would have to wallow through the stuff.

Once he reached a wall, the tough part of the job began: getting into position to use the bucket took nearly an hour. First, he would have to get to his feet and work his way around over the bucket, taking care that the traveling irons did not push it away or upset it. Then, with hands made numb by torture cuffs, he would have to work his trousers around, loosen the drawstring that held them, use the bucket and get the trousers up and the drawstring tied again. It did not take many such sessions to persuade Denton to stop eating.

He was left alone for longer periods. The torture cuffs were a hell on his wrists. He endured. He tried to lose himself in sleep, but the pain and misery were such that he could not sleep. He daydreamed. He prayed. Occasionally he would hear a cock crow, and in the far distance the sound of a streetcar moving, and he would know that it was dawn again.

He waited. He hurt. Things crawled on him, and he heard other things moving about in the room. Rats, certainly. He didn't care. Food would come; usually it would have rat feces on it and chunks gnawed out of it. It did not matter to Jerry; he was not interested in eating, only in water, and in the few minutes of freedom he was allowed from the hell cuffs. But when the cuffs were loosened, blood began circulating back through his hands. This new excruciation was worse than the cuffs. Then, when it ended, the cuffs were ratcheted down tight again. And again and again, the guards would come in, make him stand, beat him about the room.

He hallucinated. A kindly old Vietnamese woman ministered to him, tried to assuage his agony. He thanked her and thanked God for her, and then he would come back to reality and she would be gone. He dreamed and screamed in fluent French—he had been stationed in Villefranche in 1956–1958, but he had never until now been fluent in the language.

One day a guard came in to loosen the cuffs. By now, lack of circulation had turned the prisoner's hands coal black. The cuffs had ground through skin and sinew down to the bone, and blood was caked black around them. The guard tried for about twenty minutes to get them off, then left and returned with an officer. At the sight of Denton's hands, the officer displayed alarm.

"Denton," he said anxiously, "I am very sorry about this."

At this, the guard, an enlisted man, turned on the officer, snarling, and delivered a severe dressing down. It seemed clear to Denton that the guard was a party member and that the officer was not.

It took screwdrivers, pliers, and approximately three hours to remove the cuffs.

After seven days and nights Denton yielded a fanciful biography in which he admitted to having once lived in an American town where the hotel had burned down; and then had moved to another town where three more hotels had burned down. He confided that he had been a member of ship's company aboard the carrier *Independence,* and not of the air group; and that his field of expertise was blimps. Thus did Jerry Denton learn that he could not hold out on the Vietnamese.

Other inmates at the Zoo were summoned by Dog and asked for opinions as to how camp radio offerings might be made more effective. Dog offered tea, cigarettes, and a relaxed atmosphere. Bob Shumaker refused the proffered goodies. It seemed improper to him to sit sipping tea and smoking with one's enemy, and he felt that to do so might tend to lower his guard. And he certainly was not going to advise the enemy as to how better to propagandize his countrymen and himself. Impatiently, Dog shoved a half-dozen sheets of paper across the table that other POWs had written and signed, suggesting changes in the camp radio format. This did not surprise Shumaker. He took it for granted that the others had been tortured for their comments, and he was girded for torture himself.

He was not tortured, however, and learned that others had commented and signed without being brutalized. Furthermore, they could not understand why Bob had risked torture over something so trivial.

The debate over how to handle the Vietnamese interrogators preoccupied the POWs. Many clung to a strict interpretation of the Code of Conduct. They argued that to give the enemy anything "free"—without torture—is to peel away a layer of defense; that no matter how unimportant, even silly, the item might seem, it puts the enemy one step closer to the important things he might seek. Far better to make him work for everything. Hang tough as long as you can.

Others advocated a policy of deceit. Be smart. Play it by ear. Give a little where it doesn't matter. When it comes to information of military or propaganda value, lie. If you can't get away with it, then it's time to clam up.

The debate over tactics was to go on for years. Meanwhile, a policy was needed. SRO Denton ordered, "No writing. No taping. Die before giving classified information. Take torture until in danger of losing mental faculties, then give a phony story. Keep it simple and easy to remember.''

Men kept demanding to know whether the order meant they were not to write requests for such essentials as toilet paper, toothpaste and medical attention. Frustrated at what seemed an inability to apply common sense in a situation where communications were at increasingly higher risk, Denton finally issued a blanket, inviolable order: "No writing. No taping.''

Most accepted this policy, and lived by it with varying degrees of success. It depended on a man's pain threshold.

Things were getting rough all over. At the Briarpatch, Ed Davis refused to write a biography. He was seated on a stool before a desk with an oil lantern on it and left alone. A guard outside the barred window kept watch to see that he did not sleep. Ed knew he would be kept on this stool for several days and nights, perhaps even a week or more. Then, if he had not been weakened enough to do his captors' bidding, he probably would go into ropes and torture cuffs.

At night, when the guard wasn't looking, Ed would move the lantern on the desk, so that the metal lattices of the lantern container would cast shadows across the side of his face and his eyes. Then he was able to close his eyes, rest them, even occasionally to doze off. When the guard suspected he was falling asleep, he would shout, and Ed would awaken and turn and look at him, affecting surprise, as though he did not understand why the guard was shouting.

The lamp was taken from the desk and put on the window ledge, where Ed could not reach it.

After a week on the stool, Davis decided to force the issue. He felt certain that torture awaited him, and he preferred to go into it with some measure of strength. Rising from the stool, he went to the barred window and stood in it, letting the flickering rays of light from the oil lamp send shadows undulating up his neck and face. The effect, he knew, was eerie, ghostly, and he enhanced it by widening his eyes and mouth until he looked like a Halloween mask. Outside, the guard was seated on a stool, below the window, facing away from it. Ed made a noise, and the guard looked up.

"*AHHHhhhhgggg!*'' Ed screamed.

The guard leaped from the stool, jumped back, stood staring at Ed, his eyes wide with terror. Then he turned and took off, running, as though he had been shot out of a cannon!

The fun soon ended.

Ed never was certain how many guards returned. He was back on the stool, looking surprised when they entered. There were enough of them to gather him up and heave him, kick him, and beat him back and forth across the room. *This,* he thought, *is how a soccer ball must feel!*

Outside, an effeminate officer stood calling to the prisoner, in a high-pitched voice, "Attention! Attention! Attention!" Clearly, he expected Davis to disregard the pounding he was taking from the thugs and to heed his own calls to pop to attention—after all, he was an officer! Ed wanted to laugh, but was too busy protecting vital organs.

The beating went on for long minutes. Then Ed was laced into ropes, and his wrists were manacled in the torture cuffs. He had been in these straits before and thought he remembered the pain. He didn't. It was new again, unreal, a blinding, unbelievable agony. A guard hovered over him, one the prisoners called Nicely Nicely, after Damon Runyon's *Guys and Dolls* character, because he had a constant, fixed smile on his face. Nicely Nicely grabbed Ed by the hair, yanked him forward, onto his knees, set himself, and drove his fist into the prisoner's face. He returned from brief oblivion to find Nicely Nicely gripping him by the hair, pulling him upright, and smashing his face again.

Nicely Nicely kept delivering these blows, and his smile was real, his eyes full of pleasure. Ed was aware of the punches, but could not feel them—the pain from the ropes and cuffs overwhelmed all else. He kept slipping in and out of consciousness—it was as though someone kept flicking a light switch on and off in his head. Now he saw his father, standing just outside the barred window. His face was drawn with anxiety for Ed, and he was talking to him. But Ed couldn't hear him, couldn't hear over a voice that kept screaming, *You better quit! You better quit!*

For a moment, he was able to catch hold of himself, to ascertain that his vocal cords and mouth were not working, that it was not he who was screaming. But the voice went on and on, insistently: *Quit! Quit! Let go! You're too close!*

It was *not* him, but *it was inside him,* something real, screaming a warning that he was going too far, that he was slipping over a precipice, that he had to pull himself back before it was too late. He thought to himself, *I am in a place where I cannot be. I have to get out of here!*

He was not able to take any more, to allow himself to go insane. He had no choice but to submit.

He scrawled a condemnation of the American B-52 raids in South Vietnam. He was left alone for the rest of the night.

The next morning Frenchy, the Briarpatch camp commander, demanded a written biography, but told Ed he would not have to sign it. When it was done, Frenchy demanded his signature. Ed refused it. He was placed back on the stool. This time, he took no shortcuts. He remained on the stool day and night for a week. Then he was tied into ropes again, and finally he agreed to sign the biography. He drew his name in childish script. Frenchy produced his Navy ID card and made him write his name over and again, until he was satisfied that the signature matched the one on the ID card.

———

Ralph Gaither continued to have his troubles at the Briarpatch, too. He was caught communicating with a fellow POW, Air Force Lt. Edward Alan Brudno,* who had been shot down on October 18. Ralph had been caught communicating before. A religiously oriented youngster, he had one Sunday begun whistling the Lord's Prayer in hopes other prisoners would recognize the cadence and would think about paying homage to God. Suddenly, guards threw open his cell door. Surprised, Ralph stopped whistling, but the whistling continued—almost everyone in camp had been "praying" along with him.

Ralph got away with a warning that time, but when he was caught tapping to Al Brudno, he was locked in torture cuffs and led from his cell through a trench, down into a one-man "bomb shelter." This hole in the ground was perhaps four feet square and seven feet deep. The Vietnamese had been using it for a cesspool, and Gaither found himself ankle-deep in human excrement. He did not know whether the overpowering stench was worse than the pain from the cuffs, but he knew his predicament was intolerable. "Bao Cao!" he shouted.

---

*Brudno died by his own hand on June 3, 1973, the day before his thirty-third birthday.

"Keep silent!" a guard answered.

"No! Bao Cao! Bao Cao!" He kept shouting it, again and again, as loudly as he could. He thought and hoped that he would be taken from the cesspool and given a severe beating, and that that would be the end of it. A beating would be much preferable to this! He kept shouting.

He was taken from the cesspool and slammed up against a wall. Three guards pinned him there while a fourth tried to gag him with his own towel, about the size of a kitchen hand towel. Ralph fought the gag, kept shouting, "Bao Cao! Bao Cao!" Now his buddies were shouting, too: Ron Storz, Ed Davis, Wes Schierman, Brudno, Navy Lt. (j.g.) Bill Shankel.

"Let him alone, you bastards!"

"Keep your damned hands off him!"

"You sons of bitches!"

Ralph kept shouting, "Bao Cao!" Once when he did this, a guard shoved his fingers into his cheeks, forcing the insides of his cheeks between his teeth so that he could not close his teeth without biting himself. Then another guard used a sheath knife to ram the towel into his mouth and down his throat. The knife was sharp, and Ralph felt the edge cut the inside of his mouth as the guard worked the towel in past the nasal air passages. He felt himself beginning to suffocate. He was frantic. He looked beseechingly into the guards' faces, saw stupidity in them. They did not realize he was dying.

He went limp, feigned unconsciousness, fell heavily to the ground, stopped struggling for air. The guards stood around him, chattering. Ralph could tell they were worried, and he hoped one of them would figure out what to do about it, fast! Suddenly, the towel was jerked from his mouth, and he found himself gasping air.

He was taken to see Frenchy, who warned him to abide by the regulations and ordered him back to his cell.

––––––

At Hoa Lo, Jim Stockdale was taken to interrogation on a cold February night. As a torture guard stood by brandishing ropes, Rabbit and Mickey Mouse complained to the CAG that they were having trouble getting the American "criminals" to talk to them. It would be necessary, they said, for Stockdale, a well-known senior officer, to tape-record a broadcast to his reluctant countrymen, urging them to provide answers to the questions their captors were asking.

It had been only a few weeks since Stockdale had had his first taste of the ropes, and he was still down. His broken left shoulder and crippled left leg still hurt badly. A numbness persisted in his left hand, as a result of the rope torture, and he felt weak and suffered dizzy spells. The sight of the thug caressing the ropes induced a sinking sensation. He agreed to speak: "The Democratic Republic of Vietnam," he told the tape, "does not honor the Geneva Convention of 1949. The Vietnamese are not treating us as prisoners of war. The man who is addressing you is not operating under the rules which we have been taught pertain...." Then, stuffing the most flagrant grammatical errors he could imagine into a flat monotone, he said the things the interrogators demanded of him. He was sick at heart for saying these things in any fashion, but was confident that Americans who heard the message would understand how it had been obtained and would ignore it.

A guard escorting him back to Heartbreak Hotel failed to guide him past an uncovered sewer drain, and Jim's injured left leg went into the thing up to the hip. Within a few days the leg had swelled hugely and a high fever raged in him. He lay sick, aware that Robbie Risner, in the next cell, kept encouraging him and praying for him; when he felt strong enough he prayed along with Risner. A doctor came, checked his heart, and gave him a supply of pills. After about a week the infection and sickness began to subside. Almost immediately, he found himself back in interrogation, facing Major Bai, Cat.

Cat was contemptuous of Jim's taped references to the Geneva Convention, and angry about the "tricks" he had employed with the rest of the message. "You are unsatisfactory," Jim was told. "The tape is not good enough." The verbal chastisement completed, he was returned to his cell.

For the next few weeks Stockdale and Risner remained in Heartbreak Hotel, while new shootdowns staged through. They told new arrivals what to expect and how to conduct themselves. They taught them the tap code and the vital importance of communications, of prayer, of thinking positively and keeping one's spirits up. "Don't sweat it if they torture something out of you," they told the new POWs. "We have all been through it. The important thing is to get back up as quickly as you can and get set for the next round. You're going to get depressed. If it is at all possible to do so, contact someone else. Talk about it. Don't keep it to yourself. Just talking about it helps."

Then, in late February, Stockdale was moved to New Guy Village. One day he was taken into Room 18 to meet Rabbit, who wanted him to "correct" the tape he had made and the letter he had written. When he refused, he was locked in stocks for ten days, then brought back to Room 18. "You must confess your crimes and repent them, and beg the Vietnamese people for mercy," the young interrogator screamed. Jim declined, and Rabbit had him tortured in ropes until he submitted. Then, with Rabbt dictating, he wrote a "confession," repenting his crimes and throwing himself on the mercy of the people. Also, he read a short script onto a tape, urging other Americans to cooperate with their captors—again the wording was such that he knew other American POWs would not accept it as a senior officer's directive. But for having submitted, Stockdale wanted to climb out of the broken body that had betrayed him.

Two days later Stockdale was taken to a film or TV studio and ordered to make the "confession" before cameras. Rabbit handed him the script, and Jim read it. So preoccupied did the Vietnamese remain with his words that they paid no heed to his actions. Holding the script in one hand and reading from it, he kept waving his other hand back and forth. He kept this hand clenched, with the forefinger and little finger extended, a signal the world would recognize as indicating that the words being spoken were untrue.

He was returned to his cell in New Guy Village.

————

At the Zoo, Bob Purcell told his keepers that hell no, he would not stand at attention and bow to show his subjugation to the Vietnamese people. He was isolated in a cell in the Auditorium and clapped into torture cuffs and traveling irons. For five days he received half-rations of food, no water. Thereafter he got a half-cup of water with each meal.

Approximately once each week, an officer would come by to ask, "Are you ready now to bow to Vietnamese officers and guards?"

"No," Purcell would answer, "I'm not."

After thirty days Bob estimated that he had lost thirty to thirty-five pounds. He was skinny, but felt fit. Spring was coming on, the weather was warming, and he thought he could go on indefinitely in this situation.

Apparently, his captors thought so, too. On the last day of March a contingent entered his cell, put him in torture ropes, and extracted a promise to bow. He also agreed to write a biography, in which he confided that one of the U.S. Air Force's biggest military problems was that the cooler that had kept the beer cold had gone on the blink, and that the men's morale often was low because the beer was hot. His interrogators accepted this intelligence and were intrigued by it.

Out of irons and cuffs, Purcell was moved into a cell in the Pool Hall. By now, Zoo SRO Jerry Denton was also in the Pool Hall, in a cell directly behind Purcell's. From Denton, Bob learned that three other Pool Hall residents were being starved for biographies: Air Force Capts. Jon Reynolds and James Otis Hivner and Air Force Lt. Robert Duncan Jeffrey.

The trim Purcell suggested to Denton that he was unused to the full rations he was now receiving and could easily do with lighter meals. He proposed to distribute shares of nourishment to the needy three. An access panel in the ceiling of his cell gave entry into an attic, from which Bob could reach any cell in the Pool Hall. With Denton's blessing, Purcell began a catering service.

Placing himself on quarter-rations, Bob rolled his meat servings into jelly-bean-sized pellets. He tore his bread into narrow strips that could be passed through small openings. He stuffed the food into his shirt pocket. He tied loops into one of his cotton blankets, made a rope ladder of it. He placed his waste bucket on his bunk and put all of his spare clothing and his other blanket atop the lid. He stood on this makeshift platform, sprang up from it, and got a grip on a bar in a small air vent high on the cell wall. He pulled himself up and tied one end of his blanket ladder to the bar. Using the loops of his ladder, he was able to climb up and push through the access panel in the ceiling, and pull himself into the attic. From there, he hauled up his water jug—he had fashioned a hauling line out of a drawstring in his spare trousers and thread he had stripped from his blankets.

Purcell found the attic to be a treasure trove of wire and big nails, items that could be used to pick locks, scratch messages, make holes for communications drops. He gathered these up. Naked light bulbs hung in each cell on wires that fed through small holes that had been made in the attic floor. Bob quickly found Reynolds, Hivner, and Jeffrey, alerted them, used nails to enlarge the holes around the light wires. He passed food rations down to the three, who would climb up on their bunks and hold up their drinking cups, so that he could pour water into them.

Purcell entered the attic daily during siesta, for guards usually were not about then—but it was by no means a sure thing. Once he was pouring water down to Bob Jeffrey when a guard's key rattled in the cell door. The POWs disconnected in the nick of time, and the guard, who for some reason had decided to see if Jeffrey was still alive, did not notice that his light bulb was swinging back and forth. Purcell kept gambling at great risk to himself that his own cell would not be checked as he made his runs.

Denton worried about him. One day he ordered Bob not to enter the attic. He insisted that guards would enter Bob's cell during siesta that day. He said it had come to him in a dream. Purcell stayed put, and incredibly the guards did come to his cell.

Percy could have been excused for wondering about his SROs' connections. Earlier, Risner had ordered prayers for lights, sleeping mats, and outdoor time, and all these things had been delivered. Denton got messages or had visions of future events, and they came to pass.

The Vietnamese never discovered Purcell's supply service. It went defunct in mid-April, when the POWs in the Pool Hall were reshuffled.

––––––

"Letters from your family in return for answering these questions."

The offer was made to Bob Shumaker, and was real enough. The letters, one from his wife, Lorraine, and the other from his mother, were shown to him. How badly he wanted them! It had been more than a year since his shootdown, and he had received no word from home in a long time.

But the questions were not the kind one could play games with. There were thirty-five of them, and they were highly technical, dealing with antimissile warning systems in aircraft, pulse repetition frequencies, band widths, and so on. They implied a knowledge that Bob felt certain far exceeded the technological expertise of the Vietnamese—even he, with advanced degrees in two technical fields, would not have been able to answer more than half of them. Surely, the questionnaire had been prepared by others, who were not likely to be fooled by any foolish answers he might give.

The price for the letters being too high, he declined to pay it. He was seated on a stool for twelve days, and ordered to "think deeply."

––––––

Perhaps because of his effusive personality, Larry Guarino was tied, blindfolded, and transported to a building in Hanoi to meet a foreign visitor. "Be talkative," urged Dog, as he escorted Larry to the room where she waited. "Above all, be very, very polite, because she is a very old lady."

Indeed, she looked old. She smiled at Guarino through crooked teeth. In a British accent she lectured him on the virtues of communism, insisting that, among other things, the Vietnamese "have now replaced God with science." Larry thought of the filth he lived in and looked around the dirty room in which they were meeting. He wondered how anyone could be in such a place and extol the Vietnamese commitment to science. The interview ended inconclusively, and shortly he was taken to another.

This one was televised. It was conducted by Wilfred Burchett, an Australian journalist who had reported from the Communist side during the Korean War. The American POWs in Vietnam referred to him as "Wellfed Bullshit." An affable fellow, Burchett introduced himself to Guarino as "George Graham." He was accompanied by a woman he introduced as his wife. She appeared to be in her early thirties. She was blond and good-looking, but hefty.

Also present was a Caucasian TV cameraman. A strikingly handsome chap, he shook Guarino's hand warmly and said, "How do you do, Major?" as though he meant it. He looked at Larry as though full of compassion for him.

Burchett, alias Graham, his female companion, and Guarino all sat down before the lights and cameras, and the interview began. First, Burchett asked Larry his name, rank, and serial number, then, "Where were you based, Major?"

"North Vietnam," Larry said, looking straight into the camera.

"Now, see heah!" Burchett said, rising. Irritated, he ordered the cameras to cut.

"Oh, pardon me," Larry said, smiling, "a slip of the tongue."

The show was started over. On camera, Burchett insisted Larry was a criminal. Larry retorted that he was no such thing, but a prisoner of war. Burchett condemned the American aggression in Vietnam; Guarino denied it was an agression, calling it an honorable intervention against Communist aggression. The interview was no different from any of the interrogations the Vietnamese conducted with the POWs. But it got out into the world, and many, including

Larry's family, saw it and wondered how it was that he had been allowed to say such things.

————

"People all over Vietnam are having meetings and demanding trials for the criminal air pirates!"

All that spring the message kept coming through the squawk boxes in the cells. Hour after hour, day after day, the POWs heard of how the "justly wrathful people" were coming together to denounce the American aggression. At the Zoo, Rod Knutson got so sick of it that he wadded up small pieces of toilet paper and stuffed them into his ears.

On April 10, Rod was taken to interrogation and informed by Fox, the Zoo camp commander, that it was time to write his biography.

"I will give you three minutes to write it," said Fox, placing a small clock in front of Rod. Rod flipped the clock back across the desk.

"Get out!" Fox screamed. "You will be punished!"

Rod started out of the office. Fox shouted at a guard, who slammed a rifle up against Rod's chest, stopping him.

"You did not bow," said Fox.

Rod stood staring at him, then started to walk out again. Again, the guard slammed his rifle into him, then slammed a fist heavily into his stomach, grabbed him by the hair, and tried to pull his head down into a bow. Rod resisted and was returned to his cell. A few minutes later, Dum Dum arrived with three guards. These four escorted Rod to a small building behind the Pigsty, on the southern boundary of the camp. The POWs entitled this building the Outhouse. It was about fourteen feet long and eight feet wide, with a partition down the middle. There was nothing in the place but a wooden pallet, a waste bucket, a light bulb whose strength Rod estimated at six watts, and an almost tangible stench of urine. The floor was damp with it. The guards ratcheted torture cuffs onto Rod's wrists, putting one side of each cuff against the wall and slamming it to ratchet it as tightly as possible. The pain was instant and intense.

"You will say, 'Bao Cao,' when you wish to apologize to the camp commander and write your biography," said Dum Dum. Then the four Vietnamese left, locking the Outhouse door behind them.

Rod's hands went numb quickly and started to discolor and swell. After several hours blisters had formed on his wrists, under the tight cuffs. The blisters soon broke, and pus ran from them.

The Outhouse stood on swampy ground. In the light of the low-wattage bulb Rod could see mosquitoes, thousands of them, and almost forgot the agony of the torture cuffs in his constant effort to keep them off him. He had to keep rushing about the room, brushing his face and head and arms and legs and back against the walls. In a way, he was grateful for the mosquitoes, for they helped him get his mind off the agony in his wrists.

He had been in the Outhouse for perhaps six hours when Dum Dum and two guards returned. "Are you ready to make apology to camp commander?" asked Dum Dum.

"No," said Rod.

Dum Dum motioned to the two guards, two sadists whom the prisoners called Slim (because he looked like a snake) and Magoo (because he looked like the cartoon character). These two stepped forward and began slapping and punching the manacled Knutson about the cell. They had delivered perhaps a half-dozen blows when Magoo threw a body block into Rod, knocking him backward into a corner of the cell, down onto his cuffed wrists. Rod moaned as severe pain darted from his right wrist and flamed all through him. The three Vietnamese departed, locking the cell door behind them.

Rod struggled to his feet, wondered desperately how to manage the pain—the cuffs had now cut to the bone on each wrist, and he was sure the right wrist was broken. He kept walking about, continuing the fight with the voracious mosquitoes.

Most of two hours passed. Then Dum Dum and the guards returned to tie Knutson's ankles in ropes, so that he could not walk. They threw him on the urine-soaked floor. He could have gotten himself onto the pallet but decided that it didn't make much difference. The main thing was to tough it out for as long as he had to.

And so he lay there, coping, all through the night.

Dum Dum returned to ask Rod if he was ready to apologize to the camp commander. Rod called Dum Dum's attention to his injured right wrist. It was grotesque. Both hands looked like inflated balloons, and the right hand was streaked with purplish, yellowish, reddish, brown colors, painted by demons of pain. The fingers of both hands stuck straight out and were so swollen he could not bend them; when he tried to move the right hand, bursts of pain shot up through the arm.

The cuffs were left on. That night Rod sat mute through another interrogation. Then he was thrown into the black room in the Auditorium. The next night he was told that if he would write an apology, he would be taken to a hospital where repairs would be made on his wrist. Rod replied that if they would attend to his wrist, he would consider writing something. A cloth was stuffed into his mouth, and a tape was slapped across his lips. He was blindfolded and taken somewhere in a vehicle, then into a room. The torture cuffs were removed, but the blindfold and gag remained on. His injured right wrist was placed on a cold surface, and Rod heard something buzz—it could have been X-ray equipment. He was led back into the vehicle and taken back to the interrogation room at the Zoo.

"Now," said Dum Dum, "you write the apology."

"No," said Rod. "You said you would fix my wrist. You did nothing for it."

"Your wrist is broken," said Dum Dum, "and your hand is so swollen that we cannot put a cast on it. We must wait until the swelling goes down."

"In that case," said Rod, "I will not write the apology or the biography."

He was taken to the black room in the Auditorium, the torture cuffs were snapped back on, and he was left for the night.

The next day he was taken back to interrogation, where Dum Dum advised Knutson that his refusal to cooperate was intolerable, and that he would be severely punished if he did not do as he was told. Again, Rod refused to write anything. He was returned to the black room and made to lie on his stomach. His ankles were bound together, then pulled up and tied tightly to the chain that held the torture cuffs together. He was left alone in the blackness.

He lay like a rocker on a rocking chair. At first the focus of pain remained in the right wrist, but then, quickly, it began shifting. Sharp claws of pain dug into his shoulders, into the fronts of his thighs, into his groin, into the small of his back. It burgeoned in all these places, then exploded all through him. He grappled silently with it for what seemed a long time, and then he began screaming. He estimated that he had lasted approximately thirty minutes in this torture.

He sat in the interrogation room and, crushed, put pen to paper for the first time since his capture. He had to write with his left hand, because of the painful injury to his right wrist. "I have been told that I have violated camp regulations," he scrawled, "and I promise to do a better job in the future. . . ."

Dum Dum didn't like it. He told Rod that his handwriting was bad and that he must write it over again. Rod pointed out that his hands were so swollen and numb that there was no possibility that his writing would improve. He was taken to a cell, where he received food and water, the first in days.

The same night, he was returned to interrogation and told he must begin writing his biography. It was necessary, he was told, that he write down every detail of his life, beginning with the day he was born. Rod's physical strength and spirit were at low ebb, just as they had been six months earlier after sustained torture. Again he had been taken to the edge of sanity and was not sure he could keep his grip on reality if he were subjected to more torture. Again it was time for evasive tactics.

He spaded his memory for the preposterous biographical data he had supplied the previous autumn and wrote down all that he could recall. This time he revealed that as a youngster he had delighted in pineapple milkshakes and dill pickles, and that when the two were mixed together they produced a savory flavor. Also, that his father, the farmer in Montana Farm District Number One, was a chicken farmer. He wrote reams of nonsense, then was asked to make clarifications.

"You say that your father is a chicken farmer," it was pointed out, "but you do not say how many chickens he has. How many chickens he has, your father?"

Rod wrote that his father had twelve chickens.

"Oh, no, no, no," he was told, "you cannot live on only twelve chickens. It must have been more than that." The paper was handed back to him, and, obligingly, Rod scratched out the number "12" and substituted "1,000." This number proved acceptable—but what kind of chickens? "Red chickens," Rod wrote.

"Now," he was told, "write concerning your job in the U.S. Navy."

He repeated in writing the same story he had told the previous autumn, stressing the importance of his job as a ship's recreation officer to the morale of the men. This done, he was pressed for papers on survival schools, military pay, and relatives who were famous or were in government service. He refused to write on any of these subjects, but finally agreed to produce an essay on fishing in Montana. When this was completed, he was left alone.

For a week he complained to the guards about his injured wrists. Finally, a medic came and painted what looked like Merthiolate onto the open wounds around both wrists. Then the mouth of a wooden spoon was placed in the palm of Rod's right hand, with the handle placed splintlike up the inside of the arm. The medic used gauze to wrap the spoon in place. It was to be many months before Knutson could use his right hand.

Spring 1966—Hard Times Continue

Navy Comdr. James Mulligan learned to bow that spring. Executive officer of Attack Squadron 36, operating off the nuclear-powered carrier *Enterprise,* and due to assume command of the squadron on April 1, he was shot down near Vinh on March 20. During ejection from his A4 Skyhawk, he suffered a broken shoulder, a number of cracked ribs, and a badly bruised hip. He was captured immediately. He was stripped to his underwear and socks. His wrists were bound before him, a leashlike rope was attached to the bindings and he was led before a large, angry crowd in bleachers under a huge tent.

The very air in the place seemed to vibrate with noisy hatred. Thousands of people were roaring, shaking their fists, screaming, and keening. Then Mulligan heard a chant building, words that sounded like *"Boo rown!"* The man leading him joined in the chant and looked expectantly at Jim. He jerked the leash, and Jim came forward, doubled over in the agony that flooded through his shoulder and ribs. The crowd cheered, and chanted, *"Boo rown! Boo rown!"*

"Bow down!" He understood. The American must bow in submission!

"Bullshit!" replied the prospective commanding officer of Attack Squadron 36. His reaction was almost reflexive. A twenty-one-year professional, Mulligan was proud of his service, and knew how his wife, Louise, and their seven fine sons, back in Virginia Beach, would expect him to behave.

"Boo rown!"

"Bullshit!"

It went on and on. The man kept jerking the rope leash, the pain kept doubling Mulligan over, and the crowd roared in triumph.

He was exhibited in many villages during the trip to Hanoi. Once, guards noticed that the ropes binding his wrists were so tight that they had cut through the skin, and his hands had turned a deep blue. Laughing gleefully, two of them grabbed him by the hands, held the roped wounds under a spigot, and let gasoline wash over them. The ropes shrunk into the wounds, and the guards delighted in his agony.

He found no surcease in New Guy Village. Rabbit and Mickey Mouse left the shrunken bindings in the bloody gashes around his wrists. Mulligan received no medical attention, no food, no water, and was not permitted to rest. The two interrogators demanded that he write and tape-record a "confession of your crimes." He kept refusing, and after a while felt himself drifting away. Just when he thought he would escape to unconsciousness, a large cup of well-sugared coffee was poured into him, and his level of consciousness was raised and sustained. He persisted in denying his captors a "confession" until the pain in his wrists became intolerable.

He was actually speaking to the recording tape before Pigeye, the torturer, began cutting the wrist bindings away. The ropes were so deeply embedded in the gashes that it took a long time to extract them. Later, remembering as much as he could of a situation where he had not had command of all his faculties, Mulligan was satisfied that he had given nothing of use to the enemy. The script employed language Americans would not normally use, and his voice was the weak, quavering voice of someone in dire mental and physical straits.

This did not deter Rabbit and Mickey Mouse from preparing Mulligan for a "press conference." He was to make a statement that the United States was waging an "... evil, immoral war. Washington has no right to bomb the Democratic Republic of Vietnam. The people of Vietnam do not bomb Washington, so why should Washington bomb the people of Vietnam, destroying schools, and churches, and hospitals, and killing innocent women and children . . .'' When Mulligan refused, he was taken to the foot of a bunk and his arms were locked in ankle stocks. In this position, halfway between standing and sitting, the strain on his broken shoulder and cracked ribs was excruciating. He was kept like this for days.

The next thing he knew, he was in a hospital. A doctor, a man whom Jim judged to be in his fifties, was looking at him. The man's eyes were clouded with dismay. ''My God, what's this!'' he said, in perfect American English. Turning to Mickey Mouse, who was standing close by, he said angrily, ''Are you trying to kill this man?'' Then he turned to Mulligan, saying, ''Your country is bombing my country, and I don't approve of that. But I don't approve of *this,* either!''

Mulligan was bathed, and his wounds were cleansed. The doctor kept looking at the torn, tortured wrists. ''How did this happen?'' he asked.

''Well,'' said Jim, ''the ropes . . .''

''Ropes? Ropes did that?''

''Yes. They poured gasoline on them . . .''

''Gasoline?'' The doctor was horrified, incredulous. ''We are going to take pictures of all this!'' he said, glaring at Mickey Mouse. ''I'm going to make a full report to the General Staff!''

Mulligan was taken to an operating room and fed intravenously. Many photographs were taken. He was anesthetized, and when he awakened there was a cast on his shoulder. Then he was returned to Hoa Lo. A week later, he was back in the hospital, clad only in underwear and socks.

''My God!'' said the doctor. ''Aren't you cold?''

''Yes.''

''Where are your clothes?''

''I don't have any clothes.''

The doctor turned to Mickey Mouse, jabbing his finger at him, his face suffused with anger: ''You get him some clothes. Tonight! Now!''

Mulligan was issued prison garb. There was another examination, and he was told his shoulder injury would require major surgery. The operation was scheduled to take place in a few weeks. Back in his cell in New Guy Village, he made his first contact with another American. It was Jim Stockdale, three cells distant. Stockdale talked out of his cell window into the alley when there were no guards present.

He told Stockdale of his injuries and of Vietnamese plans to operate on his shoulder. Stockdale grew thoughtful, pondering the unsuccessful operations on his leg. Finally, he said, "Jim, if you can get away with it, don't go back for the operation. They're not up to this kind of medicine. You could lose your arm . . ."

On the appointed day Mulligan refused to return to the hospital. There was no pressure on him to do so. That night he was moved to the Zoo.

He was stashed in a cell in the Barn. He heard tappings on the walls but did not know the tap code and was unable to make contact with the Americans all around him. His frustration mounted. One day when he heard other Americans nearby talking to each other, he tried to whisper his way into the conversation. Nothing worked. The others went on talking, as though Mulligan did not exist. He grew furious. He wondered, *Who the hell do they think they are, ignoring me? They are probably all junior to me.* He threw back his head and howled, "You guys don't have a hair on your ass if you don't get in contact with me!"

There was a silence, and then a voice came back: "Keep your shirt on, Commander Mulligan. We know you're here."

The others finished their conversation. Then Mulligan was told, "The next time you hear someone on the wall, put your cup on the wall and listen."

His first contact was with Marine WO John W. Frederick, Jr., a radar intercept operator who had been shot down on December 7 with Maj. Howard Dunn. Using the International Morse Code, "Freddie" Frederick taught Jim the tap code. The contact restored Mulligan's spirits. After a few days Frederick was moved, and two Air Force captains were moved into his cell: Richard E. (Dick) Bolstad and Warren Robert (Bob) Lilly. Both had been shot down on the previous November 6.

Bolstad brought Mulligan up to date on what was happening at the Zoo. He described an all-out effort by the Vietnamese to stifle prisoner communications. Also, the Vietnamese seemed to be embarked on a wholesale torture program, its purpose being to extract military and biographical information and confessions of crimes. Bolstad explained Denton's "No write, no tape" policy, and said the POWs were doing their best to follow it. Recently, though, said Bolstad, Denton had disappeared. In any case, with interbuilding communications being effectively suppressed, it appeared that each building had to operate much as a separate camp. And Jim Mulligan was SRO in the Barn.

On April 20, Jerry Denton had been taken from Cell # 6 in the Pool Hall and told that he was "inciting others to resist." As he was transported from the Zoo back to Hoa Lo for punishment, he was able to reflect with some satisfaction that he was guilty as charged. The Vietnamese assault on the prisoners for biographical information had met with stiff resistance. The POW performance implied a discipline which derived from strong leadership.

He was taken to Room 18 and made to sit on one stool nested atop another, so that his feet did not reach the floor. His arms were pulled behind him, and torture cuffs were ratcheted onto his wrists. He could not get down from the stools and move about even when there were no guards in the room. He knew that to be found off the stools would supply the Vietnamese with an excuse to apply more severe torture. So he remained on the stools, suffering the cuffs, for three days and nights, during which time he received no food or water. Then he was asked if he was ready to confess his crimes against the Vietnamese people. When he refused, he was made to stand at the foot of a bunk and his arms were locked in stocks. He remained in this position, unable to stand upright or sit, for most of a day, after which he refused again to confess his "crimes." Rabbit told him, "We know we cannot break you by food or water. Tomorrow we get serious. Tomorrow we torture you." This might have been the first time the word "torture" was used by any North Vietnamese to a POW; usually the Vietnamese took care to use the word "punish."

That night Jerry told Jim Stockdale in a nearby cell, "I'm going in there to die." He asked Jim to carry a message back to his wife, Jane: "Tell her I love her, but that I want her to remarry."

During the torture in Room 18 the next day, Denton prayed to die. Pigeye, the most proficient of torturers, worked on him, along with an eager assistant whose face was covered with pimples. Jerry's wrists were locked behind him in torture cuffs, his ankles were shackled, and his upper arms were laced tightly into torture ropes. As the torturers waited for him to break, he lay back on numb hands, sought unconsciousness, relief from the engulfing pain. A large, gray doughnut formed at the periphery of vision and kept thickening, darkening, growing toward the hole in the center. He concentrated on the fattening doughnut, willed its growth, knowing that when the gray filled the hole he would be unconscious.

Pigeye would not let it happen. He pulled Denton back up into a sitting position. A long, heavy iron roller was laid across his shins, and the two torturers each put a foot on it and walked it up and down his shinbones. Jerry tried to deny Pigeye the satisfaction of seeing him react to pain. He smothered urges to scream. Pigeye put his face close to the prisoner's, searched his eyes for the telltale film of pain. Pigeye knew one word of English, and he said it with a sneering smile: "Okay?"

Jerry returned Pigeye's sneer and cursed him. The two torturers again jumped on the roller, and Jerry was amazed that his shinbones did not snap inward. The gray doughnut was at the edges of his vision, and he concentrated on it, willed it to grow faster. Pigeye hovered close, diverted him, ruined his concentration. Then Pigeye began hitting him, and Jerry now concentrated on not flinching, on keeping his eyes wide open and staring, hoping he could make the torturer think he had lost consciousness, that he was catatonic. But Pigeye was too knowledgeable in these matters to be fooled.

Denton had a high pain threshold, but Pigeye knew how to make things intolerable. He loosened the ropes on the upper arms, let the blood flow again into the lower arms and hands. When this wave of agony had spent itself, Pigeye again lashed the ropes tight around the upper arms, pulled the pain back into the chest and shoulders. He shoved his face close to Denton's. "Okay?"

"Okay!" Denton spit back, letting him know he still had not conquered him.

Pigeye lifted him by his manacled wrists, lifted the roped arms up behind his back, used them as a lever of excruciation. Again Jerry found himself concentrating on the big gray doughnut at the edge of his world, trying to make it come in upon itself. But Pigeye kept breaking the rhythm of the pain, infusing new intensities into the torture, then letting them ebb. He stopped lifting the arms, loosened the ropes, let the blood wash huge new waves of pain down into the forearms and hands, then squeezed the ropes tight again, lifted the arms, rolled the shinbones, knuckled the cheekbones. At last Jerry knew that the torturer was not going to let him escape into unconsciousness, and that he could stand no more. "Bao Cao," he whispered.

Instantly, Pigeye called off his helper and left the room. Denton was left in the manacles, shackles, and ropes. His clothes were drenched with sweat, which had puddled on the floor all around him. He lay gasping, dazed, waiting, wondering where his tormentor had gone.

Presumably, Pigeye went to confer with Major Bai, the prison system commander who had taken a special interest in Denton, to tell him that the prisoner had surrendered. A decision was made to take Denton beyond mere surrender, to break him utterly, make him totally submissive to Hanoi's will. Subjugate the leadership, and the others were bound to follow.

Pigeye returned, got the roller back onto Jerry's shinbones, and lifted the roped arms again, up his back, slowly, so as to wring the fullest measure of pain out of the exercise. Denton thought he would never stop lifting his arms! Pigeye took them higher up his back than they had been before, higher than he would have believed they could go. He saw the gray doughnut growing again, saw it darken quickly and rush in upon itself, saw Pigeye's face close to his own, saw the torturer looking into his eyes, watching the pain build its film. He heard Pigeye breathe, "Ahhhhh!" Then, merciful, merciful oblivion.

———

It was dark when Denton awakened. He was propped on a stool. His ankles were still in shackles, but the wrist manacles and torture ropes had been removed, and his arms were now tied together in front of him.

"Now, Denton," said Rabbit, "you are ready to write a confession of your crimes against the Vietnamese people?"

Jerry nodded his assent.

"And to make a tape recording of it?"

He nodded, and then agreed to write a biography.

His arms were untied and he was provided with pen and paper. Rabbit dictated, telling him to write that he often had led many American aircraft in attacks against the North Vietnamese people, bombing and destroying many schools, churches, and hospitals, killing many women and children. Denton tried to take this down, but his benumbed, discolored hand would produce only an illegible spiral. Rabbit decided he could make the tape first. But Denton had no voice—he knew he had not screamed it away in torture, but it was gone. He simply could not talk. He was given something to drink. He did not know what it was, but his captors thought it might restore his voice. It didn't work.

After a long time he was taken to a bath area, to clean himself up. Left alone, he became aware that another American in an adjacent bath area was whispering to him, asking him to identify himself. Then, somehow, he understood that it was Robbie Risner. He had been Risner's deputy at the Zoo, before Robbie had left, but this was his first direct contact with him.

"Who are you?" Risner kept asking insistently.

Jerry could not find his voice, to give his name. He tried to whisper, tried to talk, could not get it out. Finally, he tried yelling, and managed to squeak, "Denton!"

"Well, God bless you!" Robbie said. "I know what they have been doing to you, and I know you've done your best. They did that to me, too, back in November. Keep your chin up." Jerry never would have believed he would need encouragement so much.

Denton gave written and oral confessions, exactly as Rabbit dictated them in Communist jargon. In the written version he misspelled words and used bad grammar throughout; on tape he mispronounced words and used the same bad grammar. He wrote a new biography, also full of misspellings and grammatical disaster areas, in which he explained that his entire career had been spent as a flight instructor.

That was not all. The Vietnamese had him going now and meant to keep him producing. He agreed to attend a "press conference." For days, starting in the early morning and lasting far into the night, Mickey Mouse prepared him. "I realize you are a sincere man who has been brainwashed by your government," the tutor offered. "You do not undahstan your government wages an illegal and immoral war in Vietnam. Do you undahstan that?"

Just before the "press conference" Denton was warned to remember what had happened to him in recent days, and to conduct himself accordingly. Jerry did not think he was likely to forget his recent ordeal. Ever.

It proved to be a TV interview. It was conducted by a Japanese reporter fluent in English. Denton was told that the interviewer was a "socialist," and was urged to "be polite" to him. Major Bai, Mickey Mouse, and Pigeye all were present. As the interviewer briefed Jerry on the procedure, it was clear the man had been given to understand that the American had come to recognize the error of America's ways. He advised Denton that his first on-camera question would invite a condemnation of the United States for its wanton slaughter of Vietnamese innocents.

Denton's memory churned over an exchange years earlier with his wife and son, Donald, then in the eighth grade. It had involved a newspaper account of a Moscow "press conference" involving Gary Francis Powers, the American U-2 pilot shot down in Russia in 1960. Powers had been depicted as an unscrupulous mercenary, a spy who had hired himself out to the U.S. government to violate Soviet air space. His Soviet captors had implied that Powers had provided them with all kinds of vital information.

"Isn't it too bad that he wasn't able to stand up and say something in that press conference?" said Jane Denton.

"Mother," said Donald, "don't you know that they can make you say anything? If they can force a man like Cardinal Mindzenty to make a confession, they can force anyone to do it."

"Yes," said Jane, "but wouldn't it have been great if he had found the courage to say something . . ."

Now, in Hanoi, the cameras were grinding, and the Japanese reporter posed his question to Jane's husband. Jerry looked straight into the camera and summoned a resolute voice. "Let's get one thing straight," he said. "I don't know what's going on in this war. The only sources of information I have are your magazines, your newspapers, and your radio. But whatever my government is doing, I agree with it, and I will support it as long as I live."

Major Bai and Mickey Mouse stood six feet away, just out of range of the cameras, and Pigeye stood to one side, brandishing ropes. None of the Vietnamese present were fluent enough to comprehend the exchange, but Denton noted some fidgeting, some suspicious looks. The Vietnamese had assured the TV journalist that the American would say the right thing. Now, apparently, there was a reluctance to lose face by stopping the proceedings to ask the Japanese, a fellow Asian, what had been said. And the interviewer, whose reportorial instincts seemed to overpower his allegiance to Hanoi's cause, did not belabor the point, for to do so would have called attention to it. Instead, he moved on with a series of questions designed to show an American who was alive and well in Hanoi: What time did Denton rise in the morning? Go to bed at night? Did he enjoy a rest period during the day? Receive cigarettes? After several minutes of this he ended the session.

The Japanese reporter lost no time in getting the interview broadcast, and Jerry appeared on U.S. network television in June. In addition to his remarks, he had blinked out in Morse Code with his eyes a message that was picked up by American Intelligence and by many others who had been radio operators during the century's wars. The message: *torture*.

Denton's press party was not over. The Japanese reporter departed, and a few minutes later Wilfred Burchett and his female companion were ushered in. As she seated herself facing him, Denton was amused at her deliberate way of crossing her legs so as to reveal expanses of bare thigh. What was not amusing about her was the hatred in her eyes.

Burchett wanted to know why the United States was conducting a slaughter of Vietnamese innocents.

"Nonsense," said Denton, "the United States has leaned over backwards to protect civilians."

Burchett's woman sneered. Burchett snorted, "If you think that's true, you Americans must have the worst Intelligence in the world."

"The United States," said Denton, "takes great care to avoid injuring civilians. I know of no one who has ever deliberately hit a civilian target."

After a few minutes of debate on the subject Burchett moved onto broader ground, denouncing the United States for intervening in Vietnam. Denton engaged him with pleasure. The argument was bitter, waged from opposite philosophical poles, but it was good to be able to talk freely after so long. He ended the meeting with Burchett by telling him, "I can't believe that you are convinced of the justice of what you're saying. I can't believe you're that deluded."

Cat and Rabbit were agitated. They were all but certain Denton had not performed as ordered in the TV interview, and knew, of course, that far from denouncing the United States to Burchett, he had defended his country's position, had been "impolite." He was returned to New Guy Village. Rabbit spent most of two days berating him. "Den-ton," he said, over and over again, "you have been cunning. Cunning! You will be punished!"

To his great surprise, Denton was taken a few days later to meet a journalist from Chile, another "socialist." The prospect of more torture frightened him, but he decided he had to end the "press conference" business no matter what the cost.

Cat, Rabbit, and the Chilean sat in easy chairs, and Denton was seated on a stool, in front of the journalist. The Latin looked smug as he launched on a harangue about America's Vietnam involvement.

Jerry made his move.

"You're a Communist," he said, interrupting.

"I am a Progressive!" the Chilean said, drawing himself up haughtily.

Denton got up from his stool and walked from the room. A guard at the door grabbed him. But Cat had had enough. There had been another miscalculation with Denton. It had been assumed that torture and threats had induced a cooperative mood in him, but again he had caused them to lose face. There were to be no more press conferences for Denton.

A few days later Rabbit cited formal charges to Denton: communicating with other criminals; "polluting" his comrades; refusing to accept Vietnamese "education to progress"—there were nine counts, and it was stressed that chief among them was "being impolite at press conferences." "Now, Den-ton," said Rabbit, "you must be punished." Rabbit departed, and Pigeye took over.

Jerry's ankles were shackled, and his wrists were locked in front of him in torture cuffs. Then Pigeye produced what looked like a large, three-cornered ruler, but it had no markings on it. He came close and, using the sharp corners of this club, began rapping a tattoo on various parts of Denton's head and face. The blows stung and broke the skin atop the ears, above the eyes, on the knuckles, and on the nose and lips. Pigeye took care, as he bloodied the lips, not to knock out any teeth. When he had the prisoner bleeding profusely from all these areas, he began ramming the club into the kidneys. These blows hurt badly. Jerry shook the blood from his eyes and glared at the torturer, hoping he could read the hatred he felt for him. Pigeye flushed, and put something extra into his blows, and Denton felt good about arousing anger in the man.

The beating lasted for perhaps twenty minutes. Then Jerry was made to sit in a corner of the room. Jumbo irons were affixed to the shackles, above the ankles, and Denton committed a grievous error. It occurred to him that he was not sweating a storm, as he had in his previous torture, and he was anxious that anyone who looked in think him to be sweating profusely. Furtively, he began spitting into his hands, and rubbing the saliva about his head and face. In the door window, Pigeye saw the reflection of Denton trying to disguise his condition. He spun around, pointing at him, smiling evilly. "Ah hah!" he said. "Ah *hah!*"

The shackles were turned so that the brackets for holding the long iron were now behind the ankles. Denton was made to cross his right leg over his left to align the brackets so that the bar could be inserted. He could not do this; it was not possible. Four men worked for twenty minutes before the right leg was crushed down through the left to accomplish the alignment. Then the bar was run through the brackets on each shackle. The prisoner was made to lean forward until he thought his spine would snap and his left wrist was chained to the bar.

Jerry had never known pain to equal this! It was as though both ankles were undergoing a spraining process that did not end. When he tried not to think about his ankles, he found himself thinking that his back was going to kill him literally. No man could take much of this.

He said a rosary, concentrating on each word of each prayer. He finished the rosary, and no one came. He said another. And another. No one came. Sometimes he found himself losing his concentration and rushing the prayers; he would force himself to slow down, to think about each word, and the meaning of each thought.

He had gone into this rig at sunset. He was still saying rosaries when morning came. By now, his legs and feet had swollen to football size around the ankle shackles. A guard entered, and Denton whispered, "Bao Cao." The guard indicated that it was 7 AM and that torture would end at 8.

When he was released from torture, he was as pliable as his captors were ever to find him. He was made to copy a well-constructed statement he felt certain had been written by another American after severe torture. In it, he confessed to having led many destructive raids against the DRV, in which churches, schools, hospitals, and many innocent lives had been destroyed. He wrote that henceforth he would do his best to follow orders and to abide by camp regulations and advised other prisoners to do likewise, lest they, too, be severely punished.

His Vietnamese captors were satisfied that Denton was broken. But he certainly didn't impress Sam Johnson that way.

———

Air Force Maj. Samuel Robert Johnson, thirty-six, of Dallas, Texas, a graduate of Southern Methodist University, a combat veteran of the Korean War, once a member of the "Thunderbirds," the famous Air Force high-precision aerial acrobatics team, arrived at Hoa Lo prison on May 6, after three weeks on the road in North Vietnam. An F4C Phantom jet pilot based at Ubon, Thailand, he had been shot down on April 16, about forty miles north of the DMZ. On ejecting from his crippled aircraft into an approximately 600-mile-per-hour windblast, he had dislocated and broken his left shoulder, broken his right arm in two places, and suffered a compression fracture in his back. He had been captured almost immediately. Johnson received little medical attention, except that his dislocated left shoulder was reinstalled in its socket.

At Hoa Lo, two interrogators asked Johnson what targets in Hanoi the American Air Force was going to attack. Sam replied, truthfully, that he did not know. At a signal from one of the interrogators, a guard grabbed him by the left arm and ripped the shoulder out of the socket again. Sam crumpled to the floor, awash in pain. He was pulled to his feet, and the question was asked again. Again he explained that he did not know the answer; again his left arm was yanked and twisted savagely; and again he fell to the floor. After the routine had been repeated for a third time, the interrogators decided that he was telling the truth. They got up and left. After a while Sam was taken to Heartbreak Hotel. There Jim Stockdale and Jerry Denton briefed him on procedures and codes, as they did all new arrivals, and tried to keep his spirits up.

One night the indomitable Denton began loudly singing patriotic songs, and Sam Johnson found that he had to join him. The two sang and whistled until guards came and threatened them to silence. The next day Denton was clapped in stocks for two days.

On June 2, Denton, Stockdale, and Johnson were moved to the Zoo. There, Stockdale and Johnson were isolated in adjacent cells in the Garage. In the cell on the other side of Stockdale, between the two Americans and the rest of the camp, were two frightened Thais who refused to communicate. For the whole, hot summer of 1966, Stockdale and Johnson remained out of contact with other Americans.

With Stockdale, who was senior, unable to function as SRO, the mantle of leadership again fell on Jerry Denton, who was back in his

old cellblock, the Pool Hall. The day after he returned he was summoned to interrogation and told, "You have agreed to follow camp
regulations. Your first job will be to read Vietnam News Agency
news over camp radio."

If he did, Denton thought, other Americans would no doubt follow
suit. Soon the world would be listening to American military officers
explaining how, on reaching North Vietnam, they had found their
country to be guilty of illegal, immoral aggression. Still, Denton
wondered if he dared refuse. That long night of horror in Room 18
was still a bleeding scar on his memory. He was not sure how he had
kept his sanity—indeed, he was not certain he *had* kept it when he
heard himself say, "No, I will not read on the radio."

"Then," said the interrogator, "you must be sent back to the other
camp for more punishment."

The interrogator left the room, apparently to arrange for transportation, and Jerry sat down and began sobbing uncontrollably. The
thought of more torture was unbearable. He could not stop crying.
After a few hours the interrogator returned and sent him back to his
cell in the Pool Hall. There, on the walls, he learned that other POWs
had been similarly threatened to read the news, but that the
Vietnamese had not yet followed through on the threats.

Late that spring, prison broadcasts were filled with news of British
philosopher Bertrand Russell and his plans for an international war
crimes tribunal. President Lyndon Johnson and other American leaders were to be tried in absentia for "brutal treatment of the people of
Vietnam for twelve years." The tribunal was to be patterned after the
Nuremberg Trials of Nazi war criminals following World War II.
Russell urged American servicemen to submit evidence.

Thereafter, the Vietnamese talked incessantly to their American
captives of war crimes trials. Again and again, it was explained that it
was now clear to the whole world that they were criminals. In
Vietnam there would be trials for the military men, just as the Russell
tribunal would try their leaders. They would be put on stage before
the whole world.

Zoo SRO Denton promulgated policy: POWs who were threatened
with war crimes trials were to deny that Hanoi had a right to try them;
were to demand legal representation by the United States government; were to stand mute if taken to trial without such counsel; and if

forced to speak were to defend the United States' position to the best of their abilities.

> *That spring of 1966 President Johnson was firing rhetorical broadsides at domestic war critics. He warned against "Nervous Nellies," who would "turn on their leaders and on their country and on our own fighting men." He insisted that "if America's commitment is dishonored in South Vietnam, it is dishonored in forty other alliances or more that we have."*
>
> *But even the most steadfast supporters of Johnson's policies could have been forgiven for wondering at election year activities in South Vietnam. Far from democracy in action, a picture seemed to be emerging of totalitarian repression and civil war. On March 10, Roman Catholic Premier Ky had provoked the wrath of Buddhists by firing the Buddhist General Nguyen Chan The. At Da Nang, troops loyal to The had remained in a state of virtual revolt. Then, on May 7, Ky asserted that he had no intention of leaving office, following the upcoming election of a Constituent Assembly, which was to decide on the form a civilian government would take. He declared that he would stay in power for at least another year, to ensure that the policies being established by the military government were carried out. This announcement triggered wild Buddhist–labor-union demonstrations in Da Nang. On May 15, Ky sent troops into the city to put down the demonstrations. The government forces were resisted by 1st Division troops and needed more than a week to prevail. Meanwhile, Hue, the ancient imperial capital, became the center of Buddhist resistance. In violent anti-American demonstrations, Buddhist mobs burned the American library and consulate. On May 29, a protesting nun burned herself to death before a Hue pagoda, and within a few weeks nine more Buddhists had followed her example. By the end of June, the dissidents had been overwhelmed.*
>
> *There were now 285,000 U.S. combat troops in the country.*

The Hanoi Parade

Plans for POL strikes in the Hanoi-Haiphong area had been actively advanced ever since Johnson's Christmastide bombing pause in the air war proved that Hanoi was interested not in the conference table but in conquest....   *Time,* July 8, 1966

POL: petroleum, oils, lubricants. The lifeblood of a modern military force. On June 29, 116 U.S. military aircraft from Air Force bases in Thailand and Navy carriers in the South China Sea had entered the Hanoi and Haiphong metropolitan areas for the first time. They had rained nearly 100 tons of bombs and rockets into these areas, destroying at least half of the country's POL. For the Communists, it was a major disaster. As *Time* quoted Maj. James Kasler, forty, co-leader of the Air Force armada, "The whole place was going up. Every bomb that went in set off a secondary explosion."

Hanoi, said *Time* in its next edition, "responded with a mixture of fear, rage and determination...."

On July 6, fifty-two American POWs tasted the rage.

At the Briarpatch that morning, some Americans thought the war was over. For days they had been listening to "Hanoi Hannah," a female newscaster, ranting over the camp radio about the American air strikes against Hanoi and Haiphong. News of the strikes had lifted POW spirits to new heights. At last, Washington had taken off the gloves and was hitting the enemy where it hurt.

Sixteen Briarpatch POWs were awakened and fed early, and their shirts were taken from them. At siesta time their shirts were returned to them, and they were ordered to put them on. A three-digit number had been stenciled on the back of each shirt. The numbers did not run consecutively, and there seemed to be no rhyme or reason to them. Ev Alvarez, the first American shootdown, judged this to be a propaganda ploy—Hanoi continually insisted that hundreds of American aircraft had been shot down and that thousands of Americans had been killed or captured. What mattered was that the war was over, and the POWs were going home.

The POWs were blindfolded, divided into two groups of eight, and put aboard two trucks. During the thirty-five-mile ride to Hanoi, a last-day-of-school atmosphere prevailed. The Vietnamese guards enjoyed looking at the passing countryside. They talked, joked, and laughed among themselves, and paid little attention to their prisoners. There seemed little question that the American air strikes against Hanoi and Haiphong had brought the Communists to their senses, that the war had ended or was about to end, and that the prisoners were being returned to Hanoi preparatory to being released. The POWs chattered and joked. Newlywed Ed Davis was teased bawdily about his jock itch, and warned that to return home in such condition would surely ruin his marriage.

But as the trucks approached Hanoi, air raid sirens screamed, and at once the trucks stopped. It appeared that the war was not quite over. Ed Davis, peeking over his blindfold, saw Frenchy, the Briarpatch camp commander, get out of the cab and come toward the rear. To warn his friends to silence and divert the sadistic Frenchy's attention, Ed began complaining loudly.

"Debis! Debis! What do you say?" cried Frenchy, running toward him.

"I gotta go to the bathroom."

"Not now. Go later."

"No, I gotta go now."

"Shut mouth!"

"No! If ya gotta go, ya gotta go!" Ed could hear his friends around him chuckling softly.

"Shut mouth!" shrieked Frenchy. He was angry, and climbing onto the truck. Ed knew he was overplaying his hand, but the scene was bringing out the ham in him, and he could not resist baiting the hated officer. Frenchy pounded his fist into the side of Ed's head. The blow stunned him—he was amazed to see stars. *It's just like in the cartoons!* he thought.

Then, through the bottom of his blindfold, Ed saw Frenchy's foot coming at him. The kick landed hard, on the bottomside of the thigh. Frenchy backed up and kicked him again and again. The kicks hurt, but did not do serious damage. Finally, Frenchy climbed out of the truck and walked away. After a while, guessing that Frenchy was out of earshot, Davis said, "Well, I don't have to go near as bad anymore!" The truck exploded in laughter.

But optimism had dissipated by the time the trucks pulled into a big stadium in Hanoi. "Ooooh," murmured Davis, "lions three, Christians zero. I've seen this game before!"

Robbie Risner, who had been tortured several times since his first ordeal, was back at the Zoo, in a cell in the Garage. On July 6, he watched through a crack in his cell door as one POW after another was led across the grounds, blindfolded and wearing rubber-tire sandals tied on with surgical gauze or string. Soon, guards entered his cell, blindfolded him, tied on sandals, and took him to a place where he was handcuffed to another prisoner, Air Force Lt. Jerry Driscoll, who had been shot down on April 24, 1966.

Thirty-six Zoo POWs were told they were "going for a walk." Also, that they were not to attempt to communicate with one another, that the guards had orders to shoot on the spot any who did so.

Trucks took them from the Zoo to a park in downtown Hanoi. Other trucks brought the Briarpatch prisoners. English-speaking Vietnamese officers climbed into the trucks and read a prepared statement to the POWs. Today, they were told, they were going to make one of the most important choices of their lives. The time had come to decide whether they were going to repent their crimes and join with the Vietnamese people in seeking a just end to Washington's "illegal and immoral" war, or to continue on their belligerent ways. Those who did not repent would be tried as war criminals. The path for them would be the path of death.

The prisoners were left in the trucks for a long time to "think deeply." Then, in early evening, they were taken out of the trucks, still blindfolded. Ev Alvarez was led off to have his wrist tied to that of another prisoner, Robbie Risner. A guard came by asking if anyone had to make water. Risner indicated that he did, and he and Alvy were led off to some bushes. The guard stood back, and for a few minutes the two were able to whisper, exchanging information.

"Where are you?" asked Ev.

"In the Zoo," said Robbie. "I just got out of Heartbreak. Where are you?"

"At the Briarpatch. There are thirty-five of us up there."

"I thought you were at the Zoo."

"No. They took a bunch of us up there in May."

The guard approached, and the conversation had to end. All the POWs were now ordered to sit down. Bob Purcell, trying to peep over the top of his blindfold, was suddenly aware of someone standing over him, a Vietnamese officer or guard—Bob could not see well enough to identify the man. The man reached down, took Bob's chin in his hand and lifted it gently, to look into his face. He held Purcell's chin for a moment, then gave it a friendly tug, as though to reassure Bob. Then he walked away.

At last, the POWs were ordered to rise, and their blindfolds were removed. Bill Tschudy and Al Brudno, cellmates at the Briarpatch, stood at the head of the long column of twos; there were fifty-two prisoners, each pair standing approximately ten feet behind the pair in front of them. Ahead, in a large traffic circle, bleachers had been erected and were full of people. Rabbit moved along the line of POWs, speaking to them through a battery-powered megaphone: "Now you are going to see the hatred of the Vietnamese people. We are going to try to protect you, but we are not going to kill any Vietnamese in doing so. So if the people want to kill you they are going to kill you. Now I give you advice: do not look to the right or to the left, do not look behind you. Do not speak. Walk straight ahead. Show a proper attitude to the Vietnamese people. Bow your heads in shame for your crimes." Rabbit ended his monologue by demanding, "Do you undahstan? *Do you undahstan?*"

There was a silence, then Wes Schierman drawled, "Well, I guess

I understand, but I just don't think I can remember all those things, they just kind of dribble off into nothing . . .'' Several POWs burst out laughing.

Slapping at Schierman, Rabbit shouted, ''I cuff you like a cur!

Now we allow you to march!'' The guards beside Tschudy and Brudno motioned with their rifles, and the line of POWs moved toward downtown Hanoi.

''Oh, boy!'' laughed Purcell. ''A parade! I love a parade!''

The crowd ahead, in the bleachers, maintained an eerie silence as the prisoners moved toward them. The people stared, almost apathetically. Risner and Alvarez, the third twosome in the column, watched Rabbit and others with megaphones stride ahead, stand in front of the bleachers and climb into them, then begin shouting, screaming, gesticulating, exhorting the crowds like cheerleaders. Still, the crowd was silent. Then, almost as though a switch had been thrown, the crowd came roaring alive, gave itself over to an endless cacophony of rage. Men, women, and children shrieked at the prisoners and shook their fists at them. As Alvarez and Risner came close, Rabbit began leading a chant: ''Alvarā, Alvarā, son of a bitch, son of a bitch! Alvarā, Alverā, son of a bitch! Alvarā, Alvarā . . .''

Bob Purcell suggested to Jon Reynolds, ''Let's hold our heads and shoulders high. Let's look like Americans.''

''Right,'' said Reynolds.

Larry Guarino, marching with Ron Byrne, was not concerned. He had utter faith in the Communists' ability to control their people. He did not see how it could possibly benefit Hanoi to allow its American POWs to be injured or killed in public. Larry was certain the whole show was phony.

A very large truck moved along next to the column, loaded with big strobe lights, movie and television cameras, cameramen and reporters, all of them Caucasian. Jerry Denton believed he detected neutral and even friendly expressions on some of the Occidental faces. In any case, the event was being observed and filmed, and the reports could hardly fail to reach the outside world, which surely would censure Hanoi for subjecting POWs to such treatment. Denton felt it important to impress upon the outside world that the Hanoi's American POWs had not been subjugated. ''Keep your heads up!'' he shouted. ''Don't bow your heads!'' The message traveled up and down the line, became a battle cry. Denton smiled hugely at the grinding cameras and waved a V for Victory signal at them. He grinned at the crowds on all sides, extended the middle finger of his free hand and held it high in the air.

The roaring of the crowd picked up, intensified, grew angrier. Suddenly, a group of perhaps a dozen young men, some of them wearing caps, strode unopposed past the guards and, staying together, piled into the POW twosomes, slugging and kicking at them.

Their actions drew the roaring approval of the crowds and now people poured out from the sidewalks and bleachers toward the line of prisoners, howling and screaming, throwing stones, bricks, and bottles. They pressed closer and closer, pushing the guards into the prisoners, and pushing past them to kick and punch.

"Bow!" the guards screamed. "Kowtow! Kowtow!"

"Don't lower your heads!" POWs shouted to each other.

The guard next to Risner slammed a judo chop into the back of his neck, and he found himself stumbling, barely hanging onto consciousness. Alvarez held him up, carrying him along until his senses were back in place. Just then, someone hurled an uppercut into Risner's face that nearly tore off his nose. Ev kept his grip on him, kept him moving along.

Larry Guarino was taking a beating, too. His aplomb began fading rapidly when he saw that some of the guards were terrified. People in the crowd beyond the guards actually were tearing their hair out. Mass hysteria! Madness! It didn't look phony anymore!

People got between the guards and the prisoners. One Westerner who spoke English with a heavy French accent walked along next to Jerry Coffee saying, "You Yankee murderer, you filthy son of a bitch."

A Cuban photographer came in close to Alvarez, cursing him vilely in Spanish. He kept asking him if he were Cuban and calling him a "dirty Cuban traitor." Alvarez kept walking, making no response to the man. Suddenly, the Cuban landed a stunning blow on the back of Alvarez's head. Risner had to help Ev along for a while.

Up front, a crowd of Cubans ran alongside Bill Tschudy and Al Brudno, chanting, "Cuba, si! Yanqui, no!" Some came close, sneering, and, in English, called them foul names.

Larry Guarino thought that the most frightened of all the guards must be the young man next to him. The lad was white with terror and almost in tears. He stumbled along, holding his bayonet down, and with his horrified attention riveted on the surging mobs. As the crowds ahead began to hinder progress, the space between prisoner twosomes shrank rapidly, and the lad inadvertently poked his bayonet into the rear end of the guard in front of him. The offended guard turned and snarled at the youngster, who backed off, muttering abject apologies. A little farther on and again the bayonet reached the guard's posterior. This time he erupted in a long stream of what could only be the direst Vietnamese curses and slammed a number of punches into the lad.

The mobs kept swirling, thickening, closing in around the prisoners. A Vietnamese male, moving along in the crowd beside Jerry Denton, suddenly delivered a roundhouse left hook, as hard as he could, into Jerry's groin. The blow felled him, and he knelt, in blinding pain, hunched over in the street, with the crowd hooting and roaring around him. His marching partner, Bob Peel, knelt with him, offering words of encouragement and trying to help. Soon Jerry was able to walk again. A few steps, and again his antagonist slipped in close, threw another sledgehammer blow into his groin, and again Jerry went down. "I've had it, Bob!" Denton shouted. "We're gonna practice. Follow my moves." Jerry's right wrist was locked to Bob's left, but Denton, who had learned some boxing, could deliver a left jab that was nearly as powerful as his right. The two prisoners danced ahead, feinting, balancing, setting up and swinging, counting aloud, "One! Two! *Three!*" On *three* Denton would lash out with his left. They practiced this several times, and soon were moving in effective unison. Denton looked in the crowd. He saw his attacker, creeping along nearby, smiling hatred, not understanding the gyrations of the two Americans, and getting ready to dash close again.

A delicious, furious impatience seized Denton. He could hardly wait for the next assault. Then he saw Spot, one of the officer-interrogators at the Zoo, watching him closely. Spot was open-mouthed, obviously frightened at what he divined Denton's plan to be and uncertain as to what to do about it. Denton pointed at his assailant and told Spot, "If that son of a bitch comes out here one more time, we're gonna go": and again, he and Peel went through their "One! Two! *Jab!*" movement.

Suddenly Spot ran into the crowd and, with both hands, grabbed Denton's attacker by the shirtfront, just below the collar, lifted him and shook him hard, screaming into his face. Then he dropped the man, pushing him back into the crowd. The chastened citizen did not appear again, but the damage had been done. The man had inflicted a partial hernia on Denton.

Clouds of debris hurtled through the air at the POWs—rocks, clods of dirt, garbage, bottles. The crowd chanted, *"Kowtow! Kowtow!"* Vietnamese moved alongside the prisoners, screaming into their ears, *"Bow! Bow! Bow your head, filthy Yankee son of a bitch!"* The guards nudged the points of their bayonets into the backs of the POWs and banged rifle butts against their shoulders. "Bow! Bow!" they commanded shrilly, and now and then a POW would jerkily lower and raise his chin.

Dum Dum, his eyes glazed with excitement, stood in front of Bob Purcell, ordering him to bow.

"No," Bob said.

Dum Dum grabbed Purcell with both hands around the back of the neck and tried to pull his head forward to force it down. Under-nourished as Purcell was, he still was far too strong for the Vietnamese officer. Determined, Dum Dum put all his strength into the effort, actually lifting his feet from the ground in the attempt to bring Purcell's head down, but Bob walked along easily, thinking that the officer looked like a monkey; thinking, too, that he would pay later for making Dum Dum lose face. It was worth it. He kept his head up.

"Shoot the Yanks! Shoot the Yanks! You son of a bitch Yankee!"

Jon Reynolds turned to see who was behind him, and a rifle butt smashed against the side of his head. He did not look back again. A civilian dashed in front of him, grabbed him by both ears, pulled his head down and held it down. Jon was furious, but could not move his head; there was nothing he could do about it. He heard Purcell, still carrying Dum Dum on his shirtfront, laughing, "Hey, Jon, who's your friend?"

At last, Reynolds's ears were freed, and Dum Dum dropped away from Purcell disgustedly.

A Vietnamese ran past Guarino holding a small boy high in the air. The boy had his fist cocked. The man launched the youngster over a guard's head and he landed, punching, on Smitty Harris. Harris shrugged, the child fell to the street, and guards kicked him back into the crowd.

Another child, maybe eight years old, shot past guards and doubled over Wendy Rivers with a punch in the testicles. It occurred to Wendy that this was no way to spend one's thirty-eighth birthday.

The crowd jeered: *"Chonson murderer! Rusk murderer! Mocknomara son of a bitch! Fuck you, Yank!"*

Ahead, Ed Davis could see that the wide walk and steps before a hospital had been cordoned off. Suddenly a man in a white smock, cap, and surgical mask came running out of the hospital, holding a surgical instrument high in the air. Unimpeded, he dashed into the street and began beating prisoners about their heads with his instrument. The crowd milled around him, cheering. Clearly, the people understood that the surgeon had been at work, attending to the innocent victims of American bombs, and that on learning that the American criminals were passing had been unable to contain his outrage. Then, his anger apparently sated, he raced back to his patients in the hospital.

A woman walked alongside Ron Byrne, shrieking hysterically at him. She reached down and pulled one shoe off. A guard interceded, tried to hold her back. She swung her shoe at the guard. He pushed her back, warning her angrily, but she was beyond reason. She pressed in again, swinging the shoe. The guard's punch came all the way from his toes and landed squarely on one of her breasts. She seemed to fly several feet in the air, then landed, turned, and ran off through the crowd.

We might not make it through this thing, Alvarez thought. The crowds were out of control, in the grip of a powerful, unmanageable hysteria. Hundreds of thousands of people had become a lynch mob. The guards were powerless, and too frightened now even to try to retrieve control. Just ahead of him, Hayden Lockhart and Phil Butler were being pounded mercilessly. Alvarez thought they were being beaten to death.

Up front, Bill Tschudy and Al Brudno were also taking a terrible beating. They were bloody and their clothes were in shreds. For some reason Tschudy would never be able to explain, however, it never occurred to him that the prisoners might not make it. He was frightened. At the same time, he had for months been consumed with a desire to see Hanoi. This was not the sort of tour he would have selected for himself, but he was making the most of the opportunity, ducking blows and flying objects to note store windows, billboards, the modern glass front of the Voice of Vietnam, the radio station, and gathering a general impression of a French-looking city in an advanced stage of decay. Almost everything he could see was dilapidated, falling apart.

Behind, Skip Brunhaver and Jerry Singleton, Ron Storz and Wes Schierman, Jim Hivner and Ed Davis struggled through the continuing melee. Davis, his right hand locked to Hivner's left, raised his own left hand to protect his head, felt a sharp sting, lowered the hand, and found it awash in blood. Bewildered, he turned his head, looking for the cause of the wound, just in time to see a fist come smashing flush into the middle of his face. He felt himself sinking, but Hivner grabbed him, managed to keep him on his feet and moving, shouting encouragement to him. Then, as Ed regained his senses, he became aware that people were tugging Hivner, beating him and trying to pull him out of the line. Ed though the pressure on the handcuff locking him to Hivner would tear his arm off. He tugged back, hard, pulled with his free hand, retrieved Hivner and they moved on.

The POW column kept moving ahead, stopping, then moving ahead again. The shrieking fury of the mobs, the cursing, spitting, and beating of the Americans never slackened. Some guards tried to slug with their rifle butts at the pressing crowds, but it was a losing battle. The mobs remained unmanageable.

Tschudy and Brudno, leading the column, found themselves approaching partially open doors into the stadium where they and the other Briarpatch prisoners had spent much of the afternoon. An officer nearby shouted to him, made it clear that they were to enter the stadium, but it was not clear how they were to reach it. A solid wall of shrieking humanity perhaps fifteen feet thick stood between them and the stadium doors. The two young Americans lowered their heads and shoulders and began fighting their way through, punching, kicking, and ramming forward. At last, they reached the doors; Vietnamese guards on the inside reached out, grabbed their arms, pulled them through and slammed the doors.

Behind Tschudy and Brudno came Lockhart and Butler, fighting their way in. The screaming mob before the doors was thickening by the time Alvarez and Risner arrived. An officer pointed at the doors, beyond forty feet of seething, screaming thousands, and shouted, "Go!" The two lowered their heads and went. The doors opened to admit them and slammed shut again.

To Jerry Denton, it was like a football game with no rules. Ahead, POWs were getting knocked down, were crawling, getting to their feet, kneeing people, slugging them, knocking them down, throwing them down, fighting through. Denton did not know who the POWs in front of him were, but he was proud of them. With his partner, Bob Peel, he took on the mob before the stadium doors with a will.

As Navy Lt. Jim Bell and Ralph Gaither approached the stadium, word flashed through the mob that they were the last twosome. The crowd closed in behind them, and for Bell, who had suffered a terrible shoulder injury during his shootdown nine months earlier, it was an especially painful passage.

All the POWs made it into the stadium. The doors were locked. The Vietnamese officers and guards strode about sighing with relief and congratulating each other on having survived. The prisoner two-somes were ordered to keep silent, but they whispered to each other: "We did okay. Great show!"

One POW, Navy Lt. Cole Black, who had been captured only fifteen days earlier, asked, "Hey, do they do this often?"

Now, over a public address system, the POWs were told, "You have seen the just wrath of the Vietnamese people. Those of you who have seen the light and want to apologize for your crimes and join the Vietnamese people will receive lenient and humane treatment. If you are true Americans, you will follow the way of Fulbright, the way of Morse, the way of Mansfield." The alternative, the prisoners were advised, was to be turned over to the mercies of the justly wrathful Vietnamese people.

The Hanoi Parade was over. The beaten, bloody Americans, many of whom had thought earlier that day that the war had ended and that they were going home, were herded back onto their trucks, to ride blindfolded back to their dungeons at the Briarpatch and the Zoo.

At the Zoo, many were taken immediately to their cells— blindfolded Bob Shumaker was walked into a stone archway, knocked cold, and thrown onto his cell floor. Others remained in the swimming-pool area for what Bob Purcell called the "Garden Party." Guards checked blindfolds, made certain that all were on securely and that the prisoners could not see, then cuffed their wrists behind them around trees. They were gagged with towels and socks, stuffed into their mouths and deep into their throats. Then guards strolled about, taking turns inflicting savage beatings and kickings. Among those cuffed to the trees in addition to Purcell were Jerry Coffee, Wendy Rivers, Duffy Hutton, and "Pop" Keirn (Air Force Maj. Richard P. Keirn, captured on July 24, 1965).

Larry Guarino and Ron Byrne, still cuffed together, sat apart. So did others, cuffed in pairs and singly. Occasionally, guards would approach these others, pull them to their feet, to punch them about and kick them in the testicles.

Two guards were at sport with Risner. His wrists were cuffed behind him, and they would take him by the elbows and run him into things—the back of a truck, bushes, trees, concrete steps. He bled and hurt from head to toe. He thought it would never end.

Air Force Maj. Fred V. Cherry, thirty-eight, black, a distinguished combat veteran of two wars, did not march in the Hanoi Parade. He participated in a different way. He would have much preferred the wild mobs in the streets to the corridors of pain through which Vietnamese doctors escorted him that night.

During his shootdown nine months earlier, his left arm and shoulder and his left ankle had been broken. For months he had received virtually no medical attention. Early in February, as the American bombing pause persisted and it appeared that Washington and Hanoi might reach an accommodation, Fred had been rushed to a hospital. There had been an operation on the broken shoulder and arm, and he had been put in a torso cast; his ankle, too, had been casted. He had been returned to his cell in the Zoo. Shortly, Ho Chi Minh had rejected a fourteen-point peace proposal by President Johnson; the American bombing campaign resumed, and Cherry's captors lost interest in his condition.

The surgical incisions became infected, he ran high fevers, and by early March he was delirious most of the time. Finally, on March 18, he had been returned to the hospital and the cast had been removed. A cocoon of pus had caked around his arm and body and there were major sores everywhere. He had been cleaned up, given blood transfusions and intravenous feedings, the incisions had been bandaged, and he had been returned to the Zoo the same night. Three days later he was back in the hospital, where he spent the next twenty days.

The hospital care had been primitive. For days on end, his blood- and pus-soaked bandages and bedding had remained unchanged. He had been impressed, though, with the good intentions of some of the personnel. Doctors had displayed concern for him, and always made sure he had pain-killers. Two young girls, teenagers whose task was to clean hospital rooms, would bring him bananas and candy—one actually fed them into his mouth while the other stood watch at the door, ready to sound a warning if a guard came.

When fever was finally subdued, Fred was returned to his Zoo cell. Periodically, a medic had come by to change his bandages. On July 3, the medic had probed the infected area and found a mass of decayed flesh. On July 6, after the Zoo POWs were taken downtown, Cherry was returned to the hospital. He was to undergo a second operation. The decayed flesh was to be cut away, and the bone scraped clean.

The atmosphere in the hospital was different that night. The same doctors who previously had been concerned for Cherry's well-being and comfort now exhibited savagery. Fred was given no anesthetic. A small sheet was placed over his face and draped down his neck, above the left shoulder and arm. The doctors excised the decayed flesh, cutting to the bone and scraping clean infected areas of bone.

Fred lay in an immense agony. He became aware that the doctors wanted him that way. Occasionally one of them would lift the sheet over his face and look at him hopefully, waiting for him to cry out. Summoning a self-discipline he did not know he possessed, he refused to cry out. The drape would be replaced, and Cherry would hear animated, puzzled conversation whose content was clear—"He is not unconscious; he is not screaming!" They wanted him to scream, and he spent much of the evening wanting to scream; but it was important to him that he not afford them the satisfaction they sought. He gritted his teeth until he thought they would break or fuse together. But whenever the sheet was raised from his face, he made sure he was smiling widely.

He tried not to think of the pain. He thought instead about all that had kept him alive these past months, chief among them "Hally"— Navy Lt. (j.g.) Porter Halyburton, his cellmate at the Zoo. Despite the pain, Fred almost grinned thinking of their first meeting, in November. Halyburton, a handsome, dark-haired Southerner who had been educated at Sewanee (Tennessee) Military Academy and Davidson College, North Carolina, had impressed Fred as being shocked at finding himself incarcerated with a black airman. The two did not seem destined to become close. But in the months that followed, Cherry could not have asked for a better friend than Halyburton. Hally had done everything for him. He had forced him to eat when he had not wanted to, which had been most of the time. He had carried him to his waste bucket and had held him over it, all the while keeping a wet towel on his forehead to keep him from passing out. He had wiped him, bathed him, and talked to him, trying to keep his mind off his desperate physical problems, and had never once complained when the odor from Fred's decayed shoulder had been so bad that Cherry didn't think he was going to be able to stand it himself. Hally had tucked him into bed each night carefully, making certain he was covered. In Fred's healthier moments, Hally had lifted him, had forced him to get up and walk about the cell, to build his strength. Quite literally, Cherry knew, he owed Halyburton his life.

Cherry was determined to perform well for his country. America had been good to him. He had grown up poor in rural Virginia, and had suffered his share of racial indignities—the one that bothered him most had involved his older brother, who by the time he was fourteen was man of the house, their father having died. The boy had quit school and gone to work so that Fred and a sister could remain in school. He loved his family, and worked hard and uncomplainingly, and Fred worshipped him. One day, Fred had watched a young white boy drive his car dangerously close to his brother, who was returning home from work on his bicycle. The white boy reached out and knocked his brother into the street, then drove away. There had been no reason for it; it had been terrible to see, and terrible to see his brother cry. Indeed, there had been many such bad moments. But by and large, life had been good. With his family's support and encouragement, Fred had earned a degree in biology from Virginia Union University, then had done what he had always wanted to do: won entry into the Air Force's pilot training program and earned his wings and commission. By 1953, he was in Korea flying combat in F84G fighter-bombers. He got in 50 missions before the war ended. After that, he had done well in the Air Force, and the Air Force had done well by him. He had been ready and eager to fight in Vietnam, and had flown more than 50 missions when he was shot down.

He was Hanoi's first black captive. The Vietnamese had seemed surprised that a black could be an officer-pilot, and were unsure how to deal with him. There had been tentative attempts to zero in on his blackness, to find and exploit his resentments, but he had squelched them. He had made clear that he was first and foremost an American military officer, and expected to be treated as such. An angry interrogator had ripped up his Geneva Convention card, saying, "I will show you what a joke this is!"

He had persistently refused to give more information than the Geneva Convention required of him. For a lot of reasons, he meant to do well as a prisoner of war; he owed it to his family, for the years of love, help and encouragement that had been invested in him; and to the Air Force and the country for the opportunities that had been granted him and the confidence exhibited in him. And so he endured his night of horror in the hospital, he, too, refusing to bow his head to America's enemies on the night of the Hanoi Parade.

At last, his ordeal over, he was returned to his cell. A guard half carried him in. He was covered with blood and all but irrational. Halyburton, who had been downtown in the parade, took him from the guard, and, thinking that Fred, too, had marched, murmured, "Oh, my God, did they put you through that?"

"Oh, Halyburton," was all Fred could answer.

Hally got him into bed and sat up all night with him. Fred's surgical wounds would not stop bleeding. Halyburton wrapped the wounds with all their spare clothing, and by morning all was blood-soaked.

The infection that had caused the decay was not destroyed. It flared anew, the rot set in again, and in the July heat Cherry and Halyburton lived with the stench and wondered what lay ahead.

––––––

Jerry Denton had been returned to his cell, bloody, bruised, and exhausted. Yet he felt elated. He kept thinking of that truckload of cameras and newsmen. He was certain the enemy had disgraced himself before the entire world. He was about to climb onto his bunk when his cell door rattled open; guards entered and led him to the swimming-pool area. There his wrists were cuffed tightly together behind a tree. He was blindfolded and the now filthy, sweat-, blood-, and dirt-soaked rags that had been used to tie the sandals to his feet during the parade were crammed into his mouth.

Left alone, Denton coughed out his initials, in tap code, to see who was near. Back came two answering coughs. The only one he could make out was "J. C." He giggled to himself, *There are three of us here, and 'J. C.' is in the middle—I'm the repentant thief!* Then he realized that "J. C." was Jerry Coffee.

It was a long night. The next morning Bob Shumaker and Smitty Harris tapped on the wall separating their cell from Wendy Rivers's, "Please don't invite us to any more of your goddamn birthday parties!"

––––––

Radio Hanoi's report on the Hanoi Parade reached the prisoners in their cells. The broadcast was also monitored in Tokyo and relayed to the rest of the world. According to the broadcast, "American prisoners were being marched through the streets of Hanoi under armed guard . . . when tens of thousands of people poured into the streets shouting, 'Death to the American air pirates!' and 'Down with U.S. imperialism!'

"One or two of the pilots tried to put on an arrogant air, but in the face of the wrath and protests of the population, all of them marched docilely, their heads bent, their faces pale and sweating with fear. . . .

"The Hanoians, though seething with anger at the crimes committed by the U.S. air pirates, showed themselves to be highly disciplined; otherwise the sheer thought of these crimes might have prompted them to tear Johnson's 'skywarriors' to pieces!"

The parade was reported over Radio Moscow and *Isvestia,* the official voice of the Soviet Communist Party, reported that North Vietnamese government offices were being inundated with demands for the trial and sentencing to death of U.S. pilots shot down over North Vietnam.

Washington watchers in Hanoi did not have to wait long for an American reaction. Far from rallying the "true American people" to an antiwar stampede on Washington, Hanoi found itself on the receiving end of numerous somber warnings. Eighteen of the Senate's most vocal "doves" joined in a "plea for sanity," insisting that trials, executions, or abuse of any captured Americans "would drastically reduce the influence of all those in the United States who have tried to curtail the fighting. It would incite a public demand for retaliation, swift and sure. . . ." Among the signers were several of the bitterest critics of American policy in Vietnam, including Senators Fulbright, Morse, McCarthy, and McGovern.

Sen. Robert Kennedy said , "I have dissented at many points from this war and its conduct, but I am at one with all Americans in regarding any reprisal against these young men . . . as an intolerable act—contrary to the laws of war, contrary to all past practices in this war, a plunge into barbarism. . . ."

Sen. Richard B. Russell, the greatly respected chairman of the Armed Services Committee, said he believed action against the POWs would lead to an American reaction that would "make a desert" of North Vietnam.

On July 14, the Washington *Post* editorialized, "North Vietnam will invite terrible retaliation if it proceeds to try and punish captured American pilots. The measured restraint of the air attacks so far would melt in the popular passion likely to be generated in the United States by reprisals against the airmen.''

At a July 20 presidential news conference, Johnson was asked for his reaction to talk from Hanoi about war crimes trials. He answered, ''We feel very strongly that these men are American military men who are carrying out military assignments in line of duty against military targets, are not war criminals and should not be treated as such.''

Later, when pressed for what action he would take in the event of trials, the President declined to speculate, but said, ''I think the people of this country . . . would find this action very revolting and repulsive and would react accordingly.''

So Hanoi, if it sought an American reaction, had one. There had been press reports that the trials would begin in Hanoi on July 20 or August 4.

They did not begin. But if Hanoi was cowed by all the denunciations and warnings, the POWs didn't know it.

12

The "Make Your Choice" Program

"Now, all you criminals who are being asked to make their choice, you all know Robinson Reesner and Jeremeeya Den-ton, and how stubborn and obstinating they are. Listen to what we have forced them to do!"

The confessions that had been tortured out of the two in previous months were read over the camp radio. The POWs were made to understand that Risner and Denton, "stubborn and obstinating" though they were, had been made to admit to the most heinous of crimes, the deliberate murders of countless innocent Vietnamese and the destruction of hospitals, schools, churches, and homes. If these two could be forced to such admissions and made to apologize and to plead for forgiveness, surely the other Americans would realize that they, too, could be made to do their captors' bidding. Why not, then, make it easy on themselves?

"Now, you have come to the place where you must make your

choice. You must decide whether you are going to take the good path, the path of Ho Chi Minh and the Vietnamese people, the path of cooperation; or whether you are going to take the bad path, the path of resistance and death.

"Those who take the good path will receive good treatment. They will receive better food and lots of exercise and sunshine. They will have recreation. They will be allowed to read and study. When the time comes, they can expect to be released and go home to their families, perhaps even before the war ends.

"But we know that the vast majority will not be able to take the good path because they have been spoiled by the American system. They will understand the good path, but will not be able to take it because they are set in their ways. We understand that, and they will be treated humanely, because even though they do not take the good path, they will not take the bad path, either. They will receive enough food and medical care, and when the time comes they will be released to go home.

"But, also, there will be a very small group of diehards. These people will take the bad path. They will refuse to admit their mistakes and will refuse to apologize and cooperate with the Vietnamese people. They will oppose us and resist us, and lead others against us. That group will be severely punished. We are done with the diehard criminals. Theirs is the path of uncertainty and death!

"Now, it is up to you. You must make your choice. Which way will you go?"

The effect on the POWs of the Risner and Denton confessions was not what the Vietnamese hoped for. By now, most of the other prisoners were well aware of how severely the two had been tortured for these confessions. They knew what they had to do.

At the Zoo, Barn SRO Jim Mulligan instructed his men not to respond to the "Make Your Choice" program. "They have no right to require POWs to make such a choice," he insisted. "Tell them to jam it!"

It wasn't all that easy. Zoo inmates Wendy Rivers, Ray Merritt, Jerry Coffee, and Duffy Hutton were taken to Hoa Lo. From there they were taken singly to interrogation rooms in the Ministry of Justice building across the street. It was explained to each that he would have to write two open letters, one to American pilots fighting in Vietnam, advising them of his discovery that the American war effort was "cruel and unjust," and urging them to "reconsider your actions," and the other to the United States government, saying essentially the same thing.

Some worried that other American pilots and their government would not understand that such statements had been extracted under duress. All worried that others in the world would not understand, particularly those Southeast Asians whose lives were at stake. How were they to know the American pilots did not mean what they said? It was worth a fight. So, as best they could, the POWs fought. Typically, Wendy Rivers answered, "I can't do it. Not of my own free will."

For the first time, Rivers was laced into torture ropes, and left alone. As much as he had heard of the ropes, the intensity of the pain surprised him. Soon he was screaming, pleading, and praying for relief. He shouted "Bao Cao" many times, but nobody came. He stayed alone and in the ropes, sweating, groaning, and crying, certain in his agony that his arms were lost to him forever, wondering if he was to be left here to die of this agony. Again and again he shrieked, "Bao Cao!" Finally Rabbit came in, asking, "What do you want?"

"I want to get out of these ropes. I'll do what you want."

"You must think about it for a while," Rabbit said. "I don't want you to change your mind." He left.

It seemed a long time before Rabbit came back, this time with guards, who pulled at the ropes while the interrogator sat laughing. "Please!" Wendy begged. "Take the ropes off!"

Rabbit smiled.

"The ropes have been off for five minutes," he said.

Wendy's shoulders were still pulled back, as though frozen in the position they had been tied into. He couldn't move them. He tried to collect his wits. He became aware of the cries of other Americans, screaming, begging for mercy. Rabbit sat laughing at him. He presented Rivers with letters that had been written by three other POWs and told him to use them as guides in writing his own. After Wendy was able to use his arms and hands again, he produced three letters that were as innocuous as he could make them. Much to his satisfaction, his torturers kept insisting on changes that made the letters clearly recognizable as Communist propaganda. The editing completed, he read the letters onto a tape. He could hear tapes being made in other rooms, too.

Then the prisoners were returned to the Zoo. The torture sessions had shocked and subdued them. All were appalled at what had happened to them—and to Duffy Hutton, whose face was a mass of blue-red blotches: after he had been roped, his ankles and neck had been tied together, across his back. He had lost consciousness and nearly strangled. Most of the blood vessels in his face had ruptured.

They had fought an important battle and lost it, and felt the way professional military men feel when that happens. But they were to learn soon enough that their war was far from over. Like a lot of others, they had committed themselves to the bad path, and there a lot of fighting yet to be done.

––––––––

Zoo diehard Robbie Risner refused to confess to an outrage perpetrated in the bullpen, an area enclosed by bamboo fencing where prisoners were allowed a few minutes' solitary exercise each day. There, on the ground, the word "RESIST" had been scratched out in large letters. Immediately, SRO Risner was hauled in for interrogation. "You are still preaching resistance and opposition," he was told. "You must confess."

"I will not confess to something I have not done," he answered.

He was wrong.

His wrists were cuffed behind him, and he was locked in the black room in the Auditorium. In summer this unventilated room surely had to be one of the hottest places in Southeast Asia. When Robbie entered, he already was covered with heat rash and boils. He had a severe diarrhea, and with his hands locked behind him he was unable to reach the drawstring belt that held up his trousers. He was filthy, miserable. Twice each day, one cuff was removed so that he could eat and drink water, and during these moments he did what he could to clean himself.

After several days he was marched back to his regular cell in the Garage and made to listen to a broadcast. He marveled at the enemy propagandists' facility for blaming the United States for all that went wrong in Vietnam. Crops did not fail, but were destroyed when United States aircraft blew out some dikes. Floods occurred because United States aircraft were seeding clouds. A child was stillborn or born deformed because U.S. planes were filling Vietnamese air space with chemicals. There was no end to the litany of grievous American sins. It occurred to him that this was all the Vietnamese people heard, all day, every day. Most were uneducated and had no access to other information. No wonder they were so easily provoked to frenzied hatred at the sight of Americans.

During the broadcast the door to his cell had been left open, and a guard armed with a rifle patrolled back and forth before it. Robbie managed to get next to the wall and, standing with his back to it—his hands remained cuffed behind him—tap to Jim Lamar* in the next cell.

"Did you admit anything?" Lamar asked.

"No," Robbie tapped, "I never will."

Just then the guard spotted him. He came into the cell, stood his rifle against a wall, and, smiling, spent long minutes hammering the cuffed prisoner from wall to wall, beating him to a bloody pulp.

He was returned to the black room. That night a light was turned on and torture cuffs were ratcheted down to the bones of his wrists. Then another guard, obviously enjoying himself, worked Robbie over for a long time.

The next day the battered Risner was returned to the cell in the Garage for another broadcast. This time he was handcuffed to a ring on the wall opposite Lamar's so he could not communicate with him. When the broadcast ended, the guard released him from the ring. A few minutes later he found himself in interrogation.

"You secreted a nail to communicate with! This is a violation of camp regulations!"

"I did not secret the nail," Robbie replied.

"The guard said you did!"

"The guard is a liar!"

He was returned to the black room and locked in torture cuffs. The guard used both hands to force them to the last notch of the ratchet. So excruciating was the pain that Robbie could not move; he was absolutely immobile. That night the guard returned to deal with him for calling him a liar. The beating he administered was the worst Robbie had ever had. The torture cuffs were left in position throughout the night. He wanted to cry out, but did not want to give the enemy the satisfaction of hearing him scream. The sweat of torture soaked through his clothing, drenching him. Periodically guards would throw open the door, turn on the light, look at him, listen to him groan, and laugh happily.

In the morning he agreed to write a confession that he had written "RESIST" on the ground in the bullpen; that he had attempted to communicate—but he refused to name others; or to admit that he had secreted a nail on himself. It wasn't good enough. The interrogator

*Air Force Major James L. Lamar, captured on May 6, 1966.

demanded that he confess also that "I have committed crimes against the Vietnamese people, and am a criminal."

Risner refused angrily. "I am an officer in the Air Force of the United States, captured in line of duty, a prisoner of war."

He was rushed back to the black room, the torture cuffs were ratcheted back onto the agonized, swollen wrists, and he was left for another night. The next morning he wrote the confession that was demanded of him, exactly as it was dictated.

———

Larry Guarino was at Hoa Lo, in Hearbreak Hotel with Navy men Paul Galanti and Leonard Eastman, and fellow Air Force officers Alan Lurie and Darrel Pyle. On the afternoon of July 10 these five were taken from their cells and escorted into separate rooms in the Ministry of Justice building. Political cadres demanded that the pris oncrs produce letters to the U.S. Congress protesting the American war effort. Unanimously, the prisoners declined to do so, and a long night of rope torture got under way.

Guarino had not been in ropes beforc, but he thought he knew how painful they must be. He now learned that he had had no idea how bad they were—particularly when, as in his case, they were applied by amateurs. His torturers seemed very young and were wildly, almost hysterically enthusiastic for their work. He actually heard bones snap and felt a sharp pain flaming in his right arm. He felt the skin of his upper arm burning, as they ran the rope around it. Someone stood on the point of his shoulder, pulling the rope tighter, tighter, unbelievably tighter. The other arm was roped, and then, amazingly, the upper arms were pulled together behind him until the points of his shoulders were nearly touching. He could feel his ribs spreading, spreading, spreading as though they were going to break and burst out of him. He would never have believed that skin could be made to stretch so far! His wrists were tied together behind him, and another rope was run from the wrists up around his throat. Then he was left alone.

He flopped about the floor, holding his head back and gasping for air, hoping he could find the strength to withstand the pain. *Boy,* he thought, *it's a good thing Evelyn doesn't know about this! She'd have a heart attack!*

Rabbit was master of ceremonies.He went from room to room, cajoling the agonized POWs. "You are the only one who is resisting us," he would tell each of them. "The only one." Beyond him the prisoners could hear a discordant chorus of crying and screaming.

Guarino screamed. Someone came in and jammed a wet rag well down his throat, gagging him. Down the hallway the screaming went on. After a while one prisoner's screaming achieved ascendancy. Someone came into Guarino's room, pulled the gag from his throat, and left with it, and then Larry heard the other POW's screams being stifled. Apparently the torturers were having to make do with one rag.

Larry lost track of time. He wondered at the fact that the pain in his shoulders and chest did not diminish, but seemed to get worse with every passing minute. He found himself rationalizing: *Does my country expect me to die this way? Being pulled apart on a dirty floor in a distant Asian town? Just to resist saying I'm a criminal, or some other foolish thing?*

The answer, of course, was no. Indeed, Risner and Denton both had called for resistance only to the point where sanity was at stake, or permanently disabling injury or death seemed imminent. Guarino, having had all he could take, surrendered.

Rabbit would not accept his surrender. He kept him in the ropes to teach him that he should have surrendered sooner. Finally, after a long time, the ropes were removed. It was time to allow Guarino to "make your concrete act. Show your repentance." In the letter to Congress, he was to "write your true feelings about the Vietnamese people." Larry wrote:

Dear Congress:

In this past year that I have been a prisoner, the Vietnamese camp commander has given me the opportunity to study much of their literature. Of the 4000-year history of the Vietnamese people, I have seen that these poor people have always been exploited, first by the Chinese, then by the French and now the Americans. And now I ask you to stop immediately and for all time the bombing of these innocent people . . .

The letter completed to the enemy's satisfaction, Larry was now made to read it into a tape recorder. Present were Rabbit and a superior, an English-speaking officer whom Guarino did not know. For the reading, Larry affected a somber tone, speaking very slowly, like a record on a turntable that was running down.

"What are you trying to do?" Rabbit interrupted. "Are you trying to bush around the beat? You think I don't know what you are doing?

You talk like you are in a church. Don't talk like you are in a church! Talk like you are convinced!''

"No, no, no!" said Rabbit's superior, "nice and slowly. Speak nice and slowly."

A glow of angry frustration suffused Rabbit's face. He got up, tight-lipped, and left the room. Guarino completed the reading, sounding as though he were in the last stage of consciousness.

———

One day, as a new arrival confessed his crimes and apologized over the radio, a Zoo prisoner tapped to Denton, "God, I don't see how he could do that!" For some reason, the disgusted pilot, who had been downed months earlier, had so far escaped torture.

"Don't condemn him," Denton advised. "There is no telling what they did to him."

The other pilot remained skeptical. Late the next night he returned to the Zoo from Hoa Lo, where he had been tortured. He tapped to Denton, "I am humiliated. What an arrogant fool I was to say what I did."

"G B U," Denton tapped.

———

It was a long, grim season, that summer, fall, and winter of 1966. Guards now had carte blanche to abuse the prisoners. Zoo turnkeys would fail to lock cell doors after evening meals, so that guards could enter, always in twos and threes, to beat men unmercifully. No reasons were given for these beatings. Victims were selected at random, and the guards enjoyed themselves. Men who were found with nails or too many cigarettes or suspicious markings on their walls, or who refused to "make your choice," were brutalized on the spot or taken off to full-dress torture sessions.

There were small tortures, too. During the day the radio speakers filled the cells with the song "Wheels," over and over and over again; the record player or tape was off speed. The Americans came to detest the song, and the sound of Rabbit's voice, which came on periodically, to urge them to "choose one of two ways . . ."

At the Zoo, men were disappearing from their cells. They would be gone for varying lengths of time, some for several weeks. Then they would be seen again, heavily bandaged, being led across the grounds by guards. Back in communication, they would confess brokenheartedly to the other POWs that they had been unable to stand the torture any longer and had given the enemy what he wanted.

In the smothering July and August heat, Jerry Denton, Jim Mulligan, John Borling, Air Force Lt. Norlan Daughtrey, shot down and captured August 2, 1965, Al Lurie, Air Force Lt. Darrel Pyle, shot down and captured on June 13, 1966, and Navy Lt. (j.g.) Larry Spencer, shot down and captured on February 18, 1966, were all ushered into solitary cells in the Gatehouse, a long, concrete building on the north perimeter of the camp, near the front entrance. There were no lights in these cells, no windows, and no provision whatever for ventilation. The prisoners were not allowed to have mosquito nets, nor allowed out of their cells for any reason. Except for Mulligan, the prisoners' wrists were locked behind them in torture cuffs and their ankles were shackled in traveling irons.

In addition to the vermin that infested all other cellblocks, this one contained a sizable bat population. There were no ceilings in the cells, and the walls between them reached nearly to the interior roof, which was hung with thousands of bats. At night the prisoners were aware of the bats winging close to them.

The Gatehouse prisoners soon all were covered with heat rashes and boils. Borling counted some thirty boils on himself.

Apparently, Mulligan was not locked in cuffs and irons because he was very nearly dead. He had been tortured in March, immediately on reaching Hoa Lo, for a statement condemning his government's Vietnam policy. On July 8, this statement—Hanoi called it a "deposition"—appeared in an Associated Press dispatch in the New York *Times:*

> This war in Vietnam had no appeal for me, for it was an unjust war against a people who never did anything to the detriment of United States interests. My military obligation forces me to participate in this war. Many other military men share this same attitude, as do numerous other groups forming against this unjust and unlawful war in the United States and contributing to a ground swell of war opposition on the United States home front.

At the time the "deposition" appeared, Mulligan was not exactly relaxing in Hanoi and giving himself over to a long rethink on the war. As Barn SRO, he had instructed his juniors to give the enemy nothing, and had himself, that July, refused to make his choice. He had been consigned to the hot, filthy black room in the Auditorium.

After five and a half days of dehydration and starvation he was desperately ill—other POWs who caught glimpses of him during this period likened his appearance to those of the living skeletons who walked out of the German death camps at the end of World War II.

In the Gatehouse, Jerry Denton taught other POWs how to pick themselves free from the torture cuffs. He had found that a bamboo strip worked between the ratchet and the housing would uncouple them; also, that to strike the ratchet sharply with a toothbrush handle—positioned in the hands so as to use the cell wall as a hammer—would do the trick. When John Borling opened his cuffs, he was so frightened he locked them right back on. He unlocked and relocked them several times, until he was certain he could cuff himself quickly and tightly if guards came. Then, stooping to a finger-sized communications hole he and Darrel Pyle had drilled to each other, he said, "Darrel, do you want to hear the most beautiful sound in the world?" With that, he let his cuffs clank to the floor.

Later, Borling and Pyle were caught communicating and were beaten savagely, then tied tightly to their bed pallets on the floors of their cells and not allowed to rise for any reason, not even to use their waste buckets.

———

Americans fought the "Make Your Choice" program. When pen and paper were finally forced upon Howie Rutledge, he grabbed them and wrote, "Death." He spent the next month in hell cuffs and leg irons, stayed to the very edge of sanity, until he no longer could remember his children's names. Then, he confessed in writing to being "a Yankee imperialist aggressor."

Likewise, Harry Jenkins, when approached, said, "I'll take uncertainty and death." Jenkins was upset with himself. The memory of the rope torture the previous November was still vivid; psychologically he had not recovered. Thus, he had been writing when his captors demanded it of him. The previous spring, for example, he had complied when asked to outline his thoughts on Communism. "My father," he wrote, "is a very strong American. He taught me about communism. It is a dirty word. The whole history of communism is replete with bloody purges. The only place I know of where a Communist government was ever honestly elected was in Italy after World War II, and that government was thrown out in the next election."

The paper had infuriated his interrogators. Harry had been threatened with punishment for his insults, but it had not been forthcoming.

Asked to profile a U.S. naval aviator, Harry described ". . . a man who has no equal, a competitor, a man who is convinced he is better than all other men . . ."

Harry kept writing and talking, and was not tortured. He gave the enemy nothing of value—indeed, his responses kept his captors in high dudgeon. Yet, he knew he was violating the Code of Conduct, and he despised himself for his weakness. What he did not understand was that he was "rolling"—a term that would be invented later by Jerry Denton—while he searched within himself for the mental and spiritual strength he needed to bounce back from the earlier torture.

And when the Vietnamese finally told Harry to make his choice, he found he had bounced back. When he made the "bad" choice, he was made to hold up the wall for five days, then was left alone. It may have been that the heretofore articulate Jenkins had so confused his interrogators that they were uncertain as to how to deal with him. Or it may have been that they were too busy torturing other Americans.

But his time was coming.

The war waxed hot at Briarpatch, too. "You show a bad assitude!" Frenchy screamed at the prisoners. "You showed a bad assitude in the march! The people are angry at you, and want to see you *again!*"

The bloodlust in the air was nowhere more visible than in Frenchy, whose sanity now was widely suspect among the POWs. Lately he had been giving the news himself over the camp radio, and his renderings were intensely emotional, almost hysterical. He spoke to prisoners the same way, and his eyes stayed lit with a sort of mad fury.

"Now, you will make your choice!" he shrieked. "And you will confess your crimes and make apology for them!"

Jim Bell was caught communicating, and confined for thirty days to "the pit," a grave-sized hole about four feet deep, dug in the floor of the cell beneath one's bunk; it was supposed to be a bomb shelter. Bell's wrists were cuffed behind him; thus, he was unable to cope with the clouds of mosquitoes and the crawling vermin that lived with him in the dark, dank hole.

Jon Reynolds, when forced to make his choice, chose to "support

President Chonsin," and not "Fulbright and the true American people," as his captors put it. Then, squeezed for a confession of crimes, and for an apology "for the misery you have caused the Vietnamese people," he wrote, "I sincerely regret having flown the mission on November 28, 1965"—the mission on which he had been shot down—and that he was "sorry for the miserable Vietnamese people . . ."

Reynolds liked living in a cell next to George McKnight. After McKnight was broken—among other tortures, he had spent a month in the pit below his bunk—the two worried about what to do after the war. They agreed that they certainly could not return to the United States, where they would be in disgrace. It was decided that Reynolds would go to Canada while McKnight checked out Australia and South Africa. They would correspond, and join up wherever it seemed best for a couple of American "traitors." Ev Alvarez and Tom Barrett also thought of themselves as traitors. They had been broken on August 9.

There were fifty-six POWs at the Briarpatch, and Frenchy went after them all. When Rod Knutson refused to make his choice, he was ordered to sit at attention on a small concrete block. When the interrogator and guards left the room, he left the stool—it was bad enough to be mistreated by others, but he wasn't going to mistreat himself.

"But you *must!*" said a bewildered officer, who found him lounging about the room.

"Well," said Rod, "I'm not going to."

Torture cuffs were ratcheted to the bones of his wrists. His right wrist, which had been broken in the April torture and beatings in the Outhouse at the Zoo, had not yet healed and the pain of the cuff on it made him scream. He thought that this officer, who had not been involved in the April session, did not know the wrist had been broken. He was about to tell him so when the man kicked Rod in the face, snarling, "Shut mouth! We will break it again if necessary!" He kept kicking him, in the face, stomach, and ribs. Finally, unable to stand the pain any longer, Rod made his choice, writing, "I am a United States naval officer, and proud of it. I support my government . . ." He went on at length in this vein.

"Insolent swine!" snapped the officer, tearing the paper into small pieces and throwing it in Rod's face. "You will be punished!"

Guards hammered him with rifle stocks, split open his forehead, slugged away with joyous abandon, until he thought he would be beaten to death. He wrote a confession of crimes, saying, "I flew over the Democratic Republic, and from the cockpit of my airplane I could see the determination in the gunner's eyes as they were shooting their bullets at me. . . ."

It was accepted.

———

That summer in North Vietnam a lot of Americans wanted to die; some tried to.

The Briarpatch torture steamroller reached Bob Shumaker late on the afternoon of August 16—he had been transferred from the Zoo a month earlier, right after the Hanoi Parade. Frenchy called upon Shumaker to make his choice, and Bob chose the path of the "perfidious U.S. government." Incensed, Frenchy screamed some orders, and guards pulled Shu's arms behind him and ratcheted torture cuffs down to the bones of his wrists. His feet were tied together, then tied to a small concrete post. He was made to sit on the post all night. Just after dawn he again chose the bad path. The torture cuffs were taken off his wrists and reapplied farther up his forearms, again ratcheted down tightly until they felt as though they were glued to the bone. He was blindfolded, taken outside, and made to stand within a circle of guards. For a long time the guards played games with him, shoving and pushing him back and forth about the circle, throwing him down, picking him up, kicking him, heaving him across the ground, knocking him down again, all the while laughing and enjoying themselves. Then a rope was tied about his neck, and he was run from one side of the camp to the other. He would stumble, fall to the ground, be dragged along, and somehow struggle to his feet. It went on and on, with the pain mounting all the while. He found himself crying, begging the guards to forgive him, and begging his wife, Lorraine, back in California, to forgive him.

He was thrown into a small cell and left alone. The pain on his arms mounted, chewed into him, was unbearable, utterly intolerable; it pointed the way toward his only alternative other than cooperation, which was death.

He smashed the side of his head against the wall of the cell as hard as he could. The wall was embedded with small, sharp stones and rocks, some of them more than an inch in diameter. He stunned himself with the first blow, but did not lose his grip on his objective. He kept throwing his head at the wall, swinging it with as much abandon as he had ever swung a hammer, looking and hoping for death.

The blows hurt, but helped—shifted the focus of pain away from the torture on his arms. He kept smashing himself against the wall. Then, suddenly, he was aware that he was regaining consciousness, that he had succeeded in knocking himself out. A crowd of guards was at the door, chattering, and a key was in the lock. No time to lose! Bob belabored the wall with his head, smashing, smashing, smashing, but the guards entered and yanked him away from the wall. An English-speaker stood on his chest, looking down at him, saying, "Do you recognize the evil of your ways now, and do you realize that you are a criminal?"

At last, Shumaker yielded. He admitted that he was a criminal, and said he was sorry for all he had done. Still, there was no release from agony. The torture cuffs were left on, he was lifted by the rope leash around his neck and led on the run to the far side of the camp. Then, finally, the cuffs, blindfold, and rope were removed. He was surprised at how swollen his arms were, approximately twice their normal size. They were frightfully discolored, all black and blue. The cuffs had cut deep grooves into his arms. One side of his head was a mass of sticky blood.

He was made to sit with pencil and paper and was ordered to confess his crimes in writing. His hands, bloated more than twice their normal size, were unusable. He simply could not hold the pen. After a long time he managed to grip it in his fist, and tried to scrawl a statement. It was illegible, and he was made to do it again and again, draft after draft, hour after hour. Late in the day, after he had produced something that seemed to be satisfactory, a medic came to attend to the head wounds Bob had inflicted on himself, but he would accept no treatment. That night he was returned to his cell.

His cellmate, Smitty Harris, had been through a similar ordeal. He, too, had finally submitted, and had been returned to his cell only a few minutes earlier. Whispering, they told each other of their experiences. Shu began to cry, and he cried all through the night.

———

"Your fellows know you are here," Frenchy told Larry Guarino one day.

It surely seemed so. Aircraft attacking military sites around the Briarpatch kept overflying the camp, banging in their afterburners and dipping their wings. Some were photo reconnaissance aircraft. Was rescue in the offing? Larry prayed that it was.

Frenchy took countermeasures. Through his peepholes, Guarino began to see guards running through the camp and up and down surrounding hills carrying long poles. At the ends of the poles were photographs of helicopters, and when these pictures came in view the Briarpatch guards would track them with their rifles and pretend to be shooting at them.

It was soon clear that Frenchy had no intention of losing his prisoners. At dawn, their wrists were locked behind them in cuffs. The cuffs were removed only to allow the men to eat their morning and evening meals and to sleep. During daylight hours the shutters on all cell windows were closed and locked.

Then began the "runout" drills. Suddenly, a gong would sound and guards would rush into cells and rush prisoners out of them. They would run out the front gate of the Briarpatch and into a trench that had been dug into a hill facing the camp. The slimy mudbath of a trench deepened and snaked nearly two miles into the hill. There were many tributary trenches leading away from the main one, and each led to a dungeon carved into the walls of the trenches. Each had a cement facing, perhaps eight feet high and four feet wide. Centered in the facing was a heavy wooden door, secured with a strong, steel padlock. The floors, ceilings, and walls in these dark, moist recesses were all soft mud; indeed, the floors in the cells in the lower parts of the hill were ankle-high in drainage. On reaching their assigned dungeons, the prisoners were locked into them for perhaps an hour at a time and left to sweat and think about what a grim turn life had taken.

By the end of September, Frenchy's fear that there would be an American rescue attempt apparently waned. The runout drills stopped, and in the mornings ropes were tied to only one wrist—handy for a quick binding of both wrists if necessary; this practice was to continue until the Briarpatch was finally closed.

Late 1966—The Battle Rages

... to many, the hottest pilot (in Vietnam) is U.S. Air Force Major James Kasler, 40, of Indianapolis, who is dubbed by his wingmates as "one-man Air Force." A World War II tail-gunner and six-kill ace in Korea, Kasler in five months has limped home four times with his F-105 riddled by flak or Migs, has seen 30 SAM missiles zoom up in his vicinity, tangled in the longest dogfight with Migs thus far of the war. Six weeks ago, Kasler flew as co-leader of the raid on Hanoi's oil installations.

... says a fellow pilot, "he is part hawk." The four-plane flight that Kasler commands (has) destroyed or damaged 219 buildings, 66 barges, 53 railroad cars, 44 trucks, 36 fuel tanks, 28 bridges and 16 flak sites—a record for any such air unit... says he, "the best way to survive is by being aggressive." *Time,* August 12, 1966

Kasler fell into enemy hands on August 8, the day the *Time* article appeared. He had not seen it, but the Vietnamese had. They were very glad to meet him.

He had been searching the hilly landscape southeast of Yen Bai for his downed wingman, Fred Flom, twenty-five, when his aircraft was ripped by flak. His control stick had rolled back and locked across the top of his right thigh. As he ejected, the thighbone was broken and the top of it was driven well up into his groin. The pain was instantaneous and intense, and as he descended in his 'chute he could see a large lump protruding from his lower abdomen above his G suit.

He was captured by machete-wielding hill people, and four days later he reached Room 18 at Hoa Lo, sick with pain and fever. "Kasler," an officer said, "you must confess your crimes against the Vietnamese people."

"Negative," he answered. "I have committed no crimes."

"You are in our hands now," he was told. "You are very sick. If you want to live, you will cooperate with us!"

"I'd rather die," he said.

Someone threw a pile of papers on his lap, confessions written by other prisoners. Kasler tried to read them, but his misery was such that he could make no sense of what he saw.

He was left in the room all day. Every few hours, interrogators would return, and he would repeat that he had not read the confessions and was not going to produce one of his own.

Late in the day, from the next room, he heard, "Can't I even lie down?" It was Fred Flom's voice. He was groaning, obviously in great pain. His left arm was badly broken and there were torn ligaments and tendons in his right arm. Late that night the two of them were trucked to a hospital. Kasler found Flom at leave from his senses, unable to communicate.*

A doctor showed Kasler X-rays of his injury. The top of the thighbone appeared to have been pushed perhaps seven inches up into the abdomen, and was shattered, splayed open like outstretched fingers on a hand. It looked as bad as it felt. The doctor mumbled something about an operation, but Jim, looking at the dirt around him, did not feel confident the required medical competence was on hand. *Boy*, he thought, *I'm in trouble!*

He was carried to another room and laid on a beige mat whose edges were fastened to the floor with lengths of wide red tape. *The*

---

*As this was written, Flom still had no recollection of his shootdown, or of how he acquired his injuries, or of the earliest days of his imprisonment. He recalls being on R & R (rest and recreation) leave in Bangkok, then awakening in a Heartbreak Hotel dungeon with his left arm casted and his right arm splinted. He left the hospital shortly, and was returned to the Zoo, where he was brutalized.

amputation room! he thought. *This is where they're gonna' do the deed!*

A mask was cupped over his face, and he was told to count. He found himself counting the number of times hypodermics of pain-killer were needled into his leg—forty-two! They had no effect—perhaps he was too excited to lose consciousness; he did not even become groggy. The mask was taken from his face, and he spread a blanket of vitriol over those attending him. *"You son of a bitch, any quack in the States could fix this . . ."* He did not want to lose his leg, but there didn't seem much to do about it except to curse those who insisted on taking it. He laid into them.

Now he felt the cold line being drawn around the top of his thigh—*the knife! They were cutting!* He shut his eyes tightly, and hosed the place down with a stream of oaths. Finally someone lifted the back of his head and told him to look. The cold line he had felt was gauze; a thick plaster cast was being wrapped around his leg. The top of the thighbone had been pulled down, out of the abdomen, and worked into position. The cast would immobilize it, allow it to rest and heal.

Jim had never felt so relieved—he still had his leg, and for the first time in days, the intense pain was gone. He was placed on a stretcher and carried from the room. Raising himself, he grinned back at the doctors who were watching him go and threw them a salute. Some of them smiled back.

Kasler remained in the hospital for more than a month. The cast was removed, and there was an operation in which a metal pin was inserted through the middle of the thighbone, to align the broken ends. It was not, however, a restful stay. Twice he was wrapped in unnecessary body casts—later removed—solely for the edification of visiting press photographers. Once, when he refused to confess his crimes, everyone in the hospital who had had anything to do with him was brought into his room. The crowd of doctors, nurses, orderlies, and attendants screamed at him, reviled him, beat upon the bed, and danced about making menacing gestures. Kasler lay staring at them, frightened, sensing that these healers would not need much induce-ment to do him in. Finally it ended and he was moved to a cell in the Zoo's Stable. There, Dum Dum took over.

"How many airplanes did you lose on the Hanoi POL strike?" Dum Dum asked.

"One," said Kasler.

"Liar, son of a bitch!" Dum Dum retorted, irritated. "You lost seven!"

"One," Jim said.

Dum Dum left the cell, screaming wildly.

In the days that followed, the surgical incision on Kasler's leg became infected and he ran a high fever. He kept asking for a doctor, but Dum Dum and the guard would answer only that he must bow to them. He found the idea unacceptable, and inconvenient as well—after the insertion of the pin he had been encased in a body cast and had great difficulty even getting up off his bunk. He could not have bowed if he wanted to. He ignored the commands. Two guards entered the cell, took him from the bunk, stood him up, and slapped him about for failing to show proper respect.

The high fever persisted, and so did the commands to bow. Every twenty to thirty minutes, for days and nights, the guard would open the peephole in the door to Kasler's cell and call on him to rise and bow. Jim did not need any more slappings, and would struggle to his feet and nod his head. The peephole would close, and often, just as Jim was getting back down onto the bunk, it would open again, and he would have to rise and nod again. In this manner, he was denied sleep or rest of any kind for nearly a week.

Again he asked Dum Dum for a doctor. The interrogator and a guard entered the cell, lifted Jim to his feet, stood him against a wall, and demanded a written confession of crimes. When he refused to write, the guard smashed a fist into his face and began pounding away. Several minutes of this was all he could take before agreeing to write a confession.

Dum Dum then began dictating a condemnation of the U.S. government's Vietnam policy. Jim refused to write this, and Dum Dum shifted gears, demanding instead a letter warning American pilots of the danger of flak over North Vietnam. The letter was taken away, then brought back with a new demand for a condemnation of American policy. Again Kasler demurred.

"Motherfucker, you write!" Dum Dum screamed. The guard stepped forward to pound him. Kasler took the paper, rolled over on his bunk, and tried to write—it was difficult, for the guard stood behind him, slamming his fist into the back of his head. Once Jim turned his head and the guard caught him on the lip with a ring, opening a bloody gash that soon became infected. His total condemnation read, "The Vietnamese and Americans should stop killing each other and seek peace at the peace table.'' This satisfied Dum Dum, who then required Jim to tape-record the statement.

He had said nothing about the bombing and had not condemned his government's policy. Still, he was distraught at having yielded anything.

Now Dum Dum demanded a letter to Senator Fulbright, in which Kasler was to profess support for the Arkansan's antiwar efforts. Jim flatly refused. Apparently Dum Dum was not ready for another persuasion session with Kasler. Jim was left alone. By mid-October, his fever had subsided.

Navy Lt. Comdr. John H. (Jack) Fellowes reached Room 18 before dawn on September 9.

Flying an A6 attack bomber off the *Constellation*, Fellowes had been downed and captured on August 27, his fifteenth anniversary in the Navy. A Naval Academy graduate, Jack had always been aware of the possibility that he might someday become a prisoner of war. But he felt badly about his ''sideseater,'' Bombardier-Navigator Lt. (j.g.) George Coker. Only twenty-three, Coker was just out of Rutgers University and trying the Navy on for size. Fellowes wondered what their captors had done with him.

Then, there was no capacity to wonder about anything but Vietnamese brutalities to himself. Having refused to write a confession of crimes, he was shackled, locked in hell cuffs, tied into torture ropes, and left alone. All day. Only occasionally would interrogators return to ask if he was ready to write, and he would always shake his head no. All day he subdued an ever-mounting urge to scream and cry. Occasionally, his torturer, Pigeye, would return to stand on the points of his shoulders, kick him and drag him about the cement floor on his shoulders and elbows, wearing the skin away. He prayed silently for the strength to endure.

Darkness fell again. Jack was seated on a stool and again asked to write; again he refused. Pigeye slapped him in the face repeatedly. Fellowes was so immersed in pain from the ropes, cuffs, and shackles that he could not feel the slaps. The exercise struck him as absurd, so much so that despite the pain he almost laughed. Then it ended. After ten or more hours, the torture rigs were removed.

''You have got to write this,'' the interrogator said.

''No,'' said Fellowes, ''I can't.''

"Come over to the table."

He leaned forward to use his arms to push himself to his feet; the arms collapsed beneath him and he fell sprawling. He was surprised and embarrassed. His arms and hands were utterly without feeling and would not respond to his will. He looked up, saw alarm crowding the interrogator's eyes. Jack managed to get to his knees.

"Come here," the interrogator urged, "pick up the pencil and write."

Reaching the table, Jack said, "I can't pick up the pencil. I can't move my arms."

The interrogator stared at him silently, his eyes full of worry. Suddenly he rose and almost ran from the room. Shortly a guard came with a bowl of rice. He fed a spoonful to Fellowes, who immediately vomited. He was not interested in food. He was nearly dehydrated from the long hours of sweating in torture and needed nothing so much as water. He was given a cup of water, then another, then left alone. He gripped the edge of the cup with his teeth, drained it, and wanted more. Through the night when guards looked in on him, he pleaded, "Water. Water." But they did nothing.

The next morning he was taken back to a cell in Heartbreak Hotel. The camp commander entered with a medic, and Fellowes was ordered to perform some exercises with his arms. Jack explained that he had absolutely no feeling in them and could not move them. The medic took hold of his hands—they were a deep blue-black—and kept squeezing them. At length the camp commander said, "You will be all right," and the two Vietnamese left.

Then the cell door opened again and in walked Air Force Lt. Ronald G. (Ron) Bliss, twenty-three, a 1964 Air Force Academy graduate who had been downed only six days earlier.

"I'm sorry," Jack smiled, "I can't shake hands."

"What happened?"

"I've been tortured for a little while, and I can't move my arms."

"I hear you're quite a fighter."

"You do?"

"Yes. They told me, 'This man is a real fighter.' "

Jack's spirits soared. "They said that?"

"Yes."

"That's amazing. I was never a fighter. In fact, as a kid, I was kind of a coward." He laughed. "Ron, you've got to write my family and tell them this, because they would be proud to know I fought."

Bliss was a fighter, too. He stayed with Jack for the next five hundred days. He became his arms. He fed him, dressed and undressed him, helped him attend to his bodily functions, cleaned him, massaged his arm muscles, kneaded his wrists and fingers, encouraged him, and, as often as necessary, refused to let him indulge in self-pity. He simply was not going to allow Fellowes to lose his arms, or the spirit that made him a fighter.

———

At the Zoo, ''Happy'' was unhappy.

He was a guard, a nice-looking, clean-cut lad of about eighteen who did not seem to like the work in which he now was engaged. Jim Mulligan, in a Pool Hall cell, tapped to Jerry Denton, his next door neighbor, ''Happy just came in here crying like a baby. I think he is very upset at what he is doing to you.''

Denton appreciated the guard's tears, but if he were to hang on much longer he would need more practical help. He could not imagine where it was to come from.

By early October, all Zoo torture rooms were filled and were being worked in round-the-clock shifts. The Vietnamese began torturing the remaining POWs in their cells. Denton was tortured when he declined to brief his captors on prisoner communications. He was seated on his bunk, his wrists were locked behind him in hell cuffs, and his ankles were shackled to the foot of his bed. A length of iron was placed beneath his lower calves, just above the heels. A rope affixed to the middle of this iron was threaded through a pulley on a hook in the ceiling and pulled taut. With his ankles held fast to the bunk by the shackles, his legs could yield nothing to the upward pressure of the bar beneath them. With his wrists cuffed behind him, he could not lie back. There was no move he could make, nothing he could do to relieve the pressure against the backs of his legs. It was strong and constant and, as the hours wore on, his tolerance for the torture diminished.

There were no relief periods. Denton was kept in this rig through meals, and when he had to use the waste bucket, guards brought it to him, and got it underneath him. Each day, young Happy would be sent into the cell to pull the bar tighter against the backs of the prisoner's legs. It was clear that the task disgusted the boy, but he had to follow orders. Denton's distress mounted as the hours passed.

After five days and nights he capitulated.

Released from torture, he wrote, "Sometimes we communicate by talking under the door. Sometimes, we tap on the walls . . ." The Vietnamese, he knew, were well aware of these things; indeed, many POWs were convinced by now that they knew the tap code, for they would tap messages like "Hi," on the doors and walls, and wait vainly for answers. Denton continued, "When a new man comes in, we get his name and if the guy has sports news from home or news about somebody's family we get that." The way to stop prisoner communications, he advised, was to "put on more guards."

He hoped the worthless confession might pass. It failed. After a few hours of blessed, blessed freedom to move about his cell, of exercising long-imprisoned limbs and muscles, he was locked back in the rig. The torture went on and on. After three more days and nights he knew he was near the end of his endurance, approaching the point where he would trade something of value for sanity. He gave himself over to prayer again. He went at it as intensively as he had on that long night of torture in New Guy Village the previous May. . . . *I am totally in Your Hands. I can't give in again without giving something that will be compromising. . . .* He begged for Divine help.

Suddenly, as he finished his prayer, he was aware of a great comfort—he had never in his life been so completely comfortable! The pain that had been tightened and tortured into his cuffed wrists and shackled legs was gone. He was no longer desperate to be freed from the torture rig. Indeed, he felt relaxed, as much at ease as he had ever been in his life. He knew in that moment that he could outlast his tormentors.

And so he did. The mantle of comfort remained with him. Each day, Happy would be sent in to increase the tension on the torture pulley. He would do so, and it would affect Denton not at all. On the tenth day of torture, when Happy began to tighten the rope, the youth's eyes filled with tears. He dropped the rope, pushed another guard away from it, and ran out of the cell, screaming at the officer who was supervising torture, "No! No! No!" The officer spoke back sharply. An argument raged for long minutes. Then, incredibly, Happy came back into the cell and took Denton out of the torture rig.

The next day Denton was moved back to the Gatehouse, where in August he had taught others how to free themselves of torture cuffs. That morning Happy visited him and roughly—after all, a soldier could not show sympathy for his country's enemies—cleansed the wounds on his swollen legs with disinfectant.

On October 31 Hanoi insisted on "a stern and universal condemnation of U.S. crimes . . . [being] as imperative as the Nuremberg trial of the Nazi leaders." The United States was charged with crimes that "surpass those of the Hitlerite hordes in gravity, cruelty and savagery." It was asserted that President Johnson, Defense Secretary McNamara, Secretary of State Dean Rusk, and Army General William C. Westmoreland, Commander of U.S. Forces in Vietnam, all "must be tried and condemned."

In London, on November 17, Lord Russell, whose "tribunal" had been postponed until March, 1967, accused the United States of perpetrating war crimes in Vietnam without parallel in his ninety-four-year lifetime. Of the North Vietnamese he said, "I have no memory of any people so enduring, or of any nation with a spirit of resistance so unquenchable. I will not conceal the profundity of my admiration for the people of Vietnam."

His secretary, an American named Ralph Schoenman, announced that when the "international war crimes tribunal" convened, it would look for the "pattern of evidence" to support "the necessary conclusions" concerning America's guilt. Wrote the Washington *Post*'s Karl Meyer, "Some wondered whether, Lewis Carroll fashion, the 'tribunal' was delivering its sentence first and verdict later."

Schoenman also advised that the "tribunal" would concentrate on five broad areas of American criminal activity, including the torture of prisoners.

In the non-Communist world, few seemed impressed. The heads of four African governments resigned from membership in the Bertrand Russell Peace Foundation, which was sponsoring the "tribunal." One of them, President Julius Nyerere of Tanzania, was angry enough to say, "Lord Russell may not object to his name being used for other people's purposes. I do object to my name being so used. I also object to a serious matter like the Vietnam situation being dealt with by trickery and dishonesty."

The Vietnamese continued to extract "confessions" and "apologies," to be presented to someone, somewhere, sometime.

At the Zoo on December 8, Denton counted 26 sets of torture cuffs and leg irons that were brought from various cellblocks and stored in a room near his cell in the Gatehouse. Subsequently, Denton and other POWs would agree that on Pearl Harbor day, a phase of the captivity ended. Until now, the enemy had been engaged in a concentrated effort to break and subjugate the entire American prisoner population. He had attempted to destroy the will of senior officers to take command, and to destroy the will of all prisoners to communicate. In the face of this attempt, the prisoners had formulated and disseminated a strong resistance policy. In an attempt to intimidate the United States government, the Vietnamese had flaunted the prisoners, in the Hanoi Parade, in meetings with "peace delegations" and with threats of war crimes trials. Washington had not been intimidated; the reaction—both from the Administration and from antiwar leaders—had been strongly negative. By early December, 1966, the enemy was satisfied that steamroller tactics were unproductive, and abandoned them. By no means were mistreatment and torture to end; for the Americans, the worst periods of the long captivity still lay ahead. But henceforth, pressure was to be applied on a somewhat more selective basis and for specific purposes, not merely to make men utterly submissive or to cow the United States.

———

The year grew old too slowly at the Briarpatch, where the demented Frenchy and his torture guards seemed infected with a kind of joyous paranoia. The prisoners were on short rations, two daily meals of a handful of rice and a bowl of warmish water each. Men were becoming skeletons. Jim Bell and John Heilig became so ill that they were taken to a hospital in Hanoi. SRO Larry Guarino, who had twice been wrung out in torture cuffs, became so weak he could not carry a pail of water—at the slightest effort, he would pass out, and his cellmate, Ron Byrne, kept lifting him from the floor onto his pallet. The place was so heavily staffed with guards that POW communications were all but shut down. What the Briarpatch prisoners heard too much of during these months were the screams of friends in torture.

Men were returned to interrogation again and again. A confession that had been tortured out of Ev Alvarez was waved before him. "Do you really believe this?" the officer asked.

"Hell, no," said Alvarez. "I don't believe that."

"Then why did you write it?"

"Are you kidding me? Because you damn guys made me write it!"

"What do you believe of it?"

"I don't believe any of it except that my name is Everett Alvarez, Jr., 644124, USN."

The interrogator produced a book about the Democratic Republic of Vietnam which prisoners occasionally were required to read. "Have you seen this?"

"Yeah, I've seen it."

The interrogator thumbed through the book, stopped at a picture of his country's flag, got Ev to identify it.

"And what is this?" he said, turning a few more pages to another picture. It was a photograph of Ho Chi Minh. Someone had given the North Vietnamese president a black eye, the most impressive shiner Alvarez had ever seen. Unable to hide his glee, he began laughing. The interrogator shoved the book toward him. "You did it!" he screamed. "*You did it!* Berg has confessed, and told us you did it!" (Ev's cellmate, Air Force Lt. Kile D. "Red" Berg, had been taken to quiz earlier.)

"That's not true," Ev answered. "He knows I didn't do it."

"No, no! You did it! You did it!" the man was shrieking. "You must confess! You *will* confess! You will *apologize!*"

Alvarez lost his temper. "*I'm not gonna apologize!*" he screamed. He was shaking with anger. "Do anything you want with me, but I'm not gonna apologize!"

He was isolated in a cell he had not been in before—it proved to be a pit stop on the rat route through the camp; at night, as he tried to sleep, long caravans of rats ran over him. In this cell he was beaten and starved for days until he agreed to write a letter ot U.S. Navy pilots flying over North Vietnam, urging them to cease their criminal activities and to protest their government's actions. "Use a lot of adjectives," he was told.

He wrote, "Pilots, protest this long, involved, lengthy, durable, expanding, expanded, extenuated combat action . . ."

"Ahh, it's *good!*" his captors said, nodding approvingly.

"I'm tired," Ev said. "I need rest."

"But you must write. First, you must write!"

Alvarez wrote, as ordered, to the Bertrand Russell tribunal: "I protest against the long, involved, costly, controversial war, a violation of the gallant, heroic, liberated, freedom loving, independent loving Vietnamese people . . ." He was made to produce similar letters for Senator Fulbright, for American students, for the American people.

Then he was allowed to rest—if he could—back in the rats' playroom.

"News bulletin. Hanoi. President Horseshit Men proclaimed today that the hee roic Vy yet nameese people . . ."

Thus came the signal that American POWs had at last been tortured into reading the news over the camp radio. Cellmates Dick Bolstad and Bob Lilly devised the imaginative delivery and took turns performing. They soon had their starved and tortured compatriots rolling with laughter on their cell floors. There was a story about how "Horseshit Men" had come to the aid of a "hee roic little Vy yet nameese girl and her mama" whose home had been bombed. Dialogue was squeaked out: "The mama said, 'Dau, *why* do they bomb us!' And the dau said, 'Ah dunno, mama, ah dunno, mama . . .' "

Soon it was Alvarez's turn to read. His assignment was an article denouncing American chemical warfare in Vietnam. He kept struggling with the words, sounding as though he were about to strangle on some—". . . dio . . . bio . . . clarktra . . . chlorofeeee . . ."

"No, no, no!" his director kept saying, turning off the tape. "We must start again. You must try harder. You do not read very well."

"I never could read out loud," Ev confessed. "I always had difficulty . . ."

"Yes, many Americans have this problem. You must try harder."

Ev would appear to do so, but at the first reference to the "beloved and respected leader, Ho Chi Minh," he used the Bolstad-Lilly pronunciation. Off went the tape, and the exasperated director said, "You Americans find it very difficult to pronounce our president's name."

"Yeah? Horseshit Men?"

"No, no, no. Try hard. Ho Chi Minh."

"Yeah, yeah. Horseshit Men."

"No, no, no. *Ho Chi Minh.*"

Another interrogator was pleading with Red Berg for information: "I don't understand this. I am very confused. Will you explain this to me?" He showed him a Batman Fan Club card. It came out of a letter a POW's wife had sent, apparently to show her husband the sort of activity their children were now involved in. The card described Batman and his young sidekick, Robin, as "leaders of the forces for good in the world," and "dedicated to the fight against crime, corruption and evil."

"Who is this Batman?" the interrogator wanted to know.

Oh, Lord! Red thought. *How in hell am I ever gonna explain this to these people?*

"Well," he said, "he is a character in the United States . . ."

"Ah," the interrogator interrupted, "but it says here, 'Dedicated to the fight against crime and corruption.' "

"Yes," Red said.

"It says here that he is now a member of this organization."

"Yes."

"How much does it cost to join this organization? What is this Batman? Where does he live? What political party is he affiliated with? How big is the membership? What is their strength? Tell me."

Red explained as best he could and was sent back to his cell. He was not at all sure he had dispelled the interrogator's confusion.

————

Alvarez's third Christmas as a POW approached.

"We want you to write a letter to the soldiers in South Vietnam, telling them how good all of your Christmases have been here," he was told.

"No."

"You will think about it."

He was ushered back into the rat room. There, on a table, was pen and paper for him to use after he had thought about it. He was not allowed to sleep. He spent long hours watching a trail of red ants march through the cell. He discovered that when he killed any and wiped the trail clean, it wasn't long before ant ranks were solid again, and moving along the same trail; but that when he left dead ants where he squashed them, the others would detour around them, and sometimes would stop coming altogether. Methodically he began killing ants and leaving their bodies around the cell.

He studied the geckos, the small lizards that were everywhere. He watched them hunt, catch mosquitoes with their flicking tongues, watched them make love.

After five days and nights he sat down to write not what had been ordered but "What Christmas Means to Me." He wrote of pleasant memories of Christmases at home and then the words to the Christmas hymn "Silent Night, Holy Night." The interrogators accepted the paper without looking at it and Alvarez was returned to the cell he shared with Red Berg.

As always, Christmas brought on a "good guy season." In mid-December, torture stopped. Prison rules, regulations, and disciplines were relaxed. The POWs were given twigs, branches and pieces of cardboard, with which to make checker and chess sets for themselves. On Christmas Eve the men were taken by turns to an interrogation room, where they were allowed to look at a Christmas tree—it was a small tree the prisoners themselves had decorated with papier-mâché ornaments and wrapped with paper chains; there was cotton all over it that looked like snow and there were candles all around it. It looked like Christmas and even sounded like it—there were tape recordings, of Dick Bolstad singing "Jingle Bells"; Jim Ray* singing "Puff, the Magic Dragon"; Art Black doing what he called "a bass drum solo of "Jingle Bells""; and Ralph Gaither singing "Wabash Cannon Ball" and playing "Malagueña" on the guitar. The POWs were offered candy, tea, and extra cigarettes, and many were given letters from home—Alvarez got one from Tangee that had arrived the previous summer.

The next day there was a turkey dinner and then a movie in an interrogation room. Each prisoner was told that other prisoners would be present and was warned against trying to communicate with them. Ropes had been strung about the room, and blankets were hung on the ropes, so as to form individual cubicles from which the men could not see each other. Guards were stationed all around the room to forestall attempts to communicate. The film treated the prisoners to scene after scene of lovely little Vietnamese girls, their hair festooned with flowers, frolicking and laughing at play. At length there would be the sounds of approaching aircraft, and the tykes would look skyward, their faces contorting in anguish, their eyes brimming with tears; the scene would dissolve in a mammoth explosion of American bombs!

The picture failed to grip the POWs' attention, and they soon were reaching under the blanket walls surrounding them to tap out messages on each others' hands: names, locations, physical conditions of themselves and cellmates. Occasionally an excited POW would stick his head above his blanket walls, to look around, and two or three guards would come pouncing into his cubicle and the others would hear much scuffling, slapping, and hoarse, angry whispering.

———

One day just before Christmas a letter Jim Mulligan had been allowed to write in early November reached his wife, Louise, and their seven sons.

My darling wife and children:
My captors are allowing me to write a letter home. I hope it arrives before Christmas. You all know my feelings, how I like things and

*Air Force Lt. James E. Ray, shot down and captured on May 8, 1966.

what I expect you to do. This separation is difficult, but it will end and we will resume our lives together once again.

I won't discuss much about life here. Physically, I have some problems that will need attention when I get released. My left arm, shoulder and left side of my chest will need some work.

I was quite sick for a few months and lost a lot of weight. At meals, in addition to meat and vegetables, I get piles of whole grain rice, plenty of warm soup and a pot of water, and now estimate my weight at 150 pounds. . . .

To intelligence analysts, "piles of whole grain rice, plenty of warm soup, and a pot of water" would spell "POW, POW, POW," and "estimate my weight at 150" would mean Mulligan estimated there were 150 POWs in Hanoi. By year's end, this estimate was to be nearly exactly correct; there were to be 151 American POWs in Vietnam. Mulligan's outlandish description of his meals served a double purpose: it alerted American analysts that another meaning was involved; and it pleased the Vietnamese, who were anxious that the world know how well they were treating their American prisoners, and thus let it go through without change.

The letter continued:

Life is much like the religious retreat I made a few years back, only it's much more quiet here and I have more time for thinking and meditating.

To an intelligence analyst, Mulligan was saying that he was in solitary confinement.

Give my best to Father Gallagher. You know he is some athlete. He got six hits in seven at bats. Tell him his altar boy, Paul Daley, showed real promise as a tennis player. He had a good backhand but he was rough in missing his forehand . . .

To Father Gallagher, a good friend and chaplain aboard Mulligan's ship, *Enterprise,* this meant there were a total of seven *Enterprise* airmen in captivity. Paul Daley had been the backseater in the only other aircraft Mulligan's squadron lost, but the pilot, Jim Ruffin, was missing—"rough in missing."

As for you, my beloved wife, once again you must bear the harsh burden of life's cross alone. Keep your faith and spirits, my darling. Our love can do nothing but grow stronger. Thank the good Lord for sparing my life. I love you all and miss you very much, and though I am a prisoner I remain ever with you in my thoughts and prayers. A happy and joyous Christmas. Love one another.

Your devoted husband and father,
/s/ Jim

————

By Christmas, Ron Bliss had been working intensively for three months on Jack Fellowes' arms and hands, which seemed to have been ruined in an unbelievable ten-hour stay in the ropes. In long, daily sessions, Bliss patiently rubbed and massaged, pushed, pulled, and kneaded the injured limbs. After many weeks the grotesque swelling had subsided, and Jack's arms began to respond when he willed them to move—but only slightly, and very slowly. He regained no feeling in his fingers and hands and could not move them. He had begun to resign himself to a life as a partial cripple, but Bliss would not tolerate it. He kept working on Fellowes' hands, and one day he fit an injured hand around a spoon, asking, "Can you work the muscles to grip it?"

"I think so," Fellowes replied. "I don't think it's going to fall."

"Can you feel it?"

"No."

"Come on, let's keep workiung at it."

On Christmas Day, Ron watched intently as Jack got a slice of turkey onto the palm of one hand and, concentrating as he never had before in his life, slowly, ever so slowly, willed his fingers to close over the meat. Suddenly his face split in a wide grin and he said, "I'm going to make it, Ron! Everything is going to be all right!"

————

The Christmas spirit at the Briarpatch dissolved quickly. On December 28, his third wedding anniversary, Bob Shumaker was taken to an interrogation with Frenchy, the balmy camp commander. Frenchy demanded that the prisoner write that he had been shot down in the city of Dong Hoi. Shumaker wrote the truth, that he had been shot down while engaging a military target four miles northwest of the city.

"This is no good!" Frenchy wailed, "no good! You must put down that you were shot down *in the city* of Dong Hoi!"

"That's not true," Shumaker answered. He understood: the enemy was trying to get POWs to establish as fact that American aircraft were attacking Vietnamese population centers. It was worth a battle, and mentally he girded himself.

He was taken to a little house on a hill about 100 yards above the camp. Frenchy and another officer sat behind a desk. There were four torture guards and many spectators, teenage boys and girls who did odd jobs around the camp; they crowded the doors and windows. Shumaker was blindfolded and stripped to his T-shirt and shorts. The temperature was in the 30s, and he was shaking with cold. The torturers quickly got his mind on other matters. He was tied into torture ropes, his wrists were locked behind him in hell cuffs and he was made to kneel while the guards beat him about the back and buttocks with metal rifle-cleaning rods. The blows were painful, but the pain from the chest and wrists was nearly overwhelming. After many blows, a rope was tied about his neck and he was pulled to his feet, out the door and up the muddy trench that had been used in the run-out drills the previous fall. He was locked into one of the hillside dungeons, where the cold, slimy mud was perhaps three inches deep on the floor. He was shivering, bleeding from his back and buttocks, and there was a great agony in his chest, shoulders and wrists. But he was grateful for the respite in the dungeon—maybe they would forget about him, leave him here.

A few minutes later, they came back for him. The rope leash was kept taut around his neck, and whoever was leading him kept yanking it so as to throw him to the ground. The ground was uneven, muddy and rocky, and he would be dragged along for long distances, much to the delight of the spectators. Then he would almost be strangled as he was pulled to his feet, to be run a short distance and thrown down again. It lasted for a long time. Then he was returned to the torture house.

Shu had been reduced nearly to that animal-like state he had been tortured to the previous August, when he had tried to commit suicide. Again he had had far more than he could stand and agreed to make a tape-recording. This time, though, he was able to keep his grip to the extent that he mispronounced words and committed grammatical errors all through the thing, ended sentences on upbeats, called Sidewinder missiles "wide sinders" and so on. Frenchy was satisfied, but not so grateful as to return Bob to the cell he had shared with Smitty Harris. He needed company badly, but was taken to solitary confinement.

For Shumaker, it was the final cruelty of what had been a dismal year.

As the year ended, there appeared to be some reason for optimism concerning the future of South Vietnam. Through the late summer, the Communists had employed the tactics of desperation in an effort to keep people from the polls. In a bloody terror campaign, the Viet Cong had put the torch to many hamlets, blown up trains, buses, and bridges, bombed polling places, and killed large numbers of people. But the attempt to intimidate had failed, and the Communists looked like losers. Approximately 80 percent of the country's eligible voters—more than five and a quarter million people—had cast ballots, electing a 117-member Assembly charged with drafting a new constitution.

In October, President Johnson interrupted an Asian tour to make a surprise visit to the huge U.S. military base at Cam Ranh Bay. He explained to the troops that "I could not come to this part of the world and not come to see you." He awarded numerous medals, dined in an enlisted mess, and visited with many GIs. Then he resumed his tour.

PART II

Stratton, Superman, and Stockdale

On January 5, 1967, Navy Lt. Comdr. Richard A. Stratton, flying an A4E off *Ticonderoga,* became the first American pilot of the year captured in North Vietnam. He was just what the Vietnamese were waiting for, a big, heavy-set, dark-visaged, tough-looking American with a deep voice, the very model of an arrogant American imperialist. Stratton was a Communist propagandist's dream, and his captors immediately set about making the most of him.

Washington had long insisted to the world that Hanoi and Haiphong were off limits to American military aircraft. Stratton, who had been downed south of Thanh Hoa, some seventy miles from Hanoi, would be made to tell the world that Washington had lied, that he himself had rained death and destruction into the capital city. Such a confession would make for a convincing presentation at Lord Russell's "war crimes tribunal."

The decision to cast Stratton in the role of "mad bomber of Hanoi" was to prove less than fortunate. In his case, appearance deceived. Much as he looked the part of facist thug, he was an essentially gentle soul. He had spent six years in seminaries studying for the Roman Catholic priesthood. Then, acceding to a preoccupation with world affairs that struck him as too absorbing for a conscientious cleric, he transferred to Georgetown University and earned a degree in History of Government; he entered the Navy Air Corps, found it a congenial life, and settled on it as a career. Later he earned an advanced degree in International Relations at Stanford University and maintained a lively interest in world events. In short, he was well equipped for the sort of combat in which Hanoi now engaged him.

Stratton was well aware of the implications of a confession that he had bombed Hanoi: the opponents of America's Vietnam involvement at home and abroad would use it as a cudgel against the Administration. When the demand for a confession was made, he understood that he had not been blown out of the war, but merely reassigned by fate to another fighting front. But he could not know that when the enemy wanted something badly enough, he knew how to get it.

He got it. Stratton was choked, kicked, and beaten until his face and head were bloody and his eardrums were ruptured. Twice he was tortured in ropes and hell cuffs and burned with cigarettes, and there was a painful although incomplete effort to pull out his thumbnails. He was left no choice but to admit that he had bombed Hanoi. This admission soon was to reach the world, but Stratton would cause it to backfire on Hanoi. In fact, Stratton was to become such an embarrassment to his captors that eventually they would try to fatten him up and send him home early.

In early 1967, the North Vietnamese who were in charge at the Briarpatch seemed to believe the war was ending. In fact, during this period, Lyndon Johnson and Ho Chi Minh were secretly in contact, and there were high-level hopes that negotiations toward ending the war might soon begin. Doubtless, those in charge of the American POWs were ordered to ease the pressure on them. Then word came to close the Briarpatch and return the fifty-six POWs there to Hanoi. The dismal camp was never to open again.

They were moved on February 2. Two dozen went to the Zoo, where Larry Guarino became SRO. The other thirty-two were taken to a newly opened section in the northeast quarter of the Hoa Lo compound. This subcompound was christened Las Vegas by Air Force Capt. David B. Hatcher, captured on May 30, 1966. Six individual cellblocks were entitled by others, Thunderbird, Desert Inn, Stardust, Golden Nugget, Riviera, and the Mint.

The Briarpatch prisoners who went to Las Vegas joined twenty-two others who had been moved from the Zoo on January 26, making a total of fifty-four. Except for Robbie Risner, who months earlier had returned from the Zoo to solitary confinement in New Guy Village, this group included all POWs of the rank of Navy commander or Air Force lieutenant colonel—all the seniors. SRO was Jim Stockdale. Jerry Denton was his deputy. Then, by order of seniority, came Harry Jenkins, Bill Franke, Jim Mulligan, Howie Rutledge, and Jim Lamar.

Stockdale, Denton, Jenkins, Sam Johnson, George Coker, and Air Force Capt. H. K. "Bud" Flesher, captured on December 2, were installed in separate cells in Stardust, a maximum-security, no-communications cellblock on the east side of the compound. It contained seven small, module-type cells, like little huts; they were brand new—the cement was still wet. To preclude tapping, each cell was surrounded on three sides by corridors. The only walls any cells had in common were the outer walls of the cellblock. Cell doors did not face each other. The cells varied in size. Generally, they were eight to nine feet long and four feet wide. Much of this space was taken up by a double-decker bunk, each equipped with stocks. An average-size man intent on walking might take three strides forward, then turn and take the same number of steps in the opposite direction. Windows were well above eye level.

It took the initial residents of Stardust all of ten minutes to establish communications. This involved no stroke of genius. Finding that they could not tap to each other, they simply began pounding, loudly, and then began talking beneath their cell doors. They got away with it, probably because the secret Washington-Hanoi exchanges had induced a relaxed stance toward the POWs.

For a short while a relaxed atmosphere prevailed at the Zoo, too. One evening the announcement came over the radio speakers in the cells: "To show its good attitude, the Democratic Republic of Vietnam has given armistice to make a definite move to end the war."

"Hey," Larry Guarino asked his cellmate, Ron Byrne, "did you hear that?"

"Yes!" said Byrne. His eyes were big as saucers.

Guarino sat down and composed a shopping list. He would buy Evelyn a diamond ring; a man could never go wrong buying a woman a diamond! He would buy gold crucifixes for his four sons. He would buy a tape recorder, a fishing boat he had had in mind for a long time, some reels . . .

But the Washington-Hanoi talks foundered, and the war in South Vietnam resumed with renewed savagery. So did the war in the prison camps of North Vietnam.

————

Despite the enemy's best efforts to suppress communications, the Vegas POWs quickly developed new systems. When the coast was clear, communications were by voice, and were relayed from cellblock to cellblock. When guards were about, other methods were used: men could lie on the floor and look through the gap at the bottom of the cell door, "reading" tap-coded messages others sent by flashing their hands at the gaps at the bottoms of their doors. Others could do the same thing through the drainholes at the back of the cells; these openings, called "ratholes," because they were that, too, were in alignment. Prisoners manning brooms in the courtyard or in the cellblock corridors would "sweep" tap-coded messages to many listeners at once, within the sight and hearing of unsuspecting guards. Written messages were also left in notedrops in a ten-stall bath area, in the courtyard.

Soon enough, SRO Jim Stockdale had reason to begin disseminating policy over this network. Prisoners were being pressured to read on the camp radio. One day the POWs were treated to a recitation by Al Brudno of a series of newspaper articles from the New York *Times,* written by Assistant Managing Editor Harrison Salisbury, who had visited North Vietnam in December and January. To the POWs, the articles strongly implied that the United States was conducting wanton attacks against North Vietnam's civilian population. Among other things, Salisbury insisted, "One can see that United States planes are dropping an enormous weight of explosives on purely civilian targets." He paid special attention to Nam Dinh, North Vietnam's third largest city, reporting: "No American communique has asserted that Nam Dinh contains some facility that the United States regards as a military objective."*

*Predictably, Salisbury's dispatches inspired fury in Washington. Defense Department officials produced three unclassified press handouts which were said to have

Salisbury's articles obviously did not sit well with American POWs, many of whom had exposed themselves to danger avoiding civilian targets. Brudno, however, infused them with a delightful mockery. He relished every reference to North Vietnam's President "Horseshit Men," mispronouncing the name just as Dick Bolstad and Bob Lilly had done at the Briarpatch; and his tone, implying that the dispatches were the product of incredible gullibility, took much of the sting out of them—indeed, filled the cellblocks with laughter.

SRO Stockdale joined in the general merriment, impressed that Brudno, instead of letting the articles shatter morale, had cleverly used them to improve it. But Stockdale worried. Others might want to try this approach rather than accept torture, and it was unrealistic to expect everyone to be able to handle the situation so well.

And there was something else. Prior to coming to Vietnam, Stockdale had made a point of studying the brainwashing techniques the Communists had used on American POWs during the Korean War. He was convinced that it was dangerous to allow POWs freely to participate in such activity. He anticipated that the enemy's next step would be to end isolation for selected groups of prisoners and to bring them together in "open discussions" of camp life, politics, world affairs, and so on. For the skillful Communist moderator, it would be no trick to create an atmosphere in which physically and emotionally tired men could be induced to stand before their peers and confess to shortcomings. The Communists had made an art of the self-criticism session. They know that in every sizable group there are likely to be sensitive personalities who feel guilty over one thing or another, who are willing to express their regrets at their own weaknesses. Self-criticism can become contagious and is crucial to the brainwashing process.

Still, a POW could be expected to take only so much torture before acceding to demands that he read on the camp radio. Stockdale did not want to issue an order men could not follow, or to phrase policy in such a way that men who were forced to submit would feel lost beyond recall. Thus, shortly after Brudno's entertaining readings of the Salisbury articles, the Vegas contingent was in receipt of the SRO's order: *To read on the camp radio requires a license. The fee*

---

been available both in the Pentagon and Saigon. These releases listed the military targets in Nam Dinh which had been hit: a rail yard, a thermal power plant, a petroleum dump, and a collection of warehouses and assembly areas.

for this license is one week in irons. This license is good for only one week and thereafter must be renewed.

Stockdale's task, as he saw it, was to try to hold to a minimum an activity that could not possibly be stopped. He feared that to attempt to stop it altogether might well result in a net loss, with men who had succumbed in torture losing heart. As it turned out, however, none of the Vegas POWs ever read on the radio again during Stockdale's tenure as SRO.

————

Ben Casey and Superman entered the war on the American side on February 19. They were recruited by two young Navy airmen off the carrier *Coral Sea:* Lieut. Charles Nels Tanner, an F-4 pilot, and his backseater, Lieut. Ross R. Terry. These two had been captured the previous October 9. Immediately on reaching Hoa Lo, both had been subjected to nearly two weeks of heavy torture. Tanner's torturer, a sadistic amateur, had approached his work with a maniacal enthusiasm and had nearly killed him. Once he pulled him into the ropes with such abrupt savagery that Nels could hear cartilage and bone separating and cracking, and the sudden, engulfing pain had caused him to lose control of his bowels. Throughout the days and nights of his torture Tanner could hear Terry screaming in a nearby torture chamber. At length, both had yielded. Tanner had made a propaganda tape, confessing to violations of international law and of the sovereignty of the Democratic Republic of Vietnam; Terry had substantiated a false claim that they had been shot down by a North Vietnamese fighter plane. (A Mig had recently been destroyed in air-to-air combat with an American aircraft and apparently Hanoi felt that it had to square matters.)

When torture ended, Tanner and Terry were reunited. They were to remain cellmates for months, probably because Tanner's arms and hands had been rendered useless, and he could do nothing for himself. In the following weeks they received political lectures and, when Tanner regained the use of his hands, both were kept busy rewriting confessions. The confessions were hazy ramblings which contained no incidents that could be construed as war crimes, and no names of other members of their squadron, which was what their captors were demanding. Thus, the Vietnamese kept finding their confessions unacceptable.

Meanwhile, the two POWs kept conferring, trying frantically to find an effective course of resistance to follow. To both men, the thought of more torture was terrifying. But so was the thought that the enemy could take whatever he wanted from them. Together, day after day, they knelt and prayed for guidance. One day Tanner said, "Ross, if we give them a lot of phony names and ridiculous incidents, maybe they won't catch it. Maybe they'll accept it and leave us alone."

If discovered, more intense torture seemed a certainty. Still, neither man liked the feeling that came of "rolling."

"I'm game," said Terry.

They listed the names of men long deceased, others who had rotated back to the States, and still others who had never come to Vietnam. They reported that two *Coral Sea* pilots, Lt. Comdr. Ben Casey and Lt. Clark Kent, had refused to fly their missions and had been court-martialed and dishonorably discharged. Kent, of course, was Superman, dedicated to "truth, justice and the American way." Casey was then America's leading television surgeon. Tanner wrote that the bitter dissent over the war was also reflected in the fact that Lt. Comdr. Tom Ewell, overseer of the ship's "WF" squadron, had been divorced by his wife, who was enraged because he was flying combat missions in Vietnam. Ewell was an American motion picture star, not a naval aviator. And, as military analysts would know and enterprising journalists would learn, WF, or "Willie Fud," aircraft are flying radar stations charged with providing early warning of oncoming enemy air attack. They do not fly combat missions.

The Vietnamese accepted with delight the names and the gossip about the Ewells; they were pleased that Mrs. Ewell shared their rage over the bombing.

A few days later Rabbit presented Tanner and Terry with a short script, ordering them to memorize it. They were going to be interviewed on television, and the script contained the ten questions they would be asked and the answers they were to give. The questions had been manufactured to suit the answers the two had given in the Clark Kent–Ben Casey–Tom Ewell confessions, and the answers had been taken verbatim from those papers. Rabbit kept a copy of the script himself, and he warned the prisoners not to deviate from it or to answer any off-the-cuff questions. They were to memorize well, and at the interview were to make it seem that the answers were not memorized, but given spontaneously.

A month earlier, Tanner had been trotted before some Japanese

Communists. They had confronted him with a series of innocuous questions, and he was satisfied he had given them no answers that would be usable for propaganda purposes. But in retrospect he felt he had made one big mistake. He had been seated before a table full of fruit, cookies, candies, and cigarettes and, confused and frightened, had touched none of it. This time, he told Terry, he meant to dig in. The famished Terry was enthusiastic about joining in. Not only would it be a chance to sate the gnawing hunger that had been with him for the four months since his capture, but it would demonstrate to the interviewer and his audience that the POWs were being starved.

Major Bai awaited them at the site of the interview, a luxurious hotel suite. He took the prisoners aside to warn, "You know what is at stake here!" The Americans knew it was no idle threat.

They were seated on a couch behind a coffee table laden with bowls of bananas and cookies, and coffee, cream, and sugar. The two wasted no time in attending to these goodies. They set upon them with a will, peeling bananas, cramming them into their mouths, tossing the peels on the table, grabbing another banana and beginning anew. Their jaws worked mightily and their countenances were suffused with a sort of desperate pleasure as they stuffed cookie after cookie into mouths overflowing with banana, washing it all down with copious amounts of well-sugared coffee. The interviewer, a Japanese, beheld this prodigious exhibition with a faint smile of amazement. Then, realizing it was not going to end until all the food was gone, he proceeded with the script using a Vietnamese interrogator.

Apparently the interviewer had agreed to restrict himself to the questions Rabbit had constructed. Through mouths packed with food, Tanner and Terry gave the answers as though reading them off sheets of paper. Rabbit sat in a chair behind the interviewer, following the script and grinning happily to himself over his accomplishment. He was not known to be a drinker, but Tanner believed him to be half-drunk that day and guessed that the interview meant much to him professionally (indeed, shortly afterward, Rabbit was promoted to the Political Department).

Suddenly, when the interview reached the Clark Kent–Ben Casey court-martial, the Japanese came close to Tanner with his microphone and asked him, in clear, precise English, to spell the names. The surprised Tanner did so, watching the interviewer wink at the cameraman. Staying in English, the journalist now asked for spellings of the several other names, and Nels gave them. By now the table was covered with the peelings from perhaps fifteen bananas and the crumbs from a huge pile of cookies. Noting this, the Japanese asked, smiling, ''Are you very hungry?''

''Yes.'' Tanner nodded, smiling.

The journalist grinned widely. Turning to Terry, who had several nicks on his face, he asked, ''What happened to you? Run into a door?'

''No,'' Ross said, ''I cut myself shaving.'' This was the truth. He had been given a dull blade and ordered to shave prior to the interview. At the answer, though, the Japanese laughed uproariously.

Rabbit paid no heed to these departures from the script. He sat quietly reading his script and smiling to himself. The interview ended, and the engorged prisoners were returned to their cell. For approximately six weeks they were treated well.

Things seemed to be improving for Robbie Risner, too. Since leaving the Zoo on July 31, he had remained alone in a cell in New Guy Village.

''You will never be put with another American,'' Major Bai had told him. The reason, it was explained, was that Robbie was an incorrigible troublemaker who incited others to oppose authority.

The disheartening prospect of continuing loneliness was tempered by an optimism that the war had to end sometime. Meanwhile, he prayed, exercised, did his best in now infrequent interrogations.

In February, about the time of the Tet holiday, there had been a strange meeting with Cat. The prison system commander was full of wine, jovial, and determined to establish a rapport with the American ace. He kept assuring Risner that there was a bond of mutual respect between the two of them. Robbie did not deny it, but was unable to get a grip on his own end of the bond. Cat spent a long time delivering an admiring description of his own abilities as a dancer and his expertise with pistols. Then, increasingly expansive, he asked Risner, ''How would you like to go home?''

''We'd all like to go home.''

''No, I mean early.''

''Like when?''

''Sooner than the end of the war.''

''Only when the rest go home.''

"You are not very smart. How would you like a roommate?"

"Yeah, I would like a roommate."

He got one, possibly because the jails were getting so crowded, but also, Robbie believed, to provide his captors with some leverage to use against him.

On the evening of March 6, his cell door opened and in walked Air Force Lt. Ronald L. (Ron) Mastin, twenty-six, who had been captured on January 16. It was Risner's first sight of an American in more than seven months, and he was so excited he thought he might burst. But Mickey Mouse and several guards hovered in the background, grinning, obviously hopeful that they would be able to describe an emotional scene to Cat. Robbie would not let himself give them this satisfaction. He greeted Mastin quietly, showing him where to put his things, then fell silent, looking impassively at the Vietnamese. Disappointed, they left. Robbie jumped up and nearly hugged his new cellmate. He sat down and talked to him for hours, draining him of information about the war, the world, and his own background, then telling him of all that had happened to himself.

"You're just a carrot," he explained to Mastin. "They just put you in with me to try to buy something. What they are going to do is let me become attached to you, then they will threaten to snake you out unless I come through."

The two began receiving reading materials, propaganda tracts consisting mainly of atrocity stories about women, children, and innocent venerables who had been maimed by the American "air pirates." They perused these materials, hoping to find kernels of information about what was going on in the world. There were none. They began handing the materials back to the guard within an hour of having received them. This perturbed the camp officer, one called Bug, who had replaced Mickey Mouse. Bug was not much more than five feet tall, chubby, round-faced. His right eyeball seemed undisciplined; it wandered off in various directions, and the eye seemed mainly to be white. When "Bug" spoke to prisoners, he emphasized words by holding his right index finger at an angle above his head and jabbing it into the air. As the POWs would learn, he was a sadist.

Bug knew how to make certain the notorious Risner was reading the materials that were supplied him. He began taking him outside the cell and making him read the tracts aloud to him. After a few days Robbie deduced that Bug was bored and not listening to the readings.

He tested him, skipping paragraphs and then whole pages. Bug did not react. The charade continued.

———

One day in early March, Rabbit and Pigeye entered Dick Stratton's cell. Rabbit handed the pilot a fistful of papers, admissions by Stratton that he had engaged in "air piracy." Rabbit had constructed them. In these papers Stratton found himself confessing to twice having led bombing raids against Hanoi, and of having delivered napalm and fragmentation and phosphorous bombs upon the innocent residents of the city. He apologized to the Vietnamese people for having done these things and pleaded abjectly for his life.

"You will read these papers to a delegation," Rabbit advised.

"No," said Stratton, "I won't."

Indicating Pigeye, Rabbit said, "You will be punished."

Dick was scared, still hurting and sick from prior torture. The wounds from rope torture and beating were infected; he had boils that were suppurating; his broken eardrums were infected, his right wrist had seized up stiff; each midafternoon he was overcome by a fever that lasted into the night. At this point he didn't need any more punishment. Yet he was certain that somehow he had to resist. But how?

Maybe there was a more effective tactic than a head-on collision. At home he had been a member of Toastmasters International and had worked hard to overcome the common errors that mar an effective public speaking performance. He would put his Toastmasters training to work in reverse. He would get on the tape and make all the mistakes the Toastmasters had trained out of him. He would mispronounce words, speak haltingly, in a monotone, and would fall into a singsong delivery. He would make sure that anyone who heard the tape and knew English would know instantly that it was a phony.

His plan went badly. At the taping session he was monitored by three Vietnamese who spoke impeccable English. They understood what he was trying to do. Patiently, they kept erasing the tape and making him deliver the readings over and over again until they were satisfied. He managed a few mispronunciations and stretches of monotone, but he was frantic with doubt, not at all sure he had accomplished his purpose—if he had not, he had *really* blown it.

The next day he was told he was to be taken before the delegation.

He would not have to speak, but his tape would be played and he would be expected to bow politely before the visitors. It was emphasized that he would not make the humiliating 90-degree bow American criminals were required to make before their captors, but the civilized 10- to 15-degree bow Orientals generally proffer. Dum Dum arrived to tutor him in this nicety and after perhaps thirty minutes was satisfied that Stratton had learned to bow properly. That done, the prisoner was given a haircut and dry-shaved with a razor blade that felt as though it had been used to whittle the furniture. His face was scraped to a raw redness. To offset his underfed appearance, he was dressed in an extra sweatshirt.

In late afternoon of March 8, he was taken to an auditorium in the city. By this time he was at the peak of his daily fever. He felt grim and it showed—indeed, with his fever and the raw redness of his face, he could hardly have looked much grimmer. He was ushered into a room offstage. Onstage, he could hear someone, a Westerner, not a Vietnamese, holding forth in English on the inhumanity of the American CBU (cluster bomb unit), a weapon, the speaker insisted, that was being used exclusively against Vietnamese civilians.

The onstage Westerner completed his denunciation of American CBUs, and suddenly Stratton heard his own tape-recorded voice, reading the statement Rabbit had authorized for him. Listening, Dick felt relieved, for he could not believe objective observers, particularly Americans, would be able to accept that an American officer had freely offered such a statement; and certainly other Americans would not be able to believe that he had constructed the "confession." "The second of December," he heard himself say, "was to be an air wing strike on the suburbs of Hanoi. This was an extremely important mission necessary to make the people of Hanoi realize that they were not immune from the ravages of war. Anti-personnel weapons were chosen to inflict maximum damage on the population. The busiest part of the day was chosen for maximum effect on the population.

"I was horrified at the density of the buildings and population in the target. Bombs were scattered over the entire south side of the city. Privately, most of the pilots were appalled at the pacific nature of the target. Yet I not only did not have courage to refuse to go on the mission, but I did not have the courage to speak out against the mission or at the policy. I was inwardly ashamed at being such a coward."

Out front, foreign newsmen followed the tape-recorded statement through five mimeographed pages as Stratton droned on.

The reading completed, Dum Dum escorted Stratton onstage. Dick bulged his eyes, fixed a vacant stare on a spot on the rear wall of the auditorium, and walked stiffly to center stage. He stopped, facing the rear of the hall, and, keeping his arms and hands stiffly at his sides, bowed—deeply, until his face almost touched his thighs. He turned to the right and delivered another deep bow. He turned to the rear of the stage and, with his back to the audience, bowed again. He turned to the left side of the stage and did it again. He behavior caught Dum Dum off guard; he cried nastily, "Bowwww!" Stratton could not have hoped for more! Again, the prisoner bowed deeply to the four cardinal points of the compass.

The auditorium was alive with consternation. Voices were babbling, flashbulbs were popping, and cameras were clicking and whirring. Stratton finished bowing, then regained his zombielike pose. He was hustled offstage.

"Why you bowed like that?" Dum Dum asked anxiously.

"It was part of my early training for the priesthood," Stratton replied. "In my country Catholic priests always bow like that before the congregation."

The explanation was not challenged. The farce over, Stratton, having done his part, now received medical attention.

————

By the end of March, 1967, there were 178 Americans in Hanoi's prisons. The Vietnamese were running short on dungeon space. Heartbreak Hotel had become the receiving station and was fully booked most of the time. It became necessary to quarter new arrivals in Vegas near and even with old-timers. Veterans were able to brief newcomers, to install in their memories the POW roster, to advise them as to enemy tactics, to provide advice and to spell out POW policy.

Robbie Risner had not reappeared in the system since leaving the Zoo at the end of July, 1966. The Americans did not know whether he was alive. The senior POW known to be alive was Jim Stockdale, who now occupied TBW-6—he was in Cell #6 in the Thunderbird West Cellblock, at the northwesternmost corner of Vegas. From here he made policy. Working through his tough, cool communicator,

Ron Storz, now in TBW-2, the SRO had no trouble getting policy disseminated.

In Vegas the POWs were embarked on an anti-bowing campaign. Most could not abide the idea of bowing "to show your shame and subjugation" to every Vietnamese they encountered. They resisted doing so, but the guards were tireless in enforcing the requirement. They slammed rifle butts into stomachs and the backs of heads, kicked men in the groin, and pulled them down by the hair on their heads when they failed to make obeisance. Men felt so strongly about it that Stockdale did not order a no-bowing policy. He left it to individuals to develop the most disdainful and disrespectful bows guards would tolerate. For the most part, the bow evolved into a spasmlike downward jerk of the head, performed while sneering.

To his amazement, Jim Stockdale, whom his captors had assured was one of the "blackest of criminals," received a cellmate. It was twenty-seven-year-old Lt. Comdr. Danny Glenn, a *Kitty Hawk* pilot who had been captured on December 21, 1966. He was an architecture graduate of the University of Oklahoma, where, as a member of NROTC he had also earned his commission. Bright, cheerful, and intelligent, Glenn after his shootdown had suffered the typical mistreatments, and one that had not been typical: while most POWs had spent Christmas Day enjoying a relatively good meal and respite from harassment and torture, he had spent it hanging upside down from a hook.

It was during this period with Glenn that Stockdale formulated a general policy to give POWs guidance on practical questions not covered by the Code of Conduct. It was to remain in force throughout the long captivity. Its easy-to-remember acronym was BACK US. The letters stood for:

B—Bowing. POWs were not to bow voluntarily *in any fashion* in public, where anyone other than prison authorities were present. On such occasions, the enemy was to be required to force a bow. This would show objective observers that the prisoners were not subjugated, and that they were not being treated in accordance with the Geneva Convention.

A—Air. Stay off the air. Stay off radio. Stay off tapes.

C—Crimes. Admit to no crimes. Avoid using the word.

K—Kiss. Don't kiss the enemy goodbye. If forced to leave before a general prisoner release, a POW was to make no show of gratitude to his captors. There was to be no slightest indication that the Vietnamese had been generous or even civilized in their behavior toward their captives.

US—Unity over Self.   It was vital that the POWs' trust in and feel responsible for one another. Stockdale realized that there was a natural, enormously powerful temptation to try to reduce one's exposure to torture and other pressures by ducking leadership responsibilities. The Vegas SRO made it clear that no military officer worthy of his rank would dodge his responsibility to take command in order to protect himself.

To be sure, men in torture would vary in their abilities to hold to the BACK US policy. They would be forced to submit, and would "roll," and hopefully would "bounce back." But Stockdale hoped the policy would enable each to set an effective line of resistance for himself against an extortion program that was picking up steam.

———

At the Zoo that spring, Jim Kasler thought he was dying. In December he had been moved into a cell with Air Force Capt. John Brodak (captured on August 14, 1966). The two were old friends, had served together in Europe and again in Southeast Asia. Brodak had been through heavy torture at Hoa Lo. Tight, rusty irons had left his legs badly infected, and periodically Vietnamese medics would lance the leg sores and drain them.

The stench that issued from Kasler's encased leg left no doubt that it, too, was infected. The cellmates, however, saw no point in worrying over things they could do nothing about, but they enjoyed tormenting themselves with daydreams of candies and pastries. Their diet was thin: invariably, the two daily meals consisted of a watery soup, a bowl of rice, and several small pieces of boiled gourd or pumpkin. A piece of pig fat in the soup was a cause for celebration.

In January, after four months, Kasler's cast had been removed. The leg was covered with scabs the size of silver dollars and the knee wouldn't bend. He was issued a pair of crutches and ordered to write a letter of encouragement on behalf of the prisoners to someone named the Reverend Dr. A. J. Muste, an American antiwar activist. Kasler, who had refused to write such a letter to Senator Fulbright, made it emphatically clear that he would not write to Muste. He was made to "hold up the wall" for several hours, and did so, mainly on one leg and his crutches. Finally, disgustedly, his interrogators dismissed him.

In early February the surgical incision atop Kasler's thigh became infected, and the leg swelled painfully. It was lanced, he was given an antibiotic, and the infection faded, only to recur a week later. This time, it was eleven days before he received medical attention. By then the leg was swollen to half again its normal size, and the suture line stuck out like the laces on an overinflated football. In agony he was taken to a hospital. A doctor examined him, issued some instructions to a medic, and returned him immediately to the camp. For a few days the medic came in and needled injections into the infection. The leg continued to swell, until it overwhelmed the foot, almost hid the toes. Occasionally great gobs of stinking green pus would erupt from the infection. There was fever, and the pain became so excruciating that he could not sleep save from exhaustion. He lay like that for more than a month. Brodak cared for him and tried to feed him, but toward the end of March, Jim could take no food at all.

Then, one night in early April, he was again packed off to a hospital. The chief doctor awaited him, wearing an irritated expression.

"You have a bone infection," he advised curtly.

"What would cause it?" Jim wanted to know.

"Shut mouth," said the healer.

Jim was anesthetized. He awakened the next morning to find a new thirteen-inch incision in his thigh; it had been opened all the way to the bone and the wound had been filled with gauze that had been soaked in a yellowish medicine. After two nights he was returned to the cell he shared with Brodak. Thereafter, a medic appeared periodically to replace the medicine-soaked gauze in the incision. During these sessions the medic would require Brodak to fan the gnats, flies, and mosquitoes from the wound. The wound kept the place filled with a sickening sweet smell that made the prisoners nauseous. It smelled like death.

———

Bamboo walls had been erected between most of the buildings at the Zoo. Interbuilding communication was stifled. In effect, each cellblock became a separate prison camp, and guards hovered about each in hopes of catching men tapping and talking—whispering to a cellmate or even scraping a spoon against a bowl was enough to get a man punished. A guard looked through a peephole into the cell Larry Guarino shared with Ron Byrne and saw Guarino exercising, running in place atop his bunk. Shortly, Dum Dum arrived to assure the SRO that he was fooling no one, that the Vietnamese people knew him to be senior and that he had been tapping out orders to the others with his feet. Larry was locked in torture cuffs for ten days and nights.

Ev Alvarez, Tom Barrett, and Red Berg were all in similar punishment for communicating. The three shared a tiny cell in a small oven of a building called the Gym, behind the Garage. All were in rear cuffs and leg irons but were not tied to their bunks. They sat on them, side by side, with Berg in the middle. Barrett was in the throes of severe diarrhea and the other two did their best to keep the waste bucket within easy range of him. Once, Berg, working frantically with his shackled ankles to guide it to Barrett, wasn't quick enough.

"Ah, forget it," Tom said miserably.

For a long moment the three sat silently, contemplating the appalling mess, the aroma made worse by the furnacclike heat. They looked at each other and all seemed simultaneously to reach the same conclusion: things were so bad that there was nothing to do but laugh. And they laughed and laughed.

A "Spy" from the Sea, and Trouble on the Home Front

In the earliest hours of April 6, one of the most remarkable characters in American military annals came on the scene. This was Seaman Apprentice Douglas Hegdahl, nineteen, a veteran of nearly six months in the Navy. At six feet plus and 225 pounds, he was the beloved and well-cared-for son of a Clark, South Dakota, innkeeper and of a mother who did her own baking and wrote daily to her son in the Navy. Hegdahl had grown to young adulthood in a prairie society whose values, even in the cynical 1960's, were not so much taught as they were absorbed and taken for granted, values that attached preeminence to God, Country, Family, and Honor. Imbued with such values, he was to become one of the most peculiarly effective American combatants in what the POW seniors were to call, "The Battle of Hanoi."

Doug had joined the Navy to see the world, and the Navy had lost no time in its efforts to satisfy his wanderlust. As quickly as he had completed boot training in San Diego he had been hustled to Subic Bay in the Philippines, there to board the guided missile cruiser USS *Canberra*, as a member of the ship's gunnery gang. *Canberra* had steamed forthwith into the Gulf of Tonkin off the coast of North Vietnam for on-line duty, bombarding Communist military installations ashore.

For Hegdahl, it had all been fun. There had been his first trip on a commercial airliner, and stops in San Francisco, Japan, and the Philippines—an exciting itinerary for a youngster who never before had been east of his uncle's Dairy Queen stand in Glenwood, Minnesota, or west of his aunt's house, in Phoenix, Arizona. So far, the only segment of his Navy career that had been less than enthralling had been the on-line time in the Gulf of Tonkin.

As a lowly apprentice seaman, it had been Doug's lot to spend most of his time below decks, in the ammunition-handling spaces. He had never seen a night bombardment, which, his shipmates assured him, was a spectacular sight. And the night-morning of April 5–6 was to be the last on the line; following a planned bombardment *Canberra* would steam for Hong Kong. So when the guns jarred him awake just prior to 4 AM on April 6, he exhumed a cheese sandwich he had stashed beneath his mattress the night before, ate it, slipped into his clothes, and headed topside. There were sensible rules against going on deck during bombardment, but others had done it, had even taken some fantastic pictures of *Canberra*'s guns speaking, with tongues of flame issuing from their mouths. No one had been caught or hurt, and Doug wanted to see a bombardment.

The next thing he knew, he was in the Gulf of Tonkin, regaining his senses, watching *Canberra* recede into the darkness. He had walked under a battery of five-inch guns, apparently just as they had been fired, and had been blown into the sea. In all probability no one had seen him fall. The ship was pulling away fast, and in the darkness there seemed scant chance that anyone could see him. He waved his arms frantically and screamed, "Help! Help!" again and again. But with the guns booming there was no chance that anyone would hear him. *Canberra* steamed away.

Hegdahl, a powerful swimmer, trod water for a long time. He thought of the few times he had stood the man-overboard watch, thinking it was ridiculous. He didn't think it was ridiculous anymore. Now another chilling thought leaped to mind: he recalled that during the hours he had spent on that watch, leaning against a guardrail and gazing into the sea, his horrified attention had been captured by schools of snakelike creatures that stayed near the ship. *Those snakes!* he worried. *Could they be around me now? And sharks!*

He was afraid but stayed afloat. Dawn crept over a cloudy sky. There were no sea snakes, no sharks, no ships, and there was no land. There was nothing but cold and fear and loneliness.

He had been afloat for approximately five hours when he caught sight of what he thought was a buoy. He swam for it, occasionally losing sight of it in the swells. Closing on it, he saw that it was a Vietnamese fishing vessel. He stripped off his T-shirt and waved it, and minutes later he was aboard. There were six fishermen, and they seemed kind. They stripped off his soaked clothing and dressed him in a burlap sack with buttons on it. They gave him clams to eat, but hungry as he was from his long exertion, he couldn't stomach the foul-smelling things, and when no one was looking he threw them overboard.

The fishermen continued with their day's work. They showed him no animosity, and for a while he thought they must be South Vietnamese, and that he would be delivered into friendly hands when they reached shore. These hopes were dashed when other fishing boats passed close. His rescuers discarded their friendliness, pulled him to his feet, and put him on display, describing him in unmistakably hostile tones. The fishermen in the other boats shook their fists at him, snarling epithets in a language he did not know.

Ashore, he was handed over to waiting militiamen, who tied his hands behind him and led him through an angry crowd to what he judged to be a community center. Here he was seated on a stage beneath a large painting of Ho Chi Minh. For the first time, he was struck with the full realization that he was a prisoner of war.

The angry villagers piled into the place. They shook their fists, shouted at him, made him know he was a hated enemy. *Look proud,* he told himself, *keep your head up!* An old woman came close, slammed her small fist into his mouth. He was surprised that so fragile-looking a person could deliver so forceful a blow. It stunned him and opened a large cut on his mouth which began bleeding profusely. He was embarrassed that his first battle wound should be inflicted by a little old woman. Now others tried to get past the guards to hit him. The guards held them back, but people kept reaching over them and between them to slug at the prisoner, and he had to lower his head between his hunched shoulders.

Eventually the guards drove off the throng.

After dark he was blindfolded and put aboard a truck for a trip that lasted until the middle of the next day. When the blindfold was removed, he found himself in a dirty little shack in remote Vietnamese countryside. A young officer explained to him in almost unintelligible English that he must bow when approached by North Vietnamese. This did not strike the youngster as a loathsome obeisance, as it did the Americans in the Hanoi prison system. Hegdahl recalled that in movies he had seen with Oriental settings there had been all kinds of bowing and assumed it to be common custom in this part of the world. Then the officer gave him an English-language booklet to read concerning Bertrand Russell's international war crimes tribunal. Having committed no crimes that struck him as being possessed of international significance, Doug was not inclined to read the booklet. Besides, he had lost his glasses when he was blown off the ship and was half blind without them.

Two interrogators arrived. One was wizened and angry-looking. The other was younger, with huge, protruding eyes. The old one glared at Hegdahl and barked something in Vietnamese.

"I beg your pardon?" Doug asked innocently.

A guard behind him rammed a rifle butt into his head, and he remembered that he was supposed to bow.

Through an interpreter the interrogators took his name, rank, and number, then asked, "What do you fly?"

When nervous, Doug tended to stammer. "I d-don't f-fly," he said. "I f-fell off a s-ship."

The old man seemed to take on additional age as he listened to the translation. His mouth withered, as though he were eating lemons, and he fixed the prisoner with a tired, baleful stare. Again and again, Doug was made to explain how he had come here. He could see that his unlikely story was not believed, but at last the younger interrogator said, "All right. You come from the sea. You come to spy on our country?"

"No, no, no," Doug said. "I tell you. I fell off a ship."

The interrogation went on and on. The young Dakotan had never had so much as a single lecture about interrogations by an enemy. What was expected of him? He knew there were rules pertaining to American POW behavior, and he racked his brain trying to remember them. There had been that Code of Conduct poster on the wall just outside the company commander's office in boot camp. On it there had been an illustration of Nathan Hale, the Revolutionary War hero who had said he regretted having only one life to give for his country. One day the Skipper had called Hegdahl an idiot for not knowing how to present himself and chased him outside to come in and try again. As he collected his wits, he had stood in the passageway staring at the poster. Now, in North Vietnam, he again remembered Nathan Hale and what he had said. But what were the other words on the poster? How did the Code of Conduct go?

The interrogators kept insisting he was a commando. Much as he admired Nathan Hale, he did not want to be shot for being something he was not. Doggedly, he kept answering that he was a sailor who had fallen off his ship.

"You *lie!*" the saucer-eyed interrogator shouted. He launched on a tirade, and a guard stood before Hegdahl, slapping him in the face. The slaps didn't bother him so much as the visions they induced of unspeakable Oriental tortures, of his genitals being squeezed and of rusty nails poked through his eyeballs. He was scared.

Once, he made the mistake of saying, "South Vietnam." He was shouted down, and as the guard stood slapping him, the interrogator spoke and the translator intoned, "Vietnam is one. The Vietnamese people are one. Rivers may dry up, the mountains may erode, but this shining and glorious fact will always remain."

The interrogations continued, until finally he was told, "You must tell the truth or you will be shot. We now give you time to think."

He was left alone for hours. He still had difficulty believing what had happened to him, that he was not in the throes of nightmare, soon to awaken and find himself in his bunk aboard *Canberra* steaming toward carefree R & R visits in Melbourne and Hong Kong.*

But the nightmare didn't end. He was going to be shot; *he was really going to be shot!* He was frightened. The interrogation was resumed. "What is your decision?" he was asked.

"Well, I understand you're going to shoot me," he answered. He kept his voice flat, emotionless. Somehow, he knew it was important

---

*When Hegdahl's absence was discovered, *Canberra* retraced her route, searching for him. When he wasn't found, memorial services were held aboard *Canberra*. When word that he had been lost at sea reached his mother, in Clark, South Dakota, she was mending a pair of his trousers. She never accepted that he was dead. She laid the trousers atop an old flour barrel she used as a sewing table, and there they remained until the day he returned home.

that he not display his fear. "Before you do it, I would like to see a chaplain."

There was much jabbering, and one of the Vietnamese produced a Vietnamese-to-English dictionary. "Ahh, you want to see a priest." Hegdahl, a staunch Lutheran, indicated that a priest would do. His interrogators fell silent, stared at each other, and Doug knew that whatever they had in mind for him did not include his execution. At least, not yet.

His request for spiritual solace was ignored. The interrogators spent the rest of that day and much of the night and next day trying to shake his story. When it was clear he would never admit to being either an "air pirate" or a "commando" the interrogators gave up, and he was taken to Hanoi.

At Hoa Lo he was interrogated in the worst room he had ever been in. It stank of urine. Dried blood fastened patches of hair to several points on the walls and the floor, too, was bloodstained. Doug had never been in so sinister a place, had never been so frightened. Hour after hour, teams of interrogators harangued him and demanded "the truth." Sometimes guards hit him, and he was made to kneel on the floor and to hold his hands high in the air. After two days of this he understood that the only acceptable "truth" would be the "truth" his captors wanted to hear. At last, he asked wearily, "Tell me what you want me to say, and I'll say it. Just leave me alone."

"Tell us about the *Canberra*."

The demand surprised him. Apparently they had accepted that he was not a pilot—but not that he had simply fallen off a ship and swum to North Vietnam. They seemed convinced that he was on some mission and they meant to learn what it was. Meanwhile, they would learn about his ship.

"How thick are the walls?"

"Two feet."

"You *lie!* You think I a fool?" The interrogator summoned a guard to punish the prisoner.

"Sir, I don't mean the walls are solid metal. They are layers, with an outer wall, an inner wall, and a middle wall, and air spaces in between."

"Ahh, I see!" said the interrogator, smiling as though to burst. He offered Hegdahl a cigarette. "Here, you smoke and rest before continuing your disclosures."

The Vietnamese produced a small ruler. "How thick are each layer?"

"Oh," said Hegdahl, raising a thumb and forefinger, "about like that . . ."

The interrogator measured the space between the two digits and wrote into a small book.

"And how far it is from the waterline to ship's deck?"

"Seventeen feet," said Hegdahl, who did not have the slightest notion what the distance was.

It went on for days. He was made to draw the interior of the ship. His rendering looked like a small child's drawing of a tugboat. He falsely labeled spaces: "galley" and "Officers Country. No passageway." It was ridiculous, but he had begun to perceive that his captors would accept the most absurd replies so long as he appeared to be cooperating, so long as they were satisfied that he was "sincere." He resolved to make the most of it. He would inundate them with "sincerity"; he would be all farm-boy honesty, all open-faced, helpful innocence.

A few days later, "How far it is from waterline to ship's deck?"

"Ten feet," said Hegdahl, forgetting his previous answer.

The interrogator bristled. "Last time, you say seventeen feet. Now you say ten. You are not being sincere!"

"Sir, seventeen feet when the ship is empty, ten feet when the ship is loaded with supplies."

This proved acceptable.

"Now, Heddle," said the interrogator, "how large the guns were on your ship?"

"Wow!" said Doug, shaking his head. "Gee, you know anything I say will be always a guess, cuz I don't know. They don't let apprentice seamen around guns. But you know, I always try to be helpful to you. From a distance, they looked about this big . . ." and with his fingers and thumbs he made circles of various sizes. He was similarly evasive with ensuing questions. The interrogator became noticeably bored, tired of dealing with a prisoner whom he obviously regarded as an ignoramus. He walked from the room. Hegdahl was never again asked about the ship.

The interrogations continued, though. He was asked about what survival school he had attended.

"What's survival school? How do you spell that?"

"You had to go through survival school."

"You mean boot camp?"

"You tell me. You write."

Supplied with pen and paper, he wrote reams about boot camp. He had discovered that the interrogator would swell with pride on finding that he knew something the American did not know. Doug kept catering to the interrogator's ego, certain now that his best approach was in the role of good-natured numbskull. He stopped writing often to ask how to spell some word. The interrogator would tell him and advise, gloatingly, "You do not even know your own language!"

"Well, I'm only a seaman apprentice."

"Yes," the interrogator nodded, now clearly persuaded that Hegdahl was indeed of the American peasantry and thus possessed of an intelligence and education that probably were the rough equivalent of those of his own country's peasant class. But at least the American could write. "Go on," he urged, "keep on writing."

Doug filled pages with the most boring details he could recall. There was a long, stupefying instruction on how to deal with different types of burns. He spilled ink, and more had to be brought to him. He sucked on the pen, and got ink all over his tongue and face, and smudged it all over his papers. The interrogator began looking at him suspiciously, as though he could not believe him. Doug favored him with innocent grins that gleamed with "sincerity," and went on writing. But he worried that he might be going too far, that they would get wise to him and inflict the tortures he had dreaded so. He had to be careful.

His captors complained that his handwriting was illegible. He insisted that he was doing his best, but that he was frightened and nervous, and that he was only a farmhand, a peasant who could not write well and that he didn't know anything anyway. This ignited a lecture on capitalistic exploitation of the working class.

"What do you know politically?" he was asked. "What organizations do you belong to?"

"The Luther Youth League," he said, "at St. Paul's Lutheran Church, in Clark, South Dakota."

"What is the Luther League? How is it broken down? Who is the chairman?"

The days passed. The Vietnamese kept shifting subjects. "You have been insincere," Hegdahl was told. "You abuse the humane policy. Now you must do concretely for the camp. Even your commanders do for the camp, so you, too, must." The interrogator pushed a stack of papers toward him, statements signed by American officers.

"Oh, I'll be happy to sweep and clean up," Doug smiled, ignoring the statements. "Gee, I want to do my part. Just show me what work needs to be done."

"No, no, no," the interrogator said. His tone softened and he smiled, as though he were talking to a small child. "You do not undastahn. Let me show."

Together, they read several antiwar papers. Hegdahl doubted their authenticity. There was a falsity to the tone and language, and he could not believe the officers had signed the papers voluntarily. He believed they had been tortured to do so. If the officers were being tortured to "do for the camp," he would just have to be tortured, too. The game was up; he was frightened, but he toyed for a moment with the notion of letting the interrogator know that he was not as dumb as he seemed; it would be a satisfying thing to do. But before he could do so, the interrogator put on an antiwar tape that had been made by an American officer. It was hilarious, a parody, full of "thee's," "thou's," and "ye's," and Doug had to tune out the voice to keep from bursting out in laughter. Concluding, the officer intoned, "All Americans, even little old ladies in tennis shoes, opposed this war . . ."

Hegdahl had the guidance he needed. The interrogator turned to him, was delighted to find him smiling. "Now you write on morale of ship," he told him.

"What do you mean? What's 'morale' mean?"

"What the sailors thought of this war. It is illegal. It is unjust. It is immoral. They must hate it."

"Oh, they like it fine. We had checkers and Ping-Pong and boxing matches, and everybody eats steaks and drinks ice cold drinks. There's so much to do, there isn't much time to think about the war. . . ."

"Write," the interrogator said tiredly.

He wrote in detail about the meals that were served three times daily, the goodies that were available at fountains and snack bars between meals, the games that were played, the movies that were shown.

At this point, the Vietnamese gave themselves a breather from Hegdahl. He was shipped to the Zoo and ushered into a cell occupied by Navy Lieut. Charles D. (Charley) Stackhouse, an A4 pilot off *Bon*

Homme Richard. Stackhouse, who had been downed a few days earlier near Haiphong, had already been rope-tortured. He was appalled at what had happened to him and frightened at his captors' barbarism. Hegdahl was still scared, too. Each was ecstatic at being with another American.

"Where were you downed?" Stackhouse asked.

"Gulf of Tonkin," Doug mumbled.

"Really?" Not many aircraft were shot down at sea; in fact, this was the first time Charley had heard of it happening. "What were you flying?" he asked.

"Look," Doug said, "you're not going to believe this."

"C'mon, tell me how you were captured."

"Well, I sorta fell off my ship . . ." It took some convincing, but the amazed Stackhouse finally believed him.

Dum Dum demanded that Hegdahl tell him the length of his ship, the *Canberra*. Irritated, Doug replied that he did not know the answer. "I'm a bad judge of distance," he said, "and I don't know what to compare it with."

Dum Dum produced a dictionary, found the word "compare" and a flash of understanding lit his eyes. "Ohh, yes, yes," he said. He led Hegdahl into the yard and put a mark on the ground. He instructed him to stand at the mark, and to call out when Dum Dum had walked a distance from him that matched *Canberra*'s length. Hegdahl let him walk to the opposite end of the camp, then flagged him. The distance represented perhaps half of *Canberra*'s length. Dum Dum counted the paces back to the prisoner, and wrote something into his notebook.

"How far was it?" Hegdahl asked, craning his neck to look into the notebook.

"Mmmh!" Dum Dum exclaimed, leaping away, holding the notebook to his chest and shaking his finger at the prisoner. The feces collector had no intention of surrendering military information to such as Hegdahl!

———

Through 1966, Hanoi's attempts to convince the prisoners of the rightness of its cause had been totally ineffective, even a source of amusement to many POWs. But early in 1967 the enemy introduced Americans into a situation that had a powerfully demoralizing effect. Instead of Hanoi's own poorly constructed diatribes, the POWs found themselves listening to many of their most prominent countrymen, including high-ranking members of government, not only questioning America's course of action in Southeast Asia, but even condemning it in the most virulent terms. Articles from American newspapers were read over camp radios, describing how Sen. Ernest Gruening (D., Alaska) had drawn deafening applause from an audience of more than two thousand clergymen in Washington's New York Avenue Presbyterian Church when he described the decision to commit American troops to combat and to bomb North Vietnam as the "gravest kind of treason."

Sen. Wayne Morse (D., Ore.), the prisoners were told, won approval from the same congregation for expressing the view that the "great need is for the United States to start exporting bread and stop exporting bullets to the underdeveloped nations...."

No word or activity of American antiwar activists went unreported. The POWs heard Dr. Martin Luther King, the revered civil rights leader, call the war a "blasphemy against all that America stands for."

Dr. Linus Pauling, the Nobel Prize-winning chemist, was quoted to them: "I am ashamed of my country, the United States of America. This is the most powerful, most militaristic and most immoral country in the world, in waging its wicked,savage war."

Dr. Benjamin Spock reported feeling "nothing but scorn and horror for Lyndon Johnson's Vietnam policy. In the rest of the world, our ruthless actions are being compared to the Soviet Union's suppression of the Hungarian revolt and Hitler's murder of the Jews."

POWs who had been suffering torture in preference to making such statements could not understand such talk from other Americans, especially from members of their own government, for whose policies they had been committed to combat and were enduring vile captivity. They felt bewildered, depressed, betrayed. They understood political leaders dissenting from policy and opposing it; but not openly opposing it to the enemy's benefit while the country was at war.

Beyond that, many POWs could not fathom the basis for the dissent. They could not understand what was "treasonous," "blasphemous," or even questionable about helping a small, weak ally resist a forcible Communist takeover. By far the large majority of the prisoners believed wholeheartedly in the American effort, had lent themselves to it willingly, even eagerly, and did not grudge the fact that participation had brought them to their present straits. Most still believed strongly enough to keep resisting the enemy with all the spiritual and physical strength they could muster. Their most fervent prayers and hopes were that America would prosecute the war with the kind of intelligent zeal that would end it quickly, would end the Communist threat to South Vietnam, and, by no means incidentally, their own harsh imprisonment. The POWs feared that the antiwar faction at home would impede intelligent prosecution of the war and would encourage the enemy to keep fighting. In making the most of such support, the enemy seemed to be showing his need for it, and to be signaling his intention to fight on.

The POWs were told that on April 15, there were to be monster war rallies sponsored by something called the Spring Mobilization Committee to End the War in Vietnam. Sen. Robert F. Kennedy (D., N.Y.) had commended these rallies, saying that they would "provide the means for the broadest expression of the desire of the vast majority for peace." Millions of Americans would attend the rallies or support them. The camp's radio asked. "What will you contribute to the April 15 peace movement?"

Posters in the camp's bath areas posed the same question. The Vietnamese urged POWs to write letters of support to American antiwar leaders and to Congressmen and their own families, asking them to support the peace movement. Instead of complying, they scratched obscene words and illustrations onto the posters, and eventually tore them down.

They were treated to full coverage of the rallies, however. They were told how an estimated 125,000 people had jammed United Nations Plaza in New York to cheer as Stokely Carmichael, of the Student Non-violent Coordinating Committee, cried, "There is a higher law than the racist McNamara. There is a higher law than a fool named Dean Rusk. There is a higher law than a buffoon named Lyndon Baines Johnson. . . ."

In the prison cells of Hanoi something seemed terribly wrong in the United States of America.

———

But April was not a good month for Hanoi, either. *Life* magazine, in its April 7 issue, presented a full-page photograph of Dick Stratton at his March 6 press conference, bowing. It was an arresting, shocking picture, a big, husky American combat pilot in purple and cream striped prison garb and sandals, his arms and hands held stiffly at his sides, lowering himself in subjugation. The scene was not the kind Americans have ever been conditioned to expect where their fighting men are concerned, and not one they would easily believe, for it was humiliating to the American spirit. Indeed, there was a sinister quality to it—Stratton looked like an automaton, like someone who had been made into a puppet.

Americans reacted angrily to the photograph and speculated as to whether Stratton—and other POWs—had been brainwashed or drugged. Ambassador-at-large Averell Harriman, in charge of POW matters for the State Department, told *Life*, "From the photographs, videotapes and descriptions by eyewitnesses that I have seen of the so-called 'news' conference at which Commander Stratton was exhibited, it would appear that the North Vietnamese authorities are using mental or physical pressure on American prisoners of war. We all remember the ugly record of 'brainwashing' during the Korean War. It would be a matter of the gravest concern if North Vietnam were using similar means against the prisoners."

The photograph had been taken by Lee Lockwood, the only American journalist who had been present at Stratton's press conference. Along with the photograph, Lockwood supplied some text in which he described Stratton as having a "red, swollen nose" (he had a boil in each nostril), empty eyes, an expression that never changed, a puppetlike demeanor. In a New York *Times* interview Lockwood reported, "He looked straight ahead, but he really wasn't looking— his eyes never seemed to focus—he just wasn't there. It was like a robot—when they said something to him, he acted; if they said nothing, he did nothing.

"Some Vietnamese newsmen denied that Stratton had been given any orders as he stood there, but several of us heard it quite clearly. A few sharp words from the officer, then the prisoner went into this robot-like bowing."

Time magazine, in its April 14 issue, said Stratton's "Pavlovian performance" had "Orwellian impact" that "unsettled even hardboiled communist newsmen," and that he behaved "like a Manchurian candidate."

The story also called attention to many other "peculiar confessions" by American POWs, for instance, one made by Jerry Denton that Havana Radio had played months earlier: "The brave and determined workers of an antiaircraft battery shot down my aircraft," he said. Denton lauded "the kindness of heart of the Vietnamese government and people," and admitted his own "vicious, revolting crimes" in bombing "the innocent people and civilian buildings of the Democratic Republic of Vietnam."

As *Time* observed, "It made Commander Denton sound just like the boy next door—to any boy in Hanoi."

"Ho Chi Minh," *Time* judged, "still believes that he will win the war by default, and the apparent aim of his prisoners' confessions is to convince the world that U.S. fighting men are sick of the war and guilt-racked over their 'criminal' behavior in bombing North Vietnam. . . . Hanoi's efforts so far only accentuate North Vietnam's endemic ignorance of Western idiom, intellect and ideology."

———

In its article on Stratton, *Time* also reported on "One artful dodger who beat the system . . . Lt. Cdr. Charles Tanner, 34, from Covington, Tenn . . . who solemnly declared that two fellow pilots . . . (who) refused to fly their missions were court-martialed and dishonorably discharged. The officers' names, subsequently trumpeted by Hanoi: Lt. Cdr. Ben Casey and Lt. Clark Kent."

The Clark Kent–Ben Casey confession was also carried by other news magazines, by wire services, and by network television newscasts. Much of the world enjoyed it; Hanoi was not amused.

One siesta time in early April, a number of guards burst into the cell Nels Tanner and Ross Terry shared, pulled Terry up from his bunk, and hustled him roughly from the room. They returned for Tanner and took him to interrogation, where one whom the prisoners called Eel demanded, "Name for me some movie stars!"

Eel was furious, struggling to maintain his composure. Nels professed bafflement. "What do you want movie stars for?"

"Just name some," Eel said. He pushed paper and pen at the prisoner. "Write down names of all movie stars you can think of."

Tanner had no way of knowing the Ewell-Casey-Superman confession had reached the outside world. He assumed some knowledgeable Vietnamese had spotted it and that an admission of perfidy had been tortured out of Terry. He scribbled the names of perhaps 150 movie stars, but did not name Clark Kent, Ben Casey, or Tom Ewell. Eel scanned the sheet, ripped it up angrily, and marched Nels into another room. He was seated on a low stool before a table lined with the prison authority. Presiding was Cat, Major Bai; also present were

Rabbit, Spot, Eel, and another nasty interrogator called Lump, because of a sizable tumor on his forehead. Cat did the talking in Vietnamese. Eel interpreted.

"Do you know comical characters?"

"Comical characters? Could you mean funny characters?"

Cat barked angrily, and Eel said, just as angrily, "You know what I mean! Comical characters!"

Nels began naming popular comedians. "Red Skelton. Groucho Marx . . ."

As Eel translated, Cat's anger, already vast, kept mounting. Tanner thought he would explode. The American went on naming comedians, until finally Cat shouted.

"You know what I mean!" Eel translated, biting off the words. "You know, *Superman!*"

"Oh, you mean comic strips."

"No, I mean comical characters, Superman and Ben Casey, movie stars. Terry has told us all! He told us you are a liar!"

Cat waved a typewritten letter at Nels. "But you *never* fooled the Vietnamese people *for one minute!*" he shrieked in English. "We have here a letter from the Communist party of the United States! My friends in your country have written me and told me of your *deceit!*" So his spurious confession had gotten to the United States! His captors had been made to look ridiculous, had lost face.

Cat ranted on at such length that Tanner thought he would lose his voice. Nels was happy that he had scored against the enemy, but frightened, for now he would have to pay the price. He would take as much torture as he could before apologizing or "making atonement." He and Terry had made a pact that they would never again yield anything to this enemy without first taking torture.

Tanner was kept on the stool for five hours, listening to Cat declaim. The man's anger never diminished. He sat, he rose, he strode about and sat again, all the while waving the typewritten letter and assuring Tanner that he had fooled no one. At last, abruptly, he marched from the room, and the others followed him.

All but Lump. He remained in the room with Nels, sat looking at him tiredly. At length, he asked, "Tanner, do you really think that anyone outside of the United States of America would know who Superman is, and would know it was false? What about the Japanese? Surely they would not know?"

With the fat as far into the fire as it was, Nels saw no point in letting his captors think they might get off without losing face with other Asians. He drawled, "Well, Superman is on television in Japan, you know."

Lump's face sagged. To Tanner's surprise, guards were ordered to return him to his cell.

He waited for Terry, worrying over what had happened to him.

Like Tanner, Ross had been railed at and threatened, but not physically abused. He had told them nothing. He didn't return to the cell. Tanner would wait a long time to see him again—nearly six years.

The evidence suggests that Hanoi's propagandists, who wanted the world to believe their American prisoners were receiving "humane and lenient treatment," were frantic over the reaction in the United States to allegations that Stratton—and perhaps other POWs—were being brainwashed or otherwise mistreated. It was revealed that, on March 16, two other American prisoners had been interviewed separately in a villa near Hanoi by three Westerners, who had been unable to detect that the two had been treated other than humanely.

The POWs were Air Force Maj. Jack W. Bomar, who had been captured on February 4; and one who had asked to remain nameless, inasmuch as he had made remarks critical of the Johnson Administration—according to the visitors, he had said, "I don't want to go from a Vietnamese jail to an American one."

The visitors were Dr. Jean-Michel Krivine, a French surgeon; Dr. John R. Neilands, a University of California biochemist; and Maurice Cornil, a Belgian lawyer. Interviews with them appeared in the New York *Times,* stating that Krivine and Neilands were associated with the Bertrand Russell Peace Foundation and the international war crimes tribunal, and Cornil was "directing a team of jurists investigating the war" separately.

The three reported having found the prisoners "in reasonably good health and lucid in conversation." Still, the report was not altogether reassuring, for it alluded to the fact that the two POWs had performed the same sort of deep bow that Stratton had made famous—Bomar had bowed even though he had been on crutches. Moreover, he had appeared to be confused when Neilands had proffered his hand; Neilands had found it necessary to explain that he wanted to shake hands before Bomar had extended his own hand.

Bomar recalls that he had suffered shrapnel wounds to his left thigh and an injury to his left ankle when he was shot down. He had, nonetheless, been severely tortured, to the extent that he was not inclined to make an issue of bowing. He agreed to meet the delegation when he was told the lie that one of the visitors had recently seen his wife and had expressed a desire to speak personally to him. Beyond that, Bomar's most notable recollection of the meeting is that when he turned to the American, Neilands, to ask bluntly, "What are you doing here?" Neilands replied, "No son of a bitch like Dean Rusk can tell me where I can go and where I can't go. I am free to go anywhere, anytime."*

Interrogators continued to try to persuade Nels Tanner that he had written his Clark Kent–Ben Casey confession in order to protect real people who were flying combat and thus to avoid court-martial when he returned to the United States. It was suggested to him that he put this in writing and also that he admit to criminally attacking with napalm and CBUs the innocent civilians of Phu Ly, a city not far from Hanoi. Nels refused, but the Vietnamese persisted, until finally, impatiently, the prisoner seized pen and paper. He wrote for a long time, then handed the paper over and watched, with a mixture of satisfaction and fear, as the interrogator crimsoned with fury— Tanner had written the Clark Kent–Ben Casey confession all over again. The paper was torn to pieces, and he was returned to his cell to "think deeply."

In mid-April he was moved from the Zoo to a cell in Stardust, where he was locked in ankle stocks. The window in this cell was boarded over, and there was no light. He was not let out of the stocks except occasionally to empty his waste bucket. After two weeks he was taken before the same five who had assured him at the Zoo that he had fooled no one—Cat, Rabbit, Eel, Lump, and Spot.

"Now," Cat said, "you have changed your mind. You will write a rebuttal statement."

Pen and paper were provided, and Tanner wrote the bogus Clark Kent–Ben Casey story for the third time. He refused to write any more. There ensued two long days of argumentation, wild polemics, and dire threats.

---

*The use of a U.S. passport was authorized for travel to Cuba, Mainland China, North Korea, and North Vietnam only when specifically validated for such travel by the State Department, over which Dean Rusk then presided.

On May 1, Cat said, "Today you are going to pay for your crimes against the state!" Nels was locked in torture cuffs and left alone. He had not heard of this torture before. He endured the excruciating pain for nearly four hours. Then Rabbit returned to tell him, "I have written the rebuttal for you, and you must copy it and sign it."

"I refuse," said Tanner.

Apparently, Rabbit's mistake in accepting the original Clark Kent–Ben Casey confession had been noted by his superiors in the political department and they had ordered him to rectify his blunder. He now began to beat Tanner about the face—this was unusual; normally, beatings and torture were left to the guards. Rabbit was very angry, and the blows stung and stunned. The beating lasted for perhaps five minutes. Then a guard was summoned, and Nels was tortured in ropes. He lasted about an hour before agreeing to copy and sign the rebuttal Rabbit had written, and to read it onto tape. Then he was returned to his cell and locked back into the ankle stocks. Except for two occasions when he was taken out for more torture, he was to remain there for the next four months —and then things would really get rough.

No Early Release, No Repent, No Repay

Through the spring of 1967, the cell space crisis became increasingly acute. Most of the old-timers in Vegas received cellmates, always new shootdowns who were younger and junior in rank. But some veterans remained alone. Howie Rutledge, for example.

A skilled and active communicator, Rutledge was always in the mainstream of POW message traffic. But he had not had a face-to-face conversation with another American since his shootdown, eighteen months earlier. After a month-long ordeal in the Outhouse at the Zoo the previous August, when he had temporarily lost his ability to recall his children's names, Howie had been left pretty much to himself. There had been only a few interrogations. Once Rabbit had scornfully torn to pieces the confession Rutledge had written following the Outhouse session. "We don't need this!" Rabbit had said. "We have much more interesting copy!" Howie remembered that he had couched the thing in Communist jargon and had worried not that Americans would believe it, but that it might sound persuasive to Asian peasants. He had been delighted when Rabbit destroyed it.

At another quiz Rabbit had confided. "I have been told by other interrogators that you are very bad. You are a diehard reactionary. They don't like to talk to you. But I think I can work with you."

"Forget it," Rutledge advised. "You may as well torture me right now, because I am not going to give you anything until you do."

But he had not been tortured, and had not seen Rabbit again. He had been left in solitary. He was confined to a space so small it was not possible to take more than two or three steps in one direction. The space was alive with vermin. There was little ventilation, little fresh air. The place stank, and was either much too cold or much too hot. There was never enough food. There was no one to talk to, nothing to read, no writing materials, nothing to hear, and, eventually, nothing to think about. It was a depressing, dispiriting existence, and there was no end to it in sight.

Howie had quickly recognized that he had a choice: he could curse his fate and remain depressed and dispirited. If he did so, sooner or later he probably would lie down and die. Or he could pull himself together, decide to live. He opted to live.

He organized a daily routine that was so full he often had trouble meeting it. At the morning get-up gong, he would rise and spend half an hour painstakingly folding his blankets, sleeping mat, and mosquito net. Then he would spend an hour at vigorous exercise. When he was taken out to empty his waste bucket, he would simultaneously fulfill another task he had set for himself—counting the number of cell doors on one side of the passageway; fixing the location of windows in other buildings; counting the number of steps to the waste dump. Back in the cell, there was a time allotted to breakfast and then, for two hours, he would pray and work hard at mentally reconstructing scripture readings and hymns he recalled from boyhood. Howie had been raised a Southern Baptist, but it had been many years since he had had any real interest in religion. He had it now and found the training of his youth to be a source of needed comfort and inspiration.

From noon until 2 PM, during siesta, he was a key communicator in the prisoner network. There was always a great deal of business to transact: names of new shootdowns had to be received, relayed, and committed to memory. Information was passed concerning interrogations, tortures, punishments, and movements that had taken place or were in progress. Questions were asked concerning policy, and answers had to be delivered. Then, if there was time, men simply became acquainted. Men who had never seen each other became close friends, got to know all about each other, their careers and backgrounds, their plans and hopes, even became deeply involved in each others' family triumphs and problems.

Rutledge would spend hours each day squinting through cracks and termite holes in his cell door, tracking the movements and studying the habits of the various guards, things that would have to be known if anyone worked up an escape plan. He would spend additional hours planning what items of clothing he would wash on his next washday. After his evening meal he would sit on his bunk and engage in pleasant memory exercises—to start with, he spent months trying to remember the names of every member of his high school class, back in Tulsa. It had been more than twenty years since high school, but eventually he was to be 75 percent successful.

His next-cell neighbor was George McKnight, who also had been kept in solitary since his capture. Howie had first met him in Heartbreak Hotel in November, 1965, the month both had been shot down. They had not seen each other since, but each was aware of the other's reputation as an aggressive resister. Now they became close friends.

Perhaps the best measure of how cramped the Vietnamese were becoming for prisoner living space was that on April 24, Rutledge and McKnight were joined as cellmates. To Howie's amazement, his cell door opened, and in walked George, carrying his rolled-up gear. As quickly as the guard departed, they celebrated. George hurled a handful of shredded toilet paper into the air, like confetti. Their cups filled with water, they toasted their inexplicable good fortune. They could not stop talking, could not even sleep. They went on, in whispered conversation, for three days and nights. Each developed a sore throat. Each delighted in the other's being a serious "bad attitude" case for the Vietnamese—Rutledge especially enjoyed McKnight's "personality conflicts" with enemy personnel. They enjoyed being together and knew it could not last.

"Thirty days, George," Howie croaked. "I give us thirty days together. Then something will happen or they'll catch us at something, and they'll split us up."

He was optimistic, but only by three days.

Clearly, if Hanoi was to regain any of the propaganda ground lost because of all the horrified speculation as to its treatment of prisoners of war, imaginative measures were in order. Somehow, the DRV had to be cast in a humanitarian light. By May, a plan had been devised. The POWs were advised, over and over, that those criminals whose attitudes did not improve would be "severely punished." On the other hand, "those who show a good attitude, who properly accept the education provided and repent, truly repent their crimes against the Vietnamese people, may be provided the opportunity to go home even before the war is over."

The policy was repeated a number of times. During delivery, prisoners became aware that cellblock corridors were being prowled by men whom they had not seen before. Some were in uniform, others in civilian clothing. All were older and appeared to carry considerably more authority than prison staff members. They walked from cell door to cell door, opening the hatches that covered the peepholes and looking in at the inmates, as though to assess prisoner reaction to the choice being posed.

With Robbie Risner still missing, Jim Stockdale remained the senior ranking POW in Vegas, and, as such, responsible for dealing with the enemy's dangerous new approach. And dangerous it was. Stockdale had no doubt that Hanoi now meant to pit the POWs against each other in a competition for early release. Chosen to go home would be those prisoners whom the enemy deemed most likely to do him some good in the United States. Doubtless, these would be men who had suffered little or no mistreatment themselves, who had been kept so isolated that they knew little or nothing of the enemy's atrocious treatment of the bulk of POWs, or who had been made so fearful by threats of blackmail for statements yielded freely or under minimal pressure that they could be depended upon not to blow the whistle on Hanoi for its treatment of American prisoners. Moreover, Stockdale believed, no one would go free early for free; the early releasee would have to take out some sort of propaganda mortgage with the enemy, would have to say or do something on Hanoi's behalf.

There was another factor: if the Vietnamese were successful in getting their American captives to compete with each other for freedom, the fight on the Hanoi front would really be over, for mutual trust and confidence among the POWs would disintegrate. There could be no discipline, no loyalty to any cause save one's own well-being.

Stockdale issued a counterpolicy: no one, he ordered, was to accept early release. His communicators saw to it that this policy was widely disseminated in Vegas, and men who were moved took it with them to other camps.

Incumbent as it was on Stockdale to think this matter through carefully and to promulgate policy on it, he suspected and later learned that he needn't have worried. To the vast majority of POWs, the idea of early release was as abhorrent as it was to the SRO. If there was an "average American prisoner," he was as determined as Stockdale to leave only when they all left, and in order of shootdown. The only exceptions could be those who escaped, as authorized by the Code of Conduct; and the sick, wounded, and injured.

To be sure, the enemy was successful in stimulating some competition. Eventually, 12 POWs were to accept early release, 11 officers and one enlisted man. Only the enlisted man, Doug Hegdahl, was not in violation of Stockdale's order—Hegdahl's release really amounted to a reluctant escape.

———

"Criminals will be given an opportunity to atone for their crimes in a meaningful way," the POWs were now told over the camp radio. "They will be allowed to help the Vietnamese people clean up the debris of bomb damage. Work parties are to start among volunteers and the work will afford you the opportunity of fresh air and exercise. A bath will be available to each volunteer after returning from the bomb-site area. You will be approached individually."

It would be nice, Stockdale thought, to get out of the cramped cells, get some fresh air and exercise, to be able to bathe and to meet other Americans face to face. The only thing wrong with the proposition was that the enemy was sure to make propaganda yardage with it. There would be photographers all over the place, and the Americans would be shown to the world as "working together" in apparently healthful circumstances, "atoning" for their "crimes."

Stockdale ordered, "No repent, no repay. No work in town. No clearing of craters. No repent, no repay."

No Vegas prisoner ever accepted this opportunity to make "atonement."

———

France having made clear that Bertrand Russell's international war crimes tribunal was unwelcome, the tribunal finally was convened in

Stockholm, Sweden, in May, 1967. It was, at various times, comprised of sixteen to eighteen people, including three Americans: David Dellinger, editor of *Liberation* magazine; Carl Oglesby, a writer; and Courtland Cox, representing Stokely Carmichael. The "executive president" of the "tribunal" was the French philosopher Jean-Paul Sartre.

In their prison cells, the POWs heard that Russell's American secretary, Ralph Schoenman, who had made three trips to North Vietnam, had testified to the "tribunal" that the United States was engaged in genocide in that country. "It is not possible," Schoenman was quoted as saying, "to drop four million pounds of bombs every day on a country the size of New York and Pennsylvania without exterminating the population—and this is genocide."

Schoenman also insisted that the United States was conducting chemical warfare in North Vietnam. As proof, he offered what he called extracts from the diary of a Dr. Nguyen, who told of attacks by an American helicopter and two aircraft in November, 1964, which had left him nearly blind. The next day, all the poultry were dead and all the fish in the streams and lakes were floating on the surface of the water, discolored. The crops were either burned up or rotting, and all the pregnant women and animals miscarried.

The POWs heard that on May 10 the "tribunal" had found the United States guilty of "crimes against peace and crimes against humanity." Cited as accomplices were Australia, New Zealand, and South Korea.

As the "tribunal" had closed, the prisoners were told, Vladimir Dedijer, a Yugoslavian writer who was presiding, had warned that "some of us might be subjected to all kinds of pressures, particularly in the United States." But, he said, the "tribunal's" American members, Dellinger, Oglesby, and Cox, were "men of great integrity" who represented "what is best in the American tradition."

Their fulsome half-ration of news concerning events in Stockholm did not convey to the POWs that the rest of the world had paid scant attention to these goings-on. Few newspapers accorded it much space. A Washington *Post* article put the total cost of the "tribunal" at $240,000, indicating that most of the money had been supplied by Lord Russell himself. Had the Americans in Hanoi known all this, they might at least have enjoyed judging it a poor return on investment.

As the war intensified, the Vietnamese became even more cramped for prison space. On May 19 alone—the Americans would remember it as "Black Friday"—seven aircraft were downed. On May 21, Marine Capt. Orson Swindle was ushered into a cell he was told he must share with three others, Ron Storz, Wes Schierman, and George McKnight, three of the most stalwart resisters. Swindle was thrilled, but the thought nagged that he did not deserve such company, for there was no denying his treason.

"Look, you guys," he said, "I've heard about you and I just can't tell you how much I admire you. But I've got to tell you something: I betrayed you up here. I gave them a statement and didn't take torture for it."

Tears of shame filled his eyes as he explained himself: he had been shot down on November 11, 1966, near the DMZ, had been captured immediately and subjected to savage beatings. He was interrogated and pressed for information and confessions of war crimes several times during a thirty-nine-day trip to Hanoi. Resisting, he had been rope-tortured numerous times. Reaching Hanoi, he had refused to make antiwar statements and had been kept isolated, hungry, thirsty, and tired. Then ropes had been displayed to him and he was told he was to be tortured again. It had been too much, he said, and he had caved in, confessed to criminal acts against the Vietnamese people, agreed with Sen. Wayne Morse that the war was "illegal" and was sorry for having participated in it. He felt he had betrayed his country, his family, and every American who had fought and died or been captured in this war. He was inconsolable.

"Orson," said Ron Storz earnestly, "don't worry about that."

George McKnight laughed. "Orson, you're looking at the Ernest Hemingway of North Vietnam! I've written so much bullshit up here you wouldn't believe it!"

That made Orson laugh—and nearly cry with relief. He felt all right about himself again. He believed that with men like these around him he would not fail again. It would not be for lack of opportunity.

———

Other veterans came together on May 21.

"Den-ton, your attitude has not improved at all, but conditions are crowded. We must put you in with someone else. We will put you in with Mulligan."

Denton and Mulligan were old friends. Each was the only American the other had spent any time with since his capture, and they were ecstatic at coming together again. Both had been in tiny punishment cells in the Mint. Now they were moved to an eight-foot by four-foot cell in Stardust. There was no cross-ventilation, and in the smothering heat and humidity the pungent stench from two waste buckets was nearly overpowering. To make matters worse, Mulligan had virulent diarrhea. He seemed terribly ill, emaciated and so weak he had trouble moving about. Denton worried about him. But at least they were together.

Back in the communications stream, Denton found himself to be senior in Stardust. Separating Stardust from Desert Inn, to the north, was a large room, twenty to twenty-five feet wide, where the Vietnamese now were stashing new shootdowns. There were several Americans in this room, but guards were lurking everywhere. Communications had seldom been riskier, but Denton, determined to acquire the vital information on the men in the large room, chose a siesta period to initiate voice contact. Phil Butler and H. K. Flesher "cleared"—kept watch for guards in the moatlike alleyway between the cellblocks and the prison wall. Denton spoke in a loud whisper through his window and into the alley. Scotty Morgan and Air Force Maj. Tom Sima (captured on October 15, 1965), in cells between him and the new men, relayed his queries and brought answers back to him.

The room seemed to be serving as an aid station or infirmary. The senior patient was Navy Lt. Comdr. Eugene B. McDaniel, an *Enterprise* pilot who had been shot down on May 19. During ejection he had suffered a broken vertebra and a severe injury to his right knee. Despite these injuries, he had been locked into hell cuffs and shackles almost immediately on reaching Hoa Lo and tortured in ropes for military information four times in two days—once during his dehydrating travail he had grown so desperately thirsty that he had tried to smash some wounds into his head in hopes of using some blood to moisten his lips. When the pain of his injuries had been compounded in torture, he had lost control of his bowels and bladder.

After torture he had been tied up and thrown into a rat-infested bath stall. Lying there, he had listened for a long time to the agonized screams of other Americans. No torture he had yet endured was as bad as having to listen helplessly to the screaming and crying of other young Americans.

In the room with McDaniel was Navy Lt. (j.g.) William J. (Bill) Metzger, Jr., a *Bon Homme Richard* pilot who also had been bagged on May 19. Metzger was twenty-five but looked younger. He was a mess. Battle injuries included a left arm that had been split open to the bone from the wrist to above the elbow; a deep, ten-inch-wide cut in his left leg, which had yielded a two-pound piece of shrapnel; and a broken right leg. When McDaniel reached the room, he found Metzger lying on a stretcher on the floor. He was nude; the Vietnamese, thinking him likely to die, had squandered no clothing or blankets on him. But medics were dressing his wounds. The Vietnamese kept incense sticks burning to counter the awful stink that issued from Metzger's long-untended wounds. When the medics left the cell, they took the incense with them, and Metzger could hardly stand himself.

But this was to be among the least of his problems. For two months Metzger was to be left lying nude. He was issued no clothing, no blanket, no soap, no towel, no toothbrush or toothpaste, nothing. McDaniel cared for him as best he could, but Metzger steadfastly refused to accept more than an occasional use of the other man's soap. McDaniel complained daily to guards and officers about Metzger's plight, but nothing was done about it. One night, Metzger's screams awakened McDaniel: a rat was gnawing on the youngster's wounds. They drove it off, and next morning McDaniel requested an audience with the camp commander, again for an issue of prisoner gear for Metzger and to explain the necessity of closing the cell to rats.

"There's an old saying in Vietnam," the officer laughed, "when the cat's away the rats will play. Besides, they are just trying to make friends." He dismissed McDaniel. Metzger was not issued his necessities until August.

Another cellmate was Air Force Lt. Col. Thomas J. (Tom) Sterling, who had been captured on April 19. He had suffered two broken legs during shootdown and ejection.

Others were Air Force Lt. Joseph E. (Joe) Milligan, captured on May 20; he had been burned during shootdown. And Navy Lt. (j.g.) Gareth L. (Gary) Anderson, another May 19 shootdown, who had an infected leg. Milligan and Anderson had been through heavy torture.

After McDaniel completed his personnel report to Denton, Jerry wanted a briefing on the world and war situations. McDaniel reported that more and more American troops were being committed to combat and that casualties were now in the neighborhood of three hundred per week. To long-incarcerated POWs, this seemed an indication that the United States now was waging war on a businesslike basis. If so, surely Hanoi could not hold out much longer. In that sense it was good news.

In turn, McDaniel was briefed on Vegas, on the enemy's apparent aims and tactics, and on SRO Stockdale's policies. That done, Denton wanted to know, "Is that 'Red' McDaniel?"

It was, indeed, an old friend of both Denton and Mulligan; the three men's families were neighbors in Oceana, Virginia.

"Ask him if he's got any news for Jim Mulligan or me," Denton said, his voice rising.

Mulligan was nervous. Essential communication was dangerous enough. In his weakened condition, he found the prospect of more torture, or even isolation, unappealing, the more so for the sake of mere personal exchange. "Jerry," he barked, "get off the goddamn wall!"

The message came back from McDaniel: "Tell Jim his wife knows he is a POW, and that Father Gallagher says they are all praying for him aboard *Enterprise*."

Mulligan was elated, in no mood to object to further communications.

McDaniel's message continued, "Tell Jerry his family is in great shape. They know he is a POW and that he is OK. His son Billy is burning up the Little League."

"Hot dog!" Jerry exclaimed delightedly.

Flesher and Butler, who were watching the moat, began coughing, signaling that guards were approaching. To their horror, the Denton-McDaniel exchange continued unconcernedly. The guards in the moat now heard Denton's voice.

Just before noon Denton was taken to a stall in the courtyard bathhouse. The place was a storage area for garbage, and there were roaches and rats all over it. The stall was a few feet square, and the whitewashed concrete walls reflected the intense heat of the sun. Denton's ankles and lower calves were shackled into two sets of irons. His wrists were locked behind him in torture cuffs. A tight blindfold was applied and he was made to kneel. He remained on his knees in this place for hours, and then, suddenly, he was not there.

He awakened in a small, very hot cell in the building called Riviera. A doctor was examining him. His wrists and ankles were mangled, bloody, and swollen, and Jerry knew that he had a high fever. The doctor instructed that the hell cuffs and leg shackles be removed. Denton then was made to sit on a stool in this cell for five days and nights. Occasionally, he would get off the stool and lie down, but whenever he did this a guard would enter immediately, beat him, and make him get back onto the stool.

Finally, it ended. He was returned to his cell in Stardust. It was worth it all to know that Billy Denton was burning up the Little League.

———

While other American seniors had come together on May 21, Howie Rutledge and George McKnight had come apart. The two had been good for each other. Together they had analyzed the effects on themselves of the kind of animalistic life they had been forced to live. There were some things they could do nothing about, but other things that they could deal with. They did not like the language they found themselves using, and each agreed to keep track of the number of times per week the other uttered obscenities. At the end of each week the worst offender would owe the other a banana—the Vietnamese served them occasionally and they were precious to the starving prisoners.

They kept each other's spirits up by keeping the Vietnamese infuriated, offering all who looked in their direction the most exaggerated bows and the most enormous, contemptuous smiles. Finally, Bug, the Vegas camp commander, had had enough. He had Rutledge brought to interrogation.

"You have been given very good treatment," Bug said, "very humane. Look, now you have a roommate. You should show gratitude and cooperative spirit."

Howie was not impressed. He reminded Bug, "I spent a year and a half in solitary confinement before I got a roommate. That is the worst form of mental cruelty. Your government signed the Geneva Convention, yet you do not treat us as we are entitled to be treated, as prisoners of war. You are in violation of international law! I demand . . ."

Bug was in no mood to accept Rutledge's demands. On May 21, Rutledge and McKnight were split, having been together for twenty-seven days. Howie was taken to Cell #1 in the Mint, just vacated by Denton.

———

Spring burgeoned, and with it the anger of the prison camp authority. Doubtless, the primary reason was an intensification of the American air war against North Vietnam, but the attitudes of the "criminals" themselves surely exacerbated matters. None would read on the camp radio. None would avail himself of the opportunity to atone by helping to clean up bomb damage. The prisoners would not cooperate in any meaningful way.

The chief of the resistance, the prison authorities knew, was Stockdale. He was the most senior, the leader, the chief troublemaker. Stockdale had to be brought down.

Like Denton, he was locked in rear cuffs and leg irons and cooked in the Bathhouse. In the oppressive heat he found himself weakening rapidly. When he called "Bao Cao," a guard entered and slapped him hard several times on both sides of the face. An English-speaking officer arrived and Stockdale upbraided him for the behavior of his subordinate.

"The guard can do anything he wants," the officer assured him. Apparently, submission by the SRO was not acceptable; he was to be baked until the toughness was all gone.

The nights were too short and the long, shimmering hot days blended together. He was moved to various stalls in the Bathhouse. He was kept on short rations of food and water, just enough to keep him conscious of his parched misery. Occasionally he would escape into sleep. Once a guard who decided not to let him sleep accused him of dozing and slugged him savagely on both jaws. When the guard left, Jim heard a towel snapping somewhere nearby; someone was shaking the water from it to dry it and sending a tap-coded message: G B U J S. "God Bless You, Jim Stockdale."

The next day a guard locked cuffs onto the meatiest parts of his forearms, cutting off circulation. Stockdale was soon shouting for relief. The guard returned, stuffed a dirty rag into his dry mouth, and squeezed the cuffs a notch tighter. That evening he was let out of the cuffs and isolated in a small cell in Riviera. There he remained for several weeks. Then he was taken before Cat.

Cat was expansive. He graciously presented the prisoner with his enamel drinking cup, which had been denied him during his punishment. He observed that now that Stockdale had learned his lesson, he certainly would be wise enough not to "take advantage" of the situation. That night, said Cat, Stockdale would be taken to meet some visitors.

"I will not answer any questions," said Stockdale. "I will say nothing."

Cat bristled. "We will see! I warn you to use good judgment!"

He was blindfolded and driven into the city. Arriving at his destination, where his blindfold was removed, he was ordered to leave the vehicle unaccompanied and to go up into the porch of what appeared to be a large restaurant or hotel, to turn left and enter a lighted room, bowing as he did so. He decided instantly not to bow. He stayed upright as he entered and kept glowering fiercely. The room was bathed in blinding bright lights, and in the shadows behind them Jim could make out cameramen working furiously. He limped to the center of the room and stood scowling for several seconds. Then he heard Cat say angrily, *"Leave! Get him out!"*

Stockdale was seen entering and leaving the room by the junior Navy POW, Seaman Apprentice Doug Hegdahl. Earlier, an interrogator had told Doug, "I want you to go and see a delegation that is visiting and tell them how you were left to drown."

"What?" Hegdahl asked incredulously.

"You know, how your shipmates were green with fear and they left you to drown in the water."

"Hey, wait a minute, that's not what happened."

Hegdahl had kept objecting. To no avail.

When Stockdale left the room, Hegdahl was ushered in. The lights were so bright he threw his hands up to shield his eyes. He groped his way toward a table where the visitors were sitting, saw them, men and women, looking at him as though he were a circus animal and making notes. Then he was led from the room. It was over. He had been asked no questions and had said nothing. Later he would see a report the delegation produced concerning its visit, noting that, "We met James Bond Stockdale, who passes himself off as James Bond," and also "Douglas Hegdahl, a crewman on a helicopter that was shot down. Hegdahl was green with fear, and tried to swim out to his aircraft carrier. . . ."

Hegdahl was returned to his cell in the Zoo. Stockdale, to his amazement, was returned to his old cell in Thunderbird West. The SRO lost no time getting back into communication. But Cat had hardly begun.

In late June and early July an East German film company was in Hanoi to make a propaganda movie entitled *Pilots in Pajamas*. The purpose was to depict the American POWs as ordinary mortals, indeed even weaklings, who were being treated leniently and humanely by their Vietnamese captors. Much of the filming was done at the Zoo. The prison authority awarded leading roles to the fierce-looking Dick Stratton, the "Mad Bomber of Hanoi," and to Doug Hegdahl, who was well known as a young man who turned "green with fear." Perhaps half the prisoners at the Zoo were taken out of their cells to play supporting roles.

Filming was difficult. The East Germans wanted to create an impression of POWs working happily together, in healthful activity in an open compound. To show how the Vietnamese cared for their prisoners, many POWs were issued brooms, to be filmed sweeping the supposedly immaculate place; others had shovels to dig shelters in the ground for protection against American bombs; and still others were exhorted to lead each other in body-building exercises. The German filmmakers would have preferred the prisoners occasionally to exchange words and smiles, but the Vietnamese would have none of this—they had guards posted behind every tree and the corner of every building, watching, and it was tricky trying to keep the obviously predatory guards off camera. Nor did the Americans take direction well—the sweepers were forever turning their backs on the cameras and sweeping away from them; the shovelers stayed hunched over and scowled. The exercisers were ludicrous, jogging around in absurd little circles that were not a yard in diameter. The POW who led them in calisthenics stood holding up one fist, with the little finger extended, and kept time with it!

That day Stratton and Hegdahl got their first close looks at each other. They were made to take showers together. In a low voice Hegdahl muttered, "Whaddya make of all this?"

Stratton made little effort to muffle his own deep voice. "Personally, I think anybody that takes pictures of people taking showers has got to be a little queer."

Hegdahl had a hard time keeping a straight face.

Stratton could barely contain his curiosity about Hegdahl. He had caught several glimpses of the youngster, and the lad's youthful countenance had him thoroughly puzzled—he could hardly be old enough to be a pilot. When the story of Hegdahl's capture finally reached him, Stratton, like most other POWs, had a hard time believing it. But from a distance, he had developed a high opinion of the kid.

In May, Hegdahl had been placed in a cell with a young officer whose badly deteriorating morale had many POWs worried. He had been a good officer, had resisted the enemy in brutal torture as well as anyone. But lately his spiritual strength had been eroded in the Niagara of propaganda that was washed endlessly over the prisoners. The camp radio and the Vietnam *Courier,* a propaganda sheet for the POWs, constantly carried lengthy reports of massive antiwar activities in the United States. The prisoners received copies of pages from the Congressional *Record* containing increasingly virulent antiwar statements by respected and high-ranking American political leaders. All of which had driven the young officer through a tortured reappraisal of the American effort in Vietnam; he seemed almost ready to embrace the enemy's contention that the war was "unust, illegal, immoral." Beyond that, he was unable to understand why he and others should accept imprisonment and torture on behalf of a cause so many of their countrymen despised. It was assumed the Vietnamese had joined Hegdahl with this man in order to expose the youngster to his "good attitude," and there was speculation that the two of them might be relased together.

Hegdahl spent a little more than a week with this officer. Then, to the astonishment of the other POWs—and doubtless the Vietnamese—the officer had rejoined the resistance, and had vowed never to give in. Hegdahl had been rushed off to the Outhouse, the punishment cell, and put on a diet of rice, rock salt, and hot water. The camp commander had complained angrily, "You try to corrupt your roommate!"

Hegdahl had enjoyed his time with his roommate. Confused and angry as the officer was over the situation in which he found himself, he was pleasant, had an outstanding sense of humor, and certainly was not afraid of his captors. Once when a guard entered their cell for whom the officer harbored special antipathy, he had deliberately broken wind. Snarling at the insult, the guard had run to get an interpreter, who returned with him, sputtering, "You . . . you . . . you made *air* at guard!"

"No," the officer replied pleasantly, "I *farted* at the guard."

The interpreter stood staring at him. "Fart," he said speculatively.

He pulled out an English-Vietnamese dictionary, asking, "How you spell that?"

The insult was forgotten. The interpreter left, delighted to have a new English word, one not even in the dictionary!

Hegdahl observed, "I thought he kind of lost a lot when he asked you how to spell it."

Stratton and Hegdahl had had little chance to communicate on the day the East German film was made. A few days later, they were among several who were transported from the Zoo into the city, to open a new prison a few blocks from Hoa Lo. This place was situated on grounds that formerly had been the official residence of the mayor of Hanoi. It was to be the showplace prison, where visiting delegations were to meet prisoners—actually, living conditions were no better than at Hoa Lo or the Zoo, but a few cells had been spruced up for display purposes, and the mayor's mansion was available for meetings. This prison was to be called the Plantation Gardens—for short, the Plantation.

One morning shortly after reaching the Plantation, Stratton, looking through a small hole in his cell wall, studied Hegdahl, who was sweeping the street outside. The youngster worked very slowly, making the most of the opportunity to look over the camp. An armed guard was with him, obviously bored at the pace at which Hegdahl worked; eventually, the guard sat under a tree and dozed. Hegdahl then swept a pile of dirt and sand close to a parked truck. Standing with his back to the gas cap, he kept swiveling his head in both directions. Then, to Stratton's amazement, Hegdahl reached behind himself, unscrewed the truck's gas cap, knelt, grabbed up several handfuls of sandy dirt, and jammed them into the tank. Then, again standing with his back to the tank, he had trouble getting the cap screwed back on. He kept fumbling with it, swiveling his head in both directions. Stratton was frantic. *Get the damned thing on!* he prayed.

At last, abandoning caution, Hegdahl turned, got the cap on, and swept himself away from the truck in a cloud of dust.

This kid gets the job done, Stratton thought. *This place is full of hot-shot pilots, but I haven't heard of anyone else sabotaging a truck!*

Shortly, Stratton and Hegdahl found themselves attending an interrogation together with Major Bai.

"He is from the air," Cat said, nodding to Stratton and addressing Hegdahl. "You are from the sea. Now you will live together."

Hegdahl was pleased, and awestruck. He knew Stratton to be a lieutenant commander, and he had never been so close to so much rank. More impressive, though, was Stratton's fearsome appearance, the same heavy-bearded, big-nosed, bushy-browed aspect that had led the Communist propagandists to type him as a typical U.S. air criminal. Hegdahl had seen guards force Stratton to bow and had admired the way he had smiled as he had done so, rumbling, "Piss in your boot, you little bastard."

Now, turning to the officer, Cat snapped, "There is no rank in this camp, Stratton." It was as though Stratton had raised an objection to being forced to live with an enlisted man. In truth, he was elated. It would be good to have someone to talk to, and now he could get to know this amazing kid.

They were ensconced in a spacious cell, much larger than either was used to. In addition to bunks, it had a table and stool. It was lit by a low-wattage bulb. A sign on the wall proclaimed, "Clean and Neat."

"Sir," said Hegdahl formally, when the two were alone, "my name is Seaman Apprentice Douglas Hegdahl."

"I am Lieutenant Commander Dick Stratton, off the 'Tico.' "

"Sir, do you want me to call you 'sir'?"

"Hell, don't call me 'sir'; My friends call me Dick or Rich. They called me Beak on the ship. Take your choice."

"Sir, can I call you Beak?"

"Sure."

"Yes, sir, Beak."

They got on well. They told each other of their experiences. Hegdahl was appalled at the tortures that had been inflicted on Stratton, and Stratton was impressed at the way the youngster had conned the Vietnamese into thinking him dumb. One day Stratton returned from an interrogation with instructions to write the story of his shootdown for a camp magazine the Vietnamese had entitled *The New Runway*. They seated themselves under the sign on the wall; Stratton, who sat under "Clean," now called himself "Mr. Clean," and Hegdahl was "Mr. Neat." The young apprentice seaman now tutored the lieutenant commander on the production of nonsense for the enemy.

"My airplane just blowed up . . ." Stratton wrote.

"That's fine," said Hegdahl. "Now, why don't you say, 'I landed in a tree and decided to hang around for a while. . . .'"

Stratton laughed. "The guys will get a kick out of that. And I'll say I landed in *the* tree, next to *the* rice paddy, like there's only one of each in North Vietnam."

"Good. Good!" Hegdahl nodded sagely.

They labored mightily, completing the piece. It was never published.

The two made an adventure of their meals together. Stratton would give the signal to begin by pounding his loaf of French bread on the table and shouting, "All right, everybody out! Everybody out!" Tiny weevils would come crawling out of the bread.

They saved what they called "little surprises" to show each other after meals. Stratton would show Hegdahl half a cockroach, asking him if he knew where the other half was and advising him not to worry, since it was good to have some protein in his diet. Hegdahl once produced half a rat feces, explaining that he had retrieved it from Stratton's bread.

They liked each other immensely. Stratton couldn't get over the youngster's dumb-like-a-fox behavior toward the Vietnamese—and his thoughtful manners—Doug would always go to the far end of the cell and stand facing the wall when Stratton had to use the waste bucket. After learning that Stratton could not stand the smell of toothpaste, Hegdahl always held his head in the bucket while brushing his teeth.

Hegdahl idolized Stratton, for the tortures he had suffered and for his brilliant tactics in dealing with the enemy. He recognized him as an authentic American hero and viewed it as great good fortune to be living with him. In addition, Stratton was fun to be with. He seemed to sense when others needed a morale lift, and could always be counted on to deliver one. For example, one night that midsummer when Doug was feeling especially low, "Beak" sat down and put an arm around his shoulders, as though to give him a fatherly pep talk. The youngster waited, expectantly. At last, Stratton said, "Christ, Doug, if you can't take a joke you should never have joined the Navy!"

But Stratton was to see to it that Hegdahl would have the last laugh on the enemy.

17

Summer 1967—The Meanest of Times

Robbie Risner lost his cellmate, Ron Mastin, in July. They had shared a small cell in New Guy Village for more than four months. The pressure had begun building in early April, when an interrogator told Robbie, "Now you must choose to cooperate with us and live, or oppose us and die."

Back in the cell, Robbie told Mastin, "Ron, I don't know what they are after, but we aren't cooperating, no matter what."

"I'm with you a hundred percent," Mastin replied.

The next day Risner refused to make his decision. For ten weeks thereafter, through the hottest, highest-humidity period of the year in Hanoi, he and Mastin received a one-pint daily water ration for the two of them, for drinking, bathing, and washing clothing. They had been giving over their entire mornings and from two to six each afternoon to a program of vigorous exercise. It involved thousands of leg lifts, pullovers, side-saddle hops, leg kicks, push-ups, sit-ups, and jogging. When the water was cut off, the exercising had to stop. The days dragged. Unable to properly clean themselves, the two were soon covered with boils—now a common POW malady.

In May, Robbie suffered a torturous two-week siege with kidney stones. Once, as he lay in agony on his bunk, Ron tried to cool him with a fan he had made by wrapping a shirt over a broom. The waves of warm air washing softly against the kidney area caused such pain as to make Robbie scream. But it was not until after he became incoherent that he was taken to a hospital and treated until the stones had passed.

Back in New Guy Village, he was given two pictures of his wife, Kathleen, and their four sons; these had come with a letter or package from Kathleen that he had never seen. He cherished the pictures, became absorbed in them, sat looking at them for hours, lost in thoughts of his wife and their smiling youngsters. He was told that he now was expected to meet with a delegation from East Germany. When he said he would not do so, Cat came into the interrogation room, ordered torture ropes thrown on the table before the prisoner, and told him again what was expected of him. Weak from illness and from the memory of savage torture, Robbie agreed. He was told what questions would be asked and was made to memorize his answers. For example:

> *Question:* What is the solution to the Vietnam War?
> *Risner:* The only solution is for the American government to disassemble all their air bases and all other military installations and to withdraw their troops and to stop supporting the dictatorial Saigon regime. . . .

Meeting the delegation, Robbie did not perform as ordered. He remained mute to some questions and his answers to others could have been written by Lyndon Johnson. The meeting soon ended in confusion, with Cat glaring at him and advising the Germans that Risner had just received some photographs of his family. Delegation members evinced interest, wondered if they might see and make use of the pictures. Cat assured them that this could be done.

Robbie was returned to his cell. He was frightened, wondering if he could survive whatever tortures lay in store for him but determined to deny the enemy the pictures of Kathleen and the boys. The photographs were sacred to him, and he would die before allowing the Communists to blaspheme them by using them for propaganda purposes. He tore them up, put the pieces underneath a rock at the bottom of the waste bucket he shared with Mastin.

The cockeyed Bug came for the pictures, and when Robbie was unable to produce them he had him hustled into Room 18, the Meathook Room. There, a big, exceptionally ugly guard whom the prisoners called Big Ugh worked him over. He kicked and smashed the badly weakened Risner about the room, got him down on the floor and kept smashing his face against it until it was a bloody mess. Then Big Ugh applied torture ropes. When Robbie began screaming, the torturer stuffed a thickness of rags deep into his throat. A set of irons was shackled onto his ankles. He was then bent forward and tied so that the toes of his feet were pressed against his mouth.

He was left like that for what seemed a very long time. When he was finally released and ordered onto a stool, he could not get up. His legs would not support him. No one would help him. He was ordered repeatedly to get onto the stool, and finally was able to crawl to it and lift himself onto it.

Bug was in white-lipped fury. "Where are the pictures?" he screamed.

"I destroyed them," Robbie whispered.

Again he was tied back into the ropes, and his toes were fed to him. He was left in the torture much longer this time, but when he was brought out of it his answer remained the same; he could not provide the pictures because he had destroyed them.

For a third time, Big Ugh began lacing him into the ropes. This time, it was too much. He could not live with any more of it; he felt unglued, as though he were coming apart, and knew that more torture would drive him insane. He cried, pleading for mercy, and confessed that the pictures were at the bottom of the waste bucket. He was made to retrieve all the pieces and to return with them to the torture chamber. The pieces were washed and taken away.

Robbie's arms were twisted behind him and his wrists were pulled up between the shoulder blades and locked together in bone-tight hell cuffs. His ankles were shackled and a "jumbo" iron, perhaps twelve feet long and weighing a couple of hundred pounds, was laid across the tops of the ankles. He suffered the pain, praying God to see him through the night. Sometime before dawn he was released from torture and given food and drink, probably to keep him at a level of consciousness where torture would remain effective. Then he was returned to his cell. Ron Mastin was gone and Robbie knew he would not see him again for a long time, if ever. He was made to sit on his bunk. His ankles were locked into the stocks at the end of the bunk and again his wrists were pulled high and tight behind his back and locked into torture cuffs.

He was left like that for ten days and nights.

One morning, full of fatigue, pain, and misery, his whole body began twitching and then jerking, hard, convulsively. He thought of his wife and children, desperately, like a dying man—and then became more desperate in the realization that he could not remember their names! He became aware now that he had gone as far as he could go, that his reserves were used up. He had no choice but to submit. He called, "Bao Cao," and was released from torture to write an abject apology for the troubles he had caused the camp authority.

———

Cat had the notorious Risner broken to halter and meant to make the most of it. Within a few days he was trotted before a delegation from North Korea. "Do not anger me again," Cat warned.

Robbie did not want to anger Cat. He dreaded the prospect of more torture. He tried to be agreeable with the North Koreans, but could not find it within himself to accept their accusatory questions.

"How many crimes did you commit against our country?"

"None."

"How many of our villages did you bomb?"

"None. I shot down eight of your aircraft in air-to-air combat."

The questioning continued in the same vein. Robbie kept denying the substance of it but worked hard at trying to be pleasant.

Afterward, Cat was angry, but not angry enough to torture.

Robbie was taken to the Plantation, the showplace prison, for a meeting with American writer Mary McCarthy. He knew little of her and his captors did not seem to know much either, except that she had written some articles about the war and seemed to them to have the "right attitude." He was warned to say nothing that might put Hanoi in a bad light.

The interview was innocuous. When Robbie advised that he missed having a Bible and sweets, the writer proposed to send Bibles for all the prisoners and a cake for Risner. Cat declined these offers, observing that Bibles were not needed, that Risner got plenty of good food. The writer confided to Robbie that she did not think the

Vietnamese understood her. Raising his eyebrows, Robbie said, "I think they do."

The interview ended with McCarthy knocking on the wood of the table and hoping for a quick end to the war.

After she left, Robbie spent hours in interrogation trying to explain that raising the eyebrows and knocking on wood were not secret codes.

————

There never was a worse time for American airmen to reach Hanoi than that summer of 1967. There seemed to be a new madness in the air, an eagerness to hurt, to cripple, to create the kind of groveling fear that would induce a "cooperative attitude."

At Hoa Lo the chief interrogator and director of torture was Bug. Often the grotesque little sadist would affect a friendly manner as he sought to enlist his captives for Hanoi. Chain-smoking, grinning evilly, his right eyeball wandering erratically, he would inquire of new shootdowns who had just been tortured, "Now you have learned to think correctly? You have seen the truth and the light? You have seen how unjust, illegal and immoral the acts of the United States are? You have seen how they are killing the Vietnamese People? Now you must condemn the United States and its actions in Vietnam!"

When a prisoner demurred, Bug's anger would mount. He would slap him and tell him, "You have a very bad attitude. You are one of the blackest criminals that have been victoriously shot down while conducting an inhuman raid against our country. I must teach you to think correctly. I will give you more time."

Depending on the influx of prisoners or on Bug's mood, men would be given a number of short periods to think things over. Those who remained recalcitrant were then tortured anew. There were many.

————

Navy Comdr. William P. (Bill) Lawrence lay on a bunk in his cell, trying to believe that the five days of horror he had just endured had really happened and that the horror was over. He was still shocked and surprised at the torture—he had been aware of no information that the North Vietnamese were torturing POWs. Commanding officer of Fighter Squadron 143, aboard *Constellation,* he had been downed on June 28 at Nam Dinh. Captured, he had been taken to Room 18 in Hoa Lo, where he had been beaten and tortured in ropes for five days. Occasionally during this time, he would hear his young backseater, Lt. (j.g.) James W. (Jim) Bailey, screaming in a nearby room. Then Bailey's screams had stopped. Bill hoped and prayed that he was all right.

As for himself, Lawrence wanted only to be left alone. He could barely walk from all the bending, and his hands and arms were swollen and discolored. Like a wounded animal, he needed some private healing time.

"Hey, Bill Lawrence," a voice called, "are you in the corner room?"

Surprised, Bill lifted himself laboriously from his bunk and struggled down to the gap at the bottom of his cell door. The voice, he learned, belonged to Ron Mastin, solitary in a cell across the corridor. The camp, Mastin told him, was called Las Vegas, and their cellblock was Thunderbird West, which happened to be headquarters for SRO Jim Stockdale.

Mastin had come here after being separated from Risner and had quickly proved himself a dependable communicator. He explained to Lawrence that others were clearing as they talked. He gave him the danger signal: a single cough; and the all clear: two coughs. Then he told him that his backseater, Jim Bailey, had been in Thunderbird a few days earlier and that he was all right and had been taken to another camp. He gave Lawrence the names of the others in Thunderbird West cells who were not within communications range of him. Two—Jim Stockdale and Bill Franke—were old friends of Lawrence. Bill sent word to the SRO that he was known to be a POW; that he had seen his wife, Sybil, at a party six months earlier, and that all was well with her and the children; and that Stockdale had been selected for promotion to captain in the fall of 1966. It was the first time in the nearly two years since his capture that Stockdale had received any reassurance concerning his family. It was an immense relief, and nice, too, to know that they now were receiving the pay of a four-striper.

Lawrence could not find the heart to deliver a complete message to Bill Franke. Franke had been reported killed in action, after being downed on August 24, 1965. There had been a memorial service for him at the Miramar Naval Air Station in San Diego. His life insurance had been paid to his wife, and she had bought a new house and set about making a new life for herself. Then, about a year and a half later, it had become known that Franke was a POW. His wife had resettled with the insurance company, and now was awaiting his return—which, Bill Lawrence decided, was all that was important for Franke to know. "Tell Franke," he said, "that his wife is doing great, too."

He had no answers for hopeful questions as to how the war was going. Like many who had been absorbed in the day-to-day business of fighting the war, he knew only what others had long known, that the Vietnamese had mounted some very stiff air defenses and that the war raged on. Lawrence was not confident that many Americans could long survive the appalling living conditions and the torture. "Have many guys died?" he asked Mastin.

"No," Ron replied, "most of the guys seem to hacking it pretty good."

———

Another who reached Room 18 that July was Navy Comdr. Robert Byron (By) Fuller, 1 1951 Naval Academy classmate of Bill Lawrence. Fuller, commanding Attack Squadron 76 aboard *Bon Homme Richard,* was downed on the fourteenth while leading a strike against a railroad bridge not far from Hanoi. Ejecting at high speed from his A4, he flailed badly and suffered a broken left leg, a broken right arm and hand, and two dislocated shoulders. The manner in which his captors attended to the mangled officer attests to the climate of lunatic savagery that prevailed.

Fuller's injuries were ignored. In Room 18 he was quizzed immediately for military information. Several *Bon Homme Richard* airmen had preceded him to Hanoi, and his interrogators knew of him; mockingly they called him Skipper, and spoke as though they had been waiting for him. They knew a lot: the command structure of the Seventh Fleet; the names of all the Fleet's admirals and their flagships; which ships were on line in the Gulf of Tonkin; each carrier's area of responsibility. Clearly, they had extracted a lot of information, and Fuller was soon to learn how they had extracted it, for they wanted much more from him: information about a weapon called "Walleye," a free-fall bomb that is guided to its target by television. They knew *Bon Homme Richard* carried the only American air unit using such a weapon and felt certain they could get all the technical information they wanted pertaining to bomb weight, release altitudes, and so on from one so senior as Fuller—a commander, a Skipper.

They tried hard. They kept Fuller in Room 18 for seven days and nights. Four times they squeezed him in torture ropes and hell cuffs. In the end, they got him to give the names of many pilots—all those he had known who had died since 1951; and to name several future targets—bridges and power plants in various locations that had long been under continual attack; and he told them all he knew about "Walleye"—that it was a free-fall bomb that was guided to its target by television. Fuller knew that his week of hell ended not because the enemy was satisfied with what he had given, but because they knew he would die if subjected to more torture.

———

Robbie Risner remained alone in a cell in New Guy Village. Returning from an early-morning interrogation on August 1, he found his breakfast awaiting him. He had just begun to eat when indigenous convicts began nailing strips of lumber over his barred window. He was now to be denied what little light entered his cell through the moatlike alleyway. Simultaneously, he became aware of a sharp burning sensation at the rear base of his neck. The discomfort increased rapidly; it was almost as though a hot poker were being held against him. He put his bowl down, wet his towel, and held it against the distressed area. It didn't help. He put the towel aside and sat down to finish his meal. Suddenly, unaccountably, he was very nervous, too nervous to eat or to sit still. He jumped to his feet and began pacing back and forth in the limited cell space, wondering what was wrong with himself, trying to pinpoint the reason for his nervousness.

This is foolish, he told himself, wringing his hands. *Just because they're darkening your room. You've been in dark rooms before! It isn't going to make any difference. . . .*

The boarding up of the cell window was completed. Robbie kept pacing, but the nervousness seemed to keep increasing. It was as though something were piling up very rapidly inside him and he had to keep moving lest whatever it was take control of him.

He went to his bunk and lay down, but he could not stay on it. The nameless anxiety kept piling up; some screaming thing that he could feel, could almost hear, was flooding through him, trying to take control. There was only one way to keep it from doing so. He had to get up and move. There was no place to go, so he began running in place, counting his steps.

He ran and ran and ran. He could not seem to grow tired. He knew that he would not be able to sleep or even rest until he became tired, so he kept on running. He ran all day. He calculated that he had run approximately twenty-five miles by the time he was able to stop. Even then he could not rest. He dared not try to sit still, for fear the panic that surged within him would overwhelm him. He did other exercises—side-straddle hops, a thousand sit-ups, five hundred push-ups. Even when the next meal came he could not stop moving. He kept pacing the few yards back and forth in the cell, holding the bowl up to his face, eating rapidly, taking care not to spill anything. The meal finished, he resumed the exercises, went at them furiously, knowing that if he did not he would be overtaken by the terrible, nameless something that was inside him. It was very late at night and Robbie literally had run and exercised himself to exhaustion before he was able to sleep.

He awakened sometime between 2 AM and 3 AM, again full of fast-mounting anxiety. He jumped from his bunk and began running—and he ran and ran and ran. When breakfast came, he paced about rapidly, eating it, impatient to be done with it so that he could get on with what he had to do to get away from the fearsome thing that crawled inside him. He ran and exercised through the siesta and the afternoon, paced through the evening meal, and ran and exercised himself again into a sleep of exhaustion. Then, after a few hours' sleep, he was on his feet again, running and running.

Risner was to go on like this for ten months, spending sixteen to eighteen hours each day in a physical struggle to survive his private, darkened hell. During this time he saw no other Americans. He was let out of his cell only occasionally, to bathe and to clean out his waste bucket. He realized after a time that he was fighting for his sanity, and the thought terrified him, allied itself with the screaming panic that lived inside him all the time. Often it all seemed too much. Despite the marathon running and the thousands upon thousands of muscle-straining exercises, he could not induce exhaustion, could not rest, could not subdue the rising terror. Sometimes, frustrated that the battle seemed never to end, or fearing that he had lost it, he would sit on his bunk and cry until there were no tears left. Just as often, he would frantically stuff his towel and pieces of clothing into his mouth and scream and scream.

He prayed continually and fervently. He thought always of his family. And he wondered if he would ever again see another American.

————

In Las Vegas what was to become known as the Stockdale Purge got under way. The Vietnamese meant to break the stubborn resistance. The way to break it, obviously, was to break the leader, whom they knew to be Stockdale. To combat his policies, they had to know them. They set out to get these policies from Stockdale's men. They would confront him with his own men's statements and would be justified in taking action against him. Their plan, Rabbit confided to Sam Johnson in one brutal interrogation, was to "make a domestic animal out of Stockdale."

Many POWs were swept up in this purge, and the Vietnamese began to score. Nels Tanner had been in solitary and locked in ankle stocks, first in Stardust and now the Mint, for more than three months. Early on the morning of August 6 he was taken to an interrogation with Rabbit, who told him, "Now you will pay for your Clark Kent and Ben Casey crimes. You will act the part of Clark Kent and Ben Casey in a movie to help our effort."

"No," said Tanner, "I won't."

He was introduced to Pigeye, the most expert of torturers. Pigeye applied rope torture, but not with ropes. This time he used green straps that Nels recognized as strapping that American pilots carry in their G suits in case they must rappel down mountain or cliff faces. Its tensile strength, he recalled, was five hundred pounds, ample for the application of unbearable pressure to the human body. Nels was impressed at Pigeye's efficiency. The torturer took care that the victim's sleeves were rolled down, so as to prevent cutting and scarring. In applying the straps he was careful to get them on smooth and flat. All the while he spoke soothingly to Nels. He spoke Vietnamese, but there was no doubt in the prisoner's mind as to what he was saying: that it was going to hurt very badly, but that it would not last long because Nels would not be able to stand it long. He would give up quickly; then it would be over. The torturer was not trying to frighten Nels; there was no question that he meant to be comforting—but it wasn't coming off.

Pigeye looped the green strapping around the prisoner's upper arms, standing on the arms and pulling each loop tight to the bone. Then, using more of the strapping, he wrapped Nels's arms together behind him from elbows to shoulders. As though this well-remembered excruciation were not enough, the torturer then tied Nels's wrists behind him with regular hemp rope. He ran this line over the prisoner's shoulder and down between his legs and underneath him. Then, very quickly, he pulled on the rope, jackknifing Nels forward until he was certain he could bend no farther. Then he bent him still farther forward, until his face actually was pressing up into his rectum.

Nels was now a small ball of shrieking pain. Accompanying the agony was the new fear that he would suffocate, for it was nearly impossible to breathe.

Tanner was not long in this rig before agreeing to make the film. But now he learned that this would not be enough. "You must reveal your organization," Rabbit said. "You must tell who is in charge. You must tell his policies and how he communicates them."

Tanner had known Stockdale for years, as a superior officer and friend. He had always liked him and admired him, but never more profoundly than on reaching Hanoi. It had taken a special kind of courage to exercise the kind of tough leadership the injured SRO had supplied in these savage circumstances, knowing that it was only a matter of time before tortured subordinates would reveal him. Apparently the time had come.

"We know it is Stockdale," Rabbit said angrily. "You must admit it. You must tell us his policies and how they are communicated."

Squeezed and knotted into the ball of his torture, Tanner tried hard not to succumb. Pigeye ripped screams out of him until he could stand no more. Fighting for breath, hurting, sweating, Nels tried to submit. Rabbit wasn't ready. Nels was kept in torture.

"You have communicated with the man in the next cell," Rabbit charged. "Admit it! You have talked with him, in the next cell!"

Jerry Coffee now occupied the middle cell in the Mint, between Tanner and Howie Rutledge. Obviously, Nels was supposed to finger Coffee, who in turn would be tortured into implicating Stockdale. Nels could not bring himself to name Coffee, so Rabbit did it for him.

"Admit it!" the interrogator persisted. "You talked to Coffee! Admit it!"

Finally, he had to admit it. He told the truth of their conversations, that they had been mainly of families and friends. But the torture did not end until he made a tape admitting that Stockdale was SRO. He confessed that Coffee had passed to him the SRO's policies, which were to make no tape recordings or films. The few pieces of information he had yielded would fit into the mosaic of "evidence" that was being constructed for use against Stockdale.

Tanner then kept his motion picture commitment. The setting was an open field perhaps fifteen miles from Hanoi. It was a battle scene in a war movie. The field was laced with mock explosives and crowded with men dressed in ARVN (Army of the Republic of Vietnam) uniforms. Tanner was dressed in U.S. Army fatigues and heavily bandaged. On signal from the director, the explosives began going off, a group of rather romantic-looking individuals equipped with bayoneted rifles and bandoleers began advancing on the field while those playing the roles of ARVN troops began throwing down their weapons, affecting fearful expressions and rushing from harm's way. Nels, playing the part of the retreating cowards' American advisor, was required to run with them. It was not a role that either Clark Kent or Ben Casey would have relished!

The morning after Tanner's interrogation, Jerry Coffee was locked in ankle stocks.

When Tanner was returned to his cell, he quickly tapped his anguish to Coffee: "Oh, God, Jerry, I'm so sorry! They forced me to finger you."

Jerry understood.

He remained in the stocks for a week, then was taken to interrogation. Ropes and straps lay on the table. "You know about the movie Tanner was in," he was told.

Jerry denied such knowledge. To admit to it would have been to admit to communicating.

"It is your turn to be in the movie," he was told.

"No," he replied, "I'm not going to be in any movie."

He was strapped into the same kind of small ball that had been made of Tanner and the interrogation began. It had nothing to do with moviemaking.

"Who is the senior man? What are his orders? How does he pass his orders? How do you communicate from your cellblock over to the other ones?"

Coffee ignored the questions as long as he could. Finally, he answered, "Okay, I'll make the movie!"

The quiz on camp organization continued. Jerry held out for most of an hour, kept agreeing to make the movie. Then, unaccountably, the torture ended. "All right," he was told, "you will make the movie tonight."

Coffee's scene was filmed in the Vietnam People's Army Film Studio in downtown Hanoi. First, he was taken into a makeup studio and seated in a barber's chair before a large mirror. It had been a year and a half since he had seen himself and he was thunderstruck at the gaunt apparition that stared back at him from the mirror. His face seemed to have caved in around the bones; there were huge, dark circles underneath eyes that were too large; and the lips were drawn and thin. He looked very old. Bullet holes were painted onto his head, and he was made to lie down and play dead while victorious Viet Cong and North Vietnamese troops moved across a smoky battlefield.

Bob Shumaker and Smitty Harris also were tortured to participate in the evening's moviemaking. For Shumaker, whose torture at the Briarpatch once had been enough to drive him to attempted suicide, this had been the worst session yet. He had been roped, blindfolded, then savagely kicked and slugged about the room. Then he had been bent backward and tied neck to feet, like a drawn bow. After he began choking, he was bent in the other direction, until his mouth touched his feet. He had not been able to keep from screaming, and his attendants, finding his noises offensive, grabbed up a dirty rag that had been stuffed into a rathole, draped it onto a ramrod and shoved it far down his throat. Panicky, Bob fought to grab the rag with his teeth, but failed. The thing was pushed deep enough to hurt badly. He kept gagging, and felt certain he would suffocate. After an agonizing time, the gag and ropes were removed. His body snapped out of the torture position like a tightly coiled spring, and his head slammed hard against the floor. He lay coughing up blood. He became aware that he had attracted a sizable audience, bland-faced young men and women who did odd jobs in the prison. They began drifting away as he crawled about the floor, trying to regain his wits. He was returned to his cell. He felt proud that he had ruined his captors' plans to put him in the movies—certainly no film-maker would want to use anyone in his condition. He did not realize he had just done the makeup for the part he was to play—that of a wounded American.

———

It was the meanest of times. During the night of August 8 a guard opened the door to the cell Jim Mulligan and Jerry Denton shared in Stardust. Mulligan, occupying the lower bunk of a double-decker, got up to see what the guard wanted. What he wanted was to spit in an American's face, which he did. Mulligan, his Irish temper overwhelming his better judgment, spit back, scoring satisfactorily. The guard stood staring, Mulligan's spittle generously decorating his face. Then, wordlessly, he slammed the cell door shut and locked it.

"Well," said Denton, climbing down from his upper bunk, "we better use the buckets, Jim."

"Why?" Mulligan asked.

"Because," Jerry said, "we're going into irons." It was good policy to use the waste bucket before being locked in stocks.

"They wouldn't do that," said Mulligan. "The little son of a bitch had it coming!"

"Jim," Denton said reasonably, getting over his bucket, "they aren't going to tolerate spitting in a guard's face. C'mon, use your bucket."

Mulligan did so in time's nick, finishing just as the aggrieved guard reentered the cell with an officer, who ordered the two prisoners locked into their ankle stocks.

"We'll be out in twenty-five days," said Denton, remembering that September 2 was the enemy's National Day, on which all sins were forgiven and amnesties granted.

"Oh, I don't think it will be that long," Mulligan said.

"Yep," said Jerry, "it'll be that long."

It was Denton's night to be right.

———

Guards were everywhere in the cellblocks all the time, suppressing communications, selecting prisoners at random to take from their cells. Outside, they would order them onto their knees and administer bloody beatings. The ultimate purpose was to intimidate even the hardiest of resisters, to the point where prisoner organization would be destroyed. Interrogation rooms were kept occupied, and a merciless enemy kept his young captives screaming in torture and exhorting them to name Stockdale as their leader.

On the night of August 21, a runty, effeminate Vietnamese officer, whom the prisoners called Greasy, led a crowd of guards into the cell in the Desert Inn occupied by Ron Storz, George McKnight, Wes Schierman, and Orson Swindle. Greasy was in a rage, insisting that the prisoners had been communicating and, furthermore, that they had gone to bed before the go-to-bed gong, another serious infraction. Storz, the senior prisoner in the cell, began to argue, but Greasy would have none of it. At his direction the guards lifted Storz onto his upper bunk and locked him in stocks. Then they sat him up, pulled his arms behind him, and tied him into torture ropes. Storz objected. A guard grabbed a hand towel and used a sheath knife to stuff it down into his throat.

Angrily, George McKnight shouted, "He's no more guilty than I am! If you punish him, you must punish me!" Greasy and his guards were quick to oblige, inflicting exactly the same torture on McKnight. Schierman and Swindle were locked into ankle stocks in the lower bunks and tied into torture ropes but not gagged. Schierman watched in horror as two guards climbed up onto McKnight's bunk diagonally above him, slugged George, and pulled him back onto his tortured arms.

Then one guard made a trampoline of McKnight, jumping up and down on his stomach, stomping his feet hard into him. Schierman screamed, "Stop! You're going to kill him! Stop it!" He began shouting as loud as he could, *"Torture! Torture! Torture!"*

The guard stomping McKnight's stomach kept at it until George evacuated in his trousers. This was the least of his worries, for he was choking, strangling on the towel that had been rammed down his throat. He knew that he would be dead very shortly if the towel were not removed.

Schierman, now joined by Swindle, kept screaming "Torture!" Guards piled onto them, slugging and kicking them, beating them about their faces with rubber sandals. They were choked so as to make them open their mouths so that gags could be stuffed into them. Avoiding the gags, they kept shouting, and the chant was taken up by other Desert Inn POWs, who banged against their cell doors, shouting, *"Torture! Torture! Torture!"* The ruckus was heard all over Vegas.

The beatings continued. Soon most of the screaming and shouting was being done by the rampaging Vietnamese; they were in a mounting frenzy. Their prisoner victims were reduced to cries, grunts, and moans. A guard, divining that George McKnight was about to expire, took the towel out of his throat.

The merciless beatings went on for perhaps half an hour. Then the four prisoners were taken from their cell and out through a gauntlet of hostile camp personnel, other guards and civilian prison employees, both men and women, who spit, slugged, kicked, and slapped at the prisoners. The four prisoners were taken to separate stalls in the bathhouse. They were gagged and left in torture ropes, ankles bound tightly together. And ropes were pulled taut between necks and ankles. All night long, Greasy kept leading his guards from stall to stall, and he watched as they lifted the prisoners, slugged them savagely about the head and face, kicked them in the stomach, kidneys, and groin. It was a long, long night.

Early the next morning, a flight of U.S. Air Force F-105s roared low over Hoa Lo. Orson Swindle, lying on his side with his head over the door sill to his stall, barely had time to wish he were in one of them when he saw Greasy and some of his bullyboys approaching. Greasy's eyes had a glaze to them, as though he were drunk or under the influence of drugs. Nearing Swindle, he screamed, "You bomb and strafe our city!" He drew back a foot and kicked Orson, hard, in the face. He kicked him in the chest, the stomach and the groin. While he was about this, one of his thugs ground a heel into Orson's face.

By mid-morning the four prisoners were in separate interrogation rooms, faced with demands that they reveal all they knew about their organization—to name the leader, to tell his policies, to tell how these were disseminated and to name the communicators. They were kept in torture ropes, tied into balls, rolled about the rooms, beaten, kicked, told that Stockdale was their leader and that they would have to admit it. Taken beyond the limits of their endurance, they were made to yield tape-recorded and written confessions—when Orson Swindle balked at writing, he was assured that he would comply or be fed the contents of his waste bucket.

Left alone in the quiz room to contemplate this, Orson peered through a crack in the door and winced at the sight of Ron Storz, who was being led across the compound to the room that was being used as an infirmary, between the Desert Inn and Stardust. Ron was holding his arms close to his sides and shuffling and stumbling, his face a mask of agony. They had hurt him badly.*

Swindle, McKnight, and Schierman were taken from Hoa Lo and installed in solitary cells in a building next to Hanoi's thermal power plant. The prisoners called this place Dirty Bird, because it was especially filthy. These three knew it well. Along with Ron Storz, they had spent most of a month there during July and early August.

The power plant had more and more frequently been the target of American bombs. The incarceration of American prisoners next door to it apparently was meant to reassure nervous Hanoians in the neighborhood. Also, it was doubtless hoped that the presence of the Americans would become known to their own forces and that the attacks on the power plant would be stopped.

———

"The Vietnamese sure seem to know a lot about you," Sam Johnson told Jim Stockdale one day. Sam had just returned from interrogation to the Thunderbird West cell he had been sharing with the SRO since early July. Johnson advised that Rabbit knew all of the SRO's policies and had revealed his intention to "make a domestic animal" out of him.

Stockdale mused on this and on information he had gleaned from a book his captors had made him read. Entitled *An Heroic People,* the book was mainly propaganda, but it also contained the interesting fact that approximately half of the senior political officers of the government, including Premier Pham Van Dong, had spent five years and more as prisoners of the French, probably in these very cells. As prisoners, these Communist leaders had understood that to survive and eventually to prevail, they had to organize, and that to organize they had to communicate. They had gone to extreme lengths to do so, even to the point of inflicting serious wounds upon themselves in order to gain admittance to hospitals, whence they could disseminate information and resistance policy to comrades in other cellblocks and prisons. Their overriding theme, Stockdale discovered, had been essentially the same one he had adopted and promulgated as policy: organization above all—Unity over Self.

From the French the Communist jailbirds had also learned to be jailers. They knew that to suppress prisoner resistance it was neces-

---

*Among other injuries, Storz had suffered numerous broken ribs.

sary to keep men separated as much as possible, to keep communications down, to move swiftly and ruthlessly to crush anything resembling organized resistance.

Stockdale was not angry that other Americans had told the enemy his policies. He had expected that in brutal torture sessions such information was sooner or later bound to be extracted. He reflected that eventually he and other leaders would be found out and their organization smashed. They would be sent to different camps, carrying the gospel of resistance with them, and the process would begin anew. They would organize again, knowing that they would be smashed and dispersed again, because they would understand they still were combatants on their country's behalf and that organization offered them their best chance to survive with honor. So Stockdale, while he was resigned and apprehensive, was not angry or even particularly concerned about the POW organization. One night, Rabbit, in the company of three guards, entered the SRO's cell, sputtering furiously about "you and your communications!" and drove a fist hard into Jim's jaw. Stockdale charged the interrogator with a rush that sent him scurrying from the cell! Shortly, Rabbit came on the camp radio, announcing that a "provocation" had been committed against a camp officer, that camp discipline had broken down to an intolerable level.

The next night Stockdale was stashed in Cell #1 in the Mint. Sam Johnson was in Cell #3, in punishment because he had been with Stockdale and therefore had to be considered dangerous. Ron Storz, after the severe torture and beatings he had suffered through the night of August 21, had been scheduled for Cell #2. From this position, his captors told him, he was expected to inform on the communicating that took place between "the two black criminals, Stockdale and Johnson." Apparently the Vietnamese thought the tough-minded Storz had finally been brutalized to the point of pliability and would cooperate to avoid more savaging. Storz, fearing they might be right, had got hold of a pen and used the point to lacerate his wrists and chest over the heart in an attempt to commit suicide. He'd gone to the infirmary, and his place in Cell #2 was taken by Howie Rutledge, who had left the Mint only hours earlier, having been there since splitting with George McKnight in May. At interrogation Greasy had told Rutledge grandly, "We are going to permit you to have a roommate, Captain McKnight."

Howie's elation at the prospect of a reunion with George soon turned to anger as Greasy explained, "Before he moves in, you must promise to tell us all that he says and does."

Rutledge stared balefully at the officer, making no effort to hide his revulsion. Then, speaking in measured tones, he assured Greasy, "Neither I nor any other American would ever spy on our fellow American prisoners. Even the thought of doing such a thing makes me sick!"

Rutledge was returned to Mint Cell #2, where his ankles were locked in stocks. He was not asked to spy on Stockdale and Johnson. He confirmed to Stockdale that many prisoners had been tortured to give information on him and his policies.

Stockdale was amazed at the lengths to which the enemy was going to build the case against him. But they would not move against him, he knew, until they caught him red-handed at some "black activity." It all seemed so childish.

They would catch him soon enough, and the consequences would not seem childish.

Hoa Lo Prison, above, became known to its American inmates as "The Hanoi Hilton." Most newly captured Americans were brought here for interrogation and torture. Below, Cu Loc Prison, which the Americans called "The Zoo," is located in southwest Hanoi. Formerly, it had been a film studio.

Xam Ap Lo, above, a grim prison located about 35 miles north of Hanoi, was known to its American prisoners as "The Briarpatch." It was ruled by a lunatic camp commander who tortured men to near-insanity and attempted suicide. Alcatraz, below, is behind Hanoi's Ministry of National Defense. Its tiny, tomb-like cells were home for more than two years for a handful of Americans who were identified as leaders of prisoner resistance.

ALCATRAZ

Above, a prison known to its American inmates as "The Plantation Gardens" was formerly the residence of the mayor of Hanoi. POWs often were taken to rooms in the mansion to meet visiting press and antiwar delegations. Below, a prison called "The Rockpile," in thick jungle about 40 miles south of Hanoi. Jim Thompson, a prisoner of war longer than any other American in history, attempted his final escape from here.

ROCKPILE

From the air and closeup, the prison camp at Sontay, 20 miles from Hanoi, site of a Green Beret attempt in November, 1970, to retrieve some POWs. The Sontay Raiders, organized, trained and led by Army Col. Arthur "Bull" Simon, killed many Vietnamese, but found no Americans on the premises.

A photograph that startled the world and raised angry fears that Hanoi was brainwashing its American captives. The prisoner, Navy Lt. Cdr. Richard Stratton, performed a number of such bows before a sizable press conference in hopes of eliciting just such a reaction. (Photo: Lee Lockwood, Black Star.)

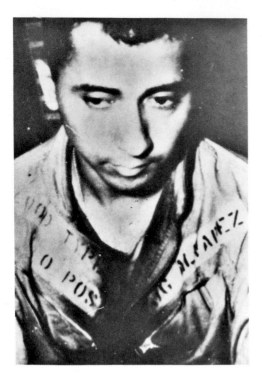

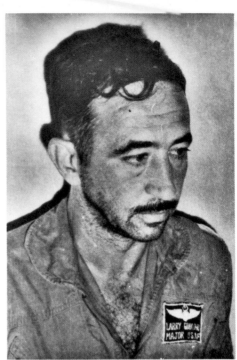

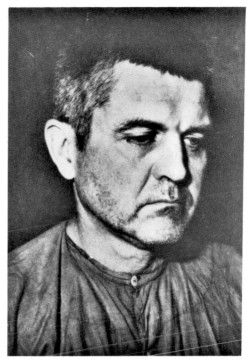

Some early shootdowns and leaders, from left to right across both pages: Ev Alvarez, Larry Guarino, Jerry Denton, Jim Stockdale, Robbie Risner, Jim Kasler, and Doug Hegdahl. Stockdale had led the August, 1964, Gulf of Tonkin raids, in which much of North Vietnam's navy was demolished. Risner, a famous air ace of the Korean War, was the subject of a *Time* magazine cover story not long before his capture. Kasler, also a Korean war ace, had likewise been well publicized just prior to capture for having led the first air strikes against Hanoi, in which vasts amounts of North Vietnam's POL (petroleum, oils and lubricants) was destroyed. Hegdahl, a 19-year-old apprentice seaman when he was captured, was ordered to con his captors into releasing him, did so, and brought home the names of hundreds of prisoners and gave the first public accounts of Hanoi's systematic torture program.

Some notorious prison camp personnel: Top left, Rabbit; top right, Spot; bottom left, Soft Soap Fairy; bottom right, Pigeye, the master torturer, also known as Straps and Bars, for his favorite working tools. He is escorting Robbie Risner. (Photo: Thomas Billhardt.)

A Joke, a Dream, and a Trial

Throughout that spring and summer of 1967 pressures had been mounting at the Zoo, too. Brick and bamboo walls had been constructed between a number of cellblocks to prevent interbuilding communications. Physical strength was eroded by an abominable diet—an ounce or two per week of a liverish meat paste, occasionally some tiny pieces of pork fat, but mainly a watery pumpkin soup and the small loaves of French bread, heavy with weevils and rat feces. Guards were everywhere all the time, listening, opening peepholes, making certain that Americans were not communicating, shouting orders at them through squawk boxes in their cells.

"Hello, put on your clothings! Sit on your bed, be at attention! Listen! The policy of the Democratic Republic of Vietnam toward the treatment of U.S. criminals is from our policy of Communistic humanitarianism. This is not a system of punishment, but a system of education. We will educate you. You must try to learn. If you show a good attitude by concrete acts and obey all of the orders of the camp authority, you will be given deserved treatment. But if you show a bad attitude and still cling to your old ways, then you must be severely punished. . . .''

There ensued interminable lectures on the glories of communism, on the necessity to criticize others and to self-criticize. After each one many prisoners would be randomly selected and taken individually to interrogation, where it was ascertained whether they had paid attention. Then prisoners were advised that they were now free to make their concrete acts, to confess to crimes, condemn the United States, call for an American withdrawal, laud the struggle of the Vietnamese people, and thank the Vietnamese people for their humane and lenient treatment.

The prisoners fought a delaying action. All that summer the interrogators at the Zoo heard nothing but, ''I really didn't understand. . . .''

''You see, I have been thinking this way for many years, and it is going to take a long time for me to change. . . .''

''I really have to know a lot more about Vietnamese history. . . .''

Unanimously, the prisoners continued to eschew ''concrete acts.'' The camp authority became thoroughly irritated, and the quality of life, already poor, began to deteriorate. The sadistic Magoo and Elf, a diminutive, equally sadistic interrogator, frequently entered the Pool Hall cell of Jim Kasler and John Brodak to beat the two of them bloody.

Apparently it had been decided that Kasler, the senior ''criminal'' in the building, was now well enough to be beaten. The April operation on the Korean War ace's infected right leg had reduced the swelling, and for a time he had been placed on an improved diet. For two weeks he had received a cup of hot milk each morning. His meals had consisted of meat and potato soup and he got two loaves of bread each day. He had shown his gratitude by communicating. This was intolerable. Brodak was guilty by association with Kasler.

Kasler and Brodak always knew they were in deep trouble when, peeking through the cracks in their cell door, they would see Magoo and Elf smoking what was either marijuana or opium. Finishing the smoke, the two invariably came to the cell and, their eyes glazed, would enjoy themselves by laying into the prisoners with long, savage beatings. One day as the cellmates lay on the floor assaying damages Brodak laughed, ''No disrespect intended, sir, but I sure would like to move away from you!''

By early August, Pool Hall prisoners were being tortured in ropes and hell cuffs for extensive autobiographical information, then for intelligence on prisoner communications, for codes, and for the orders Pool Hall SRO Kasler had issued. Soon, Magoo was locking Kasler into torture cuffs: Jim's right arm was rolled clockwise away from him, his left arm counterclockwise, the arms were pulled behind him and the backs of the wrists were forced flat against each other and ratcheted tightly into torture cuffs.

The hands went numb quickly. The intense pain in the shoulders and arms did not subside. Brodak tried holding Jim's elbows together, in hopes of relieving the pressure. It didn't help. Kasler was left in this torture for perhaps 12 hours. Then, in the middle of the night, food was brought and the cuffs were removed. The wrists were torn, raw, bloody. There was no feeling whatever in his hands, and they were swollen hugely and discolored, a sickening purplish black. He could not move his arms. Brodak had to feed him. But it was a blessed relief to be out of the cuffs, to have the awful tension removed from the shoulders and arms.

He was given about 15 minutes to eat. Then Magoo returned, pulled his arms behind him again and reapplied the torture cuffs, but this time the sadist was merciful; the arms were not rolled to the outsides, but to the insides, the normal torture—that first application had been the chuckling Magoo's unique little joke. Jim's wrists were so swollen that Magoo had trouble locking the cuffs back on. He vented his rage in several blows to the prisoner's ear and the side of his face. Kasler was to remain in the cuffs for the next 32 days—released from them twice each day for about 15 minutes at a time for meals.

———

"C'mon, Larry," said Ron Byrne, "let's pray."

"Ron, I can't," Guarino answered. "I'm all prayed out."

The two had been sharing endless days and nights of hell in a small cell in the mosquito-infested building called the Gym. They had refused to confess to a variety of "crimes," such as communicating, urging other "criminals" to communicate, and advising them to refuse to write antiwar statements. At night, the culprits were locked into leg irons and torture cuffs that precluded sleep. In the morning, the cuffs were removed, but teams of guards entered every few minutes, all day, to beat them. The beatings mostly consisted of slappings around the prisoners' heads and faces. The slaps stung, and the constancy of the harassment wore on the nerves. It was almost a relief each evening when darkness came on and they were again locked into the leg irons and torture cuffs. Soon, though, their attentions again were focused on the grinding pain and the voracious mosquitoes.

Morale ebbed. The cellmates, both of them devout Catholics, had sustained themselves and each other by praying together. Now, to Byrne's dismay, Guarino seemed to be despairing. "I've prayed ten million prayers, Ron," he said. "We're not getting any help, and I don't think we're gonna get any. I think He just worries about big things, like whether the world is gonna continue or not. I don't think He gives a damn about you and me anymore. You pray. You pray a lot better than I do anyway."

Shocked, Byrne pondered Guarino's words. Then he said, "Aw, I think I'm all prayed out, too."

They fell silent. Guarino would never be certain whether he then lapsed into a brief sleep of vivid dream, hallucinated, or engaged in some other mysterious exercise of the psyche. Whatever, there ensued one of the most intensely real experiences of his life. He suddenly found himself alone in a fancy glassware shop. Crystal was a passion with Guarino, and now he began moving from counter to counter, absorbed in the beauty of what he saw. Glass tinkled musically in the background. A set of especially attractive cocktail glasses caught his eye. Looking around, he still saw no one in the shop. Furtively, he picked up the glasses, one by one, opened the zipper of his flight jacket, and secreted them inside. Moving on, he came to a beautifully cut Dresden piece, a boat which, when it was turned over, somehow became a fuel truck. He was about to tuck this piece into his flight jacket when he felt a presence behind him. Turning, he found himself under the scrutiny of a kindly-looking elderly gentleman with a white beard. The man was smiling, knowingly, at Larry, and he spoke: "Is there anything I can do for you?"

"Well," said Larry, "I'm just curious, and I see this lovely piece of Dresden."

"Do you like it?"

"Yes, very much."

"You can keep it. Why don't you put it in your jacket?" The man continued to smile and there was no question that he wanted Larry to take the piece.

"Oh, no," said Larry, "I couldn't do that! Really, I'd like to pay for it."

"Oh, no, no, no," the man insisted. "You go ahead and take it."

Larry opened his jacket zipper and tried to slip the piece in without revealing the cocktail glasses he had shoplifted. The man kept smiling at him and Larry felt sure he knew about the cocktail glasses. Unable to get the Dresden piece in, he decided to carry it in his hand. He zipped up his jacket, and suddenly the cocktail glasses began expanding, growing all out of size and shape, pressing ever more tightly against his chest. He could hear them grinding against each other, then breaking inside his jacket. The pressure against his chest continued to mount, and his breath came shorter and shorter. He was gasping for air and felt the beginnings of panic.

"Don't you feel well?" the old man asked solicitously.

"No," Larry managed to answer, "I can't breathe."

"Perhaps you ought to go outside and get some air."

"Yes, yes." Larry felt himself growing weak. He held onto the edges of the counters, and made his way to the door. The glasses inside his jacket kept growing and growing and he felt as though he was suffocating.

"You had better hurry!" the old man urged, and there was real concern on his face and in his voice.

Larry fell to his knees as he got a hand on the doorknob but he managed to get the door open and to crawl outside. He felt himself continuing to weaken.

"Hurry up!" the old man pleaded. "Hurry up!"

Larry turned and looked back at him. Over the man's head, above the door to the shop, was a huge, golden gong.

"Hit the gong, Larry!" the old man said, pointing to it. "Hit the gong! Before it's too late! Hurry!"

The old man's voice was receding, getting farther and farther away. Larry felt himself losing consciousness, could almost see the life rushing out of his body. A rock lay in the street where he knelt. It took all his strength to reach down and pick it up. With a last, desperate gasp he heaved it at the gong. It made a tremendous clanging noise when it struck and a great ray of golden light shone outward from it. Then, as strength and breath flowed back into Larry, the gong and light disappeared, and now hanging over the door where the gong had been was a string of rosary beads. Then, motion-picture-like, the scene dissolved and Larry was back in his cell in Hanoi, whispering excitedly to Ron Byrne, telling him of his experience. When he finished telling his tale, Ron was silent for a moment. Then he said, "The hair is standing up on the back of my neck!"

They began praying the rosary. Neither had ever prayed harder.

To both, the message seemed plain: to despair meant to die. Prayer was the only thing they had, a lifeline and weapon, and they had better make the most of it.

———

At the Plantation, Major Bai, Cat, asked Doug Hegdahl, "How would you like to be released?" Then, smirking, he held up his hand, saying, "No, you must not answer me now. It is only a thought. I just wanted to see your face. You are dismissed."

As Doug turned to leave, Cat said, "You must not tell Stratton, for he may be an evil man, who could cause you many hardships."

Back in the cell he shared with Stratton, Hegdahl immediately briefed him.

"Oho," said Stratton. "Now I think we are starting to see a little bit of the big picture!"

In early August the food ration for the two had been improved dramatically. Along with the watery pumpkin soup and the foul French bread, there had been plates of meat, French fried potatoes that looked as tempting as any they had ever seen, and bowls of sweet milk. For two days they had enjoyed themselves, assuming that all the prisoners were now receiving such fare. But by the first mealtime of the third day, Stratton was worried. Squinting through cracks in the cell door at meal deliveries, he found that other Americans were not being so well fed. He turned to Hegdahl, who sat waiting politely, anxiously—the French fries were getting cold.

"Something's up, Doug," Stratton said. "They're fattening us up for some reason. I don't like it."

Hegdahl shifted in his seat hungrily, watching the pacing, worrying Stratton. At length, Stratton said, "If you think you are sick and need this food to get better, go ahead and eat. But I'm eating only the bread and soup. That's all the others are getting. I'm not letting them build me up so they can use me for propaganda purposes."

Hegdahl studied the food in silent agony, then said, "Okay, Beak, I'm with you." Then, wistfully, "But couldn't we eat the French fries and give 'em back the bread and soup?"

Stratton chuckled.

Hegdahl wondered, "What will we do with the food? Throw it in their faces?"

Stratton ruled out such dramatics. The Vietnamese would know he had a way of ascertaining what others were being fed. There would be an inspection and the cracks and holes in his cell door would be found and sealed up. The main thing was not to play hardnose, but to forestall being made comfortable and sleek while fellow POWs were still enduring privation. He decided that they should dump the extra rations in their waste buckets. Most of the Vietnamese had a strong aversion to getting near the American criminals' buckets and would never look inside them.

Hegdahl tortured himself, pushing the succulent-looking French fries one by one into his waste bucket, enjoying and grieving over the memory of the taste. Before reaching Hanoi, the big, husky youngster had never in his life wanted for food. Now he had never wanted food so much. But he knew Stratton was right. There could be no accepting food the others were not receiving—Doug knew that if he tasted so much as one more French fry, he would not be able to live with himself. Still, it hurt to throw them away.

Stratton pondered the situation: Cat had warned Hegdahl not to tell Stratton that he was being considered for early release; he had told the youngster that Stratton "may be evil." Yet, Stratton, too, had received special food. Clearly, Cat, despite his warning, had wanted Hegdahl to tell all to his cellmate in hopes that Stratton would do all possible to prove that he was not "evil" and would try to win early release for himself. The Vietnamese, Stratton deduced, *wanted* to release him, wanted to send him home plump and healthy so that the American people could see that he had not been brainwashed or drugged.

"Doug," said Stratton one day, "if they offer you release, I want you to accept it."

Hegdahl was shocked, silent. Then he said, "No, Beak! I want to go home with everyone else."

Stratton understood. The youngster had been a first-rate POW. It was unfair to tell him to accept early release when he wanted to carry on. There was also the risk of grave and undeserved injury to his reputation; other POWs, who could not know the details of his departure, were likely to think harshly of the lad. But Hegdahl was quick, smart, and had committed to memory the names of scores of POWs. If he got the chance, he had to go: Stratton would make it his first order of business when the war was over to repair any damages to Hegdahl's reputation.

"Doug," he explained, "I don't believe the American people, or the military for that matter, know a damned thing about what's happening to us up here. I think a lot of people at home have been shocked by some of the confessions POWs have made. They don't know about the systematic torture, or that the Communists have come close to killing Americans for propaganda. There are horror stories that ought to be told. You can get the word out.

"You've got a lot of names," Stratton continued. "You will take them back. Many wives have no idea whether their husbands are alive or dead.

"You *will* accept early release if it is offered to you, Doug. That's an order."

Hegdahl did not like the idea. He wanted to go home with the others, as one of them, holding his head high. Stratton reasoned with him: "Look, Doug, you've made fools of the Vietnamese. You've done a damned good job as a POW. Now here's your chance to do something really important."

Disconsolately, Hegdahl wondered, "What about you, Beak? You've been getting this special food, too. They must have ideas about letting you go."

Stratton shook his head. "I worked too hard creating those brainwashing charges. I'm not letting them off the hook. They aren't sending me out of here early. I'd be playing right into their hands."

In the days that followed, Hegdahl was summoned repeatedly to interrogation with Cat and Rabbit. They wanted him to write propaganda statements, attesting to his good treatment and to his hope that America would cease its immoral aggression. He kept producing gibberish.

"Heddle," Rabbit asked him one day, "what is your greatest aspiration?"

"Aspir . . . what? I-I don't know what you mean," he said, smiling innocently.

"What do you want?" Rabbit said, exasperated. "What do you want more than anything else in the world?"

Doug thought, *I'm supposed to say that I want to go home. Then he'll tell me how to get there. All I'll have to do is write down what he tells me to write, give them written and probably taped propaganda . . .*

He grinned at Rabbit. "Oh, jeez," he said, "food, I guess. I'd like a bowl of sugar!" He rolled his eyes.

"No, no, no, Heddle!" Rabbit said impatiently. "What do you want most *to do* in the whole world?"

Doug sat looking at him dumbly. Then he drawled, "Well, to tell you the truth, I'd like a lot of toilet paper. We ran out a couple of days ago."

Rabbit stared at him, open-mouthed, as though unable to believe his ears. Finally, he said, "You may go."

The next day Hegdahl and Stratton received enough toilet paper to last them for months.

Hegdahl's interrogations continued. There were frequent references to release, and hints that Stratton, too, would be leaving.

"Gee whiz, Beak," Hegdahl said one day. "How are we gonna keep them from just kicking you out of here?"

Stratton said, "I'll do what I have to do, Doug. Don't worry about it." He affected calm, but he was frightened. Somewhere along the line, when he did what he had to do, he would have to pay a price. It seemed odd, the thought of paying a price for voluntarily staying in hell. In any case, he didn't want Hegdahl concerned with it. He talked endlessly to the youngster about the importance of his own imminent departure. At the same time, Stratton made clear that Hegdahl was not to leave at any cost, that he was not to repent for crimes no one had committed. Stratton had a notion that no matter how rigid the Vietnamese were about their release conditions, Hegdahl would bamboozle them somehow.

Stratton's time to do what he had to do came on August 17, as he was getting ready for bed. He was summoned to a quiz with Rabbit. Rabbit produced a copy of *The New Runway* magazine, written and illustrated by American prisoners at the Zoo. The cover illustration was ludicrous. It had aircraft taking off straight into a three-story building at the end of a runway; other aircraft were landing on the same runway. None of the pilots were paying any heed to windsocks that showed them all to be—in defiance of the fundamentals of aerodynamics—taking off and landing downwind. The magazine was full of such articles as one entitled "Though We Are Pilots, We Cannot Use This As An Excuse To Commit War Crimes Against The Vietnamese People." Rabbit advised Stratton that he wanted him to copy the articles in this magazine, so that they could be published in a Plantation edition of *The New Runway*.

"No," said Dick.

He was hustled back to his cell. He was certain, now, that the Vietnamese wanted to release him. After all, he had caused Hanoi grievous difficulty. It would be a great propaganda plus to send him home so that the American people could see that he had not been brainwashed or drugged. But first, his captors had to know that the good food and treatment had had its effect, that Stratton was grateful, and anxious enough to go home so that it would be safe to release him.

So Stratton had done what he had to do. He waited. He had a need to tell someone how frightened he was, a need for encouragement. But he couldn't tell Doug—the youngster would worry himself sick. Stratton tried not to show his fear to Hegdahl. Guards came for him at about noon two days later.

He proffered his hand to Hegdahl and said, "Doug, I won't be seeing you again. Remember everything I have told you." At the door he turned again to Hegdahl. "Doug, tell Alice exactly what has happened to me and why you have to go public with our story. If it means more torture for me, at least I'll know why and will know it's worth the sacrifice. Good luck and God Bless."

The door opened, and a guard motioned for Stratton to follow. "And, Doug, tell Alice that I love her."

When the cell door slammed shut, Hegdahl pressed an eye against a crack and watched Beak go. The youngster had a lump in his throat the size of an apple.

This time Cat awaited Stratton in interrogation. He reprimanded Stratton for refusing to obey Rabbit's orders. Then, smiling expansively, he said, "But this time, we will forgive. Now *I* will order you, so you can accept *my* order."

They haven't given up on me! Stratton thought, amazed. *They want me out of here so bad they are giving me another chance!*

He told Cat firmly, "I will accept no orders from you."

Cat shook his head. "That was a very unwise choice," he said. "For I stood to smooth your path out of here."

"Thank you very much," Dick said evenly, "but I don't need your help. I've got people back in the States who will do that for me."

Cat said nothing. He did not seem angry. To Stratton's surprise, he smiled and gestured to guards, who led the prisoner from the room. He was not tortured, but locked in a vermin-infested, totally blacked-out cell. There he could only wonder if his plan for Hegdahl would succeed.

———

"You told our secret to Stratton," Cat said accusingly.

"No, no!" Hegdahl lied. "I would *never* disobey the orders of the officers."

Cat and Rabbit sat staring at him in wondering disdain. Doug smiled at them dumbly, knowing what they were thinking: *Heddle, you stupid ass, you really didn't tell Stratton, did you? If he had known there was a chance he would go home, he surely would not have behaved as he did!*

Cat said, "Then you want to be released?"

"Gosh, sure!" Doug smiled. "Gee, I'd *love* to go home! Who wouldn't?"

The next day Rabbit entered Hegdahl's cell with pen and paper. The prisoner was to write a letter to Ho Chi Minh requesting release. The young Dakotan struggled for a long time. Rabbit paced impatiently, occasionally looking over Hegdahl's shoulder. Doug imparted the impression that he did not know how to spell most of the words in the English language and that he could barely write. His letters were crudely formed, and most of the words were illegible. At length, though, he managed to convey to Ho Chi Minh that he wanted to go home.

"This will not do," Rabbit said. "You must ask for amnesty."

"What is that word—am-testy?" Doug asked. "What does that mean?"

"It means your release," Rabbit snapped. "Now write!"

Doug wrote again. He produced a somewhat neater draft but did not use the word "amnesty." Instead, he asked for "my release." Rabbit accepted this version and departed with it.

————

At the Zoo, Jim Kasler had been in torture cuffs for more than two weeks. His wrists were grossly swollen, and he was worried about them. Several times each day Magoo entered the Pool Hall cell Kasler and John Brodak shared to beat the two of them insensible. But there was not much to be done about it.

In the hot August misery, despite the short rations, the cellmates found themselves lacking appetite. Uneaten food was to be returned so that the Vietnamese could feed it to the hogs they raised on the prison grounds. One day, Brodak, who disliked helping his captors feed their hogs, dumped some excess rice into the single waste bucket the two prisoners shared, certain the Vietnamese would never look there. Shortly, Magoo entered and, inexplicably, as though directed by some malevolent mental radar, went directly to the waste bucket, lifted the lid, gazed down at the rice. The prisoners knew they were in for a rough time.

Kasler was taken to be interrogated by Elf. "You have committed another crime against the Vietnamese people by throwing away food," Elf said happily. "Now you are going to be punished!"

He was returned to the cell. Brodak was standing outside, holding the waste bucket, surrounded by several armed guards. The two prisoners were marched to an area where waste buckets were emptied. The place was rotten with filth, and the senses reeled in the nearly overpowering stench. Kasler was handed a bamboo screen and he and Brodak were ordered to enter this place and to sift the excrement in the waste bucket until they reclaimed all the rice they had thrown away.

Slug, the large guard who especially enjoyed beating people, entered with them. Before they began the reclamation of the rice, Slug was allowed several minutes of freedom with them. He administered frightful beatings. Taking the prisoners one at a time, he made bloody, bruised, aching messes of both of them. Then they were ordered onto their knees, to begin screening the contents of the waste bucket. Kasler and Brodak both had severe diarrhea, and the stinking, sloppy task took a long time. At first, Kasler tried to avoid plunging his torn wrists into the stuff, for fear of infection, but it was no use and he gave up.

"Jim," said Brodak, "I think they're gonna make us eat the stuff!"

"Negative!" Jim grunted. "We're gonna *die* first!"

They were kept at it for hours, long after every grain of rice had been screened. Then, to their vast relief, they were made to dispose of both the contents of the bucket and the rice. They were given bars of soap and allowed to clean themselves. That done, Kasler was locked again into torture cuffs. Brodak, who was not in cuffs, would have to care for him—would have to help him with his trousers when he had to use the bucket and would have to clean him. It was not a pleasant late summer for them. But things would get worse.

———

On August 31, Air Force Maj. Norman (Norm) Schmidt (captured on September 1, 1966) had been in ankle stocks for ten days, in the Desert Inn cell he shared with Harry Jenkins, Bob Shumaker, and Air Force Capt. Lou Makowski (captured October 6, 1966). His offense: looking through a crack in a bath stall wall. When the sentence was completed, he was let out of the stocks and ushered away by guards, to what his cellmates assumed would be a routine quiz—some interrogator would read him the riot act for his "black activity"; he would be back soon.

Privately, Shumaker reflected that the stocks, which were a bad enough punishment for anyone, seemed to be a particularly hateful torture for Schmidt, who had been very active physically and had always kept himself in excellent condition. Bob and Norm had become close friends. Shu admired the Air Force officer for his intelligence and for his behavior as a POW. He was a smart, tough, escape-minded resister; and he was nice, the best of company.

A little while, and guards came to the cell and collected Norm's belongings. No one ever saw him again. Later, the camp radio reported him dead.

————

While many were being tortured and beaten regularly at the Zoo, Ev Alvarez and Tom Barrett, who now shared Cell #2 in the Auditorium, were impressed into service as groundskeepers. With Magoo overseeing them, they spent two weeks in August sweeping streets clean, picking up rubbish, cutting grass, moving and trimming bushes, trimming the hedges that surrounded the swimming-pool area, and cultivating flower gardens. Alvarez would never have believed the place could be made so attractive, and surmised the camp was being spruced up for the visit of some big shot.

The notable arrived in a green sedan, a Russian-built car, just after sunset on August 27. The prisoners had all been locked up, but were able to hear how enthusiastically the man was greeted by the camp officers and numerous guards. They had escorted the visitor off to their rooms, where revelry could be heard into the late hours.

The next day, at approximately the same hour, the V I P arrived again in the green sedan. The car and driver—an officer!—underscored his importance; not even the camp commander enjoyed such a perquisite—he rode to work on a bicycle. Shortly, Alvarez and Barrett saw Ray Vohden and then Larry Spencer marched off to interrogation.

Soon guards came for Alvarez. He was taken to an office in the headquarters building, on the north side of the camp. Seated behind the center of a table, facing him as he entered, was a tall, young Caucasian. He had a fair complexion, but very black hair fashioned in a sort of long crewcut, and he wore short sideburns. He had on a clean white shirt, unbuttoned at the neck, neatly pressed blue trousers, and black shoes with pointed toes.

Flanking the notable on one side was Lump, the Zoo's political commissar, sucking on a pencil and looking smug; and on the other side, another Caucasian, a smaller, older man, with graying hair, gray eyes, and a few facial freckles, a less arresting, obviously less important individual.

There was no question that the two Caucasians were Latin Americans. "Sit down!" the important one ordered, glaring at Alvarez. It was a command, not an invitation, and Ev was surprised. POWs who had seen visitors to Hanoi, even Communist visitors, usually found them to be congenial. This one behaved like a member of the prison system staff. Indeed, he seemed to be running this show.

"What's your name?" he demanded. His English was excellent, although delivered in an accent Ev could not pin down. Preoccupied with the accent, he didn't answer.

"I asked you a question!" the interrogator reminded him nastily. "Don't you hear well?"

"My name is Alvarez."

"Ah, Alvarez. Alvarez. What's your first name?"

"Everett."

"What's your rank?"

"Lieutenant, junior grade."

"How long have you been here? When were you shot down?"

"I was shot down on August 5, 1964. I have been here three years."

"What were you flying?"

Ev had never given the Vietnamese any military information and had no intention of supplying any to their visiting friends.

"Well?"

"I was flying an airplane."

"An airplane!" the man said sarcastically. "An airplane! He says he was flying an airplane! A wise guy! Okay, wise guy!" He rose, glowering menacingly at Ev, who was impressed at his size. He seemed huge!

"You're looking for trouble," he continued. "Well, I can give you all the trouble you want, wise guy! You want trouble, you got it, right here!"

The interrogator looked at his older sidekick. "He's a pretty wise guy, isn't he?"

"He sure is," the older one replied. His English was authentic American; he could have come from Miami.

Turning back to Alvarez, the important one suddenly affected a conciliatory tone. "Look, Everett," he said, "I don't want to give you any trouble. I don't want any trouble from you. I'm just asking a few questions, like a decent human being. Why can't you answer my questions?"

"Well," said Ev, "I don't know who you are or what you are or where you're from."

"It doesn't make any difference who I am." He offered a Vietnamese cigarette. The prisoner declined, with thanks.

"You're not very cooperative. I offer you a cigarette, you don't even take it. What's wrong?"

"I don't smoke much."

"You don't smoke much. You don't smoke much." He seemed to be getting angry again. "Here," he said, offering the pack a second time, "have a cigarette!"

"Okay," said Ev agreeably. He took one and lit it up.

"They're much better than those fucking perfumed-up Chesterfields," the interrogator said.

Abruptly, his tone changed again, and he began lecturing Ev on his behavior. "You gotta show a good attitude," he said. "Get along. You gotta realize your position and where you are. You Americans think you're so shit hot; really, really hot shit! But you sons of bitches, you take something from everybody, the best from everybody else. Do you know where the Guernsey cow comes from?"

"From the island of Guernsey," Ev said.

"You go to Cuba or Puerto Rico and those other countries and you take the sugar and the bananas, and what do you sell 'em back? You sell 'em back Coke! And milkshakes! Rotten stuff! And the women, everywhere you go, you make prostitutes out of them! You take the good from everybody, and what does the United States have? You got the coyote, you got the rattlesnake!

"I want you to realize your position. What kind of car you got?"

"A Buick. A 1964 Skylark."

"How much you pay for it?"

"Thirty-two hundred."

"Are you Mexican? Do you speak Spanish?"

"Yes."

In English, the important one proceeded to lecture Ev on the despicable treatment the United States accords its ethnic minorities. Then, still in English, he engaged in whispered conversation with Lump. Somewhere, Ev could hear the familiar clanking of leg irons. He heard Lump ask the Latin if he wanted Alvarez locked up in another cellblock. "Oh, no, no, no," the newcomer said, turning back to Ev. "You go on back to your room, and maybe I'll see you again."

As Ev made to leave the room, the Latin demanded, "Aren't you gonna bow?" It was more a command than a question. The prisoner stopped, turned, bowed, and departed.

Alvarez could not make sense of what had happened. Who was this man? Where was he from? What was that accent? How did he fit into the picture? He reached his cell lost in thought. For a few minutes he remained heedless of Tom Barrett's insistent questions: "Well? Well? Did you see him, the dignitary? Who is he? Ev, who is the guy?"

Finally, Alvarez briefed his cellmate, told him all that had happened. Tom listened avidly. Then he said, "I think it's going to be a good deal for us."

In the next few days a number of other prisoners, Barrett included, were interrogated by the Latin. The consensus was that the newcomers were Cuban. Alvarez now felt certain that the accent was Cuban. The prisoners labeled the important one Fidel, and his older sidekick Chico. Soon enough, Tom Barrett was to be proved wrong—Fidel was not a good deal.

———

One morning in early September, Vegas SRO Jim Stockdale, still in a punishment cell in the Mint, was caught red-handed communicating with Sam Johnson in the next cell. He was marched off to an interrogation room, where ropes and irons were produced and it was demanded that he reveal the substance of the communication with Johnson. Stockdale told the truth, insisting there had been no exchange. He and Sam had just put their drinking cups against the wall separating their cells preparatory to beginning a "telephone" conversation when a guard in the alley had looked through his cell window and spotted him. When it was clear Jim meant to stick to this story, he was blindfolded, his hands were tied behind him, a rope leash was looped around his neck, and the guard who had caught him was awarded a period of complete freedom with the prisoner.

The guard took him outside and ran him about the yard for several minutes. Unable to see or to move well on his game leg, Jim kept stumbling and falling, and the guard would pull him to his feet with the leash, nearly choking him. After several minutes of this, the guard stood him against the wall of the Desert Inn and piled several hard blows into him, bruising him and knocking the wind out of him.

He was then taken to New Guy Village, to the large room where Bob Shumaker had spent so much time in early 1965, which had for a time been known to the POWs as Shu's Corner. Since then, the walls had been covered with fist-sized knobs of plaster and it had become known as the Knobby Room. Along with Room 18, nearby, it was now one of the most infamous of torture chambers—the knobs of plaster had the acoustical effect of absorbing the screams of prisoners in torture. Here Stockdale was locked in leg irons and tortured in ropes until he confessed to having communicated with Sam Johnson. He admitted they had speculated as to how long they would remain prisoners, and had traded information about their families— trivialities he knew were of no interest to his captors. It was announced that Stockdale would be brought to trial the next day.

Jim was scared. His moment of truth was at hand. His confession had given the Vietnamese the excuse, the moral justification they seemed to need, to wring more important stuff out of him. Primarily, they would want the names of the key men in the communications network. They would isolate these men, torture them for more information, perhaps kill them. To fail now, Stockdale believed, would mean the end of everything; his reputation and self-respect would be gone.

The "trial" took place in the Knobby Room. Presiding was a husky, impressive-looking officer whom the prisoners called Mao. Jim had caught glimpses of this man around the camp and believed him to be a front-office man, probably a troubleshooter. Mao was flanked by a number of other officers. Pigeye was there and so was Big Ugh. Jim stood facing this group with his hands tied; seven guards stood in a semicircle behind him, holding rifles with fixed bayonets.

"I have not been the commander of this camp long," Mao said, opening the proceedings, "but I have heard a lot about you. All of it has been bad. Now we have come to the place where we must investigate you and your urging others to resist the camp authority. What do you have to say?"

Stockdale did not deign to answer. He knew it was essential that he show no fear, for surely the enemy would know how to exploit fear. He had spent the night psyching himself up for this confrontation, and had come to it on a surge of adrenalin. He was still frightened, but ready for whatever came.

The "trial" proceeded. The presiding official instructed Pigeye, who stepped forward and delivered two solid blows to the prisoner's face, then threw him to the floor and tied him into torture ropes. The torturer was efficient, and soon had the SRO tightened into a ball of pain. He was kept in this torture until he agreed to tape-record another confession. Then he was released from the ropes, but Pigeye kept him on his good right knee and kept twisting his arm behind him as he spoke: "I am a war criminal who has wreaked destruction on your country, and now I have violated the good treatment you have given me by urging others to oppose the camp authority. I confess my guilt and I beg the authority for mercy."

That done, guards were paraded into the room to gaze upon Stockdale, the criminal who had been "apprehended and punished." The showing of Stockdale completed, Mao, obviously pleased with the day's accomplishments, ceremoniously adjourned court and took his leave, accompanied and escorted by the other officers, the torturers, and the guards. Stockdale was left alone for two days. Then daily interrogations began. They were conducted by Greasy, who had supervised the terror in the Desert Inn on the night of August 21. "Your instructions have even been understood at camps many kilometers from here," he shouted angrily. "You set our treatment regime back two years!" He rose from the table and circled around Stockdale, who had been required to sit on the floor before the two interrogators. "You are stupid, crippled, and old," he assured the prisoner, "and you are a troublemaker!" Having worked himself into a rage, he kicked Stockdale in his ruined and still-tender left knee.

The interrogators demanded that Stockdale provide the names of all the members of his "central committee," the policy-making body that directed prisoner resistance. Stockdale kept insisting, futilely, that he was the entire policy-making body. His interrogators would not believe this. To the trained Communist, it appeared to be an article of faith that important policy always had to be made by a group, a "central committee."

"I issued the orders," Stockdale said. "They were carried out. The men to whom I addressed the orders had no choice but to obey them; that is military law."

The interrogation lasted for hours and went on in the same vein, day after day. Finally, one morning, Pigeye arrived and stood by waiting, until Stockdale again insisted there was no central committee. Then the torturer stepped in and tied Jim into ropes, while the interrogators paced about the room screaming, "Tell us who! Tell us who!"

With the prisoner's upper arms tourniqueted and roped together behind him, Pigeye then ran a rope over the shoulder and down the front of him, underneath his legs, yanked it tight, and fed him his toes. Jim heard the cartilage pop loudly in his injured left leg; he knew it had broken. There was no focal point of pain, however; it was everywhere all through him, and now the interrogators were chanting, "*Who? Who? Who?*" He took as much as he could stand, then agreed to name names. "I will write it out," he said. "Give me some time." He was left alone with pen and paper.

He put his own name down first. Then, in order of seniority, he listed the names of every American he had ever heard of as being in Hanoi, men whom he knew to be imprisoned as well as the names of men who might or might not have been captured.* He omitted Risner's name because he had caught a glimpse of him through a hole in his cell door and did not want the Vietnamese to know that he knew Robbie to be alive. His list contained 212 names.

The Vietnamese found the list unsatisfactory. According to Stockdale, they pointed out, all but a handful of the Americans in Hanoi were members of the central committee.

"This is the organization," Stockdale insisted. "It is an unbroken line. It is like a living organism. There is no way you can destroy it. Take me away, and Denton will take command. Take me and take

---

*Members of two-man aircrews would supply the names of crewmates who often did not make it into the prison system, having been killed during ejection or after capture, or having died of injuries.

Denton, and Jenkins will take charge. Franke, Mulligan, and Rutledge are all ready to assume command. Take a man out of the middle, and the next senior man will fill in. Nothing will change no matter who you take. This is the American military organization. There is no central committee. Take it or leave it.''

The interrogators departed with the list, for ''study.'' Stockdale tried to anticipate the enemy's next move. They were after the names of key men, and he had provided them, but had buried them in an unwieldy crowd. The Vietnamese had time and were determined. Would they go after everyone on the list? Or pick a few at random? Had he been smart, after all? All he knew was that he had taken as much torture as he could and was fighting the battle as well as he could.

Greasy returned, angry that he had not named ''the ringleaders.'' Stockdale was full of relief, for this seemed to mean they were not going to torture their way through the entire list. At the same time, there was no question that more torture was in the offing for him unless he named some ''ringleaders.'' He decided that it would be better to appear to give them something than to go into torture again and risk losing everything to them. He now wrote statements on the dozen most senior officers, men already known to the enemy as tough resisters. These statements read as though the officers involved were being recommended for medals. For example, ''Jeremiah A. Denton, Jr., Comdr., USN, served under my command . . . has carried out all of my orders in a forthright manner, and thereby opposed the camp authority. He organized communications in his cellblock so as to execute my orders—''

He wrote virtually verbatim reports on Jenkins, Franke, Mulligan, Rutledge, Johnson, and others.

As he proceeded through these repetitions, the interrogators became increasingly irritated.

''You are obscure,'' Stockdale was told. ''You have not given details on what these people did, and when they did them.''

''I would not know such details,'' Stockdale replied. ''I issued general orders. The details are up to my subordinates. That is our military custom.''

''You have left out a very important element from these statements,'' the interrogator said. ''You have not said which of these men has the capability of doing damage to the Democratic Republic of Vietnam.''

Stockdale now understood that the prison authority wanted him to finger the natural leaders among the POWs, the strong personalities, the idea men, the planners. These qualities, of course, were not to be found in uniform measure in all the seniors, and some of the most outstanding resisters were junior officers, men like George Coker and Ed Davis. Stockdale had no intention of naming them. He merely added to each of the statements he had already written on the most senior officers, "He also has the capability to do damage to the Democratic Republic of Vietnam."

At last he was told, "Now you must beg the mercy of the Vietnamese people." He was shown a draft of a plea for mercy which had already been composed for his signature. It was crude, the work of authors unfamiliar with American English. He was allowed to add a few ridiculous lines: "I want to thank you for saving my life from death." Also, "I ask that I be afforded clothes, shelter and particularly food so as to sustain my health." Then he signed it.

He was left alone in the Knobby Room. Now he spent most of the time sitting still, for his knee continued to hurt badly. Once he discovered a spot on his leg he thought to have been a bruise to be moving—it was a colony of black ants, which had affixed itself to him. He brushed them off disinterestedly.

Promises To Keep

Air Force Maj. George H. (Bud) Day, an F-100 squadron commander, had been downed and captured on August 26, 1967, just north of the DMZ. During ejection he had wrenched his left knee, and it was badly swollen; had somehow torn up the right side of his face—he could only see out of his left eye; and had broken his right arm in three places. Day hurt all over, but his injuries were of little consequence to him. All that mattered was escape. He had promises to keep, and could not abide the thought of captivity. Tonight was the night.

Day had four adopted children, two sons, eleven and six, and two-year-old twin daughters, and he was determined that they should have a father.

The son of a day laborer who had rarely been able to find work, Day had grown up in desperate poverty—during the Depression years the family had survived by growing vegetables in vacant lots around Riverside, Iowa. His father had done his best to fit him with a sense of values and self-worth. Thus, during World War II, Bud, as quickly as he had turned seventeen, had rushed to a Marine recruiting office to enlist in the crusade against facism. Following the war he had earned a college degree and then a law degree at the University of South Dakota. He had accepted an Air Force commission, had been activated during the Korean War, had learned to fly, had loved the excitement of Air Force life, and had stayed with it. He had no regrets, and meant to have none—he would return to his children and provide for them as his father had for him. Nothing would stop him.

And there was Doris, warm, smiling, spirited, lovely, full of all the strength and support a fighter pilot needed in a wife. Bud had a rest and rehabilitation (R & R) leave coming up some days hence, on September 13, and a date to meet Dorrie in Honolulu. He meant to keep that date.

After his capture, a North Vietnamese medic had given him three shots of Novocaine, then pulled his broken right arm nearly a foot beyond its normal length and molded on a bulky shoulder-to-fingertips cast. Then his ankles had been bound loosely together and he had been stashed in a tiny underground bunker. There he had planned his escape. He was familiar with the region, having over-flown it daily for months. He would travel by night, navigating by the stars. The Ben Hai River, which separated North Vietnam from the DMZ, was only about eighteen miles to the south. He would reach it in three nights, ford it, then walk through the DMZ to a South Vietnamese town he knew. He calculated that the whole journey should be accomplished in a week.

It was to take two weeks, and was to stand as one of the epic stories of the war.

When darkness fell, he untied the loose bindings about his ankles and rubbed dirt over his face and cast. He crawled out of his dungeon and slipped away from the camp, past guards who were chatting perhaps twenty yards from his dungeon. A few yards from the camp, he moved into a rice paddy, lost his footing, and crashed loudly into several inches of water, landing on his broken arm. He cringed in pain and for fear the guards had heard him. They had not. No one came. The pain subsided. Noiselessly, he picked himself up and moved off. Miles to the southeast, lightning from an isolated storm played on a mountaintop. Day kept moving toward it, through the mud and silt of the rice paddies, hoping by dawn to reach the cover of some woods he had spotted earlier. He felt exhilarated—he had es-caped! He had put perhaps two miles between himself and the camp when he heard an uproar behind him and knew that his escape had been discovered. Looking back, he saw flashlights flickering and moving in all directions. He pushed on faster.

He was in the woods by first light. They were a disappointment, little more than a thicket of thin, scrubby trees. He had looked forward to hiding, sleeping, rejuvenating himself for another night's travel. He was tired, and his wrenched knee hurt badly, but he had no choice but to keep moving. Ahead, perhaps twenty minutes' walk beyond a lake, was thick jungle foliage. Suddenly, overhead, there was a faint whining; it mounted quickly in intensity until it became an ear-piercing shriek. Bombs falling! B-52s! He flattened himself against the ground, heard the roaring explosions, felt the world quaking beneath him. Then, as suddenly as it had begun, the bombing stopped. Immediately, from a position not a hundred yards distant, a large-caliber artillery piece began hurling shots toward South Vietnam—the gun position must have been what the B-52s were after.

He lay motionless all day, desperate for sleep but not daring to indulge himself. He remained alert, yearning for an end to this longest day he had ever lived. At last darkness came and he moved out, slowly, carefully, making a wide swing around the area where the artillery piece had revealed itself to be. He waded across a narrow river, then walked through some hilly, hard-packed terrain. Soon it began to rain. Exhausted, he crawled beneath a large bush and slept.

He would never be able to explain what happened next, never be certain whether he heard an ear-shattering blast or saw a blinding flash of light, or both. Suddenly he seemed to be lifted high in the air, then slammed against the ground. He found himself hunkered down into a fetal position, vomiting. Blood ran from his nose and ears and his head was full of a loud, insistent ringing. He kept vomiting until there was nothing left to throw up. Even then his stomach continued to heave uncontrollably.

He lay dazed, semi-conscious, struggling to regain his senses. Had it been a bomb? A mortar round? What? At dawn he struggled to his feet, but found that he could not take a single step. He let himself down under the bush again and slept fitfully through the day and night.

Dawn came again. He was anxious to move on and decided not to wait for darkness. He went on slowly, keeping close to cover. He was dizzy, feverish. His broken arm ached and so did his swollen left knee; and now there was new pain, in the lower right leg—a large, bloody scab covered the calf. He limped on.

He collected water off the leaves of banana trees—and threw it up. He had not eaten in days. He was not hungry, and in any case there was no food to be found anywhere. Nothing. Not a single banana. He walked for a long time and saw not a living creature, not even a bird. There was nothing anywhere but the evidence of warfare, and this was all around him: broken and charred trees, craters, occasionally piles of empty mortar boxes with Russian markings on them.

He kept moving, sleeping, awakening, and moving. He recovered from the dizziness and fever. His spirits rose; he was going to make it. He knew it!

He moved quickly along jungle trails; these, he knew, were highways for enemy troops, and he traveled quietly, always ready to dive into underbrush. There were no troops, however, nothing to hinder him, and he moved at a good pace. Days passed. One late afternoon he judged he had made a dozen miles and was close to the Ben Hai River. Reaching a clearing, he mounted the top of a ridge, looking for a porkchop-shaped hill that had been his objective since early morning. He found it and stood staring at it, stunned, muttering aloud to himself, *"It can't be! It can't be! It can't be!"* The hill stood at least two miles farther to the south than when he had first sighted it that morning. With the sun hidden from view above the jungle canopy, he had spent an entire precious day and much energy walking in circles! He was shattered.

Suddenly, he was weak, near exhaustion, on the verge of tears. For the first time, he found himself wondering seriously if he was going to make it. Both legs ached fiercely, as though they had been pierced by arrows, and the broken arm throbbed. He felt sick with frustration—it was as though his heart would break. Then he thought of the children and of Dorrie—her family was from Norway and during World War II had fought heroically in the Resistance, had never given up. Nor would he! Discipline asserted itself. He knew that the tides of battle ebb and flow, that a reverse need not be a defeat. Tomorrow was another day. He had promises to keep, and would keep them. He crawled back into the jungle and slept. In the days that followed, he made progress.

His stomach growled with hunger. He found purple berries and ate them; they were delicious. So was a single, small tangerinelike fruit he found hanging from a vine. Once he caught a small frog, perhaps four inches long, shoved the whole squirming thing into his mouth, and swallowed it. It left a dreadful, slimy aftertaste—but it helped. He felt good. He kept moving, kept looking for the Ben Hai.

He traversed steep bluffs, moved along ill-defined trails through thickly forested valleys, and became dangerously preoccupied with hunger—a number of times he found himself standing still, staring into bushes, dreaming of finding berries that were not there. Remonstrating with himself, he moved on.

At last he mounted the crest of a ridge and found himself looking down at the Ben Hai. Not far to the east, he could see a large, white, French colonial mansion he had often looked down upon from the air. He was elated.

The river was approximately eighty yards wide, the current swift. He found thick lengths of bamboo to float himself across, and with his good arm worried small branches off trees to use as camouflage. He slipped and slid down a steep, muddy bank and plunged into the water. The bamboo gave good flotation, and he sped downriver looking for a likely exit point on the opposite bank. Suddenly, he saw a lone North Vietnamese sentry atop the bank, staring at him, straining to see him, obviously uncertain as to whether his eyes were deceiving him. Then he began to lift his rifle. Bud cringed in the water, lowered his head, waited for the shot. It didn't come. Long seconds passed. He looked back, saw the soldier lowering his weapon. Then he was lost to view. He could not imagine what had caused the rifleman to decide not to shoot, but the breaks surely seemed to be with him.

He worked his way into a V-shaped opening in the opposite bank, then climbed up and away, through jungle, and then suddenly onto open terrain—he was in the DMZ! It was a barren landscape, cratered, burned, almost surreal. There was nothing alive here. The carcass of a water buffalo lay decomposing but no carrion eaters were in sight, not even a single buzzard. It was a deathly land. He moved on, starving.

Food! A large cache of K-rations! Cans of ham, turkey, lima beans, raisin pudding, sourdough crackers—he couldn't believe his eyes. Their markings showed that they had been left by a U.S. Marine patrol. He almost cried his prayer of thanks. Then, as he picked up one can after another, he found that the Marines had left nothing usable for the enemy—each can had been slashed through with a bayonet, and the contents had spoiled. He hobbled on.

He reached some jungle, managed to catch and swallow another small frog. It only seemed to stimulate his appetite. Occasionally, small contingents of enemy troops passed close by, moving northward, and he hid himself behind thin, defoliated brush, not even daring to breathe until they were gone. He kept moving. He tried to pray but his mind kept turning to food. Once he was startled to hear the voice of another American praying, loudly thanking God for His help and imploring Him for deliverance. Then, appalled, he realized that the voice was his own.

He stopped, tried to clear his head, take stock: the tormenting hunger was no worse than the pains that agonized his broken arm and his legs; the wrenched left knee hurt terribly, and the wounded lower right leg was now swollen to about twice its normal size. These problems now appeared to be affecting the mind. *Pull yourself together!* he commanded. *Keep moving. Get on with it. Get out of here!* There were promises to keep.

Days and nights blended together. Now the sky seemed to be full of American aircraft. In one jungle clearing he waved frantically with a three-foot length of aluminum from a napalm canister as an O-1 spotter plane searched the clearing for enemy targets. He was certain that his rescue was at hand. But the plane flew off, and he watched, trying not to believe what he knew to be true—he had not been seen, the plane would not come back. He moved on, unwittingly into the middle of an enemy encampment, then, slowly, carefully, out of it.

He longed for food. Occasionally, he became frightened at himself, as when he caught himself in a loud argument with a Sunday school teacher. Sometimes he found himself seeming to regain consciousness, staring at bushes or trees, yearning for berries or bananas that were not there.

Late one day he stood on the bank of another stream, suddenly alert, his senses sharp. Another O-1 came overhead—it had just taken off and was in climb-out; the airfield could not be more than a mile or two away! He crossed the stream, moved through jungle. Just ahead, he could hear the unmistakable *whop! whop! whop!* of American helicopters, and now he could *see* them, less than a mile off! A gunship hovered at 1,500 feet, and another chopper was landing.

The American camp was so close that every instinct was to make for it, running. But he was in command of himself now, thinking clearly, coolly; night was falling fast. Surely, the approaches to a forward-area airfield would be mined. Perimeter sentries at such a base were more likely to shoot than to ask a lot of questions of a lone figure emerging from the jungle, the more so if the figure happened to be baked dark brown and to have a desperate look about him. Far better to lie low until morning than to lose everything because of foolish haste. He crawled into the bush and tried to sleep—freedom was so close!

He awakened early and moved down the jungle trail through a devastated, deserted village. He was nearing the jungle on the opposite side of the village when he heard a shout—the words were Vietnamese, but he knew with chilling certainty that he had been ordered to stop. He looked back and saw two young men holding AK-47s on him from a distance of about a hundred yards. Without moving his head, he searched with his eyes for cover. Dense jungle was not fifteen yards away. He had to try for it. He lunged into a stumbling, limping dash. He heard the shots, felt two creases break across the back of his right hand, then felt a hammer blow into his left thigh that drove him hard against the jungle wall. He fell against it, got to his hands and knees, and crawled into the densest cover he could find.

He lay waiting, his head pressed hard against the ground. He heard them running after him, their sandals flopping. They came close, kept firing, spraying the area; overhead branches were splintering and twigs were snapping off trees. Then all was silent. Had he escaped them?

Then, again, underbrush and twigs were snapping around him. A voice called out only a few feet from where he lay. He dared to turn his head, quietly, look up. He could see the face and eyes of one of his pursuers—the lad stood not eighteen inches from where he lay, but so thick was the foliage that he had not seen him. Then the young man did look down and their eyes met.

After fourteen days and nights, Bud Day's epic escape attempt had fallen less than a mile short.

20

Women Strike for Peace, and Fidel

Doug Hegdahl had not been released, but the mild treatment had continued and he thought his release had merely been delayed. On September 9 he got a new roommate, Air Force Lt. Joseph (Joe) Crecca, Jr., who had been captured on November 22, 1966. The move was fortuitous. Crecca was a memory bank, who carried in his head the names of all 264 Americans then in the prison system. On learning that Hegdahl was under consideration for early release and had orders to take it if offered, Crecca set about filling the youngster's head with all the names—by service, rank, and alphabetical order.

Early on September 11, guards marched into the cell and went to work, sweeping the place out, scrubbing with soap and water. The boards were taken from the window, and the shutters received a fresh coat of whitewash. The rusted waste bucket was replaced with a new, porcelain one. After lunch, Hegdahl was marched off to meet "an American delegation."

Cat was in the room and so was Rabbit. Seated behind a table laden with colorful fruits, candies, and peanuts were three American women, who were introduced to the prisoner: Mrs. Dagmar Wilson, Mrs. Ruth Krause, and Mrs. Mary Clarke. They represented an organization called Women Strike for Peace.

"They come to observe the lenient and humane treatment of American war criminals," Rabbit explained.

En route to the meeting, Hegdahl had hit on a plan of behavior he hoped would impress upon the American visitors that the POWs were being starved and reinforce his captors' belief that he was the lowest form of American peasant, invincibly stupid. He wasted no time launching upon this plan. He did not look at the women as they were introduced to him. Instead, he moved ravenously into the goodies on the table, seizing an orangelike fruit and biting into it, hugely, sloppily, chewing it peel and all, letting the juice squirt about and dribble down his chin. Continuing to chew the fruit, he grabbed pieces of candy, stuffed them into his mouth without bothering to remove the rice paper wrappings, chewed at them, occasionally spitting out a scrap of paper. He went on chewing and slurping at the fruit and adding more candy and peanuts as quickly as there was room in his mouth.

Stealing a quick glance at Cat, Doug satisfied himself that he was accomplishing his purpose; Cat looked disconcerted. Now, looking at the women, the prisoner addressed them through a mouthful of food: "Well, I suppose you're a bunch of Communists."

The remark seemed unremarkable to the Vietnamese in attendance, who doubtless saw nothing objectionable in anyone being Communist; the visitors, however, seemed startled at the young man's assumption that they were Communists, and the atmosphere was suddenly, unmistakably tense.

"We're not Communists," one of the women said.

Then, somewhat contentiously, another asked, "And what's wrong with Communists?"

"Oh, nothing," Doug answered. Privately, he reflected that he was having enough trouble with the Vietnamese and hardly needed an argument on the subject from visiting Americans.

He kept shoveling the fruit and candy into his mouth, noting that Cat and Rabbit looked most unhappy. He concentrated on the goodies and let the ladies do the talking—a lengthy, bitter complaint about Lyndon Johnson's war policies. Doug continued to eat and soon demolished the entire serving. He felt bloated. He now began chain-smoking Vietnamese cigarettes from the table. As the ladies droned on, he smoked, ostentatiously, as though he had not had a cigarette for months, dragging on each one until it was down to the last shred of tobacco, then lighting another with it.

At a signal from Cat, the session ended, and Hegdahl was led from the room. As he left he caught a glimpse of another prisoner being led in. He thought it was Larry Carrigan, an Air Force lieutenant who had been shot down only recently, on August 23, 1967. He occupied a cell a few doors from Hegdahl and Crecca.

The Vietnamese had offered to let Carrigan write a letter to his family if he would agree to allow delivery by visiting members of Women Strike for Peace. Carrigan had never heard of the organization, but assumed that it must be sympathetic to the enemy's cause, or at least unsympathetic to the American war effort. He appealed for advice to cellmate and military superior Air Force Maj. Elmo Baker, who had been shot down the same day as Carrigan. Not yet briefed on POW policy, Baker left the decision to Carrigan, but assured him he saw nothing wrong with sending a letter home with the visitors so long as he was careful to say nothing in it that might lend itself to antiwar propaganda.

Carrigan was presented to Wilson, Krause, and Clarke, who asked if there were anything he wanted to know about them.

"Yes," he said. "Are you Communists?"

He was assured they were not Communists.

"Are you here with the permission of the United States government?"

They admitted, sheepishly, he thought, that they did not have such permission, then said that they were very concerned about the civilian targets in the DRV that the United States had been bombing. The Vietnamese, they explained, had taken them to a village that had been struck, and they were most distressed at the indiscriminate American slaughter of civilians.

Carrigan could not determine whether the American women were naive or simply wanted to believe the enemy's assertions that their country had nonmilitary targets under attack. The women may have seen a bombed-out village, but would have had no way of knowing whether there had been a missile site there prior to the American attack, or an antiaircraft artillery site or a truck park. After a strike, the military target could have been removed, leaving nothing but a bombed village. How to convince these Americans that American pilots did not toss bombs about indiscriminately? He decided to tell them of a personal experience.

Once, he explained, he had participated in an air strike against a North Vietnamese Army base near Sontay. Excellent reconnaissance photography showed a road just south of the base and a Vietnamese hospital perhaps a hundred yards south of the road. During several pre-strike briefings, Carrigan's wing commander, Col. Robin Olds, had emphasized the presence of this hospital and insisted that the pilots study the aerial photographs carefully to fix its location. Moreover, Olds had ordered photography of the strike—two of the sixteen attacking aircraft would be carrying cameras—and warned that the photos had better show that no bombs fell on the hospital side of the road. After the strike, Olds had studied the photography carefully and confirmed that no bombs had been dropped anywhere near the hospital.

Carrigan assured the women, "That's typical of the lengths American force commanders are going to to make certain that bombs are placed on the proper, military targets, and away from the civilian population."

The visitors seemed gratified at this story. At which point, Cat insisted that Carrigan was tired, and had to return to his room.

The next night Carrigan was roused from sleep by an officer who wanted to know, "What does 'a wayward individual' mean?"

"I don't know what you are talking about," Carrigan said.

"It is an American term. You must know what it means."

Another interrogator was summoned. Carrigan was told that the camp commander was very upset at what the prisoner had told the three American women the day before, and about his refusal to admit to them that he had been bombing civilian targets. He was told several times that these women had later described him as "a wayward individual," and the Vietnamese did not understand the meaning of this. By now Carrigan understood the context of the characterization and was not inclined to be helpful. He was marched off to an interrogation room, where a dictionary was produced. Hovering over it, the interrogators found that "wayward" meant "... willful ... perverse ... disobedient ... stubborn ..."

Carrigan was taken from the Plantation to a torture chamber in New Guy Village. Here, two guards administered a savage beating. Then he was tied into torture ropes, locked into leg irons, and beaten again. Then he was seated on a stool, and a length of the rope that held his arms in torture was run through a hook in the ceiling and pulled taut. Without warning, the stool was kicked out from underneath him. Enveloped in a miasma of pain, he could hear a guard chuckling—the sound seemed far off, and didn't matter. What mattered was somehow getting to his feet, relieving the agony that raged in his shoulders. After he finally succeeded in reaching his feet, he was again seated on the stool, and the process repeated. Carrigan had never known or even imagined such pain. He wondered how much of it he could survive.

At last, it ended. A medic applied a salve to his tortured shoulders. An interrogator lectured him sternly that he should not have been bombing civilian targets. He was told that he must repent his crimes. Still in leg irons, he was returned to his cell at the Plantation.

It had been a memorable evening. Larry Carrigan would be a long time forgetting it; and a long time forgetting three Americans named Dagmar Wilson, Ruth Krause, and Mary Clarke, and something called Women Strike for Peace.

———

September was eventful at the Zoo, too. Except for the few hours Pool Hall SRO Jim Kasler and his cellmate, John Brodak, had spent screening rice from their excrement bucket, Kasler had remained in torture cuffs for thirty-two days and nights. In mid-September the cuffs were finally removed. His wrists were badly swollen, dark and purplish. He was taken to an interrogation by Elf and a large, lantern-jawed guard whom Kasler had not seen before. The man had badly bucked teeth and looked upon Kasler as though he were a meal about to be enjoyed.

Elf demanded to know what orders Kasler had issued to the other American "criminals" in his building, and also that Kasler explain the tap code to him. Kasler declined to answer. He knew that Elf already had this information. Other Pool Hall prisoners had returned from torture and had reported in detail what had been extracted from them. Elf's plan now, the prisoner realized, was simply to break him, establish himself as his master, get him started in the business of "cooperating"—in the Vietnamese mind, once a prisoner had cooperated in any way at all, even if the cooperation had been tortured out of him, it would be difficult for him to stop; it would be like turning a ratchet backward.

At Elf's signal Lantern Jaw pulled the prisoner's arms behind him and squeezed the torture cuffs back onto the tender, swollen wrists, ratcheting them down to the last notch, against the bone. Then he threw him to the floor and tied him into torture ropes. This was his first experience with ''the rope trick.'' The pain was excruciating, but he promised himself that he would not give the enemy the satisfaction of hearing him cry out, and he did not.

He suffered in silence, sweating through his clothing, for perhaps half an hour. Then the ropes and cuffs were removed. The wrists were a shredded, bloody mess; strips and pieces of purplish skin hung from them. The same questions were put to him again; again he refused to answer. This time the cuffs were applied diagonally, across the wristbones, adding a degree of pain Jim would not have believed possible.

He lasted for perhaps fifteen minutes before agreeing to talk. The ropes and cuffs were left on him as he was dragged to a stool, seated upon it, and the questions put to him again. After providing information he knew the enemy already had he was stashed in solitary in the Carriage House and locked in leg irons. He was urged to write a paper explaining why the United States was in Vietnam. He wrote, ''The United States is in South Vietnam to stop the spread of militant Communism in Southeast Asia.'' This seemed to be accepted and he was left alone. One day he sat on a sawhorse in his cell, looking through a crack in the door, and he saw the man the other prisoners called Fidel. He was a husky, good-looking man, and he certainly appeared to be Latin. In times to come, Kasler was going to get to know Fidel far better than he would have liked.

''One of your countrymen is here to talk to you,'' said Dum Dum to Jack Bomar. Bomar had seen no visitors since the previous March, when he had been duped into seeing the French doctor Krivitz, the Belgian lawyer Cornil, and Neilands, the American professor from Berkeley who had referred to Dean Rusk as a ''son of a bitch.'' In fact, since the end of June, Bomar had been in solitary in the Pigsty and had not seen much of anyone. Now Dum Dum was making it clear he was going to see this ''countryman.''

''You will be polite,'' Dum Dum advised. ''If you are not polite, if you embarrass the Vietnamese people, you will be severely punished.''

He was presented to Fidel, who impressed him. He was well dressed, in a sport shirt and slacks, and, despite his accent, had good command of English. Bomar assumed him to be a Latin American.

Fidel was stern with the prisoner. He spoke of the ''grave crimes'' the United States was perpetrating against ''the peaceful Vietnamese people,'' who were ''trying to unify their fatherland.'' He assured Bomar that he was a ''criminal from the day you hit the ground,'' and not entitled to the protection of the Geneva Convention. Therefore, Bomar was to be ''tried for your crimes by the Vietnamese people.''

''I can help you with your defense,'' Fidel said, ''but you will have to be very honest with me. Are you an honest man?''

Bomar confided that he was, to be sure, honest.

''Good,'' said Fidel, ''because I want to give you a break.''

After perhaps an hour of this, Bomar was returned to his cell. He was shaken. Like most of the POWs, he had heard many threats that the Americans were all to be tried, but it had always been said in a general, unconvincing way. But this had been specific—Fidel had left no doubt that Bomar was to be placed on trial. He was scared.

The next night, a Friday, he was again brought before Fidel. The Latin reminded him that he had claimed to be honest and said that now he was going to give him a chance to prove it. He produced a pad of paper and a pencil. He numbered the pages, from ''1'' to ''20,'' handed the pad and pencil to Bomar, and said, ''Write all you know about the EB-66 aircraft. They don't really need this, intelligence-wise. They know all about the airplane. This is just to prove you are honest so that I can trust you and help you in your trial.''

Bomar was given the weekend to compose the essay. The EB-66 was an electronic intelligence collector, used in North Vietnam to locate SAM sites and communications centers for attack by other aircraft. Bomar had been navigator aboard one when it had been shot down. He was frightened. He certainly could not provide any military information. He spent the weekend wondering whether to write twenty pages of nonsense—or nothing. Fidel had impressed him as being smart and might not be fooled by nonsense; and he was tough—he might not put up with nonsense, or with nothing. He worried, and wondered what Ed Hubbard was going to do, or had done. Air Force Lt. Edward Lee Hubbard, another EB-66 navigator, had been downed on July 20, 1966, and Bomar assumed that Fidel, who seemed to want EB-66 information, was also pressuring him.

All day Sunday, guards kept looking into Bomar's cell, pointing to the empty paper that lay on his bunk and warning him that he had better start writing. He wondered desperately how to reach Ed Hubbard. If they could get together on their stories, they stood a good chance of selling spurious information; but if their stories contradicted each other, they would both be in serious trouble.

Hubbard occupied a cell in the middle of the Stable, just to the north of the Pigsty, adjacent to the Pool Hall. A bamboo wall now stood between the Pigsty and the Stable, and there was no possibility of communicating directly with Hubbard. Bomar tried an end run. Early on Monday morning he started tapping his wall. His message quickly reached the cell at the northwesternmost end of the Pigsty. From here, it was hand-flashed, beneath the gap at the bottom of the cell door to the cell at the southwestern corner of the Pool Hall, just to the north, where the bamboo wall did not block the view between these cells. The message was then tapped from the southwesternmost Pool Hall cell to the cell directly behind it, at the Pool Hall's southeasternmost corner. From here, it was flashed across the courtyard to the Stable. In the Stable, it was tapped along to Hubbard. Hubbard responded immediately.

Bomar had surmised correctly. Fidel had already grilled Hubbard on the EB-66, and the other navigator had provided nonsense.

Fidel was not present for Bomar's Monday interrogation. The prisoner presented the interrogator with various childish sketches of an aircraft. He had drawn arrows to various of the appendages, describing them as "wheel," "wing," "window," "tail," and "fuselage." The interrogator was not amused. Bomar was returned to his cell and ordered to gather up his gear.

He was moved into a cell in the Stable with Ray Vohden and Air Force Maj. David Duart, who had been shot down on February 18, 1967. Bomar was appalled at the condition of Vohden's right leg. During shootdown, nearly two and a half years earlier, the Navy pilot's right shinbone had been snapped just above the ankle. There had been a good deal of amateur carpentry on the injury, and now about three inches of the shinbone were missing. Vohden had suffered a lot of infection in the leg, and was still in considerable pain and on crutches.

Vohden and Duart also had been interrogated by Fidel and did not know what to make of him. All were nervous about the Latin. Vohden said, "I think we're in deep shit."

Deep trouble, indeed, for about a dozen POWs who were now entering into a terror that came to be known as the Fidel Program.

By September 15, the round-the-clock harassment of Larry Guarino and Ron Byrne had continued for a full month. Every few minutes during the day, guards entered their cell to slap and punch them about; at night they were locked into torture cuffs and leg irons and tied down to the benches, sometimes with the lower legs extended beyond the end, with heavy iron bars laid across them. Then the guards kept looking in to make sure they did not sleep. Except for moments when they had been knocked unconscious or had simply passed out, they had not been able to steal much sleep—Guarino estimated that he had had perhaps an hour and a half during the entire month. The two prisoners were in indescribable misery. They were on the edge of nervous breakdowns. During the days, when the cuffs and leg irons were off, they would sit together between beatings and embrace each other, and cry, and console each other, and pray together. Then, when a month had passed, they were separated, and both went into solitary confinement.

"If you want to show a good attitude," Dum Dum told Guarino, "you should write a letter to your wife."

An unusual suggestion! Larry hoped it meant they had given up on torturing him. In any case, he was willing to write Evelyn. Dum Dum provided writing materials, saying, "Now, I will tell you exactly want to write!"

> Dear Wife:
> I am feeling fine, and now you must answer certain questions. Number One, what is the extent of the anti-war movement in the U.S. of A? Number Two, what is the extent of the black militant movement in the U.S. of A? How long do you think it will take for the black movement to stop the bombing of the Democratic Republic of Vietnam?
>
> /s/ Your Loving Husband,
> Lawrence

Dum Dum exhibited pride in having extracted this letter from the stingy Guarino. Larry could not believe Evelyn would ever see it. Surely, one of the pompous waste collector's superiors would have to read it and would junk it instantly, recognizing how ludicrous it sounded. Apparently Guarino guessed right, for the letter never reached Evelyn.

After ten days Guarino and Byrne were reunited. They were together only a few minutes when they were marched off separately for complete physical examinations by a doctor. Returning to the cell, Byrne muttered ruefully, "C.F.T., Larry. Cleared for torture."

It began the next morning and continued throughout that day and night. Both were badgered for the confessions they had failed to yield during the previous month. They continued to resist and that night they were locked again in torture cuffs and leg irons. The following morning Guarino was taken to interrogation. He again refused to confess. Byrne was brought into the room in time to see Larry ordered down onto his knees. There were fifteen to twenty guards in the room. At a signal from Dum Dum all of them began savagely beating Guarino. Soon he was insensible. Byrne was moved to another interrogation room.

When Guarino regained consciousness, Dum Dum ordered him tied into torture ropes. Again, consciousness slipped away fast. When he awakened, the ropes were being removed. He saw some women at the door. Their faces were contorted with hatred for him, and they were urging the torturers on. Guarino was made to kneel. Dum Dum came around from behind his desk, sliding a bullet into the chamber of a pistol. "Now I give you your last chance," he said. "If you do not confess, I kill you."

He held the pistol to Larry's temple. "Confess, Guarino, or I kill you."

Larry looked up at him. Death seemed so inviting. Quietly, he answered, "Please, do me a favor, will you?"

Dum Dum seemed to understand and became enraged. Larry never knew what hit him, a fist or the hand holding the pistol. There was another painful explosion in his head. He rolled on the floor all the way across the room. Dum Dum followed him, kicking him and yanking him up to punch at him. Then Larry was again tied into torture ropes. Dum Dum grabbed him by the hair and said, "Now I give you opportunity. You can speak. Say anything. Go ahead. I allow you to speak."

Guarino was drained, whipped, a sodden lump of aching, despairing humanity. But some warrior instinct surged, induced an alertness, insisted on further resistance. Through eyes blurred with bloody sweat and hatred, Larry regarded the little sadist, understood that the offer to let him speak was to establish the groundwork that would enable Dum Dum to save face before an audience that had failed to see him extract a confession from the prisoner. Guarino knew that no matter what he said, Dum Dum, the only Vietnamese present who knew any English at all, would advise the onlookers that the prisoner had confessed. Larry lowered his head and remained silent. Furious, Dum Dum smashed him again.

Guarino was rope-tortured four times that day, with brutal beatings sandwiched in between. He did not confess. At last, when there seemed nothing left to do with him but to kill him, Dum Dum ordered a guard to give him a cigarette, explaining this to Larry as an example of the humanity of the Vietnamese people. Guarino, a heavy smoker, tossed the cigarette aside. A guard was ordered to return him to his cell. On the way, another guard approached, demanding that the American criminal bow. Larry was too weak. He was beaten senseless.

He was barely strong enough to sit up on his bed pallet when Ron Byrne returned, looking like a wet, bloody, dirty rag. The two prisoners hugged each other and cried, and described their all-too-similar days. The next morning they were separated. Each had a long way to go before torture would end, but now he was to journey alone.

———

"I'm tired of fucking with you," Fidel snarled to Jack Bomar, seated before him on a low stool. "This is it. You're either going to surrender or I'm gonna surrender you like you've never been surrendered before. It's up to you, you make your choice. Which is it?"

Bomar shook his head. "No way," he said firmly.

"Okay," said Fidel, nodding to Magoo, who was standing over the prisoner. Magoo sent Bomar sprawling with a roundhouse blow to the head. This particular room had many windows, and these were crowded with the eagerly interested faces of spectators, guards and women who worked in the camp. They seemed settled for a good show.

Fidel had initiated his association of the "Fidel group" of POWs like a Westerner who espoused Oriental ways. On coming before him, prisoners were required to bow deeply, and when they failed to do so were required to back up, come through the door, and bow again. They were made to sit before the Latin on a low stool or on the floor. "That's where criminals should sit," he would say, "there in the dirt."

Fidel kept a silver cigarette case and a matchbox on his desk, and would tell prisoners, "You're gonna be the cigarette case, or you're gonna be the box of matches. Now it's your choice. If you're the box of matches, you're gonna be punished so badly that you're gonna beg me to be this case." At each meeting, Fidel would push the matchbox away from the cigarette case and observe that Bomar was the matchbox, heading for serious trouble. "You're either gonna surrender completely, or you're not," he explained. Then, leaning forward, he would confide, "Let me tell you, you *are* going to surrender to the Vietnamese people! You *will* surrender! You will do anything you are asked to do. Anything!"

This went on for weeks. Fidel kept the prisoners off balance. He came in a different mood to every meeting. He would quiz, cajole, warn, threaten. Sometimes, angrily, he ordered a guard to slap the prisoner about the room. Sometimes he confided that there was to be an early release, that a prisoner was to be sent home, implying that the men with whom he was dealing were under consideration.

Once Fidel told Bomar, "Today you will make a tape to that fucker, Lyndon Johnson. That fucker ought to be sitting there instead of you. You will tell President Johnson your views on the war."

Bomar stalled for long minutes, dreaming up a meaningless message to put on the tape. Finally ready, he picked up the microphone and turned on the recording switch. Fidel intervened, turned the machine from "Record" to "Play," and Bomar found himself listening to a Frank Sinatra tape. "What are you trying to do, ruin this beautiful tape?" Fidel laughed.

Bomar was allowed to hear several Sinatra ballads. Fidel sat laughing at him, at how funny it had been to watch him sweating it out when he had thought he was going to have to make a tape for "that fucker, Johnson."

Bomar and other Fidel POWs surmised that the Latin did not want to torture them; torture was dangerous, because it could yield propaganda that backfired, like the Clark Kent–Ben Casey confession. Fidel's mission, it was speculated, was to make the Americans cooperative without physically torturing them; to break them to Hanoi's will with some sort of psychological attack. To be sure, the Latin was keeping Bomar nervous. Bomar set himself on defeating his antagonist, on forcing Fidel to torture him for anything he got from him.

As the weeks passed and Fidel continued to come up empty from his bouts with the Americans, he became increasingly impatient and nasty. Clearly, he was running out of time. He had to show some results, and soon.

Now, the sparring had ended. At Fidel's signal, Magoo sent Bomar sprawling, now put him back on the stool and teed off on him perhaps ten times. The crowd loved it; they babbled, happily. The blows stunned, but Bomar did not lose consciousness. A rage built up inside him. There was a pause in the proceedings, as Fidel explained, "These are really rough people you're dealing with!"

Bomar looked around, making no effort to hide his contempt.

"I told you one time I was gonna give you a break," Fidel said. "Okay, today I give you a break." He reached to the floor, picked up a set of leg irons, and slammed them on the desk. Then he slammed a pair of torture cuffs beside them. "You wouldn't make the choice between the cigarette case and the matchbox. Now I allow you to choose. Which will it be? If you choose the manacles, I guarantee I will break both your wrists. The leg irons are not going to be too bad."

Bomar, who had broken an ankle during shootdown, was not interested in the leg irons. "I'll take the manacles."

"You make a big mistake. You're the dumbest guy. You should never do that."

The cuffs were ratcheted on tight, and then he was tied into torture ropes—the green rappelling straps were used. Fidel stood by watching, and as the pain tore into Bomar, a rage seemed to mount in the Latin. Suddenly he slapped the tortured prisoner in the face and shouted, "*Surrender!*"

Bomar did not answer. Fidel slapped him again. "*Surrender!*"

The prisoner kept silent.

Another hard slap. "*Surrender!*"

A rhythm developed, and the spectators became caught up in it, chanting and shouting excitedly. A guard stepped in and dug the fingers of one hand deep into the prisoner's throat; he had a grip on the windpipe and seemed intent on pulling it out of him—he was crushing it, choking him.

"*There are four things I won't do*," Bomar had once told Fidel. "*I won't say anything against my country. I won't say anything against my President. I won't say anything against my family. And I won't say anything against my religion.*"

Angrily, Fidel had replied, "*There are four things you are going to do for me after I break you apart: You will speak against your country. You will speak against your President. You will speak against your family. And you will speak against your religion.''*

Bomar had known instantly that it had been a mistake to challenge the Latin and had felt a sick, sinking feeling, knowing that sooner or later Fidel surely would take such statements from him. The memory haunted him. Now, apparently, the time had come.

The guard kept tearing at his throat, choking him. Fidel kept slapping him and shouting, *"Surrender!"* On and on. Then, finally, Bomar, frantic for air, nodded. The Latin kicked the guard's hand away from his throat, and the ropes and cuffs were removed.

"I don't think you've had enough," said Fidel. "I'm too easy on you!" The Latin seemed to be seething, having difficulty containing his rage. He ordered the guards to administer an additional beating to the prisoner. When it was over, Bomar was stashed in solitary and locked into leg irons. He was bruised and bloody. His chest and shoulders ached, as though they had been torn apart, his arms were numb from the straps, and a tooth had been broken. He sat on the floor of the cell, thinking about the torture. It was not the worst day he had endured. The worst day had been the one he had spent in the cell the prisoners called the Ho Chi Minh Room, Cell #3, in the Auditorium. The open window in this cell had been close enough to the open window of Fidel's quiz room so that he had had to spend hours listening while Fidel and a torture crew worked on the crippled Ray Vohden. The badly injured Navy pilot was as tough-minded and tough as anyone Bomar had ever known, but Fidel had known how to make him scream. And there had been nothing, nothing that Bomar had been able to do to help him. Except pray.

Thus, one by one, the Fidel prisoners made war with the Latin. The American "criminals" "surrendered," but the Vietnamese could see that they were doing so only because of physical torture.

There now were some 480,000 U.S. combat troops in Vietnam. At home, America was polarizing on the war issue. For many, the Administration's purposes were clear-cut and vital; it seemed essential to halt the spread of communism in the world, and the farther the job could be done from America's shores, the better.

But for many others, the Administration's purposes remained unclear, and the price was too high and much too personal; too many American youngsters were being drafted to die in far-distant jungles. Nor did the immense sacrifice appear to be accomplishing much.

Certainly, it was not stemming the flow of enemy troops and supplies into South Vietnam; indeed, in this strange conflict American forces sometimes seemed unable even to defend themselves. One July midnight, for example, the Viet Cong delivered a devastating attack on the big airbase at Da Nang, killing twelve Americans, wounding forty-five others, and destroying eleven airplanes and a dozen helicopters—more than seven hundred American aircraft had now been lost.

Moreover, there was a great deal of hostility and confusion in high places. Antiwar congressmen were continually engaging in disagreeable public debates with members of the Administration. Administration supporters were accusing dissenters of appeasement, of aiding the enemy by their opposition, and of promoting "another Munich."

In September, General Nguyen Van Thieu and Premier Ky were elected President and Vice President of South Vietnam. They received nearly 35 percent of the vote, the rest of which was divided among ten civilian tickets. Civilian candidates charged election "irregularities," but a group of twenty distinguished Americans sent to observe by President Johnson disagreed. One of the twenty, Oregon's Gov. Thomas McCall, said the election was "as good as any in the United States," and the group reported to Johnson that it had found no evidence of election rigging.

United Nations Secretary General U Thant advised reporters of his fears that the world was witnessing the opening stages of World War III, described a Washington-Peking confrontation as "inevitable," and insisted that the U.S. air campaign against North Vietnam was the main obstacle to peace talks.

Gov. George Romney, a highly popular candidate for the 1968 Republican presidential nomination, revealed that during a 1965 visit to Vietnam, "I just had the greatest brainwashing that anyone can get . . . not only from the generals but also from the diplomatic corps over there."

21

Late 1967—The Crown Prince, The Alcatraz Eleven, The Fink Release Program

In a jail in Vinh, approximately 150 miles south of Hanoi, a short, stocky North Vietnamese was introduced to the recaptured Bud Day as a "nerve doctor." He was not encumbered by any of the instruments most medical doctors seem to need for the conduct of a physical examination. The prisoner was made to be seated, and the "nerve doctor" proceeded, relying solely on his eyes. He peered deeply into Day's eyes, and then into his ears. He took considerable time gazing into these orifices, but finally the examination was completed. The "doctor" advised the interrogator that the American's memory certainly was still there, and that there was not a thing wrong with it.

"Now," the interrogator told Day, "you must remember. What was the name of your squadron? Where were you based?"

Day shook his head. "My head was injured when I ejected. I can't remember anything about my life before that."

The interrogator was a thin man with a thin, dour face and ears that stuck away from a narrow head. He displayed a great contempt for the American, and spent three days lecturing him on "the people's struggle in Vietnam," plying him for military information. He refused to credit Bud's protestations that he had amnesia and assured him that his only hope for badly needed medical attention lay in his willingness to provide "the people" with military information. "We will teach you to remember," he said.

The interrogator motioned to a guard standing nearby with lengths of rope. Loops were placed around Day's shoulders and armpits, and the ropes were pulled and tied as tightly as possible behind his back—the shoulders nearly touched—and the pain that leaped and raged in the shoulders and chest was worse than anything Bud had yet imagined. Then a stick was looped into the rope, like a turnbuckle, and the rope was made still tighter. Still Bud bore the pain, refusing to answer the interrogator's questions. He writhed and sweated in the ropes for most of a morning. Then the ropes were removed. The interrogator said, "I do not have unlimited time. You are not a young man, Day. You must have the limbs of your body to place food on the table of your family. You will talk, or I will turn you into a cripple!"

Back in his cell, Day's ankles were chained to the floor. After siesta he was rope-tortured again. He yielded nothing, continuing to insist that he had amnesia. He was returned to his cell. That evening the interrogator brought to Day's cell a strikingly handsome Vietnamese officer in a new, well-pressed uniform. Bud could smell liquor on both of them. The interrogator introduced his companion as the camp commander and said, "He orders you to tell all you know about the imperialists in the South."

Again, Bud claimed amnesia, wondering, somewhat fearfully, how the liquor would affect his captors. He did not have to wonder long. A guard was sent for a thick, green willow stick, nearly an inch in diameter. It was given to the commander. The interrogator asked a question about American bases in South Vietnam.

"I can remember nothing before my shootdown," Bud said.

Employing a wicked backhand, the commander slashed the willow strip across the prisoner's face.

The interrogator repeated the question, and Day repeated the answer. Again the commander whipped his face with the willow rod.

The interrogator kept repeating the question, Day continued to refuse to answer, and each time the commander would lash his face. The blows raised welts and opened bloody wounds all over the prisoner's face, head, shoulders, neck, and wounded left hand, as he tried to ward them off. They came faster and harder, and through eyes blurred with blood Bud could see that the commander now seemed feverish, as though in the grip of some sadistic insanity, raising the willow stick again and again and whipping the defenseless prisoner's head with all his might. It went on and on, until Bud's brain seemed to be going dead on him. He could not think—he was aware only that he could not think, and of something inside that was screaming, *Tell them something! Anything! Make them stop!* Some other something fought this screaming urge, and overcame it.

After an endless time the beating stopped. The prisoner stood shredded, bloody, in an envelope of agony, but undefeated. The camp commander's impeccable uniform was soaked through with sweat, and perspiration poured from his face. He was out of breath and exhausted by effort and excitement. The interrogator was angry. He told Day, "I will absolutely turn you into a cripple! Tomorrow, you will see!"

The interrogation the next day took place in an ancient pagoda. A crowd of civilians was present, apparently invited to witness the humiliation of the American "air pirate." As the interrogator asked questions, guards slipped the rope loops around the prisoner's shoulders.

"There is no need for you to be crippled," the interrogator said.

Day did not reply. He was girding himself mentally for the pain that now came, as the ropes pulled his shoulders tight behind him, and then were turnbuckled even tighter. He stood silent, trying not to think about the smothering pain. But there was no way not to think about it. Now he was made to climb onto the seat of a chair. An end of the long rope that held his shoulders in torture was tossed over a rafter and pulled taut. The interrogator turned to the audience, smiled, waved an arm, and the chair was yanked from beneath the prisoner.

Bud hung in the air by his agonized shoulders, immersed in a hell of pain worse than any that had been inflicted before. The interrogator stood beneath him, looking up at him, sneering, shouting, "Now, you imperialist pig, now you will answer my questions!"

The interrogator seated himself at his desk. Bud tried to come to grips with the agony—his shoulders were literally being ripped from his body; the muscles and bones in his chest seemed about to explode out of him; sweat rolled out of him, drenched his clothes, dripped onto the floor almost as though it were coming from a hose. How,

Bud wondered, to divert his mind, retain his sanity? He began count-ing the drops of perspiration rolling off his nose—each drop a second in time he would not have to live again.

For a while the interrogator sat gazing up at the hanging prisoner, a look of satisfaction on his face. Then he began peppering him with questions. Through the shrieking pain, Bud finally found the diver-sion that gave him the strength of will to go on. The desk concealed the lower part of the interrogator's anatomy from the audience. But the prisoner, from his perch, could see that the interrogator's arm was moving vigorously beneath the desk. At first, Day had paid no atten-tion, assuming that his tormentor was scratching or rubbing his leg. But now he could see that his tormentor was massaging his genitals, masturbating! Day realized now that he was in the hands of a pervert, a genuine sadist, one who achieved sexual satisfaction from inflicting pain on others.

It was the incentive Day needed. He summoned the strength to focus a disdainful smirk on the hateful degenerate, one that let him know that he had been seen, that his victim knew. It might have been a mistake.

The sweaty seconds became minutes and then, incredibly, hours. Bud did not want to die, yet did not see how he could go on living in this agony. He wondered, prayerfully, how long it would take the pervert to achieve sexual satisfaction, to tire of the torture and release him from it.

He estimated he had been hanging for from two to three hours when one member of the audience, apparently bored by the show, rose to leave. The interrogator, sensing that the show was losing interest, rose from his desk, shouting angrily that he would give Day a last chance. When Bud did not avail himself of this opportunity, orders were snapped in Vietnamese. A guard reached up and grabbed Bud's right wrist, protruding from the cast. He began to twist the arm slowly. Bud's world went dark blue, and there seemed to be brilliant white lights flashing on and off. The arm kept twisting, and there was enormous pain and a long, splintering, shattering, sound. He was seized with nausea; he had an intense urge to urinate. But the pain overwhelmed him, blocked his capacity to do anything. Anything but—at last!—to scream.

The interrogator came close, sensing victory, snarling, "If you do not give me the information I seek, I will make you a double cripple. I will break your other arm. Talk, Day! You must answer!"

Bud knew the threat was not an idle one. To his immeasurable disgust, he heard his own voice quivering out of him, agreeing that he would talk. He was lowered and released from the ropes. He sat in the chair before the desk. His arms hung uselessly, his chest and shoulders ached, and a bloody pus ran from the infection in his lower right leg. He was questioned anew. He gave only false answers, naming a base he had read of in the newspaper *Stars and Stripes* shortly before his shootdown and describing another flying job—one with which he was unfamiliar, hence, could not describe accurately—as his own.

He could not stand himself for having been broken by the perverted interrogator. He sobbed uncontrollably as he was returned to his cell, then screamed obscenities. He ignored the guards' warnings to be quiet. He shouted his name and described what had happened to him in a voice other Americans, if they were in the place, could not fail to hear. He heard a faint, distant cough.

———

On October 11, Doug Hegdahl was given his opportunity to "do for the camp." His captors had listened to a tape he had made for his family, in which he had adjured them to read *Masters of Deceit*, J. Edgar Hoover's account of Communist conspiracy. To his surprise, the Vietnamese found no fault with the message. The tape was given to him, and he was told that he must present it to a visiting American delegation, through which it would be delivered to his family.

He met the delegation in a room in the Big House, the mansion on the Plantation grounds which once had been the residence of the mayor of Hanoi. Hegdahl was seated on a hassock, and about a half-dozen visitors sat on the floor around him. He felt like a monkey on display. The delegation leaders were antiwar activists Tom Hayden and Rennie Davis. Another man, small and skinny, whose neck seemed awash in his high collar, purported to be an Episcopalian minister. He boasted of having attended many antiwar riots. "My wife would pack me a lunch," he said, "and if I didn't come home she'd assume I was in jail and would come down and bail me out."

There were four girls, all of them dressed in worn, patched blue jeans. Disagreeable body odors emanated from them. It was Hegdahl's distinct impression that the Vietnamese were ashamed of these allies; there certainly was no question that the Vietnamese women who served them tea found them repulsive—their eyes were full of contempt.

Hegdahl knew nothing about these people other than that their presence in Hanoi implied sympathy for the enemy's cause. They were, therefore, his enemies. Spotting Hayden as the leader of the group, Doug smiled at him, balled his right hand into a fist, extended the middle finger and ran it along his hairline. The gesture startled Hayden, who smiled and returned it. Hegdahl could not help smiling at this, but silently berated himself for yielding to poor judgment; if the Vietnamese detected him making obscene gestures at their friends, he would be in for it.

"What are you doing here?" he asked Hayden.

"I thought it would be a gas," Hayden replied.

"What are the Beatles doing?" Hegdahl asked.

"Oh, the *Beatles!*" the minister interrupted. "They've got a new album, 'Sergeant Pepper's Lonely Hearts Club Band. . . .'" In the background, Hegdahl could hear the puzzled mutterings of Vietnamese interrogators: *"Beatles? Beatles? Sahjent Peppah?"*

The conversation remained innocuous. Nothing was said of the war. After perhaps forty minutes, Doug was led from the room. Outside, he was berated for not applauding the visitors for their antiwar activities and for allowing the conversation to proceed at such a rapid pace that it had been impossible for the Vietnamese to follow it. Privately, he wondered if the tape he had given Hayden for delivery to his family would ever reach them. It never did.

———

On the evening of Columbus Day, two Americans named George— Coker and McKnight—departed their cells in Dirty Bird prison, near the Hanoi thermal power plant, on a journey they hoped would take them to the New World.

They had not been much more than a week planning the break, but it was well thought out. The seed had been planted in Coker's head a year earlier, when he had lived in a cell in the Zoo adjacent to Jerry Denton, the escape-minded senior officer, who had explained to him how to remove the lock on his cell door. Denton had wanted to leave then, but Coker had found his escape plan unimpressive, had characterized it as "honorable suicide," in fact, and had elected to await a more likely opportunity.

Coker had once complained to Denton that the Vietnamese seemed to be torturing everyone but him. Not long afterward, the feisty Coker had been accommodated. He became the first prisoner in Las Vegas to be locked in ankle stocks; he was caught up in the Stockdale purge and rope-tortured twice. Then he had been isolated in Dirty Bird for ten days. During the siesta hours of these days he was locked in handcuffs and leg irons and, because of the intense heat of the cells, allowed to sleep in a small courtyard behind his cell. He was sleeping in this courtyard one afternoon in late September when the shaven-headed George McKnight shook him awake and introduced himself.

McKnight had been isolated in Dirty Bird since the atrocities of August 21 and 22 had been visited upon himself, Ron Storz, Orson Swindle, and Wes Schierman in Las Vegas. He did not know what had become of Storz. Swindle and Schierman had been transferred to Dirty Bird with McKnight. McKnight, too, was permitted to spend the siesta hours in a yard behind his cell, but in circumstances that hardly induced sleep. Each day his turnkey would shackle a wrist to an ankle and leave him until sundown. McKnight had found a piece of wire and picked the lock of the shackles. Coker, too, had a wire and was soon free of his own irons. The two communicated daily during siesta.

One day, Coker, a navigator who had frequently flown over the Hanoi area, listened with great interest to McKnight's descriptions of the neighborhood—McKnight was often sent to the power plant to bring back a water supply. Among other things, McKnight talked of a bridge a few blocks distant with distinctive structural grillwork. This, Coker knew, could be only the Paul Doumer Bridge, one of the best known in North Vietnam. It crossed the Red River, and its location told Coker exactly where in Hanoi they were.

Coker suggested to McKnight that conditions seemed right for an escape. He explained how Denton had taught him to remove the locks on the cell doors at the Zoo, and pointed out that the locks at Dirty Bird were the same, primitive, cotter-pin-type arrangements. Coker proposed that McKnight, on his trips for water, could case the streets and plot a course for them over the three to four blocks to the Doumer Bridge. Once at the river, Coker could take over. He knew all the major bends and confluences of the river and could guide them to the coast. They would have to swim approximately sixty miles, traveling by night, hiding and resting along the riverbank by day. At the coast they would steal whatever they could find that would float, hopefully a fishing boat, and Coker would navigate them to waters where Seventh Fleet ships operated.

McKnight was not immediately enthusiastic. The scheme struck him as harebrained—a couple of Caucasians swimming sixty-odd miles along a heavily trafficked river through one of the world's most densely populated regions, then somehow stealing a boat and sailing off to good-guy country. It seemed implausible. Then he remembered a former squadron commander who, when subordinates would propose apparently impossible ideas that appealed to him, was fond of saying, "They said it couldn't be done, so let's try it!"

Turning to Coker, McKnight said, "Let's try it, George!"

They talked, planned, prepared. On the afternoon of October 11, Coker and McKnight tested their cell door locks, to make certain they could get out quickly the next night. Near disaster! McKnight's lock got away from him; the shanks of the cotter pin slipped through the door and the lock on the outside of the door fell away, dangling on a chain down the front of the door. McKnight was in a cold sweat. He forced open the hatch that covered the peephole in the door, jammed his right arm thourgh the peephole, reached down, praying there was no guard outside, half expecting that at any moment his arm would be sliced off. For long moments he searched with his fingers, blindly, frantically. Then, at last, he felt the lock, lifted it back into place, found the hold in the door the shanks had slid through, pushed them back into it, grabbed the ends on the inside of the door and jammed a nail into the hole with them, securing them. Then he sat down, still sweating, saying prayers of thanksgiving.

Columbus Day passed at a tantalizing crawl. Peculiar things happened. Guards normally paid little attention to the prisoners, but today they entered McKnight's cell five times, to paw through his gear and search the place. McKnight spent the day fearing that the nail holding his lock assembly together would fall out and that the lock would come free in some guard's hands.

After dark, when the nightly propaganda began issuing from the speakers in their cells, the two prisoners arranged their extra clothing, extra blankets, and bowls under another blanket, dummy fashion, to make it appear that they were sleeping—hot as the season had been, Coker and McKnight both had been sleeping in their long pajamas and under blankets to condition the guards to the idea that they did so. When the dummies were made, Coker slipped out of his cell door, replaced the lock, stole to McKnight's door, and called to him. McKnight led him along an arcadelike corridor that ran along the inner side of the prison building. There was no moon, but the night was clear, the sky billiant with stars. They climbed onto a low wall and crept along it to a point where they could climb onto the roof of the building. There they gathered up soot that emanated from the power plant and covered everything in the neighborhood, and blackened their hands and faces with it.

They dropped off the roof onto another wall, moved across it to the roof of another building. At the far end of this roof, they slid down a metal pipe into a coal bunker. Now they had to cross an open yardlike area. McKnight led them, staying low and in the shadows, to a slag heap against a wall. Quickly they climbed the slag to the top of the wall and held strands of barbed wire apart for each other as they slipped through. Below the wall was a street. It was nearly deserted, but there were a few people passing. They waited for them to pass, then dropped onto the street, and, keeping to the shadows, scurried to the doorway of a deserted building. There they hunkered down to catch their breath. They were free!

They moved on, down a side street, up an embankment, across one of Hanoi's main boulevards, down an embankment on the opposite side, and onto swampy wetlands near the Red River. In the distance a dog barked. Back on the highway an occasional bicyclist passed. Ahead loomed the Doumer Bridge. It had taken considerable bomb damage, and repair crews were all over the thing, shouting above the racket of riveting hammers and the noisy hissing of dazzling-bright acetylene torches.

Suddenly, there was a rustling in the grass nearby. A man with a gun was emerging from the shadows—no! It was a cow; a glint of light on one of its horns had made it appear to be a gun barrel.

They moved on, found a ditch, got into it, and followed it to the river's edge. They stayed in darkness, moved along the riverbank until they were directly beneath the bridge. High above, a train on the bridge backed, clanked, and squealed. Coker and McKnight stripped off their pajamas, removed the drawstrings from the trousers and tied themselves together. Coker tied one end to his left wrist, and McKnight tied the other end to his right wrist. If they could avoid it, they did not want to get separated. They buried their pajamas, and slipped into the river.

The water was warm, and the current a swift four to five miles per hour. The river was perhaps sixty yards wide. They got out into the middle and drifted past sampans nested on both banks. Lanterns glowed and cooking fires burned here and there on the levees. It occurred to McKnight that they had not even discussed the fact that they might have to obtain food during the tremendous exertion of the escape. It didn't matter; somehow they would find food if and when they had to. The main thing was that they were on their way. He felt strong enough to swim to San Francisco.

Coker was the stronger swimmer. By first light, he estimated that they had come approximately fifteen miles. They made for the north bank, to find a hiding place for the day. The bank was nude, with no foliage, no rocks, no cover of any kind. The same was true of a considerable area above the bank. They went back into the river and continued downstream. Daylight was coming on with a rapidity that began to alarm them; they had to find cover fast. They scrambled ashore, up onto a high, steep bank. There was no cover here, either, but they dared not stay any longer on the river. They began digging furiously, with their hands, tearing at the hard, clay earth.

There was a sound on the water behind them. They kept digging. Coker looked back. A sampan was coming by. Vietnamese on deck were staring straight up at the two Americans. The escapees kept their backs to the river, hunkered down, stayed motionless, tried to make themselves invisible, prayed. The Vietnamese did not point or cry out; they simply stared as the boat drifted off into the fast-dissipating morning dusk.

Coker and McKnight dug out a crevice and crawled into it, satisfying themselves that they could be seen only from one direction: straight up. Above the bank was a mudflat, and there seemed no reason why anyone would cross it at this exact spot just to look down at the river.

The Americans lay resting, but adrenalin surged and they did not sleep. Carefully, in great detail, Coker began briefing McKnight on the forks of the river, so that in case they were separated he would know how to proceed. McKnight found himself tiring. He heard Coker say, "Hey, you know something? It's Friday the thirteenth!" Then sleep overtook him.

Suddenly, Coker was shaking him. "It's all over," he said.

"What do you mean?"

"Old gook came along with a fishing pole. Looked right down at us."

"Maybe he didn't see us."

"No, he saw us. He let out a yell and took off. He's gone for the militia."

The two had agreed from the outset that the most dangerous situation they could encounter would be armed, frightened peasants, and that in such an eventuality they would not resist. They climbed out of their crevice, looked for somewhere to run. But a crowd of jabbering civilians appeared above them, looking down. One had a rifle and was so excited he was trying to jam a cartridge sideways into the breech. Slowly, deliberately, the Americans raised their hands high above their heads and climbed to the top of the bank. The Coker-McKnight escape had failed.

———

By mid-October, the chronic optimist Jerry Denton was all but certain that the war was over. There could be no other explanation for the things that had been happening.

Weeks earlier, word had reached Denton of the Stockdale purge. He knew men were being hammered hard for information about the SRO and his policies. He assumed his turn for torture would come up again soon. At last, Greasy, the sadistic runt who had supervised much of the late summer–early fall horror at Vegas, hauled him into Cat's quiz room, locked him in rear cuffs, and ordered him onto his knees on the rough, brick floor. Denton had psyched himself up for a long session and was determined to yield nothing. He had not been on his knees an hour when the despised Greasy said, "Den-ton, I think no matter what we do to you, you not tell us anything."

"That's right," Jerry replied.

For a moment, Greasy studied the prisoner fixedly. Then, to Denton's amazement, he heaved a sigh of frustration, waved an arm, and said, "Get up. Go back to your room."

The rear cuffs were removed. He was returned to his cell in the Mint. He was not locked back into the stocks. He could not understand what was happening. One possible answer was that the war was ending. He began to persuade himself that this was so. It became a conviction when suddenly he was moved back into the cell in Stardust he had shared with Jim Mulligan.

Mulligan was no longer there. He had been moved in August to the Desert Inn. But with the war ending, it didn't really matter to Denton that he did not have a cellmate. He would be seeing everyone soon.

The two Georges, Coker and McKnight, had reason to feel optimistic, too. After being recaptured, they had expected heavy torture. Coker was cuffed about and both of his eardrums were broken, but that had been the extent of it, a punishment he considered surprisingly mild. McKnight had not even been beaten. Then, after brief stops at Heartbreak Hotel and Dirty Bird, they were stashed in separate cells in the Mint. They could not imagine what the Vietnamese were up to.

They found out on the evening of October 25. The Vietnamese plan involved eleven American archcriminals, including some of the highest ranking: Jim Stockdale, Jerry Denton, Jim Mulligan, Harry Jenkins, Howie Rutledge, and Sam Johnson. Of lesser rank but equal criminal stature were Ron Storz, Nels Tanner, Bob Shumaker, and Coker and McKnight. These eleven had been identified by their captors as men to whom the other criminals looked for guidance, for inspiration, for leadership. This leadership was now to be removed. Without it, the Vietnamese obviously believed, the bulk of the prisoner population would become more pliable.

By evening, the eleven were in their new home, a prison approximately ten blocks from Hoa Lo, in a courtyard behind Hanoi's Ministry of National Defense. The courtyard was perhaps sixty feet square. A long, low building against one east-to-west wall contained ten cells. A much smaller building containing three cells stood in the middle of an adjoining wall, at a right angle to the long building. Across the yard, a few feet from the last cell in the longer building, was an open cesspool. Near the cesspool was an earth-covered bomb shelter. Beyond, in the far corner of the yard, stood a pigpen. And there was a small bath area a few feet beyond the small three-cell building.

It was a stinking, depressing place. The most arresting thing about it was the cells—concrete tombs, perhaps fifty inches wide. Just inside each door was an area slightly more than a yard square, for exercising and walking—a single stride in any direction. Beyond this, there was an eighteen-inch step up onto a raised area about six feet long, where the inmate was to sleep. None of the cells had a window. Above the doors were closed metal transoms punched with a number of small ventilation holes, each about the diameter of an ordinary pencil. There were also gaps of about three inches at the bottoms of the doors.

Into the first eight cells in the long building went Rutledge, Jenkins, Johnson, Shumaker, Storz, Tanner, Coker, and McKnight, in that order. Cell #9 remained empty, and Denton went into Cell #10. Mulligan and Stockdale went into the small building, Mulligan into Cell #11, closest to the long building; and Stockdale into Cell #13, with Cell #12, between them, left empty.

The prisoners named this place Alcatraz. Stockdale was to remain

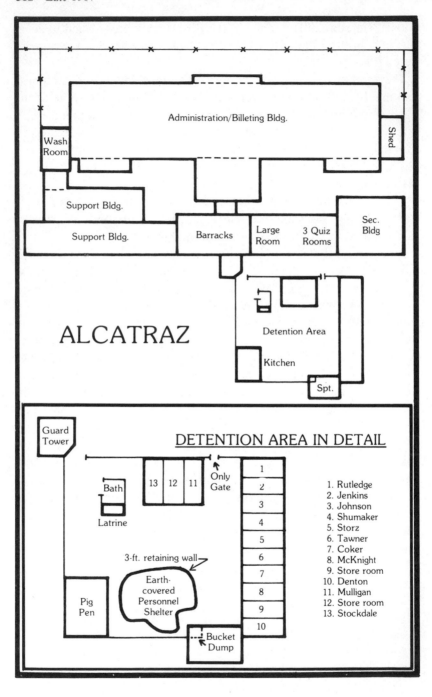

ALCATRAZ

Administration/Billeting Bldg.

Wash Room

Shed

Support Bldg.

Support Bldg.

Barracks

Large Room

3 Quiz Rooms

Sec. Bldg.

Detention Area

Kitchen

Spt.

DETENTION AREA IN DETAIL

Guard Tower

Bath

Latrine

13 12 11

Only Gate

3-ft. retaining wall

Earth-covered Personnel Shelter

Pig Pen

Bucket Dump

1
2
3
4
5
6
7
8
9
10

1. Rutledge
2. Jenkins
3. Johnson
4. Shumaker
5. Storz
6. Tawner
7. Coker
8. McKnight
9. Store room
10. Denton
11. Mulligan
12. Store room
13. Stockdale

here for fifteen months; nine others were to remain for twenty-six months; one was never to leave.

The security measures surrounding the Alcatraz Eleven were stringent. At sundown each day, each prisoner was locked in leg irons until 8 AM or 9 AM the next day; this was to continue for sixteen months. The prisoners were allowed out of their cells only briefly, and always singly, four times daily, to dump waste buckets, visit the bath area, and collect their morning and evening meals. Because of the constant presence of guards, voice communication was not possible. Except in a few highly unusual instances, none of the prisoners was to hear another American voice during their long Alcatraz confinement.

But there was to be plenty of communicating, using the respiratory-system version of the tap code: a single cough meant one; two coughs meant two; clearing the throat meant three; hawking meant four; spitting or sneezing meant five—a spit was good for close-range communicating, but a sneeze was better for longer range. Also, there was light wall tapping and a great deal of hand-flashing under doors between the two cellblocks.

Beyond installing them in Alcatraz, the Vietnamese seemed to have no program for the eleven. They were simply locked away in their tiny, filthy cells, kept under heavy guard, and allowed to languish.

—

"We have the crown prince!"

The jailers crowed the news to their captives. On October 26, a surface-to-air missile had downed Navy Lt. Comdr. John S. McCain III, son of four-star Admiral John S. McCain, Jr., commander-in-chief of U.S. naval forces in Europe. The Vietnamese had not been quick about identifying this prisoner, and had nearly let him die. McCain's crippled A4 Skyhawk had been upside down when he had ejected. His arms and legs had flailed badly, and he had been fished out of Western Lake, in the middle of Hanoi, with two broken arms and a broken left leg. Ashore, someone had smashed a rifle butt into his left shoulder, breaking it, and another had bayoneted a deep wound into his left foot.

No American reached Hoa Lo in worse physical condition than McCain. Despite his wounds, he was carried on a stretcher immediately to a cell in Desert Inn. Here Pigeye and Big Ugh stood over him while the cockeyed Bug interrogated him. Bug wanted McCain to tell him what kind of aircraft he had been flying and to name future targets. McCain kept replying with name, rank, and serial number. Each time he did this, Pigeye or Big Ugh would seize him by the neck of his T-shirt—he had been stripped to his underwear—and smash a fist into his face. McCain was knocked unconscious a couple of times, in which state, Bug deduced, it was not possible to interrogate him. The torture guards were instructed to soften their blows. Bug advised the broken pilot of his criminal status, assured him that he had no rights and that if he failed to provide satisfactory answers he would receive no medical treatment. This surprised McCain. He could not believe that his injuries would be left untended. All he had to do, he decided, was to hold out for a couple of days. Then the interrogator would give up on him, and he would be taken to a hospital.

Holding out wasn't easy. He was weak and feverish and in great pain. The interrogations and beatings continued. Twice each day, at mealtimes, a guard would attempt to feed him, but his stomach would accept nothing. No one bothered to clean up the vomit. No provision was made for his body wastes; he had no choice but to relieve himself where he lay and to lie in the waste. He became aware that he was losing consciousness more often and that he was staying unconscious longer. He began to wonder how long he could survive. His left knee was the size, shape, and color of a football. After four days, realizing that his physical reserves were fast diminishing, he summoned Bug and told him, "I will give you military information if you will take me to the hospital."

Bug brought a medic to the stretcher, representing him as a doctor. The medic took McCain's pulse, chattering with Bug. McCain asked, "Are you going to take me to the hospital?"

"It's too late," Bug said. The two Vietnamese left. McCain felt himself slipping away.

The next thing he was aware of was Bug, standing over him, shouting, "Your father is a big admiral. We take you to the hospital!"

In the days that followed, as McCain drifted in and out of consciousness, he became aware that he was in a room that was perhaps fifteen feet square. The place once had been whitewashed but did not look as though it had been cleaned since. There were cobwebs everywhere and clumps of mud and dirt all over the floor. The room was in a low spot, apparently a basement, for there was a dank smell to it and, when it rained, an inch or more of water would cover the floor. McCain lay on a bed that was essentially some boards covered with a half-inch-thick foam-rubber pad. A clear fluid was being inserted into his veins, and he was told that he had been given a great deal of blood. He had never felt so miserable.

One day McCain was told that a Frenchman who was visiting Hanoi wanted to see him and would like to take a message back to his family. He agreed; it seemed a good idea to get word back to his family that he was alive. First, though, a cast was to be affixed to his shattered right arm. A Vietnamese using a fluoroscope spent nearly three hours trying to align the broken bones. The patient was given no anesthetic to ease his way through this exercise. A guard stood behind him, holding him in a sitting position on the bed, and he was able to watch and to feel the agonizing and unsuccessful manipulation of his bones. Occasionally a shout of pain would escape him and sometimes the pain would engulf him and cause him to lose consciousness. At last, the job was given up. A cast was wrapped around him from his neck to his waist and down to the wrist of his right arm.

"Now," he was told, "you are going to be in your new room." He was installed in a commodious room, in a bed with clean white sheets. Cat, the prison system commander, soon arrived. He was eager to show McCain the identification card of a high-ranking American Air Force officer, Col. John Peter Flynn,* who had been bagged on October 27, the day after McCain.

Then, through an interpreter, Cat said, "The French television man is coming."

This was the first indication to McCain that the visiting Frenchman was a member of the press. "I don't think I want to be filmed," he said.

Cat pointed out, "You need two operations. If you don't talk to him, you won't get any. You will say that you are grateful to the Vietnamese people for the humane and lenient treatment, and that you are sorry for your crimes."

"I won't do it," McCain replied.

The TV correspondent, François Chalais, arrived with two French cameramen. Chalais appeared to be about forty and was most friendly. One of the cameramen, when he was introduced to McCain,

*Flynn was to remain the highest-ranking American military officer captured.

winked at him. The interview was to reach the United States on February 13, 1968, over the CBS evening news. Chalais established that McCain was indeed the son of his famous father, got him to recount the details of his shootdown and injuries, and to say, "I almost died. I am going to receive an operation on my leg."

Chalais asked McCain how he was being treated. The pilot, judging that the truth would get him more trouble than he might be able to handle, replied, "I am treated well by the doctors and the people here."

"How is your food?"

"It's not like Paris, but I eat it."

Chalais then invited McCain to speak to his loved ones. "I would just like to tell my wife that I'm going to get well," he said. "I love her, and hope to see her soon. And I'd appreciate it if you'd tell her that. That's all I have to say."

During the interview Cat and two interrogators stood behind Chalais. As the interview proceeded, they became increasingly agitated. They began urging McCain to tell the Frenchman that he was grateful for the humane and lenient treatment, and that he hoped the war would soon end. McCain ignored them, and they became more and more insistent. At length, Chalais turned to the Vietnamese and said, "I think what he told me is sufficient."

When the French TV crew was gone, Cat said, "Now you will not receive any operations. And you go back to your old room. This is because you have a very bad attitude!"

A number of people came to visit the son of the American admiral. An elderly man who was introduced as one of North Vietnam's most famous writers wanted to talk about Ernest Hemingway. McCain told him that Hemingway was anti-Communist and that he disapproved of Castro so strongly that he had vowed never to return to Cuba while Fidel was in power. He went on documenting Hemingway's anti-communism until his revelations had the Vietnamese distraught. He launched upon a denunciation of the pilot, reminding him of his criminal status, then departed.

Gen. Vo Nguyen Giap, Hanoi's hero of Dienbienphu and Minister of Defense, came into the room, spent several minutes looking wordlessly at McCain, then left.

Bug came and played a tape-recorded statement that he said had been made by one of the prisoners. There was no question that the voice was American, and McCain was surprised at the enthusiasm with which the speaker denounced his country. First, he gave a detailed history of himself, explaining that he had joined the Marine Corps, gone through flying training, had flown in the Korean War. Then, he said, he had become aware that the United States government is not really democratic, because southern senators and congressmen who do not really represent the people stay the longest and control everything. The marine insisted the country had to be changed and that America had to be extricated from Vietnam. The war, he said, was unconstitutional, and the United States was illegally interfering in the affairs of another nation.

The tape went on at great, boring length. McCain remained amazed at the eagerness with which the prisoner parroted the enemy's propaganda line. He wondered who this marine was, and how it was that he so willingly would say such things.

Bug wanted McCain to make such a tape.

"No," John answered, "I don't want to say anything like that."

"This man gave his true feelings about the war," Bug insisted. "You should not fear to do this."

"I don't feel that way about the war," McCain said.

Bug kept after him, but the prisoner remained uncooperative. His condition deteriorated. He spent most of his time in feverish sleep. Interrogators seemed constantly to stay at his bedside, to grill him through most of his waking hours. He remained unwilling to supply the information they sought. Occasionally an interrogator would lean over the bed and slap him and punch him; once, one of them landed a blow on his broken left arm. John screamed loudly and the interrogator backed off, obviously fearing the wrath of hospital authorities. Thereafter, when someone struck him, McCain would unleash a blood-curdling scream, which always seemed to dampen the interrogators' inclinations to violence.

An operation was performed on his broken right leg. He was told that he needed another operation on his leg, but that because of his "bad attitude" it would not be forthcoming. Nor was anything done about his broken left arm; it was left to heal by itself.

In mid-December he was discharged from the hospital and taken by ambulance to the Plantation, where two Americans, Bud Day and Norris Overly, another Air Force major, who had been captured on September 13, awaited him in a cell that was approximately fifteen feet wide and nine feet deep.

Day was appalled at McCain's appearance. Word of his capture had been trumpeted over the camp radio, and Day knew him to be a young man (he was thirty-one). But he appeared very old. His hair was snow white. He looked like his own skeleton. Day guessed his weight was less than a hundred pounds. His eyes were bright with fever. A Vietnamese guard and Overly carried him into the cell.

McCain's frightful physical condition notwithstanding, Day and Overly found him to be a spirited and engaging companion. He was elated at last to be with other Americans. The three men spent the entire night in whispered conversation.

Day and Overly had come to Hanoi together from Vinh. Day, despite his interrogation and vicious torture, was brought to New Guy Village and subjected to intensive interrogation again by Bug. In an apparent paroxysm of emotion, Bug had insisted that Day had mur- dered his mother* and therefore had to be shot. Day had remained unresponsive to the interrogation, and Bug had ordered Pigeye and an assistant to beat him. The beatings were savage, and went on for two and a half days.

The cast on Day's rebroken right arm was pulverized. The wounds on his left hand had not been tended and the hand had become a virtually useless claw; he could get only slight movement out of the thumb and forefinger. When he had asked for medical attention, Bug told him that both of his arms were going to be allowed to rot and then would be cut off. Eventually, though, the old cast was replaced with a new one. Bud protested that the new cast was crooked and would cause his arm to heal in a deformed manner. The Vietnamese doctor poo-pooed these fears, but they were to prove well founded.

McCain could do absolutely nothing for himself. Without help, he could not feed himself, wash himself, take a drink of water, shave, relieve himself, or clean himself. His only operating equipment was an unflagging optimism and an unquenchable will to survive. Day, who was all but helpless himself, looked on admiringly as Overly tirelessly lavished attention upon the desperately injured Navy pilot.

An endless parade of dignitaries came to the cell, mainly to stare at McCain, ''the crown prince.'' The visitors were mostly older men. They wore civilian clothing, but prison staff members attested to their exalted rank by bowing deeply to them as they came and went. These dignitaries would look upon the young son of an American admiral

---

*Bug commonly told American prisoners, "You have murdered my mother!"

with something close to awe. Once a translator asked McCain, "How many corporations does your family own?"

Puzzled, McCain wondered if he had heard the question correctly.

"Yes," said the translator, "I know that your father, since he is a big man in the military, is bound to have many companies under his control."

"You've got to be putting me on, man," John laughed. "My father is a military officer. His income is confined to his military salary."

The translator repeated this for the attending dignitaries, who all smiled, knowingly. Watching this, Bud Day exulted inwardly. *Honest Communists!* he thought. *In their system, you can't be a general or admiral without getting involved in graft and corruption.*

Now the Vietnamese exhibited an intense concern for McCain's well-being. "How are you feeling?" an officer would ask. "Are you getting enough to eat? Would you like to have something special?"

"No," McCain answered, "I'll just take what everybody gets."

"Would you like to have some fruit?"

"I don't want anything that everybody is not getting."

"We always give the sick men fruit."

The next day, when Overly brought back the food tray for the three of them, it contained, in addition to bread and weed soup, fifty-seven bananas. The three prisoners consumed them ravenously. The next day, fifty-seven more were delivered, and they ate them all. That was the end of the banana treats; apparently the Vietnamese judged that there were not enough bananas in the jungle to satisfy the three.

As Christmas approached, Day grew uneasy. He could not understand the comparatively good treatment, could not reconcile it with the horrors of the recent past. It seemed clear the enemy was trying to curry favor with McCain. What would they want in return: And what did it have to do with him? And with Overly?

By December, Byron Fuller had recovered to the extent that his captors felt free to engage him again in combat. Fuller was alive because of Air Force Maj. Dewey Wayne Waddell, thirty-two, of Bremen, Georgia. An F-105 pilot, Waddell had been captured uninjured on July 5, nine days prior to Fuller. He had found Fuller lying in untended misery—the Navy pilot, on ejecting, had suffered a broken left leg, a broken right arm and hand, and two dislocated shoulders. On reaching Hoa Lo, he had been tortured in ropes and hell cuffs for seven days and nights. He was nearly dead. Waddell had instantly taken charge.

For a hundred days the cheerful Georgian nursed Fuller. He made him comfortable on his pallet. Gently, he got the broken leg set and tightly wrapped bandaging around it, to hold it in place. Waddell washed Fuller thoroughly and regularly. During the intense summer and fall heat, he sat by his side and kept mopping up the perspiration that bathed him. He fed him and gave him water. He helped him to relieve himself, and cleaned him afterward. When the cold weather came, he kept him well covered with blankets. All the while, he steeped Fuller in the lore of Georgia Tech football.

In late October the Vietnamese separated the two. Waddell went to the Zoo. Fuller, who was now on his feet, was moved into one of the small punishment cells in the Mint. He was interrogated daily for biographical information. He steadfastly refused to supply more than name, rank, and serial number. He was warned that he would never see his family again, that he would stay in solitary confinement forever. He remained uncooperative. There was only one way to handle Fuller. On December 9, he was again tortured in ropes, and his right shoulder was rebroken.

He was returned to solitary in the Mint. A medic came and put a sling on his arm. He was to remain alone for more than two years. He had to learn to take care of himself. He wondered what had become of his good friend Wayne Waddell.*

It was nearly Christmas and at the Zoo, Dum Dum entered Larry Guarino's cell saying, ''And now I have come to show you the good heart of the Vietnamese people for the holiday time. I give you another blanket.''

It was cold, and Guarino was glad to have the blanket, but wanted something more. "Listen," he croaked to the retreating stool gatherer, "I think you've forgotten something. Do you know that I'm still in irons? I've been in irons since last August."

"I know," said Dum Dum. He slammed the cell door shut and left.

*The two did not meet again until February, 1973, more than five years later.

After the futile August-September brutalizations of Guarino and Ron Byrne for confessions, Dum Dum had scaled down his assault. The two prisoners had been separated, isolated, and kept in leg irons. For forty-four days, each time Larry's cell door opened—twice each day for meals, once to empty his bucket, and sometimes just for fun—he was made to kneel, while Dum Dum denounced him and guards beat him.

Once during this time Guarino was served a substantial meal of chopped pig meat. He was amazed. He calculated that there were 150 to 200 POWs in the camp and that the Vietnamese were serving them a total of fifteen to twenty pounds of meat at this one meal. Therefore, he deduced, the war was over. The Vietnamese wanted the prisoners to go home thinking well of them and felt required to serve them a few good meals first. He lay down and began giggling and then laughing uproariously. "The war is over!" he told himself aloud. "I've beaten Dum Dum! The poor son of a bitch has me in torture and doesn't know how to get me out without losing face. Now I'm gonna get up and thumb my nose at him, because he never broke me, and I'm gonna go home, and is he gonna be embarrassed!" Larry laughed until he cried.

Of course, the pig meat was not served generally to the prisoners; it was given to Guarino to help keep his strength up for the daily beatings. As these continued, Larry fought desperately for sanity and life with the only weapon he had: prayer. Each day he would go as far as he could on his own, withholding his last resource until the misery and frustration and fear overwhelmed him. Then he would use it. He would enter into a "max [maximum] prayer session" and would pray for hours on end. In each such session he would reach a point where he could actually feel the burden of his misery growing lighter. The weight never was lifted entirely but it was always lifted to the extent that circumstances became bearable and Larry knew he could survive another day.

Guarino was administered his last beatings on November 7. Thereafter his greatest misery was the leg irons. Besides hobbling him, the irons drained all of the body heat out of him, and as winter deepened he found himself shivering all the time. The irons became a horror. At last, on Christmas Day, Dum Dum brought guards in to remove them. Now, Larry thought, he might last the winter.

At the Plantation, Doug Hegdhal was lonely. He had been separated from the effusive Joe Crecca. The two had had their differences. Crecca had been a "circler," one who paced the cell in circles, while Doug had been a "pacer," one who strides back and forth in a straight lines. There had been many traffic jams and arguments, but they had become close friends. Doug missed Crecca and prayed that all would go well with him.

As Christmas approached, the interrogator the prisoners called Smoothie wanted Hegdahl to tape-record his reminiscences of Christmases past. There had been two false starts to the taping session. Each time, just as they had started, there had been American air raids in the Hanoi area and it had been necessary to hustle to bomb shelters. Now, again, Hegdahl appeared to be sitting patiently as Smoothie prepared the recorder. Actually, the young Dakotan was full of contempt. The interrogator had a nice, new Sony recorder which he was unable to plug in, since there were no electrical outlets. Smoothie was required to cut the plug off the recorder lead, unravel the wires, and attach them to wires that protruded from the wall. Then, he had to go outside and turn on the power.

The fools, Doug thought. *They don't have anyone in the whole country who can build them a plug. Someday this guy is going to electrocute himself.*

At last Smoothie got the machine working, sat down, and said, "Now, Heddle, tell me, what did you do for Christmas?"

Suddenly the roar of jets was in the air, bombs were falling, gongs were gonging, and Smoothie was in a rage of frustration. He glared at Hegdahl and shouted, "Ah, fuck war!"

That was the end of Hegdahl's reminiscences, but not of his Christmastide interrogations. The interrogator known as Chihuahua summoned him to ask, "Tell me, Heddle, how was your stay with Stratton?"

"Oh, fine!" Doug replied. "We spent last summer together. Is he okay? I'd really like to see him."

"He is well. Heddle, did Stratton tell you anything about his past?"

"Oh, yeah. He was captured on the fifth of January, and he has a wife named Alyce, and they have two children, and . . ."

"Heddle, could you regard anything that happened to Stratton as—ah—torture?" Chihuahua giggled nervously.

Hegdahl and Stratton had long ago agreed when talking to their captors never to use the word "torture." It seemed to inflame their captors and often caused prisoners who used it needless additional grief. The acceptable description of the miseries that were inflicted upon Americans was "resolute and severe punishment," for this implied that the "criminal" had only received his just desserts.

"Oh, no," Doug said, "but he did receive some resolute and severe punishment."

Chihuahua looked bewildered. Then he said, "Oh. Yes. All right, Heddle, you can go back to your room."

A few days later Smoothie confided, "I am not supposed to tell you, but are going to get a new roommate."

Doug was overjoyed. The days and nights of imprisonment crawled especially slowly when there was no one to talk to; having a roommate, another American who had lived a life he could talk about, was almost like having a television set. He could hardly wait.

Doug never saw Smoothie again.* On December 10, another interrogator, whom POWs called Soft Soap Fairy, introduced him to his new cellmate, Air Force Capt. John Black, thirty, of Johnson City, Tennessee.

———

On Christmas night, an interrogator known as Rat came to Jim Mulligan's Alcatraz cell, filled his drinking cup with rice wine, and told him, "On Christmas, the camp always permits you to go to mass."

He was blindfolded and transported a distance of perhaps a city block to a small room where some guards were shooting pool. There seemed to be a press conference under way in another room. The place was full of reporters, all of them Asian so far as Mulligan could see. He counted a dozen American POWs entering the room where the press conference was being held. At length, he heard American voices singing Christmas carols. Then suddenly the press conference seemed to be over, and the reporters were milling about all over the place. One of them approached Jim and asked, "Are you receiving humane treatment?"

"No," said Mulligan.

*Smoothie later showed up at the Paris peace talks as an interpreter for the North Vietnamese delegation.

"Why? What's wrong?" the reporter asked. He was surprised, anxious that Mulligan elaborate.

Mulligan began telling him what was wrong, but Rat intervened. "You cannot talk to this prisoner," he told the reporter, steering Jim away. He hustled him across the street, into an auditorium–like building.

Up front, rows of folding chairs faced a beautifully decorated, candlelit altar. A dozen other American prisoners were seated in these chairs, three in each of the first four rows. From behind, Mulligan was unable to recognize any of them. Guards stood watch all around. Rat ushered Mulligan onto a seat in the fifth row, which he occupied alone. He wondered how to let the others know that he was there and how to get word to them of the Alcatraz Eleven. Suddenly another prisoner stood as though to go forward and look at the manger scene near the altar. An interrogator ordered him to be seated, advising that he would be allowed to look at the manger after the mass. Mulligan stood up and, in a loud voice, said, "Will I be permitted to go after mass to see the crib? I understand I can't go now. Is that correct?"

The other prisoners all turned and looked at him. He recognized none of them, but up front he could see one man's lips forming words to the man next to him: "That's Jim Mulligan." It was Jerry Coffee. A year earlier, Coffee had lived in a cell behind Mulligan at the Zoo, had often talked to him through the wall and recognized his broad Boston accent.

Rat hustled to Mulligan, shushing him and assuring him that he could see the crib later.

A legitimate Catholic priest whom the prisoners called Father Ho Ti Minh said the mass. Wizened with age, he appeared to be a kindly man. The POWs had been advised by their captors that the priest was head of the "Peaceful and Patriotic Catholics of Hanoi."

When Mulligan got in line to go to Holy Communion, he kept mumbling word to the others that he was one of eleven who were imprisoned one block north, all of them solo and in irons. He was the last to receive Communion. As he left the rail he looked at Jerry Coffee, whom he had seen mouthing his name. Coffee mumbled, "Merry Christmas, Jim."

Guards and interrogators stood close by as the prisoners visited the manger scene. Then Jim noticed that there were cameras operating in the darkness to the rear. *So*, thought Mulligan, *we paid for our mass. They get movies and photographs of us at Christmas worship, and the*

*fact that we are permitted to worship demonstrates their humane and
lenient treatment.*

———

On January 19, 1968, Doug Hegdahl was treated to a quick look at
his friend and hero Dick Stratton. By now, Hegdahl had two
cellmates, Navy Ens. David Matheny having joined him and Air
Force Capt. John Black. The three were marched into a room where
Stratton was seated on a stool. No conversation was allowed and
Stratton and Hegdahl could only trade smiles. Doug was relieved to
know that Beak was alive and apparently well. And that, the young
Dakotan realized, was the point of the exercise—when the
Vietnamese released him, they wanted him to go home and report
that the "brainwashed" Stratton was in good condition.

The sight of Stratton heightened Hegdahl's contempt for the role he
was playing; he wanted to go home, but not early—not ahead of all
the others. But Beak had long since given him his orders and no word
had ever reached him that they were rescinded. So Hegdahl would
leave, as Stratton had ordered.

The next day was John Black's birthday, and his captors provided
him with a gift of a bowl of sugar. The interrogator who brought it
was the one whom the prisoners called Soft Soap Fairy, for his
effeminate mannerisms and for his assignment to play the "good
guy" role. Invariably, after a prisoner had been threatened or mistreated, Soft Soap Fairy would approach him as a friend, full of
consolation and assurances that whatever had happened would not
have happened had he been on hand. Then he would urge the prisoner
to avoid further trouble by cooperating with him. In short, Soft Soap
Fairy was a con man.

Dave Matheny had joined Hegdahl and Black in the cell on January
17. Matheny was twenty-three, boyishly handsome, six feet tall, and
with blond hair and blue eyes. He and Hegdahl hit it off well.

As Soft Soap Fairy offered Black his birthday sugar, he asked the
three prisoners, "What is your great aspiration? What do you want
most?"

According to Hegdahl Black, the senior man in the room, answered
first. He wanted to go home. Matheny, who was troubled with an
untended infection, voiced a preference for medical attention. Hegdahl, who had heard the question before and whose previous answer
had netted him a couple of months' worth of toilet paper, asked for

eyeglasses; his own had been lost on his abrupt departure from the *Canberra* and he was having trouble reading the hand-flashing that was going on around the Plantation.

On Saturday, Matheny returned from an interrogation and announced, "I'm going home. I think they really mean it. All I have to do is write a letter."

A few days later Soft Soap Fairy came in and proffered pens and paper to the three, inviting them to write to President Ho Chi Minh and request release. Black and Matheny wrote. Hegdahl declined the writing materials, explaining, "I wrote last fall." Indeed, he had written the previous fall, abiding by Stratton's order not to use the word "amnesty." He could not find it within himself to keep asking Ho Chi Minh to let him go home.

On February 3, Soft Soap Fairy advised Matheny that Hegdahl was not to be released.

Now Hegdahl worried. What of the 260-odd names he had memorized? Many wives and families had no idea whether these men were alive or dead, and he had been ordered to bring word of them. Had he allowed his own pride to ruin an operation? How would he explain himself to Stratton? At least he had better be able to tell Stratton that he had sent some names out. Black claimed to be poor at memory work. The youngster went to work with Matheny. In two days, the Navy pilot had nearly seventy names down pat. Then Hegdahl was moved to another cell.

Major Bai, the Cat, prowled the Plantation. He presented himself to Bud Day, John McCain, and Norris Overly. The three were allowed outside one balmy winter day for some sunshine and fresh air because, they were told, McCain and Day had been badly injured. McCain in recent weeks had been deathly ill, too weak even to sit up. He had developed a brain-rattling cough that shook his broken right arm inside its rough cast to the extent that the cast dug two holes in the back of the arm all the way to the bone. McCain's cellmates had not been at all sure that he would survive, but they had worked determinedly at keeping him alive, and he seemed to be recovering.

Cat impressed Bud Day as no other Vietnamese officer he had seen. He did not know that he was the prison system commander, but the deference accorded him by guards and officers alike made plain his importance. Moreover, unlike most Vietnamese military personnel around the camps, this one seemed to care about his appearance. He wore an immaculate, well-tailored uniform. He was self-possessed and spoke English well enough so that he needed no translator, although he often relied on one.

"What is your name?" he asked Day.

"I am Major George Day," Bud replied.

"Oh," said Cat, "we don't use rank here. You do not need to say 'Major.'"

Turning to McCain and then to Overly, Cat engaged in similar exchanges. The conversation remained innocuous. The Vietnamese officer seemed to be looking very carefully at the three Americans, as though they were sides of beef he might buy.

A few days later, on February 4, Overly returned from an interrogation to advise McCain and Day that he was scheduled that evening to meet with some high-ranking Vietnamese to discuss his being released. Apparently, Overly had been selected to replace the recalcitrant Hegdahl to be released with Black and Matheny.

Day recalled that a number of times Soft Soap Fairy had referred to Overly's "good attitude." Day thought, too, about Cat's recent visit; it now seemed clear that the prison system commander had come while the prisoners were sunning themselves to have a look at Overly's physical condition, to assure himself that Norris had no visible scars or marks, that he would make a presentable early release.

The next day Overly left the cell he shared with Day and McCain. They did not see him again.

But Doug Hegdahl saw him. Hegdahl, who was practically blind without glasses, had been given a new pair. Now he spent virtually all of the daylight hours looking through a peephole in the door, studying the grounds, the guards, and the POWs who came in view. He got frequent looks at his former cellmates, Black and Matheny, and the man who had been selected to replace him on the early-release contingent, Major Overly. Doug watched the three at mealtimes, when they got their food—special, "fattening-up" food.

Hegdahl, when he had been separated from Black and Matheny, had been told by Soft Soap Fairy, "You will find yourself more comfortable where you now move. You will live with a seaman."

The "seaman" was Air Force Maj. James F. Low, who had indeed been a seaman during World War II. Low had long since entered the Air Force, and had become an ace during the Korean War. He had been captured two months earlier. He was entirely disenchanted with North Vietnamese imprisonment, and according to Hegdahl made no secret of it with him that he was anxious to depart the premises and the country as quickly as possible.

Hegdahl was taken to be photographed wearing his glasses and saying farewell to the three who were leaving. He was worried that he might have failed to give Matheny some names. He got next to the Navy pilot and, as the flashbulbs popped, asked, "Dave, did I give you Phil Butler? Tom Browning? Dick Bolstad?"

"Yeah, yeah," Matheny kept saying. "I got him. I got him."

Black, Matheny, and Overly departed Hanoi on February 16. They had tape-recorded messages to the POWs who remained, the gist being that the Americans should cooperate with their captors.

When they were gone, Hegdahl was escorted to the cell they had occupied and made to empty and clean their waste buckets. Then, his head was shaved, signifying that he was in disgrace, having failed to qualify for early release. He did not feel disgraced. He worried about Stratton's reaction to his having blown it.

The news that the three had accepted release came as a shock to many POWs, and the departure statements sparked bitter anger at the Plantation. Indeed, the effect on morale was so devastating that Doug Hegdahl got word that his orders to leave if he got the chance were rescinded. The message came from Stratton, through a note dropped in the bath area. Stratton explained that while he still favored sending Hegdahl out, the camp SRO, Air Force Maj. Hervey Stockman (captured on June 11, 1967) would not go along with the idea. Stockman felt that it was not worth the damage to the spirits of those who remained.

The departure and departure statements of Overly, Black, and Matheny, broadcast in all camps, ignited a weeks-long policy discussion among the eleven POWs isolated in the quiet world of Alcatraz. SRO Jim Stockdale presided. Nels Tanner, centrally located in Cell #6 in the long cellblock, was his chief communicator. He and Stockdale, in Cell #13 at the outside end of the little building that stood at a right angle to the long cellblock, could flash to each other beneath gaps at the bottoms of their doors. Tanner would tap Stockdale's thoughts and ideas to the walls on both sides, would receive the tapped comments and ideas of the others, then would flash everything back to Stockdale. Stockdale would tap everything to Jim Mulligan in Cell #11 on the inside end of the little cellblock.

The consensus of the Alcatraz Eleven was that the three releasees had broken faith with the POWs who remained, had disobeyed orders of the prisoner leadership, and had done violence to the Code of Conduct. In working for and accepting parole, they had supplied the enemy with the most damaging kind of propaganda ammunition. Stockdale and the others christened the enemy's early-release tactic the "Fink Release Program."

But there were policy questions to resolve. What if the enemy offered a man his freedom while demanding nothing in return? This was by no means idle speculation. Hanoi might well bank on the fact that such a humanitarian gesture would generate enough goodwill for itself to offset anything damaging the releasee might say. There was considerable "conversation," but the answer was straightforward: except for those sick, wounded, and injured who clearly required medical attention their captors could not or would not provide, no one was to leave out of turn. The POWs would go home together.

But what if the enemy opened one's cell door and said, "You're leaving." How was one to know that the United States government, for reasons of its own, had not made a deal for him?

No matter; in this kind of situation, it was decided the POW would be required first to demand from his captors a meeting with his SRO. Pending such a meeting, he was to drag his feet while trying to ascertain the answers to three questions:

1. Are all the POWs leaving?

2. Is the release being made to the United States government?

3. If not, is it being made into a propaganda-free environment such as Hong Kong rather than the U.S.S.R. or the Peoples Republic of China?

If the POW knew the answers to any two of these three questions to be no—or if in his judgment they were no—he was to fight to avoid release, to do everything possible to make it plain that he was being expelled from the country against his will.

Alcatraz feeling ran high about the fink releasees. There was an abundance of "conversation." At the end of one long day, the over-worked Tanner flashed to Stockdale that he had that day processed some ten thousand words!

As policy was discussed and set, Stockdale's loquacious deputy, Jerry Denton, ensconced in Cell #10 at the far end of the long cellblock, had plenty of comments and questions. He wanted to be certain that if he or others were transferred to other camps, they had things exactly straight. He banged question after question at Stockdale, through empty Cell #9 to George McKnight in Cell #8, George Coker in Cell #7, and Tanner in Cell #6. At length, Coker tired of relaying Denton's incessant questions, most of which he felt Stockdale had already answered. He began answering the deputy's queries on his own; he would accept a question from McKnight, wait a reasonable interval, then tap back what he thought would be a common-sense answer from SRO Stockdale.

Coker's "Stockdale" answers prompted new questions from Denton. Some of them, Coker realized, required answers based on a maturity of experience and judgment he did not yet possess. However, these questions could not be forwarded to Stockdale lest the SRO deduce, from absence of the necessary prefatory questions, that Coker had been clarifying policy in his behalf. Coker found himself getting in deeper and deeper. His impatience with Denton's interminable questions gave way to a nervous anxiety—who was he, a young j.g., to be telling Commander Denton what Commander Stockdale thought or meant about anything. The prospect of a postwar court-martial haunted him.

At length, he decided he had no choice but to confess all to the SRO and take his medicine. Through Tanner, he asked for a private flashing session with Stockdale; it was personal, he explained, and he wanted no one else to be privy to the exchange. Stockdale could not imagine what the young officer might have to say that the others could not know, but he finally agreed to a private conversation that would involve dangerous flashing angles.

As Coker confessed, Stockdale had all he could do to keep from laughing aloud. Fortunately for discipline's sake, Coker could see only the SRO's hands. These administered a severe dressing down, warned him not to "ever try to come between Denton and me. We were in this outfit together before you were born!"

Repentant and chastened, Coker felt better. The fink release policy discussions continued and he faithfully transmitted every question and answer.

PART III

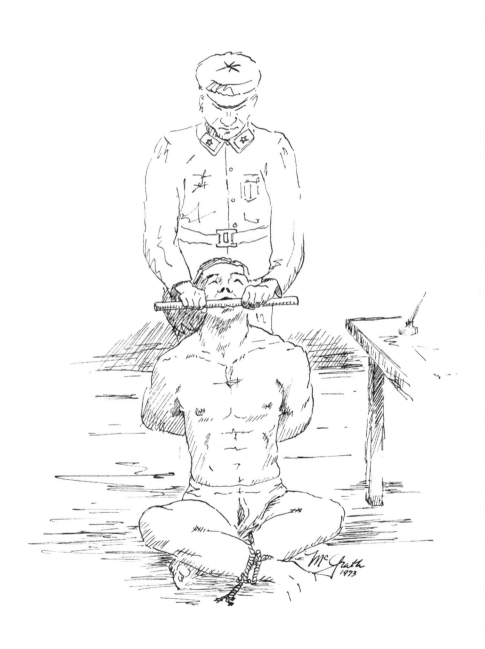

"Dying Is Easy.
Living Is the Difficult Thing."

A changeless misery lay over the prison camps of Hanoi. Meanwhile, in South Vietnam, other captured Americans lived horror stories of their own. U.S. Army Capt. Floyd James Thompson, thirty, had been commander of a Special Forces (Green Beret) detachment at Khe Sanh, in Quang Tri province, the northernmost province of South Vietnam. He had been captured on March 26, 1964—nearly five months before Ev Alvarez was shot down at Hon Gay.

Thompson, a tough, professional soldier, had been on a reconnaissance flight in an O-1 "Bird Dog," a light plane piloted by Air Force Capt. Richard Whitesides. At Thompson's direction, they had been flying low over a suspect jungle area and were downed by automatic weapons fire. There had been the crash, explosion, and oblivion. Jim had awakened to such intense pain that he had lost consciousness again—he would learn later that his back was broken. It had been late afternoon when he again regained consciousness. He found himself surrounded by Viet Cong guerrillas, one of whom was about to amputate his ring finger with a knife. He wanted Jim's birthstone ring, a July ruby, and he had been unable to get the thing off over the middle knuckle. Jim quickly twisted it off and give it to the man. There was no sign of Whitesides.*

Again, Jim passed out, and when he next awakened he was tied to a litter and being carried down a mountainside. The next several days were a jumble of swimming in and out of consciousness, of being carried from one jungle village to another, of being tied by the wrists and ankles to stakes in the dirt floors of huts.

During these travels Jim's captors were solicitous of him. A facial bullet wound inflicted during the shootdown was cleaned and treated; a badly burned and infected leg was debrided; and he was treated with penicillin and other medicines. There was no capability, though, for diagnosing or treating his back problem. He was told, therefore, that there was nothing wrong with his back, Even so, he remained unable to walk, and was carried from place to place.

As quickly as his physical condition began to stabilize, a mental torture began. Jim's wife, Alyce, and their three daughters awaited him at Fort Bragg, North Carolina. He had been looking forward to going home in June, especially since the arrival of a new baby was imminent. He prayed that Alyce would deliver safely before word of his capture reached her. (She was informed that her husband was missing in action at 5 AM the day after his capture; the baby arrived at 6 PM the same day.) He prayed for the strength he would need to endure the deep melancholy that assailed him as he contemplated indefinite, perhaps even permanent separation from a deeply loved family.

Thompson had never figured on going to war, much less on becoming a prisoner. As a youngster, he had suffered a broken neck in a horseback riding accident, and doctors had insisted that one of the things he never would be able to do would be to enter military service. Thus, he had been bitterly unhappy when in 1956 he had been drafted. Then twenty-two, he was already happily married and had a good job with high expectations in Dumont, New Jersey, with a major grocery chain. A letter and X rays from his doctor had made no impression on the Army's examining physicians, and he soon found

---

*He was never seen again, and was later declared to have been killed in action.

himself aboard a bus to Fort Dix. Infuriated, Thompson had passed the hat among the other inductees, bribed the driver to stop at a liquor store, and the draftees had begun their Army careers fully loaded.

At Fort Benning, Georgia, Thompson's recruit training platoon had performed poorly. When Thompson was discovered to be the main reason for the shabby record, his superiors' solution had been to charge him with responsibility, naming him training platoon leader. He had tried his best to dodge the job, insultingly advising his first sergeant that he had no intention of doing his work for him, and interspersing the refusal with what he felt certain were enough four-letter words to ensure a court-martial and dismissal to civilian life. To Thompson's immense dismay, the first sergeant had ignored his profane reaction, and reluctantly Thompson had taken command. A little power had corrupted—he soon knew he was hooked, a thirty-year man. Following basic training, he had been selected for Officer Candidate School, earned his commission, had become an airborne ranger, and then joined Special Forces.

Now he worried, too, about the survival of his jungle camp. With him in enemy hands, there was no one knowledgeable enough to keep things moving. He had to escape.

First, he had to make himself walk. He got no argument from his captors, who had been carrying him from place to place. At first, it was almost unendurably painful, and he moved very slowly, but he kept on with it. Somehow, his back began to repair itself. By the end of April, he was able to move along the trails for a few hours at a time without help. The odyssey continued.

He tried to escape. Once, he was installed in a lean-to on a riverbank. He was not twenty miles from his camp at Khe Sanh and knew the area well. On the second day, his guard put down his rifle, waded into the river, and went swimming. Jim immediately got up and shuffled away onto a jungle trail a few feet from the lean-to. He had traveled perhaps fifty yards when he came upon another armed guard coming uptrail. Using sign language, Jim explained that he had merely stepped into the jungle to relieve himself. The guard nodded, smiled, and escorted him back to his lean-to.

When several more attempts to escape failed, he gave himself to prayer. And soon he was aware of a great difference—nothing wrong, just different. Something about his recent life had changed rather drastically. Suddenly, he had a lot of important knowledge: he *knew* that his son, Jimmy, had been born, and that all was well with both mother and son; and he *knew* that he would make it, that he would survive this captivity, would return to his family. He *knew* these things with an absolute certainty that was the source of an utter peace of mind—in that moment he felt as secure about the future as he had ever felt in his life. What he did not know was that he was to remain a prisoner of war for nearly nine years, longer than anyone else in American history.

"The Vietnamese people have no desire to keep you long," Jim was told. "They realize that you are not an imperialist aggressor, but just a man who had been duped by the Administration in Washington into following its imperialist ways. We only wish to educate you. Once you understand the truth, you will be released and allowed to go home."

Two political cadre members explained this to him in excellent English during the first week in June. He had reached a small camp in Thuy Tien province, in northwesternmost South Vietnam. The camp had been constructed especially for him—he was then the only American officer in captivity, and a Very Important Prisoner. They insisted that they were not "interrogators," "indoctrinators," or "brainwashers." They said they were "teachers." For as much as eight hours daily, he was made to sit and listen to an endless, stupefying, Communist version of Vietnamese history. It sprawled back over thousands of years, dealt with Mongol invasions, the oppressions of Chinese dynasties, and French colonialism. The boredom and the pain in his damaged back, exacerbated by having to sit up for long hours, were almost equally excruciating.

At first he was well treated, but the atmosphere abruptly changed. One morning long before dawn, after perhaps half of a much needed night's sleep, he was awakened roughly, handed a machete, and told it was necessary for him to clear away the brush around his hut. The effort was exhausting. As he cut away at the undergrowth, he kept passing out. A guard kept shaking him back to consciousness, pulling him to his feet, ordering him to continue.

That day he was advised that he could not be allowed to bathe. No reason was given. Also, that he would have to build his own fire and cook his own meal. On his knees and squatting around the fire he discovered that he had to take care to move extremely slowly, that if, for example, he tried to rise quickly to his feet he would pass out.

Once when he lost consciousness, he fell into the fire and had to be pulled out of it by a guard. And, for the first time, his "teachers" showed anger at his refusal to provide personal information.

The next day there was a reversion to the good life—it was as though the previous day had never occurred. He was allowed a long, rejuvenating night's sleep. On awakening, he found his breakfast fire crackling. He was taken to bathe, then given a hot bowl of rice soup. At the day's lectures his "teachers" were their old, genial selves.

From his study of psychology in college, and his Army intelligence training, Jim understood what his captors were trying to do: they were well aware that one of the first principles of interrogation is to get the captive talking—about anything at all. And the best way to get the captive to talk is to present him with a variety of what he deems to be safe subjects—his childhood, his schooling, his favorite sports. Once a prisoner started talking, much could be learned simply by noting the subjects he avoided.

Also, a talking prisoner rarely failed to give insights as to his state of mind. His mental toughness could be measured, and determinations could be made as to how much effort would have to be invested in breaking him. Things that weighed heavily on his mind could be used to tempt him—for example, a prisoner concerned about his loved ones, say a wife in the ninth month of pregnancy and three daughters, might cooperate if allowed to write home or to receive mail. Jim forced himself to stay alert, continued to resist on the strength of training and professional instinct.

The bad life began again a week later. He was awakened in the middle of the cold, rainy night and told that he must gather wood for his morning fire. The small efforts of groping through underbrush, reaching down and picking up pieces of wood, and carrying them back to his hut caused him to lose consciousness again and again and to fall sprawling into the mud. Each time, a guard would revive him and order him to keep searching for wood.

The interrogators were now impatient, nasty, threatening. He was told he was not progressing satisfactorily with his "education." They said that their policy of humane and lenient treatment was reserved for "reasonable people," people who showed a "good attitude." But Thompson's attitude was that of a "stubborn diehard," an "imperialist aggressor." The interminable lectures continued.

After two days and nights of the bad life, the good life came again. Then, six days later, the bad life resumed. This time it lasted three days and nights. Jim began to recognize what his captors were doing: subject a captive to sustained bad treatment, and he will adjust to it, learn to live with it. Knowing what to expect, he will be able to cope from day to day for a long time, perhaps indefinitely. But start out by treating him well, by giving him only good days, and then, gradually, begin giving him some bad days, and an enormous mental pressure begins to build. Alternate the treatment in random fashion, so that he never can be sure what kind of day tomorrow will be and he will not be able to properly adjust. Thompson knew the tactic to be tried and true, that ultimately the prisoner so treated would crack, that he would give his captors what they wanted or would go insane. The program could not be allowed to continue. He had to escape.

He knew that he was approximately in the waist of Vietnam, or perhaps just across the western border in Laos. The countryside around him was controlled by the Viet Cong. But the sea was not more than thirty miles to the east. If he could reach the coast, chances would be excellent that he could find friendly forces. Between him and the coast was mountainous jungle, jungle so thick that given even a few minutes' start, he would be hard to find. He reasoned that his pursuers would quickly divine his plan and would scour the geography between the camp and the sea. Therefore, he would spend his first day moving northward, putting a margin of formidable real estate between himself and the likely search areas. In his weakened condition it would be slow going, especially since he would have to stay away from trails and make his own way through the dark, green jungle. He estimated that it would take him two weeks to reach the coast.

The opportunity presented itself on July 21. He awoke, as usual, at about 5 AM. No one else in the camp seemed to be awake. He wondered why no one called him out for breakfast. He thought that perhaps they had decided to let him rest; in recent days he had been ill with dysentery. Outside his door, a young guard sat asleep on a bench, a submachine gun cradled in his arms.

Jim pulled on his boots and slipped out the door like his own ghost, moved around to the back of the hut, past his latrine area and into the jungle. He picked his way ahead, quietly, as quickly as he dared, up a hillside so heavily jungled that by the time he had taken a dozen steps he could not see the camp behind him. He kept moving through the dark foliage, hoping, praying, listening—every step counted that he could put between the camp and himself, before his captors started after him.

Five minutes, and he still had heard nothing from the camp behind him. He pushed on, his amazement mounting and his hopes beginning to soar. His pursuers were going to need dogs to find him, and they had none. He kept moving. Occasionally he was aware of stabbing pains in his back, but he ignored them. He was perhaps ten minutes into the jungle when he heard the uproar in the camp, signaling that his escape had been discovered.

They could not know where he was, could not track him; the jungle was too thick. He had seized an edge on them. He savored his freedom; when one was free, even the air smelled different. He came upon a banana tree, stuffed his pockets with bananas, and ate two of them. He had to keep up his strength.

It was slow, torturous going. So dense was the mountain jungle that progress required something more than walking—rather, a kind of climbing, picking, sliding, snaking through it. In recent weeks much less effort had consistently cost him his consciousness, but now he was so full of mounting hope and excitement that, as the day passed, he seemed to keep gathering strength.

He daydreamed about reaching the American base at Da Nang. What a welcome there would be for him! Surely there would be a big beer bust at the club. How surprised and happy Alyce would be when he telephoned her. He pushed on.

In midafternoon he came out on the crest of a ridge. Ahead and below lay the loop of a river, perhaps thirty yards wide. Jim assumed that at this time of year it would be shallow enough to wade across. The jungle lay thick on the landscape down to within about fifty yards of the riverbank. These last fifty yards appeared to be abandoned fields, and were overgrown with scrub brush. He selcted a crossing point on the river. He would work his way down through the jungle to the scrub field before that point, crawl through the scrub to the sandy riverbank, wait until dark, then cross.

He sat in the scrub before the riverbank for a long time, watching and listening. He heard nothing, saw nothing. He was anxious to move on, to cross the river and turn east. At dusk he decided to chance it. He stood, moved out onto the bank and down into the river. As he reached the water, the bank on the opposite side of the river came alive with people. They exploded into view, came walking out onto the bank shouting and howling at him. There were two dozen or more of them, bearded old men and little boys, some of whom were carrying old, flintlocklike rifles.

Jim got back on the sandy riverbank, turned upstream and began walking fast. The noisy crowd on the opposite bank made no move to follow him. He had walked perhaps fifty yards when he learned why. Still another clamorous group emerged on the bank opposite him. Clearly, Jim's captors had figured out what he had meant to do. They had outposted the riverbank every thirty to fifty yards with friendly members of the local Montagnard population and had waited for him. Suddenly bullets were splashing into the water and along the riverbank in front of him. He stopped and waited, and they came across after him. He was heartbroken.

Hands tied behind him, he was taken onto a jungle trail. It had taken a full day to reach the river; the walk back to the camp took about thirty minutes.

The camp commander was in a fury. It was obvious to Jim that the man had lost much face, and meant to exact a price for it. A crowd of perhaps fifty people formed a circle around the two men. The camp commander paced before the prisoner, speaking, snapping off each word with a continually mounting anger. Jim's "teachers" translated, explained that by his attempted escape he had proved that he still had a hostile attitude. The Vietnamese people, he was told, had treated him humanely and leniently, because they had believed him to be a dupe. However, if Thompson was going to "follow the policies of the brass hats," then it would be necessary to treat him "like one of the brass hats."

Whereupon the camp commander smashed his fist into Jim's face and sent him sprawling onto the muddy ground. Guards lifted him, and the commander slugged him again. He kept after him, driving his fists into Jim's face and sides, knocking him down again and again. Jim was dazed, on the edge of consciousness. He could taste the blood in his mouth, could feel his eyes beginning to close, and felt sure his ribs would cave in if it didn't end. Finally there was merciful oblivion.

He awoke in a mire of bloody mud. His two "teachers" and a political officer were ministering to him. All seemed concerned at his condition and were apologetic and anxious for his welfare. He was allowed to bathe, and a large, warming fire was built in front of his hut. He was given a bowl of hot soup. Then his well-wishers took him to the hut where they had been instructing him and promptly threatened to have him shot. "According to our policy," he was told, "any prisoner who attempts to escape can be shot." Some guards with rifles lined up outside the hut, apparently awaiting orders to perform the execution. But Jim learned that before that drastic action was taken he was to have a chance to "atone" for his transgressions by answering some questions and making some statements.

They began by asking many questions that could have been answered only by staff members of the American high command: how many U.S. aircraft in Vietnam? How many ships in the U.S. Seventh Fleet? How many aircraft in the 15th Air Force? How many radios?

Jim would answer no questions, and his "teachers" seemed to expect no answers. Nevertheless, the session lasted all night. Jim knew that they wanted something from him that was most important to them, but even in his weakened condition he was not ready to yield.

He held on for weeks. More and more, he was denied sleep, given exhausting, makework tasks. His diet consisted only of thin rice gruel, occasionally seasoned with a little salt. He continued to lose weight. Soon he found himself passing out from the exertion of blowing on coals to get a fire started. It took massive concentration and a huge effort merely to walk, to put one foot in front of the other.

Periodically, he was reminded that once he understood the "situation" he would know what he had to do. When he continued to fail to understand the "situation," he was warned, "We still have French prisoners, from our war with France. They were not fit to return to their families, so we never released them. Don't you ever want to see your family again?"

Jim was made to stand at interrogations, and a guard with a length of bamboo was stationed behind him. When his interrogators wanted to emphasize points, they would nod at the guard, who would lash him across the back or the legs. The blows hurt, but did not draw blood or cause him to lose consciousness.

Then, one day in August, when Jim went into the interrogation hut, he found that a small desk had been placed in front of his seat at the interrogation table. On it were a pen and a blank sheet of paper. He was ordered to write a statement to the effect that he had been well treated by the Vietnamese people; he was to make it clear that he had never been humiliated, maltreated, or tortured; he was to observe that the National Liberation Front was comprised of thoughtful people who were dedicated to freedom and peace; and he was to assert his conviction that Vietnam should be for the Vietnamese people, and that the Americans should stop interfering and go home.

Jim refused to write the statement.

"Pick up the pen in your hand!" one of the "teachers" shouted.

He did so.

"Now write the statement!"

He refused. The "teacher" signaled to a guard behind Jim, and he winced under the lash of the bamboo stick across his back. Again, he refused to write anything. Another blow. Another refusal.

"Why will you not write?" the interrogator demanded to know.

"Because they are all lies, all of them," Jim answered, "and you know it as well as I do."

"They are *not* lies!" the "teacher" shrieked. "They are the *truth!*"

All that day Jim was made to sit with pen in hand, poised over the paper as though at any moment the light would dawn and he would want to begin writing. He wrote nothing.

It went on like that for many days. These sessions lasted for as long as four hours at a time, and there were three sessions per day. The interrogators kept alternating their approach. The would spend long hours cajoling Jim. Then, abruptly, they would turn tough, order him to write, have the guard behind him beat him with the bamboo stick when he failed to comply. It went on and on. Jim became aware that he was losing touch with the situation; suddenly he would realize that he had no memory of what had transpired for the past hour, that his interrogators were saying something entirely unrelated to the last thing that had registered with him. He worried that he might be losing his sanity.

He marveled to himself that his captors had gone to all this trouble for a statement from him: they had built a special camp and staffed it with sixteen people; sent accomplished interrogators and spent nearly five months applying mental and physical pressure to him for a propaganda statement! It was unbelievable! They were desperate for this statement. This was what it had all been about. How much the world's good opinion meant to Hanoi!

On August 18 he was presented with a detailed statement and ordered to sign it. He was amazed to find himself in the role of spectator; it was as though he had nothing to do with what was happening. He had the sensation of watching himself sign the statement that had been placed on the desk before him. A psychiatrist would have understood: the overly stressful situation had lasted a long time, and there was no end in sight. When this happens, the mind sometimes does what it must in order to save itself—it will displace or subdue the strongest of wills and accede to previously unthinkable demands.

At last, Jim Thompson "understood the situation." He had done "what he knew he must do." Now, surely, he would be "released and allowed to go home."

———

U.S. Army Capt. Floyd Harold Kushner, still, after two months, had trouble comprehending the unbelievable turn his life had taken.

Flight surgeon for a First Air Cavalry Division helicopter squadron, Kushner had been captured on November 30, 1967. He had spent the afternoon at Chu Lai in his capacity as squadron safety officer, lecturing helicopter pilots on the dangers of night flying. That night, anxious to return to his own base in the coastal highlands, he had boarded a helicopter. The chopper had been downed in the jungle, not by Communist gunners, but by violent monsoon weather. In the crash Kushner had suffered some crushed teeth, a broken left wrist, and some cracked ribs. Flames had engulfed the chopper and cooked off some M-60 machine gun rounds that had been stored aboard. One of these had caught Kushner in the left shoulder. With the pilot dead, an uninjured sergeant had been sent for help while Kushner stayed with the copilot, who had suffered a broken leg. Then, after three days, when the sergeant had not returned and aid had not come, Kushner had gone for help.

He had not traveled far when the Viet Cong found him. Looking back, he could see helicopters hovering near the crash site.

Despite his broken wrist, his arms were bound behind him and he was marched for days through rugged, jungled mountains. The wrist and cracked ribs throbbed with pain and a green pus drained freely from his shoulder wound. He knew that the slug had to come out soon.

Somewhere he awoke to find himself lying on a plastic-covered bed of elephant grass. A Vietnamese woman wearing a surgical mask stood over him, probing his shoulder. He had been given no anesthetic and the excruciating pain caused him to cry out. "Morphine!" he begged. The woman stared down at him, her eyes full of icy hatred, and shook her head. She kept on with the probe, pushing the instrument around inside his shoulder until she found the bullet and removed it. Then she took a hot iron rod from a nearby fire and held it against the wound, cauterizing it. Kushner heard himself scream, and then he passed out. He awakened to find a nurse sprinkling a crushed penicillin tablet onto the wound.

He was given a C-ration can of turkey loaf to eat and a package of Salem cigarettes. He needed clothing to replace the burned and bloodstained uniform he wore. Stealthily he approached a clothesline and helped himself to a set of North Vietnamese fatigues. No one challenged him. Shortly, Kushner was marched to another camp where he was locked in a cell and made to stay on his bed. Except to empty his waste bucket, he was not allowed off the bed for any reason. He was fed three small cups of rice per day. He began to believe that he was going to die.

The camp commander "interrogated" him with a lecture on the "criminal war of U.S. aggression" in Vietnam. Kushner was told, "Thieu is a puppet of Lyndon Johnson."

He retorted, "Ho Chi Minh is a puppet of Mao Tse-tung!"

The commander slapped him across the face twice. Extracting a small tape recorder from his jacket, he invited Kushner to display the progress he had made by making an antiwar statement.

The doctor glared at the interrogator. "I will never disgrace my family or my own honor by cooperating with you," he declared. "I would rather die than make a statement against my country!"

The commander studied the prisoner. Then he smiled and uttered words that were to ring in Kushner's mind for years:

"Dying is easy. Living is the difficult thing."

On January 8, 1968, he reached a small jungle prison compound. There were many South Vietnamese prisoners here, and a few Americans. Two were Puerto Ricans who had been captured nearly a year earlier: Army Sp4c Luis A. Ortiz-Rivera and Marine Cpl. Jose Agusto-Santos; and there was Roberts,* a Marine lance corporal, who had been a prisoner for two years.

The compound was surrounded by a bamboo fence. The place was

---

*Not his real name.

dark green—not a ray of sunlight penetrated through the thick jungle canopy to the ground. A stagnant creek was the sole water supply. The latrine was an open hole in the ground and the stench was pervasive. Flies and mosquitoes swarmed everywhere. The prisoners slept together on a long communal bed made of flattened bamboo slats. Each prisoner had a single sackcloth blanket to protect himself against the winter cold, but there were no sleeping mats, no mosquito nets.

Diet consisted mainly of three cups per day of rice for each man. The rice was rotten, and full of rat feces, weevils, and small stones. Every few days, when prisoners were strong enough, guards would escort them on manioc runs: manioc—the Vietnamese called it *komi* (pronounced ko-mee)—is a starchy, tuberous root that affords little nutrition. Kushner worried over the near total lack of protein—it could reduce strong men to ravening animals.

To the young doctor, the most depressing thing about the place was the Americans he found in it. The men were pale, drawn, hollow-eyed. They regarded Kushner with unmistakable hostility. Roberts told him, "We don't go by the Code of Conduct here. I know you're an officer, but you will learn." Then the marine launched upon a bitter condemnation of the American "aggression" in Vietnam.

"Dammit, shut up!" Kushner snapped. He walked off with the Puerto Ricans, Agusto and Ortiz, questioning them: "What's going on here? Have you been brainwashed? Do you feel as Roberts does about the war?"

Ortiz did not speak English. Agusto, who did, answered for both of them: "I know only three things: I am an American. I am a Catholic. And I want to go home. And that's all I'm going to tell you."

Roberts, although an eleventh grade dropout, seemed intelligent and possessed of leadership characteristics. He was extraordinarily well schooled in military history, and was a Civil War buff. He took fierce pride in being a marine, was a parachute-qualified underwater demolitionist, and had been a member of one of the Corps' crack units. It seemed apparent that his problem was that he had been captured too long ago, and had too long been denied proper treatment or any hope of freedom.

"What about escape?" Kushner asked him. "How can we get out of here?"

Escape was impossible, said Roberts. Only VC knew the trail routes out of the place. Moreover, the trails were full of VC, and there were punji traps everywhere, small camouflaged holes in the trails in which lay banks of sliced bamboo so sharp they would easily penetrate an American combat boot—and often the tips of the slices were covered with human excrement, to ensure infection to a victim. In emotion-laden tones Roberts told how he and an Army Green Beret captain whom he deeply admired had escaped one night in October, 1966, and wandered lost in the jungle for two days before being recaptured. They had been locked in ankle stocks, Roberts for three months, the captain for six, and not allowed out for any reason. As the excrement had piled beneath their bamboo slats, it had attracted clouds of jungle flies and vermin. The two prisoners had taken to evacuating into their hands and throwing the waste as far as they could. During those months Roberts had seen the captain, who once had weighed nearly two hundred pounds, fade to less than one hundred pounds and die. The marine was nearly in tears when he finished telling this story.

Kushner persisted: "There has got to be a way out of here." Roberts insisted escape was impossible. Nor, he said, was there any hope that the war would end soon. He insisted his only chance for freedom was for the Vietnamese to release him. Kushner could not dissuade him.

One morning it was announced that sixteen South Vietnamese officers were to be released, having learned "the truth" about the war. There was to be a celebration and the Americans were to share in it. The humane and lenient camp authority had killed two pigs and there was to be meat for all. But for Kushner, it proved to be a day of bitterness and disappointment.

Just prior to the celebration, he was summoned by the camp commander, who revealed that he was aware that the doctor was plotting an escape and warned him not to try it. The commander confided that Roberts had told all. Confronting Roberts, Kushner angrily assured him that he was of a mind to stuff him in the latrine. Roberts admitted that he had ratted on Kushner because the Vietnamese knew everything their prisoners said and thought anyway. Roberts advised, "They have a mystical power over us. If you don't want them to know anything, don't tell it to me. I want to be released so badly that I'll tell them anything you tell me."

Kushner was unable to partake of the celebration feast, which consisted mainly of entrails, blood, fat, and gristle; the sight of it sickened him. His fellow prisoners gratefully consumed his share.

He was sickened, too, at Roberts's betrayal of him, and at the bitterly anti-American and antiwar speeches of the ARVN officers who were being released. If they were not authentic turncoats, Kushner thought, they certainly were unreasonably good facsimiles.

———

Bloody Tet, 1968! As the sacred Lunar New Year observance was getting under way, large, strong North Vietnamese Army and Viet Cong forces simultaneously launched massive surprise attacks on thirty provincial capitals in South Vietnam. The completely unexpected action caught Allied forces with their defenses down. There ensued some of the bloodiest fighting of the war, much of it in the streets of Saigon and Hue. In Saigon, Viet Cong units invaded the grounds and buildings of the American Embassy, and it took hours to drive them out. In Hue, block-by-block and house-by-house fighting went on for weeks; it was late February before well-entrenched North Vietnamese main units finally were defeated. Other cities throughout the country fell into Communist hands for short periods.

American officials were quick to pronounce the Tet offensive a military and psychological failure. In fact, it won the Communists no new ground and failed to ignite the popular uprising Hanoi had hoped for—indeed, the ferocious assault seemed to unite the South Vietnamese people as nothing else had in their determination to resist the Communists. On the other hand, there were severe repercussions in the United States. Many, including Administration supporters, felt they had been misled concerning the progress of an American military effort that had become hugely expensive in terms of both blood and treasure. People were startled and disheartened at the enemy's ability to mount so widespread and powerful an attack, especially in many supposedly secure areas—one being the American Embassy. Grisly combat scenes on nightly television newscasts and in full-color news magazine coverage further eroded psychological strength. The Administration's conduct of the war came in for heavy criticism.

The Communists reaped a new harvest of American prisoners. "Surrender! Humane and lenient treatment!" The demand and promise were issued in strained English to Michael D. Benge, an American agriculturalist with the Agency for International Development (AID) who made his home and headquarters in Ban Me Thuot in South Vietnam's Central Highlands. A dozen North Vietnamese Army regulars, all of them armed with AK-47 automatic rifles, had risen to face him from a culvert not fifteen feet away. He had no choice but to raise his hands and climb out of his jeep.

His hands were tied behind him, a soldier appropriated his sandals, and he was marched off barefoot in the company of a fourteen-year-old Montagnard boy who had worked for him the previous year. The next day they reached a village, where a "People's Court" was in session.

Benge recognized many of the Vietnamese who awaited trial. Mostly they were young men, some of them boys still in school. At one time or another, all had worked for the Saigon government or for the Americans. To their Communist captors, this constituted treason. Charges were read, the accused were browbeaten into "confessing," and they were led into a nearby field and shot. Recognizing the hopelessness of the situation, the fourteen-year-old at Mike's side suddenly bolted and ran for the trees. A guard shot the boy in the leg and he crumpled into the dust. The officer-judge muttered a command. The guard walked to the downed youngster, put the muzzle of his rifle in his ear, and fired.

The bloodbath lasted through the afternoon. Benge was not "tried." Through a translator, the officer-judge interrogated him. Benge played dumb, answering in negative monosyllables when asked the locations of the American 23rd Division and the billeting places for South Vietnamese troops. He was only a farmer, he said, an agriculture advisor. That night his captors led him onto the jungle trails.

Within a few days Benge was joined by two other captured Americans: Betty Ann Olsen, a nurse of the Christian Missionary Alliance, who had been working in the leprosarium in Ban Me Thuot, and Henry F. Blood, a missionary of the Summer Institute of Linguistics, who had been translating the Bible into Montagnard dialects. Both had witnessed horrors similar to those Mike had seen. Three missionaries emerging from a bunker, their hands high in the air and calling out in Vietnamese, trying to surrender, had been gunned down in cold blood. Another missionary's home had been dynamited before he had been able to get out of it. Betty Ann Olsen knew of seven others in her mission group who had been killed. But the deepest anguish was Flood's, who told of being led away from his wife and three children. He had no idea what had become of them.

The three prisoners had not known each other before, but their common plight and the tragedy of recent days bound them together. They talked when they could, consoled each other, prayed together, wept for each other. And they walked and walked. Once, reaching a small village, their captors staged another "People's Court"; seven tribesmen were led off to execution. They kept on moving, into high mountains and trending southwesterly. Their captors had to keep them moving, for in the wake of the Tet offensive South Vietnamese Army patrols were everywhere, and American spotter planes constantly prowled at low altitudes. And so they kept walking, wondering where they were going and what was going to become of them.

———

Floyd Kushner was full of hope. Nine newly captured American infantrymen had arrived in the jungle camp, among them Army 1st Sgt. Benson,* forty-two, a seventeen-year man with a lot of combat time in both the Korean and Vietnam wars. Benson was a born leader, and his men accorded him a respect that bordered on hero worship. They called him Top, and told how, even after he had been badly wounded, he had fought and had directed them in a battle in which for four hours they had stood off an enemy regiment. On reaching the jungle prison, Benson's first words to Kushner were "I'm going to get these men out of here."

The new arrivals were herded into a meeting room strung with cloth banners proclaiming, "Welcome the lenient and humane policy towards COWs"—COW meant "Criminal of War." Agusto and Ortiz sat up front, wearing white pajamas—"Liberation" pajamas, it was explained; the new arrivals were told that the two Puerto Ricans were going home, that they had shown sufficient progress in their thinking about the war to warrant being "liberated." Statements were read in which the releasees denounced the American aggression and heaped praise upon their "lenient and humane" captors. The marine Roberts, bitterly disappointed at being retained in captivity, also spoke, denouncing himself for having failed to make good progress with his own thinking about the war.

*Not his real name.

Kushner devoutly hoped that "Top" Benson would live to lead Roberts and the rest of them out of this hellish place, or at least create the climate of resistance necessary to healthy morale and to the development of a community strength of spirit essential to survival. But the doctor was not optimistic. Top's left hand and arm had been mangled by gunfire and during the eight days it had taken him to walk the jungle trails to this prison, no medical attention had been provided. Now the wounds were exuding a creamy, sweet-smelling pus and were alive with maggots. The damage was beyond repair, and Kushner feared that gangrene would set in; the arm needed to be amputated.

Kushner, who had been forbidden by his captors from practicing medicine, put the problem to the camp commander. The commander merely advised that a Vietnamese surgeon soon would arrive.

Kushner went to the camp nurse. She supplied penicillin, and Kushner was at least able to treat the wounds with it and clean them up. But precious days passed and Top's condition deteriorated. At night, as he slept, he would scream for relief from pain. Eventually Top's tolerance for pain was reduced to the point where he could not allow Kushner even to clean the wounds.

It took two weeks for the Vietnamese surgeon to arrive. He agreed with Kushner that amputation was in order, but after Benson mentioned—erroneously, Kushner believed—that he had once had a heart attack, the surgeon refused to do so. Instead, he simply excised all the shattered pieces of bone and infected tissue, leaving the arm withered and the hand a useless bag of fluid.

Amazingly, as the days passed, Top improved, and mainly because of him, so did prisoner morale. Even the despairing Roberts responded to the first sergeant's leadership. At night the prisoners actually joined in singing such songs as "God Bless America," "America the Beautiful," and "The Star-Spangled Banner."

Small groups of newly captured prisoners, all of them American enlisted men, kept arriving. One day they were astonished to see five more Americans being herded into camp by an American. He was well over six feet tall, dark-haired, and with a nice, healthy, All-American boy look to him. He wore a "liberation" hat, much like the hat worn by the typical movie cowboy, with a drawstring under the chin. He held a rifle on his charges.

This, Roberts advised, was Bobby Garwood, formerly a U.S. Marine. He had been captured by the VC in August, 1965, and for a time had been imprisoned in this camp with Roberts and the Green Beret captain who had died. Garwood had argued bitterly with the two of them, Roberts said, and had often informed on them to their captors.

According to Roberts, Garwood had joined Viet Cong ranks when his captors had offered him his freedom for enlisting in "the people's struggle." A prerequisite for release was that he prove his sincerity by fighting with them for a time. He had agreed to do so, and the longer he had remained with them the more deeply involved he became. Now the VC insisted that he was indeed one of them and that he stay.

Garwood was fluent in Vietnamese and seemed as at home in the jungle as any other VC guerrilla. When, occasionally, he was put in charge of the American POWs, he had no qualms about barking orders at them. At the same time, he seemed to enjoy talking to the Marine prisoners, swapping tales of Camp Pendleton and the good life in California. Often he indicated that after the war he had every intention of returning to live in the United States and sometimes suggested to prisoners that he hoped to visit them.

Big, nice-looking, well-fed Bobby Garwood was hard to believe, but he was real, a living, breathing traitor who had taken up arms on behalf of the enemy and had no compunctions about helping to hold American troops in vile captivity.

Storybook Soldiers

The American-led camp at Langvei, near the heavily defended U.S. Marine stronghold at Khesanh, fell today after it had been assaulted by Soviet-made tanks. It was the first use of Soviet armor in the war.

South Vietnamese military headquarters reported that 316 Allied defenders, including eight Americans, had been killed or wounded, or were missing. . . ."   New York *Times,* February 8, 1968

Langvei, close to the Laos border, was the most exposed base in South Vietnam. It was militarily important to the Allies in that it was a springboard for disruptive operations along the Ho Chi Minh trail, the Communists' supply lifeline to the South. Langvei had been manned by some five hundred Montagnard troops, supervised by twenty U.S. Army Special Forces advisors, Green Berets. Among the advisors who were captured were a pair of storybook soldiers who might have been invented by Rudyard Kipling: S./Sgt. Dennis Thompson and 1st Sgt. Harvey Brande.

Both grew up on the West Coast. Both were products of poverty and broken marriages, high school dropouts who had found their own ways in the world since their early teens. Both had a penchant for barroom brawling. Both were free spirits, neither of them amenable to the discipline of garrison life. Nonetheless, both were superb soldiers.

Special Forces—the Green Berets—seemed to have been designed for such soldiers. Brande was on his third tour in Vietnam, and Thompson on his second.

At Langvei, Brande and Thompson took a lot of capturing. Brande had been hit by one Soviet-made tank while attacking another, intent on stuffing a pocketful of grenades down its open hatch. Escaping the scene with a badly ripped left leg and wounded right hand, he had found refuge in a small underground bunker. An enemy squad methodically "sanitized" his hiding place by heaving grenades into it. Fragments further ground up his torn left leg, more tore into his right leg, and a big chunk penetrated his chest just below the armpit. Miraculously, he remained alive; he had been captured while trying to escape the overrun outpost.

He did not fear for his life. An inveterate intelligence gatherer, he could get along in the Vietnamese language and had learned in recent days that North Vietnamese troops had orders to keep captured Americans alive for use as propaganda tools. What Brande had not considered, however, was that the severity of his wounds made him a burden that at least one young North Vietnamese captain did not want to suffer. He ordered Brande decapitated. Two guards, one with a rifle, the other with a machete, marched the now-anxious prisoner toward an area where some graves had been dug. Brande, with nothing to lose, had knocked the one with the rifle to the ground and tried to wrest the machete from the other. Unable to do so, the prisoner ran off on his shrapnel-torn legs into a field of tall elephant grass. He was quickly recaptured and the captain, now furious, ordered Brande shot on the spot. Brande had resigned himself to death when suddenly there appeared a senior officer, who ordered the American removed to a prisoner of war camp.

The camp was in Laos, perhaps thirty miles southwest of Langvei. It was primitive, a clearing carved out of the jungle. Brande was stashed in one of three bamboo huts, and about a hundred South Vietnamese and Laotians, many of them captured at Langvei, lived in small lean-to's around the clearing. There was no latrine, no medical facilities.

After a few days of total rest Brande felt well enough to try to escape. Then Dennis Thompson showed up. Brande was appalled at Thompson's appearance. He looked as though he had been in the ring with a homicidal Jack Dempsey. Still, Thompson walked with an irrepressible spring, a nonchalance that made Brande feel better. Brande could not imagine what had happened to Thompson, but was glad to see him. There was no one he would rather escape with.

"You gonna be ready to make it when I give the word?"

"Yeah. But give me a couple of days. They really did a job on me."

Thompson was ushered into his own hut. A little while later, he slid under the bamboo wall into Brande's hooch.* "Got any smokes?" he asked.

"Just smoked my last one."

"Wait here. I'll see what I can find."

Brande laughed inwardly. It was just like Thompson to tell him to "Wait here," as though he might go somewhere. In a few minutes Dennis returned with a cigar. With no tobacconist or corner drugstore in the neighborhood, he had called upon skills developed during his deprived childhood and relieved one of his unwary hosts of the stogie.

Now Brande learned what Thompson had been up to for the past week. When the enemy had overrun Langvei, Thompson and a half-dozen other American advisors had decided to try to escape to the north, then to head east toward the Marine position at Khesanh. Moving out, Thompson had found that fragmentation wounds in his back and legs made it impossible for him to keep up. Unwilling to slow the others down, he had silently detached himself, dropping back to the center of the camp to continue the battle, to be killed or to be captured. Eventually, he found himself the leader of a large group of Montagnard soldiers who were pleading with him, the only American present, to get them out of the place.

American planes and helicopters were now all over the sky. Dennis found a radio, described the situation to the airpower above, and was himself ordered to board the next evacuation helicopter that landed. He began organizing the troops into four groups, to be carried out by incoming choppers. Then, suddenly, he was shouting into his radio, "Don't let those helicopters land! NVA [North Vietnamese Army] on strip! Hit it with everything you've got!"

---

*A hooch is a grass and/or palm thatch hut.

In seconds, Communist soldiers were everywhere. Thompson, armed with a grenade launcher, found himself face to face with one of them. He squeezed off his last round and saw the thing make a hole in the man's chest. Then he turned and ran down a hill, away from the airstrip, and heaved himself into a ditch along a road. An Air Force A-1 flew low along the road, and he saw what he thought to be a napalm canister fall from it. *Oh God!* he thought. *Anything but that stuff!* Out of ordnance, the pilot had dropped not napalm but a fuel tank. It landed less than twenty feet from Thompson and exploded into a large ball of fire. Thompson felt a blast of heat, then lost consciousness. When he awoke, Communist troops were dragging him along the road.

Thompson had been a less than cooperative prisoner. Once, as he was shepherded down a jungle trail with some Montagnard prisoners, he had scampered off into the bush—straight into an enemy troop encampment. Recaptured, he was bound hand and foot and beaten unconscious with shovels, rifle butts, and fists. Regaining consciousness, he found himself bruised, bloody, aching. A rope was tied around his neck and a guard yanked him down the trail.

At dawn the prisoners reached a jungle holding camp. Thompson was taken immediately to interrogation, where he blundered. Before a crowd of interested subordinates, the interrogating officer tried to quiz him in less than rudimentary English. Thompson replied in Vietnamese. Clearly angered at having lost face to the American, the officer asked questions about the Langvei encampment. When Thompson refused to answer, the officer ordered him beaten again. It was brutal.

In the next three days Thompson was beaten to unconsciousness countless times. He thought he might be beaten to death, until finally an elderly officer halted the proceedings, pointing out to the angry interrogator that more punishment might kill the prisoner, and that orders were to keep Americans alive.

Now, in Brande's hut, Thompson's eyes searched for the source of the foul stench which even his odoriferous cigar could not overwhelm. Finally spotting the infected wounds on Brande's left leg, he felt small for having complained of his own tribulations. He exclaimed, "Jesus, Harv, you can't travel on that!"

"The hell I can't," Brande snapped.

Thompson reflected that there was another American back in the camp he had just left, Army Sgt. John A. Young. Young had been captured on January 31, a week before the battle. AK-47 fire had shattered one of his legs below the kneecap, and he had not yet been able to walk to the camp in Laos. He would be coming soon, though, and if he were here when Brande and Thompson escaped, it had to be expected that Young would pay a terrible price for it; he might even be executed, as an example to other prisoners. For Young's sake, they had to go before he arrived.

They slipped away in midmorning, three days later. On the trail, Brande, who did not trust Thompson's sense of direction, stepped into the lead; then, to Thompson's amazement, he broke into a run.

They headed for Langvei. Even if the outpost had been cleaned out by the Communists and bombed out by U.S. planes, the bunkers would contain hidden packages of emergency rations, enough to sustain them as they moved on. Also, it was possible that by now, ten days since the battle, Special Forces had reoccupied the base. They reckoned the trip to be about twenty miles.

They moved through dense jungle, forded rivers polluted with the bodies of dead people, dead fish, dead dogs, and with the bloated carcasses of dead water buffalo. They sidestepped numerous enemy patrols and crawled past enemy encampments. They starved. Once they came upon a small mound of rice, probably spillage from a bag that had once been stored in the jungle. Brande declined to eat the raw rice, warning Thompson that he could get worms from such a diet.

"Yeah, Harv," Dennis mumbled through mouthfuls of the stuff, "I'm sure gonna quit eatin' so I don't get worms."

Brande's leg infection worsened. The leg became rosy pink and painful to the touch. The holes the shrapnel had made seemed to be larger and were full of pus. After four days the rapid pace that had carried Brande out of Laos and back into South Vietnam was reduced to a slow hobble and he needed long rest periods—too long to suit either of them. So Thompson carried Brande piggyback.

Starvation began to influence their thinking. Once, after they had crawled directly through a North Vietnamese Army encampment where all were asleep or absorbed in campfire conversation, Thompson tapped Brande's shoulder, saying, "Wait a minute, Harv, I'm going back and steal a rifle and pack."

"The hell you are!" said Brande, who was senior. They pressed on.

After seven days they were on a hillside looking at Langvei, less than a mile distant. "Jesus, Harv," Thompson exclaimed, "we've made it!" He heaved Brande up onto his back and hurried down the trail to the bottom of the hill. As they came down onto an open stretch, they found themselves face to face with two North Vietnamese soldiers, walking straight toward them.

"NVA!" shouted Brande. He estimated that there was just time for the mobile Thompson to make it back into jungle cover; he released his hold on his neck, so that Thompson could drop him. "Make it, Tom!" he said urgently. "Get out of here!"

In the three days that he had been carrying his friend, Thompson had anticipated such a moment and had thought about it: the Communists were likely to kill the emaciated and crippled Brande if they captured him alone. He could not allow that. "We'll stick it out together," he said.

"Get going!" said Brande, the senior sergeant. "That's an order!"

Thompson smiled at the first sergeant. "No," he said. "I think I'll just stay with you, and see that you're all right."

They were recaptured, and soon found themselves in a camp just north of the DMZ.

But Thompson was more than determined. Twice more he escaped—and was quickly caught. Then, on March 20, he told Brande, "I'm going to make it tonight." It would be his fourth escape attempt.

He also told Brande that Sgt. Bill McMurry (William G., Jr.), another member of the Langvei Special Forces contingent, was in camp, as was Marine Pfc. Ronald L. Ridgeway,* eighteen, who had been captured February 25, near Khesanh. McMurry was badly injured. John Young, the Special Forces sergeant who had been captured on January 31, was there too. Brande did not think the prison authorities would now take it out on the remaining prisoners if Thompson escaped; there were too many American witnesses. He wished Thompson well.

At night Thompson was locked in handcuffs; his left ankle was locked into log stocks at the foot of his floor-level bamboo bed. When all was silent, he managed to break the cuffs. Then he stuck a long, hollow bamboo stick, issued as a urinal to prisoners in stocks, between the log stocks, levered the logs apart, and twisted and turned his left ankle until finally he was able to pull it through. Stepping from the hut, he took it as a good omen that there was no moon.

---

*U.S. Military authorities believed Ridgeway was one of 43 marines killed in an ambush near Khesanh. A memorial service was held for him at Jefferson Barracks, Mo. The Communists did not release his name as a prisoner of war until early 1973. Only then was he known to be alive.

Then, suddenly, a stream of automatic weapons fire was splattering the ground all around him!

He raced back to his bed, got onto it, and, in an instant, replaced the handcuffs. Desperately he tried to push his left foot back into the log stocks, but a flashlight was on him.

Guards spent hours that night beating Thompson nearly to death. Bill McMurry was amazed that he survived the punishment. Before dawn, the two of them were moved into another hut and locked in stocks that held both ankles. Thompson's wrists were tied tightly behind him, and he was handcuffed. The pain was intense, but at length he fell into a semi-conscious stupor. Then he became aware of a gnawing on his ear. It was a rat. He came up screaming and the rat hustled away.

But the rats wouldn't stay away. They raced over the two prisoners' bodies, stopping occasionally to sniff and appraise and to try to nibble. Thompson and McMurry shouted and jerked about on their beds, and the rats would back off; but they kept coming back, day and night. The constant battle to keep the rats off them began to exhaust the prisoners, but they dared not give themselves to exhaustion—in another hut lay a Vietnamese whose face had been disfigured by rats while he had been unconscious.

After ten interminable days the nightmare of the rats ended. One evening the five Americans were loaded onto a truck. Reaching a jungle terminal, they left the truck to proceed on foot. Brande and Young, whose severe leg injuries precluded their walking, were placed in hammocks and carried by South Vietnamese prisoners. The Communists took no chances with Thompson; the upper half of his body was wrapped mummylike in ropes pulled so tight as to cut off blood circulation to his hands. As they walked, Ridgeway stationed himself next to Thompson, tugging and pulling at the bindings, trying to relieve the pressure. At night he stayed close, loosened the ropes, and massaged Thompson's arms and hands, trying to restore circulation. At daybreak he would help Thompson retie the ropes around himself—but each morning, before marching, guards would come and wrap yards of new rope over the old.

They walked for eleven days before they reached their destination and Thompson finally was unwound. More than 250 feet of rope had been wrapped around him, and it was to be several days before feeling was restored to his hands and lower arms.

They were now in a jungle prison camp, approximately ninety

miles north of the DMZ and twenty miles inland from the coast. In this camp was a series of thatch-roofed bamboo buildings whose interiors had been divided into cells. The new arrivals were ushered into these cells.

There were other American captives in this camp, military and civilian. One was Army Capt. Floyd James Thompson. The Green Beret officer had now been a prisoner of war for more than four years.

The years had not been kind to Thompson. After being brutalized for a propaganda statement in the summer of 1964, he had been left much to himself for a very long time. His back, broken during the observer plane crash that had yielded him up to the enemy, still troubled him painfully and he developed malaria.

To pass the time and save his sanity, he engaged in demanding mental exercise. Mainly this involved the design and construction of houses; he did not merely *think* about these creations, he actually put them together in his head, idea by idea, piece by piece, step by step, using knowledge he had gained years earlier while working for a building contractor. Each house took months to design and build, for it was vital that everything be perfect. He would dwell for long periods on every detail, computing the precise amount of board feet of lumber he would need, the number of bricks, the flagstone, the plastering, the electrical wiring, the plumbing. He became obsessed with figuring all costs down to the last penny.

After five houses, Jim built a church, a small rustic chapel. It was constructed mostly of pine and oak. There was a large stained-glass window behind the altar, and smaller ones along the sides of the building. The benches had red-upholstered cushions. The altar had only a simple cross on it. He placed this church on a cloud—it seemed an appropriate place for it—and called it the Chapel in the Sky. Each Sunday, he would meet his wife Alyce and their children at the chapel, and they would attend services. Having been a faithful lifelong attender, Thompson knew the entire order of worship and would listen in memory to his favorite hymns: "The Old Rugged Cross," "What a Friend We Have in Jesus," "Jesus Loves Me." The prayer Jim cherished most in the Chapel in the Sky was the Twenty-third Psalm. As a POW he knew what it meant to walk in "the Valley of the Shadows." He remembered "green pastures" and knew he would see them again; he had to believe that his Lord was "preparing a table for me in the presence of mine enemies." The

Sunday services sustained him. He looked forward to them as the months and years passed.

Thompson had arrived at the North Vietnam camp the fall of 1967. He suffered from disease, starvation, and intense physical and mental torture, and for the next several months he lived in a cage that was not more than thirty inches wide, thirty inches high, and sixty inches long. He had to bend himself to fit into the thing. Such confinement was necessary, he was told, because of his penchant for escape—he had last attempted to escape more than three years earlier.

A few days before Christmas, he had been moved to a newly completed cellblock. The building had solid board walls and floor. It stood in a hole that had been dug perhaps four and a half feet into the ground—only the thatch roof protruded above ground level. It contained nine cells. Jim's was thirty-six inches wide, seventy-two inches high, seventy-two inches long—a gymnasium compared to the cage. Jim could scarcely contain his excitement at being able to stand up and to pace back and forth a few steps. It did not matter that since he was below ground it was dark and he could not see outside; this was the best thing that had happened to him in a long time.

Thompson remained alone in the underground cell for about two months. He saw daylight only occasionally, when he was taken to the latrine. The winter seemed especially cold underground and the ill-clothed, ill-nourished, emaciated prisoner shivered all the time.

In March he was moved into a drier, warmer, above-ground cellblock. His hands swelled terribly and excruciating pains kept shooting through them. He thought the damp winter had induced rheumatism, but these were symptoms of malnutrition. The condition was now exacerbated by a digestive disorder; he was so run down that his stomach could not accept food.

Thompson was interrogated, as he had been periodically over the years, and ordered to write of the "humane and lenient treatment." He refused. The interrogator ranted, "It is only because of our humane policy that we permit you to live. You must remember that there are still Frenchmen in our prisons who did not reform their mind. We can keep you in prison forever."

He was advised that his captors had contacts in the United States who would "take action against your family." He was threatened with starvation, torture, and execution, but he would not write anything. And somehow, despite his miserable and declining physical condition, he knew he would survive.

During Jim Thompson's ordeal, and into the spring of 1968, more and more Americans had arrived at the camp—which many of them called Portholes, for the shape of the small, round windows in the buildings. All except Harvey Brande and John Young were consigned to one of three newly built cellblocks. Brande and Young, neither of whom could yet walk, were stashed together in a cubicle within a large bamboo storage shed, which the Vietnamese called the "dispensary." It had three walls and no door. An intense hatred was to develop between the invalid twosome.

English-speaking officers began visiting the "dispensary." At first they were friendly. They asked that the two prisoners issue laudatory statements about the quality of the medical attention they had received and offered packages of cigarettes in return. Brande and Young refused. The treatment soon turned harsh. Each day, as the prisoners denied them the statements they sought, the officers would beat them with sticks and with their fists. It went on for weeks. Brande, already in frightful physical condition, went into a decline.

On June 13 the two invalids were ordered to another building for interrogation. Brande could not make it. "Crawl!" an officer kept shouting, cracking him with a walking stick. Brande lost consciousness. When he awoke, his old friend, Dennis Thompson, was lifting him. "They've been torturing us," Brande croaked hoarsely.

"It'll be okay," Thompson soothed. "What's your name?"

Brande, thunderstruck that his friend did not recognize him, was silent. Then he said, "It's *me*, Brande!"

Thompson was horrified. The most substantial part of Brande was his head, and that seemed but a skull wrapped too tightly in skin. He was light as a ghost. It was difficult to believe that anyone in such condition could long continue to live. Gently, Thompson put him in the quiz room on a bench next to Young and left.

Brande and Young offer conflicting versions of this interrogation. According to Young, an officer entered, opened a briefcase, handed each of the prisoners a list of questions, put a pistol on the table, and advised, "You can either answer these questions or you will never live to see the sun go down."

"Brande and I just looked at ourselves," Young recalls. "We just weren't going to take any chances. We decided there is no reason to get killed for something like that. We agreed."

The questions, Young was to remember, amounted to "basically nothing. They asked a biography about ourselves. If we were married and how many children we had, how much money we earned each month, stuff like that.''

The prisoners were also queried for their opinions on the war. Young was later to say that he wrote what he felt, that ''the war was wrong, but I also felt that what the other side is doing is just as wrong. And I'm an American citizen and I've gotta do what my government tells me.''

This, Young says, was not the first time he had written an antiwar statement; he had authored one about a month after being captured, while on the trail to the jungle camp. There was no duress involved; he had written it because it was ''just the way I felt.''

Brande's recollections are at odds with Young's, beginning with the list of questions they were handed. The enemy, Brande was to recall, sought a great deal of military information. According to Brande, they answered none of the questions. They printed their names, ranks, serial numbers, and dates of birth, and handed the papers back. Ignoring this, the interrogator now handed each man a blank sheet of paper and ordered him to sign it at the bottom.

''Ain't signin' no paper,'' said Brande.

The interrogator lifted his pistol and pointed it at Brande's head. ''If you do not sign,'' he said, ''I will kill you myself.''

''No.''

The interrogator now turned the pistol on Young and repeated the threat. In a quavering voice Young asked Brande, ''Is it all right if I sign, Sarge? He's gonna kill me if I don't.''

Brande was flabbergasted. Surely Young knew what he had to do when the enemy demanded that he sign a blank check!

Young asked again, ''Is it all right if I sign, Sarge?''

The interrogator wheeled on Brande, shrieking, ''You are the cause! You are the cause! You have ordered him not to sign!'' He turned back to Young. ''Is it true?'' he demanded. ''Has he ordered you not to sign?''

''Yes.''

Young was taken from the room. The interrogator told Brande, ''Today, you receive extra punishment because you have defied the regulations. You will get ten days of unannounced beatings. One-quarter rations. No medicine. No wash.''

Brande was returned to the ''dispensary.'' He recalls teams of guards entering the place at all hours, to beat him with their fists and with clubs, to kick him and to spit on him. He was beaten at least three times and as often as eight times daily. During these ten days he never was taken to the latrine, nor was he allowed to use a waste bucket. He was forced to eliminate onto his bed. Afflicted with dysentery, he evacuated a great deal of pus and blood. He would try to press the waste down through the cracks of his board bed, and would scoop up the excess with his hands and fling it as far as he could.

Terribly wounded, terribly sick, terribly weak, Brande knew he was dying. He did not want to die; he wanted to live for many reasons, not the least of them, he recalls, to settle accounts with John Young. His will to live notwithstanding, Brande believes he could not have survived these ten days without help. His guards were unable to take seriously the task of watching a charge who clearly was not going anywhere. As quickly as security became lax, a peasant worker named Nguyen Nam, with whom Brande had made friends, appeared with two potatoes and some fruit. Nervously, Brande warned him that the situation had changed, and that he must be careful. Nguyen nodded. He understood the danger involved, yet he advised that he meant to keep coming; if he was unable to gain entrance to the building he would distract the guard outside and send food in with his young son. He reached for Brande's hand and grasped it tightly, uncaring that it was soiled with bloody excrement. Then, as quickly as he had appeared, he was gone.

During the ten days of Brande's horror, Nguyen Nam or his young son reached him five times with food and encouragement.

Brande recalls that when the beatings ended, he was shaved, bathed, and moved into a cellblock with the other American enlisted men, into one of the telephone-booth sized cells. He remembers that he was so weak that he barely could hold up his head. He wondered if his friend, Nguyen Nam, would be able to find him now. But he was never to see Nguyen again.

———

Dennis Thompson's captors were entirely dissatisfied with him. Irascible, disruptive, escape-minded, he required a great deal of close attention. He seemed never to tire of insulting the guards, officers, and interrogators. He spoke deprecatingly of their antecedents, and suggested that it could not have been possible for authentic members of the human race to reproduce such faulty specimens as these. Frequently and loudly, he insisted to each and all of his keepers that they were given to incest, sodomy, and bestiality, and encouraged them to go have sexual intercourse with themselves.

He remained determined to escape. This determination was reinforced one day at mealtime, when Dennis was dispatched with a cart to the kitchen to collect rice for the cellblock. Capt. Jim Thompson ladled out the rice. Dennis was appalled at the sight of him. He was skeletal, ash gray; his ears seemed greatly oversized for his head, but his nose was the biggest thing about him, and huge bags drooped on his face below the sunken eyes. He looked ancient as death, a skinny, decrepit wisp of a man. Dennis tried to talk to him, but there was no response. When the four-year-prisoner had finished ladling the rice, he fainted. Dennis moved away, certain the man could not live long, and thinking, *Damn! That's what I'm going to look like if I don't get my ass out of here!*

At Dennis's urgings, others refused to answer questions or to make statements. His jailers' impatience began to mount. They warned Thompson, through other prisoners, that they would feel justified in killing him unless he cooperated. The warning had little effect. One midnight in June, officers accompanied by several guards removed Dennis from his cell and marched him out of the place, announcing to all that he was now to be executed.

He was frightened. His hands were tied behind him, he was blindfolded and taken into a field. There he was asked, ''Who is right?''

''I don't know what you are talking about,'' he answered.

''Your attitude.''

''My attitude is my attitude.''

The officers and guards stood away. The fear crawled in Dennis, dried out his throat and mouth; but he sensed somehow that the enemy was bluffing and it was important that he not let the fear show now. He reasoned to himself, *If they are serious, they're gonna kill me anyway, so why give 'em the satisfaction of seeing me grovel?*

He told them, ''I am a soldier. I came to Vietnam in defense of my country and of the South Vietnamese people. As a prisoner of war, I am entitled under international law to a standard of civilized treatment I have not received. I will continue to resist you. I will instruct and encourage all other enlisted men, officers, and civilians I come into contact with to do the same.''

The Vietnamese were enraged. They stalked about, shrieking at him, shoving him, stamping their feet, and threatening him with death.

The fear ebbed. If they had meant to shoot him, he thought, they would have done it by now; they would not be standing out here, in the middle of the night, arguing with him. It was all a bluff to cow him into submission.

The Vietnamese kept screaming and promising to shoot him. Dennis, now confident that he had the game figured correctly, said, "Well, shoot, fucker, do me a favor!"

He was not executed. He was beaten severely for a long time. Then he was isolated in a cell in a distant building.

"Illegitimae Non Carborundum"

The jungle camp in South Vietnam, where Dr. Floyd Kushner, Top Benson, and a crowd of other American enlisted men languished, had become a living hell. The mere act of existing was torture. For a time, after Top had arrived, morale had been good. But their meager diet of a handful of rice daily and a little manioc soon reduced them to near starvation. They became gaunt, skeletal, their abdomens distended. Afflicted with dysentery, Kushner was defecating fifty to a hundred times daily. He weighed perhaps ninety pounds now, and each time he stood to make for the latrine, he would momentarily black out. Anxious to keep himself clean, he would periodically bathe in the creek that passed through the camp; it was little more than a hundred yards from the hooch, but every crawling, stumbling, falling trip took most of two hours each way.

All soon had a painful skin disease that covered them with frightful sores, the worst of them in the underarm and pubic areas; these ran with blood and pus and attracted swarms of jungle flies and mosquitoes; they itched so dreadfully that when men scratched they would claim a relief akin to sexual satisfaction. The sores soon were overflowing with feasting maggots.

Men tried to keep clean and to keep the encampment clean. When his dysentery did not allow a man time to reach the latrine and left him no choice but to soil the ground, he would try to clean up his mess quickly. Still, the stuff lay everywhere, all the time.

The prisoners were made to sleep crowded together on a single community bed made of hardwood boards overlaid with pieces of flattened bamboo. There were no mats to soften the surface, and the hard bamboo wore large bedsores into some men. There were no mosquito nets. There were no blankets to ward off night chill. The men were not issued clothing, and the clothes they were captured in soon were in tatters; some were left nearly naked.

Tormented by the painful symptoms of starvation and by illness and nightmares, most found sleep to be elusive. They hovered on the edge of exhaustion.

The men tried to keep each other entertained with stories of their pasts. The same stories were told again and again, and changed a little with each telling until they had changed a lot. The men didn't care, for the stories got better and better. The story they liked to hear most of all was Top Benson's account of how the Korean War POWs had been repatriated. He supplied vivid descriptions of men being taken aboard luxurious hospital ships where they had been fed the most delectable meals and taught the newest dance steps by gorgeous Red Cross girls. He told how, on reaching the United States, the POWs had been received as heroes and honored with ticker-tape parades. The men gloried in his memories of how things had turned out for the POWs of the earlier war.

One thing the young enlisted men in this camp did not get was the leadership to which they were entitled from the highest ranking prisoners. Kushner, the medical man who was the highest-ranking officer, correctly gave himself no marks as a military leader. And the second-highest-ranking prisoner, Army WO Francis G. Anton, a helicopter pilot who had been captured on January 5, 1968, displayed no leadership competence. His long suit seemed to be a sense of humor, for which there was a desperate need. He was well liked, for he could make people laugh.

Top was unable to do much work after the Vietnamese doctor

removed most of the bones in his shattered left arm and hand. Still, he was knowledgeable in survival techniques and taught them to the men. He designed and supervised the building of bamboo shelving in the prisoners' lean-to-kitchen, organized cooking schedules, showed the prisoners how to conserve wood and to bank coals, kept spirits up and remained dedicated to the thought that he had to lead the Americans out of the jungle captivity.

Benson had a profound effect on Roberts, the marine who after more than two years in the jungle camp was determined to gain his release any way he could. Roberts heard the stories of Top's leadership in combat and of how he looked after his men after capture. The proud marine saw in the Army sergeant a kindred spirit, the kind of military leader he admired. He was drawn to Top and fell under his influence.

Periodically, more Americans would arrive. One was Marine Pfc. Earl Weatherman, nineteen, big, friendly, outgoing, who knew and cared nothing about the politics of the war. He had committed some transgression which had landed him in a marine brig at Da Nang and wanted out of the brig and out of the war. While resident in the brig, he had heard that the Viet Cong would give safe passage to neutral Cambodia to Americans who defected to them. Escaping from the brig, he had scouted out some Viet Cong, delivered himself unto them, and had received safe passage to the jungle prison camp. The Vietnamese thought that, like Bobby Garwood, Weatherman was a "crossover."

Except that Weatherman never really understood the deal. He did not consider himself a "crossover" but a "dropout." He thought the Viet Cong owed it to him promptly to escort him to Cambodia and turn him loose. If the Viet Cong ever planned to do so, however, they certainly intended first to extract some service from him. In the camp they fed him well and treated him well. He lived with some South Vietnamese prisoners, separate from the other Americans, and was at liberty to roam the camp. Occasionally he was able to steel cans of milk and smuggle them to the starving Americans.

Weatherman did not take kindly to his hosts' efforts to educate him in the cause in which they felt he had enlisted. He bickered constantly with his keepers. He was made to attend a political course with the other Americans, and when asked for his opinion of the just struggle of the Vietnamese people, he would not say, as he was supposed to, "The just struggle of the Vietnamese people has lasted four thousand years, and now the U.S. imperialists have come and must be thrown out.'' Instead, he would say, ''The Vietnamese have been fightin' all their lives, it's a civil war, and now the Communists are comin' down and tryin' to take over and the U.S. is gonna kick their ass back up into North Vietnam.''

Bristling, Mr. Hom, the Viet Cong in charge of the Americans' political development, would urge, ''Look at Garwood. Look at Bobby. He is a good example. You ought to be like him.''

But Weatherman became increasingly rebellious and disrespectful. His liberties were withdrawn and he was treated more and more like a prisoner. He began making the day-long hikes with the other Americans to gather manioc. He was on such a trip on April 1 when he overpowered a guard, took his rifle, and disappeared into the jungle with another American hoping to make it to Cambodia. Within fifteen minutes guards had tracked down the two. Weatherman threw out his rifle and he and his companion emerged from cover with their hands over their heads. A guard walked to Weatherman, placed the barrel of his rifle between his eyes, and blew the young man's head away. The other American, realizing that he, too, was to be murdered, began running. The guard fired, but the round went low, striking the prisoner in the leg. It downed him, and he writhed on the ground as the guard approached, lifting his rifle to complete a double execution. The other guards stopped him. The prisoner was beaten savagely, returned to the camp, tried before a kangaroo court, and sentenced to ninety days in stocks.

These stocks were made of bamboo. Each set was contained in a hooch just large enough for a single prisoner. The prisoners were kept in the stocks day and night, not allowed to leave for any reason. They were forced to urinate and defecate through the slats of the bamboo beds. They were never allowed to wash, or to clean themselves.

The conditions of captivity did not improve. Dr. Kushner began to notice that men were exhibiting bizarre mental symptoms. He diagnosed Acute Brain Syndrome, a mental disorientation that occurs when the brain is denied proper nourishment over a prolonged period. Men were forgetting where they were and who their companions were. Sometimes a man would get up to do something, walk a few steps, and forget where he had been going and what he had intended to do.

Top Benson began to fantasize. He talked of crossing over to the Viet Cong so that he could take charge of the prisoners and lead them to freedom. And gradually he changed. The once proud soldier who had cared only for his men showed less and less concern for them. He whined constantly and begged his captors for more food, tobacco, and clothing. He hoarded things and began to steal tobacco from the others. Once selfless, he made it clear that he now cared for no one but himself. He took a perverse pleasure in disputing Kushner's medical advice. When Top's abdomen and extremities began to swell, the doctor warned him to stop eating salt. Instead, Benson began stealing salt from the kitchen and eating it voraciously. Even his appearance changed. His face withered and sank in around its bones. His once steady blue eyes became shifty. With his bald head and white beard, he had the look of an ancient Shylock. Roberts, who admired him so, cajoled him day after day, angrily imploring him to recover himself. To no avail.

In the mornings, Roberts, whose habit it had been to remain abed until he felt like rising, now fairly leaped into action at the first discordant note of the get-up gong. He would stand in the center of the compound, shouting loudly for all to rise and shine, to join him in calisthenics, to get busy sweeping and cleaning up. He sounded for all the world like a Marine boot camp drill instructor. Men joined him, did as he ordered, some because they thought exercise and cleanup seemed a good idea, some because he insisted on it. Others did not join him, cursing him for his loudness and arrogance. All wondered what had gotten into him.

What had gotten into him, they learned, was word from Bobby Garwood that the political commissar of the region was coming to the camp, and that if Roberts showed progress he was to be included in a release. The man's name was Ho. He was reputed to be a political general. He would conduct a fourteen-day course. When it ended, some prisoners would be released.

––––––

That midsummer, Army Capt. Jim Thompson departed Portholes. Air Force Capt. Edward W. Leonard, Jr.—friends called him "J. R." for the "Jr."—felt certain that Thompson had been taken somewhere to die. Leonard, a search-and-rescue pilot who had been downed on May 31, had occupied a cell in the same building as Thompson. He did not believe the Green Beret officer could live long. There was nothing left of the man. What skin and tissue hung on his bones had a grim, grayish, dead look to it—almost as though he were decomposing.

One day Leonard had seen Thompson collapse, the victim of an apparent heart attack. Guards had summoned a medic, who had plunged a long hypodermic needle straight into Thompson's chest. He had been carried away, and when Leonard had made inquiries he was told that Thompson had been taken to a hospital and that he was going to be released.

Shortly afterward, Thompson and a few others were taken to another prison camp, about ten miles southwest of Hanoi. It was a penitentiary the French had built, a grim place, all heavy masonry, iron bars, and small, dark cells with heavy doors. Even by the standards of the other camps the prisoners had been in, the place was filthy. There were no lights, ventilation was poor, bathing facilities were practically nonexistent, and guards were everywhere all the time, to smother communications. Later American inhabitants were to call this prison Skid Row, for to them it would seem the end of the line. Thompson was placed in solitary confinement.

Six weeks later, the remainder of the Portholes inmate population were trucked to a camp in the countryside, perhaps fifteen miles southwest of Hanoi. They were to remain in this camp for more than two years; it was to be known to them most commonly as D-1, because one of the buildings was so marked.

———

In the camp in the South Vietnam jungle, the man named Ho arrived in style. Apparently a commissar, he was attended by several guards and porters, who carried his luggage and generally made him comfortable. He brought his own cook along. Vietnamese camp personnel accorded him a puling subservience.

He was taller than most other Vietnamese, and thin. He had a long, scrawny neck and buckteeth, his bespectacled eyes gleamed with fanaticism, he spoke fluent English, and displayed a talent for attracting and holding his pupils' attention. "Let me tell you criminals one thing," he said. "I can release you or I can have you killed. No one in your country knows where you are or anything about you. Each of you is at our mercy. You will learn. You will do as I say, or you will be executed for your crimes against the Vietnamese people."

School began. In the mornings Ho lectured on "The Vietnamese People's Cause," "The Americans Have Broken the Geneva Agreements," "The Vietnamese People Surely Will Win, the U. S. Surely Will Lose," and so on.

In the afternoons the prisoners were divided into several groups in separate classrooms. Ho and Mr. Hom, the camp interpreter, were teachers and moderators; Bobby Garwood was an assistant teacher.

In a discussion one day Top Benson committed the grievous sin of referring to the Saigon army as "ARVN."* Ho seized the moment. "This militarist seeks to sabotage your course," he told the others. "He calls puppet troops 'ARVNs'!" Ho declaimed for long minutes, wondering how anyone could even think in words that connoted legitimacy to the Saigon government. When he finished he ordered Top taken away. He told the others to prepare to join in a public criticism of Top for his crimes and his attitude.

Before the session began, the other POWs managed to convey to Top that he was to pay no heed to the criticisms they were to heap upon him, to understand that they were forced to say these things and did not mean them. Top himself was made to get things started. He advised the others that he was an old-line, hard-core militarist, that he still was thinking like a first sergeant. It would be necessary, he said, that he change his ideology.

When he finished, it was announced that henceforth no one was to call him Top; he was to be called only by his last name. Kushner was also to be called and referred to by his last name; no one was to call him Doc. No terms connoting rank or respect were to be used.

The criticism session disgusted Kushner. Most of the prisoners merely went through the motions and were easy on Top, assuring him that "you must change your way of thinking," and "constructive criticism is good." But there was a trace of bitterness in the tones of some, who told him that he was "obstinate," "stubborn," "greedy," "uncouth." His personal habits and manners were deplored, and it was pointed out that he ate with his hands and made sloshing noises with his mouth when he chewed. He was called "reactionary" and an "imperialist."

He was a pathetic figure, sitting on a low stool before the group. His uniform by now was in rags, and he looked aged and weak. He made no move to brush away the flies that swarmed about the running sores on his body or to wipe away the mucus that dripped from the end of his nose into his dirty white beard. Kushner felt an enormous sadness for him.

Top spent several long nights in the camp commander's hooch, where he was threatened and hounded for a written apology for his

*Army of the Republic of Vietnam.

attempt to sabotage the course. It is known that during these sessions Ho several times held a pistol to Top's head. At length, Top produced a written apology that included a condemnation of the American intervention.

Four other prisoners, including Kushner, were designated to write statements to the U.S. government demanding an end to its aggression. When the statements were written, the political course ended and Ho delivered a valedictory. "As a result of this course, you have learned about our culture and about our country. You have learned that we fight many aggressors: Genghis Khan and the Mongols, the Chinese, the Thais, the Japanese Fascists, the French imperialists, and the American imperialists. Now that you know the right road, you must follow it. Now you are no longer criminals but prisoners of war."

Most of the prisoners were immensely relieved at his departure. But there was no prisoner release, and Roberts was crushed. Bobby Garwood had assured him that if he behaved correctly he would be freed, his hopes had soared; now he kept to himself, avoiding contact with the others.

Notwithstanding Ho's decree that they now were POWs, the men remained deprived, hungry, sick. Nothing was done to improve their lot. They also remained leaderless. Some were unable to work; others simply refused to work; and others found themselves carrying what they deemed an unfair share of the burden, gathering all the firewood and manioc and making all the fires. There was constant and increasingly vicious bickering over the division of labor. The prisoners divided into factions—cliques. Physical strength became all important. For long periods, the strong would not provide manioc for those who were too weak to gather their own, and some even took from others the rice that their captors provided.

Life continued to deteriorate, and so did the prisoners. Once, a prisoner who was roasting a piece of manioc left it untended for a moment and returned to find a small bite missing from it. He demanded to know who had eaten it.

"I did," Kushner confessed. The doctor was nearly sick with remorse.

The man was enraged. "If you weren't so small and skinny," he said, "I'd kill you."

Kushner nodded. He was nearly in tears, and seemed almost to be speaking to himself. "You know, I probably regret doing that more than anything else I have ever done in my life."

The man stood staring at him. Then, mollified, he said, "Forget it."

But Kushner could not forget it. The thought that he actually had stolen food from a fellow prisoner was almost more than he could bear. He began telling himself and repeating to them all, "You must be above your environment. Don't let it make an animal out of you."

But the environment wore men down. Kushner warned the camp commander that prisoners would die unless conditions were radically improved. The warning was ignored. Shortly, when the first man to die expired in Kushner's arms, the camp commander sent emissaries with white burial clothing. Tearfully, angrily, Kushner refused to accept it. "You wouldn't give him clothing when he was alive," he shouted. "We'll bury him as he lived. Why don't you give clothing to the living, who need it?"

Then, Top died. Then a young Marine began to swell up, as Top had swollen. A stinking serum ran constantly from his scrotum, from the insides of his thighs, and from his calves. He stopped eating altogether. Kushner warned him, "If you don't eat, there is no way you can survive. You've got to try. You've got to want to live." Finally, one night, Kushner was awakened and told the boy was in distress. He cradled the lad's head in his arms and asked, "Do you know what's happening to you?"

"Yeah, Doc, I'm dying."

"Is there any message that you want me to give to your loved ones?"

"Doc," the boy breathed, "just tell them where I've been. Just tell them where I've been." Then he was gone.

Again, angrily, tearfully, Kushner warned the camp commander that all his prisoners would die unless proper medical attention and a proper diet were forthcoming.

And nothing changed.

————

After being captured during the Tet offensive, Mike Benge, the AID agriculture advisor, Betty Ann Olsen, the missionary nurse, and Hank Blood, the missionary linguist, had walked the jungle trails together for months. At first, the three were kept chained together, but their North Vietnamese Army escorts, who ate well themselves, kept the prisoners on a starvation diet until they were too weak to attempt escape. Then the chains were removed. The diet was not improved, though; it was always a small serving of rice and manioc, only occasionally a small piece of fish or meat—terrapin, iguana, or gibbon ape.

That spring of 1968 the party camped by a river. Here, Benge contracted malaria. For most of thirty-five days, he remained delirious or blind. Betty Ann cared for him, keeping him warm when the chills shook him, feeding him, bathing him. At length, the attacks began to subside.

Betty Ann was seized with a fever, headache, and severe pains in the joints and muscles. She diagnosed dengue fever. She rested as much as she was allowed to, increased her fluid intake, and recovered within a few weeks.

The party kept moving all summer, trending southwesterly. Betty Ann and Hank both developed malaria; Hank, who at fifty-three was sixteen years older than Mike and twenty years older than Betty Ann, seemed to get much sicker than they did and to have more difficulty recovering. In addition to the malaria, the terrible jungle skin disease tore ugly running sores into him, and these itched maddeningly. Their North Vietnamese captors would do nothing for them, and there was little the Americans could do for each other except to huddle together for warmth against the cold monsoon rains which now were upon the land.

One morning Blood complained of chest pains. Betty Ann examined him and told Benge the older man had pneumonia. A short walk away was a Communist base camp, complete with hospital facilities. Mike pleaded with the officer in charge of the group that Blood be taken there. His pleas were denied. It took Hank three days to die. He was buried in a shallow, unmarked grave beside a jungle trail. Mike and Betty Ann were allowed to say prayers over the grave. Then the party moved on.

They crossed into Cambodia, turned north, then east. By late summer, they were back in the vicinity of Ban Me Thuot, where they had been captured. By now, scurvy had loosened their teeth, and their gums bled constantly. Mike and Betty Ann were covered with running sores; their hair had turned white and came out by the fistful. Betty Ann was anemic and suffering terribly from dysentery. They wondered to what purpose they had traveled and suffered all these months; they seemed to be going nowhere.

Still, they encouraged each other and tried to keep each other's spirits up. Mike told Betty Ann of his family's ranch in Oregon and of his three-year hitch in the Marine Corps. Betty Ann told Mike of growing up in Africa's Ivory Coast, where her parents were missionaries. They starved. They chewed at pieces of buffalo hide they found on the mountain trails; and they grabbed bamboo shoots and munched at them.

Ill and tired himself, Mike worried more and more about Betty Ann. She seemed to be giving out. Their captors showed her no mercy. When she lagged on the trails, they would slap her, knock her down, pick her up, drag her. She kept getting to her feet, moving on.

The monsoon rains hatched out the worst scourge of the Asian jungle, the bloodsucking leech. By September the jungle foliage was covered with them. They were shiny black, and some were enormous. They brushed off by the hundreds onto all who passed. One day Mike found himself following a trail of blood—anemic, dysentery-wracked Betty Ann's. When they made camp that evening, she was too weak to pick off the leeches that covered her. Mike removed them, then tried to carry water from a nearby creek to bathe her. He was not strong enough, though, and could get no help. Again he implored the officer in charge, pointing out that there was a North Vietnamese battalion encamped close by. Surely, it would have a doctor or a medic who could help Betty Ann. Perhaps he would have some medicine, some food for her, something. She was dying. The officer in charge was not interested.

Betty Ann was five days dying. Like Hank Blood, she was laid in a shallow, unmarked grave near a jungle trail. Mike prayed over her. Then the party moved on.

Alone now, Mike developed beriberi. His legs swelled so that he could barely lift them. When he came to a log he had to sit down and lift one leg at a time over it with his hands; and he dared not sit down unless there was a tree close by, so he could pull himself up again. His captors continued to do nothing for him but to keep him moving and to feed him a small ration of rice daily. It occurred to him that they were waiting for him to die. But, suddenly, he knew something they didn't know; he was not going to die. Someone had to survive, to make it known what had happened to Hank Blood and Betty Ann Olsen. It was up to him and he would do it, no matter what it took. He would do it by putting one foot ahead of the other, living one hour at a time, for as many steps and years as it took. He was going to do it.

They walked on, into a village near the Cambodian border. The wretched prisoner was displayed to the locals. "Look at this American,'' his guards shouted. ''He's been riding in cars and airplanes too long. He can't walk.''

Benge, who was fluent in Vietnamese, spoke up in reply: ''It is not true,'' he shouted. ''I have walked halfway across your country. These men have starved me almost to death. I have beriberi and dysentery and malaria, and they have given me no medicine, no care of any kind. And yet I am alive, and I go whereever they take me.''

The villagers muttered among themselves. The soldiers hustled Benge out of the place. They took him back into Cambodia, which they called the Land of Milk and Honey. Large numbers of North Vietnamese troops were on the roads of the supposedly neutral country. In his determination to survive, Mike became expert at spotting, snatching, and gulping down edible nuts and fruits, as he moved along jungle trails. For protein, he ate certain of the insects he found beneath the bark of trees. He discovered, when he was allowed to bathe in streams, that fish would clean the running sores on his arms and legs, nibbling away the dead flesh; then he would grab the fish and eat them raw.

One day the party reached a large clearing in the Cambodian jungle. It was a major North Vietnamese base with a sizable hospital. The doctors used Benge for demonstration purposes in training a group of combat medics. Benge was diagnosed as having acute malnutrition, beriberi, and scurvy. He was also badly dehydrated, and the first order of business was to rectify this condition. An attempt was made to infuse a bottle of sugar water into him intravenously. A doctor had great difficulty finding a vein in the patient's bony arm, and so shrunken were the veins that the fluid was accepted only very slowly. When after an hour little more than a spoonful had gotten into Mike, a doctor removed the needle, poured the remaining contents of the bottle into a bowl, and ordered the patient to drink it.

The demonstration completed, Mike was ushered to a cagelike hut in a stockade area of the base. U.S. Army Lt. Steve (Stephen R.) Leopold (captured on May 9, 1968), a Green Beret officer who occupied a cage of his own, watched Benge approach. He guessed him to be sixtyish, with his white hair and beard, and the way he used a stick to help himself walk. Soon, the two were communicating. Benge discovered that Leopold knew Latin, and was anxious to learn the language.

Leopold's presence in a Communist cage was ironic. Only twenty-four, he was not long away from the campus of Stanford

University, where in 1965 and 1966 he had been editor of the *Daily*. In that capacity, he had mounted cogent stands against the conduct of the war, and had favored restricting the American involvement to military advisors, to train the South Vietnamese to fight their own war. Like many other editorialists of the time, he had not had his way.

Finishing at Stanford, Leopold had been accepted by graduate schools at both Harvard and Columbia, to study international relations. He had been tired of school, though, and despondent after his girlfriend jilted him. An idealist, Leopold had thought hard about joining the Peace Corps; he had not done so because he had been unable to see any value for underdeveloped countries in his educational background of history and political science. It had occurred to him that Army Special Forces, the Green Berets, were a sort of armed Peace Corps, engaged as they were in civic action programs that included teaching people to defend themselves. And so here he was, encaged in Cambodia, his camp in South Vietnam's tri-border area with Cambodia and Laos having been overrun by North Vietnamese regulars a month after his arrival in the country.

He began teaching Latin to Benge: *"Illegitimae non carborundum"*—"Don't let the bastards wear you down!"

Fidel, Kasler, and the Faker

At the Zoo, in Hanoi, the one whom the prisoners believed to be Cuban and whom they called Fidel had been busy. The prisoners were never to be certain of the Latin's mission, but they generally agreed that it was to teach the North Vietnamese how to handle captured American military men; and to learn as much as possible on the same subject on behalf of his own government, whatever it was.

Fidel had selected a dozen or so American prisoners and had dealt with them one by one. He attempted to browbeat the men into yielding military information and cooperating in Hanoi's propaganda campaign. It seemed clear, at first, that he did not want to brutalize the men; perhaps Hanoi's mysterious ally wanted to demonstrate that mind and will were more effective than hell cuffs and torture ropes. In any event, the prisoners judged this to be the case, and one by one set their own minds and wills to frustrate Fidel. And he thus proved unable to show his hosts, the Vietnamese, any results. Defeated, furious, he turned to savagery, directing horrendous torture and beatings. So intense was the mistreatment that each prisoner had finally acquiesced to Fidel's enraged demand to "Surrender!"

But not unconditionally. For example, the senior ranking officer of the group, Air Force Maj. Jack Bomar, a navigator, when asked to write on the Doppler method of navigating aircraft, produced two pages of spurious biography on "the system's inventor, a German named Erick Von Doppler, who used to listen to trains. . . ."*

Fidel insisted that the American criminals become more self-sufficient. Therefore, he said, they would raise their own fish. They were made to dig two "breeding ponds," each about ten feet long and four feet wide. When each hole had been filled with water, Fidel produced a supply of approximately 350 tiny fish, each perhaps an inch and a half long. These fish, Fidel explained, would grow to a length of three feet and would weigh twelve pounds.

When Fidel finished speaking, someone noticed that the water in the ponds was so muddy that the fish could not swim in it; they were clustering at the surface, dying. At Fidel's frantic commands, the prisoners tried to use mosquito nets to lift the fish out of their mud-baths. It didn't work; the netting engulfed the fish in sticky mud, and soon there was mud all over the prisoners, the guards, Fidel, and the yard. Washtubs were brought out. The prisoners descended into the mudpits with pails and bailed them out. They picked fish out of the mud, cleaned them off and threw them into the washtubs. About 120 fish were salvaged. Like the American prisoners, whom the fish were eventually supposed to nourish, the fish were to find themselves occupied mainly with survival. They were to do none of the spectacular growing Fidel predicted, and no American was ever to taste any of them.

Fidel was full of ideas for prisoner self-sufficiency. He decided that the inmates should build a bakery and bake their own bread. Two of his criminals, Norlan Daughtrey and Ed Hubbard, immediately represented themselves as bakery-building experts and were placed in charge of construction. The project consumed most of two months. A sort of mud-adobe oven was built, with a chimney about eight feet high. It was an impressive-looking structure, but midway through construction, an amazed Jack Bomar observed to Hubbard, "Ed, that will never work. You don't have the chimney connected with the oven."

"That's right," Hubbard mumbled, nodding vigorously. "Never work."

---

*The Doppler effect was discovered by Christian Johann Doppler, a nineteenth-century Austrian physicist.

The prisoners, while they enjoyed being outside, breathing fresh air, getting exercise and a chance to communicate with each other, had no intention of producing construction their captors were sure to cite as examples of Hanoi's "lenient and humane treatment."

As construction of the oven advanced, Daughtrey and Hubbard kept feeding Fidel's pride in the project, assuring him that his brainchild would produce more bread than the miracle of the loaves and fishes. When construction was completed, Fidel and the camp officials gathered before it for a ceremonious first-baking. Cooks built a fire. The fire immediately went out, and a large cloud of stinking, black smoke billowed forth and rolled into the sky. The prisoners and some anxious cooks fiddled for at least an hour with the oven, trying to get the fire going again. Finally Fidel stormed away. The Latin knew that somehow he had been had, but he never was to figure out why the bakery wouldn't work.

Fidel's prisoners made coal balls for cooking. These were about the size of snowballs and were made by kneading together coal dust, mud, and small amounts of water. When the going got slow, the prisoners complained that they needed additional help and more prisoners were asigned to the task. The communications network spread. Soon the Fidel prisoners knew the names of the entire inmate population of the Zoo and Zoo Annex, a prison compound that had been built directly behind the west wall of the Zoo.

The Fidel prisoners shared a large cell in the Stable and were allowed to speak to each other. One day, when the group returned from a work session, a message was flashed from the Pool Hall, a few yards to the west: "While you were gone, there was a lot of activity in your room and the room next to it. We could not see, but we heard an electric drill going all day."

The prisoners gathered in the center of the cell and, in whispered conversation, decided that Fidel probably had bugged the place. Silently, they went over the room inch by inch. They found nothing. Still, most felt certain that listening devices had been installed, that Fidel hoped to show the Vietnamese how to keep themselves abreast of prisoner communications. Then someone in the Pool Hall flashed a message that Fidel and two Vietnamese had just moved stealthily into the room next to them. The Fidel prisoners instantly devised a new communications policy: no talking about anything even remotely important. All such conversation was now to be hand-flashed back and forth across the room, or, when speed was essential softly whispered while others engaged in loud conversation about innocuous matters.

One day Fidel, clearly frustrated, blurted to Jack Bomar, "Everytime you want to talk about something important, you talk secret. Everything else is very loud!''

For the most part, however, life with Fidel was worse than grim. Once, when the Fidel prisoners were divided into small groups and taken off to different work projects, Bomar and Daughtrey found themselves listening to the sounds of an awful beating being administered inside a stall in a small bath area. It went on and on, amidst shrieks of unrestrained rage and the sounds of fists and other things smashing against flesh and bone. The noise chilled the blood and spirit. After a long time, Fidel emerged from the stall and, spotting Bomar, shouted, "We've got a fucker that's faking! Nobody's gonna fake and get away with it!'' The Latin launched on a lengthy tirade, describing how the prisoner had been pretending illness and injury to avoid interrogation and work. "I'm gonna teach you all a lesson,'' he vowed. "I'm gonna break this guy in a million pieces! He's gonna eat, he's gonna bow, he's gonna work, he's gonna do everything we say! He's gonna surrender, just like all of you surrendered!''

A Vietnamese guard brought the man from the stall. The sight of the prisoner stunned Bomar; he stood transfixed, trying to make himself believe that human beings could so batter another human being. The man could barely walk; he shuffled slowly, painfully. His clothes were torn to shreds. He was bleeding everywhere, terribly swollen, and a dirty, yellowish black and purple from head to toe. The man's head was down; he made no attempt to look at anyone. He was taken into the cell the Fidel prisoners shared, and Fidel grabbed Bomar by the arm and hustled him in, too, ordering him to "Shake hands with your comrade!'' Bomar introduced himself, offering his hand. The man did not react. He stood unmoving, his head down. Fidel smashed a fist into the man's face, driving him against the wall. Then he was brought to the center of the room and made to get down onto his knees. Screaming in rage, Fidel took a length of black rubber hose from a guard and lashed it as hard as he could into the man's face. The prisoner did not react; he did not cry out or even blink an eye. His failure to react seemed to fuel Fidel's rage and again he whipped the rubber hose across the man's face.

Bomar was nearly physically ill at what he saw happening, and at his helplessness to stop it. Again and again and again, a dozen times, Fidel smashed the man's face with the hose. Not once did the fearsome abuse elicit the slightest response from the prisoner. Bomar began to realize that the man was not really there, that somehow his brain had tuned out the pain and damage—and everything else. At last, Fidel ordered, "Take him down and clean him up!"

Bomar helped the battered prisoner to a bath stall. In the stall was a concrete tank containing some dirty water, and a pail. Bomar had some soap. He got the man undressed and found that he had been through much more than the day's beatings. His body was ripped and torn everywhere; hell cuffs appeared almost to have severed the wrists, strap marks still wound around the arms all the way to the shoulders, slivers of bamboo were embedded in the bloodied shins and there were what appeared to be tread marks from the hose across the chest, back, and legs. Horrified, Bomar was afraid to touch him, for fear of causing him more pain. He spoke softly, trying to comfort the man, to let him know that he was now in friendly hands, that he wanted to help him and make him comfortable.

The man did not react. He did not open his eyes or say anything. He simply sat, head down. Gently, Bomar cleaned him up as best he could. Then, suddenly, Fidel burst into the stall, grabbed Bomar, pushed him out of the place, and began beating the man again. He kept driving his fist into his face, slamming him against the walls and down onto his knees. Then he stalked away, leaving Bomar to get him back to the cell.

The other Fidel prisoners returned from their work details. As Bomar described what had happened, the new man remained mute, his head down, his eyes closed, his teeth clenched tightly together. It was as though he were alone in a world of his own. None of the others knew him or anything about him. All that was known was that he was an American, that unspeakable horrors had been done to him, and that he needed all the solace and help they could provide.

His belongings were delivered. His blankets and clothing were covered with dried blood, pus, and waste matter. A bed was made for him and he was made to lie down. The others discussed what to do. Somehow he had to be brought back from wherever it was that Fidel and his colleagues had driven him. He needed to be kept clean, to be fed, and to be nursed back to physical and mental health.

The bowing program was in full swing. Guards were opening cells dozens of times daily just for the pleasure of seeing the American criminals bow to them. The Fidel prisoners lost no time coming to their feet and bending in obeisance, but the new arrival would not so much as acknowledge that the cell door had opened. Unfailingly, the offended guard would stride to his bunk, grab him by the neck of his shirt, pull him up, and slap him hard across the face. The others winced with every blow; some muttered fears for their own sanity if the assault on the man continued.

The man would say nothing and do nothing. The others took turns feeding him, trying to talk to him, soothing him, and offering encouragement. He ate, and at length he opened his eyes. But he kept his head down, staring blankly, and kept his silence, keeping his teeth clenched tightly when he was not eating.

Then, suddenly, he spoke. Somehow, someone had come by a banana—a prize!—and proposed to feed it to him. Through teeth that remained clenched, he said, "There is a microphone in the banana."

The others gathered round, certain that a turning point had been reached and that important ground was about to be gained. Eagerly they broke the banana open in front of him, showing that there was no microphone in it. He refused to accept this, and refused to eat the banana. Again he fell silent, unresponsive.

Days later, he spoke again, muttering as if to himself, that the room seemed to be full of people who "look like Americans."

"We *are* Americans," Bomar assured him. "We have gone through a lot of what you have gone through. We are all in the same boat."

"They changed your hands," the man replied. "They changed your face. They needed your face and hands. There are gas jets in the wall."

"Our hands are okay...."

"You are all Russians, Russian actors on a stage. The sun goes too fast. There it goes, across the sky."

Now he refused to eat. Bomar and the others could get nowhere with him. Only occasionally would he say, "I know what you are doing. I know you want my hands. I know you are going to kill me. Why don't you go ahead and do it? Kill me."

"He's faking!" raged Fidel. The Latin took the man out onto the porch of the Stable along with Bomar, to warn him that he had to stop faking. The man did not answer. He stared downward, behaved as though Fidel were not present. Fidel's rage mounted. He ranted at the man, screaming. "He's faking. I know he's faking, and I'm gonna prove it!"

The man was removed to a hospital.

———

The events of March 31, 1968, the halting of the American air campaign against North Vietnam and President Johnson's announcement that he would not seek another term in the White House were trumpeted to the American POWs as evidence that Hanoi's cause was prevailing. The antiwar movement was succeeding beyond expectations. There was no other way to interpret events.

Generally, however, the American prisoners interpreted the news differently. Most took it for granted that the Communists had come to terms with Johnson, that some sort of acceptable agreement had been reached, that the war was in its climactic stages, and that they soon would be home. The prisoners were full of optimism. Typically, Jack Bomar found himself speaking freely to one whom the prisoners called Pancho. Pancho, too, was Latin, of average height, but powerfully built and with a big, shaggy black beard. Whatever his purpose in Hanoi, he was not an interrogator. He merely wanted to talk to Americans, and sought Bomar's reaction to the bombing halt.

"The President didn't stop the bombing without concessions," Bomar told him. "There is no doubt in my mind about that. And I'm the concession. I don't know what the other concessions are, but the release of the POWs is primary. We'll be out of here within ninety days."

Fidel entered the room where Pancho and Bomar were talking just as the American uttered the word "concessions." He grabbed Bomar by the shoulder and threw him to the floor, roaring furiously, "*Concessions?* Never! The Vietnamese have absolutely defeated the United States. You will never leave here!"

The next morning Bomar was summoned from the cell. The long Stable porch was crammed with Vietnamese, armed guards and men and women who worked around the camp. Bomar knew he was in for a brutal session. He was made to kneel on the ground, hands in the air. Fidel strode before him, delivering a long, angry lecture on "concessions." At last he said, "Now, we are going to teach you what concessions really are!" With that he drove a roundhouse blow straight into Bomar's face, sending him sprawling. Guards brought him back up onto his knees. Again Fidel smashed him in the face, and again the prisoner was brought back up onto his knees.

The spectators appreciated the show, laughing and shouting encouragement to Fidel.

Now the Latin stepped behind Bomar with the length of rubber hose and lashed him hard, just below the kidneys. Then a second blow. Bomar was down again, writhing in the dirt, wondering how much of the rubber hose he could stand. He was yanked up onto his knees again, and Fidel was screaming for Daughtrey.

Daughtrey was made to kneel in the dirt beside Bomar. Fidel smashed a fist into his face, guards pulled him back onto his knees, and Fidel lashed him across the back with the hose. Then the Latin stood behind Bomar again, lashed him again with the hose, and screamed for Rice (Navy Ens. Charles D. "Chuck" Rice, captured on October 26, 1967). Rice was smashed in the face and lashed with the hose. Then, again, Fidel stood behind Bomar and laid the hose across his back.

One by one, each of the Fidel prisoners was brought before the crowd, made to kneel, smashed in the face, and lashed once with the rubber hose. Each time, Bomar was lashed once again.

At last the physical punishment ended. The Americans all were on their knees, their hands high. Down the steps came Lump, the Zoo camp commander. He walked to Bomar, poked a finger close to his face, and shouted, "Jackasses, these are your concessions!" Then he disappeared.

The prisoners were kept on their knees for perhaps thirty minutes while Fidel harangued them, warned them to put out of their minds any thoughts that they might be leaving soon. Then all but Bomar were ordered back into their cell. Bomar was treated to additional histrionics, and finally Fidel smashed him sprawling one last time and ordered him back to the cell.

After most of two weeks, the man whom Fidel said was "faking" was returned from the hospital to the cell the Fidel prisoners shared in the Stable. He was an unkempt, malodorous mess. He had several huge boils on his back and hip. The camp medic, a Vietnamese whom the prisoners called Slasher, tore the cores out of the boils. Using some sort of rusty instrument, he cut deeply, drawing blood, ripping out patches of skin and draining pus. The prisoner never winced. When the medic left, the others ground up sulfa pills they had begged and stashed away and dusted the powder into the gaping wounds.

Within a few weeks many of the group were covered with boils. Ed Hubbard had more than two hundred, from the top of his head to the soles of his feet. He was in an agony that worsened when he moved;

he could not walk, sit, or lie down without causing himself terrible pain. Still, he kept moving, helping with the cleanup chores, trying to take care of himself.

Bomar had forty-four boils, including four in one armpit and an especially painful one on a little finger. Using a bamboo needle he opened this one to drain it. Soon angry red streaks painted the arm, signaling blood poisoning. He became terribly ill. Slasher carved into the little finger, the poison flew out of it, and the illness receded.

Amazingly, Larry Spencer, who was waiting hand and foot on the "Faker," developed no boils. He scrubbed the man's clothing, bathed him, and stayed close to him, tending to his every need, but remaining free of infection. He kept looking after the man in the face of enormous frustration.

The bowing program remained in effect, and the guards enforced it with what the prisoners called "fan belts"—actually rubber whips cut out of old tires. One day the door to the Fidel prisoners' cell opened thirty-nine times, requiring seventy-eight bows, one each time a guard entered, a second when he indicated that he was leaving. All delivered these bows except the Faker. Each time he failed to bow, the offended guard would slap him, punch him, or lash the rubber whip across his face. His face and head were ripped bloody, but he never once gave the slightest indication that he felt any of these blows.

The others kept caring for the man, worrying about him, worrying about their own abilities to maintain emotional stability while being forced to witness such grisly treatment and wondering how to stop the slow murder. SRO Bomar pleaded with Fidel time and again to make the Latin believe the truth, that the man was not faking, that no one who was faking could suffer such punishment without reacting. "Give up on him," Bomar urged. "Let us take care of him."

Fidel would have none of it. "The fucker is faking," he insisted. And the horror continued. Apparently Fidel needed some "victories." He remained determined to break the Faker, to win his "surrender."

———

"The food has gotten much better," the interrogator Spot observed, smiling, to Jim Kasler. Kasler, the Korean War ace who had led the first strikes against Hanoi's oil depots two years earlier, studied Spot. He knew him to be a sadist, and judged him to be homosexual. He hated him, with a quiet, intense hatred, and knew that the feeling was mutual. He wondered why Spot was attempting to be friendly; why the smile and the inane conversation?

Suddenly Spot announced: "My major has directed me to find a man to meet a delegation and make a TV appearance on the occasion of the downing of the 3,000th enemy airplane over our country. And so who should I think of but you, of course, which is quite an honor for you."

"Bullshit. I'm not going to see any goddamn delegation."

"You have no choice. You are in our hands now. We have kept you alive, now you owe this to us."

"I owe you nothing." Kasler was terribly ill from the infection in his leg. Nonetheless, he had been subjected to prolonged, brutal torture and beatings. Only recently, Spot had beaten him to a pulp, then had kept him on his knees for the rest of the day, allowing him a five-minute rest break each hour because of his leg infection. This, the sadist had explained, was in keeping with the humane and lenient treatment.

Spot got up to leave the room, handing Kasler an English-language Vietnam *Courier*. Kasler read of the assassination of Sen. Robert F. Kennedy. He was trying to digest this shocking news, when Spot returned to demand his "final decision." Kasler advised that he already had it. He would make no appearances, before people or cameras.

Spot clapped him in the Ho Chi Minh Room, the filthy, darkened cell in the Auditorium. The next day he was summoned again to interrogation. The table was laden with torture paraphernalia—ropes, leg irons, and three different sets of cuffs, all of them different sizes.

"You can torture me, you can drag me before that delegation," Kasler said, "but I'm not going to say a goddamn word when I get there. And I'm not making a TV appearance."

Spot supervised the torture. Lump came in to observe, as guards lashed Kasler's arms behind him so that the backs of the wrists met, and hell cuffs were ratcheted on down tò the bones. Then ropes were pulled on, bone-tight, from the elbows to the shoulders and his arms pulled tightly together. The prisoner suffered this excruciation in silence. Spot kept urging him to put an end to his discomfort; all he need do was agree to meet with a delegation.

Kasler tried to concentrate on not thinking about the awful pain in his wrists; other prisoners, he knew, found the pain in the shoulders and chest to be the worst, but for him the hell cuffs were the worst.

After perhaps forty-five minutes, the cuffs and ropes were removed, and Kasler was made to kneel for a beating. Then another, smaller set of hell cuffs was ratcheted on. The pain was worse this time; after about half an hour it was intolerable, and he lost consciousness. When he awakened, the cuffs were being removed. He was allowed fifteen minutes' rest, then was given another beating. Hell cuffs were reapplied and this time, somehow, the pain was intensified. He passed out within a few minutes.

"Do you surrender? Do you surrender?" Spot was asking him when he regained consciousness. The cuffs had been removed. A guard stood over him, holding them.

Sick, bathed in pain, Kasler could take no more. He muttered, "Okay, I surrender."

Abruptly, the torture guard pulled him up onto his knees, pulled his arms behind him, and ratcheted the cuffs back onto his wrists, down to the bones. Again he passed out.

He was awakened and again asked, "Do you surrender?"

Again he surrendered, but again it was as though he had not spoken; again he was tortured to unconsciousness. This happened several times. At last the torture guard pulled him up onto his knees, threw a rope around his neck, and began garroting him. Unable to breathe, he lost consciousness. He awakened to find the guard slapping his face, and Spot continuing to ask, "Do you surrender?"

"Yes," he said again. Finally the torture ended. Kasler judged that he had been tortured as long and as intensively after first saying that he surrendered as he had been before.

It took him several hours to regain the use of his hands. Then he was instructed to copy out the questions that would be put to him, and the answers he was to supply:

    Q. Who captured you?
    A. Mostly unarmed women and children.
    Q. What have you observed since you have been in this camp?
    A. I have seen hundreds of new prisoners arrive in this camp, and it is obvious that our bombing has been fruitless because Vietnamese production is up on all fronts. We now get fruit, sugar, beer and a lot of extras with our diet.

Another question required that he assert that the United States was waging an "illegal, immoral and unjust war."

On July 2, he was brought before Lump, who advised that Kasler would be presented to a visiting delegation. Kasler replied, "You can torture me all you want and take me before the delegation, but when I get there I'm not going to say a goddamn word.''

Lump pushed a set of glossy photographs across the table, inviting Kasler to look at them. These were ·pictures of large antiwar demonstrations in the United States. Protesters held high placards inscribed "End the War," "Stop the Slaughter," "Get the Troops Out," even "Communist Party USA." But in one photograph Kasler spotted two elderly gentlemen wearing American Legion caps who had worked their way into the middle of a howling, antiwar mob. They smilingly held up a placard inscribed "Drop the Bomb." Grinning, Kasler repeated that he would not be cooperative in any appearance he was forced to make before a delegation. Confused, Lump returned him to the Ho Chi Minh Room.

The next dawn, July 3, the camp medic entered Kasler's cell to bandage his draining leg. Jim knew what this meant; it was always done prior to torture, to keep. the blood and pus from staining the interrogation room.

Within an hour he was in torture. Lump entered, pulled up a stool, and sat down next to the prisoner's head. "Now, Kasler," he said, "I am going to enjoy this." Kasler was alternately put in hell cuffs and ropes, then beaten. Once, guards were standing on his wrists, trying to squeeze them into a smaller pair of cuffs, when a voice said, "Kasler!"

It was Fidel. Jim had seen him in the street once the previous September examining torture equipment and talking with Lump. And he had heard much about him from fellow prisoners. Now, it seemed, he was to be handed over to the Latin. Fidel reached down, grabbed Jim by the neck of his shirt, and shook him like a rag doll. "What do you think you're pulling, you motherfucker? What kind of shit are you trying to pull?"

Fidel seemed beside himself with rage. He kept screaming obscenities. Then he slammed the heel of his boot down into the center of Kasler's chest. Intense pain exploded up through the shoulder and down the arm to the hand. Jim gasped, fought for air, felt certain he was having a heart attack and was going to die.

Torture guards kept stuffing rags into his mouth. He had not cried out, but many did in torture, and the Vietnamese did not like it. He kept spitting the rags out onto the floor, and guards kept trying to replace them in his mouth. After a while, when he still had not screamed, they stopped trying to gag him.

"Why are you doing this, you motherfucker?" Fidel shrieked. "Why won't you cooperate?"

"You won't make a traitor out of me!" Kasler muttered. "You're not going to make me betray my country!"

After a while Fidel ordered the cuffs and ropes removed. Kasler sat at the table before him. "Who knows you're here?" the Latin asked.

"Nobody."

"Then why are you pulling this shit? You don't have to go through this. You'll go before the delegation."

"I refuse," Kasler said.

Shifting psychological gears, Fidel asked, "You want a drink of water?"

"Yes." Having sweated through the tortures, Jim was completely dehydrated.

Guards brought water. Fidel turned a small table fan on Kasler and gave him a cigarette. At length the Latin said, "Okay, when you go before the delegation . . ."

"Forget it," said Kasler. "I'm not doing anything."

"Back on your knees!" yelled Fidel.

Guards administered another beating. He was squeezed again into hell cuffs and torture ropes. He lay in agony, trying to concentrate on something other than the pain that assailed him. He tried to fling his mind into the past; he thought about pies his mother used to make, picnics with his wife and children. He recited the Lord's Prayer to himself, thinking through the meaning of each word and thought. Then Fidel was low on the floor next to him, asking, "Do you want to take a bath?"

"Yeah."

"Are you gonna surrender?"

"No."

He was taken out of torture. Fidel ordered him to go to the bath area, clean up, and "change those filthy clothes. You smell like a pig!"

Jim turned to leave. Fidel leaped from behind the table, grabbed him, whirled him about, and slapped him hard across the face. He pointed out that Kasler had started through the door ahead of one of the Vietnamese guards. "Show a little respect," said the Latin.

After the bath he was returned to the interrogation room. Kasler again advised Fidel he was not going before any delegation.

"On your knees!"

This time, after the hell cuffs were on, Jim's thumbs were wired together. Ropes were tied around his elbows. A guard stood in front of him, put a foot on his head to hold him down, and lifted his arms slowly, until they seemed to be in a ball behind his head. The pain was the worst he had known yet. It engulfed him, yet he could feel it all, the wires cutting the thumbs, the cuffs biting through the skin and into bone, the shoulders turning, turning, agonizingly, in a direction they were not meant to turn. But he did not cry out—he would not give his tormentors that satisfaction. And so it continued—and got worse. Even tighter torture cuffs were applied and fists were smashed repeatedly into his face.

He was returned to the Ho Chi Minh Room. There Lump met him with another guard who, having been awarded ten minutes to work over the prisoner, beat him unmercifully. That done, Kasler was made to kneel in the center of the floor, so that guards could observe him from the peephole in the cell door. He lost consciousness, fell, awakened, crawled toward his water jug. He needed water desperately. Before he could reach it, though, the cell door opened and a guard took the jug away. Kasler was made to get back onto his knees. He passed out several times. Each time, guards would enter, revive him, and get him back up onto his knees. Fidel arrived and made him lie face down on the wooden pallet that served as a bed. The Latin unlimbered a heavy rubber whip. Lifting it, he shouted, "The best way to survive is by being aggressive!" With that, he laid the lash across Kasler's buttocks. Then, "Strike the enemy first, before he has a chance to hit you!" Another lash. More quotes, from various newspaper and magazine interviews with Kasler prior to the ace's capture. Kasler writhed under the lash that slammed down into him over and over again. Lost in pain, Kasler paid no heed to what his torturer was saying. He counted the blows, fought down a mounting urge to scream, to vomit. The flogging went on and on, and he was unable to lose consciousness.

After thirty-six lashes, Fidel asked, "Are you going to surrender?"

"No."

"I'll talk to you tomorrow, you son of a bitch!"

Kasler's buttocks, lower back, and legs hung in shreds. The skin had been entirely whipped away and the area was a bluish, purplish, greenish mass of bloody raw meat. Lump came to warn, "Tomorrow, we show you the determination of the Vietnamese people!"

But the next day was July 4 and, in deference to the American holiday, Fidel gave Kasler respite. He was given cigarettes, a beer, and a piece of peanut-brittle-like candy.

Early on the fifth, he was taken to an interrogation room. Fidel was not present, but the ropes were, and a pair of hell cuffs so small that it took the guards about thirty minutes to get them locked onto the emaciated prisoner's wrists. This pain exceeded all that had gone before. Kasler began to fear for his sanity. He was tied back into torture ropes, and his arms were pulled straight out behind him, then pulled upward, toward his shoulders. The ropes were drawn across his shoulders and down around his feet. Then they were pulled tight, until his toes were against his mouth. He remained tied into this agonized ball for a long time. Guards kept slapping him and punching him. He would not surrender. He knew that the torture that came after surrender lasted as long as that which preceded it.

After a long time he was returned to his cell and made to strip down to his shorts. He was locked in leg irons and made to sit on the bed pallet. His hands were left free but they were useless now. The wrists, torn and bloody, looked as though they had almost been severed by the hell cuffs, and the discolored hands and fingers remained so swollen that he could not move them.

That night guards stayed at his cell door, looking in on him every few minutes to make certain he did not lie down or sleep, and that he did not abuse the clouds of mosquitoes that feasted on him. He was kept like that all the next day and next night.

Then, early on the seventh, there was another session with Fidel. "I'll tell you what I'll do," said the Latin. "We'll give you a symbolic torture. I'll bring ten other POWs into this room and we'll torture you. They will see it, then you can surrender. Everyone will know you have been tortured and you will be an honorable man."

"Bullshit," said Kasler.

"You motherfucker!" Fidel shrieked. "You son of a bitch! What kind of shit are you trying to pull, you bastard?"

"I'll never surrender," said Kasler. It occurred to him that he had made a mistake, that he should have agreed to being tortured in front of ten other prisoners, then refused to surrender.

"All right," said Fidel, "you're going to go in front of that delegation if we have to carry you. Either that or I am going to beat you to death!"

That night he was again fed to the mosquitoes. At dawn the next morning, a Vietnamese guard whom the prisoners called Cedric entered the cell. Cedric apparently had been assigned to Fidel as his batman, bootlicker, and errand boy; he fawned on the Latin, and Fidel despised him. Cedric had his own rubber whip. He ordered Kasler to lie on his stomach, then lashed him seven times across his already ravaged buttocks.

Kasler was made to remain in position on the bed pallet. For three days, every hour on the hour from 6 AM until 10 PM, Cedric would supervise as a different guard came to deliver three to four lashes with the rubber whip. Each time, Cedric would treat himself to an additional three to four lashes. Cedric always took his time, extracting enormous pleasure from the exercise and heaping upon the prisoner all the appellations he had heard his idol, Fidel, use on Kasler.

In the three days Kasler was flogged with approximately three hundred more lashes. When he was not being flogged, he was made to sit up on his terrible wounds. At night he was locked in leg irons, and was not allowed to sleep or to do anything against the mosquitoes and flies that were drawn to his blood.

During the flogging at noon on the third day, he knew he was going mad. Suddenly, involuntarily, he said, "I surrender." He had not meant to say it; some conspiracy of mind and body had overcome the will, and the words had escaped him, like a scream. It didn't matter. The flogging continued. He was flogged six more times that day. At each flogging Cedric kept saying, "My commander does not believe you. He believes you lie. Why do you lie?"

That evening he was made to sign a letter in which he assured his captors that he would do everything he was told to do "to the best of my ability." He was locked again in leg irons but he was given a mosquito net and allowed to sleep. The sleep restored him to the extent that by the next morning he was distraught with himself for having surrendered. But for the next several days he kept replying affirmatively when guards opened his peephole to ask if he still surrendered. He hurt so badly that he could not find it within himself to say something that might lead to a resumption of the torture.

Once the peephole opened and he was startled to see an American face. It was Jack Bomar who, along with other Fidel prisoners, was unloading a truck full of melons into another room in the Auditorium. The group had been wondering for days who it was that Fidel had in torture and now, with the guards all in sight and preoccupied, Bomar was finding out. He talked to Kasler for perhaps five minutes, then returned to tell the others who it was and to say, "He looks bad. Bad. Bad."

The guards kept coming to the cell, to ask Kasler if he still surrendered. One day he answered, ''No.''

Within minutes Cedric was in the cell with a crowd of guards. The prisoner was made to kneel with his hands behind his back, and the guards took turns slapping him in the face. Kasler was able to note that several younger guards were unable to contain their disgust at what they saw happening and stole away. The others enjoyed it. Cedric took out his rubber whip and flailed away at him, lashing with abandon across the face, chest, back, and legs. Kasler's left eardrum was ruptured and blood streamed down the side of his face and neck. Once, when he was driven off his knees and fell back against the bed pallet, a guard kicked him in the back; Jim felt a rib break, felt the sharp, breathtaking pain flood through him, overwhelming all the other pain. He rolled on the floor, his arms crossed over his chest, trying to protect himself as the guards continued to kick at him. The floor was puddled with blood and pus, most of it from his infected leg. The guards became aware that the leg was bleeding and draining, and began jumping up and down on it. Only half-conscious now, Jim felt a sharp pain above the hip, where the pin had been inserted down through the thighbone. The guards seemed caught up in a bloodlust; they kept screaming, kicking, and spitting at the prisoner. They would smash his head against the floor and occasionally would pull him to his knees to slug at his face. Periodically Cedric would manage to get the others to stand back so that he could lay away with the whip.

It went on and on, and the prisoner, weak and broken, wondered when death would come; he knew that he surely could not suffer such treatment much longer.

The savagery continued, though, and death did not come. The guards howled and slugged and kicked and spit and whipped, but the prisoner would not die. After what seemed like hours, he lay sprawled, in a stupor. He became aware of an intense physical struggle which did not involve him. Then, suddenly, he was alone. He surmised that other guards had been sent in to pull off those who had seemed bent on his destruction. He lay motionless, wondering whether that was good or bad—what else did the enemy have in store for him?

An hour passed. Guards entered and ordered him onto his knees, hands high in the air. The broken rib filled him with pain, and as he raised his hands this pain intensified. He was warned that if he failed to do as commanded, the beating would be resumed. He stayed on his knees, hands high, until early evening—eight or nine hours. Then he collapsed. He did not lose consciousness. He fell to the floor and lay there, unable to move. Guards entered and threatened him.

"Go ahead and beat me," he muttered. "I don't care."

They lifted him onto his bed pallet, put down a sheet of paper. He wrote, as ordered, "I apologize for surrendering five times and taking back six."

He lay alone for several days in a semi-coma, uninterested in the meals that were shoved into the cell; in any case, his face was so terribly swollen that he could not open his mouth; it was as though his teeth had been cemented shut. Many of the teeth were broken.

Then he found himself in interrogation again, facing Fidel.

"Do you surrender?" the Latin asked.

"Yes."

He was taken to a bath area and allowed to shave and clean up. He was returned to his cell and a bowl of soup was brought to him. There was a large, hard lump in the broth. He poked at it, then lifted it out of the bowl. It was the head of a dog, complete with all the anatomical appurtenances—eyes, nose, ears, teeth, hair. He put the head aside and downed the broth.

There was another interrogation with Fidel in which Kasler replied affirmatively when asked if he still surrendered. That was the end of it. There were no demands to write anything, no insistence that he appear before a delegation. Fidel said, "We're going to take care of your leg."

Kasler said, "Bullshit. You haven't done anything for it for two years and you're not going to now."

Fidel insisted that treatment was in the offing. He tossed a package of Viceroy cigarettes and a package of Juicy Fruit gum on the table and told Kasler to take them. Kasler declined. Fidel grabbed him by the shirtfront and began shaking him. "You take 'em," he shouted, "or I'm gonna beat the shit out of you!" He took them.

He was moved into Cell #11 in the Pigsty. It helped immensely to be able to make contact with other Americans. His old friend and squadronmate, Air Force Capt. Norman L. (Norm) Wells, who had been flying with him the day he was downed and who had been captured himself three weeks later, asked, "Did you hear about Low, Carpenter, and Thompson?"

"No," said Kasler.

"They were released while you were in the Ho Chi Minh Room."

On August 2, the Vietnamese had released Jim Low and two other Air Force officers, Maj. Fred Neale Thompson and Capt. Joe Victor Carpenter, to American antiwar visitors.

———

Having failed to persuade Kasler to write an acceptable paper or to appear before a delegation, Fidel concentrated on breaking the Faker. Jack Bomar told Lump that if the brutal mistreatment of the man continued, he was certain to die. Lump would have none of it. The guards continued their horrendous physical abuse of the prisoner, slapping, punching, or flogging him with the rubber whip whenever he failed to bow. But he would not bow, and now he removed himself as far as possible from association with his fellow prisoners, whom he continued to regard as sinister. He went underneath his blanket, folded himself into a fetal position, and tried to stay there.

Bomar ordered the man to bow to the guards, to eat, to stop withdrawing. He would comply with none of these orders. The Fidel prisoners began dragging him from beneath his blanket and sitting him up on his bunk, against the wall. Men would sit on either side of him and would hold conversations across him on every subject they could think of, hoping that something someone said would capture his attention, draw him out, bring him back. Day after day, the men took him on in teams, talking, watching, waiting, hoping. Nothing worked; nothing was ever said that caused the slightest flicker of interest.

The men had better luck physically exercising him. They would take his arms and legs, push them so as to bend them at the joints, then pull them out. They would stand him up, walk him, sit him down, and force him to do sit-ups. Whatever the exercise, the man resisted strongly. For all concerned, it was a beneficial, sort of isometric, exercise.

Bomar decided that somehow the Vietnamese abuse of the man had to be stopped, that he had to be made to bow when the cell door opened. The others now learned that it is very difficult to bow the head of one who does not want to be bowed. Several men had to exert great effort to accomplish this, lifting him to his feet when a guard entered, then holding him so that one man could put a full nelson on him, hands looped under his arms and up around his neck, forcing his head down. The man would lift his feet and drive his heels against the shins of the one who applied the full nelson. But it worked. The

Vietnamese accepted the forced bowing as a face-saving compromise. The pounding of the man ended.

These efforts to save the Faker induced in him a massive and active hatred for his saviors. As the others continued to exercise him, he kicked them, elbowed them, spit in their faces, slapped and punched at them. Frustrated, the others, some of whom were often sick, all of whom were always weak and hungry, managed to restrain their anger. Now the man refused to eat. He would not be persuaded and after fourteen days he had wasted so that the others decided he had to be force-fed.

There were many unsuccessful experiments, but the man could not be made to open his clenched teeth. He kicked over plates of rice and sent the food lying all over the others and the cell. When he could get his hands on a plate, he would throw it at those who were trying to feed him. He was skin and bones, but when efforts were made to feed him he was always, for a few moments, full of a tremendous strength. Then the energy would ebb and they would feed him, but it still required teamwork, great effort, and patience. For the only way he could be made to open his teeth was to hold him down, hold his nose, and choke him. Then food would be stuffed into his mouth. As often as not, he would spit the food out and come up swinging and kicking.

Fidel departed sometime in August. He was not seen again. Now the Vietnamese concluded that the Faker was not faking. Frequently, a few bananas or cookies would be delivered for him. When the other prisoners would urge these extras upon him, he would sometimes accept them only to fire them back at those who had proffered them. The Vietnamese seemed increasingly frightened over the man's condition. Lump kept asking the other Americans, "What do you want us to do? What is needed?"

One of the group, Navy Lieut. Al Carpenter,* had a plan which Zoo SRO Larry Guarino approved. "Release him," Carpenter suggested. "See that he gets back to the United States, where he will receive proper treatment and care. Do that, and we'll see that the story never gets out about what we saw happen to him here."

The plan was rejected. It seemed clear the man's captors did not want him on view to the world. Lump kept badgering Bomar to write

*Captured on November 1, 1966, Navy Lt. Allen R. Carpenter is not to be confused with Air Force Capt. Joe Victor Carpenter, who was released on August 2, 1968, along with Air Force Maj. James Low and Air Force Maj. Fred Neale Thompson.

of the good treatment the man had received. Bomar kept producing such unsatisfactory statements as "He received two oranges after they stopped beating him with a fanbelt"; or "He was allowed a cookie after they stopped hitting him"; or "Since the beating stopped, he has been given a banana."

Dissension began to seethe within the Fidel group. Some of the men, sick and weary themselves, reached the end of patience with their deranged compatriot. Tired of trying to cope with him, they urged Bomar to demand that he be taken back to the hospital. Bomar agreed that hospital care was in order, but not in Hanoi. He thought it vital that the group retain physical possession of the man. Bomar felt certain that if the man were removed from the company of other Americans, he would never be seen again. Still, for the sake of some of the others, Bomar wanted him in another cell, preferably nearby, with some Americans who would look after him. Larry Spencer and Ed Hubbard volunteered for the job. Bomar, having divined that all good ideas must originate in his captors' heads, tried to emplant this one in Lump's cranium. It didn't take. The disaster continued.

26

Yankees Who Won't Go Home

It seems apparent that the August 1968 Low-Thompson-Carpenter release was not all that Hanoi had hoped for; the Communists had had a Fourth of July propaganda spectacular in mind but despite intensive efforts had failed to enlist the cooperation of the one whom they had scheduled to be the star performer.

In May it had been announced in Washington that on July 4 Adm. John S. McCain, Jr., would succeed Adm. U. S. Grant Sharp as commander-in-chief, Pacific. In Hanoi, at the Plantation, Admiral McCain's POW son, John, was soon visited, separately, by a pair of North Vietnamese generals. Both desired that the younger McCain brief them on his father's career, personal life, family relationships, habits, and so on. The prisoner was generally unresponsive and untruthful with his replies.

McCain mused often on these meetings. He suspected, rightly, that the enemy would maintain a keen interest in him. One night in mid-June, he was summoned to interrogation with Cat, the prison system commander. Cat rambled on at stupefying length about a French prisoner whose release he alleged he had secured years earlier. This

Frenchman, said Cat, had later returned to Hanoi as a member of a peace delegation, and Cat had met him on the street. The man had thanked Cat profusely for obtaining his release and had invited the jailer to visit him at his home in Paris. It was, Cat seemed to think, a heartwarming tale of how two military men who once had been enemies had become friends in humanity. Cat observed that Norris Overly, who, until his release earlier in the year, had shared a cell with McCain, had returned "with honor" to the United States.

Finally, bluntly, Cat asked, "Do you want to be released?"

McCain was thunderstruck. For months, his captors had belabored him with assurances that he was a war criminal, that he was to be tried for his crimes, and that he was never to be allowed to go home. Now he was being offered early release.

Severely injured and in dire need of competent medical attention though McCain was, he felt certain that many in the United States would not believe he had been released for any reason other than that his father was a four-star admiral. And he knew the Vietnamese would use the fact that he had accepted release as a selling point to the remaining POWs.

Still, he was tempted. There seemed no possibility that his captors could or would provide proper medical care for his broken right leg and two broken arms. He now had dysentery and was rapidly losing weight he could ill afford to lose. He was not confident he could long survive if he remained in Hanoi. He told Cat, "I will have to think about it."

He was returned to his cell, where there now was no one with whom he could discuss the matter. After Overly's departure, Bud Day had remained with him until early spring, when McCain's casts had been removed and it was possible for him to hobble about on crutches. Then Day had been moved to the Zoo. He had to make his own decision, and all he was certain of was that he had better be right.

Over the camp radio came the announcement that prisoners were to be released on July 4, in tribute to the American Revolution, which was likened unto the "Vietnamese people's struggle for liberation."

Several nights later, McCain was back in interrogation with Cat and Rabbit. There were cigarettes, tea, and what Communist propagandists would have described as "an atmosphere of happiness and goodwill." After half an hour of pleasant inanities, Cat asked, "Have you considered my offer?"

"Yes."

"What is your answer?"

"I can't accept it."

"Why?"

"Our Code of Conduct tells us that we must not accept parole, or amnesty, or special favors."

"President Johnson has ordered that you go home."

"Show me the orders."

"We don't have them."

"Show me the orders and I will believe it."

Cat handed the prisoner a letter from his wife, Carol. Referring to the Black-Matheny-Overly release, she had written, "I wish you had been one of the three who got to come home." McCain remained adamant; Carol could not know all that was involved in early release.

Cat advised, "The doctors say you cannot live if you do not go home."

"The prisoners must be sent home in the order in which they were captured, starting with Alvarez," said McCain.

The meeting was inconclusive. Cat seemed determined to persuade McCain to leave. On the morning of July 4, there was a final conference in the interrogation room. Rabbit came quickly to the point. "The senior officer wants to know your final answer."

"My final answer is no."

Cat remained silent, stared at the prisoner through rimless glasses. There were papers on the desk before him and he held a fountain pen between his two hands.

"That is your final answer?" Rabbit asked.

"That is my final answer."

Cat snapped the fountain pen in half. Ink spurted onto his fingers and the papers on the desk. He came to his feet, knocking his chair over backward, glaring at McCain and hissing, "They taught you too well! They taught you too well!" Then he stormed from the room, slamming the door behind him.

Rabbit said, "It is going to be very bad for you now, McCain. Go back to your room."

Rabbit was right. Shortly after the Low-Thompson-Carpenter release, which was a month delayed, McCain was taken before a brutish officer whom the prisoners called Slopehead, who was now the Plantation camp commander. Slopehead advised McCain that he was "guilty of black crimes against the people," that he had been "disrespectful to our guards," and that it was time he confessed to his sins.

"Why are you disrespectful to our guards?" Slopehead demanded.

"Because they treat me like an animal," McCain answered.

With that, Slopehead uttered a command and eight or ten guards piled into the prisoner. Howling with laughter, they tried to outdo one another, pounding McCain in the face and body with roundhouse blows, slamming and kicking his mending limbs, battering him from wall to wall and corner to corner. By the time the guards' appetite for inflicting punishment seemed sated, the prisoner lay on the floor, unmoving, a bloody, aching mess. Slopehead asked, "Are you ready to confess your crimes?"

"No."

Guards sat him up on a stool, tied his arms behind him in torture ropes, and left him alone. It was his first time in ropes. He had heard from others how bad they were, but while he found the torture painful it was not intolerable; he thought he might be able to withstand it. Every few hours all through the night he was asked if he was ready to confess. Each time he replied that he had nothing to confess. In the morning the ropes were removed and he was led to a small cell that contained only a waste bucket. Three guards entered. One held him and the other two savaged him, pounding him to a bloody pulp. This exercise was repeated every two to three hours, day and night, for four days. Once when guards entered, he lay exhausted on the floor, full of pain, unable to move. During the beatings, some ribs had been cracked. The abuse had caused his right leg, broken during shoot-down, to become extremely swollen and he could not stand on it. His broken arms, both of which had mended improperly, were too weak to help him to his feet. Still terribly ill with dysentery, he lay in his own waste, unable to reach the bucket. A guard yanked the suffering prisoner to his feet, held him, smashed a fish into his face and sent him sprawling toward the bucket. His left arm landed on it, and broke again.

Left alone, he knew that he was beaten, that he could take no more. He contemplated suicide; had there been a way successfully to take his own life, he would have ended it. There was no way to achieve death, though, and the alternative was to yield. In writing, McCain confessed, "I am a black criminal and I have performed the deeds of an air pirate. I almost died, and the Vietnamese people saved my life, thanks to the doctors . . ."

It was unsatisfactory. "You must put in that you bombed a school," he was told. He refused to do so. The badgering and rewriting went on for a dozen hours. At last a confession was produced in

Communist jargon that was full of generalities, and the weary prisoner signed it. He was distraught with himself; he tried to convince himself that he had been left no choice but to sign, but he could not make himself believe it.

Having thus enlisted the cooperation of the "crown prince," his captors, doubtless comfortable in the certainty that they could rely on him for additional contributions in the future, allowed him to rest. This was a mistake. For two weeks he gathered his strength and mobilized his spiritual resources. Then they came to him for another statement, and he was able to refuse. They were never to be able to break McCain again.

———

For young Doug Hegdahl, 1968 was proving to be an interesting year. In February, after Black, Matheny, and Overly were released, Dick Stratton had sent word to Hegdahl rescinding the orders to leave if the chance presented itself. When he had not gone out with the first three releasees, his head had been shaved, apparently signifying that he was in disgrace. Then he had been installed in a cell with Air Force Maj. Jim Low. After Low, Thompson, and Carpenter had departed, Hegdahl's head was again shaved. Soft Soap Fairy adjured him smugly, "One day you will learn, Heddle. It is not the extent of your crimes, it is the degree to which you repent!" The youngster was led away to solitary confinement.

Later he was summoned again before Soft Soap Fairy, who was visibly upset. Hegdahl knew why. Word had reached him that the Vietnamese had learned that Low had been an ace in the Korean War. "Heddle, what do you know about Jim Low?"

"Jim Low? Well, er . . . ah . . . he's an Air Force major. He was married and divorced and married again. He was a jet ace in the Korean War. He's about six fee . . ."

"What? What do you say about Korea?" Soft Soap Fairy was agitated.

"He was a jet ace. They called him 'Jimmy the Mig-Killer.' You know, I never understood why the Vietnamese people released that man. He hated them. He used to call them gooks. He used to walk around saying, 'The only good gook is a dead gook.' He used to . . ."

"Heddle, Heddle," Soft Soap Fairy shouted, "why did you not tell me of these things?"

"Jeez, I would of, but you never asked!"

He was clapped back in solitary. Lonely, he kept asking for a roommate. He was taken back to interrogation and shown a striped French sailor shirt and a pair of dungarees. "What do you wear in your navy?" he was asked. "Do you wear something like this?"

"Yeah. That's what I wear in my navy."

He was ordered to dress himself in these clothes. He kept asking about a roommate, until he finally was told, "Perhaps. If you do everything properly, you may get a roommate."

Blindfolded, he was led up onto the back of a truck. There were two young guards aboard, the friendliest he was ever to know. As quickly as the truck cleared Hanoi, they pulled up his blindfold, plied him with beer and sandwiches, and tried to talk to him. After a few beers, Hegdahl delighted them with a rendition of "Old MacDonald Had a Farm." The ride lasted most of a day, ending in a village near the seacoast. He was stashed in a pagoda for the night.

The next morning he met the villagers, crowds of friendly, laughing people. At a film director's instructions, the crowds lined up on opposite sides of a path. An interrogator instructed Hegdahl to remove his shoes. Then he stood between his guards and ran down the pathway, and the people jeered him and shook their fists. That done, the crowds moved happily to the seashore. Here it was explained to Hegdahl that he was to climb out of a small boat, anchored a few yards from the shore, and wade "humbly" ashore. The director signaled, and an assistant dumped a pail of water over Hegdahl's head.

Doug did not like the way things were going. He felt uneasy about helping the enemy produce a piece of propaganda and decided against a show of humility. On cue, he came out of the boat, beaming, waving to the delighted crowd, and striding ashore as though he were MacArthur returning to the Philippines.

The director shrieked and the cameras stopped grinding. The director danced before the interrogator, jabbering angrily at him. Again the interrogator explained to Hegdahl that he must come ashore "humbly." Again Doug came wading in smiling and waving, the picture of a conquering hero. The frantic director berated the interrogator. The scene was revised. Doug was made to stand a few feet into the water with two soldiers who were to capture him and bring him ashore.

"Act like you are struggling," Hegdahl was told.

He struggled. Unleashing months of pent-up anger, he pushed one soldier away, dragged the other down into the water, and set about drowning him. The other soldier came back at him, but Doug fought him off, trapped his prey underwater, and gave himself to the joy of doing him in, this representative of all those who had so mistreated the POWs. Then reason overcame emotion and he let the frantic soldier up.

Another scene. Hegdahl's wrists were tied behind him with twine and he was made to march down a path before a small girl armed with a stick. Told to poke at him with the stick, she did so, lightly. Doug looked back at her and winked, and she burst out laughing. The director shrieked, and the little girl started crying. The little girl's mother burst through the crowd, swept the youngster up in her arms, and delivered a blistering tongue-lashing upon the director.

There was a lunch break. Village children surrounded the American, chattering and laughing. He played with them. They would jump back, giggling, when he reached for them, but finally one shook hands with him; Doug lifted the youngster onto his shoulders, and the others crowded in. A member of the filming crew, a man with a Pentax camera, brought his small son to the actor. Doug lifted the lad, and the man took pictures. The kids swarmed on Hegdahl. Large numbers of parents stood close, beaming approval. Then a stony-faced cadre, taking note of the atmosphere of goodwill, strolled into the crowd of parents, glaring and muttering at them. The parents moved in, grabbed their children, and left, some of them shaking their fists in the face of the American commando or air pirate or whatever he was.

The moviemaking resumed. The director continued to find fault with Hegdahl's performance. Once, he spent several minutes screaming angrily in Vietnamese. He strode about, gesticulating, shouting, stamping his feet, slapping his clipboard against his thigh, and delivering himself of opinions to which he clearly thought the American should respond. Then he was silent, though by no means satisfied. There was no question that he wanted Hegdahl to understand every word he had said. He glared at the interpreter, waiting impatiently. The interpreter sighed deeply, turned to Hegdahl, and said, "He is very angry."

That night Hegdahl was returned to solitary confinement in the Plantation. "Where is my roommate?" he asked. "I was told if I did everything properly, I would get a roommate."

"You not satisfactory," he was told. "No roommate!"

———

Endure. Survive. Most who reached captivity were managing to do so.

"Please don't make a widow of me," Navy Lt. Comdr. Dale Osborne's wife had said when she kissed him goodbye. And so he endured. He survived.

An A4 Skyhawk pilot operating off the carrier U.S.S. *Hancock,* he was shot down on September 23 in countryside north of Vinh. He awakened face down in a rice paddy and could recall nothing more recent than a squadron party at Cubi Point in the Philippines two weeks earlier. To be sure, a great deal had happened. His mouth was full of blood and he could not understand why his hands seemed incapable of removing the oxygen mask. He discovered that his right wrist had been shattered; jagged, bloody bone ends had torn through the skin and protruded in various directions, and the hand and arm were full of shrapnel. His left hand and wrist were broken. He dragged his face along the ground, tearing the mask away. He spit out gobs of blood. Exploring with his tongue, he found that two teeth were gone, and there was a large hole in the roof of his mouth.* He seemed to be alone. He knew he was in deep trouble. He breathed deeply and lost consciousness.

When he awakened a group of North Vietnamese troops were ripping away his clothing. One of them held his survival radio close to Osborne's mouth, indicating that the American should speak. The Navy man surmised that the troops had set up a flak trap; his distress call would attract rescue aircraft, which could be shot down. He shook his head and passed out.

When he awoke again, he found himself lying alone on the ground in his shorts and undershirt. The troops were walking away, doubtless thinking him to be dead or nearly so, and wanting no part of the burial chores. Osborne knew that he surely would be dead soon if he were left here. "Hey," he shouted, "don't leave me here." The troops, now perhaps seventy-five yards distant, looked back, stopped, returned. One of them produced a syringe and shot something into Osborne's left arm. Then he was placed on a stretcher and carried a long distance. He kept losing and regaining consciousness.

It was nighttime. He lay on his stomach on a wooden table in a small hut. Two Vietnamese, doctors or medics, were working on his legs—it felt as though one-inch strips of skin were being ripped off his legs and feet. The pain was unbearable. He screamed and pleaded for them to stop, pleaded for morphine. But they did not stop, and he

---

*A sliver of shrapnel had gone through his jaw, taking out the teeth, puncturing the roof of the mouth and lodging in his head, where it still remains.

passed out again. It was to be several days before he would discover that, during shootdown, most of the calf of his left leg and much of the thigh had been blown away, and that those who had been attending him had not been torturing him but had been removing shrapnel. Both legs and his right arm were bandaged; his left arm was in a splint.

For several days he was cared for by a family. Two of the daughters—he guessed them to be twenty and eighteen years old—seemed to have had some training as nurses; they were kind to him and looked after him. Neighbors, sometimes twenty-five or thirty of them, kept coming to stare at the American. One day the man of the house began to harangue the visitors, to point to the American and speak of him in angry tones. As the diatribe continued, the visitors became increasingly agitated, until finally they surrounded the table where Osborne lay, snarling epithets he did not understand, slapping him and punching him. They did him no serious damage, but it was frightening.

After that the atmosphere was different. The girls were not gentle about changing his bandaging. It took about an hour and a lot of water to rip the blood-soaked stuff off and by the time it was off Osborne was soaked with the sweat of great agony. During this hour, the girls kept pointing to his damaged limbs and making sawing motions, indicating that they were to be amputated. Full of pain and terror at the prospect of amputation, Osborne at last got a look at his left leg; everything seemed to have been blown away—he actually could see most of his thigh and shin bones. He felt certain gangrene would soon set in. He had no medical training but amputation certainly seemed in order. He was frightened; he could discern nothing resembling the sort of medical competence the situation seemed to require, and the closest thing to an appropriate instrument was a dirty bamboo saw in a corner of the room. Then, to his amazement, the girls rebandaged his legs. But they kept telling him the leg and an arm had to come off. He wondered when the deed would be done.

Days passed and there was no amputation. One of the girls advised him, in sign language, that he was to be shot through the head. She pointed to the straw thatch ceiling. A rifle barrel had been poked through it and was aimed at his head. He got his broken arms around a post next to his table-bed and began to pull himself up into a sitting position. Then he lost consciousness.

When he awakened it took a few moments to ascertain that he was still alive. He could see through the door of the hut. Outside, a hole was being dug in the ground. The two girls and others kept coming in to make him understand that the hole was his grave. Again he lost consciousness.

It was night when he came to. He was on a stretcher now and he was being lowered into the grave. Above, several Vietnamese faces were framed around the edges of the grave. He began shouting, pleading, waving his bandaged broken arms. The faces above began chattering and he was lifted out of the grave and taken back into the hut. Apparently, he had been thought to be dead.

One day a man in uniform arrived, looked at Osborne, and said, "Hanoi." The American nodded his head vigorously and repeated, "Hanoi." He thought that in Hanoi he might have a chance; there, surely, would be a hospital, doctors. Almost immediately, he was hallucinating: he was in Hanoi, in a first-class hotel named the Royalle. The place was full of good food and doctors, and he had been assigned a plush room with a shower. He could not understand why there were no other Americans in the place.

Then he was placed on a stretcher and put aboard a truckbed. There was a long, torturous ride to somewhere; the truck seemed to have no springs, and the roads were atrocious. For endless miles the patient, lying on his back and unable to use arms or legs, kept bouncing, high in the air. Painful, raw wounds were opened on his back, hips, and buttocks. He pleaded for water, but none was given to him, and his lips cracked and his tongue swelled. Finally he was taken off the truck and into another hut.

He knew that he was dying, and so did his captors. Some indicated, by sign language, that this was so. A black, rubberized plastic bag about six feet long was placed near him, a body bag; he was given to understand that his remains would be inserted into it when he died. An elderly man came into the hut and offered him some rosary beads. Osborne indignantly refused them; he was determined not to die, not to make Donna a widow. Then, as quickly as the man left, he realized the rosary had been offered in Christian kindness, and that he should have accepted it. He wished the man would come back so that he could apologize and thank him; but he did not return.

He thought he would go mad with thirst. He hallucinated: he stood next to a swimming pool at some home in the United States and drank water from a hose. It was delicious, lifesaving; he luxuriated. Then he was back in North Vietnam, literally dying of thirst—his urine had turned almost black, a sure sign of dangerous dehydration. He cried for a guard, for water.

A man in a white smock came in and ripped off the bandages. It was a painful session. Then the man departed, leaving the frightful wounds open to all manner of things that flew and crawled and infested this place. Weak though he was, Osborne knew it was essential that he keep his wounds clean. He spent most of a day trying to keep the flies and other things out of his wounds. He kept seeing his wife's face and hearing her voice: *"Please don't make a widow of me."*

In late afternoon a guard entered, sat down, and stared malevolently at the American. He seemed consumed with a visible hatred. He threw new bandaging on the bed and indicated to the prisoner that he must wrap his own wounds. But Osborne's broken and lacerated hands would not function. He could not wrap the bandages. The guard got up and left.

The wounds remained open. That night there was more to worry about than flies, bedbugs, cockroaches, and the like: large rats skulked everywhere, eyeing the helpless man. He needed to evacuate his bowels; he could not get up and knew there was no point in calling for help. He did not know what to do. His body solved the problem for him. There was no stopping the movement, and it proved a blessing. The excrement acted as a cushion between some of the festering wounds on his back and hips and the bedboard. Discovering this, Dale slid around in the stuff, distributing it to other wounds, some of which were now agonizing to the touch. Achieving a measure of comfort he had not known in many days, he slept. Later he awakened to find a big, black rat feasting on the open wound in his left leg. He managed to chase the rat off, then passed out. He awakened to find the rat gnawing at him again. He spent the night losing and regaining consciousness and fighting off the big rat.

Days and nights passed. Sometimes at night he would awaken, screaming, from nightmares. Guards would come in and beat him for making noise, and he would apologize and promise to try not to make noise.

One day a compassionate soldier entered and helped him into some clean clothing, wrapping his legs so expertly in the bandaging that Dale judged him to be a medic.

Occasionally now he was given a small cup of water, but not nearly enough to satisfy his mounting thirst or even to enable him to salivate. Obsessed with thoughts of water, he left the food, small bowls of rice, untouched. The guards stopped bringing it.

He would not die. He kept remembering her words: *"Please don't make a widow of me."*

He was told he was to be taken to Hanoi. Apparently the thought was abandoned that he might die in this place. He was a problem that others were glad to pass along. Again his hopes flared. He remained convinced that his best chance to survive lay in reaching Hanoi.

It was a raw night, cold and raining hard. He was placed in the open back of a small truck. He had no blanket, no protection against the weather save the T-shirt and shorts in which he had been captured. He was freezing but was more interested in the falling rain than in warmth. He lay with his mouth open, trying to catch the drops. He was not getting much water, though, and when he heard the rain splashing into the puddles on the ground below the truck, he tried to crawl off the truckbed to get down to the puddles. A guard heard him moving, came to the truckbed, and beat him until he promised to be still.

He hallucinated again: he was in a roadshow and went from village to village in North Vietnam, putting on a feathered costume, behaving like a rooster, and trying to earn enough money to buy an airline ticket to Manila. These episodes seemed as real to him as any he had ever lived.

He remained in the truckbed in the freezing rain. The truck did not move until the next day, when a civilian couple arrived and climbed into the cab. Dale shivered in and out of consciousness. The truck kept stopping, so that civilian wayfarers could climb aboard. The American was shoved to one side and someone threw a blanket over him. He was grateful for the kindness. The blanket kept falling off, and then he discovered that it had not been given to him out of kindness, but rather to smother the terrible stench that emanated from him. His fellow travelers kept a distance from him, and whenever the blanket slipped they would use a long pole to lift it back over him. They rode on, and, somehow, Osborne slept.

He awakened wet and freezing in a muddy ditch alongside a road. It took him a few moments to gather his wits. It was dark, raining. The truck was gone, the blanket was gone; there was no sign nor sound of life anywhere. Apparently, while Dale had been asleep or unconscious, his traveling companions had tossed him to his fate. He wondered how to stay alive. He could neither care for himself with his shattered limbs, nor travel on them. But the only alternative was to lie here in the muddy ditch and die. *"Please don't make a widow of me."*

A light shone from a distant building. He pushed himself up on his knees and elbows and began crawling, working his way through the puddles and mud and rain. He passed out, fell face down into the mud, regained consciousness, crawled on. He passed out many times, then awakened and resumed the crawl. Dawn was coming on by the time he reached the building. There was a loud whistle, like a policeman's whistle, and then people were taking him inside.

Dale arrived in Hanoi on October 10, seventeen days after being shot down. He had made it! Here, surely, he would be hospitalized, and his injuries would be attended. Instead, he was taken directly to Room 18, the Meathook Room, on the main courtyard at Hoa Lo.

Nothing was done for him. He was immediately interrogated by Bug, the cockeyed camp commander of Vegas, who ranted at him, accused him of multiple murders, and insisted that he sign a tableful of confessions and statements. Osborne pointed out that his broken and wounded wrists made it impossible for him to write. He was made to make a tape, but garbled everything he was supposed to say: the tape was useless.

Finally, after two days and nights, he was taken to Vegas and stashed in a cell with Navy Lt. Comdr. Brian Woods (captured on September 18, 1968). At last, he was in the hands of one who would see to his survival; he was not going to make Donna a widow.*

————

By the fall of 1968 nearly all the Americans in Hanoi were unhappy with the Johnson Administration's conduct of the war. Few, if any, POWs believed that Hanoi could long hold out once American military power was properly applied. Yet Washington, apparently fearful of Soviet or Chinese intervention, stuck to a demonstrably ineffective policy that prohibited meaningful air operations anywhere in the country's "Northeast Quadrant," where the bulk of war-supporting industry and activity lay. The really vital targets were not

---

*Osborne credits Woods with saving his life. Woods force-fed him until Dale had reawakened his appetite, and did all the things for him that one without limbs cannot do for himself. Eventually the Vietnamese operated on Osborne. He retains all his limbs, but a four-inch section of his right forearm was removed.

being hit: the port facilities at Haiphong, where 80 percent of North Vietnam's war matériel was received; the railroad yards in Hanoi; the docks in Hanoi along the Red River; the Hanoi thermal power plant; important matériel and petroleum storage facilities; command and control centers. And since March 31, when Lyndon Johnson had announced that he would not again run for the Presidency, there had been no bombing at all above the 20th parallel, far to the south of Hanoi.

Most POWs, who had become captives while attacking relatively unimportant targets in the countryside and while trying to stop the infiltration of men and supplies along the jungle trails into the South, hoped for a change in Washington. They feared that the Democratic candidate, Sen. Hubert Humphrey, would, if elected, continue with Johnson's policies. They hoped that the Republican, Richard Nixon, would do what had to be done to end the war quickly and get them home.

At the Zoo one day in late October, Bud Day found himself in receipt of an election prediction from another prisoner in a nearby cell: on the Friday before the election, President Johnson would halt all bombing in North Vietnam. The act would be so timed as to receive a full measure of treatment from America's daily press. Since most of the largest American dailies apparently opposed the war, the Administration could expect favorable notices for its "statesmanship" in the four days immediately preceding the election. This might well be enough to win the election for the Democratic candidate.

So infuriated was Day by this cynical assessment that he refused even to discuss it. It struck him as beneath contempt even to speculate that an American President might play politics with a war, that he would take a step potentially injurious to his forces in the field merely for the sake of winning an election. Day was positive no President would ever do such a thing, and he resented, bitterly, the suggestion that he might.

On the Saturday prior to the election, it was announced to the prisoners that President Johnson had ordered an unconditional halt to all bombing of North Vietnam. Like many other POWs, Day was stunned. He could not believe there were no conditions, it made no sense. He waited to be told of the *quid pro quo;* surely the POWs— there now were approximately four hundred of them—were to be released. At the very least, the sick and injured were to go home.

That must be it. As the election had approached, there had been an easing of the mistreatment; people dressed in medical smocks had come and conducted a lot of cursory physical examinations.

For weeks, Day kept insisting to his fellow POWs that the bombing halt could not possibly have been unconditional. Prisoners throughout the system generally shared Day's belief. They kept waiting and hoping for something to happen.

———

By December, the Alcatraz Eleven had been languishing for fourteen months in their tiny cells behind the Ministry of National Defense. Having isolated these disruptive influences, the Vietnamese seemed at a loss as to what to do with them. Occasionally, a man would be taken up into rooms in the Ministry for desultory interrogation, but there had been no real pressure for information or propaganda. It was almost as though the enemy had given up on these men and was content to have them out of the way.

For the prisoners, it was a grim existence. The only sunshine, fresh air, and exercise they got was when they were taken out, singly, for a few minutes each day to empty their waste buckets and to wash. Each evening at about 5 PM they were locked into leg irons and remained in them until 8 AM or 9 AM the next day—unless, like Harry Jenkins, they were caught communicating with another American "criminal." Jenkins was sentenced to eighty-five days around the clock in irons; Howie Rutledge got ten days for listening.

Despite the tight security, the prisoners kept up a constant communications flow. They tapped, coughed, and flashed to each other about everything: backgrounds, careers, families, and plans. They formed close friendships.

SRO Jim Stockdale worried increasingly about Ron Storz. He felt a special regard for the big, handsome, young Air Force captain, who back at Vegas had attempted suicide rather than betray Stockdale's leadership. He found Storz to be attractive in all ways, in his appearance, his friendliness and optimism, his steel courage, his unswerving devotion to God, country, family, and fellow POWs. But now Storz seemed to be failing, physically and mentally. He seemed to have stopped eating, yet would argue angrily with the Vietnamese for more food. He had become even skinnier than Jim Mulligan, who looked like a walking skeleton. The spring had gone out of his step; he shuffled laboriously and the friendly grin he had once flashed to the different cell doors when he went to the bath area had been replaced by a vacant, hollow-eyed stare. No mail had been received, yet when Storz communicated he delivered long, detailed descriptions of events that were taking place back in Portsmouth, New Hampshire, where his wife, Sandra, and their son and daughter lived. His deterioration was plain to the others, too, and along with Stockdale they kept after him to eat. He replied that he would do so.

That December the Vietnamese decided what to do with the Alcatraz Eleven. One day a guard slipped unseen into the empty cell between Jerry Denton and George McKnight and caught them communicating. McKnight was taken from his cell and not seen again for several days. When he returned he told the others that he had been in heavy torture. "It's a purge," he tapped. Every prisoner was to be bent. The enemy was after apologies for war crimes and requests for amnesty. SRO Stockdale messaged, "It looks like we're going to take it on the chin, one by one. So let's go in and take it on the chin."

Denton was next. In a room in the Ministry of National Defense he spent a night standing against a wall with his arms stretched high above his head. The next morning he was tortured in ropes for hours; then again for several hours in the afternoon; and again that night. During these tortures, howling guards beat him and dragged him about the room, while officers stood by explaining that it was not possible to contain the "just wrath" of the enlisted men. Denton was tortured until he finally screamed. He yielded a request for forgiveness and for release at the end of the war.

There was a time out for Christmas.

———

On Christmas Eve approximately fifty POWs found themselves attending a religious ceremony in a room at the Plantation. An organ was playing, and Air Force Maj. Quincy Collins (James Q., Jr., captured on September 2, 1965) led a small choir of Americans in seasonal hymns. English-speaking Vietnamese officers bustled about, trying unsuccessfully to get the other prisoners to stop passing information to one another. Photographers crowded the sides and rear of the room, popping bulbs, grinding away movie film, talking, and calling out. A sort of low-key pandemonium reigned.

Soft Soap Fairy, conscious that he was being filmed, stood smiling in an aisle and calling, "McCain, stop talking."

"Fuck you," called John McCain, who resumed briefing Doug

Hegdahl on all that had happened to him. "I refused to go home. I was tortured for it. They broke my rib, and rebroke my arm . . ."

McCain was deathly pale, his eyes were sunken, and his arms looked twisted, as though he had suffered polio. But Hegdahl, who now had been months in solitary, was thrilled at the size of McCain's spirit.

"Our senior ranking officer is Colonel Larson," McCain continued (the reference was to Air Force Lt. Col. Gordon A. "Swede" Larson, captured on May 5, 1967). Someone else passed the word that there now were 130 POWs at the Zoo; that men were now being tortured for good-treatment statements; and that Larry Guarino was Zoo SRO.

Even the members of the choir—Quincy Collins, Norm McDaniel (Air Force Capt. Norman A., captured on July 20, 1966) and Mike Kerr (Air Force Lt. Michael S., captured on January 16, 1967)— were flashing signals with the facing congregation. They advised that an Annex had been constructed beyond the west wall of the Zoo, that there were nine cells, each of them containing eight Americans, most of them junior officers.

Doug Hegdahl was full of pride at being a member of such a company of men. He found it hard to concentrate on the sermon. A "Reverend Pastor" who was introduced as "Chairman of the Evangelical Church of Hanoi" was offering a homily in which he likened "the beloved and respected leader, Ho Chi Minh" to Jesus Christ, and Lyndon Johnson to Herod, the baby killer. He asserted that just as Jesus Christ had led the Jewish people to a great victory over the Roman imperialist aggressors, Ho was leading the Vietnamese people to a great victory over the U.S. imperialist aggressors.

John McCain, who was of no mind to speak softly, kept attracting the attention of a non-English-speaking guard who apparently did not understand that the event was being filmed. He stood in the aisle, making ominous noises and motions at McCain. Delighted, McCain called out, "Fuck you, you son of a bitch!" Cooler heads hauled the angry guard off.

For some, it was a great Christmas.

For some it was not.

On Christmas Day there was a relatively good meal. At Alcatraz some prisoners received letters from home. Eagerly, Jim Stockdale struggled in his dark cell to read one from his wife, Sybil. Written months earlier, it told of the death of his mother. Silently, the SRO wept.

That Christmas many at the Zoo received packages from home, including the one whom Fidel had believed to be faking and had so brutally savaged. The Faker still lived in a cell in the Stable with several other Fidel prisoners, of whom Air Force Capt. Jack Bomar was senior. The others had continued to care for him, but it had been difficult. He remained deeply suspicious of them all, full of hatred and prone to violence. He would never leave his bunk, and in order to clean him the others had to pick him up, carry him to the bath area, and wash him, usually fighting and struggling throughout.

The Vietnamese left it to Bomar to deliver the Faker's Christmas package to him. Bomar felt certain he would violently reject the contents, mainly candy and chewing gum, would regard them as an enemy trick. But there were pictues of the man's handsome family, too, and Bomar thought and hoped that these might be the lifeline that would bring him back, save him. Bomar took the pictures out of the package, and assigned Larry Spencer to try to persuade the Faker to accept the remainder of the contents; Spencer had worked harder and done more for the man than anyone else, and while the Faker displayed no trust or affection for him, he seemed more likely to accept something from Spencer than from anyone else. But when Spencer offered the package, the Faker flung it away.

The pictures were handled with care. Using bamboo scraps and pieces of twine from blankets, Ed Hubbard fashioned handsome frames for them. Carefully, Spencer approached the Faker with them and showed them to him, explaining that the photographs were of his family, assuring him that his was indeed a beautiful family. The Faker stared vacantly at the pictures. There was not the slightest flicker of recognition or interest. Nothing. He looked away.

The pictures were hung on the wall behind the Faker's bunk. No one ever saw him look at them.

––––––

Another year was dying. In a jungle encampment in South Vietnam, Army Capt.-Doctor Floyd Kushner wondered how many more Americans would die with it. Some were in bad shape and getting worse.

One was Roberts, the Marine who already had been a prisoner for two years when Kushner arrived. When he had not been released after the midsummer political course given by Ho, the regional commissar, the effect on Roberts had been devastating. For a time he had kept to himself, had refused to work, and had displayed little interest in what little food there was. As the months had passed, though, he had seemed to be recovering. In November, when some of the others had decided to make a meal of one of their captors' pet cats but had proved themselves incompetent to slaughter it, Roberts killed the animal for them. Then, when guards had found them out and they all had insisted on sharing the blame, Roberts stepped forward and proclaimed himself the guilty one. He got a severe beating.

After this beating Roberts went into a decline. He would not leave the bed, he stopped eating. Worst of all, he regressed to infancy, sucking his thumb and calling for his mother. He continually dirtied his clothing and the bed, and the others had to clean him and clean up after him. They did so uncomplainingly. They kept fires around him all the time. They heated water and bathed him. In order to feed him, they had to communicate with him, and in order to get any response at all they found that they had to cuddle him and kiss him and talk to him as though he were a baby. Then they were able to spoon-feed him.

Kushner was astounded and immensely proud of the way the others, starving and ill-cared for themselves, took care of Roberts. Many had not liked the man, for he had been overbearing and something of a bully, and had made no secret of it that he would betray any or all of them to secure his own release. Still, they worked tirelessly to save him.

One day after a warm bath, Roberts regained himself. He began to talk as though he merely had been ill, but that the crisis had passed. He promised that he was going to eat his food and take care of himself. Kushner and the others were proud of themselves that they had saved Roberts. It had been a tough battle and important things had been learned: Roberts had demonstrated how bad it could get if a man let go; at the same time, each man had learned the lengths to which the others would go to save him—knowledge that made everyone feel better.

But two days after emerging from his regression, Roberts suffered a severe relapse and became utterly infantile. For hours, Kushner kept him cradled in his arms, trying to talk to him. Then, abruptly, in the middle of the night, Roberts's eyes focused on the doctor. He called him "Doc," gave him a post office box number and a message: "Mom, Dad, I love you very much." Then he closed his eyes and died.

It had been a tumultuous year. Following the Tet offensive, in February, the Administration had remained under severe criticism for its conduct of the war. In response, President Johnson had expressed his continued faith in General William C. Westmoreland, Commander of U.S. Forces in Vietnam. But on March 22, Johnson had named Westmoreland Army Chief of Staff, a post that removed him from the war zone, and replaced him with General Creighton Abrams.

Then, on March 31, Johnson had halted all U.S. bombing above the 20th parallel, called on Hanoi to reciprocate by agreeing to peace talks, and announced that he would not be a candidate for and would not accept the Democratic nomination for the Presidency in 1968.

In early April, Dr. Martin Luther King, the revered civil rights leader, was murdered.

The war raged on. By April 6, U.S. Army units had fought through some 60,000 enemy troops to break a seventy-six-day siege of a U.S. Marine base at Khesanh, denying the Communists what some feared would be a decisive, Dienbienphu-like victory.

In early June, Sen. Robert F. Kennedy, a leading contender for the Democratic Presidential nomination, was murdered.

Hanoi had responded to Johnson's dramatic peace initiative in March by agreeing to meet in Paris for talks. Through the spring, summer, and fall, the two sides had haggled interminably. For openers, the Communists demanded an unconditional end to all American bombing of North Vietnam. American Ambassador-at-Large Averell Harriman kept insisting on some sort of reciprocal move. Neither side would yield. On November 1, Johnson halted all bombing of North Vietnam, and asked Hanoi to get serious. Now, there was a drawn-out debate over the shape of the conference table.

Republican Richard Nixon was elected President of the United States by a narrow margin over Democratic Sen. Hubert H. Humphrey.

During his campaign Nixon had alluded frequently to a "secret plan" for ending the war in Vietnam. The world, and America in particular, hopefully awaited its implementation.

27

Warriors, Antiwarriors, and Death

At Alcatraz, Jerry Denton, who had been tortured just before Christmas, knew he was in trouble again. On Christmas Eve, he had behaved badly toward Cat, refusing the prison system commander's insistent plea that he help himself at a table full of goodies. Denton had been able to hear cameras whirring somewhere and had declined to cooperate. He knew he would be made to pay and had been wondering when the bill would arrive. On January 8 he was told, "You are going to read the news, from the Vietnamese News Agency, for your camp."

"No way," said Denton, shaking his head. He was determined that if his captors were going to make him read the propaganda they called "news" to other Americans, he would make them dig for it.

"You remember what happened to you the last time," the interrogator said. Denton nodded; he remembered, all too well. "And you still refuse to read?"

"I refuse."

Several guards administered a long, severe beating. Then he was made to spend the night standing facing a wall, holding his hands high in the air. The next morning he was taken to two windows that looked down over the Alcatraz cells. Torture guards brought in ropes and the windows were opened. Denton girded himself for what he knew was to be a grim session: they were going to try to rip screams of agony out of him that the others could hear, screams that would intimidate them, make them malleable.

He was rope-tortured four times that day. The torture had been refined. After the ropes had been cinched bone-tight around the upper arms, the same thing was done to the thighs. Then, the lower legs were bent over a bamboo pole, and somehow, the prisoner's elbows were hooked to the outside extension of the pole, so that he was pulled far forward, into a small, tight, painful ball. The struggle lasted all day. It was nightfall before he was made to scream. The enemy succeeded, finally, by twisting the leg irons that were locked tightly around his ankles. When he was removed from the torture rig, he could not rise. He was seized with convulsions that had him bouncing about the floor like a decked fish. The convulsions wracked him for most of an hour. Denton was conscious throughout, though hazy; he was aware that his torturers were alarmed, and afraid to touch him. A doctor was brought to the scene, but he only chattered fearfully, like the rest of them. Clearly, Denton was thought to be in his death throes.

When the seizure passed, the prisoner was made to tape-record the "news." Now too weak to offer physical resistance, he tried to make a farce of the tape, distorting his voice, mispronouncing words and the names of political leaders, and generally attempting to create an unusable product. But it was used. His tormentors, none of whom were expert in English, played the broadcast to Denton's Alcatraz compatriots, who had heard his tortured screams. Some laughed at what he had done on tape, but all felt badly at what they knew had been done to him. And indeed, a long season of torture got under way at Alcatraz.

———

In the small hours of January 25, the others heard Harry Jenkins call out, "Bao Cao! Bao Cao!"

Jenkins had a bad case of worms. For hours a pain had been

building in the center of his chest. Sleep had been impossible, but he had not wanted to ask for medical attention, especially in the middle of the night; he thought that the pain might ebb by morning, but it had intensified until now it was like a spear of flame inside him, stunning, breathtaking. He could not lie down, sit still, roll over, walk—it was becoming increasingly difficult to breathe. He thought that whatever it was was going to kill him and at last he had no choice but to cry out, "Bao Cao!"

A guard answered, "No Bao Cao! No doctor!" He went back to his post in the middle of the yard.

Again Jenkins cried out, "Bao Cao!"

Jim Mulligan was awake by now and knew that Jenkins must be desperate to be calling for help at such an hour. He began kicking and pounding at the inside of his own cell door, shouting, "Bao Cao! Bao Cao!"

The guard looked through Mulligan's peephole.

"Get a doctor!" Mulligan roared at him. "There's a sick guy over there."

"No, Bao Cao!" said the guard.

"Yeah, Bao Cao!" Mulligan screamed, banging and kicking at the door. "Bao Cao! Get a doctor, you lazy son of a . . ."

The guard banged against the outside of the door with his rifle, shouting at Mulligan. But Mulligan would not be shouted down. He cursed the guard and kept yelling at him until finally he fetched another guard, one who spoke English. The two guards entered Jenkins's cell; the next thing anyone heard was Jenkins's voice, "Go ahead, hit me."

It was as though someone had thrown a switch and started a riot! All the other Alcatraz prisoners joined Mulligan now, screaming, howling, and hammering at their doors. They warned their captors in the most pungent terms that they were liable to criminal penalties for denying medical attention to a sick prisoner of war. The din overwhelmed the two guards. Confused and frightened, they did not know what do do. The prisoners sustained the intimidating uproar for long minutes, until the yard was full of officers and more guards. A doctor was finally brought to Jenkins's cell, and the prisoners quieted down; weak from years of maltreatment and starvation, the exercise had drained them. While the doctor examined Jenkins,* officious

---

*Nothing was done for Jenkins. The pain disappeared within a few days, leaving him terribly sore. It recurred a little more than a year later, but receded immediately when he was inoculated. He does not know what caused the pain and was not told what the

guards went about taking down the names of all but Rutledge, who was listening from what was soon to become his torture chamber.

The next morning SRO Stockdale ordered the Alcatraz prisoners: "For 48 hours, nobody takes chow." To Stockdale, the guards' refusal to provide Jenkins needed medical attention was the last straw. For fifteen months the Alcatraz prisoners had been kept locked in their dark hovels and treated like wild animals. If the SRO could do nothing to improve their lot, he could at least let the enemy know what he thought of such treatment. Correctly, he reckoned that a short hunger strike would get him a confrontation with the camp commander. When the prisoners were let out of their cells, one by one, to approach the food table in the yard, each helped himself to a cup of water but turned away from the rice. The refusal of food caused excited murmurings among the guards.

That evening the prisoners were taken one by one to interrogation. Stockdale, when his turn came, read the riot act to the camp commander, detailing the prisoners' grievances and recalling the 1949 Geneva Conventions as they pertain to prisoners of war. The camp commander took copious notes and Stockdale surmised that he had to prepare a report on the "riot" for Cat.

Before dawn the next morning a half-dozen guards entered Stockdale's cell, blindfolded him, tied his wrists together behind him with baling wire, and placed him in a jeep. There was a short ride to Hoa Lo prison—he recognized the place by its smell. When his blindfold was removed he found himself in Room 18, the Meathook Room, to the left of the main entrance. He was left alone. A few minutes later, through a crack in the door, he saw Rabbit approaching; and with him was Stockdale's old antagonist Pigeye, the master torturer.

———

When Stockdale left Alcatraz that morning, Jerry Denton immediately assumed command. His first message to the others was "Steady as you go," navalese for "Continue what you are doing." What they were doing, of course, was not eating, and Denton meant that they should stay on their hunger strike.

Before the prisoners had a chance to turn their backs on the morning meal, a team of Vietnamese doctors and medics arrived. They moved from cell to cell, spending perhaps fifteen minutes with each

———

medication was. The American doctors who examined him on his return to the United States did not speculate.

prisoner, conducting a cursory physical examination of each, handing out aspirin, medication for athlete's foot, and the like and assuring the weak, emaciated men that they were in good condition. They spent perhaps forty-five minutes with Harry Jenkins, then departed.

The enemy having caved in on the major point of the Alcatraz "riot," the provision of medical attention, George McKnight advised Denton, "Jerry, I know what your hard head has in mind, but the rest of us feel we ought to knock off the fast now. We have won our main point. We have shown them that when we have an issue we'll take action. Let's show them that when they give in, we don't act 'unreasonable' in the way this game is played. If we keep fasting now, we think they will hurt Stockdale more. Let's stop while we're ahead."

Denton disagreed. He thought it important to show the Vietnamese that it did them no good to remove a tough SRO from the scene, that his place would be taken by another tough SRO, and that prisoner behavior might even get worse instead of better.

Bob Shumaker sent a message agreeing with McKnight, expressing particular concern for Ron Storz. It seemed vital to Shumaker that the skeletal Storz eat, especially in view of the bitter cold weather.

With minutes to go before mealtime, Denton rescinded the fast. He might not have if he had known what the enemy was doing that day to Howie Rutledge, Jim Stockdale, and Jim Mulligan.

Ravaged by illness and fasts he had imposed on himself, "just to show my goddamn displeasure," Mulligan was pitifully weak. He could hardly walk unassisted. After the Jenkins "riot," he was taken again up into a room in the Ministry. There, after he had spent the day refusing to write a letter of apology for his behavior the night before, it was demanded of him that he write a request for amnesty. Refusing to do this, he was locked in two set of leg irons, was made to kneel, was tied into torture ropes and beaten by guards. They dragged him about the room by his ears, punched him, kicked him, pulled out handfuls of his hair. Earlier, Mulligan had laughed at Cat when he had threatened him with torture, pointing out that he would lose consciousness as quickly as torture was inflicted. But, amazingly, he did not pass out; perhaps it was the sheer power of his fierce Irish rage that kept him conscious—he wanted to outlast, overcome, destroy the hated enemy! In any case, he endured, defiantly, howling, cursing, and spitting at his tormentors until about 7 AM. Then, finally, he could take no more. He wrote a request for amnesty.

He was kept in the torture chamber. A day passed, then he was told to write a letter to the new American President, Richard Nixon, condemning the war and insisting that he withdraw U.S. forces. He refused. He was rope-tortured. He wrote to Nixon.

The next day he was ordered to write a letter to his old ship, the carrier *Enterprise,* pleading with the men to lay down their arms and refuse to fight. He would not write such a letter. He was rope-tortured. He wrote the letter.

The next day another letter to *Enterprise* was demanded of him. Again he refused to write it, and was rope-tortured. He wrote the letter.

The following day, when he refused again to write a letter of apology for his part in the Jenkins "riot," he was rope-tortured again. He wrote the letter.

He was rope-tortured the next day for information on Cecil Field, Florida, a naval air station he had last seen in 1965.

He was made to read the apology and the amnesty request to the camp commander, who then assured him, "Great things are going to happen to you. You will get your health back . . ."

He could hear Howie Rutledge screaming in another room, down the hallway.

———

In Room 18 at Hoa Lo, Rabbit stormed at Jim Stockdale: "My superior has taken me away from my job because of this mess that you have caused! I do not want to go into the details of what happened at that other camp. I have only one question: Will you be my slave or not?"

Stockdale was strongly negative to this proposal, and at Rabbit's signal Pigeye threw the maimed leader to the floor and squeezed him into torture ropes. The torturer was perhaps quicker and more competent that he had ever been. The excruciating pain came on quickly and rose toward a crescendo it seemed unable to reach. Rabbit paced around the suffering prisoner, demanding, "Do you submit? Do you submit?"

At length, Stockdale whispered, "I submit."

He was made to sign a prepared statement: "I understand that I am a criminal. I have opposed the camp authority and incited others to oppose the camp authority. I know the nature of my sins and I now submit to you to do whatever you ask, write, say, or tape."

The next morning Rabbit grilled Stockdale for the "names of

everybody in your wing, numbers of personnel in your squadron, numbers of men on your ships.'' Stockdale would not answer, and Pigeye inflicted rope torture again. Finally, Stockdale gave a hodgepodge of fictional names and numbers.

Each day Rabbit would probe in a new area of interest. He would quiz Stockdale on aircraft carrier air defenses or on flight tactics and targets. Each day Stockdale would refuse to answer and would be given to Pigeye for intensive rope torture. Then he would reveal such intelligence as that American aircraft carriers are defended by fighter aircraft and antiaircraft guns of unknown caliber; that when carrier aircraft approached Vietnam, the fighters turned north to guard against enemy Mig fighters, while the bombers bombed in the south; and that targets were usually enemy supply convoys on the roads.

These answers proved acceptable.

After six days Stockdale was made to sign a memo to ''the senior staff officer,'' to the effect that he would be glad to provide him with all the military information he desired.

Now, suddenly, Rabbit was solicitous, pretending concern for Stockdale's appearance and condition. ''Why don't we take a break and get some rest?'' he said. ''It is time for you to have a bath and shave.''

Pigeye escorted the prisoner to the bath area and handed him soap and a new razor. Stockdale knew he was not getting a bath and shave for free, or for what Rabbit might think of as services rendered. Rabbit hated him and could not have cared less about his need for rest or his appearance. Stockdale deduced that Rabbit wanted him spruced up for photographic purposes or some sort of public display. As quickly as Pigeye turned away, he began hacking the razor into his hair, carving wildly down the middle of his head, cutting what he hoped resembled a ''reverse Cherokee,'' a wide bald streak down the middle with bushy, uneven, unkempt outcroppings on the sides. The hair was thick and matted with dirt, and as he dug away at it he opened several bloody wounds in his scalp. *So much the better,* he thought. Blood streamed down into the mattings of hair at the sides of his head and down over his forehead, eyebrows, and nose, splashing in large drops to the ground.

While Stockdale hacked away at his head, Pigeye remained preoccupied outside the bath stall. By the time the torturer looked in to check the prisoner's progress, Stockdale appeared to be bathing in blood! Horrified, Pigeye hustled his charge back to Room 18. The quick return caught Rabbit by surprise. He was down on the floor with another interrogator. The two of them were trying to tie a tape recorder to the underside of the table. Stockdale had to stifle a smile.

The utter surprise on Rabbit's face faded quickly when he saw the bloody Stockdale. He came to his feet raging, and Stockdale seated himself on the floor, pulling back his shoulders and arms, preparatory to rope torture. Rabbit stood staring down at him, as though puzzled, then said, "No, no, get up!" The interrogator stormed about the room, ringing his hands, shouting at the prisoner. "Why are you taking your own life? You have appointments to keep!"

Stockdale learned that he had been scheduled that night to star in a movie. He was to have worn civilian clothing and played the role of a visiting American businessman, advising a young American prisoner that peace was near, and that he must be cooperative. The "senior officer," said Rabbit, was going to be angry.

A medic was summoned to deal with the head cuts. He painted them with iodine. A guard with barbering instruments was brought in, to try to reshape the butchered hair; it was hopeless. Suddenly, Rabbit announced, "We'll get a hat!" The Vietnamese all departed in search of one.

The hat would beat him! Frantically, Stockdale raked his imagination. He shuffled to his waste bucket, examined its sharp edges. The edges would cut his wrists easily—he was not intent on suicide, only on forestalling his use as a propaganda tool. Bloody wrists would do the job, but the rusted, filthy edges of the bucket would certainly infect him. He shuffled to the glass windows, to break a pane, but there were Vietnamese just outside. He shuffled back to the middle of the room, picked up his small but heavy stool, and began pounding it into his face. He had always bruised easily and soon felt his eyes swelling. He kept pounding as hard as he dared. Soon his eyes were closing and blood was dripping from cuts on his forehead, eyebrows, and face. He became aware that a group of Vietnamese civilian workers were crowded at the door, staring at him, horror-struck, obviously certain that he was mad. Rabbit, Pigeye, and the other interrogator came bursting through the door, grabbed the stool from him, and stood around him, staring in utter, grief-stricken dismay.

"Now look what you have done!" someone shrieked. "What are we going to do? What are we going to tell the senior officer?"

Peering through the huge, dark swellings around his eyes, Stockdale found himself smiling as he suggested an explanation Rabbit might offer his boss, Cat, Major Bai. "You tell the major," he said, "that the commander decided not to go."

————

Back at Alcatraz, the extortion-blackmail program continued. One by one the prisoners were taken to the torture chambers in the Ministry of Defense. Shumaker, Coker, McKnight, and the badly failing Ron Storz. In these chambers they were savaged for each of the written papers the others had produced, the apology, the request for amnesty, the plea to men in the old unit to quit fighting, and the letter to President Nixon. All were made to yield these things, but none yielded a usable tape recording.

In February, after they had been sixteen months in Alcatraz, their humane and lenient captors finally yielded on one of Stockdale's complaints; they stopped locking the prisoners in leg irons during the nights.

After the leaders and communicators who comprised the Alcatraz Eleven were removed from Camp Vegas in late 1967, the Vietnamese cracked down hard on communications. The camp was kept under close scrutiny at all times by teams of alert, sadistic guards who were eager to find excuses to take their American prisoners to torturers. Campwide communications were wiped out. In effect, Thunderbird, Stardust, and Desert Inn cellblocks became separate camps; and even internal communicating was dangerous. Men were unable to hold to the letter of Stockdale's BACK US policy, promulgated in March, 1967, and reading the "news"—propaganda—over the camp radio had become routine. The most arresting performance of the season was "The Bob and Ed Show." That was how many referred to a lengthy conversation between two American senior officers which was tape-recorded by the Vietnamese and played back in many prison camps. For its Communist producers, the tape was a propaganda triumph. For the most part, its American listeners, when they first heard it, were incredulous, unwilling to believe that such remarks could be extracted from two of their seniors for less than the most severe torture. But as the relaxed conversation proceeded, incredulity degenerated into profound disgust.

The tape was introduced to the prisoners as a discussion of the war between two American pilots who were meeting for the first time. It was unlike anything the others had heard before. To be sure, they had often heard other American prisoners broadcast denunciations of the war, the U.S. government, and themselves, but it had always been apparent that such statements were coerced; if they were not read in the awkward, poor English the Vietnamese wrote, they were delivered in voices that were full of the pain of torture. But there was nothing awkward about the conversation in "The Bob and Ed Show," and no pain in the tones of the men's voices. There was an easy spontaneity to the conversation, a quality of sincerity and conviction.

The conversationalists were Marine Lt. Col. Edison Wainwright Miller, who had been downed on October 13, 1967; and Navy Comdr. Robert James Schweitzer, who was bagged on January 5, 1968. Miller had been an F-4 squadron commander, based at Chu Lai; Schweitzer had been flying off the carrier *Kitty Hawk.*

On tape, these two emphatically assured each other that America's Vietnam intervention was deplorable, that the undeclared war was illegal, that their captors had every right to call them criminals, and that they were indeed subject to prosecution as such. They agreed that since the American prisoners in North Vietnam were criminals, the U.S. military's Code of Conduct did not apply, that the captives would be foolish to abide by it. They made it clear that they had no intention of adhering to the Code, and reminded each other that imprisoned criminals in the United States got time off for good behavior. Miller said he felt disgusted by the American bombing of peaceful peasants and children.

The broadcast lasted for most of an hour. It puzzled, enraged, demoralized most of the Americans who heard it. Old hands who had suffered unbelievable torture for refusing to say such things could not believe that two senior officers would sell out in such fashion.* Many worried about the effect of the broadcast on the younger, junior

---

*Later, when other prisoners confronted Miller and Schweitzer about the tape, both men expressed surprise that it had been broadcast—they had not heard the "show"—and readily explained how it had been extracted: Miller and Schweitzer both were living alone in cells in the Desert Inn when one day in October, 1968, each was told that he was to have a cellmate. Their captors explained to each man that they wanted to make certain the two of them would be compatible. Therefore, they were brought together in an interrogation room and told to feel free to converse; to talk about anything and to get to know each other. An interrogator stayed in the room, but appeared to be disinterested in the Miller-Schweitzer conversation. No pressures of any kind were brought to bear on the two prisoners to say the things that were said, and Miller later professed amazement that the Vietnamese had considered anything that was said to be worth taping and using.

officers, who had been resisting the enemy's brutal attempts to enlist them in this propaganda campaign.

Jim Stockdale had been moved from Room 18 and was now isolated in another cell, near the Vegas courtyard. "The Bob and Ed Show" had infuriated and depressed him. He felt it imperative that he do something, say something to counter it, but he was not in communication with anyone; since the morning of his departure from Alcatraz, no one knew he was alive. The frustration intensified his angry depression. Then a guard came, indicating that it was time for Stockdale to empty his waste bucket. As he was escorted through the Vegas courtyard toward the dump area, he rattled tap code on the bucket, a loud "BS," which meant "Bullshit!" From the cellblocks around the courtyard came a good deal of cough code that all spelled "R," meaning, "Roger!" He felt a little better.

Another American who was intensely interested in Ed Miller was Marine Lt. James Howie Warner, who was his radar operator when they were shot down. Warner recalled that whatever dislike Miller now professed for the war, he had flown combat with zeal and fervor. It seemed to Warner that, far from exhibiting any notable compassion for the Vietnamese, Miller had displayed an intense preoccupation with distributing ordnance upon them. Warner felt that this was why he and Miller were now in prison. On the day of their shootdown, as they had pulled out of an attack run, Miller had announced the loss of the aircraft's flight control hydraulic system. Standard operating procedure, on which they had been briefed only a few days earlier, was to head for home or for an area where they might be easily rescued, such as the sea. When Miller had reported the problem, Warner had assumed that they would do as instructed, and was amazed when the squadron commander elected to remain in combat. He had several bombs left, and meant to use them. In a post-release interview, Warner recalled that he tried to dissuade Miller, but to no avail. Likewise, Miller recalled that, had he followed instructions, he would have gone home. Minutes later, in any case, both men were hanging in their parachutes.

———

Up until this point, things had been going well for Ed Miller for a long time. As a small boy, he had been extracted from a Davenport, Iowa, orphanage by a woman attorney, who raised him. Graduating from high school in 1949, he enlisted in the Navy. By the time he was twenty, he had earned his wings and a Marine Corps commission. He flew more than fifty combat missions in the Korean War, and advanced through the ranks quickly, developing a reputation as a good officer. By the time he was thirty-five, he was a lieutenant colonel.

Taking advantage of a military educational program, he earned a degree in political science at the University of Maryland, then got command of a squadron based at Chu Lai. Miller recalls that while studying at the University of Maryland, he contacted the Fulbright (Senate Foreign Relations) Committee for information on Indochina, and that he was given "a big fat book with a lot of speeches and handouts"; he also solicited and received the views of the Soviet Embassy in Washington, and the Soviet Mission in New York on the USSR's views on the war. He says that it was soon obvious to him that the United States was in violation of the Constitution in that it was waging a war in the absence of a congressional declaration of war. Nonetheless, says Miller, he was not at the time overly concerned with such matters. He was concerned with delivering the kind of successful performance in a combat command necessary to become a general.

Miller remembers that in the era of the then Defense Secretary, Robert McNamara, the key to success was statistics, the numbers of sorties and hours flown, the bomb tonnage dropped, and so on. Miller recalls that, bent on success, he drove himself and his squadron in an effort to outfly all the competition.

In less than the two months that passed between his date of arrival in Vietnam and his shootdown, he flew seventy missions. The capture of Miller and Warner may be attributable to the fact that Miller, with several hundred hours of experience in flying the F-4, was overconfident of his ability to continue to control the disabled aircraft and preoccupied with his bomb tonnage statistics.

On landing, Miller suffered a broken vertebra, a broken shinbone and a crushed ankle. Captured immediately, he was forced to walk many miles with these injuries. Soon, he developed a blood infection and contracted malaria. Deathly ill by the time he reached a prison camp near Vinh, he slept 18–20 hours per day. Warner, who was with him, feared he would die.

Recovered but much weakened, Miller reached a cell in Hanoi, which he shared with Warner and two Air Force officers, Capt. Kenneth Fisher and Lt. Leon Ellis, both of them captured on Nov. 7,

1967. The four lived together for about nine months. Miller puzzled his younger cellmates. Although he was the senior officer in the cell, he displayed no interest in assuming leadership. He was taken to interrogation far more frequently than the others. He impressed his cellmates as being very frightened. He seemed to exhibit a willingness to cooperate with the Vietnamese. In a post-release interview, Miller recalled that during his interrogations he was deprived of food and water, and that occasionally he was slapped, hit from behind with rifle butts, forced to kneel for hours on end, tied with ropes and sometimes locked in leg irons and handcuffs. He said he gave erroneous information or none at all. He claimed a high tolerance for pain. He said that when he returned to the cell from quizzes, he played down any physical abuse because the others were "scared to death." Miller said that when he and his three cellmates were taken together to interrogations, he found it necessary to warn them that "the hate is oozing out of you . . . try to sit there calmly, without all this emotion and expression." He felt that some Americans who suffered severe torture brought it on themselves with their belligerent attitudes.

One day, says Warner, Miller told his cellmates that he had acceded to a Vietnamese request that he make a tape recording in which he gave autobiographical information.

John McCain would later identify Miller's voice as the one on the tape that was played to him at about this time in late 1967 when he was hospitalized. The speaker, McCain would recall, had identified himself as a Marine aviator who had flown during the Korean War. The Marine had not liked the way southerners dominated the Congress, and had no sympathy for the American Vietnam involvement. To McCain, the most impressive thing about the tape was the quality of conviction with which the speaker infused it.

In a post-release interview, Miller insisted that he never made such a tape recording, that he made no tape recordings for several years following his capture.

Warner, Miller's cellmate, says that he warned Miller against making tape recordings, but that Miller said that it "was only for the camp commander. They promised me that."

Miller argued often with Warner about the war. When challenged as to why he was in Vietnam, he bluntly advised that he had come to promote his career, to make general. Warner says that when he suggested that Communists were involved in the antiwar violence in the United States, Miller exploded, "Lieutenant, don't bother me with your opinions, and I won't trouble you with the truth!" Warner was annoyed at Miller's continual counsel to him to be less disagreeable toward their captors. On July 18, Warner, Fisher, Ellis, and others were transferred to a camp approximately twenty miles west of the city, just across a river from another city called Sontay. It was a grim place, but Warner felt immensely relieved to be away from his former commanding officer.

As the joyous Tet Lunar New Year holiday approached, there was little joy in the South Vietnamese jungle camp where Army Captain-Doctor Floyd Kushner and others continued to survive. Sick, starving men clung to life, did what they could to help one another, and wondered, hopefully, what sort of celebration meal their captors would provide them at Tet. They gazed longingly upon the livestock and poultry that roamed their compound.

There was one sow who spent all her time helping the dysentery-ridden American prisoners clean up their messes. To her, it was a by no means distasteful chore. She waddled purposefully about, lapping up the stuff. She relished it. Often, when a desperate prisoner was unable to reach the latrine in time and was forced to drop his trousers in the compound, he suddenly would feel the sow's cold snout plowing up into his underside, snorting and slurping as though she had found a cornucopia. The prisoners were grateful for the sow's help, and were entertained by it. Not illogically, they called her the Shit-eater.

One day the animal was found dead in the latrine. She had buried her snout in a pile of her favorite food and blissfully suffocated. The camp commander was distraught, and Kushner, who was not allowed to practice medicine with people, was asked for an opinion—might the sow be revived? Kushner proposed that the commander try mouth-to-mouth resuscitation.

"Give him what? Give him what?" the camp commander demanded. "Yes, yes! You give it to him!"

Instead, the pig was cleaned up, butchered, and served for Tet. The prisoners were presented with the head. They ate all its parts with gusto—the snout, the mouth, everything. In all ways, the sow had been of service, and they remembered her gratefully.

There were chickens in the compound, too, and they were small and scrawny, but the prisoners, when they became aware that their captors were not keeping close track of how many birds they had, were emboldened to start snatching them. Surreptitiously, they would grab one, kill it, pluck it, boil it—everything had to be boiled.

The prisoners developed such a taste for chicken that one day, after rations had been especially sparse for a while, someone suggested that they make a meal of Snoopy, a little rooster who had become the camp pet. While there was not exactly a cry of protest against putting a friend on the diet, the famished prisoners did agree to a referendum. The vote went overwhelmingly against Snoopy. He was decapitated and boiled to a turn.

By the end of April, eight Americans had died in this camp. Their VC captors feared that more might soon die, themselves included. For American spotter planes were overflying the area almost constantly, and a continuing rain of aerial bombs and artillery kept falling in the neighborhood. Guards and officers became increasingly nervous. Sometime between midnight and dawn on May 1, the prisoners were awakened and made to walk for approximately two hours along rugged mountain jungle trails to another campsite.

They were engaged in the construction of new hooches when German prisoners arrived. One was a handsome girl with short, blond hair, who looked to be in her mid-twenties. There was a young man, also blond, who limped badly and appeared to be very tired; and another man with long hair and bushy beard who was struggling to walk. These were nurses, members of the Maltese Aid Service, a German Catholic charity mission. They had voluntarily come to Vietnam to help the civilian victims of the war. They had been captured while on a picture-taking expedition near Da Nang and now they were moved into a hooch the prisoners had completed a few days earlier. There was a bamboo fence around the building, and the Americans and Germans were warned not to communicate with each other. When guards were not watching, though, they talked.

The blond girl came to the fence. She spoke broken English. Kushner learned her name was Rika; the blond young man's name was Bernhard; and the bearded man's was George. Rika and Bernhard seemed healthy enough, but George had a rheumatic heart and had contracted malaria; he was very ill, and Rika and Bernhard feared he might die. But what really puzzled her, she said, was the Americans. Most appeared to be mere shadows of men, weak enough to die; yet they continued to work hard at getting the encampment built. She could not imagine the source of their strength. Kushner had no answer for her, nor did any of the others. The Americans knew only that, somehow, they did what they had to do.

One thing some of the Americans felt they had to do was help the failing George. He was filthy; his clothing was foul and his hair and beard were encrusted with lice. But he could not make himself bathe in the cold water of the creek that ran through the camp. The Americans waited for an opportunity. When there were no guards about, they smuggled George into their compound, bathed him in water they had heated over their fire, and dressed him in clean clothing. George cried in gratitude at this compassionate treatment.

Another German girl arrived, a member of the same group. Her name was Monika, and crying hysterically, she delivered word that another of their company, a girl, had died on the trail, from malaria.

Rika, the healthiest of the Germans and the strongest personality, took charge of them. She cooked for them, sewed their clothing, and nursed them. Bernhard was helpful, but he soon had malaria and became terribly weak—once, when he collapsed in the compound, Rika came out and carried him back to his bed in the hooch.

Kushner wondered how many Germans they would be burying, and how soon.

––––––

In March, Jim Thompson and a few other prisoners from Portholes were transferred to a grim prison just west of Hanoi—later inmates would name the place "Skid Row," because it seemed the end of the line. On March 31, Thompson was moved into a cell with three other Americans: Lewis E. Meyer, Lawrence Stark, and Charles E. Willis, all of them civilian employees of the U.S. government who had been captured at Hue during the Communists' Tet offensive in February, 1968. It was the first time since Thompson's capture, on March 26, 1964, that he had been face to face with other Americans, and free to talk with them. At the jungle camp, Portholes, there had been occasional glimpses of other Americans, and a few snatches of whispered conversation. But that had been all; beyond that, he had remained in the solitary confinement for more than five years. Now he was no longer alone.

The three civilians were appalled at Thompson's appearance; he still looked like walking death. And they were astounded to learn how long he had been a prisoner and of all that had happened to him. In turn, Thompson was amazed to hear from them of many things: progress in space exploration, men's hairstyles, women's miniskirts, topless waitresses. He was discouraged to hear what his captors had been telling him of the antiwar movement in the United States was not all "garbage," that the movement was supported by some of the country's most prominent and respected people. He could not understand it.

Thompson and Lew Meyer were kindred spirits and quickly became fast friends. Together they mapped out a program for Thompson's physical restoration. It was immediately apparent that it was going to be a long, slow process, for he was incapable of performing even the lightest limbering-up exercises—deep-breathing exercises made him dizzy. But he kept working at it, and Meyer kept working with him and encouraging him.

At the Plantation one spring day, a new, young interrogator tried to establish a rapport with John McCain.

"What is Easter? Why do you celebrate Easter?" the interrogator asked.

"At this time of the year, a very important thing happened: Jesus Christ, Who was the Son of God, was crucified and died. Three days later, on Easter Sunday, He rose from the dead and went to heaven."

The interrogator stared fixedly at McCain. Then he asked, "You say, He die?"

"Yes, He died."

"Then, three day, He was dead?"

"Yes, that's right."

"You say, He went to heaven?"

"Yes, He came alive again. People saw Him. Then He went up into heaven."

The interrogator fell silent for a long moment, clearly wondering if he was hearing the prisoner correctly. Then he left the room, muttering to himself. He returned some minutes later, full of stern demeanor, saying, "McCain, the officer tell me you tell nothing but lies! The officer told me about you! Now, go back to your room."

Elsewhere, interrogators did not allow themselves to become so bemused. At Alcatraz it was demanded of the prisoners that they complete what they called the "blue book biography." This was a questionnaire in a booklet with blue covers. The prisoners were impressed with the slick printing job, the good English, and the thorough familiarity with American life and the American military that was indicated by the questions. It would have surprised none of them to learn that the "blue book" had been put together in the United States. It was by far the most searching probe their captors were to conduct of their personal and professional lives. It dealt with all facets of the respondent's background: the circumstances of his birth, his upbringing, his family, his economic status, his education, his political philosophy and the political philosophies of other family members, and every conceivable aspect of his military career.

One by one, members of the Alcatraz group were taken to the torture chambers in the Ministry of Defense and ordered to fill out the questionnaire; one by one, they refused to fill out the "blue book"; one by one, they were savaged until they yielded. Mainly they yielded lies, mixing them with a small measure of innocuous truth.

———

To Jim Mulligan, now a faded wisp of skin hanging on bone, the most memorable thing about that long springtime was the deep friendship that flowered with Ron Storz in Cell #5 of the long Alcatraz cellblock. Storz had been worried about Mulligan, alone in the small cellblock since Stockdale's departure, and had worked hard to keep up his morale, a hand-flashing conversation through the gaps at the bottoms of their cell doors.

Storz by this time was the only Alcatraz prisoner who looked worse than Mulligan. He had decided that the most effective way to combat his captors was to fast, to confront them with the prospect of losing a prisoner for whom they would have to account, or at least of releasing one whose horrendous physical condition would give credibility to his reports of incredible mistreatment. So he starved himself. Well over six feet tall, it was estimated that he now weighed between ninety and a hundred pounds. SRO Denton ordered him to eat, threatening him with court-martial upon release if he failed to comply with the order. Storz replied that he was trying, but that he had lost interest in food and that his stomach seemed unable to accept any.

The Alcatraz prisoners continued to live from day to day, trying not to let themselves think about how long their captivity might last.

But occasionally they could not help themselves. One day Denton found himself saying to an interrogator, "I want the truth: when do you think this war will end?"

"Den-ton," said the interrogator, "if you want the truth, I will tell you: you will fall down here."

"What do you mean?"

"I mean you fall down, like Jesus Christ. He fall down and He rise again, ha ha. You fall down and you no rise again. I mean, you die. You will die here."

There appeared to be no question that the interrogator believed what he was saying. The SRO wished he hadn't asked.

At the Zoo, SRO Larry Guarino was not above trying a little blackmail. When the "blue book biography" was brought to the Zoo, he ordered, "Resist to torture." Subsequently he found himself facing an interrogator he had not dealt with before, one whom the prisoners identified as Zoo Rat, to distinguish him from the "Rats" in the other prison camps. Zoo Rat struck Guarino as a less-than-forceful personality. He had a girlish, limp-wristed manner, and Guarino set out to make the most of it. He refused to fill out the "blue book" and when Zoo Rat ordered him onto his knees, he refused to stay on them; after a few minutes he got up and sat down and would not kneel again. Zoo Rat did not press the matter. He scolded the SRO for refusing to obey the authority, but kept it friendly and tried to win his cooperation through persuasion rather than force.

After several days of this, Guarino was convinced Zoo Rat was a homosexual. He decided to try to entice him into making an advance, then threaten to betray his sexual weakness to the camp commander. In such manner he thought to turn the tables on Zoo Rat and make the interrogator his own prisoner.

One morning when Zoo Rat came to his cell, Guarino gushed, "Oh, come in! It's so nice of you to visit me! I've been so lonely." Folding his blanket, he placed it on the bunk, sat down next to it and patted it. "Sit down here, near me. What do you want to talk about?"

Zoo Rat giggled like a little girl. "I want to talk about you, Guarino," he said.

"Oh," said Larry, "let's talk about you. My, you're a little fellow, aren't you? Just look at how small your hands are."

Zoo Rat laid a hand alongside Guarino's to compare them. Larry lifted the interrogator's wrist, as though to measure it, saying, "Oh, your wrist is so fine compared to mine!" Zoo Rat giggled and squirmed delightedly, and Guarino told him, "Gee, you're really a nice fellow; one of the few Vietnamese I can understand."

Guarino went on and on in this vein, and Zoo Rat loved it. After a time, he left, regretfully, making it clear that he could not afford to be seen being friendly with the American. He left him pen, ink, and a "blue book," asking him to fill it out and promising to return later to pick it up.

Instead, Guarino wrote a note and tied it to the handle of his waste bucket. Later the bucket would be placed in the yard, and another prisoner would pick it up to empty it. The note would be found and the SRO's message distributed: *If I've ever seen a queer, Zoo Rat is one. I'm going to suck him in, and when he makes a move for me, I'll nail him. I'll threaten to tell the camp commander. Don't sweat me, I'm doing fine. YKB.* (YKB meant "Yankee Boss.")

When he heard the shouting in the yard next morning YKB knew the wrong people had found the note. Soon his cell door flew open, and there stood Zoo Rat in his shorts, holding the note high and shouting, "Jackass! *JACKASS!* We caught you. *We caught you!*"

Frightened, Guarino approached him contritely, muttering, "Oh, sir, that's bad, very bad!"

To Guarino's amazement, Zoo Rat handed him the note. "Here, jackass," he said gloatingly, "read it to me!"

Not one to look a gift Zoo Rat in the mouth, Guarino took the note and edged backward into the cell. Zoo Rat and the guard stood in the cell doorway, bestowing congratulatory smiles and chatter upon one another. Larry ripped the note, shoved the pieces into his mouth, and started chewing, hard! When the two in the doorway saw what he was doing, they grabbed him by the hair, slapping at him, taking him to the floor, and trying to retrieve the note. Guarino, chewing and swallowing, managed to force the dry paper down his throat.

The guard regarded Zoo Rat with contemptuous disbelief, clearly unable to fathom the interrogator's stupidity in having handed the note to the prisoner. Zoo Rat was crushed, literally quivering at his loss of face. He left the cell, screaming imprecations.

After a while Zoo Rat returned, still trembling. "I know what was in the note," he assured Guarino. "Here is a piece of paper. You write the note again, word for word, and if you do not write the truth it will be very bad for you!"

Guarino said, "Sir, please don't make me write that note. You're not gonna like it. It's very embarrassing."

"Write the note!"

"If I write it, you will know why I didn't want to write it. Please."

"Write the note, or you will be punished severely."

"All right, sir, if you insist."

He wrote: *Hello, out there. You don't know who I am and don't try to find out. It is not important. It is just that today I am so happy that I want everybody out there to know that at last I have found a little Vietnamese that I really like. I call him General Lee because he is such a stately little fellow. And I am happy because I have found out that an American and a Vietnamese can truly be friends. Don't worry about me. I am okay. And please don't try to communicate with me.* He signed it, *A Yank in Uncle Ho's Court.*

Meekly, Guarino handed this note to Zoo Rat saying, "Here, sir. I didn't want you to see this note, because now I am afraid that you must show it to the camp commander, and he will know that you and I are friends. It will look very bad for you."

Zoo Rat stormed away. A little while later he returned, angrily demanding that Guarino fill out the "blue book biography." Judging that he had pushed things far enough with Zoo Rat, Larry filled out his "blue book" with lies, and got off the hook. But not for long.

Summer of Horror

On May 10, 1969, two Air Force officers, John A. Dramesi (captured on April 2, 1967) and Edwin L. Atterberry (captured on August 12, 1967), escaped from the Zoo Annex.

It was a well-organized operation, more than a year in planning and preparation. It had an abundance of opposition from other prisoners, who maintained that even if Dramesi and Atterberry got over the wall, chances were nil that a pair of Caucasians would long go undetected in the densely populated countryside. They would be recaptured, possibly killed, and those who remained behind would pay dearly in torture for the leave-taking.

Some favored the attempt, pointing out that the Code of Conduct called for escape if at all possible. Moreover, it was argued, if Dramesi and Atterberry could make it to freedom they would be able to tell the world about the enemy's "humane and lenient" treatment.

Dramesi and Atterberry had built themselves up physically by running a mile and a half daily in small circles around a cell they shared with six others, and by adhering rigidly to a program of calisthenics.

By departure time they had altered their appearances so as to look as much as possible like the Vietnamese peasant in the street. Using a dye made of a mixture of iodine pills—their captors had issued them to combat diarrhea—brick dust, and water, they changed the color of the visible skin on their heads, necks, and hands. They wore conical hats they had woven from bamboo strips taken from sleeping mats and straw taken from brooms. They carried stolen chogi sticks—carrying poles—across the shoulders, with stolen baskets at the ends. The also carried knives, pieces of metal they had found in the yard, honed razor-sharp.

Ready to go in April, they waited for a rainy Saturday night. On Saturdays most prison personnel departed to spend the weekends with their families; only a minimal guard force was on hand. They reckoned that with rain falling, the duty force guards would be keeping to shelter.

They were right. They slipped out of the place easily. They went through the roof, through tiles they had loosened. They saw no guards on the ground below. They jumped down quickly, one at a time, handing down the chogi sticks and baskets, then stole across a small garden area toward a shed that stood against a wall. They heaved their gear over the wall and climbed up onto the roof of the shed. Atop the wall, metal posts held several strands of barbed wire; and there were separate posts, with insulators on them, holding two more strands of wire, one above the other, that the prisoners assumed to be electrically charged. Atterberry, who once had been a telephone company lineman, knew how to deal with such things. He hooked a small piece of copper wire to the top strand and let it fall against the bottom strand. This short-circuited the wires and also put out half the lights in the camp; this was a common occurrence on rainy nights and did not bring any guards to the scene.

Outside the wall, they checked their makeup and dress, shouldered their chogi poles, and padded down the road, past the guard at the Zoo Annex gate, past a policeman on a bicycle, and past numerous other Hanoi citizens, along the dark, rain-puddled thoroughfares to the northern outskirts of the city. They hoped to reach the Red River while several hours of darkness remained to them; if they could do so, they would steal a boat. By first light they wanted to be several miles downriver, toward the sea. Then assuming a lost-boat alarm would prompt a river search, they would destroy the boat, so that it could not be found, find a hiding place ashore, then, at night, steal another boat, and move on.

They passed through the populated areas at the northern edge of the city, swam across a canal, and lost track of time. They became convinced that first light was coming on and that they had to hole up. They crawled behind some thick bushes, against the wall of an abandoned church. Actually, they had been making good time and there were several hours of darkness left to them.

By first light, there were heavily armed search parties all around them. Soon, a guard crawled into the thicket, saw them, and screamed.

"What do we do now?" Atterberry whispered.

"Nothing," Dramesi answered resignedly. "That's it."

They crawled out, to find themselves facing a dozen weapons. The escape was over.

The Dramesi-Atterbury escape attempt touched off the most brutal torture period of the long captivity. The Vietnamese treated this much differently from the Coker-McKnight breakout of October, 1967. Many POWs speculate that it was clear to their captors that the latter was a spur-of-the-moment thing: Coker and McKnight, having found a way to open their cell doors, had simply run away. Their escape did not involve elaborate props and disguises, homemade knives, the expertise to short-circuit a security system—all elements of real planning. Hence, the theory went, there was no important information to be squeezed out of Coker and McKnight, and their punishment had been relatively mild.

With Dramesi and Atterberry, it was different. They were returned to the Zoo and kept there for five days. Each was isolated. Dramesi was placed on starvation rations, a small piece of bread and a cup of water twice a day. He was made to spend long periods on his knees. Teams of guards took turns beating him. He was slapped, punched, flogged with a rubber whip, and rope-tortured numerous times.

Then the two prisoners were transferred to Hoa Lo, Dramesi was installed in Room 18, the Meathook Room, and Atterberry was quartered in Room 5 across the courtyard. At Hoa Lo, Bug presided, and things got rough. Dramesi was locked in jumbo irons, the kind that locked on with a long, heavy bar that precluded walking or even much moving. He spent the next thirty-two days and nights in these irons, with his hands tied tightly behind his back. He was beaten continually. He was rope-tortured approximately fifteen times. When beatings and tortures were not being administered, he was made to sit on a stool. He was not allowed to sleep. He listened to Atterberry screaming on the other side of the yard.

The two men had agreed that if they were recaptured and tortured, they would yield the details of their escape attempt. Most of the details were, of course, obvious, and the two of them had done all of the planning and preparing. There was no one else to implicate.

After Dramesi had yielded on the escape, Bug kept at him for a statement lauding the humane and lenient treatment; for a letter of apology for the escape attempt; for a written and tape-recorded denunciation of the American intervention; and for a letter denouncing President Nixon. Dramesi yielded only the letter of apology for the escape attempt and a letter about Nixon which was hardly the denunciation Bug had demanded. Instead, he wrote a page and a half explaining why he believed that someday Nixon would be recognized as one of the greatest of American Presidents.

Presumably, Ed Atterberry in Room 5 was playing it as tough as Dramesi—certainly Bug was inflicting more punishment on him than he was built to take, for he did not survive the torture.

Atterberry's death may have brought the Vietnamese to the realization that Dramesi, too, was nearing the end of his endurance. In any case, his heavy torture, which had continued for more than a month, ended. He received his first full meal since before the escape attempt and was allowed to bathe. Then he was locked in leg irons and kept in solitary confinement. In the smothering heat he was made to sit fully-clothed on a stool and was not allowed to lie on his bed or sleep. He was hurting, and the torture had had its psychological effect; he was frightened.

Opponents of the Dramesi-Atterberry escape attempt were soon proved correct in their surmise that many would pay dearly for it. By nightfall on Sunday, May 11, the day Dramesi and Atterberry were returned to the Zoo, the place had become the closest thing to hell on earth many Americans were ever to know. Through the cracks and gaps in their cell doors, many watched as the others were marched off to torture chambers in the Auditorium, in the Carriage House, in the Chicken Coop, next to the Auditorium, and in the Gook House, which was what the prisoners called the administration building. Men listened, fearfully, prayerfully, to other Americans' screams, to their shrieked pleas for mercy. And they waited themselves to be taken to torture.

The torture went on for months. Twenty-six men were taken. They were locked in hell cuffs and leg irons. They were beaten with fists and clubs. They were rope-tortured. But the primary instrument of torture now was the "fan belt," the rubber whip that was cut from an automobile tire. Using these, the Vietnamese literally flayed the hides off their American prisoners.

The procedure was to require the prisoner to drop his trousers and to lie on the floor, spread-eagled on his stomach. Two guards stood a distance away, each in a different corner of the room, each holding a rubber whip. On signal, one whipper would come out of his corner, lunging toward the spread-eagled prisoner, screaming unintelligibly, bringing his whip from his heels, up over his shoulder, and lashing with as much force as he could muster down across the prisoner's lower back, buttocks, and upper thighs. Then he would withdraw and the other whipper would run in and lash the prone prisoner. The whippers kept on coming, screaming, lashing, flogging the skin from their prisoners' bodies.

The Vietnamese were heedless of the men's cries. It made not the slightest difference that a man had been ripped open, that a large expanse of him had been turned into a quivering mass of oozing hamburger. Occasionally there would be a brief respite from the floggings; the prisoner would be lifted onto a table, and a guard would use a bamboo club to break all of the cartilage in his shins—the guard would keep cracking the club along the shinbones, feeling with his fingers to find cartilage that had not been broken, then slamming the club into it. Then the flogging would be resumed, to continue until the interrogator began to hear answers to the questions he was asking: Who were the senior prisoners in the camp? Who had been giving the orders? What were the orders? What were the various prisoner committees? How many were involved in the Dramesi-Atterberry escape attempt?

Tortured to the brink of insanity, men gave up all they knew.

One of the worst things that happened was that someone was made to confirm Vietnamese suspicions that Navy Lieut. James J. Connell was faking his injuries. Captured on July 15, 1966, Connell, a 1961 Naval Academy graduate, had been through severe introductory tortures. Since his first rope torture, he had insisted to his captors that his arms were unusable, and had put on a most convincing act. His arms always dangled and flopped about as though he had no control over them. Connell had used the conditions of his arms and hands to fend off enemy attempts to get him to write things. His captors had not tortured him again, but with the passage of time had become highly suspicious. Guards had taken to knocking J. J. about when he would have to come out of his cell, pushing him down to see if he would use his arms to break his fall. He did a superb acting job, often going down on his face and head, never once betraying the fact that his arms and hands were quite operable.

Meanwhile, in a lonely cell in the Gatehouse, near the main gate, he had been one of the Zoo's supercommunicators. Coal balls for cooking were made in the yard opposite the Gatehouse, and Connell would flash with POWs as they worked. He learned who occupied the various cells in each cellblock, collected health reports, learned who had been in torture and what had been extracted. He passed information from group to group, infusing it with an irrepressible optimism. Zoo SRO Larry Guarino called J. J. "our worldwide communications net."

Now, in the intense torture that followed the Dramesi-Atterberry escape attempt, his central role in the camp's communications system was exposed.

The Vietnamese were in no hurry to reach the seniors—"the heavies," as the POWs called such as Guarino, Bud Day, and others of high rank. They let them stew in their own worry, listening to the endless screaming and crying. Rabbit was in camp and one day he told Guarino, "I will be seeing you in a couple of weeks. We will be all set for you then, and I will be your officer-in-charge."

Once he was taken to a meeting with Cat, who smiled and said, "We think you know many things. Everyone obeys your orders. Have patience. In a few weeks, I personally will see you again."

Guarino was frightened and angry. He had known nothing of the Dramesi-Atterberry escape plan. As senior officer in the Zoo and Zoo Annex complex, he would have vetoed it. He accorded such a plan no chance to succeed and erroneously believed it to be a direct violation of Robbie Risner's years-old order not to try to escape without outside help. (Actually, Risner's order had been directed at a specific individual who had announced plans to go over the wall with no plan.) Guarino also felt certain that any escape attempt would trigger a brutal reaction.

On the other hand, Bud Day, who was SRO in the Barn, was exhilarated when he heard of the escape attempt. He was full of pride at the imagination and daring Dramesi and Atterberry had exhibited. He estimated the chance of successful escape from the Hanoi area to be very low. At the same time, he felt strongly that attempts should be made to bring word to the American people of the brutal treatment of the POWs; he did not believe that the six men who had been released early had gone home with any real knowledge of the horrors of confinement.

Guarino and Day listened for weeks to the screaming, crying, and pleading. Then, on June 12, it was Guarino's turn. He was savaged for many weeks. He was denied sleep, once for a solid week. He was rope-tortured. He was repeatedly flogged with rubber whips. Guards were set upon him to administer long, terrible beatings with their fists. Bamboo clubs were used to smash the cartilage in his shins. He was denied water until he was nearly dehydrated. He was kept in leg irons and on his knees until they were swollen to basketball size, with holes gouged out to the bones. He was torn and bleeding all over. Guards rubbed their dirty shoes in his wounds, so as to induce infection; they were successful. The truly incredible thing about what happened to him was that he survived.

During brief periods of respite he listened to the screams of other Americans in nearby torture chambers. There was nothing the SRO could do but pray, for the others and for himself.

Rabbit identified Guarino to himself as "YKB," read all his policies to him, told him he was responsible for the Dramesi-Atterberry escape attempt, and demanded a confession. Guarino refused to confess and the torture went on. Once, when no guards were in the room, he attempted suicide, breaking a window with a fist and trying to cut his wrists with shards of glass. He did not want to die; he hoped he would be found before he could bleed to death, and that his captors would stop the torture. But he was caught before he could even get a couple of good slices into his wrists, and the torture continued.

When he confessed to all the things his captors demanded he confess to, he was accused of lying, and the torture went on.

By the end of July, Guarino had yielded an acceptable confession, a letter requesting amnesty, and had agreed to write a series of eight articles for the camp magazine. He wrote all these things in the Communists' own jargon, or else tried to couch the material in Western-style humor the Vietnamese were unlikely to recognize. For the time being, at least, he had taken all the torture he could take. He needed time. He was "rolling." He agreed to see a delegation and to make a movie.

———

Barn SRO Bud Day's turn came on July 16. Day's arms had remained unusable since he had been hanged in ropes two years earlier. But at torture time that midsummer, the condition of his arms made no difference.

He was locked in leg irons and hell cuffs and flayed nearly to insanity. He hallucinated, heard Americans in extensive conversations, heard a great deal of popular American music, and knew he was losing his mind. When he could not stand the flogging anymore, he began confessing, just as the others had, to the existence of various nonexistent prisoner committees, such as the transportation committee, whose task, he explained, was to arrange for trucks for the evacuation of the prisoners; and the pass and identification committee, charged with the manufacture of travel papers.* To his amazement, this intelligence was accepted.

But it wasn't enough. His torturers wanted an escape committee. There had not been one in the Zoo, but when he was flogged for an answer he named himself as the one and only member. This proved to be unacceptable, and the flogging continued. He named his cellmates, Navy Lt. Comdr. Arvin R. Chauncey, captured on May 31, 1967, and Robert R. Sawhill, captured on August 23, 1967. The next day, full of grief at the certainty that he had betrayed his friends into torture, he insisted to his interrogators that all he had told them had been lies. Later, checking with Chauncey and Sawhill, he learned to his immense relief that neither man was ever approached for complicity on an escape committee.

The flogging of Day continued—he stopped counting after about three hundred lashes. Among other things, the enemy demanded to know what messages Day had been receiving from "the new senior American officer, Rivers," since the departure of the old leader, Guarino.

When Guarino disappeared into torture, Wendy Rivers, the

---

*Other prisoners described an athletic committee, a historical committee, an entertainment committee, an awards committee, a camp beautification committee, a reunion committee, an investments committee, a car-buying committee, an airmen's promotion committee, and others.

second-highest-ranking American in the camp, assumed command. In hopes of getting the dreadful torture siege ended, Rivers issued orders to give the enemy anything he demanded short of security information. He authorized men to read the news over the camp radio, to make tape recordings, and to admit that he, Rivers, was now acting SRO. When the terror ended, he said, they were to resume a normal resistance posture.

Day did not know Rivers to be SRO, however; he had never had a message from him and was of no mind to invent something that would bring him to grief. He gave nothing on Rivers. The flogging continued. He vomited blood and passed large amounts of it into his waste bucket. The flogging continued.

After six weeks the torture ended, and he was locked in a cell in the Pool Hall. He sent a warning to Wendy Rivers, in solitary in the same building, that the Vietnamese were torturing for information about him. Rivers sent word back that Day was to take no more torture for anything involving him—that if pressed for more he was to tell what he knew, or, if possible, to make something up.

————

Late on the Sunday afternoon of the recapture of Dramesi and Atterberry, guards boarded up the window at the back of Cell #1 in the Garage, overlooking the wall separating the Zoo from the Zoo Annex. The three occupants of this cell were Navy Lt. Comdr. Eugene "Red" McDaniel, Air Force Maj. Albert E. Runyan (captured on April 29, 1966), and Air Force Maj. Kenneth R. Fleenor (captured on December 17, 1967). Somehow the Vietnamese discovered that the cell was the primary communications channel from the Zoo into the Zoo Annex. It followed that the three Americans in the cell were important communicators, in a position to know everything.

In fact, the communicators knew nothing of the escape. In the months of contact with the Annex, no hint of it ever had been transmitted. The information was held in the Annex on a need-to-know basis, and there had seemed no need to spread it into the Zoo; what Zoo inmates did not know could not be extracted from them and could not hurt others. But in the post–escape purge, the three who had occupied the communications cell were ravaged. "Red" McDaniel was taken to torture on June 14 and remained two weeks. The torture-flogging that was inflicted on him is believed to have been the worst to which any American prisoner was subjected.

As days and nights tumbled past, McDaniel took approximately seven hundred lashes with the rubber whip. One inexperienced torturer tied him into ropes with such force that the bone in his upper right arm snapped, loudly, and a jagged end ripped through the flesh. Heedless, the torturers continued with the roping and left him tied in an unspeakable agony for three hours. His back, buttocks, and legs swelled hugely. His wounds, raw, purplish, red, oozing blood, became infected. He developed a high fever. He vomited blood. His inquisitors wanted him to name the escape planners. For a long time, McDaniel gave them nothing. Then, during one flogging session when he knew he was approaching the edge of sanity, he gasped, "I am the escape committee! I am planning an escape right now!"

The whipping stopped. Camp officers and interrogators crowded into the torture chamber, firing questions at him: How did he plan to get out of his cell? What supplies would he carry with him? Where had he hidden them?

He said that he would leave his cell simply by knocking down the door; that he would carry rice, weapons, a mirror, and some iodine; and that he had hidden these things under the brick flooring in the bath area.

Guards were sent to the bath area. They ripped up the flooring, searched the walls and nearby cistern. They found nothing. But the search afforded McDaniel enough time to gather his wits, and when the lashing resumed he was ready for it.

He hallucinated. He heard Christmas music, songs that played over and over again, day and night. His ankles were locked in irons, the U-bolts fastened around them so tightly that soon they became embedded in skin and bone and the legs swelled to at least twice their normal size. The pain became unbearable and after a while he imagined that he had a key to the leg irons and was able to open them and remove them and thus achieve a degree of comfort. It was as real an experience as he had ever had.

He prayed. Deeply religious all of his life, he gave himself to his God—. . . *not my will, but Thine be done . . .*

He was quizzed. Electrodes were placed in his hands and, when he failed to answer questions, painful charges were shot through his hands and arms.

Somehow, he endured. And on June 28 the torture ended. He was taken to share a cell with Wendy Rivers, who had been told, "Today, you will meet a new man. You should watch this man very closely and learn from his mistakes."

Rivers was horrified at McDaniel's appearance. He could not imagine how a man possibly could survive such punishment as had been inflicted on his new cellmate.

McDaniel could do nothing for himself. Rivers cared for him, and heeded his plea not to say or communicate anything sensitive in front of him. For McDaniel explained that he could take no more torture. He said, "I will tell them anything they want to know." In fact, says Rivers, it took Red McDaniel only about a week to bounce back.

———

The prisoners at the Zoo and Zoo Annex were tortured for many things that summer. Tough men who had been stalwart resisters were tortured until they yielded thorough biographies of themselves, letters of fulsome apology for having attended the war, letters of support to such as Senator Fulbright for his opposition to the war, letters to Ho Chi Minh, pleading for amnesty, letters of surrender to the Vietnamese, in which they agreed to do whatever their captors asked of them.

Kasler, Guarino, Rivers, Ray Vohden, Navy Lieut. Peter V. Schoefel (captured on October 4, 1967), and others were made to memorize what their captors apparently believed to be typically American answers to a series of questions, then were trotted before what was said to be a Japanese delegation.*

"And how are you feeling?" came the question.

"Oh, all right."

"And what is your physical condition?"

"Oh, I am fine. Look at me." (Prisoners who had been in heavy torture wore long-sleeved shirts and trousers that hid their injuries.)

"Do you think the Vietnamese people have a formidable air defense system?"

"Oh, I rather guess that is true."

And so on.

———

Kasler balked when Eel, the slimy-looking interrogator, demanded that he tape-record a letter another American had written to his wife: ". . . and, darling, I want you to continue working at home for peace, and I will do my best here to cooperate with the Vietnamese . . ."

---

*It probably was a Vietnamese film company, with actors made up to look like Japanese. The same people were later involved in the making of a movie with Guarino and Rivers.

"I'm not gonna tape that," Kasler said, tossing it back to Eel.

"But why?"

"You would put my name on it and say it's mine."

"You believe we would do a thing like that?" Eel affected shocked surprise.

"Damn right I think you'd do a thing like that!"

Eel said sternly, "You will tape-record this or you will be heavy punished."

"I refuse."

Kasler was ordered back to his cell. He was not approached again on the matter, but heard another American read the letter a few days later on the camp radio. A lot of good strong men were hurting, and were frightened.

"Unless you agree to be in the movie, we are going to start your torture all over again," Rabbit told Larry Guarino.

Guarino, who could not bear the thought, agreed to an acting job. He was to play the part of an American colonel in Saigon, in the year 1957, planning the infiltration into the DRV of "lackies in the form of South Vietnamese officers" for the purpose of toppling the government.

Through a crack in his cell door, Guarino saw Wendy Rivers being escorted into the Gook House. A few minutes later he heard the flogging begin, and after a while he heard Rivers screaming. Then Rabbit came and told him, "So now, in the movie that we are going to do, you are going to be helped by your deputy commander."

"Who's that?" Guarino asked.

"You know, your deputy, Reevers."

"Oh, is that right?"

"Yes. He said he was very happy to hear that you have consented to play in the movies with Reevers."

Rivers played the part of the colonel's deputy, a smooth, ambitious lieutenant colonel who encouraged and aided his senior in the development of his sinister plan.

The film was never shown to any American prisoners but guards and officers were later to needle Guarino and Rivers about it.

For one reason or another, the heat was on everywhere that July. The Americans in the prison camp across the river from the city of Sontay did not hear about the Dramesi-Atterberry escape attempt. Instead, they were hearing a great deal more than they wanted to hear about such American political figures as Senators Fulbright, McGovern, and Kennedy, and the powerful opposition these men continued to mount against the prosecution of the war. The Vietnamese insisted the prisoners write letters of support to these senators. The prisoners strongly resisted.

Typically, Marine Capt. Orson Swindle simply would not write Sen. Edward Kennedy assuring him that he agreed with him about the war. He did not agree with the senator, had been badly demoralized by the statements he had made, and had no intention of sending him words of encouragement and support. Nor, he said, would he write a statement to the American people assuring them that he was being well treated. The Vietnamese decided that Swindle must "sit and think deeply."

He was taken to a room furnished only with a stool and single, naked light bulb, hanging from the ceiling. He was locked in leg irons that were wired to the stool, and guards were instructed to see that he did not sleep. He remained on the stool for ten days and nights. Whenever he even appeared to be slipping away into sleep, the guards would slap him awake.

Then he would be left alone again. The days were not so bad, for then there were the sounds of life around him—doors opening and closing, plates clattering, men walking, and distant, muffled conversation. But he came to dread the nights. After the go-to-bed gong, a deathly stillness would overtake his world and he felt alone, in a terrible, melancholy void. He could not stop thinking about his wife, Gail, and their son, Kevin. Tears would well up in his eyes and stream down his face.

One night he was astounded to see his cell door open to admit several Marine officers of various ranks, in clean, fresh-pressed uniforms. He squinted at them, unbelievingly, in the dim light, his heart pounding. One of them said, "We've come to tell you what a good job you're doing. How are you getting along?"

He poured out his heart, answering every question, even some that were not asked. He was asked how he communicated with other prisoners, and he explained every technique, told what circumstances dictated the use of each, and offered judgments on the effectiveness of each. The visiting Marines listened avidly. Then he began asking them questions about friends in the Marine Corps. The visitors became evasive and seemed anxious to leave. Then it dawned on him that these were not U.S. Marines, but Russians! As they filed out of the cell, he realized that he had given away to the enemy all there was to know about the camp's communication system. Only later would he realize that he had been hallucinating.

Nor was the session with the Marines the worst of his nightmares. Next came a group of Chinese doctors in white surgical smocks, rolling a table full of hypodermic syringes. Swindle was told that his attitude was so bad that a decision had been made to perform an operation on his brain that would render him tractable. "If you don't believe it," someone said, "we'll show you some Americans we have already done it to." With that, Marine Capt. Harley Chapman and Navy Comdr. Bill Franke were led into the room. Swindle had never seen either of them; still, he knew them—there was no question about who they were. They wore white gowns. Their eyes were opaque and they moved like zombies. Each had a small white bandage on the back of his head.

Quickly, Swindle leaped at the table full of syringes, knocked it across the room, picked up his stool and flung it! The doctors scattered, ran in all directions, raced around the room, and struggled to get out of it.

Then, suddenly, he came back to reality. He found himself in a corner of the cell, where he had made a little barricade of his stool and waste bucket. He had removed the wire holding his leg irons to the stool and tied some of it around the neck of his water jug; now he was swinging it, like a mace, threatening advancing guards with it, and screaming at them. The guards subdued him, placed him on a sleeping mat, put a mosquito net over him, and left him.

He awoke in broad daylight after several hours of sleep. He felt refreshed. An interrogator came to see how he felt. There was no antagonism, no pressure for letters and statements. For three days he was fed, given all the water he wanted, and allowed to sleep. Then the interrogator said, "Surely, you will write today?"

"No," said Swindle, breathing deeply, "I'm not going to write."

He was put back on the stool. After ten more days and nights, he wrote.

In the spring, the American inmates of Portholes, the jungle camp, were transferred to another prison about 15 miles southwest of Hanoi. Most called this place "D-1," because one of the buildings was so marked. The chief interrogator was called "Cheese," because some-one had once referred to him as "the big cheese." Actually, he was a small, slight man, fortyish and remarkably clumsy for his size. He was full of hatred for his American prisoners, and soon revealed himself to be a sadist. He would break out in sweat and salivate when he tortured men. Dennis Thompson came to know Cheese well early on, when the interrogator demanded an autobiography and an apol-ogy to the Vietnamese people. Dennis refused to provide them, and was tortured for forty days. He was made to kneel through the days, holding his hands high in the air, and to stand at attention through the nights. When the pain in his knees became unbearable and he fell off them, he would be beaten by guards.

Often as Cheese paced about the room, lecturing the kneeling Thompson and asking questions, he would keep jabbing the pointed end of a cheap plastic pen into the prisoner's eye sockets and advis-ing him to "think your mind carefully."

Then he would kick Thompson's knees, forcefully enough to move them, scrape them along the floor, and would ask, "Do you hurt?" He would keep kicking, and the saliva would leak out of his mouth and he would sweat, kicking harder and harder, until the prisoner would fall over. Then he would order guards to beat him for failing to remain on his knees.

Sometimes, Cheese would fasten his small fingers on Thompson's upper and lower eyelids, pull them out and twist them and roll them between the ends of his fingers. He would engage in this exercise for long minutes, salivating and sweating, pleasurably.

After forty days and nights Thompson wrote:

> The Vietnamese people throughout my captivity have been giving me the treatment real good. It has been brought to my attention, after my captivity, that the Vietnamese people have been revolting throughout their 4000-year history. The Vietnamese people have proven them-selves to be the most revolting people I have ever met in my life. I hope that soon the Vietnamese Communists and all of those who have taken care of me and my friends as prisoners will get what they deserve. . . .

Cheese accepted this. Thompson's torture ended, and the paper was forwarded to higher headquarters. There, a few months later, someone got around to reading it and, apparently, sent word to Cheese that it was no triumph for the Vietnamese people. So, it was no surprise to Thompson when, in the grim summer of 1969, Cheese included him on a long list of D-1 prisoners to undergo intensive interrogation. After sixteen days and nights of suffering comparable to what he had endured the previous fall, he agreed to write a letter to "the peace movement in the United States." He tried to keep it unusable—". . . heard all about you marching mothers . . . compatriots, it is time that we rose up in the spirit of the October Revolution . . ."

———

In March, at the Plantation, Doug Hegdahl had received a message from Dick Stratton: "The Fox says go home with his blessing."

Fox was the code name of Air Force Lt. Col. Theodore W. Guy, who was senior to Hervey Stockman and had succeeded him as SRO. Guy had not been immediately agreeable to Stratton's proposal that Hegdahl leave early, but Beak, now code-named Wizard, had been persuasive. With Guy persuaded, Hegdahl had only to sell the Vietnamese on the idea.

On June 3, at the height of the Dramesi-Atterberry post–escape purge, Hegdahl was taken to an interrogation where it was demanded of him, "Who is Fox?"

He was frightened; he knew that his time for torture had come. He was in a dilemma; he was not going to give up code names, yet knew that a failure to cooperate would destroy his chances for release. Would he then be in violation of orders from Guy as well as Stratton?

"A fox," he stammered, "is a small red animal found in a forest . . ."

His interrogator slammed a hand down on the table, shouting, "Code! Fox. Who is the Fox?"

"I don't know what you're talking about."

He was thrown on the floor, his hands were tied behind him, and he was wrapped tightly head to foot in a straw mat. He was left alone, full of panic, terrified at the thought of what would happen to him when his interrogator returned. After about an hour, his bindings were removed and he was seated at the table again, facing the interrogator.

"We do not like to do unpleasant things to you," the interrogator said, "but you must tell us, who is the Fox?"

Hegdahl was amazed. There was no show of anger. He was now being treated almost gently; he surmised that his captors had reminded themselves of his stupidity and had decided to deal differently with him. Pencil and paper were placed before the prisoner, and the interrogator ordered, "Write, Fox is SRO."

Hegdahl wrote this, smiling brightly and saying, "Want to tell me his name; I'll write that down, too?"

The interrogator shook his head, smiling grimly; he had no intention of giving away military information to Hegdahl. He said, "Write down, 'Beak is Lieutenant Commander Stratton.'" Hegdahl felt a surge of relief. Beak was the old code name. They seemed to have the old code and fragments of the new, and with the pressure on, code names were all sure to be changed again immediately. The interrogator produced a map of the Plantation, pointed at a building, calling it by the name the prisoners called it, and said, "Write 'Warehouse' here." Then, pointing at another building, he ordered, "Write, 'Corncrib' here."

That was the end of it.

On July 4, Hegdahl was taken to a large room where Cat, the head jailer, sat with two other prisoners, Navy Lt. Robert Frishman (captured on October 24, 1967) and Air Force Capt. Wesley Rumble (captured on April 29, 1968). Tea and bananas were served to the prisoners, and Cat was expansive. "You three are being considered for release," he said, "if you show a strictly correct attitude."

When the tea party ended and the three prisoners were leaving the room, Cat called Hegdahl back. He laid before the Dakotan the sheets of paper on which he had taken the dictation a month earlier. He said, "It is true, Heddle, this time you are going home. But mind you, Heddle, if you say anything bad about the camp authorities or about the Vietnamese people when you return, I will see these documents fall into the hands of your government. According to your code of conduct, you will go to prison for revealing secrets of your comrades."

Hegdahl recalls that when he first joined the two officers, Frishman and Rumble, he felt required to remind them that ". . . you understand that you are not to accept early release," and to explain that he had been ordered to leave. He remembers that neither officer made any reply.

Prior to departure Hegdahl came to know the two well, and to like them. Rumble had an extensive, revised list of POW names, men who were known to be in captivity because they had actually been seen and heard by others. Many of Hegdahl's names were of men who had not been positively identified, had come from third parties who had only seen names on identification cards and the like. It was decided that Rumble's list, clearly the more reliable, was the one that should be given to the U.S. government.

On August 4, Frishman, Rumble, and Hegdahl were released to an American antiwar delegation. On reaching Washington, Hegdahl, disregarding Cat's threat to expose him to his government for ''revealing the secrets of your comrades,'' had much that was ''bad'' to tell his own government about the camp authorities. He delivered all the intelligence he held; he was even able to pinpoint for startled debriefers the precise location of the Plantation, which, he assured them, ''is located at the intersection of Le Van Binh and Le Van Linh''—he had collected this information one day while sweeping around the front gate of the place. The ''dumb'' Dakotan didn't have to play dumb anymore.

''Don't worry about me,'' Stratton had told Hegdahl two years earlier. ''Blow the whistle on the bastards!'' At a press conference, Hegdahl and Frishman were allowed for the first time to tell of mistreatment and brutal torture in Hanoi's prisons. During the Johnson Administration, when the first six POWs had been released from Hanoi, it had been feared that public testimony might trigger a violent reaction against the prisoners who were still in captivity, so nothing was said. The Nixon Administration was persuaded that the information would bring a weight of world opinion to bear against Hanoi that would result in improved treatment for the prisoners.

Later, when Hegdahl was discharged,* Dallas computer magnate Ross Perot, a 1952 Naval Academy graduate, sent him to Paris to press Hanoi's peace-talk delegates to allow inspection teams in the camps. During one meeting a Hanoi representative protested, ''Our policy is very humane in the camps.''

''Look,'' Hegdahl retorted, ''I was there.''

''Ohhh,'' the delegate murmured. ''Humane and lenient treatment'' was not mentioned again.

At Camp D-1, Cheese took the senior American prisoner to torture on July 20. This was Air Force Capt. Edward W. Leonard, Jr.—called ''J.R.'' by his friends—captured May 31, 1968. Leonard resisted for

---

*He was subsequently hired by the Navy to teach survival.

a long time, but Cheese was patient. Eventually, Leonard was drained of all sorts of confessions and antiwar statements. Nothing seemed to please Cheese, however, and the torture continued. In the deep of night, he would enter the torture chamber with a half-dozen guards, who would take Leonard down flat on his back and hold him. Cheese would then reach deep into the prisoner's eye sockets, fasten his small fingers on the eyeballs, and would squeeze and roll them for long, agonizing minutes, sweating, salivating, and telling the prisoner in wheedling tones, "You must trust me. You must rely on me. You are mistaken in your beliefs, and I will help you."

Then Cheese would stand up and wash his hands. Completing his ablutions, he would take a rough branch which had been whittled narrow at one end. He would insert this end into one of Leonard's nostrils and twist it and push it about, sweating, drooling, and wheedling. When he became satisfied that he had exercised one nostril sufficiently, he would transfer his branch and attentions to the other. Cheese would indulge himself in this activity for perhaps fifteen minutes at a time, then would put the branch down and resume squeezing the eyeballs.

At length, Leonard decided that he could endure no more. He looked about the chamber for an instrument of suicide. There was nothing. Then his bruised eyes fell on the waste bucket. Cheese had denied him any water for a long time; he was dehydrating and could not remember when he had last urinated. But the bucket was full, and he vaguely recalled having heard that urine would kill.* In odd moments, when guards were not present, he began stealing over to the bucket and drinking the urine, a cup at a time; it was warm, extremely salty, disgusting. He had consumed perhaps a quart and a half of the stuff before guards caught him drinking it. It was explained to him that he proved himself to be a "filthy pig." The bucket was taken from him and he was beaten.

On September 2, the DRV's Independence Day, he was told, "We will give you two days of rest. We will allow you to bathe."

Two days later, early in the morning, he was ordered down onto his knees again, with his hands high in the air. He had been at it for about an hour, was wondering when torture or life would end, when guards entered and escorted him back to his cell. He was told, "Sit down on the end of your bed. Shut up." A little while later, Cheese

---

*In fact, urine is not a poison, but Leonard did not learn this until he was repatriated.

entered, supervising the delivery of a pitcher of water and a bowl of thick green soup. The torture was over, and it was soon clear to Leonard that his captors were trying to restore him physically. About three weeks later, he learned of the death that saved him—that of Ho Chi Minh.

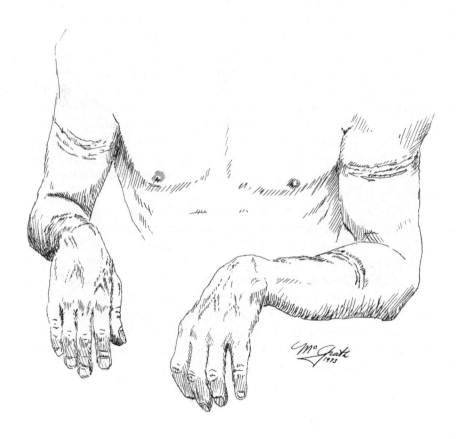

The End of the Terror

For most of Hanoi's American prisoners, 1969's summer of horror was the darkness before dawn. At the Zoo, in the Pool Hall, Jim Kasler perceived the faint beginnings of first light early on September 4. The sounds came as from far off, not over the radio speakers in the camp's cells, but through the speakers that were installed in the trees and on the utility poles and rooftops of the city. The sounds were funereal, a mournful, off-key dirge accompanying a chanted wail: *"Ho Chi Minh . . . Ho Chi Minh . . . Ho Chi Minh . . ."* Kasler tapped to his next-cell neighbor, Ray Vohden, "I think something's happened to old Ho."

As morning broke, guards appeared wearing black and red patches on their tunics. The prisoners surmised that these were mourning patches; indeed, they hoped they were and that Ho was dead—life could scarcely be any worse with him gone. The guards seemed quiet that day, distracted, almost disinterested in the prisoners. But it was clear that they were short-tempered, of no mind to brook any misbehavior. The prisoners sensed that it was not a time to provoke them. It was a time to wait and wonder—and to hope.

———

At Sontay that morning, Jim Warner heard the dirges and the chanting, too. Then there was the voice of "Hanoi Hanna," in Vietnamese now, slow, full of sad nuances and repeated references to Ho. Warner, who had suffered terrible torture that summer, thought, *The old goat's dead. Best news I've ever heard. I know where he is now, he's getting the benefits of the People's Democracy. Only this time, down there, he gets to be one of the people. He's not the President. He gets to live just like he made everybody live up here, the old son of a bitch!* Warner was as happy as he had been in a long time.

———

By nightfall on September 4, most of the POWs were rejoicing at the news coming over their camp radios, that Ho had indeed died. But John Young recalls that at D-1, he was grief-stricken. Young says he took some consolation from the fact that Ho, "who gave up everything for his people, had at least lived to see this Independence Day." He says that Cheese entered his cell that day for some reason and asked, "Why are you crying?" Young remembers that when he explained his tears, Cheese turned around and walked out. "He was crying, too."

For the most part, though, the prisoners were delighted and wondered how Ho's death would affect their own fortunes. There seemed reason for hope. But for Jim Stockdale, it seemed to make no difference. A few days after Ho's death, he found himself again in Room 18, facing Bug. Stockdale had been caught trying to communicate, and Bug was furious.

"Do you know where I have just been?" Bug shrieked. "I have been to the funeral. Do you know what that means to the Vietnamese people? Do you know what it means to have our country destroyed by criminals like you? And here you are again, trying to incite others to disobey the camp authority!"

Stockdale was tied into torture ropes. Bug lashed him across the face with a rubber hose. He harangued, lectured, worked himself into a frenzy, sustained it, and kept lashing the hose across Stockdale's face.

Stockdale could at least reflect that he had had a pretty good summer. In May he had thwarted Rabbit's plan to use him in a propaganda film by disfiguring himself; had been moved out of his torture chambers to make room for the recaptured John Dramesi and Ed Atterberry; had been stashed alone and had been pretty much left alone in a cell the prisoners called Cat's Quiz Room, where the prison system commander sometimes interrogated people; and he had been able to establish communications with Stardust Cell #3, about 40 yards to the northeast, by hand-flashing.

Stockdale immediately had assumed command. He had instructed that his BACK US policy, formulated in 1966, remained in effect except for "A," which meant, "stay off the air."

Since returning to Hoa Lo from Alcatraz, he had heard a score of different voices reading the news-propaganda. Surmising that men had suffered greatly before doing this, he judged that a blunt command to stop reading would be impossible to follow as well as demoralizing to men who had yielded and were "rolling." Where broadcasting was concerned, he now instructed, men were to be told to "get off the hook as soon as you can."

On the day Ho Chi Minh died, Stockdale had been caught communicating. Now Bug had him in torture ropes and under the lash. By nightfall, he agreed to write a confession of guilt, an admission of his "intention to oppose the camp authority." He was almost euphoric, for he was not required to name any other Americans or to write any propaganda concerning the war. Then Bug said, "Tomorrow, you will see some real punishment."

Stockdale feared he was to be squeezed for the names of those with whom he had been communicating. In his weakened condition, he was not confident that he could long guard any names, but was determined not to give any away. That night he broke a windowpane and slashed his wrists with shards of glass. After years of confinement and torture, he was not certain whether he wanted to die or was running a high-risk bluff. In any case, he meant to demonstrate to Bug that he was not afraid to die; that, indeed, he preferred death to more mistreatment and misuse, that further torture and demands would be futile. He had milked his wrists of perhaps a quart and a half of blood and was fading away by the time he was discovered. His calculated risk was successful. Bug, much aggrieved, backed off.

———

At Sontay on September 15, Jim Warner was engaged in conversation by a Vietnamese officer he had not seen before. The man claimed to be a general, a member of the General Staff and the General Political Department. He said, "I understand that you have had some trouble here."

"Yeah, that's true," Warner replied, "only that's not the half of it . . ."

"Don't worry about it anymore," the general said. He spent perhaps twenty minutes explaining that he had come "to ameliorate your living conditions. You are not going to have trouble anymore."

Warner was delighted to hear this and began to believe it even as the general spoke. Cell windows, which had been bricked up or boarded over, were being opened, and one had only to walk to them to be able for the first time to exchange waves and smiles and thumbs-up signals with other Americans, who were going to or coming from the bath stalls.

At the Zoo on October 1, a guard entered Jim Kasler's Pool Hall cell, pointed at the bricks in the wall where the window had once been, and made motions to the prisoner to pull them out. Unable to believe that he understood the guard correctly, Kasler made him repeat the sign-language instructions several times. Then, still uncertain, he pulled at a single brick; the mortar was weak and the brick came loose easily. Kasler let it fall to the floor. He looked at the guard, who nodded his head, pointed again to the window area, and indicated that Kasler should proceed. Kasler went to work with a will, slamming bricks to the floor. He could hear bricks hitting the floors of the other cells. Soon he was in contact with others. Word came that the prisoners in the other cellblocks were tearing open their windows.

A few days later Kasler was moved into a larger cell, with Ray Vohden and Jim Bell—he had hardly left his own cell when a crew of Vietnamese entered and started knocking down the wall, to make a larger cell that would hold a number of people. Word came from the Pigsty that cell walls were being torn down.

Each prisoner received what the Vietnamese called a "tea basket"—some Americans called it a "cobra basket"—a small bottle within a padded wicker covering to keep tea water warm during winter. The cigarette ration was doubled, from three to six smokes per day.

At Alcatraz, Ron Storz, who had been in torture since July, was returned to his cell when Ho Chi Minh died. Storz looked in desperate condition, hollow-eyed, thin as a rail. Through the gaps and cracks in their cell doors, the other prisoners watched as their captors, clearly worried now about the prisoner they had been brutalizing for nearly two months, took him out to sunbathe. Medics or doctors came and examined him and he was given intravenous feedings.

SRO Jerry Denton was caught communicating and was taken to interrogation in one of the rooms up in the Ministry, where he had suffered so much abuse. He fully expected more torture, but Soft Soap Fairy told him, "You were caught communicating, but you will not be punished."

Flabbergasted, Denton asked, "What did you say?" He made Soft Soap Fairy repeat the astonishing statement three times. "It is true," the effeminate interrogator insisted. "You will not be punished as long as I am running the camp."

The next day he told Denton, "Johnson and Jenkins have just been caught communicating, but they will not be punished. You see, what I tell you is true!"

In the days that followed, Soft Soap Fairy kept assuring the SRO that things were going to improve. There would be more and better food, sunshine, fresh air, and exercise. Eventually the ever-optimistic Denton concluded that the war was coming to an end.

Change was certainly in the air. By late fall, a third meal, breakfast, was added to the menu in Hanoi's prisons. Suddenly, soups were thick with vegetables, there was always plenty of bread, usually a side dish of potato or a vegetable, and often a plate of sugar and hot tea. It remained forbidden to communicate between buildings, but there was no effort now to stifle communications within cellblocks. At the Zoo one night, prisoners were astounded when they were taken to see a movie about the antiwar movement in the United States and found themselves in a well-lit room with a crowd of Americans: no effort was made to hide them from each other with darkness and blankets. The prisoners roared at the film with unrestrained, gleeful derision. The movie struck them as hilarious, full as it was of scenes of unkempt crowds waving placards inscribed, grossly, "Spiro Sucks," and "Pull Out Dick Now." They laughed, hooted, and shouted catcalls in a display of contempt that earlier would have resulted in brutal reprisals. But now their hosts only glared at them.

Following Jim Stockdale's suicide play, he was isolated in a black hole of a cell called Calcutta. This was a tiny, single-cell building, an unlit, filthy, unventilated oven of a dungeon. He was not allowed out of this sweltering, stinking cell for any reason for more than a month.

Then, in mid-October, his lot was vastly improved; he was transferred to a cell in the Mint. Here he remained under intensive surveillance. But he was allowed out to the bath stalls occasionally, so was soon back in communication. For whenever Stockdale emerged from the Mint, the air reverberated with coughing, hacking, and sneezing—Jerry Denton's cough code. Soon, note drops were established in the bath stalls and the bucket dumping area.

One late afternoon in November, Stockdale was summoned before Cat, who inquired, "Are you well?"

"I am fair," Stockdale replied. Cat seemed anxious, genuinely concerned about Jim's wrists. Stockdale guessed that his apparent attempted suicide had caused the prison boss some serious trouble.

Cat said, "I have something for you." He handed over five letters from Stockdale's wife, Sybil. Stockdale returned to his cell to read through each of them, again and again.*

———

In a jungle camp in South Vietnam, release was in the air. The Germans, the two women and two men who were nurses of the Knights of Malta, were gone. They had arrived in early May. Their leader, the handsome, blond woman named Rika, who had taken good care of the others, nursing their various illnesses, sewing their clothing, cooking for them, had died first. She had contracted severe dysentery and wasted away very quickly, and the Americans buried her one day in late June. Within a week, one of the German men, George, had joined Rika in death. The other two Germans, Monica and Bernard, had survived at least until October, when they departed

———

*It was surprising enough that the Vietnamese should give mail to Stockdale, whom they knew to be a leader of prisoner resistance. But what made it all the more surprising—and what Stockdale could not know at the time—was that, by now, Hanoi surely knew that vivacious, outspoken Sybil Stockdale was one of its most formidable opponents on the propaganda front in the United States, the front on which the Vietnamese had often told prisoners that they fully expected to win the war. It was Sybil Stockdale who invented and organized the National League of Families of POWs and MIAs and mobilized it to keep public attention focused on the plight of the prisoners.

the camp. According to their captors, they were to be taken to Hanoi, where they were to be released.*

That fall the American prisoners were told that some of them were also to be released, in conjunction with a big antiwar moratorium in the United States. The prisoners waited, each hoping against hope that he would be one of the lucky ones chosen to go home. Unlike the American prisoners in Hanoi, this leaderless group was not governed by an anti-early-release policy. They saw nothing despicable about accepting early release; far from it, each of them, officers included, hoped for it, believed it was the only way to survive.

In October the prisoners were told that the three who were to be released were Army Spec. 4 Willie A. Watkins, and Pfcs. Coy R. Tinsley, and James A. Strickland. These three were moved into a separate hooch, the one the Germans had occupied. They were placed on a special, fattening-up diet, received a good deal of medical attention, were injected with vitamins, and were no longer required to work. For the other Americans, nothing changed. They continued to gather their own manioc and their own wood for cooking fires, and were kept on an insufficiency of rice. They were allowed no further contact with the three who were to be released, but some managed it anyway. Those who were to remain now looked forward to the release ceremony, for a pig would be killed and there would be much to eat.

At the release party, Watkins, Tinsley, and Strickland went through the required motions, making tape-recorded statements in which they thanked their captors and condemned the American war effort. Another prisoner, chosen by the camp commander, rose to denounce himself and all the others who were to remain for having failed to demonstrate enough progress in their thinking to be worthy of release. Then captors and captives sat down to eat their fill of pig, rice, and bananas.

The release party was an emotional event. Some who were to remain were full of genuine joy for the releasees. At the same time, they were profoundly depressed at their own prospects—at thoughts of remaining in this hell of a jungle prison for God only knew how much longer. Some, they realized, would never make it home.

And in this camp, nothing changed.

———

*In fact, they were thrown into solitary confinement in Hanoi, and were not released until all of the prisoners were released, in early 1973.

On December 9, nine of the remaining ten prisoners in Alcatraz were returned to Vegas—two years and two months after they had departed the place. Ron Storz did not return with them. The others had heard him arguing bitterly with a Vietnamese officer who insisted that Storz was too ill to move with the others, that his health required that he be moved into larger quarters—Howie Rutledge thought he heard the officer say that Storz was to be moved into one of the interrogation rooms, up in the Ministry of National Defense. Wherever it was, Storz had flatly refused to be moved and had not been forced to do so. When the others were taken out, he had remained in his cell. He was never seen again.

———

Major Bai, Cat, kept inquiring after Stockdale's health. One day he confided to the SRO, "I am now the commander of this camp." Stockdale could not have been more amazed. It was as though the admiral of a fleet were announcing that he had been reduced to command of a single ship. Indeed, the mighty seemed to be falling! Stockdale, who had lived in solitary for most of his more than four years as a prisoner, longed for the companionship of a fellow American. He was about to tell the new camp commander that if he really was concerned about his health, he should give him a cellmate when Cat said, "You have been alone. I am going to put you with a roommate. You will meet him soon." Stockdale was overjoyed.

Major Bai was full of surprises. "I have a letter for you," he continued, handing it over. "It is from Jeremiah A. Denton." The letter advised that the nine had returned to Vegas from Alcatraz. In guarded language, Denton advised Stockdale that Cat had told him that life was to improve for the prisoners, and asked if Stockdale believed this. Cat indicated that Stockdale could write a reply. In similarly guarded language, the SRO simply warned Denton to watch his step. Stockdale suspected that Cat's purpose in allowing the letter was to impress upon the two leaders that the camp commander truly was possessed of humane and lenient instincts.

When Stockdale finished writing his reply to Denton, Cat said, "I am thinking of getting Denton a roommate. Perhaps Mulligan. What do you think of that?"

Stockdale lauded his judgment. "That is a very good idea," he said. Cat nodded solemnly, apparently satisfied that Stockdale appreciated his kindness.

Denton was in a state of near shock at what Cat had told him: that for thousands of years, the official policy of his country toward its war prisoners had been humane and lenient treatment but that, in the case of the Americans, he and a number of other officers and guards had misinterpreted and misapplied this policy. He said that he and the others had been required publicly to criticize themselves and to confess their mistakes. He indicated that these mistakes would not be repeated.

Shortly, Jim Mulligan was being taken from his cell in Stardust to empty his bucket when he saw Cat, and sought confirmation of his demotion, asking him, "Are you the commander of this camp?"

"Yes," Cat replied. "But I want you to know that I have volunteered to come here."

"Oh?" said Mulligan speculatively.

"Yes. You know, there are very many bad crim . . . prisoners in this camp, and I have volunteered to come here and see that we have the right type of camp."

There was no question about it, times were changing.

———

It is not possible to do more than speculate on the reasons for the treatment change in late 1969. There appear to have been two major factors: the death of Ho Chi Minh; and, by the time of the dictator's demise, the enormous and growing concern in the United States over the fate of those American fighting men who had fallen into Hanoi's hands. Ho seems badly to have misjudged the feeling of the American people for their captured military men. Thus, bitterly divided though America was about the war, he provided the one rallying point around which the most ardent protagonists on both sides of the war issue could unite, the well-being of the POWs. Indeed, it is difficult to imagine how Hanoi, whose purpose with its American prisoners was to exploit them for maximum political gain, could have managed the situation worse than it did. The constant references to the prisoners as war criminals; the threats of war crimes trials; the stilted language with which so many prisoners delivered so many unbelievable confessions of criminal activities and antiwar statements; the adamant refusal to allow International Red Cross inspections of the prison camps; the senselessly cruel refusal to supply the United States government with a list of American captives—all of these things succeeded only in arousing the darkest suspicions. A terrible anguish was needlessly inflicted on the prisoners' loved ones, and a terrible anger was ignited in millions of other Americans. And in the late summer of 1969, the Hegdahl-Frishman revelations of brutality and torture seemed to confirm all the worst suspicions.

The speed with which Ho's political heirs moved to improve life for the prisoners seemed to indicate some degree of understanding that the old regime's policies had been counterproductive. Ho's successors were never to yield on Red Cross camp inspections—doubtless they judged that in view of the four years of savagery the prisoners could report, it was much too late for that. Nor were they ever to supply a prisoner list—by now, there might have been too many for whom they were not prepared to account, such as Ed Atterberry, the Faker, the dying Ron Storz, and others who were tortured to insanity and death. Nor were the prisoners ever officially advised of a treatment policy change—perhaps such an announcement might have seemed to imply that the treatment ever had been less than humane and lenient.

So the prisoners had no way of knowing for sure that, for most of them, the long terror had ended.

PART IV

With Nixon in the White House, Henry Cabot Lodge had succeeded Averell Harriman as chief U.S. negotiator at Paris. The peace talks had been expanded to include both the Viet Cong and the Thieu government. There had been no discernible progress, a fact which fueled American impatience–there now were more than 540,000 U.S. combat troops in Vietnam, and more than 30,000 Americans had been killed.

In May, the Viet Cong had offered a ten-point plan for ending the war which required that the United States unconditionally withdraw its forces and cease its military and financial support of the Saigon government. The proposal was deemed unacceptable.

Nixon proposed that the United States and Hanoi each withdraw their combat forces over a twelve-month period. Hanoi, which had not acknowledged that its forces were in South Vietnam, could not agree to such a plan.

In July, Thieu proposed that the Viet Cong participate in internationally supervised elections. The Viet Cong denounced this plan as "trickery."

In August, American antiwar sentiment increased when it was re-vealed that a number of Green Beret officers and enlisted men were to be court-martialed for the murder of a Vietnamese colleague. A de-fense lawyer told newsmen that the Vietnamese had been ''a danger-ous Communist double agent.'' The case was dismissed when the C I A refused to allow its agents to testify against the defendants.

On October 15, hundreds of thousands throughout the United States participated in a war moratorium, demonstrating against continued American involvement. There were church services, rallies, and parades. Counterdemonstrators drove with their car lights on and marched with placards—one group of war supporters parachuted into New York City's Central Park to plant a flag in the middle of an antiwar rally. In Washington, the widow of Dr. Martin Luther King led a candlelight procession of 30,000 past the White House.

On November 3, Nixon made public a plan to ''Vietnamize'' the war: all American forces were to be withdrawn from combat on a secret timetable, depending on how quickly the burden of the war could be transferred to trained and capable South Vietnamese forces. He warned that he would react strongly against increased enemy activity during Vietnamization, and asked for support from ''the great silent majority of Americans.'' The White House reported that it was being inundated with telephone calls and telegrams in support of the President's program.

Congressional leaders groused at the secrecy of the withdrawal timetable and began demanding ''a date certain'' for American disen-gagement.

On November 15, upward of 250,000 antiwar protestors marched in the nation's capital in the most massive such demonstration in American history.

The same month, the American people learned that American troops were being charged with wantonly gunning down more than one hundred defenseless men, women, and children in a Vietnamese ham-let called My Lai.

30

Some Antiwar POWs

The improved diet and the fact that many prisoners were being granted cellmates did not make the Hanoi prison camps resemble Easy Street. Hard-eyed guards continued to roam the premises, keeping a tight lid on communications, and men were thrown into solitary confinement for getting caught. The propaganda harvest had been bountiful, and the camp authorities were determined that it should continue. And the Vietnamese knew that resistance would stiffen and the harvest would thin, badly, if a prisoner organization got a chance to develop.

Prisoners had been writing letters and making tape recordings, some of them praising their captors' treatment of them and lauding Hanoi's military capabilities. Some expressed the view that there was no way the United States could win in Vietnam and that in any event the war was not in the national interest. The Administration was urged to heed the demands of the antiwar movement, to accept the generous terms Communists were offering at the Paris peace talks, to withdraw from Vietnam, to withdraw support of the Saigon government, and to allow the Vietnamese people to settle their own differences.

Men had been yielding for various reasons: Some were "rolling," unable to tolerate the thought of more torture. Some had only heard of the torture, had been threatened with it, and found the price too high. Some were anxious to get their names out so that loved ones would know they were alive. Some had heard the statements of officers—including several who were much senior to themselves—over the camp radio and assumed they were free to make similar statements. There were at least a few officers who apparently thought it their right and duty to express their genuine antiwar sentiments.

But most of the POWs continued to resist the enemy's efforts to enlist them on the propaganda front. They were ruled by the traditional notion that the active-duty military man, regardless of his opinion of the merits of the war, had no business inserting himself in a political argument. They considered that, as prisoners of war, they remained at war on behalf of their government's policies and were required to support these policies to whatever extent possible.

Thus, the leaders kept passing the word, insistently, that prisoners were to stop writing and to stop making tape recordings for the enemy. Gradually, resistance to the Vietnamese threats began to stiffen, and men were amazed to find that they were not tortured for declining to do things they had done before.

But a peculiar situation obtained in Desert Inn. The place was known to be full of senior officers. High-risk contact efforts had been made, but the place had remained mute. The participants in "The Bob and Ed Show," Navy Comdr. Bob Schweitzer and Marine Lt. Col. Ed Miller, shared a cell there. They followed their long antiwar broadcast with a series of antiwar statements that were heard over the camp radio. From Stardust, to the south of Desert Inn, Jerry Denton sent word to Schweitzer and Miller, "Stop writing, stop taping, communicate with us." There was no response.

The Vietnamese built a series of bamboo screens in the Vegas courtyard, installed tables behind them, and during the warm, pleasant days of early spring brought numerous Desert Inn prisoners outside to dine together. By late February, Schweitzer and Miller were dining frequently with Navy Comdr. Walter Eugene "Gene" Wilber, who had been captured on June 16, 1968.

Wilber, also a resident of Desert Inn, had been a squadron commander aboard the carrier *America*. He had been flying along the 19th parallel, far to the south, when he had been hit. The ejection system in his F4J had malfunctioned, and he had to fight his way out of the aircraft; his young Backseater, Lt. (j.g.) Bernard Rupinski, 25, had not made it. Wilber had been taken prisoner immediately. It had taken him nine days to reach Hoa Lo.

During the trip to Hanoi, Wilber was fed little, and despite the intense midsummer heat was given little to drink. During the last hours of the journey he felt in the grip of a vertigo attack; it was almost a pleasant sensation, as though he were flying. On reaching Hoa Lo, he was unable to keep his feet. He kept falling down, and guards kept pulling him up and had to drag him into Room 18. He had no pain, but became aware that the entire right side of his body was numb, utterly without feeling; he could pinch himself and pull hair, and feel nothing. At the same time, the left side of his face seemed paralyzed; he was unable to close the eye or move that side of his mouth or tongue. Years later, competent medical authority was to judge that Wilber had suffered a stroke (or infarct) of his left brain stem. He lived in Room 18 for about three weeks, during which time he was interrogated but not mistreated. He recalls that he responded to all military questions with false answers. A doctor attended him regularly, and he received numerous shots of something that smelled like Vitamin B_1. Within a day he was able to walk, and within a few weeks all his muscles were beginning to function properly. He was able to move about and take care of himself. He was then moved out of Room 18.

Wilber had spent twenty-one months isolated in various cells in the Hoa Lo complex. During this time he was interrogated periodically and lectured extensively, washed with the same endless flood of propaganda that was poured through the radio speakers in all the prisoners' cells. But he never was physically mistreated.

Wilber, a woodworking hobbyist, had passed the time in Hoa Lo by mentally remodeling the Pennsylvania farmhouse where he planned to retire with his wife, Jean. Also, he mentally tinkered with automobile and aircraft engines. He had never been much interested in international affairs or politics—he had voted only once in a national election. But there came a time during the long emptiness at Hoa Lo when he ran out of houses to remodel and tired of tinkering with engines. He decided to try to educate himself, to try to understand the history that had landed him in a jail cell in Hanoi.

As a military officer, Wilber had not questioned the Administration's judgment concerning the necessity for military action in Vietnam, though he had wondered why there had been no declaration of war. Now, alone in a cell at Hoa Lo, he began thinking about the things his captors told him and about what he read in the literature they supplied. He also began listening hard to the views that came over his radio, paying close attention to Senators Fulbright and Mansfield, and to other prominent Americans. He was shown movies of the massive antiwar demonstrations in the United States. Apparently, it never struck him that he never was given anything to read in support of the American intervention. By autumn of 1969 he had satisfied himself that the American involvement had no constitutional sanction, and therefore was illegal; and that it lacked the support, and properly so, of the American people. That fall, at his captors' invitation, he tape-recorded a message of encouragement to participants of an antiwar moratorium in the United States. Also, he began meeting antiwar delegations to Hanoi and handing over letters full of his own antiwar sentiments for delivery in the United States.

In a post-release interview, Wilber insisted that, having in conscience found the American intervention to be illegal, he felt compelled to engage in anti-war activities, to do all possible to help effect the withdrawal of American forces. He said that, when he accepted his commission, he did not surrender his right of free speech.

Wilber had first met Miller and Schweitzer on Christmas Eve, 1969. Another officer then quartered with them was Air Force Lt. Col. John S. Finlay (captured on April 28, 1968). Finlay had been with Miller and Schweitzer for only about a month, but already had clashed angrily with Miller over the latter's strongly expressed antiwar views, and had warned the marine to keep his opinions to himself.

In post-release interviews, Finlay recalled that Miller displayed little interest in his views, and said that he fully expected to be court-martialed when he returned to the United States; but Miller said that he had no idea whether he would be court-martialed, only that he did not discount the possibility.

Miller's recollection is that Schweitzer, Finlay,* and Robbie Risner† had been among the most prolific in the authoring of antiwar

---

*After capture, Finlay had been subjected to prolonged and severe torture, including rope torture, beatings, and stompings.
†Risner's extensive tortures are described elsewhere in detail.

statements; and that his cellmates, Schweitzer and Finlay, indicated that they did not believe that they would be court-martialed for what they had done. Miller said that he sought to disabuse them of this naïveté, that he cautioned them that to write antiwar statements from a prison camp was indeed to risk court-martial. He recalled that he warned them against meeting peace delegations or making antiwar statements unless they were acting out of conviction, pointing out that to do so would be to risk their careers and futures. As for himself, he could not recall in a post-release interview ever having said that he expected to be court-martialed; only that he did not discount the possibility. He took his own risks with a will. He became annoyed at his captors' efforts to persuade him to employ their jargon in his antiwar compositions. He assured them that Americans do not use phrases like "the imperialist war" and "the aggressors." He insisted to his Vietnamese hosts that "If I am writing an antiwar statement, I'm writing it. If you want to write one, you write it."

Finlay was soon moved into a cell with John McCain. He was happy to be separated from Miller, and the feeling was mutual.

As spring moved closer, there was a pronounced change in Cat. Formerly lordly and aloof, the prime architect of the long terror now seemed nervous, full of anxiety. Jim Mulligan insisted that he actually trembled and that he had developed facial tics near the eyes.

One day in April, Jim Stockdale was summoned before Cat. It seemed to him that Cat had grown thin and that he had lost much of his self-assurance. When he spoke, he almost pleaded: "I have an obligation to get someone to talk to a professor from MIT who is visiting Hanoi. I assure you there will be no propaganda. The old days are gone; no longer do we dictate. All I want you to do is see him."

"No," said Stockdale, "you know I won't do that."

Cat now observed that he and Stockdale had much in common and that therefore Stockdale should help him out. "You and I are the same age," he said. "We have some college, and I just hoped you would do this. You know I have obligations to meet, and I have pressures on me, just as any military man does."

When Stockdale again refused, Cat called a guard to return the prisoner to his cell. To Stockdale's surprise, Cat walked to the door with him, chatting amiably, like an old and troubled friend—for a moment, Stockdale thought Cat actually was going to put his arm around his shoulder.

"How long has it been?" Cat wondered.

"It's been four and a half years," Stockdale replied.

Cat stood pondering this, then said, "I am afraid it's going to be a while longer."

Neither Stockdale nor any other American prisoner ever saw Cat again.

————

The improved treatment was applied selectively. Americans from camps in the South were finding little to cheer about. Steve Leopold arrived at Camp D-1 on Christmas Day, 1969, and met Cheese, the tiny brute whose mouth actually watered as he indulged his sadism, to the extent that the saliva spilled down over his chin. Leopold knew nothing of Cheese, but just looking at the man made his skin crawl. There was something terribly wrong about him. He walked mincingly, from the knees down, like a woman wearing a tight skirt, and often holding his hands shoulder-high, palms out. The effeminate mannerisms would have been laughable except for something in the eyes, the set of the jaw, the weak mouth, some furtive malevolence of expression that chilled the blood.

Leopold had been imprisoned for nineteen months in a large, remote North Vietnamese Army base in Cambodia, a hellish place where the prisoners were kept in cagelike cells. There had been starvation and sickness, but none of the deliberate tortures that had been inflicted on Americans in North Vietnam.

At the time of his capture Leopold had estimated that the war would be over by late 1969. In early November the prisoners had been made to start walking north, and he had thought that the war was ending, that they were being taken to North Vietnam for release. They had walked for nearly two months and had reached D-1 on what Leopold would remember as "Black Christmas."

Leopold was placed in solitary confinement. His cell was about ten feet square and blackwashed—walls, ceiling, and door were painted black. There were no windows. There were two small air vents near the ceiling, about twelve feet off the floor, which admitted no light. There was a large hatch in the center of the cell door, which guards could open whenever they wanted to look in at the prisoner. On the floor there was a board about six feet long and three feet wide, to be used as a bed. And there was a waste bucket. It was a hot, dark, dirty, stinking place.

That "Black Christmas" there was a sparse turkey dinner. After that, the menu deteriorated. There was even less food than there had been in Cambodia—two small bowls per day of thin cabbage soup and some bread. The food was filthy, full of fingernails, hair, rocks, rodent feces, weevils; once Leopold found half a rusty razor blade in his bread.

Most prisoners in this camp never left their cells except to visit the latrine or to attend interrogations, where the repulsive Cheese would try to enlist them in the antiwar movement. American prisoners were continually heard making antiwar statements over the camp radio. Once, one who introduced himself as "Colonel Robinson Risner" delivered himself of some sentiments that struck Leopold as "gung-ho" on Hanoi's behalf. Leopold assumed Risner had been forced to yield the statement and gave it no credence. But when two of the enlisted men who had come north with him broadcast antiwar statements, he was disappointed and depressed. Then he became ill with malaria, fell into delirium, and lost track of time.

In March, while Cambodian Prince Norodom Sihanouk was abroad, one of his generals, Lon Nol, deposed him in a coup d'etat, and demanded that Communist troops vacate the country–Sihanouk had permitted the Communists to establish bases in eastern Cambodia from which for years they had been conducting military operations in South Vietnam. When the Communist forces did not leave, Lon Nol called for foreign assistance in expelling them. On April 30, President Nixon advised the world that strong American and South Vietnamese forces had joined in a drive into Cambodia to destroy the Communist supply and staging bases. Nixon explained that the enemy bases contained the headquarters for the entire Communist war effort in South Vietnam. He insisted that it was intolerable that the enemy should continue to enjoy sanctuary in the Cambodian bases, whence he could continue to mount attacks in which Americans were killed. He said that American forces would be withdrawn into South Vietnam as quickly as the task was accomplished.

Sweeping into the "Fish Hook" and "Parrot's Beak" regions of Cambodia, the Allied forces quickly captured hundreds of tons of food, weapons, and ammunition. Communist troops faded into the jungles to the west and north.

In the United States reaction to the Cambodian incursion was explosive. Many supported Nixon's decision, but many did not. Antiwar sentiment on college campuses in particular reached new peaks. Some four hundred schools were shut down in the first general student strike in American history. In many places police and National Guard were sent onto campuses to keep order. At Ohio's Kent State University, Guardsmen fired at demonstrating students, killing four of them. The killings shocked the nation. The following weekend more than 100,000 angry protestors flooded into Washington to demonstrate.

Ten days after the Kent State deaths, two more students were killed and ten wounded in a confrontation with police at Mississippi's predominantly black Jackson State College.

By the end of June, American forces were out of Cambodia, as Nixon had said they would be, and the furor had subsided.

———

These were tumultuous times at D-1. The place seethed with bitterness and suspicion. Many of the inmates had known each other since Portholes, the jungle camp in southern North Vietnam, where seeds of distrust had been sown. Harvey Brande felt that he had been casually betrayed by John Young, whom he regarded as a traitor and the basest kind of opportunistic coward. Brande also had deep misgivings about others, particularly Army Sgt. Robert Chenoweth (captured on February 8, 1968), who had confided to Brande his conviction that communism was the answer to the world's ills.

Others were suspicious and wary, too. One was Marine Pfc. Robert Ray Helle, nineteen years old and only ten months in the Corps when he was captured on April 24, 1968. In a postrelease interview Helle was to recall that by late 1969 he was feeling distinctly uneasy about some of his fellow prisoners at D-1. Helle had been stashed in a cell with nine others, including Chenoweth. One day in November, 1968, Chenoweth had disagreed with Marine Cpl. John A. Deering (captured at Hue on February 5, 1968). Deering had grabbed Chenoweth and was about to punch him when the athletics were discovered and broken up by a guard. Chenoweth was marched off to explain the unseemly activity to the camp authority. When he returned, Deering was summoned to give his version of events. To his amazement, Deering discovered that his captors were not so much interested in hearing his version of the near brawl as in repeating to him several thoughts he had freely confided to his cellmates, to the effect that he was implacably opposed to his captors and had no intention of ever going along with their program.

Deering also claims to have been supplied with information on other "diehards' in the cell. They were rated in order of their attitudes. Burgess* and Lenker† were nearly as bad as he; Ridgeway, who was younger, was bad, too; so was Helle, who had volunteered that he would take advantage of any opportunity to kill his Communist captors. Others held similarly reactionary views and desires.

Deering's interrogator did not reveal the source of his material. The prisoner was returned to his cell, where, full of anger, he announced, "Evidently, we have a rat in the room!"

At this point Chenoweth told the others that he had briefed his captors on each of his cellmates. According to Deering, he claimed that in his revelations to the enemy, he had only thought to help his fellow prisoners. Several who did not feel they needed any such help took angry umbrage; some expressed a desire to kill him.

It is not clear how Chenoweth might have supposed that his reports on his cellmates would be helpful to them. Nor was it to become clear in a post–release interview with him. He admitted that "from time to time" he discussed with Cheese the political attitudes and conduct of other prisoners, but "just sort of in a general kind of way." He advised that he did not feel at the time that his revelations to Cheese would cause harm to anyone, "even if I told them that somebody hated the Vietnamese or wanted to kill all the Vietnamese." He denied that he said anything "that extreme," but said he did not think it would have made any difference: "What kind of excuse is that for the Vietnamese to take somebody out and shoot him? It's crazy. The Vietnamese knew already that we come from a racist country. They understand what the American military does to get GIs to kill Vietnamese."

Following Chenoweth's revelations to Cheese, Deering was removed to solitary confinement. He remained there for two years.

In June, 1969, Helle and Chenoweth became cellmates. As they came together, Helle recalled that Chenoweth was nervous; that he seemed to feel badly over having discussed the others with their captors. Helle recalled that one day in late October, Chenoweth re-

*Marine Cpl. Richard G. Burgess was captured on September 25, 1966.
†Army Sgt. Michael R. Lenker was captured on February 8, 1968.

turned to the cell from an interrogation in a state of extreme anxiety, "all shook up, sweating." Helle said Chenoweth told him that he had asked his captors for political asylum, that he now thought that "the Vietnamese are right in what they are struggling for... we should leave them alone and not interfere." But mainly, said Helle, Chenoweth confessed to being "very scared" at having betrayed his nine cellmates the previous November. He believed he would be charged with treason if he returned to the United States.

Chenoweth said he did not feel he had done anything wrong, but that he was concerned at what others thought he had told the Vietnamese about them, and that he was frightened at the prospect of treason charges. "Everybody was," he said.

Shortly, Chenoweth was moved out of the cell. A few days later, Helle was moved in with an old friend, Marine Sgt. Abel Larry Kavanaugh, with whom he had been captured. Helle next saw Chenoweth at Christmastime, working with Marine Sgt. Alfonso Riate as masters of ceremonies at a party involving many prisoners, a well-filmed propaganda extravaganza obviously aimed at promoting the notion of humane and lenient treatment.

Chenoweth denied that he ever sought political asylum, although he said he did consider not returning to the United States. He described the evolution in himself of a political philosophy that involved an "intense hatred" for the United States and shame at "being an American, because you know that the United States is ripping off the world. That's why we have the living standard that we do, because we've stolen it from the rest of the world." He said he found communism superior to capitalism, but had "misgivings" about the way "some countries," the Soviet Union, for example, had "messed up" their "socialist development."

As for Helle, Chenoweth described him as "the kind of person that would preach 'my country right or wrong.' He believes in America no matter what." Chenoweth reflected that Helle is from a well-to-do family, and felt that "his class background has a great deal to do with his attitude." He insisted that Helle was a "classic example of a victim of an affluent society."

When Helle and Kavanaugh came together, they were raucous cellmates, beating on the cell walls, singing loudly and otherwise violating camp regulations. Shortly after the New Year they were separated, and both were placed in solitary confinement for five months. During this time they were interrogated and tortured. By early summer of 1970 they were together again, but Helle found that Kavanaugh had changed. Never excessively religious, he now announced that he had been visiting with the Lord. He said that he knew himself to be a saint—"the thirteenth disciple." He insisted that he was absolutely opposed to the war, that he was opposed to all violence and the taking of life.

Helle and Kavanaugh shared a cell in a building just inside the main gate at D-1. This building contained four cells, all of them interior rooms with no windows to the outside. Hence, the prisoners called this cellblock the Drum. Dennis Thompson was alone in another cell. In another, larger cell were John Young, Michael Branch, Richard Burgess, and Army Pfc. John G. Sparks (captured on April 24, 1968). Beyond them, in the fourth cell, were Chenoweth and Riate.

By this time, Dennis Thompson had been alone and out of contact with other Americans for twenty-two months. He had seen a good deal of Cheese and his torture guards, though. Beaten, tortured, and starved, he was in bad shape. He had been kept in the dark so long that his eyes were going bad. His teeth were loosening and falling out. His hair, once thick and black, came out by the handfuls whenever he ran his fingers through it. And he was now paranoiac to the extent that when the others in the Drum tried to make contact with him, he ignored them, fearing an enemy attempt to trap him in communications. For what seemed a long time, he sat quietly in his dark cell, listening to the others whispering and sometimes singing messages back and forth, and trying to get him to communicate.

Then one day Thompson, feeling near the end of his endurance, decided he had to talk. He began whispering with Helle and Kavanaugh in the next cell. They code-named him Bullwinkle, brought him up to date on who was in the camp, and told him what had been happening to themselves and others. They advised Thompson that interpreters had assured them that approximately fifty prisoners were to be released, as evidence of the humane and lenient treatment, and in hopes of promoting the antiwar movement in the United States.

Thompson replied, "If you guys get out, take word back that Captain Leonard, Captain Montague, Lieutenant Archer, and John Deering and myself are getting the shaft. Bad." He briefed them on all that had happened to himself, and on what he knew the others had suffered. This information infuriated Helle and Kavanaugh and they resolved to do something about it.

They decided to mount a demonstration they hoped would result in an audience with higher-ups, to whom they could describe the torture and mistreatment Cheese was inflicting on the prisoners at D-1. One day they broke down their cell door, sent two frightened armed guards running, lifted the bars on the door to the cell Chenoweth and Riate shared, walked into the cell, and sat down. Helle recalls that Chenoweth and Riate were incredulous and shaken. Shortly, a crowd of thirty-five to forty Vietnamese entered the cell to take him and Kavanaugh out. The two of them were tied and beaten savagely.

Cheese spent the month of August brutalizing Thompson. He called him Bullwinkle, demanded to know what orders he had issued to the others in the cellblock. Thompson assumed that Cheese had tortured others for his code name and for information on communications. He refused to yield anything. He was kept on his knees, locked in leg irons, and beaten regularly and savagely. Sweating and salivating, Cheese pulled out his eyelids and rolled them, painfully, between the ends of his fingers. He stomped on Thompson's hands and feet and pulled large locks of hair out of his head. It went on and on until finally, on September 1, Thompson agreed to write a confession Cheese dictated. The gist of it was that he had communicated with the other prisoners, had informed them of the details of his own detention, and had tried to influence their thinking.

Following a few days of respite, Thompson again found himself before Cheese, who ordered him to "kneel down, put up your arms."

"No," said Thompson. He had had enough. He was deathly tired and did not much care whether he lived or died. It gave him immense pleasure to see the shocked surprise on Cheese's hateful face.

"What?" Cheese asked, clearly unable to believe he had heard the prisoner correctly.

"I said, 'No.' Do you understand? I'll write it down for you." He grabbed Cheese's pen and scribbled the word "No" across the top of his notebook. He glared at the runt and said, "I don't kneel down anymore."

Cheese stared at him, obviously uncertain as to how to proceed. Finally he said, "Then sit down. I permit you to sit down."

Thompson decided against sitting on the stool, thus placing himself lower than Cheese, who sat in a chair behind the table. Instead, he reached for the empty chair next to Cheese, pulled it out in front of the table, and sat on it, telling the inquisitor, "You don't *permit* me to do anything."

Visibly upset, Cheese gathered his wits and said, "You are going to write a letter to the Congress protesting Nixon's policy in Vietnam, and you will record your voice for the radio."

"No way."

"Do you want to continue to be punished?"

"Let me tell you something, you little motherfucker, there's only two of us in this room right now. I guarantee it, you insult me one more time, you call me one more name, you shake your fist at me or threaten me one more time, you bastard, and only one of us will walk out of here." Thompson stood, picked up his chair, slammed it down onto the floor, cursing Cheese.

"Calm down!" Cheese pleaded. "Calm down! Return to your room!" He stood and moved back into a corner, pulling his chair with him, keeping it between himself and Thompson. He shouted for the guards. None came. Apparently they thought that Cheese meant to spend the day enjoying himself with Thompson; expecting no trouble, they had disappeared in pursuit of their own interests.

Thompson kept railing at Cheese, cursing him, until he was nearly exhausted. Then, finally, he acceded to Cheese's earnest plea, "Return to your room and nothing will happen to you."

He went back to his cell. He felt a little better for having bested Cheese. He wondered what would happen to him now. But he didn't much care.

The Sontay Raid—A Huge Success

Life went on, better in some camps than others, but always tedious and dehumanizing. The days seemed endless. So did the war. Then, on November 21, 1970, something happened that at least signaled to the POWs that they were not forgotten.

That evening, a team of seventy U.S. Army Special Forces troops raided the prison camp at Sontay, twenty miles from Hanoi, in hopes of rescuing American prisoners. The raid was led by Col. Arthur "Bull" Simon, a thirty-year professional and a veteran of three wars. Simon had handpicked his force, the cream of some three hundred Green Beret volunteers. Nearly all were senior noncoms. The average age was thirty-two. All but three had served combat tours in Vietnam; some had served as many as three tours.

Simon had been pushing his men unmercifully since August, training and preparing in a secret corner of Florida's vast Eglin Air Force Base. He did not reveal to them what they had volunteered for until 6

PM on the night of the raid, by which time they were ensconced in a secret place in Southeast Asia. When they learned what they were about to do, there was, first, dead silence; then murmuring; then, spontaneously, Simon's raiders stood and applauded.

"Those are Americans they've got in there," the force commander reminded his men. "They've got it coming to them to have somebody try to get them out of there. You just don't let your people rot in a place like that without trying to do something about it. So we're gonna try to do something about it. That's what we've been getting ready for."

He gave a final word of instruction: "I'm sure you're all concerned about what will happen if the enemy knows we're coming in. You'll know that thirty seconds after you get on the ground. If they know we're coming, they'll have about two battalions around that place; they'll let us land and they'll nail us. And there we'll be. Don't picture yourself walking out of North Vietnam. So we keep this force together, we keep its firepower together, we back up to the river and we make 'em pay for every goddamn foot of ground between us and them.

"That's all."

The helicopter ride to Sontay took three hours and fifteen minutes. The raiders were on the ground for twenty-six minutes. They went into the prison camp as they had trained to go in, with great and precisely directed violence, killing many Vietnamese soldiers— Simon estimates 30, but he had emphatically assured his Raiders that he was not interested in body counts, that there would be no time for "feeling pulses." Quickly, they "pacified" the camp and conducted an exhaustive search of the cellblocks. To their immense dismay, the Americans they had come for—Orson Swindle, Jim Warner, Leon Ellis, Ken Fisher, Jon Reynolds, SRO Render Crayton, and the others—had been moved on July 14 to a place called Camp Faith, a few miles closer to Hanoi.

Disappointed, Simon and his force withdrew, having suffered one casualty—a badly sprained ankle. Shortly, the Sontay raid was made known to the public, and Simon and his force were properly honored. There was a great deal of public wonderment, however, at the quality of American military intelligence. People wanted to know why, four months after the POWs had been transferred, Military Intelligence was still unaware of the move.

Bull Simon answers, "I was as vitally interested in the intelligence as anyone in the world. I knew all that it was possible for us to know about Sontay. We were well aware there might be no prisoners there. The only way we could have known positively what the situation was was to have an agent in the camp. The Vietnamese could have moved the prisoners out of there twenty minutes before we arrived, as well as four months before. We only knew that there was a chance that Americans were there and, given one chance in ten that we could take one prisoner out of there, it was worth trying. Given the intelligence we had, I would try it again.''

From the standpoint of the POWs, at least, the Sontay operation was a huge success. Short of freedom, what they wanted most was the company and moral support of other Americans. As a result of the raid, most soon had this. Within a few days, all the outlying prison camps were closed and their prisoners transferred to the camps in Hanoi—Hoa Lo, the Zoo, and the Plantation. Clearly, the Communists were deeply worried that they could lose their hostages, their most important bargaining tool.

———

Conditions at Hoa Lo had been improving slowly. Cell doors were being unlocked during daylight hours so that prisoners could visit with other prisoners in contiguous cells. Occasionally, men were even allowed into a large room separating Stardust and Desert Inn to play Ping-Pong and pool. Also occasionally, the food would take an unbelievable turn for the better; soups would be full of cheese, sometimes there was fresh fish, and, in the mornings, marmalade. Many began receiving letters and packages from home and were allowed to write home.

The vastly improved life-style induced in many an assumption that the end of the war—or at least the release of the prisoners—was imminent. Some were less optimistic. Vegas SRO Jim Stockdale, believing it best to be realistic, sent out what he correctly anticipated would be an unpopular suggestion: "Pace yourself for a 1973 release." Two years and more away.

That Christmas many received packages, letters, and pictures from home. Stockdale was given two pictures of a house. At the bottom of them, in his wife, Sybil's, handwriting, was an address on Western Avenue, in Washington, D.C. He assumed this now to be the family residence. "Where's the letter?" he asked Bug.

"You do not deserve the letter!" Bug snapped. As far as anyone knew, Bug had not tortured any POWs during 1970, but he was still nasty.

Air Force Col. John Flynn, the senior American officer in captivity,* received a roll-your-own cigarette device from his wife—but the paper was missing.

"Where's the paper?" he demanded.

"You cannot have the paper," he was told, "because of the black schemes of your government."

Others received all kinds of things they had almost forgotten existed—American toothpastes, toothbrushes, soaps, and vitamin pills. They luxuriated in these items.

Some wondered what their families had been thinking of when they sent some items. John McCain received a bag of marbles from his wife, Carol. Another officer received packets containing the makings of thirty gallons of "Goofy Grape Koolaid."

For the Vegas prisoners, the best was yet to come. On December 26, teams of inspectors appeared. The prisoners had seen none of the inspectors before. Obviously police-trained, they were politely impersonal and extremely competent. They used floodlights and conducted the most exhaustive inspection any of the prisoners had ever experienced. Corners, walls, overheads, floors, and beds were carefully searched. The prisoners were made to strip to the buff, and the inspectors went through each item of clothing, then actually looked into every orifice in each man's body, even between his toes. All kinds of things were confiscated—razor blades, pencils, pieces of string, paper, and so on. These inspectors exhibited no interest in how a man might have come by such contraband or in punishing those who possessed it.

That evening, the POWs of the various Vegas cellblocks were herded, each in turn, into the courtyard and blindfolded. Then guards led each group to the western side of the Hoa Lo complex.

This large area was nearly in the shape of a right triangle with its base on the eastern side, the northern side perpendicular to the base, and the third side angling up from south to northwest. (Diagram p. 15.) The center was a large courtyard, in the middle of which was a sizable octagonal building containing bath stalls; there were smaller, rectangular-shaped buildings on the eastern, northern, and western

---

*He had been kept out of contact with the main body of prisoners since his capture three years earlier.

sides. A few yards to the south was a medic shack. The courtyard was surrounded at its edges by a series of connected buildings, cellblocks of various sizes, some of them quite large. On the east side of the compound, to the south of Building 7 and abutting it, stood the infamous Heartbreak Hotel cellblock, the dreary dungeon where most of the Americans had lived for a time when they had first arrived at Hoa Lo.

When the prisoners reached the courtyard, their blindfolds were removed. Bug, smiling benevolently, told them that a new regime was now in effect, that henceforth they were to live together in the large rooms in this camp, that together they would obey the camp regulations. For most of the Americans in North Vietnam, the long loneliness was over. Compound living had begun.

It was a day of jubilation. Men who had consoled and supported each other through years of adversity at last came face to face, shook hands, embraced each other, talked, laughed, and kept wiping away tears of happiness. Navigator George Coker and his pilot, Jack Fellowes, met for the first time since they were shot down together four and a half years before. In the lore of the camps, both were legend now, Coker for his dramatic Columbus Day, 1967, escape attempt with George McKnight; and the deceptively mild-manner Fellowes for an incredible record as a tough resister. On that long-ago day when they had been captured, Fellowes had mumbled a heartfelt apology to Coker, telling him how sorry he was to have gotten him into this, and the feisty Coker had replied, "No sweat. We'll make it!" Now Fellowes told his backseater, "Hey, I'm sorry about keeping you here this long."

"No sweat," Coker replied.

Tough, thoughtful Bud Day could scarcely believe what was happening. He had spent the previous six months alone in a cell in Heartbreak Hotel, having been moved from the Zoo in June, 1969. Now, suddenly, he found himself among many friends, touching them, talking and laughing with John McCain, whom he had last seen at the Plantation nearly three years earlier; old Air Force buddy Jim Kasler; and Larry Guarino, who had provided such admirable leadership at the Zoo for so many difficult years.

Members of different services who had not known each other prior to Vietnam but who on this battleground had become beloved to one another sought each other out—Air Force leaders Robbie Risner and Larry Guarino, Navy men Jim Stockdale and Jerry Denton.

Orson Swindle was thrilled at meeting so many men he had known only by the reputations they had forged for themselves—Risner, Stockdale, Denton, Day, Fuller, Coker, McKnight, McCain, Alvarez, Knutson, Fred Cherry and the others. To him, they were all giants. He kept muttering to himself, "Wow! All the bad guys in one place. You've got to get in line to get in trouble around here!" Swindle had no idea that many considered him to be one of the giants.

It seemed to Bob Shumaker that no one, himself included, could stop smiling; everyone's face seemed to be frozen in a look of genuine pleasure. Nor could anyone seem to stop talking—yet everyone seemed to be listening, too, and hearing what everyone else said.

Bug and his guards moved about the clusters of men explaining that the camp regulations prohibited them from gathering together in groups of more than six and that it was not permissible for one man to address a group. For the most part, these efforts went ignored, but eventually the guards got the prisoners inside. Forty-six men, including all the seniors, went into Building 7. This room was perhaps fifty feet long and twenty feet wide. Quarters were close, but no one cared. It was good to be near friends, to be able to see them and hear them and touch them. It was so good.

For most of three days, few would want to sleep. Despite the guards' protests, they talked and talked and talked.

The prisoners called this place Camp Unity. By nightfall, its cellblocks contained 342 prisoners. The prisoners in the various cellblocks were not allowed to intermingle. Within a few days, however, those in Building 7 were communicating with those in other buildings. In Building 7, leadership was quickly established. The rank-at-date-of-shootdown formula made the camp SRO Air Force Lt. Col. Vernon P. Ligon, Jr., who had been captured on November 19, 1967.* Ligon's deputy was Robbie Risner. Jim Stockdale, third ranking, was in charge of plans and policy. And Jerry Denton was current operations officer, responsible for the development of tactics. The others called these the Four Wise Men.

Under their guidance, the cellblocks were designated as squadrons, each with a squadron commander and staff, all appointments predi-

*Actually, the highest-ranking prisoners were Air Force Colonels John Flynn, David Winn, and Norman Gaddis. They had been moved together into another cellblock in Camp Unity, isolated from the others.

cated on rank-at-date-of-shootdown. Squadrons were further broken down into eating groups of six to eight men, and each eating group became a flight, with a flight commander.

From top to bottom, the Camp Unity prisoner population became a well-organized, tightly disciplined military organization. Squadron commanders soon queried the Wise Men as to how to confront an enemy now employing drastically changed tactics. The wing command had not yet settled on an approach, and Stockdale, playing for time, replied, "Our basic posture will be one of oblique envelopment."

From Building 6, next door, came the response, "Are you shitting me, sir? Orson [Swindle] can't even spell it!"

For the most part, said the Wise Men, the men were to continue to abide by the policies by which they had guided themselves thus far. The enemy, despite his change in tactics, was still after all the propaganda help he could extract from the Americans. Men were still being taken to interrogations, where they were exhorted to write and make tape recordings about the humane and lenient treatment, and to meet "peace delegations" from the United States and elsewhere. The men were ordered to take torture to the limits of their mental capacities before acceding to such demands.

But at Hoa Lo there was no more torture. Many prisoners were peacefully content with the new regime, anxious at last to enjoy "prosperity." But some Americans, full of long-smoldering rage at their captors, were full of an understandable hunger for revenge. They seized every opportunity to bait guards and officers, some of whom had not even been in attendance during the lean years.

Others were plagued with concern over what they now judged to have been their own earlier weak behavior. These were men who had yielded information or statements under merely the threat of torture, or perhaps after minimal punishment. Later, having learned of the much tougher performances of others who had been equally frightened, they were determined, as one prisoner put it, "to carve out reputations for themselves, to kick a gook in the ass every night to show how tough they were." The treatment change notwithstanding, the Vietnamese were of no mind to accept gratuitous abuse from their captives. One day, when an Air Force officer whose performance as a POW had been notoriously weak took occasion in the yard to shout loudly and obscenely about Ho Chi Minh, guards beat him to a pulp.

The Camp Unity prisoner leadership had important business to discuss with the Vietnamese. Bud Day, Jack Fellowes, and Air Force Maj. Ben M. Pollard (captured on May 15, 1967) all had spent the last half of 1969 in cells in Heartbreak Hotel. They knew of three others who had been sharing a single Heartbreak cell: J. J. Connell, who had been Guarino's "worldwide communications net" at the Zoo until he was found out in the frightful aftermath of the Dramesi-Atterberry escape; the Faker, whose total mental destruction had been so brutally supervised by Fidel, the Latin torture master; and Navy Comdr. Kenneth R. Cameron (captured May 18, 1967). All three men were thought to have been taken to a hospital the previous October. They had not been returned to Heartbreak prior to the move to Camp Unity. Day, Fellowes, and Pollard wanted to know what had become of them.

They pressed Bug and other interrogators for information about the three. They proposed to their captors that the three be returned to Room 7 and that the Americans be allowed to care for them. But no answers were forthcoming, and the three were never seen again.*

On February 4, 1971, a Viet Cong jungle prison camp in South Vietnam was closed down, and its American prisoners, Army Capt.-Dr. Floyd Kushner and others, began walking north. For some time, the war had been moving closer to the jungle encampment, and their captors, fearful of losing them, were moving them to North Vietnam. The Americans were overjoyed. For years they had listened enviously to American pilots who were imprisoned in Hanoi sending broadcast messages home in which loved ones were thanked for packages and told of turkey dinners which had been served on holidays.

The walk to Hanoi took fifty-seven days, but Kushner found it actually pleasant, the best time he spent as a prisoner. The prisoners were fed well and were sympathetically treated by passing North Vietnamese soldiers and civilians. By the time they arrived, in early April, Kushner was observing that the men were in better health than they had been when they started.

They were incarcerated at the Plantation. They soon found that

---

*The prisoners did not hear of the three men again until 1973, when the Vietnamese reported they had died in captivity.

imprisonment in Hanoi was not all that they had imagined it would be. The worst thing about it was being confined in cells so much of the time. Still, most found it far preferable to life in the jungle camp.

———

On Sunday, February 7, 1971, the Camp Unity Americans rejoined the war as a unit. Time and again Bug and his guards had warned them against gathering in groups of more than six and against one man speaking to groups. Bug even forbade religious services. This incensed many of the prisoners, and it was decided that Bug must be challenged. SRO Vern Ligon advised the cockeyed warden of forthcoming services in Building 7, and was warned that they had best be cancelled. Ligon insisted the men would worship together.

Robbie Risner, Howie Rutledge, and George Coker took turns quoting scripture, giving inspirational homilies, and leading the faithful in various prayers. A small choir held forth with a number of hymns. As the services proceeded, Bug entered with a crew of guards. Whenever Risner, Rutledge, or Coker spoke, a guard would be sent forward to advise each man in turn, "No talk." Each man in turn ignored the guard and completed his assigned portion of the service. The guards ordered the choir to stop the hymn singing, but the choir ignored them. The service was completed.

Risner, Rutledge, and Coker were marched out into the yard. Bug was enraged, threatening. Suddenly, in the building, Bud Day began singing loudly "The Star-Spangled Banner." In the next instant he was joined by the others in Building 7; and in the next few moments, by the Americans in the other buildings around the compound. The prisoners were roaring the anthem! The grounds reverberated with it. The guards stood away from the cellblocks, nonplussed, clearly frightened, and the prisoners sang all the more loudly, trying to force their enthusiasm for their country to spill over the walls and into the alien city around them.

Outside in the courtyard, Risner, Rutledge, and Coker stood quietly, enjoying the music and grinning at Bug, who was perplexed, comically aghast—his stray eyeball seemed to be wandering all over his head!

The anthem was completed, but the prisoners were hardly finished. Their combative instincts awakened, they were now in a mood to sing, and full of thoughts of home and patriotism. They gave themselves with loud vigor to many songs, over and over again: "God

Bless America,'' ''America the Beautiful,'' ''My Country, 'Tis of Thee,'' such state songs as ''California, Here I Come,'' and ''The Eyes of Texas,'' and a few popular hymns.

Between songs, Larry Guarino led a chant that was quickly picked up by the others.

> This is Building Number Seven, Number Seven, Number Seven.
> This is Building Number Seven,
> Where the hell is Building Six?

Immediately, the chant was picked up by Building 6, then 5, and so on, all the way around the compound. As each building reported in, the others cheered and applauded.

The singing and chanting went on and on, and as it continued a virtual army of police filled the courtyard and surrounded the buildings. They wore riot helmets, carried gas masks and all kinds of weapons, including tear-gas guns and canisters, and rifles with fixed bayonet. At length, the uproar at Camp Unity subsided.

Risner, Rutledge, and Coker were locked together in a cell in Heartbreak Hotel. Operations Officer·Denton immediately called a hunger strike in protest. There were some strong differences of opinion with Denton over the fast. It had been expected that the leaders of the religious services might be arrested, and many felt that to protest this was to dilute the primary issue, which was the right to worship. Also, that it was not conducive to an improved prison life-style— which was the point of the exercise—to keep piling one challenge to their captors upon another. But Denton felt that the prisoners at last were playing a winning hand and that it was time to raise the betting. He made the fast stick.

In the week that followed, all the Camp Unity seniors were interrogated about the ''Church Riot.'' All complained bitterly at the prohibition on religious services. As protests continued all the senior officers were removed from Building 7 and placed in punishment in Building 0.

Ligon, Stockdale, and Denton were crowded into a small, two-man cell. Ligon and Stockdale were locked together into a single set of stocks at the end of one of the one-man bunks, Stockdale by the left leg and Ligon by the right leg. There they remained for the next thirty-eight days, during which time neither man was let out for any reason. It could have been miserable but for the good-humored company. Denton delighted in the gentlemanly Alfonse-and-Gaston manner in which the other two, locked together, attended to calls of nature.

"Excuse me."

"Certainly."

"Sorry about that."

"Don't give it another thought."

The three enjoyed being together. In fact, it occurred to Stockdale one day that they actually were having fun.

Risner was soon transferred from Heartbreak into another cell in Building 0. Also in this cellblock were the Air Force "bulls"—full colonels, the seniormost American military men in captivity. In order of seniority, they were John Flynn; David W. Winn (captured on August 9, 1968); Norman C. Gaddis (captured on May 12, 1967); and James E. Bean (captured on January 3, 1968). Now the bulls, out of communications since capture, learned the dreadful history the others had lived. When Denton told of the Hanoi Parade, in July, 1966, Flynn recalled watching film excerpts of it on television at an Air Force base in Germany, and remarking to his wife, "I can't understand why those men didn't hold their heads up." Now he told Denton of his reaction, ruefully advising, "After I got here, I understood why you guys couldn't hold your heads up."

Immediately, Flynn realized he had made a mistake. Denton seemed crushed, agitated. He remembered every detail of the Hanoi Parade so vividly, and how he and others had kept shouting encouragement to the Americans in all directions, "Don't bow your head!" and "Hold your head up!" and how they literally had fought to do so. For five years Denton had believed that the prisoners had won that propaganda contest, that the outside world had seen them smiling and triumphant, not defeated and subjugated. Now he learned that the world had seen what the enemy wanted it to see. He was despondent, nearly to the point of tears, at what he was sure the American people must think of the POWs. Flynn spent days trying to reassure him.

Soon Howie Rutledge moved from Heartbreak into Building 0. Then came Jim Mulligan and Harry Jenkins, whose sin had nothing to do with the worship of God—he was guilty of fomenting "a riotous party" in Building 7 on the night of February 11. It had been the sixth anniversary of Bob Shumaker's shootdown and capture, and Jenkins had organized a "This Is Your Life" surprise party. Navy men who had known Shumaker for years kept rising to reveal outlandish and not necessarily truthful things about him. Shumaker was decorated with a huge hero medal that had been fashioned out of toilet paper and tin. Everyone enjoyed the party but the Vietnamese.

In the week following the Church Riot, Soft Soap Fairy, the con man, was about Camp Unity explaining that it was well known throughout the world that religious freedom was permitted in the Democratic Republic of Vietnam, that it had always been the policy of the government to allow religious services, that indeed the national leadership supported church services. Therefore, he advised, the American air pirates would be permitted to have fifteen minutes per week for church services. But these services, he warned, were not to be "used for black schemes against the Democratic Republic of Vietnam or against the camp authorities." To ensure that no "black schemes" would be planned or perpetrated, the services would have to be written out in their entireties, every word of every prayer, hymn, scriptural reading, and homily, and submitted in advance to the camp authority for approval.

By now, communications had been established with the seniors in Building 0 through Building 1, just to the north. Queried on the Vietnamese concession, the seniors surmised that it was an attempt by the enemy to save face on the issue. But the Americans were angry, weary to death at always having been treated as criminals, never as prisoners of war. It was recalled that, in most countries, even the most dangerous criminals are allowed to worship. The juniors were instructed not to accept the conditions. They were authorized to advise the enemy when services were to be held, who would officiate, and, generally, what the program would be—the sort of information that appears on any church bulletin board. Nothing more. Some juniors went so far as to invite Bug and Soft Soap Fairy and others of their captors to join them in worship. Some guards came, but only to monitor the services, to see that no "black schemes" were hatched.

Unlovely as the facilities were in Building 0, there was, from the American standpoint, a positive aspect that overrode all inconvenience. The innkeepers at the Hanoi Hilton had now unwittingly managed to do something they had spent years consciously trying not to do: they had installed their ten seniormost American guests in a single suite. The top ten quickly made the most of the opportunity.

John Flynn assumed command. The 4th Allied POW Wing was

formally established. The Wing motto became "Return with Honor." To that end, policy was made and disseminated.

During captivity, vitually all the prisoners had yielded something to the enemy, most under varying degrees of duress, but some few under no duress at all. In the latter grouping were men who had agreed openly with the enemy that the American intervention was wrong and had been propagandizing for Hanoi. Official POW policy now called on all to rejoin the fold without prejudice, to come into the Wing with a clean slate. This was an offer of unqualified amnesty, a call to "come home, all is forgiven." Most had no distance at all to come, and many were not happy about those who had strayed. But the seniors reminded them, "It is neither American nor Christian to nag a repentant sinner to the grave."

The amnesty offer was to remain open until the moment the war ended; only a few would fail to heed it.

Official policy also called on the prisoners to "take torture before writing or tape-recording propaganda, making public appearances (meeting "peace" delegations) that might advance the enemy's cause, or bowing." The men were told to make use of all their physical resources and moral courage, to use their imaginations, to concoct stories that involved only themselves, or others only if they had been previously briefed. A man could excuse himself from torture only for "urgent health reasons." It was made known that prisoners who denied the applicability of the Code of Conduct and who failed to try to live by it would be stripped of all military authority. Also grounds for relief was apparent emotional instability so serious as to impair one's judgment. It was made clear, however, that since so drastic a measure as relief from command would almost certainly affect one's reputation and future career, hearsay would be impermissible in a relief-from-command inquiry. All testimony would have to come directly from witnesses to alleged violations.

The objective was to give the enemy nothing, or at the very least to minimize his net gain.

Squadron commanding officers had full power of awards and courts-martial. Men with especially retentive memories were designated "memory banks"—historians. Committees were established for such purposes as medical and sanitation procedures, athletics, and communications and escape.

The need for strong military organization was clear. Many of the men had been in captivity for many years, and the war showed no signs yet of ending. By this time, at least 30 percent and perhaps as many as 50 percent of the prisoners were disillusioned about the war and becoming increasingly cynical about it. The primary reasons were that the policy governing the conduct of the war ensured that it could never be won, and the now apparently enormous strength of the antiwar movement in the United States. From the newscasts the prisoners heard and the films their captors showed them, it seemed to many that most of their countrymen were now on the enemy's side. Many prisoners were now wondering, quite understandably, why they should be different, why they should remain indefinitely in an unspeakable captivity, why they should not at least make things easier on themselves by giving the Vietnamese the propaganda help that seemed so vital to ending the war. After all, at home, countless numbers of prominent people, including many members of Congress, were providing the enemy with all kinds of moral support—and for free, without suffering any torture. Pondering this, many POWs had been developing a "to hell with it" attitude. The seniors recognized that if these men were to be able to live with themselves in the years beyond captivity, and that if other young Americans were to be expected to perform well in future POW situations, it was crucial that the men again be made part of a tight, tough, military unit, responsible to their senior officers and accountable for their actions.

And so they organized, and the organization worked so effectively that their captors were soon trying to break it up. In March, thirty-six younger officers whom the Vietnamese adjudged to be "bad attitude" cases were extracted from the various Camp Unity buildings. Their compatriots called these men Hell's Angels. The group included Bud Day, John McCain, Jack Fellowes, and others. They were taken to another prison camp about ten miles west of Hanoi, the grim place they called Skid Row. It was a dark, filthy place, and guards were everywhere, all the time, to smother communications. Except for a short period of time during August, 1971, when Skid Row was threatened by floods, the Hell's Angels group remained in the mean place for eight months, returning to Camp Unity in November.

In May the senior bulls Flynn, Winn, and Gaddis were transferred from Building 0 to Room 18 off the main Hoa Lo courtyard. They were not tortured; apparently the Vietnamese hoped by removing them to deny the prisoners the leadership they had been getting.

Thus, through the summer of 1971, all the Vietnamese had to deal with in Camp Unity were such as Risner, Stockdale, Denton, Mulligan, Jenkins, Rutledge, Guarino, Kasler, and a Wing which, although it was in a slightly reduced size, seemed possessed of improved morale and a heightened taste for resistance.

———

To make room for the Hell's Angels, Green Beret Capt. Jim Thompson, Lew Meyer, and other Americans at Skid Row were moved to a prison camp about forty miles south of Hanoi. They were installed in a commodious cellblock, which appeared to have been newly built for them. The place was the most comfortable they had known as prisoners. There were two large sleeping rooms, a dining room with tables and stools, and a separate latrine-bath-dishwashing-laundry area. The cellblock stood in a compound that was approximately 125 feet long and 60 feet wide. It was surrounded by sixteen-foot-high stone walls, hence, the prisoners called the place Stonewall, or the Rockpile. There were iron bars in the windows, and the entrance to the cellblock was through big double doors consisting mainly of iron bars. But the prisoners were free to intermingle and were granted a great deal of outside time. The food, by past standards, was good. Security was lax; there were only a half-dozen guards assigned to the compound, but only infrequently were more than one or two in view. Adjacent to the Rockpile, beyond the walls, was a large prison complex full of indigenous prisoners.

Jim Thompson had restored himself physically. For a year and a half he had been working religiously at the body-building program he and Meyer had worked out. At the start, even heavy-breathing exercises had made Thompson feel dizzy and faint. Now, in a single session, he could do as many as eighty-seven push-ups and more than two hundred sit-ups. He and Meyer would jog and run around their cell for more than an hour at a time, until they were drenched with sweat.

Thompson was feeling good again, like the airborne soldier he was. It had been seven summers since he last had tried an escape, and with security as lax as it was in this place, the chances for a successful escape did not seem bad—not bad at all.

———

Camp Unity almost literally hummed with communications. Mostly it concerned Wing business but, in addition, a formalized highly energetic educational program got under way. Qualified men like Bob Shumaker, who held degrees in two different technical fields, taught classes in such subjects as electronics, higher mathematics, engineering principles, and thermal dynamics. Nels Tanner offered a popular course in automobile mechanics. Others taught history and such languages as French, German, Spanish, and Russian. Dick Stratton, who had a master's degree in international relations, taught the subject. Under the noses of Communist jailers, he placed special emphasis on communism and the Communist threat.

The men used a mixture of cigarette ash, diarrhea pills, and water to produce red ink. Writing on the coarse toilet paper the Vietnamese supplied, they produced minitextbooks in various subjects and English-foreign language dictionaries three thousand words long. Occasionally guards would find these books and would confiscate them, whereupon the men would immediately set to work to reproduce them.

There is little question that Hanoi was now painfully aware that the United States was POW-conscious. Indeed, the plight of the prisoners seemed to have ignited a major movement in America. Millions of people had written letters, signed petitions, and helped to finance newspaper advertisements demanding improved treatment for the prisoners and International Red Cross inspection of the prison camps. Hanoi seemed unsure how to react to this outpouring.

One policy change that did occur is that the prisoners were now being urged to write letters home. It occurred to John McCain that the prisoners might profit from this desire of the enemy's. Improved though conditions were, they did not begin to approach the standards required by the Geneva Convention. Men were still being punished unreasonably, kept in stocks and in solitary confinement or in cramped, two-man cells for extended periods for such "crimes" as keeping score in a duplicate bridge tournament or communicating with a man who lived in another building. Sanitation facilities were abominable. In the intense tropical heat men developed a miserable heat rash, and an epidemic of conjunctivitis—pink eye—swept through the camp.

McCain proposed to the seniors that since the enemy hoped to improve its image by allowing letters, the prisoners should engage in a letter moratorium. No one should accept an invitation to write home. If the overly anxious enemy turned ugly and punishment or torture seemed in the offing, men shoud write negatively—that is, tell the awful truth. McCain had no fear that such letters would upset the prisoners' families, since the Vietnamese would never send them. And he thought the no-letter policy might improve their conditions.

The seniors approved McCain's proposal, but made participation in the letter moratorium voluntary. For some men, who had not been in touch with their families for many years, it almost seemed that continued sanity depended on being able to write, to let someone know they were still alive, and someday would be coming home. By midsummer, though, nearly all were refusing to write.

––––––

Another who was moved into Building 0 that summer was Lt. Nguyen Quoc Dat, a native North Vietnamese. Born in Hanoi in 1941, he had lived in the city with his family until he was thirteen years old. Then, in 1954, when the Communists took over, he had moved with his family to Saigon. When he had been old enough to do so, he had joined the South Vietnamese Air Force and had been sent to Randolph Air Force Base, Texas, for pilot training. Returning to Vietnam and the war, he was shot down on May 14, 1966.

Among the items his captors had taken from him was a U.S. Air Force ring, which he had bought himself on completion of pilot training; a Texas driver's license; a card identifying him as an honorary citizen of Texas; and a picture of his niece, the Eurasian daughter of his brother, who had married a European wife. In addition to all this, Nguyen spoke Vietnamese with a Hanoi accent, and fluent English as well. The evidence was sinister. His captors felt justified in concluding that he was in fact a naturalized American, that he had been sent to the United States while still a small child, had been handled with special care until he had grown up, then had been returned to Vietnam to help in the "imperialist aggression" against his native land.

For a year after capture, efforts were made to reconvert Nguyen, to explain to him the monstrous thing that had been done to him, to show him the errors of his ways, to "unbrainwash" him. Finally, in 1967, he managed to convince his captors that he was what he appeared to be, a Saigon "air pirate." He also made it clear that he would never yield the propaganda statements his captors wanted from him for use in the South. Nor would he be used as a spy against the

American prisoners. When that had been firmly established, there had been the full measure of maltreatment—tortures, beatings, and forty-nine consecutive months of solitary confinement in Heartbreak Hotel.

The Americans in Building 0 found the newcomer to be a bright and credible extrovert. There was no question about his loyalty: Norm Gaddis could vouch for it, having spent thirty-seven months in solitary in a neighboring Heartbreak cell. So could Navy Lt. (j.g.) Paul E. Galanti (captured on June 17, 1966), who had spent more than seven months in the next door cell in Heartbreak and whom Nguyen thought of as his closest friend. Nguyen was code-named Max. He proved to be a source of invaluable information. He advised his American friends that there was very little mortar between the bricks in the center sections of the cell walls and that small holes could easily be drilled through them, greatly facilitating communications. He taught them how to mold pieces of bread dough, charcoal, and soap together to make serviceable grease pencils.

Max would listen to the Vietnamese-language newscasts that came over the camp radio; these were not meant for the Americans but, since none understood Vietnamese, their captors rarely turned them off. Max was able to tell his American allies what Hanoi radio was saying—once, for example, that a group of POW wives had traveled to Paris to challenge Hanoi's delegation to the peace talks for word of the prisoners.

32

Wilber, Miller, and the Outer Seven

Almost a year earlier, in the fall of 1970, Gene Wilber, Bob Schweitzer, and Ed Miller had been transferred to the Zoo. There they had taken up residence in the Garage, along with four others: Air Force Maj. Roger D. Ingvalson (captured on May 28, 1968); Marine Lt. Paul G. Brown (captured on July 25, 1968); Navy Lieut. Markham L. Gartley (captured on August 17, 1968); and Navy Ens. William J. Mayhew (captured on August 17, 1968). These latter four had not been subjected to the same sort of brutal interrogation and torture with which so many other Americans were greeted on arriving in Hanoi. They had been kept isolated and remained unaware of the severe maltreatment of the other prisoners. They had supplied anti-war statements that their captors found useful. Reaching the Zoo, they were advised by Wilber that he was senior, but that he wanted no strong military organization, that any problems that might arise were to be resolved in "democratic meetings."

In fact, Wilber, Schweitzer, and Miller were all much senior to the other four. It was quickly apparent to the four juniors that tne three seniors shared a pronounced lack of enthusiasm for the American war effort. They were continually writing and tape-recording antiwar statements for their captors, and infusing them with tones of conviction. In the ensuing months they met often with visiting "peace delegations." Miller once suggested that the four juniors write a joint letter to the other prisoners, urging them to cooperate with the Vietnamese. The juniors declined, and Miller did not press the matter.

In mid-December, 1970, members of Hanoi's delegation to the Paris peace talks handed over to representatives of senators William Fulbright and Edward Kennedy a list of 339 American POWs in North Vietnam. Secretary of State William Rogers described this as a "contemptible maneuver," insisting that it was aimed at drawing attention away from Hanoi's failure to abide by international law in its treatment of the prisoners.

In a Christmas Day interview in Hanoi, North Vietnamese Premier Pham Van Dong assured Canadian newsman Michael Maclear that the list was a "full and complete account" of all the Americans who were prisoners of the North Vietnamese, and added, "I swear to you that these men are well treated." Then Maclear and reporters from Algeria and Japan met the seven Americans who lived in the Garage at the Zoo. Only Wilber and Schweitzer were allowed to speak. The interview was taped and filmed, and Maclear's account appeared in the December 28, 1970, New York *Times*. In the interview, Wilber advised, "We get letters about every month, packages every two months; my packages contain candy, various food items, special little snacks, like peanuts, and sometimes some underwear."

Schweitzer said, "We really don't need any clothing, but you know what wives are."

The two explained that they wrote letters to their families once a month, and on such special occasions as Christmas and Mother's Day. "And," said Wilber, "we make many radio messages each year—many." Wilber observed that on anniversaries and children's birthdays, "all we've got to do is say we want to send a message, and it's transmitted. I understand these things go through Cuba."

Wilber indicated that the diet was ample and said that mornings usually were given over to volleyball or "other sports."

Schweitzer continued, "The volleyball court and basketball facilities are available to us all day. We also have a great deal of literature, notable among which are many books by American authors." Maclear noted that the books he named were all critical of American policy in Southeast Asia.

According to the Maclear article, Wilber and Schweitzer went on to describe a near idyllic existence in Hanoi, lives full of interesting films, Shakespearean plays, and visits to museums. The two also contributed some thoughts on the war. "We've got to grip the facts as they lie and stop the war," Wilber said. "We must withdraw our troops to stop the war. That's a condition we have to face. Then the Vietnamese can solve their own problem."

———

With hundreds of other POWs, the Zoo Americans had been moved to Camp Unity on December 26, 1970. The seven from the Garage were installed in Building 8, in Unity's southeastern corner, a small building set back from the others and walled off from the main courtyard. Inside the wall there was a tiny courtyard, and the building contained several small rooms.

Contact was made briefly with other Americans in the camp. All but Wilber and Miller were eager to stay in touch with the others, but the Vietnamese stationed guards in a room between Building 8 and Building 9, a few yards to the west. Cut off from communications, the men in Building 8 became known to the others in Camp Unity as the Outer Seven.

After several weeks the Vietnamese had invited the Americans in Building 9 to play volleyball against those in Building 8. Building 9 advised the prisoner leadership next door in Building 0. Word came back to seize the opportunity in order to pass communications codes and techniques to the Seven, to brief them on the Wing and Wing policies: to follow the Code of Conduct, to accept no special favors, and to refuse any offer of early release.

The volleyball games were played on two consecutive Sundays. The Building 9 prisoners prepared meticulously. As men from the two buildings stood together on the sidelines (the Seven could have only one man out of the game at a time) or chased wayward shots, the Seven were briefed quickly. It fell to Jerry Coffee to brief Ed Miller. Coffee quickly discerned that Miller did not share his sense of values. The marine would acknowledge what Coffee said, but Coffee thought he seemed vague, distant—in fact, uninterested.

After the second Sunday of volleyball, the Outer Seven again fell out of contact. Months passed and there were no communications from Building 8; no contact could be made with them

During these months Building 8 seethed with bitterness and turmoil. Five of the seven—Schweitzer, Ingvalson, Gartley, Mayhew, and Brown—wanted to communicate with the Wing and to be part of it. Wilber and Miller strongly opposed this. Dissension ripened into hatred. It was a long winter and spring, followed by a hot summer.

The three senior bulls, Flynn, Winn, and Gaddis, were still in Room 18, and Robbie Risner, still in Building 0, was acting wing commander.* In June, he directed Building 9 that if there seemed even a fifty-fifty chance of making contact with the Seven without getting caught, the chance was to be taken. He wanted the Seven brought into the Wing.

On June 21, all other attempts to communicate with Building 8 having failed, the Building 9 communicators simply yelled out the back window of their cellblock into the surrounding moat, hoping that their shouts would be heard by the Seven. There was a window in Building 8, perhaps fifty feet away, and the shouts got through to the five men who were eager to respond.

The Building 9 primary communicators were Jerry Coffee, John Borling, and Lt. (j.g.) David J. Carey (captured on August 31, 1967). Building 8 was advised that 9's code name was Buckeye and that 8's would be Roadrunner. The primary Roadrunner communicator was Rog Ingvalson, with Mark Gartley and Paul Brown assisting.

The Roadrunner communicators were hungry for news. They wanted detailed information expanding on the quick, cryptic messages they had received during the volleyball games. They wanted to know all about the Wing, made it clear they wanted membership, wanted the names of all in camp and an updating on the situation. Buckeye supplied the desired information.

In the following days messages came through Buckeye to Roadrunner from elated friends of the Seven all over Camp Unity, expressing delight that they were in contact at last and welcoming them into the Wing. Two of the seven were distressed at the contact. Wilber said disconsolately, "I don't see how you can enjoy it. The Vietnamese tell us not to do it, so why do you do it?" Once he became angry when a greeting was relayed to him from a former squadronmate and sent word back that he wanted no more personal messages.

*It had been ascertained that Risner actually had outranked Vern Ligon all along.

Nor did Miller want any part of the Wing. For months he had been resentful over the message that had been sent out in early 1971, when the Wing was being organized, to "come home, all is forgiven." Miller believed that this message originated in Washington, either with the Department of Defense or with President Nixon, and constituted a form of bribery; that in exchange for support of Nixon and the war effort, the government would forego court-martialing prisoners such as he, who had given voice to their antiwar convictions. Miller did not feel that he had done anything requiring anyone's forgiveness, and was infuriated at what he conceived to be an attempt to bribe him.

The Wing command was puzzled at the behavior of the Roadrunner seniors. Wilber, Miller, and Schweitzer continued to produce all kinds of the most virulent antiwar, even anti-American, material for the enemy. Their letters and tape-recorded messages to families and friends, congressmen and antiwar organizations were presented often over the camp radio—for example a Mother's Day message Ed Miller had tape-recorded in May. Some excerpts:

> Mothers have been suffering for the loss and injury of sons in time of war since time began. But I think this war is different. . . . Today, America's mothers must face the fact that their sons are killing fellow human beings and destroying foreign countries for an unjust cause, making our actions not only illegal, but immoral . . . immorality is the rottenness which is consuming us. . . .
>
> We are a militaristic nation of the first order . . . our foreign policy is predicated on militarism . . . our leaders offer no hope for change, only more of the same. . . . My personal participation in this war is my personal shame and tragedy. My country's immoral and illegal actions which are now culminated in the tragedy of Vietnam is America's shame and a blight on the world's conscience. . . .

The prisoner leadership did not dispute any American's right to harbor such thoughts. However, they felt it inappropriate that American military officers—and worse, senior officers—should willingly and frequently deliver themselves of such remarks from an enemy prison camp. Wilber, Miller, and Schweitzer, all members of the Department of the Navy, received a message from Jim Stockdale, the senior Navy officer in Hanoi: "Write nothing for the V. Meet no delegations. Make no tapes. No early releases. Are you with us?"

The next day Wilber and Miller replied jointly, "We actively oppose this war."

Schweitzer replied, "I feel that the causes and effects of this war are such that every man should make his own decision. However, I am in general agreement with Commander Stockdale."

At this point, Buckeye interposed a question: "Are you obeying the Code of Conduct?"

"In general," answered Roadrunner communicator Ingvalson, "I would say no." Strictly speaking, all members of Roadrunner had violated the code in that they had supplied their captors with anti-war statements. But the juniors, Ingvalson, Gartley, Brown, or Mayhew, had not engaged in anything like the energetic antiwar activities of Wilber, Miller, and Schweitzer. The four Roadrunner juniors advised that henceforth they would hold fast to the Code. Schweitzer advised that he had agreed to write a letter to Senator Fulbright, but that once that was done he would not cooperate with his captors anymore.

Wilber and Miller refused to communicate.

Buckeye passed the Wing policies to Roadrunner, explaining that policies now were called Plums, and that the word had no significance—it was simply that it was said quickly and easily.

It was a grim time in Building 8. Wilber and Miller were angrily opposed to the Plums, which Miller kept derisively calling "prunes" or "cherries." The two senior officers made it clear they had no intention of living by such policies, that they would live by their own consciences. They spent more and more time alone together and seemed to become more and more vehemently opposed to the idea of the Wing.

Wilber and Miller collaborated on a tape-recorded, July 4, "Open Letter to the American People." It was broadcast on July 3 to American servicemen in South Vietnam. Taking turns speaking, they described themselves as patriotic American officers who had dedicated their lives to the service of their country who now had discovered that they had been "excessively politically naive, career-oriented and guilty of what is correctly termed a military mentality." Their leaders, they said, had deceived them, they had "committed aggression in Indochina," and they characterized American actions as "barbaric" and "immoral." They charged that American policy "is to economically divide and dominate the world," then ended with an Independence Day wish for "continued successes" to those who were struggling to end the Vietnam War.

Over a period of several weeks, the Wing command sent several messages to Wilber and Miller. In late July, Stockdale asked, ''Are you doing any more work for the V?''

Through the Ingvalson, the two Roadrunner seniors replied, ''We are working for peace.''

''Do you mean opposing the war?''

''Yes.''

The other five made it known that *they* were doing nothing for the V, and that prior to July 4 they had made it clear to their captors that they would have nothing more to do with their antiwar program.

On August 2, Acting Wing Commander Robbie Risner initiated a dialogue with Wilber and Miller that was to culminate in the stripping of the two of their military authority. Roadrunner communicators wrote out the Risner messages word for word and checked their accuracy. Then the messages were delivered to Wilber and Miller orally—the writing was destroyed so that the Vietnamese would not find it.

Risner offered the two ''a chance to rejoin the team.'' He advised them that they were being disloyal to their country, their services, and their fellow prisoners of war. He ordered them to abide by the Code of Conduct, and specifically to write nothing for their captors nor make any public appearances nor meet any delegations. He warned them that they faced courts-martial if they disobeyed his order, and asked whether or not they would comply.

The next day Wilber and Miller gave the Roadrunner communicators separate written messages for Risner. Wilber called Risner's attention to the illegality of the war, but said that he would obey all legal military orders.

Miller assured Risner of his pride in being a loyal American, of his certainty that the war was immoral as well as illegal, and of his uncompromising dedication to high moral principle and Christian teaching. He was sure, he said, that Risner did not mean to deprive him of his right of free speech.

On the same day these messages were sent to Risner, a tape-recorded Wilber-Miller message ''to the Congress of the United States, via Representative McClosky and Senator McGovern''* was broadcast to American servicemen in South Vietnam. In this message the two officers commended to Congress a July 1, 1971, seven-point

---

*By this time, Rep. Paul ''Pete'' McClosky (D., Calif.) and Sen. George McGovern (D., S.D.) had become leaders of the antiwar faction in Congress.

proposal that had been advanced by Viet Cong delegates at the Paris peace talks. Chief among the points was that the United States announce a 1971 date by which all American forces would be out of Vietnam. Wilber and Miller said this was ''the only honorable way out'' and called on Congress to support it.

On August 6 Risner sent another message to Wilber and Miller, demanding a yes or no answer to his order to abide by the Code. The next day Wilber and Miller replied jointly that there was no simple yes or no answer to Risner's question. They said they would obey all lawful military orders and suggested that, if Risner wished to pursue the matter, he obtain permission to ''communicate directly with us.''

Throughout their confinement with others Wilber and Miller were to contend that the war was illegal, and to imply that orders issued to them within the context of the war were illegal. In a post–release interview Wilber was to point out that at the post-World War II Nuremberg trials, the United States and its Allies tried, convicted, and even executed some Axis military officers for acting upon orders from their superiors they knew or should have known to be illegal.

On August 11 Risner sent a final message to Wilber and Miller. He expressed his sorrow at their refusal to join the Wing. He pointed out that Plum One established, as grounds for disqualification from command, failure to obey or recognize the application of the Code of Conduct. He advised, ''You are hereby relieved of military authority.'' He assured them that they would be considered for reinstatement upon receipt of word from them that they would obey and enforce the Code.

Risner also sent a short message to Schweitzer appointing him Roadrunner squadron commander. Within a few days Schweitzer asked Risner to clarify his status. Wilber and Miller, both of them senior in rank to Schweitzer, had assured him that they would not accept him as their commanding officer, that he had no jurisdiction whatever over them. Risner responded that Schweitzer indeed had military authority over all the American prisoners who occupied Building 8, including Wilber and Miller. Whereupon Schweitzer took command, warning the two seniors against interfering with his exercise of command.

Angrily, Wilber told him, ''You want to be a commanding officer? Okay, I'll show you what it's like to be a commanding officer. I'll put you in a box every chance I get!''

Wilber and Miller were tireless in ridiculing Wing policy. When

Schweitzer would speak to one of his juniors, Miller invariably would sarcastically point out to the junior that it was no less than his commanding officer who was addressing him and that he had best be quick to heed. When a Vietnamese would approach, Wilber and Miller would tell Schweitzer that the man was an "enemy," and would ask for orders, wanted to know if the "commanding officer" wanted the squadron to kill the Vietnamese and take over the camp. Pointing to approaching guards, Wilber and Miller would tell the others, "Here comes the enemy! Hate him! Kill him!"

Wilber went on a hunger strike, and a few days later Miller joined him. They explained to the others that they wanted to be separated from them. The Vietnamese interrogated the two privately. They returned to the building and resumed eating.

In late September the Roadrunner Seven were transferred back to the Garage in the Zoo. Their empty cells in Building 8 were occupied by the three senior bulls Flynn, Winn, and Gaddis. The bulls were joined by Stockdale, Denton, Jenkins, Mulligan, and Air Force Lt. Col. James L. Hughes (captured on May 5, 1967). Thus Building 8, recently notorious as a nesting place for collaborators, now took on a reverential aspect. It was headquarters, the abode of leadership, a place deserving of special trust and confidence.

Robbie Risner remained in Building 0. With Flynn resuming command of the Wing, Risner reverted to deputy wing commander.

At the Zoo the camp authority found that with the exception of Wilber and Miller, the Roadrunner group was uncooperative. Shortly, it was divined that Schweitzer was a bad influence, and in mid-October he was ordered to gather his belongings for a move. Schweitzer instructed the next senior ranking officer, Roger Ingvalson, to take command. His parting instruction to the three juniors was to "Back up Rog."

Schweitzer was returned to Hoa Lo and assigned to Building 7, where Larry Guarino was in command. If he was happy at last to be away from Wilber and Miller and in a more agreeable environment, the feeling was not altogether mutual. There was practically no one who had not heard "The Bob and Ed Show" or heard all about it. The very thought of the two American officers, Schweitzer and Miller, freely alluding to the illegality of the American war effort and the criminal status of the POWs induced livid anger in many. However, Schweitzer seemed recently to have turned himself around—after, as he put it, he had "learned the other guys had been getting screwed."

For the most part, the men in Building 7 remained wary of Schweitzer, but were inclined to give him the benefit of the doubt and a new chance.

It was soon established that Schweitzer was senior to Guarino. There being no question about the sincerity of Schweitzer's repentance and his determination to abide by the Plums, he was deemed by the Wing leadership to be worthy of command.

More Escape, More Torture, and Bitter Dissension

On October 2 at the Rockpile, south of Hanoi, the prison camp commander was about to conduct one of his periodic inspections. The Americans were ushered into the dining room in their cellblock, and sat on stools which all had been placed on one side of the table. The camp commander's usual practice was to lecture them for a few minutes, and then listen to any grievances the men might have. Just as he was about to enter the cellblock, however, a guard from the main camp, where indigenous prisoners were held, came rushing into the compound. Sweating, clearly distraught, pointing back to the main camp, he advised the commander that one of the American prisoners, none of whom was known to be missing, had just turned himself in. Apparently, the man had departed this place yesterday, then, after failing to make progress through the jungled countryside, had given up the escape as hopeless and had returned. The prisoner was a civilian named Clodeon "Speed" Adkins, a construction worker who had been captured during the 1968 Tet offensive.

The camp commander was visibly perturbed at the loose security the Adkins leavetaking seemed to indicate. But at least the man had returned. Apparently deciding to deal with the situation later, the commander proceeded with the inspection. Stalking into the dining room with intepreters and guards, he demanded a head count of the prisoners to ascertain that the returned escapee was indeed one of his 14 American inmates, and that 13 others remained. Counting in Vietnamese, the interpreters could not get past the number 11. They counted again and again, and to their mounting dismay kept coming up with 11.

An enormous rage suffused the camp boss. He kept pacing the room, his hands clasped behind his back. He kept looking at the prisoners, appeared to be counting them with nods of his head, kept looking at the interpreters and guards and saying in increasingly loud and angry tones, "Eleven? Eleven? Eleven!" Then, unable to hold back the tides of fury, he was seized in a shrieking, arm-waving monologue. Soon armed guards with dogs were scurrying into the jungle.

By this time, the other two escapees, Jim Thompson and Lew Meyer, were in a small cave on a jungled hillside overlooking the prison. They saw the search parties moving out, but were not frightened. Rain was falling, and would blunt the dogs' effectiveness, and no guards were going to find them in this jungle except by sheerest accident.

Thompson and Meyer had been planning the escape for months. Each had feigned illness a few times, and had acquired aspirin, merthiolate, and medications for the treatment of fungus and for the eyes. They had stolen a cooking pot, matches and a machete. They meant to head southwesterly, toward a special forces camp Thompson had once known—a better bet, he thought, than trying to move in other more densely populated directions. He did not believe the chances for success to be even remotely good. He had long ago assured Meyer that he felt certain they would be recaptured and perhaps executed. Meyer shared this view; but also shared Thompson's feeling that the potential rewards outweighed the risks.

For security reasons, Thompson and Meyer had told no one of their plans. During outside time on October 1, they had enlisted the help of other prisoners in getting over the wall. "Speed" Adkins had persuaded them to take him with them. It turned out that Adkins, too, had long been planning to leave, and was determined to try to make it to the coast. He feared the security crackdown that would follow a Thompson-Meyer escape. After about 20 hours in the hopelessly impenetrable jungle, he had given up and returned to the prison.

Thompson and Meyer decided they needed guidance through the mountains and jungles to the southwest. As dark fell on the second night, they slipped down into the indigenous penitentiary, found a lone Vietnamese prisoner in the latrine of a cellblock and tried to persuade him to come along. They assured the man that they could make short work of the single guard in view, could open the cellblock and free all its inmates into the jungle. The man smiled, shook hands through the barred window and made it emphatically clear that he deemed the plan a bummer. He wished them well but declined to join up. They moved out of the prison yard, back up into the jungle—and suddenly found themselves amidst about 20 irascible guards. The escape was over.

There was no severe retribution for the Thompson-Meyer-Adkins escape attempts, although the Rockpile prisoners lost their outside time for about a year, the food took a turn for the worse and the guards became a trifle nastier.

————

The start that was made in October, 1969, toward better treatment for most of Hanoi's American prisoners was a long time catching up with some. At the Plantation, torture remained much in vogue through early 1972.

SRO at the Plantation was Air Force Lt. Col. Ted Guy. The combative Guy had been downed in Laos on March 22, 1968. He was captured after shooting it out with some North Vietnamese soldiers, killing at least two of them. After capture he had been subjected to all the tortures which by this time the Vietnamese were routinely inflicting on their American prisoners. He had spent the next thirty-seven months in solitary confinement—first at the Plantation, then in Vegas, on to D-1, and back to the Plantation on November 25, 1970. He remained isolated, but was now in a cell from which he was able to at least see other Americans. He did not always like what he saw. Among the fifty-odd prisoners were some of the most disgustingly obsequious Americans in Guy's knowledge, men who could not seem to snap to attention fast enough when a Vietnamese approached, who bowed and scraped to their captors in the most servile fashion. The feisty Guy was sickened at this and, in his isolation, frustrated at being unable to provide the kind of leadership that might get it stopped.

The men with whom Guy was primarily concerned were a small group who were showered with all sorts of favors and special treatment by the enemy. They were free from early morning until late at night to do much as they pleased in their corner of the yard. They visited at will with one another, played basketball, exercised in other ways, seemed free to bathe whenever they wished, and sunned themselves, eventually acquiring nice suntans. While the quantity and quality of the food most of the prisoners now were receiving was much improved over what they had been getting at D-1, it was poor fare compared to what these eight were to receive as time passed: thermos jugs full of steaming coffee, sugar, and condensed milk; ample supplies of eggs, beef, pork, and fish; cigarettes, fruit, candy, and, occasionally, beer. These men gladly accepted this preferred treatment. Guy would later identify them as Robert Chenoweth, Alfonso Riate, Michael Branch, John A. Young, and Abel Larry Kavanaugh.

In April, 1971, Guy got his first cellmate, Army Maj. Artice W. Elliott, a Green Beret officer who had been captured at Pleiku on April 25, 1970. Elliott had also observed these men and had come to the same conclusion as Guy. Other prisoners watched, too, and now referred to the five as the Ducks, for the way they would scamper to and follow Vietnamese bearing goodies.

During the first half of 1970 at the Plantation, it seemed to Ted Guy that prisoners were on the camp radio all the time, propagandizing for the enemy. Most spoke in strained voices and used Communist jargon—it was clear they had not written the stuff and were speaking under duress. But the propaganda material issuing from the Ducks was far from halfhearted. It was also heard over Hanoi's "Voice of Vietnam" and the Viet Cong's clandestine "Liberation Radio." Typical was a May 14, 1971, memo signed by "Michael P. Branch, deserter," which was broadcast to American GIs in South Vietnam. The memo advised, "I've joined with a group of captured servicemen who are against the war in Vietnam." This group, said the memo, sought to "put pressure on Mr. Nixon to end the war immediately." The way to do this, the memo advised GIs, was

"Together with a squad, platoon or company, refuse combat or just botch up all your operations." The memo also urged GIs to desert and told them to "get in touch with the local people who will notify the Viet Cong. They will get you to a liberated area and then they will help you to go to any country of your choosing." The memo gave assurances that no harm would befall any who opted for this course of action, explaining, "I know this for a fact, for I chose this way of getting out of the war three years ago...." The memo did not explain how it was that "Michael P. Branch, deserter" had, oddly enough, chosen to go to jail in North Vietnam.

The five delivered many such offerings over the camp radio. In a postrelease interview John Young claimed credit for "only thirty-three," explaining that Cheese vetoed "quite a few" he thought to be "too strong." Among the Young creations Cheese apparently did not judge "too strong" was one that flabbergasted most of the Americans who heard it. In this one, delivered in late June, 1971, Young confided that "Sergeant First Class Brande at Langvei Special Forces camp told me that he was probably the only man to kill fifteen VC with fifteen rounds from his M-16 rifle. These men all had their hands tied behind them and were on their knees."

No one was more surprised at this revelation than Brande. Brande hotly denies that he ever did any such thing. He says he did not know Young prior to capture, that he had never served with him prior to Langvei, that he spoke to him only once at Langvei, briefly and casually, and that he certainly never confessed to Young that he had committed a cold-blooded, multiple murder.

Young insists Brande admitted the murders to him back in Port-holes, the jungle camp. He claims that the information had "upset" him, that he had remonstrated angrily with Brande, but that all he had received in return "was a smile." Young says his prison camp confession on Brande's behalf was made "not in an attempt to discredit him, but to bring it out that Americans are doing it . . . as a man, I don't think it's in him, but he was taught and forced to do stuff like that . . . just like me."

Most of the Americans who heard Young's allegations thought that, regardless of Brande's guilt or innocence, it was inappropriate that such charges be broadcast in the middle of an enemy prison camp. Brande himself was so fearful for his life that he thought it imperative to escape. He figured he might as well die while trying to save himself as to simply wait for the enemy to execute him. Making his decision known, he put out a request for information about the local area, the prison's location, the lay of the land, any props used in previous escape attempts, and general advice about the best course of action.

Word came back from SRO Guy that Brande was not to attempt to escape. Guy feared strong enemy reprisals against the Americans who remained, possibly multiple executions. He further advised that he did not believe Brande to be in any real danger; there were too many American witnesses to all that had happened.

So Brande stayed put, waiting nervously. Guy's judgment proved to be correct.

On June 13 the New York Times *began publishing the so-called Pentagon Papers, a secret Defense Department history of the American involvement in Vietnam. Stretching from the Truman through the Johnson administrations, the voluminous report appeared to be full of sensational revelations, among them prior U.S. government knowledge of the 1963 coup that had brought down the Diem regime; and the existence as early as 1964 of plans for the systematic bombing of North Vietnam. The Papers seemed to indicate an outrageously cynical disparity between the government's public policy concerning Vietnam and its actual military intent. According to Daniel Ellsberg, a Defense Department consultant and one of many authors of the report, this cynical disparity justified his delivery of the secret report to the press.*

Furious at what it deemed a gross breach of national security, the Nixon Administration on June 15 obtained a court order enjoining the Times *from publishing further excerpts. Three days later the Washington* Post *began publishing the history, and was similarly enjoined. On June 30, the Supreme Court ruled the material to be in the public domain and permitted the newspapers to publish it.*

Subsequently, Ellsberg and an associate, Anthony Russo, Jr., were charged with espionage, theft, and conspiracy and brought to trial. During the trial it became known that White House agents had broken into the office of Ellsberg's psychiatrist in a futile attempt to find incriminating information about Ellsberg; and also that during 1969 and 1970 the FBI had tapped Ellsberg's telephone. The presiding judge ruled that the government's behavior made a fair trial impossible, and dismissed the case.

On July 8 six more Americans were transferred from Hoa Lo to the Plantation: Ernest C. Brace, a civilian who had been captured on May

21, 1965; Navy Lt. Henry J. "Jim" Bedinger, captured on November 22, 1969; Air Force Capt. Jack M. Butcher, captured on March 24, 1971; Air Force Maj. Norbert A. Gotner, captured on February 3, 1971; Air Force Capt. Stephen G. Long, captured on February 28, 1969; and Air Force Maj. Walter M. Stischer, captured on April 13, 1968. They were moved into cells adjacent to the one Ted Guy shared with Art Elliott.

What these men had in common with Guy was that all had been captured in Laos. Guy surmises that the Communists thought the war soon might come to an end and, at least at this point, had no intention of ever releasing any prisoners who had been captured in Laos. Throughout the war Hanoi had insisted that there were none of its military forces in Laos, and Guy believes that the Communists meant to hang onto all who could say otherwise. He points out that none who were captured in Laos ever were permitted to write any letters. In any case, "the Laotians," as this group of prisoners came to be called, were gathered together in the Plantation that midsummer.

The Plantation soon was alive with communications. SRO Guy found that the bulk of the prisoner population was enlisted men and that they wanted nothing so much as strong leadership. He promulgated policies virtually identical to the BACK US policy Jim Stockdale had established at Hoa Lo years earlier, but urged a gradual buildup of the resistance campaign in order to soften the Vietnamese reaction.

The campaign began far from gradually. One July day seven Americans advised their captors that they had no intention of again bowing to any Vietnamese, nor would they write or tape-record anything more for them. SRO Guy's fears proved to be well founded. The enemy launched a vicious round of beatings and torture. Guy watched through the gaps and holes in his cell door, full of angry pride, as defiant Americans were marched into torture chambers. Each man who went in would emerge days later, pale, drawn, barely able to walk. The effeminate Vietnamese officer whom the prisoners called Cheese was happily supervising the program.

"J. R." Leonard was now living in a large cell with Paul Montague, Bruce Archer, Jim DiBernardo, and Dennis Thompson. In June all had been shocked to hear John Young on the camp radio accuse Brande of the cold-blooded murder of Communist prisoners of war. No one knew what to do about it. Leonard, as senior officer in the room, felt that he should do something if the chance presented itself—he worried that, following release, the Ducks might be able to return to the United States and escape accountability for their behavior by pleading ignorance, by insisting that no one had ever told them what was required of them as American military men.

His chance came one day when Leonard and his cellmates were outside shaving. Bruce Archer, next to him, suddenly said, "Hey, J. R., here they are."

Looking up, Leonard saw that the Ducks were about to pass within easy range of his voice. Leonard was terrified. His own horrendous torture at Cheese's hands in 1969 was still vivid in his memory, every millisecond of it, and the thought of more of it filled him with dread. He hated himself for what he deemed his own cowardly fears. Yet there was something that had to be done, and the moment was now. He put down his razor, fixed his attention on the oncoming Ducks. Recognizing only Kavanaugh, he addressed himself to him, speaking loudly enough so that all could hear: "Kavanaugh, you and your men are to stop all forms of cooperation and collaboration with the enemy."

"We'll do what we want," Kavanaugh replied.

"Fuck you, Captain Leonard," shouted one of the others, whom Leonard later would identify as Alfonso Riate.

Despite their response, Leonard felt that something important had been accomplished: he had issued a direct order, and the men to whom he had issued the order had indicated by their response that they knew him to be an officer and also that they had understood his order. There was nothing more that he could do but wait, and wonder what would happen to him. He watched the Ducks walk on.

Shortly, they passed Camp SRO Guy's cell. Guy had not heard the exchange, but he heard them laughing and joking about it with each other, and with a Vietnamese guard who was with them. He heard an American saying, ". . . told me to stop collaborating with the enemy. I asked him who the enemy was."

As quickly as Guy learned what had happened he ordered all other Plantation Americans to break off any contact that might have been established with the Ducks. To the SRO it seemed clear that within the group were men who were at least as dangerous to the other captive Americans as the most dedicated of their Vietnamese enemy. At the same time, Guy directed that all other Americans observe the group as much as possible and report all pertinent information on them directly to himself. Foreseeing the possibility of future legal action against members of the group, he made it plain that he was interested only in firsthand knowledge, that no hearsay would be accepted.

Leonard did not have long to wait to learn what would happen to him. Within an hour of his confrontation with the Ducks, he was in solitary, locked in leg irons. He was to remain in solitary for the next eight months.

———

Guy's order did not reach some Plantation prisoners for many months. The Army doctor, Capt. Floyd Kushner, for example. Kushner and others who had been with him in camps in the South had reached the Plantation on April 1, 1971, after a two-month trek. By this time, Kushner was like a robot. After three years of the horror of the jungle camps, the will to resist had been squeezed out of him. He was compliant. His captors commanded, and he obeyed. On reaching the Plantation, he was interrogated by Cheese as to his views on the war, and told the sadistic runt what he correctly thought he wanted to hear, that he opposed the American involvement; by now, this was certainly true. Kushner hated the war because of what it had done to him, because it continued to threaten his survival, because of what he thought it was doing to America.

Soon Kushner and his companions from the southern camps found themselves in rooms adjacent to one occupied by the men with whom SRO Guy had ordered communications cut. As yet, Kushner and those with him knew nothing of Guy, nor of this group, which was now known to many other prisoners as "the PCs"—Peace Committee. (The group had entitled itself the Peace Committee of Southeast Asia.) At night the PCs shouted out the window of their room, engaging the Kushner group in conversation, advising of their anti-war activities in language so bitterly anti-American as to appall Kushner. Kushner shouted back to the PCs, warning them against the things they were saying and telling them to stop what they were doing. One of the enlisted men with Kushner also shouted, saying, "You guys are still Americans, you know."

In late 1971, Guy's policies were finally passed to Kushner and his men by the "Sergeants," John Anderson, Donat Gouin, Harvey

Brande, and other senior noncommissioned officers. The Sergeants advised that mistakes of the past were to be forgotten, and that all were to band together behind Colonel Guy. Despite his antiwar views, Kushner was glad to comply, to become part of a team, united behind a strong leader. He told his captors that he was through making statements and reading over the camp radio.

———

While Kushner and others from the southern camps seemed to firm up behind Guy's leadership, some in other cells found the PCs' appeal persuasive. The PCs now became eight. The three new additions were Army Pfcs. James A. Daly, captured on January 9, 1968; King David Rayford, Jr., captured on July 2, 1967; and Marine Pfc. Frederick L. Elbert, captured on August 16, 1968.

Daly, eighteen years old, black, deeply religious, a conscientious objector who opposed all war, had once toyed with the idea of making a life's work in the Jehovah's Witness ministry. He had no business being in any war. But when an aggressive recruiting officer assured him that the Army had a special noncombat program for conscientious objectors, he signed up. Not long afterward, Daly found himself a member of a combat infantry unit in Vietnam. He would not fight; he would carry a weapon but, because of his religious convictions, would not use it. He had been three months in Vietnam when his unit was ambushed and he was captured.

As a prisoner, Daly became a prime target of Communist propaganda. Yet, despite his background, he was no pushover. At least once, in the South, he had been one of a handful who had refused to sign one of the enemy's antiwar tracts. In Hanoi, though, he thought he had found kindred American spirits in the antiwar PCs, whom he met at a 1971 Christmas party. He judged them to be sincere. They opposed the war. He opposed all war. He thought it best, for himself, for America, for Vietnam, that he join the PCs and do what he could about ending this war.

Fred Elbert, the marine, had been in the same southern camps as Daly, and in Hanoi crossed over to join the PCs shortly after Daly. Elbert mystified Daly. He was given to sleeping through the days and staying awake at night. During his waking hours he spent a great deal of time sitting alone, daydreaming, almost in a trance—people would speak to him, and he would not hear a word. For some reason no one understood, he insisted that his name was John Peter Johnson—when captured he had two shirts with the different name tags on them—and no one was really certain who he was.

King David Rayford, Jr., twenty-one, a black, had suffered bitter racial experiences while growing up in Chicago's ghetto, and also in the Army.

According to some PCs, a number of other American prisoners confided to them that they shared their antiwar views, but would not join them for fear of postwar courts-martial, disgrace, possible imprisonment in the United States, and loss of the substantial amounts of pay that were accumulating.

————

Ted Guy knew that the long period of brutal interrogations would end with him. He was taken to Cheese at 7 AM on January 22, 1972. The torture chamber was filthy. For the first three days and nights Guy was allowed no sleep. He was stripped naked, locked in leg irons, and made to lie on his stomach. A guard stood on the backs of his legs, Cheese kept a foot on his neck, pinning his head to the floor, and another guard flogged him with a rubber hose. The beating lasted a long time. Guy lost control of his bodily functions, he vomited, and when the pain became more than he could bear, he screamed. Rags were crammed into his mouth and the flogging continued.

In the long days and nights that followed, torture guards who enjoyed their work took turns inflicting long beatings with their fists; one of them had a habit of napping in a chair while the other indulged himself with the prisoner. When he was awakened to take his turn, he would approach his prey rubbing his hands together.

During one stretch Guy was kept kneeling for approximately eighteen hours. His knees were swollen to the extent that he could not pull his trouser legs over them. When he refused to author a confession of crimes, he was made to kneel again, this time atop an iron bar.

Cheese was ever on hand, directing activities, watching and often participating, sweating, salivating, and laughing. He was having a ball.

The torture ended for Guy when after ten days and nights, he produced an acceptable confession, an apology, and an agreement to do anything that was asked of him. Then he was asked to write a letter of "solidarity" and encouragement to the Vietnam Veterans Against the War. When he balked at this, he was ordered back onto his knees and offered another round of torture. Unable to tolerate the prospect, he yielded.*

———

The winter of 1971–72 was a bad one at the Zoo, too, not so much in terms of mistreatment as in aggravation.

In the fall the Buckeye twenty, who had occupied Room 9 in Camp Unity and who had been the communications link between the Wing commander and Roadrunner, were transferred to the Zoo. There they had been put into the Pigsty with the remaining Roadrunner Six (Schweitzer having departed in October). It was immediately apparent to some in Buckeye that there was no love lost between the antiwar seniors, Gene Wilber and Ed Miller, on the one hand, and the seniors and the four juniors on the other—in some cases, there seemed an almost tangible hatred.

The combined squadrons included twenty-six men. Wilber and Miller far outranked the others, but had been relieved of their military authority in August. Thus, Rog Ingvalson, the next senior officer, was in command. Of Scandinavian extraction, he took the code name Viking for the newly formed squadron.

The Pigsty was now divided into a half-dozen sizable rooms, each of them running the width of the building. Wilber and Miller were installed in a room at one end of the building, and the other twenty-four men were assigned more or less evenly into the other five rooms. From the outset, the accommodations accorded Wilber and Miller and the conditions of their confinement were a source of intense irritation to the others. The two seniors had a flush toilet, which remained off limits to the others—they were still required to use waste buckets. Wilbur and Miller enjoyed many other niceties that were denied the others; a table, a bench, writing materials, potted plants, an aquarium containing several goldfish, curtains on the windows, extra blankets, extra clothing, extra food. Most annoying to the others, though, was the extra freedom the two were granted. Their door was unlocked at 5:30 AM, and they had the run of the compound until bedtime at 9:30 PM. The others were allowed out of their cells from 8 AM until 10:30 AM, then were locked up again until siesta was over at 2 PM. They were locked up again for the night at 4:30 PM. On

———

*Guy was to see these letters again. After release, he filed charges against eight other returnees. Pickets patrolled Homestead Air Force Base, where Guy was stationed, handing out copies of the letters as proof that he, too, had collaborated.

Sundays, because of a reduced guard force, all prisoners save Wilber and Miller remained locked in their cells all day; the two seniors were free as on any other day.

Wilber had a garden in the compound, where he was permitted to grow vegetables. Once he offered lettuce to the others, but they refused it, insisting that they could eat nothing that was not being offered to all American prisoners. This seemed to anger Wilber, who left lettuce at the windows of each of the Pigsty cells. The others threw it away.

Wilber and Miller continued to produce written and tape-recorded materials their captors found useful. They also continued to meet with visiting antiwar delegations. Ingvalson kept cautioning them against these activities. Frequently he would take Wilber, the senior of the two seniors, aside to say, "I am the direct representative of the Wing commander, and it is my duty to ask you to stop cooperating with the Vietnamese."

Invariably, Wilber would respond to the effect that the illegality of the American intervention justified the dissenters' activities. He would point out that "your treatment depends on your attitude" and would give assurances that all the prisoners could enjoy the same benefits that were accorded him and Miller if only they would develop a "better attitude." Clearly, Wilber thought the others were foolish to behave as they did toward the Vietnamese.

For a while relations between the Buckeye group and Wilber and Miller remained reasonably friendly. Wilber was always pleasant, and Miller was a superlative storyteller who could keep listeners convulsed with laughter. And the careers and records of the two men deserved respect. But the Pigsty atmosphere changed as, more and more, the two men expounded their antiwar views. Often, during siesta periods, they would come to the barred windows of the cells containing the other prisoners to assure the others at great length of the illegality and immorality of the American intervention, and to assert that the best thing that could happen would be the expeditious and total withdrawal of American arms from Vietnam.

Generally, their listeners were amazed. It was as though they were hearing Hanoi's "Voice of Vietnam" propaganda broadcasts. Wilber and Miller delivered these offerings as though they were their own original ideas; it was apparent that they believed the things they were saying.

This was old stuff to the four who had been with Wilber and Miller since the fall of 1970—Ingvalson, Gartley, Mayhew, and Brown. But the others, the twenty who formerly had been Buckeye, as much as they had heard the two over the camps' radios, could scarcely believe what they were seeing and hearing in the visits with them.

During the early 1971 volleyball games at Camp Unity, Buckeye had told the Outer Seven something of the long years of torture and systematic mistreatment of many Americans, but it had not been possible to pass detailed information. Now, in the Pigsty, it was discovered that the six remaining members of the Seven had no conception of what others had endured. Buckeye put together a lengthy oral POW history, each man contributing all that had happened to himself and what he knew had happened to others. The history related the experiences of Robbie Risner, Jerry Denton, Ray Vohden, John McCain, Jim Kasler, and many others. It told how, for years, Hanoi had withheld from the United States government the names of men known to be dead, thus cruelly keeping alive the hopes of loved ones, and fully recounted the horror of all the incredibly brutal purges through the years; of Fidel and the year of hell he had imposed on a group at the Zoo, and what he had done to the Faker; and of Americans of whom nothing had been heard for a long time, who had not arrived at Camp Unity at the end of 1970 and who were feared to be dead: Ed Atterberry, Norm Schmidt, Ken Cameron, J. J. Connell.

Nothing pertinent was omitted. The history took several hours to relate. First, Jerry Coffee and Ev Alvarez delivered it to Ingvalson, Gartley, Mayhew, and Brown. The four listened, quietly, intently. They were badly shaken by the revelations, seemed almost unable to grasp the magnitude of the brutality that was described to them or to understand why they had been treated so differently. It seemed to Coffee that, for several days, the four remained unnaturally quiet, morose.

Then Coffee and Alvarez gave the history to Wilber and Miller separately, in deference to their senior ranks. Like the others, Wilber and Miller listened closely to the history, occasionally asking questions.

The Buckeye group had hoped their revelations would bring Miller and Wilber back into the Wing, but the POW history had no effect on them. They continued with their antiwar activities. "Viking" SCO Rog Ingvalson thought the situation hopeless, but granted Jerry Coffee permission to approach Wilber alone. Coffee had known Wilber slightly in the years before the war and judged him basically to be an attractive personality, introverted but warm and likable; he thought there was a chance Wilber could be reached. In long, private meetings with him, Coffee observed that, like many others, Wilber had for several years been pumped full of Communist propaganda and that he seemed to have reached some "significant conclusions" on the basis of limited information. This, said Coffee, struck him as an unfair way to deal with his country, his family, and himself. He suggested to Wilber that several factors might have affected his ability to judge soundly what he had been hearing: unjustified guilt feelings over his backseater, who had died during shootdown; the illness he had suffered on reaching Hanoi; the nearly two years he had spent in solitary; deep anxiety over his health; and worry at the thought that he would never see his family again. "That hasn't been Gene Wilber we've been hearing over the camp radio," Coffee said. "That's been the 'Voice of Vietnam.' You've been listening to them for years. Now, listen to me: they don't care anything about you. Their only interest in you is in what they can get out of you. They don't care what happens to you when you get home. *I* do. *I* care what happens to you, and so do the other guys in this building. We're not looking for a pro-war stance from you. Just join us."

Wilber thanked Coffee for his concern and trouble and assured him that he would think about all that he had said. It seemed to Coffee that the conversation had gone well and that there was reason to be hopeful. Shortly, however, Wilber told Coffee that there was no blinking the fact that each day the war continued innocent people were being killed to no good purpose. He revealed that the Vietnamese people did not bomb and strafe California, and the United States had no right to bomb and strafe Vietnam, destroying hospitals and churches. To the disappointed Coffee, it sounded like another "Voice of Vietnam" broadcast.

Wilber and Miller continued their antiwar activities and continued to enjoy the extras their captors gave them. The patience of the others began to wear thin. Locked behind their barred cell windows while the two seniors were in the yard sunning themselves, they chided them, "Doesn't it bother you guys at all to be out there while we're in here?"

In a post–release interview, Wilber insisted that it did bother them, that he and Miller would have preferred that everyone be granted maximum outside time. However, he said, since the door to the room they shared was left open, there seemed no point in not taking advantage of it.

High walls now stood between the various Zoo buildings, to prevent inter-building communications. At night, the doors in these walls were left open so that guards could patrol freely through the grounds. It became Wilber's routine in the early morning to close the door in the wall between the Pigsty and the Pool Hall and Stable, just to the north. In a post–release interview, Wilber maintained that he did so because, as long as the door remained open, the Vietnamese would not unlock the other Americans in the Pigsty and allow them into the yard. But Jerry Coffee observed that Wilber was closing the door long before the others were allowed into the yard, that he was denying them a couple of hours of inter-building communications. Coffee asked Wilber to stop closing the door. Wilber speculated that, if he did so, it might cause trouble. Exasperated, Coffee assured him that the others were willing to risk trouble and said, "Look, you're closing doors on your fellow Americans. If the enemy came around at night and handed you the key and told you to lock us in, would you do it?"

According to Coffee, Wilber pondered this for a moment, then said, "Yes, I probably would."

"There is a basic difference here between your fellow Americans and the enemy . . ." Coffee began.

But Wilber interrupted: "Wait a minute! They are not my enemy. My enemies are the ruling circles in Washington who keep this war going, who cause hundreds and hundreds of deaths every month. That's who my enemy is!"

Many of the other Americans voiced a strong desire to have nothing further to do with Wilber and Miller. The intensity of feeling may have had some effect on Wilber, who tried, with some difficulty, to explain that he had not meant what he had said the way it had sounded. In any case, he stopped closing the door, and when the door was open he kept calling Coffee's attention to it, inviting him to communicate with the Americans in the other buildings.

One evening Wilber and Miller were observed leaving the camp wearing civilian clothing, suits and ties. The next day, when other Americans inquired of them as to their destination and activity of the previous evening, the two refused to answer, insisting that they had been engaged in matters which would have no effect on the others. Dave Carey pressed the matter, demanding answers. He reproved the two men for their conduct. According to Carey, Wilber confided to him that he thought it likely that charges would be filed against him when he returned to the United States, and that therefore he had to be careful about what he said. Wilber asked whether, in the event charges were filed, Carey would testify against him. Carey assured him that he certainly would. Wilber replied that, in that case, he would indeed be foolish to tell Carey anything, that in doing so he would be "cutting my own throat."

In a post–release interview, Wilber, charging that the war was illegal, and citing public anti-war opinion, said that he did not expect to be court-martialed.

Wilber and Miller left the camp on several occasions. Wilber says that they visited Reunification Park, in the middle of Hanoi, attended a circus and also several museums. He insists that these entertainments were freely given, that he and Miller acquired no obligation to their captors in accepting them.

Viking SCO Rog Ingvalson also remonstrated with Wilber and asked him to stop accepting special favors and to stop cooperating with the Vietnamese.

Rabbit kept summoning Ingvalson to interrogations to warn him, "Stop trying to influence Wilber and Miller to discontinue their cooperation with the Vietnamese people. If you do not, I will send you to a punishment camp where you will be tortured."

Confronting Wilber, Ingvalson told him of the interrogation, and told him that if he persisted in his antiwar activities and in telling Rabbit what other Americans said to him, others might well be made to suffer for it. But, says Ingvalson, nothing changed.

Jerry Coffee recalled that prior to the 1972 Tet Lunar New Year, he remarked to Wilber that he and Miller seemed to be working hard for a Tet release; he wondered if they would accept early release, despite Wing policy.

"I will do anything I can possibly do to end this war," replied Wilber. "If I can cut one second off the war by going home early, all the hardships and sufferings I will have to endure will be justified. I can work much more effectively at home to end the war than I can here."

Other prisoners speculated that the two men were now more valuable to their captors in Hanoi than they would be if released. In December, 1971, the American bombing campaign against North Vietnam had been resumed, and many new shootdowns were reaching the Zoo. The Vietnamese were not greeting the new arrivals with anything like the mistreatment the old-timers had suffered. But they were exposing men to the blandishments of Wilber and Miller, and this worried many of the veteran prisoners.

By now the old hands knew the United States to be riven with dissension over the war. They guessed that a lot of the new shoot-downs did not share the hardline attitude toward the war of most of the old POWs, that some, perhaps even many of them, opposed the war. The old-timers hoped that any new arrivals who opposed the war would be military men enough to keep their opinions to themselves, at least until the war ended and they were free. But it would not be easy, especially for the younger men, when urged by two senior officers, Wilber and Miller, to join them in the antiwar movement. Viking squadron kept trying to get word to the new prisoners in the Zoo that Wilber and Miller were "bad news," had been stripped of their military authority, had no claim to their obedience, and were to be ignored.

The Last, Bitter Months

On Sunday, April 16, 1972, the American bombing campaign reached Hanoi. It was the first attack on the city since March, 1968. Then, on May 9, naval air units mined the harbor at Haiphong. These decisive strategic moves delighted most of the American prisoners, but not all of them. Jim Daly recalls that at the Plantation the members of the Peace Committee were distraught. Daly says that some, himself included, cried at thoughts of bombs falling on heavily populated Hanoi. He explains that by this time the PCs felt close to the Vietnamese and were infuriated at the attack. Alfonso Riate sat down and wrote a letter to his captors. The other PCs read it, and all signed it. According to Daly, the letter advised that its American signers lamented that the antiwar literature they were producing was not enough; it expressed a desire to do more, "to do anything," Daly says, "even if it meant joining the Vietnamese Army."

At first, says Daly, he was shocked at the notion of bearing arms against the United States. However, as a conscientious objector, he felt that if accepted into the North Vietnamese Army he would be able to wangle a noncombatant assignment. "So," he says, "I signed it, too."

In post–release interviews Robert Chenoweth and John Young both denied having signed such a letter. Following release, Daly described the incident in a book he wrote. He reports that he showed the manuscript to the other PCs at a reunion in Denver, and that they became most agitated and were anxious that the passage be excised. He remembers that Chenoweth was particularly upset; he was now active in the antiwar movement and insisted that if people read that he had been willing to bear arms against the United States it would ruin his credibility—he would no longer be able to stand up in front of groups and talk about Vietnam.

Daly did not delete the passage.

A few days after Haiphong harbor was sealed off, Gene Wilber, Ed Miller, and a half-dozen new shootdowns issued a denunciation of the American "escalation" of the war and called on Congress and the American people to press for acceptance of Communist terms and to "Bring us home now!"

These eight Americans then held a press conference with correspondents from Hanoi, the USSR, China, Germany, and France. The prisoners expressed "shock," "amazement," "terror," and "fear" at the new air campaign, denounced Nixon, and insisted that the bombings be stopped and that America withdraw from the war.

The six junior officers whose names were attached to the statement and who were involved in the press conference all had come into captivity between late December, 1971, and February, 1972. Thus, in the minds of the old-timers, their fears concerning the effect that senior officers Wilber and Miller might have on new arrivals were confirmed.

Whatever the motives of these six juniors, the Americans who arrived in Hanoi in late 1971 and early 1972 had been taught in survival schools that in order to get their names out they should allow themselves to be photographed and otherwise exercise their own good judgment insofar as participation was concerned in enemy propaganda exercises. These rules were at considerable variance with those the old hands had been taught and under which most had taken terrible torture in an attempt to comply. Thus, while it was understandable that some new arrivals violated Wing law, it was difficult to avoid a sense of betrayal, a feeling that the Department of Defense and the services had broken faith with men who long had been fighting hard on the POW "extension of the battlefield."

The bombing continued, and most of the American prisoners continued to rejoice. There was some rejoicing for different reasons. In a postrelease interview John Young said, "I clapped my hands when I saw American planes get shot down . . . when they were shot down, it seemed like something really relaxed in me. I really felt good." He went on to explain that he "viewed the airplanes as machines of death and destruction," but that "I cried at the same time" because "an American was being killed . . . dying for nothing."

On May 13 a strange move occurred. The Camp Unity prisoner population was reduced by 209. The men were loaded onto a caravan of trucks and transported to a camp in the northern mountains, approximately 150 miles from Hanoi and only five miles from the China border. Most of these prisoners were relatively young men; there were no officers above the rank of major or lieutenant commander.

It was explained to these 209 that the new American air campaign now threatened to destroy Hanoi and that it was therefore necessary to remove them from harm's way. It is still not clear whether the Vietnamese really believed this, or by what process the 209 were selected.

The Americans entitled the mountain camp Dogpatch, and indeed it was rustic. The countryside was pretty enough, but the camp was dismal. There were a number of stone buildings, each containing two to four rooms. Approximately twenty men were assigned to each building. There was no electricity; the rooms were lit with small kerosene lanterns. By past standards, the food was excellent: a lot of cornmeal rice, usually containing large chunks of canned fish or buffalo meat, and milk every day. The prisoners were given playing cards and chess or checkers sets with which to keep themselves occupied; but the residents of the various buildings were not allowed to intermingle freely.

The war was far removed from this place and no serious demands were made of the American inmates. All but one* of the 209 were to live out the remainder of their war here.

In July, 1972, the American movie actress and antiwar activist Jane Fonda visited North Vietnam. During her visit she made numerous broadcasts in which she denounced the United States for the crimes it continued to perpetrate in Vietnam, called on American servicemen to lay down their arms, posed for at least one picture of herself wearing a North Vietnamese combat helmet at an antiaircraft missile site, and visited with Gene Wilber, Ed Miller, and a few other prisoners.**

Ramsey Clark came to Hanoi in August. Most of the prisoners regarded his visit as more serious than Fonda's. Clark, after all, had been Attorney General of the United States, a cabinet officer in the Administration that had committed the nation to war in Vietnam. He, too, saw some POWs—Gene Wilber, Ed Miller, and a few others. The meeting was tape-recorded and played over the camps' radios so that the other prisoners could all hear him offer legal aid to the antiwar prisoners should any require such help following their return home.

Back in the United States, Clark advised at a press conference that he had urged his hosts to release some prisoners. "But what they tell you," he said, "and I have a little difficulty arguing with it, is 'We can't release pilots when pilots are bombing our children.'" Clark lauded the prisoners' living conditions, treatment, and health. His remarks would have been interesting to men who had spent years in vermin-infested dungeons and who had been starved, tortured, and shackled to their bunks for long periods and forced to live in their own wastes.

That summer new arrivals at Hoa Lo were briefing the old hands on an America they did not know, a land of long-haired boys, mini-skirted women, X-rated movies, Detroit's newest automotive wonders, pro-football's superbowl, and the moon landing. There seemed no end to the things the old shootdowns did not know about their

---

*Marine CWO John W. Frederick, Jr., died in captivity.
**Following release, when the returnees shocked the nation with tales of the tortures and degradations they had suffered, Fonda called them "hypocrites and liars."

country, and their thirst for knowledge about it was insatiable.

On September 27 Hanoi released three more Americans: Mark Gartley, Norris Charles, and Air Force Maj. Edward K. Elias (captured on April 20, 1972) departed Hanoi in the company of several prominent leaders of the American antiwar movement, including Cora Weiss, Prof. Richard Falk, of Princeton University, the Rev. William Sloan Coffin, Jr., of Yale University, David Dellinger, and Gartley's mother, Minnie Lee Gartley.

––––––––

At about the time the antiwar delegation arrived in Hanoi to accept the early releasees, a woman's voice, distinctly American but never identified, was heard on the camps' radios, expressing shock at what she had seen in Hanoi, and hoping that all the POWs would have the "opportunity" to see the destruction they had visited upon the country.

Shortly, a number of younger prisoners were summoned from their cells, each having been given to understand that they were going to interrogation—apparently the Vietnamese knew of the Plum prohibiting the Americans from leaving the camp, and knew they would not leave willingly. Outside their buildings, guards muscled them aboard a bus. They were taken to the War Museum, where they were forced to look at a display of American "atrocities." The tour was photographed and filmed.

Back at Hoa Lo, the prisoners went to their cellblock walls to report how they had been tricked. From Building 8 came instructions to all: "As soon as you see you are being lured out, stop and tell them 'no go.'"

On the night of September 25, guards entered Building 8 and took Wing Commander Col. John Flynn from his cell for "interrogation." In the next few minutes guards returned for Dave Winn, Norm Gaddis, Jerry Denton, Jim Mulligan, and Howie Rutledge. It took twenty-six armed guards to wrestle the six seniors onto the bus and get them to the War Museum. There the seniors required the guards to drag them from the bus and into the building. Inside, the prisoners maintained a continuous loud uproar, refusing to look at exhibits or to listen to lectures. They would not stop shouting and refused to budge when ordered to move from one exhibit to another. Guards had to push them and pull them. At length, Jim Mulligan, peering through the gloom away from the exhibits, saw that a number of Vietnamese officers were observing them. He saw the one who had been known as Dum Dum—he had not seen the little sadist since 1967, when he had tortured with abandon at the Zoo. Mulligan moved toward him, but was restrained by guards. "I remember you," he shouted. "You people haven't changed! You're the same barbarians! You're still doing the same things you were doing at the beginning!"

At length the prisoners became so unruly that guards were forced to beat them. It was the last time any Americans were taken downtown.

———

By the end of 1971 fewer than 160,000 American combat troops had remained in Vietnam, and Vietnamization was proceeding apace. President Nixon announced that the withdrawals would continue, but that approximately 35,000 U.S. combat troops would remain until all the American prisoners of war were freed.

On March 30, 1972, the North Vietnamese launched a powerful offensive across the DMZ. In response, Nixon ordered a resumption of the bombing of North Vietnam; then ordered the mining of the harbor at Haiphong, the port through which the Communists received most of their supplies. These actions touched off a new antiwar furor in the United States and throughout the world, and there were many warnings that Nixon was virtually forcing the Soviet Union and/or Communist China to intervene.

As the fighting raged inconclusively on in Vietnam, Washington and Hanoi embarked on a series of secret talks in Paris. The conferees were Dr. Henry Kissinger, Nixon's chief foreign affairs advisor, and Le Duc Tho, a member of Hanoi's Politburo. In May, Washington proposed an internationally supervised cease-fire, to be followed within four months with the repatriation of all American prisoners of war and the removal of all U.S. forces. Saigon and Hanoi would be left to negotiate a political settlement with each other. In October, Hanoi agreed to this proposal. The world held its breath hopefully, prepared to heave a sigh of relief.

In October—almost abruptly, it seemed—the world was given to understand that the Vietnam War was about to end. American Secretary of State Henry Kissinger let it be known that "peace is at hand." The American bombing campaign was halted.

At Camp Unity the disposition of the Vietnamese jailkeepers improved. The interior walls of buildings were torn down to make bigger, more comfortable rooms. The food improved. Except for the seniors in Building 8, the prisoners were allowed much more time in the yard.

Mild as the treatment had become, it wasn't easy staying in Hanoi. In late 1970 the men had been overjoyed to move to Camp Unity, to be together at last. But after years of a solitary or near-solitary existence, some had difficulty adjusting to compound living. Thrown together in close quarters over long periods of time, even the best of friends eventually began to get on each other's nerves. Discussions involving even slightly controversial subjects frequently degenerated into nasty arguments. In addition, men who had served long years of honorable captivity were now saying that it was unreasonable to expect them to continue resisting indefinitely. They had suffered indescribable tortures trying to avoid saying things that were now being volunteered daily on the floor of the United States Senate. All of which prompted the development of an elaborate new escape plan. It involved the talents of numerous men in support of three carefully selected volunteers. Participants believed the plan to stand a reasonable chance of success. For the POW leadership that would be a bonus. Their primary aim was to focus the prisoners' unified efforts on an outside objective, in hopes of stopping internal bickering. There was no question that an escape would trigger a Vietnamese reaction against the prisoners who remained. But whatever the cost, it seemed necessary to preserve the spiritual strength the Wing would need to carry out its mission, to return with honor.

But when peace loomed, the escape plan was cancelled.

––––––

Then, in December, the peace that had been at hand in October somehow managed to slip through the diplomats' fingers. Through the camp radio the Vietnamese poured new vitriol on Richard Nixon. Some guards became a trifle nastier, but there was no drastic change for the worse in the treatment. The food remained relatively good, most prisoners were allowed a lot of outside time, and they were even being provided with selected articles from *Stars and Stripes,* the American military newspaper. One was an interview with Ev Alvarez's former wife, Tangee, in which she explained that she simply didn't love Ev anymore, that she loved someone else and that she was happy.

The past two years had been desperately unhappy ones for Alvarez. In July, 1970, he had received a letter from Tangee in which for the first time she complained about the length of the war. He was surprised at her bitterness. It had been a long time for both of them, and he had sustained himself on dreams of a life with Tangee when the war was over. The dream had grown sweeter with the passing years. He wrote her back, but there had been no further word from her. Packages and mail had come from his mother, including photos of the family; but no pictures of Tangee, not even a mention of her.

Alvarez's mother fended off all his inquiries concerning Tangee with the information that she was "fine" but that "we haven't seen her." All manner of dire possibilities occurred to him. Had Tangee, in loneliness, suffered some sort of breakdown? Had she been physically injured? Finally, desperate for information, he wrote his mother demanding straight answers. His mother was left no choice but to tell him that Tangee had divorced him.

He was stunned. It was as though he were back in torture. He hurt inside, so badly that for a long time it was actually painful for him to breathe. He retreated into himself, fell into a morose silence.

It had been nearly a year now since Alvarez had learned that Tangee had divorced him. Suddenly one day it occurred to him that this was no place for a man to behave like a disappointed lover, that his withdrawal had made him a worry and burden to his friends, and that he was doing himself and them no good. There was, after all, a lot of living left to do, a future to look forward to. Thus, he had put Tangee out of his mind and, in effect, rejoined the Wing. When the *Stars and Stripes* article reached him, it reopened the still-tender wound, but not for long. He had conditioned himself to reality by now, and his thoughts were soon focused again on the future.

———

On the evening of December 18, in Camp Unity's Building 8, the seniors were looking forward to "movie night"—it was someone's turn to stand up and "tell" a movie. Those responsible for offering such entertainments prepared themselves well, spent days raking their memories to be able to vividly describe scenes and develop themes.

In the other buildings of Camp Unity, some had already gone to bed, some were preparing to do so, rigging their mosquito nettings over their mats. Others were involved in bridge games, studying, or engaging in quiet bull sessions. At approximately 8 PM Hanoi's air raid sirens began to shriek and the lights went out. There ensued several minutes of near-silence. Guards armed with automatic weapons manned battle stations before cellblock doors and windows, ready to defend against any attempt to recover prisoners. Many prisoners assumed that the enemy was conducting a drill; certainly none expected anything more than the relatively mild, ineffectual tactical bombing in which most of them had been engaged when shot down. Prisoners groused over their interrupted activities and waited impatiently for the alert to end.

Suddenly, the whole sky flashed white and stayed white. There was a sound unlike anything the prisoners had ever heard in previous air raids against Hanoi, a strong, gutteral rumble that went on and on and on as the sky throbbed with new surges of whiteness. Soon it was possible to separate the sound into its component sounds, a seemingly endless staccato of long, fearsome explosions that overlapped one another. There were no sounds of aircraft—the ordnance was being delivered from altitudes beyond the range of the human ear. The white sky cast a glow into the cellblocks of Hanoi's prisons, and the Americans who shared these cellblocks found themselves looking quickly at each other, open-mouthed and with widening eyes. They were astounded! Elated! Frightened! Depressed!

In Building 2 at Hoa Lo, Jack Fellowes guessed that ten tactical bombers each had released a 1,000-pounder on some vital target. Someone quickly pointed out that there had been considerably more than ten big explosions. In fact, the whole world still seemed to be exploding. Antiaircraft artillery could be heard all around, pumping the Vietnamese response to the awesome assault from the heavens. Standing on the raised slab of the community bed that ran the length of the room, the men looked westward through windows, up over the wall that surrounded Hoa Lo and saw telephone-pole-sized missiles leaping away toward unseen aerial targets.

Someone claimed to have counted 105 bombs in a single string. Even the Navy men knew that the only aircraft capable of carrying such loads was the B-52. Men in all the different cellblocks reached the same conclusion at about the same time: for the first time in the long history of the war, the Strategic Air Command heavyweights had been sent to Hanoi. Men ran up and down in their cellblocks looking for better vantage points, clapping each other on their backs, shaking hands, shouting encouragement at the skies, shouting to each other about packing bags and making ready to go home. The concussion of falling bombs seemed to edge closer to the prisons. The ground shook, the buildings shook, the very air seemed to shake. Incredulous, happy prisoners warily eyed the ceilings of their cellblocks—privately, nervously, Navyman Allan Brady reflected that the bomber crews were only human, that anyone could make a mistake; at the same time he was thrilled, did not want the assault to end until the enemy capitulated.

Red McDaniel, whose captors had flogged him nearly to death following the Dramesi-Atterberry escape, was depressed. He had thought peace to be close, but there was nothing peaceful about this. Such an immense assault seemed to him to signal a serious break-down in the negotiations. On the other hand, he felt certain that the Vietnamese could not long withstand such pressure, and hoped the United States would keep applying it until serious negotiations were resumed. A man of deep Christian instinct and charity, McDaniel prayed for the North Vietnamese people.

The bombers came on in wave after wave after wave. Someone noticed that the Vietnamese guards all had abandoned their battle stations, probably hunkered down in shelters somewhere. No one could blame them.

The storm of destruction lasted for perhaps twenty minutes. Then, abruptly, it was over. The unseen bombers were gone. So was the whiteness that had bathed the sky. But now secondary explosions shattered the night—fuel dumps, perhaps, or ammunition storage depots—and in all directions long tongues of fire licked at the sky. The night was full of a fierce, red glow.

At 9 PM it started again. In Building 2, Jim Kasler, Ray Vohden, Larry Guarino, Bob Schweitzer, John Dramesi, and others cheered and danced. In Building 8 the seniors were cheering too.

The B-52s came again at 10 PM, then again at 11 PM, and every hour on the hour all through the night.

During the daylight hours, while the B-52 crews were resting and their aircraft were rearmed and refueled, Air Force and Navy tactical aircraft continued the assault, giving the defenders no rest. When darkness fell, the B-52s came back, again and again, every hour on the hour, dealing sledgehammer blows to Hanoi's ability to wage war.

———

For the next seven nights they came. In Camp Unity even skeptical Americans became convinced that the bombing would bring peace and their freedom. Some were so excited that they simply could not bring themselves to lie down, and went several days without any sleep. Others slept all day, through the tactical aircraft assaults, so as to be able to stay awake all night and watch the big B-52 show. And as evenings came on, men began jockeying for positions on the raised sleeping slabs.

There was no outside time for the prisoners now, and the menu had reverted to rice and sewer-greens soup. For the most part, the prisoners did not mind so long as the B-52s kept coming.

And come they did, their bombs falling closer and closer to the prisons. The ground shook, the prisoners in their buildings watched the walls and ceiling beams shake and sway and watched chunks of plaster fall to the floor. Most prisoners, though elated, were nervous. Howie Rutledge assumed a position over his waste bucket and shouted happily that he hoped he would not be blown off the thing; almost instantly a bomb landed in close enough proximity to send him flying. He regained the bucket, chuckling delightedly. One day Jim Mulligan warned a new guard, a pleasant young lad to whom Mulligan had taken a liking, not to leave the prison grounds, explaining that Hoa Lo was the safest place in town. The lad nodded solemnly, and did not leave. Those in charge of Hanoi's rolling stock reached the same conclusion independently. Every night, hundreds upon hundreds of military trucks crowded into the prison grounds or competed for position in the streets around Hoa Lo. They remained close to their American guests until the all clear was sounded in the mornings.

The wisdom of truckers and of Mulligan's advice to the young guard was soon confirmed by downed B-52 crewmen who were brought into Heartbreak Hotel. New arrivals sent word to the old residents to take heart, that the enemy could not much longer withstand what was in store for him and that there was no doubt that the war would end shortly. They assured the prisoners they were in no danger; the B-52 crews were all well briefed on Hanoi and were using the prisons as aiming points, applying their bomb loads to various targets around them.*

---

*Postattack, high-resolution aerial photography clearly showed that North Vietnam's cities were not "mass bombed," as the Vietnamese and others claimed. The B-52 attacks were restricted to militarily valuable targets, such as airfields, power plants, antiaircraft artillery and missile sites, communications centers, rail yards, bridges, military storage depots, maintenance depots, and port facilities. Experts consider it history's most surgically precise bombing campaign.

North Vietnam's air defense system was formidable. The B-52s bombed from altitudes close to 40,000 feet. The POWs could not locate them in the night sky until the Russian-built missiles reached that altitude. Then the sky was filled with a bright orange glow, and it took stricken bombers a long, long time to fall to earth. Fifteen B-52s were hit. Ten fell in North Vietnam, and the prisoners below watched in silence as they came down, praying for the crews. Sixty-two B-52 crewmen bailed out of the bombers that went down in North Vietnam; thirty-three reached captivity in Hoa Lo, four are known to have been killed, and twenty-five are classified as missing in action.

The B-52 bombers came for the last time on the night of December 29, 1972. Along with the other Air Force and Navy aircraft, they had hurled a total of 20,370 tons of bombs against military targets in North Vietnam. The defenders had fired more than a thousand missiles at the air armadas. Apparently, that effort exhausted North Vietnam's antiaircraft capacity. During the last two days of the raids, the American aircraft had a free ride; no missiles were fired at them.

For a while at Hoa Lo, the prisoners were told nothing. Most sensed that some sort of climax had been achieved. Shortly, the POWs were advised that Hanoi's chief delegate to the peace talks, Le Duc Tho, was returning to Paris and that negotiations were to be resumed. And so they waited.

Hanoi's Bac Mai hospital was said to be destroyed, and Ramsey Clark and others immediately launched a fund-raising campaign for its restoration. But the aerial photos revealed only a few sections of the hospital to be damaged. The damaged sections were near the edge of an airfield where Mig-21 interceptor aircraft were based, and which was also the central control center for North Vietnam's air defense system.

Going Home

The peace agreements were signed in Paris on January 27, 1973, but the prisoners were not immediately informed. On the evening of the twenty-eighth Wendy Rivers stood in the doorway of his cellblock, noting that the lights had been turned on in a television tower about a hundred yards to the northwest of Hoa Lo, and that North Vietnam's flag had been run up to the top of the tower.

"Looks like the war must be over," Rivers said to a passing guard.

The guard grinned and said, "In a few days you will hear important news."

In response to a question from someone else, the guard said that the television tower lights would be on at night henceforth. Someone else inquired if henceforth the DRV flag was to be flown upside down, as was the case at present. Within a few minutes someone was climbing the tower to right the flag.

The next day the prisoners were called into the yards of their various camps and the peace agreements were read to them. The yards were full of photographers, prepared to capture for Hanoi the spontaneous burst of joy that was sure to come when the men were told that hostilities had ended and that they would soon be leaving for home. In all camps the American seniors, expecting the ploy, had warned the men not to give their captors for free something that they had suffered torture and privation to deny him in the bitter years of captivity now ending. The men listened impassively as they were told that they were all to be repatriated within sixty days. Then, to their captors' obvious dismay, the prisoners looked around at each other blankly, shrugged, and shuffled back into their buildings. Only when the Vietnamese officers and propagandists were gone did the men yield to feelings of boundless joy.

———

But in Vegas things were tense. The prisoners from the Plantation had been moved into this compound after the bombing had got under way. By that time, SRO Ted Guy had done a lot of thinking about the eight PCs. They had collaborated notoriously with the enemy. It seemed clear that their allegiance was to Hanoi, not to the United States or to their fellow American prisoners. As a result, their captors had amply rewarded them, with better food and treatment, and all manner of special favors. Not only had they enjoyed virtually unlimited access to the yard, but on a number of occasions they had left the premises dressed in civilian clothing to attend entertainments, make sightseeing tours, and so on. Some of them had helped the Vietnamese dig combat positions in the prison yard, and had constructed crude model aircraft to hang in the trees for antiaircraft drills—on signal, guards would swing their weapons toward the models, presumably to practice aiming for vulnerable points. Guy had come to regard these eight Americans as being as dangerous as enemy troops. He had thought it possible during the bombing that, for security purposes, the Vietnamese would open up the camp and bring all the prisoners, including the PCs, together. In that event, he felt that the PCs would pose a distinct threat to the other Americans under his command. He had sent a combat order to the senior noncoms: they were to organize a squad to keep a close watch on the PCs. Should the PCs be observed in any way to be threatening the survival of other Americans, they were to be eliminated. The senior noncoms had assured the SRO that they would see to the matter.

Now, with hostilities ended, rumors reached Guy that some remained strongly disposed to proceed with plans to liquidate the PCs.

Moving quickly to forestall such action, Guy emphasized that his had been a wartime combat order, and that since the war was now over, the order was now void. His order, moveover, had not been a directive to seek out and kill, but to observe and to take appropriate defensive action if it seemed clearly warranted. He would not tolerate murder. He insisted that the PCs be left to him. Asserting his faith in the American judicial system, he vowed that justice would be done, that he would file charges and would see that the eight were court-martialed. Tough and persuasive, the SRO prevailed.

The PCs, who remained ignorant of all this, were unhappy with the peace agreements, specifying as they did that all Americans be repatriated. They had been confident that their applications for asylum in other countries would be honored. Now, the Vietnamese, who had assured them that this was so, made clear that it was not to be. The eight were now described to themselves as "newborn revolutionaries," and were told that if they were really interested in Marxism and in helping the American people they should return to the United States, go to school, study. It was pointed out to them that if they returned to America they would always be free to go anywhere, but that if they refused repatriation, they could never return to their native land as free men. Besides, they were told, if they were not repatriated, the United States would be able to use it as an excuse to break the peace agreements.

Guy, who knew of the PCs' requests for asylum, designated responsibility for their safety to Harvey Brande. Incredulous, Brande wondered how it was that he should be chosen for the assignment. Guy advised him that it was because he was a professional soldier, as was the SRO, and that the SRO was confident that he would behave like one. He directed Brande to tell the eight how the SRO expected them to look and to conduct themselves while in the camp, and how he wanted them to look and behave at departure.* Brande delivered

---

*Concerning his return to the United States, John.Young, who says he did not seriously consider seeking asylum, says that, "After long and hard deliberation, I found that even though I wanted to stay there [in North Vietnam], I wouldn't be happy. I figured out that if I came back here, faced whatever I had to face and fought it out to the finish, then I could go back and do what I wanted to do."

Robert Chenoweth, who denies having sought asylum, says he returned so as to work for change within the United States.

Jim Daly insists that he had decided to return home regardless of what the others did, but that the primary reason all the PCs returned was that the Vietnamese were "convincing" about it. In his book Daly says that when the PCs pressed the matter,

these instructions. Then, as senior noncom responsible for the PCs'
security, he felt it incumbent on him to warn them to retain attorneys
when they reached the United States.

———

On the morning of January 28, Army Green Beret Capt. Jim
Thompson and a dozen civilians at the Rockpile were fed a breakfast
that was the best meal any of them had had since capture—generous
portions of goose, pork, vegetables, fried potatoes, all sorts of spicy
sauces and apricot wine. For Thompson it was now just fifty-eight
days short of nine years since his spotter plane had gone down, and he
had been taken in the jungles of western South Vietnam.

After breakfast there was a drive to Hanoi in a Land Rover. For the
first time a trip with no blindfolds, and in broad daylight! The effects
of the American December bombing campaign were visible in railroad tracks that were twisted like spaghetti and occasionally what
appeared to be a ruined factory or warehouse. Along the way there
were some hostile glances, but, amazingly, most of the people who
saw the Americans waved and smiled at them. There was a ferry ride
where many civilians crowded around, seeking to shake hands and to
offer cigarettes. It seemed to Thompson that they were sick to death
of the war, ecstatic that it was over, and anxious to demonstrate to the
Americans the joy they felt that they were no longer enemies.

The Rockpile prisoners remained isolated for several days in New
Guy Village. Thompson was later to learn that the other Americans in
Hoa Lo had long been on a much better diet than those from the
Rockpile, and surmised that the Vietnamese wanted to fatten up his
group before the others saw them. At any rate, they were kept apart
and gorged for nearly two weeks with all the excellent food they were

———

they were told that if they wanted to stay, "You must make this move on your own,
with no official help from us. At the airfield, in front of all the newsmen and
cameras, you can be certain that if you refuse to walk over to the waiting Americans,
no violence will take place. The United States would look very bad trying to force
you on a plane."

Daly also gives an account of a private farewell party the Vietnamese held for the
PCs the night before their departure. It was attended by all the guards and several
officers, including the camp commander. There were several hours of revelry, of
"drinking beer and wine and singing... the Vietnamese songs." Then, as each
officer and guard rose to wish the PCs well, Daly reports that the party turned sad,
and "more than one wiped away tears. Finally, we all exchanged addresses and said
goodnight."

able to eat, and were allowed all the candy, fruit, and cigarettes they could consume.

On February 9 the Rockpile prisoners were moved into Vegas. For some there, the appearance of Thompson was almost too much—nearly three years had passed since J. R. Leonard, Bruce Archer, Paul Montague, Jim DiBernardo, and others had last seen Thompson at Portholes, the jungle camp. There, he had been a walking skeleton, a mobile corpse, and not very mobile at that; none of the brutalized wretches who had survived Nazi Germany's World War II death camps had looked any worse than Thompson had, and the others had long assumed him to be dead. Yet, incredibly, here he was, a healthy, smiling, walking, talking, living soldier of a man! It was unbelievable.

It was *all* so unbelievable—the long nightmare of the war and captivity was ending; people actually were coming back from the grave.

As for Thompson, a deeply religious man possessed of a truly tenacious will to survive, he had sustained himself through the long years mainly on hope and prayer. Sometime during the spring of 1964 he had acquired the certainty that he would survive; after that the question had never really troubled him again. Now, at last, he was going home, to meet the son he knew had been born shortly after his capture, and who now was nearly nine years old.

Robbie Risner, Jim Stockdale, John Flynn, Jerry Denton, and others were summoned to interrogations. The camp authority simply wanted to warn them, "for their own good," against revealing anything of the mistreatment they had suffered in the past and to assure them that they should they do so, it would be necessary to publish the incriminating statements they had made and papers they had signed while imprisoned in the Democratic Republic of Vietnam. In all cases, the Americans replied that, unlike their captors, they had nothing to hide and they fully intended to apprise their government and their countrymen of the mistreatment that had been inflicted upon them. They invited Hanoi to publish anything it liked.

———

During February and March the prisoners departed Hanoi in three increments, approximately in the order in which they had been captured. The first group, which included the earliest shootdowns plus some sick and wounded, left on February 12. Dressed in drab civilian clothing that had been issued the night before, the men were bused to Hanoi's Gia Lam airport, reaching it in time to watch three glistening silver Air Force C-141 Jetstars land. Debarking from their buses, the Americans followed departure procedures they themselves had planned. Lining up in columns of twos in the order in which they had reached captivity, they stood at attention, trying to look sharp. By and large, they felt they had done a good job for their country in Hanoi. They wanted to come out of the place looking the way they felt—proud.

Rabbit and Spot called out names and service numbers and, one by one, the men walked away to freedom—Ev Alvarez, Bob Shumaker, Hayden Lockhart, Scotty Morgan, and the rest of them.

Rod Knutson did not know that he had been promoted twice and that he was a lieutenant commander now. Like the others, he stopped before the Air Force colonel who waited to greet them, perhaps seventy-five yards in front of the transports, rendered him a smart salute, and identified himself—the words were almost the same as those that Knutson, the first American tortured in Hanoi, had repeated again and again to his inquisitor on an October morning more than seven long years before: "Sir, Knutson, Rodney Allen; lieutenant junior grade, United States Navy." But this time he added one thing more: "Reporting my honorable return as a prisoner of war to the United States."

Another officer took him by the arm and ushered him aboard the C-141. There were Air Force flight nurses aboard. They were beautiful. Rod stood staring at them as though thunderstruck. Then he took one of them by the shoulders and kissed her soundly. He found a seat next to a window in the back of the aircraft. George McKnight sat down next to him. The two were good friends, but at this moment neither had much to say. They sat quietly, gripping the edges of their armrests, waiting. At last, three stretchers were put aboard, carrying B-52 airmen who had been injured during the December raids. The hatches were closed, the engines were started, and the plane taxied to the end of a runway. Then the pilot poured on the power and they were moving, rolling, picking up speed.

It wasn't until they were airborne that Rod Knutson knew that he was crying. He waved a gesture of contempt through his window, down toward the scene of his long travail. Then, with the others, he tore off his seatbelt and jumped up into the aisle, exploding with happiness, shaking hands, patting backs, laughing, kissing the nurses, and trying to understand that it was over. It was all over.

The senior U.S. Government official on the aircraft, Doctor Roger Shields, advised Jerry Denton that millions of Americans would be looking on, via television, as the POWs debarked at Clark Air Force Base in the Philippines; as the senior man aboard the first returning aircraft, it might be appropriate for Denton to say a few words. Denton wrote out what he felt; then, with some difficulty, he got the others to listen to his brief statement, to approve it. They quickly agreed that he should speak for them, and when he reached Clark, he did so:

"We are honored to have had the opportunity to serve our country under difficult circumstances. We are profoundly grateful to our Commander-in-Chief and to our Nation for this day. God bless America."

POSTSCRIPT

Many of the prisoners who returned after the peace agreements were signed expected to find that those who had accepted early release had been disciplined, or that at least they would now face disciplinary action. The early releasees, it was reasoned, had broken faith with their fellow POWs and had done violence to the Code of Conduct,* accepting parole from their captors, disobeying the lawful orders of lawful military superiors, and aiding the enemy.

No disciplinary action had been taken against the early returnees, however, nor was any to be initiated. For one thing, the Department of Defense under then Secretary of Defense Melvin R. Laird, had long since decreed as policy that any alleged offenses by any POWs during the time of their captivity were to be forgiven. At the same time, it was made clear that while the Department of Defense would file no charges, individual POWs were free to do so. But as far as the

---

*On returning to the United States, most of the POWs were amazed to learn that the Code of Conduct did not carry the force of law.

first nine early releasees were concerned, the statute of limitations had expired by the time the other POWs had returned, foreclosing the legal possibility of disciplinary action against eight of them— Hegdahl having been ordered to accept early release—and the moral possibility of action against the last three.

What also complicated feelings was that a number of the early releasees had provided a great deal of information, aid, and comfort to the families of men who remained in Hanoi.

Air Force Col. Theodore W. Guy filed charges against the eight PCs: Chenoweth, Young, Branch, Kavanaugh, Riate, Rayford, Elbert, and Daly. He charged them with aiding the enemy, disrespect to a superior officer, disobeying a superior officer, conspiracy, and carrying out a conspiracy.

While Guy's charges were pending, one of the eight PCs, Abel Larry Kavanaugh, died.

Claiming lack of evidence where the five Army men were concerned—Chenoweth, Young, Branch, Rayford, and Daly—Army Secretary Howard H. Callaway dismissed the charges against them. Previously, Callaway had delivered himself of the amazing opinion that, in prison camps, Air Force officers have no legal authority over Army enlisted men. In dropping the charges, Callaway said, "We must not overlook the good behavior of these men during the two to three years each spent under brutal conditions in South Vietnam, before they were moved to the north . . . they had a very hard time, and they behaved admirably during this period."

Navy Secretary John W. Warner dismissed the charges against the two surviving Marines, Riate and Elbert, noting that they, too, had suffered "deprivations and maltreatment."

As quickly as Guy's charges were dropped, Air Force Maj. Edward W. Leonard, Jr.—"J. R."—expressed the view that a proper investigation had not been conducted, and charged the surviving seven PCs with mutiny. These charges were also dropped, and the PCs were discharged from the services.

As the senior Navy returnee, Rear Adm. James B. Stockdale filed charges against Navy Capt. Walter E. Wilber and Marine Col. Edison W. Miller. The charges included mutiny, aiding the enemy, conspiracy, soliciting other prisoners to violate the Code of Conduct, and causing or attempting to cause insubordination and disloyalty.

There ensued a three-month-long investigation. Navy Secretary Warner personally interviewed nineteen other returned POWs who were familiar with the matter. Warner found merit in Stockdale's charges, but dismissed them, judging that courts-martial would be unduly disruptive to the lives of other returnees who would have to testify, and upon the lives of their families. Instead, he issued letters of censure to Wilber and Miller, charging both with failing to meet the standards expected of officers of the Armed Forces of the United States. He also announced that both officers would be retired "in the best interests of the naval service."

"Above and Beyond..."

The Medal of Honor, the nation's highest award for bravery, is awarded by the President in the name of the Congress *for conspicuous gallantry and intrepidity at the risk of his life above and beyond the call of duty.*

On March 4, 1976, President Gerald R. Ford awarded three POW Medals of Honor. The recipients were Navy Rear Admiral James B. Stockdale, Air Force Colonel George E. Day and Air Force Captain Lance P. Sijan.

Stockdale's citation was, simply stated, for heroic leadership, specifically for disfiguring himself to avoid exploitation by enemy propagandists; and for inflicting a near-mortal wound upon himself to convince his captors of his willingness to die rather than to implicate other Americans in a possible communications purge.

Day was cited for his epic escape attempt in August, 1967; and for nearly six years of maximum resistance and stalwart leadership despite numerous horrendous injuries and several bouts of severe torture.

Sijan's award was made posthumously to his parents, Mr. and Mrs. Sylvester Sijan, of Milwaukee, Wisconsin. An authentic American hero, Sijan was in the POW system less than a month. He was two years out of the Air Force Academy when he was shot down on November 9, 1967. Despite numerous severe injuries, including a brain concussion, he evaded capture for six weeks. Weak from starvation, he was captured on Christmas Day. His condition notwithstanding, he quickly overpowered a guard and escaped again. Recaptured hours later and tortured for information, he gave only name, rank and serial number. By the time he reached the company of other Americans, he was unable to sit or stand without help. His compatriots worried over his untended injuries, but Sijan reassured them and asked only that he be kept in a sitting position so that he could exercise his muscles for another escape attempt. He died of pneumonia on January 22, 1968. In his brief time with his fellow prisoners, he provided them with an inspirational example of resistance.

APPENDIX

Personnel returned from captivity, February–March 1973

Name	Branch of Service	Date of incident
ABBOTT, JOSEPH S. JR.	US AIR FORCE	67–04–30
ABBOTT, ROBERT ARCHIE	US AIR FORCE	67–04–30
ABBOTT, WILFRED KESSE	US AIR FORCE	66–09–05
ACOSTA, HECTOR M. I.	US AIR FORCE	72–12–09
ADKINS, CLODEN	CIVILIAN	68–02–01
AGNEW, ALFRED H.	US NAVY	72–12–28
ALBERT, KEITH ALEXANDER	US ARMY	70–05–21
ALCORN, WENDELL REED	US NAVY	65–12–22
ALEXANDER, FERNANDO	US AIR FORCE	72–12–19
ALLWINE, DAVID FRANKLIN	US ARMY	71–03–04
ALPERS, JOHN H. JR.	US AIR FORCE	72–10–05
ALVAREZ, EVERETT JR.	US NAVY	64–08–05
ANDERSON, GARETH LAVERNE	US NAVY	67–05–19
ANDERSON, JOHN THOMAS	US ARMY	68–02–03
ANDERSON, JOHN W.	US AIR FORCE	72–12–27

Name	Branch of Service	Date of incident
ANDREWS, ANTHONY CHARLES	US AIR FORCE	67–10–17
ANGUS, WILLIAM KERR	US MARINE CORPS	72–06–12
ANSHUS, RICHARD C.	US ARMY	71–03–08
ANTON, FRANCIS GENE	US ARMY	68–01–05
ANZALDUA, JOSE JESUS JR.	US MARINE CORPS	70–01–23
ARCHER, BRUCE RAYMOND	US MARINE CORPS	68–03–28
ARCURI, WILLIAM Y.	US AIR FORCE	72–12–20
ASTORGA, JOSE M.	US ARMY	72–04–02
AUSTIN, WILLIAM RENWICK II	US AIR FORCE	67–10–07
AYRES, TIMOTHY R.	US AIR FORCE	72–05–03
BAGLEY, BOBBY RAY	US AIR FORCE	67–09–16
BAILEY, JAMES WILLIAM	US NAVY	67–06–28
BAIRD, BILL A.	US ARMY	68–05–06
BAKER, DAVID E.	US AIR FORCE	72–06–27
BAKER, ELMO CLINNARD	US AIR FORCE	67–08–23
BALDOCK, FREDERICK CHARLES	US NAVY	66–03–17
BALLARD, ARTHUR T. JR.	US AIR FORCE	66–09–26
BARBAY, LAWRENCE	US AIR FORCE	66–07–20
BARNETT, ROBERT WARREN	US AIR FORCE	67–10–03
BARRETT, THOMAS JOSEPH	US AIR FORCE	65–10–05
BARROWS, HENRY C.	US AIR FORCE	72–12–19
BATES, RICHARD L.	US AIR FORCE	72–10–05
BAUGH, WILLIAM JOSEPH	US AIR FORCE	67–01–21
BEAN, JAMES ELLIS	US AIR FORCE	68–01–03
BEAN, WILLIAM R. JR.	US AIR FORCE	72–05–23
BEDINGER, HENRY J.	US NAVY	69–11–22
BEEKMAN, WILLIAM	US AIR FORCE	72–06–24
BEELER, CARROLL ROBERT	US NAVY	72–05–24
BLENS, LYNN R.	US AIR FORCE	72–12–21
BELL, JAMES FRANKLIN	US NAVY	65–10–16
BENGE, MICHAEL	CIVILIAN	68–02–01
BERG, KILE DAG	US AIR FORCE	65–07–27
BERGER, JAMES ROBERT	US AIR FORCE	66–12–02
BERNASCONI, LOUIS H.	US AIR FORCE	72–12–22
BISS, ROBERT IRVIN	US AIR FORCE	66–11–11
BLACK, ARTHUR NEIL	US AIR FORCE	65–09–20
BLACK, COLE	US NAVY	66–06–21
BLEVINS, JOHN CHARLES	US AIR FORCE	66–09–09
BLISS, RONALD GLENN	US AIR FORCE	66–09–04
BULSTAD, RICHARD EUGENE	US AIR FORCE	65–11–06
BOMAR, JACK WILLIAMSON	US AIR FORCE	67–02–04
BORLING, JOHN LORIN	US AIR FORCE	66–06–01
BOYD, CHARLES G.	US AIR FORCE	66–04–22
BOYER, TERRY LEE	US AIR FORCE	67–12–17
BRACE, ERNEST C.	CIVILIAN	65–05–21
BRADY, ALLEN COLBY	US NAVY	67–01–19
BRANCH, MICHAEL PATRICK	US ARMY	68–05–06
BRANDE, HARVEY G.	US ARMY	68–02–07
BRAZELTON, MICHAEL LEE	US AIR FORCE	66–08–07

Name	Branch of Service	Date of incident
BRECKNER, WILLIAM J. JR.	US AIR FORCE	72–07–30
BRENNEMAN, RICHARD CHARLES	US AIR FORCE	67–11–08
BRIDGER, BARRY BURTON	US AIR FORCE	67–01–23
BRODAK, JOHN WARREN	US AIR FORCE	66–08–14
BROOKENS, NORMAN J.	CIVILIAN	68–02–04
BROWN, CHARLES A. JR.	US AIR FORCE	72–12–19
BROWN, PAUL GORDON	US MARINE CORPS	68–07–25
BROWNING, RALPH THOMAS	US AIR FORCE	66–07–08
BRUDNO, EDWARD ALAN	US AIR FORCE	65–10–18
BRUNHAVER, RICHARD MARVIN	US NAVY	65–08–24
BRUNSON, CECIL H.	US AIR FORCE	72–10–12
BRUNSTROM, ALAN LESLIE	US AIR FORCE	66–04–22
BUCHANAN, HUBERT ELLIOTT	US AIR FORCE	66–09–16
BUDD, LEONARD, R. JR.	US MARINE CORPS	67–08–21
BURER, ARTHUR WILLIAM	US AIR FORCE	66–03–21
BURGESS, RICHARD GORDON	US MARINE CORPS	66–09–25
BURNS, DONALD RAY	US AIR FORCE	66–12–02
BURNS, JOHN DOUGLAS	US NAVY	66–10–04
BURNS, MICHAEL THOMAS	US AIR FORCE	68–07–05
BURROUGHS, WILLIAM DAVID	US AIR FORCE	66–07–31
BUTCHER, JACK M.	US AIR FORCE	71–03–24
BUTLER, PHILLIP NEAL	US NAVY	65–04–20
BUTLER, WILLIAM WALLACE	US AIR FORCE	67–11–20
BYRNE, RONALD EDWARD JR.	US AIR FORCE	65–08–29
BYRNS, WILLIAM G.	US AIR FORCE	72–05–23
CALLAGHAN, PETER A.	US AIR FORCE	72–06–21
CAMEROTA, PETER P.	US AIR FORCE	72–12–22
CAMPBELL, BURTON WAYNE	US AIR FORCE	66–07–01
CAREY, DAVID JAY	US NAVY	67–08–31
CARLSON, ALBERT E.	US ARMY	72–04–07
CARPENTER, ALLEN RUSSELL	US NAVY	66–11–01
CARRIGAN, LARRY EDWARD	US AIR FORCE	67–08–23
CAVAIANI, JON R.	US ARMY	71–06–05
CERAK, JOHN P.	US AIR FORCE	72–06–27
CERTAIN, ROBERT G.	US AIR FORCE	72–12–18
CHAMBERS, CARL DENNIS	US AIR FORCE	67–08–07
CHAPMAN, HARLAN PAGE	US MARINE CORPS	65–11–05
CHAUNCEY, ARVIN RAY	US NAVY	67–05–31
CHENEY, KEVIN J.	US AIR FORCE	72–07–01
CHENOWETH, ROBERT PRESTON	US ARMY	68–02–08
CHERRY, FRED VANN	US AIR FORCE	65–10–22
CHESLEY, LARRY JAMES	US AIR FORCE	66–04–16
CHIRICHIGNO, LUIS GENARDO	US ARMY	69–11–02
CHRISTIAN, MICHAEL DURHAM	US NAVY	67–04–24
CIUS, FRANK E. JR.	US MARINE CORPS	67–06–03
CLARK, JOHN WALTER	US AIR FORCE	67–03–12
CLEMENTS, JAMES ARLEN	US AIR FORCE	67–10–09
CLOWER, CLAUDE DOUGLAS	US NAVY	67–11–19
COFFEE, GERALD LEONARD	US NAVY	66–02–03
COKER, GEORGE THOMAS	US NAVY	66–08–27

Name	Branch of Service	Date of incident
COLLINS, JAMES QUINCY JR.	US AIR FORCE	65–09–02
COLLINS, THOMAS EDWARD III	US AIR FORCE	65–10–18
CONDON, JAMES C.	US AIR FORCE	72–12–28
CONLEE, WILLIAM W.	US AIR FORCE	72–12–22
COOK, JAMES R.	US AIR FORCE	72–12–26
COPELAND, H. C.	US AIR FORCE	67–07–17
CORDIER, KENNETH WILLIAM	US AIR FORCE	66–12–02
CORMIER, ARTHUR	US AIR FORCE	65–11–06
COSKEY, KENNETH LEON	US NAVY	68–09–06
CRANER, ROBERT ROGER	US AIR FORCE	67–12–20
CRAYTON, RENDER	US NAVY	66–02–07
CRECCA, JOSEPH JR.	US AIR FORCE	66–11–22
CRONIN, MICHAEL PAUL	US NAVY	67–01–13
CROW, FREDERICK AUSTIN JR.	US AIR FORCE	67–03–26
CROWSON, FREDERICK H.	US ARMY	70–05–02
CRUMPLER, CARL BOYETTE	US AIR FORCE	68–07–05
CURTIS, THOMAS JERRY	US AIR FORCE	65–09–20
CUSIMANO, SAMUEL B.	US AIR FORCE	72–12–28
CUTTER, JAMES D.	US AIR FORCE	72–02–17
DAIGLE, GLENN HENRI	US NAVY	68–12–22
DALY, JAMES ALEXANDER JR.	US ARMY	68–12–22
DANIELS, VERLYNE WAYNE	US NAVY	67–10–26
DAUGHERTY, LENARD EDWARD	US ARMY	69–05–11
DAUGHTREY, ROBERT NORLAN	US AIR FORCE	65–08–02
DAVES, LAWRENCE G.	CIVILIAN	68–02–01
DAVIES, JOHN OWEN	US AIR FORCE	67–02–04
DAVIS, EDWARD ANTHONY	US NAVY	65–08–26
DAVIS, THOMAS JAMES	US ARMY	68–03–11
DAY, GEORGE EVERETTE	US AIR FORCE	67–08–26
DEERING, JOHN ARTHUR	US MARINE CORPS	68–02–03
DENTON, JEREMIAH ANDREW JR.	US NAVY	65–07–18
DESPIEGLER, GALE A.	US AIR FORCE	72–04–15
DIBERNARDO, JAMES VINCENT	US MARINE CORPS	68–02–03
DINGEE, DAVID B.	US AIR FORCE	72–06–27
DONALD, MYRON LEE	US AIR FORCE	68–02–23
DOREMUS, ROBERT HARTSCK	US NAVY	65–08–24
DOSS, DALE WALTER	US NAVY	68–03–17
DOUGHTY, DANIEL JAMES	US AIR FORCE	66–04–02
DRABIC, PETER E.	US ARMY	68–09–24
DRAMESI, JOHN ARTHUR	US AIR FORCE	67–04–02
DRISCOLL, JERRY DONALD	US AIR FORCE	66–04–24
DRUMMOND, DAVID I.	US AIR FORCE	72–12–22
DUART, DAVID HENRY	US AIR FORCE	67–02–18
DUNN, JOHN GALBREATH	US ARMY	68–03–18
DUNN, JOHN HOWARD	US MARINE CORPS	65–12–07
DUTTON, RICHARD ALLEN	US AIR FORCE	67–11–05
EASTMAN, LEONARD CORBETT	US NAVY	66–06–21
ELANDER, WILLIAM J. JR.	US AIR FORCE	72–07–05
ELBERT, FREDERICK L. JR.	US MARINE CORPS	68–08–16
ELLIOTT, ARTICE W.	US ARMY	70–04–26

Name	Branch of Service	Date of incident
ELLIS, JEFFREY THOMAS	US AIR FORCE	67–12–17
ELLIS, LEON FRANCIS JR.	US AIR FORCE	67–11–07
ENSCH, JOHN C.	US NAVY	72–08–25
ESTES, EDWARD DALE	US NAVY	68–01–03
ETTMUELLER, HARRY L.	US ARMY	68–02–03
EVERETT, DAVID A.	US NAVY	72–08–27
EVERSON, DAVID	US AIR FORCE	67–03–10
FANT, ROBERT ST. CLAIR JR.	US NAVY	68–07–25
FELLOWES, JOHN HEAPHY	US NAVY	66–08–27
FER, JOHN	US AIR FORCE	67–02–04
FINLAY, JOHN SEWART III	US AIR FORCE	68–04–28
FISHER, KENNETH	US AIR FORCE	67–11–07
FLEENOR, KENNETH RAYMOND	US AIR FORCE	67–12–17
FLESHER, HUBERT KELLY	US AIR FORCE	66–12–02
FLOM, FREDRIC R.	US AIR FORCE	66–08–08
FLORA, CARROLL E. JR.	US ARMY	67–07–21
FLYNN, JOHN PETER	US AIR FORCE	67–10–27
FLYNN, ROBERT J.	US NAVY	67–08–21
FORBY, WILLIS ELLIS	US AIR FORCE	65–09–20
FORD, DAVID EDWARD	US AIR FORCE	67–11–19
FOWLER, HENRY POPE JR.	US AIR FORCE	67–03–26
FRANCIS, RICHARD L.	US AIR FORCE	72–06–27
FRANK, MARTIN S.	US ARMY	67–07–12
FRANKE, FRED AUGUSTUS JR.	US NAVY	65–08–24
FRASER, KENNETH J.	US AIR FORCE	72–02–17
FRIESE, LAURENCE VICTOR	US MARINE CORPS	68–02–24
FRITZ, JOHN J.	CIVILIAN	69–02–08
FULLER, ROBERT BYRON	US NAVY	67–07–14
FULTON, RICHARD J.	US AIR FORCE	72–06–13
GADDIS, NORMAN CARL	US AIR FORCE	67–05–12
GAITHER, RALPH ELLIS JR.	US NAVY	65–10–17
GALANTI, PAUL EDWARD	US NAVY	66–06–17
GALATI, RALPH W.	US AIR FORCE	72–02–16
GAUNTT, WILLIAM A.	US AIR FORCE	72–08–13
GELONECK, TERRY M.	US AIR FORCE	72–12–20
GERNDT, GERALD LEE	US AIR FORCE	67–08–23
GIDEON, WILLARD SELLECK	US AIR FORCE	66–08–07
GILLESPIE, CHARLES R. JR.	US NAVY	67–10–24
GIROUX, PETER J.	US AIR FORCE	72–12–22
GLENN, DANNY ELLOY	US NAVY	66–12–21
GOODERMOTE, WAYNE KEITH	US NAVY	67–08–13
GOSTAS, THEODORE W.	US ARMY	68–02–01
GOTNER, NORBERT A.	US AIR FORCE	71–02–03
GOUGH, JAMES W.	US AIR FORCE	72–12–28
GOUIN, DONAT JOSEPH	US ARMY	68–02–03
GRANGER, PAUL L.	US AIR FORCE	72–12–20
GRANT, DAVID B.	US AIR FORCE	72–06–24
GRAY, DAVID FLETCHER JR.	US AIR FORCE	67–01–23
GREENE, CHARLES E. JR.	US AIR FORCE	67–03–11
GRUTERS, GUY DENNIS	US AIR FORCE	67–12–20

Name	Branch of Service	Date of incident
GUARINO, LAWRENCE NICHOLAS	US AIR FORCE	65–06–14
GUENTHER, LYNN E.	US AIR FORCE	71–12–26
GUGGENBERGER, GARY JOHN	US ARMY	69–01–14
GUTTERSEN, LAIRD	US AIR FORCE	68–02–23
GUY, THEODORE WILSON	US AIR FORCE	68–03–22
HAINES, COLLINS HENRY	US NAVY	67–06–05
HALL, GEORGE ROBERT	US AIR FORCE	65–09–27
HALL, KEITH NORMAN	US AIR FORCE	68–01–10
HALL, THOMAS RENWICK JR.	US NAVY	67–06–10
HALYBURTON, PORTER ALEX	US NAVY	65–10–17
HANSON, GREGG O.	US AIR FORCE	72–06–13
HANTON, THOMAS J.	US AIR FORCE	72–06–27
HARDMAN, WILLIAM MORGAN	US NAVY	67–08–21
HARDY, WILLIAM H.	US ARMY	67–06–29
HARKER, DAVID NORTHRUP	US ARMY	68–01–08
HARRIS, CARLYLE SMITH	US AIR FORCE	65–04–04
HATCHER, DAVID BURNETT	US AIR FORCE	66–05–30
HAWLEY, EDWIN A. JR.	US AIR FORCE	72–02–17
HEEREN, JEROME D.	US AIR FORCE	72–09–11
HEFEL, DANIEL H.	US ARMY	70–02–05
HEILIG, JOHN	US NAVY	66–05–05
HEILIGER, DONALD LESTER	US AIR FORCE	67–05–15
HELLE, ROBERT R.	US MARINE CORPS	68–04–24
HENDERSON, ALEXANDER	CIVILIAN	68–02–01
HENDERSON, WILLIAM J.	US AIR FORCE	72–04–03
HENRY, NATHAN BARNEY	US ARMY	67–07–12
HESS, JAY CRIDDLE	US AIR FORCE	67–08–24
HESTAND, JAMES HARDY	US ARMY	71–03–17
HICKERSON, JAMES MARTIN	US NAVY	67–12–22
HIGDON, KENNETH H.	US NAVY	72–12–21
HILDEBRAND, LELAND L.	US AIR FORCE	71–12–19
HILL, HOWARD JOHN	US AIR FORCE	67–12–16
HINCKLEY, ROBERT BRUCE	US AIR FORCE	68–01–18
HITESHEW, JAMES EDWARD	US AIR FORCE	67–03–11
HIVNER, JAMES OTIS	US AIR FORCE	65–10–05
HOFFMAN, DAVID WESLEY	US NAVY	71–12–30
HOFFSON, ARTHUR THOMAS	US AIR FORCE	68–08–17
HORINEK, RAMON ANTON	US AIR FORCE	67–10–25
HORIO, THOMAS TERUO	US ARMY	69–05–11
HUBBARD, EDWARD LEE	US AIR FORCE	66–07–20
HUDSON, ROBERT M.	US AIR FORCE	72–12–26
HUGHES, JAMES LINDBERG	US AIR FORCE	67–05–05
HUGHEY, KENNETH RAYMOND	US AIR FORCE	67–07–06
HUTTON, JAMES LEO	US NAVY	65–10–16
HYATT, LEO GREGORY	US NAVY	67–08–13
INGVALSON, ROGER DEAN	US AIR FORCE	68–05–28
JACKSON, CHARLES A.	US AIR FORCE	72–06–24
JACQUEZ, JUAN L.	US ARMY	69–05–11
JAMES, CHARLIE NEGUS JR.	US NAVY	68–05–18
JAMES, GOBEL DALE	US AIR FORCE	68–07–15

Name	Branch of Service	Date of incident
JAYROE, JULIUS SKINNER	US AIR FORCE	67–01–19
JEFCOAT, CARL H.	US AIR FORCE	72–12–27
JEFFREY, ROBERT DUNCAN	US AIR FORCE	65–12–20
JENKINS, HARRY TARLETON JR.	US NAVY	65–11–13
JENSEN, JAY ROGER	US AIR FORCE	67–02–18
JOHNSON, BOBBY LOUIS	US ARMY	68–08–25
JOHNSON, HAROLD E.	US AIR FORCE	67–04–30
JOHNSON, KENNETH R.	US AIR FORCE	71–12–19
JOHNSON, RICHARD E.	US AIR FORCE	72–12–18
JOHNSON, SAMUEL ROBERT	US AIR FORCE	66–04–16
JONES, MURPHY NEAL	US AIR FORCE	66–06–29
JONES, ROBERT CAMPBELL	US AIR FORCE	68–01–18
KARI, PAUL ANTHONY	US AIR FORCE	65–06–20
KASLER, JAMES HELMS	US AIR FORCE	66–08–08
KAVANAUGH, ABEL L.	US MARINE CORPS	68–04–24
KEESE, BOBBY JOE	CIVILIAN	70–09–18
KEIRN, RICHARD PAUL	US AIR FORCE	65–07–24
KERNAN, JOSEPH EUGENE	US NAVY	72–05–07
KERNS, GAIL M.	US ARMY	69–03–27
KERR, MICHAEL SCOTT	US AIR FORCE	67–01–16
KEY, WILSON DENVER	US NAVY	67–11–17
KIENTZLER, PHILLIP A.	US NAVY	73–01–27
KIRK, THOMAS HENRY JR.	US AIR FORCE	67–10–28
KITTINGER, JOSEPH W. JR.	US AIR FORCE	72–05–11
KJOME, MICHAEL H.	CIVILIAN	68–01–31
KLOMANN, THOMAS J.	US AIR FORCE	72–12–20
KNUTSON, RODNEY ALLEN	US NAVY	65–10–17
KOBASHIGAWA, TOM Y.	US ARMY	70–02–05
KOPFMAN, THEODORE FRANK	US NAVY	66–06–15
KRAMER, GALAND DWIGHT	US AIR FORCE	67–01–19
KROBOTH, ALAN J.	US MARINE CORPS	72–07–07
KULA, JAMES D.	US AIR FORCE	72–07–29
KUSHNER, FLOYD HAROLD	US ARMY	67–11–30
LABEAU, MICHAEL H.	US AIR FORCE	72–12–26
LAMAR, JAMES LASLEY	US AIR FORCE	66–05–06
LANE, MICHAEL CHRISTOPHER	US AIR FORCE	66–12–02
LARSON, GORDON ALBERT	US AIR FORCE	67–05–05
LASITER, CARL WILLIAM	US AIR FORCE	68–02–05
LATELLA, GEORGE F.	US AIR FORCE	72–10–06
LATENDRESSE, THOMAS B.	US NAVY	72–05–27
LATHAM, JAMES D.	US AIR FORCE	72–10–05
LAWRENCE, WILLIAM PORTER	US NAVY	67–06–28
LEBERT, RONALD MERL	US AIR FORCE	68–01–14
LEBLANC, LOUIS E. JR.	US AIR FORCE	72–12–22
LENGYEL, LAUREN ROBERT	US AIR FORCE	67–08–09
LENKER, MICHAEL ROBERT	US ARMY	68–02–08
LEONARD, EDWARD W. JR.	US AIR FORCE	68–05–31
LEOPOLD, STEPHEN RYDER	US ARMY	68–05–09
LERSETH, ROGER G.	US NAVY	72–09–06
LESESNE, HENRY D.	US NAVY	72–07–11

Name	Branch of Service	Date of incident
LEWIS, EARL GARDNER JR.	US NAVY	67–10–24
LEWIS, FRANK D.	US AIR FORCE	72–12–28
LEWIS, KEITH H.	US AIR FORCE	72–10–05
LEWIS, ROBERT III	US ARMY	68–01–05
LIGON, VERNON PEYTON JR.	US AIR FORCE	67–11–19
LILLY, WARREN ROBERT	US AIR FORCE	65–11–06
LOCKHART, HAYDEN JAMES JR.	US AIR FORCE	65–03–02
LOGAN, DONALD K.	US AIR FORCE	72–07–05
LOLLAR, JAMES L.	US AIR FORCE	72–12–21
LONG, JULIUS WOLLEN JR.	US ARMY	68–05–12
LONG, STEPHEN G.	US AIR FORCE	69–02–28
LUNA, JOSE DAVID	US AIR FORCE	67–03–10
LURIE, ALAN PIERCE	US AIR FORCE	66–06–13
MACPHAIL, DON A.	US ARMY	69–02–08
MADDEN, ROY JR.	US AIR FORCE	72–12–20
MADISON, THOMAS MACK	US AIR FORCE	67–04–19
MAKOWSKI, LOUIS FRANK	US AIR FORCE	66–10–06
MALO, ISSAKO F.	US ARMY	71–04–24
MANHARD, PHILLIP W.	CIVILIAN	68–02–01
MARSHALL, MARION A.	US AIR FORCE	72–07–03
MARTIN, EDWARD HOLMES	US NAVY	67–07–09
MARTINI, MICHAEL R.	US AIR FORCE	72–12–20
MARVEL, JERRY WENDELL	US MARINE CORPS	68–02–24
MASLOWSKI, DANIEL F.	US ARMY	70–05–02
MASTERSON, FREDERICK J.	US NAVY	72–07–11
MASTIN, RONALD LAMBERT	US AIR FORCE	67–01–16
MATSUI, MELVIN K.	US AIR FORCE	72–07–29
MATTIX, SAM	CIVILIAN	72–10–27
MAYALL, WILLIAM T.	US AIR FORCE	72–12–22
MAYHEW, WILLIAM JOHN	US NAVY	68–08–17
MCCAIN, JOHN SIDNEY II	US NAVY	67–10–26
MCCUISTION, MICHAEL K.	US AIR FORCE	67–05–08
MCDANIEL, EUGENE BARKER	US NAVY	67–05–19
MCDANIEL, NORMAN ALEXANDER	US AIR FORCE	66–07–20
MCDOW, RICHARD H.	US AIR FORCE	72–06–27
MCGRATH, JOHN MICHAEL	US NAVY	67–06–30
MCKAMEY, JOHN BRYAN	US NAVY	65–06–02
MCKNIGHT, GEORGE GRIGSBY	US AIR FORCE	65–11–06
MCMANUS, KEVIN JOSEPH	US AIR FORCE	67–06–14
MCMILLAN, ISIAH	US ARMY	68–03–11
MCMURRAY, CORDINE	US ARMY	67–07–12
MCMURRAY, FREDERICK C.	US AIR FORCE	72–09–12
MCMURRY, WILLIAM G. JR.	US ARMY	68–02–07
MCNISH, THOMAS MITCHELL	US AIR FORCE	66–09–04
MCSWAIN, GEORGE PALMER JR.	US NAVY	66–07–28
MEANS, WILLIAM HARLEY JR.	US AIR FORCE	66–07–20
MECHENBIER, EDWARD JOHN	US AIR FORCE	67–06–14
MECLEARY, READ BLAINE	US NAVY	67–05–26
MEHL, JAMES PATRICK	US NAVY	67–05–30
MEHRER, GUSTAV ALOIS	US ARMY	68–12–25

Name	Branch of Service	Date of incident
MERRITT, RAYMOND JAMES	US AIR FORCE	65–09–16
METZGER, WILLIAM JOHN JR.	US NAVY	67–05–19
MEYER, ALTON BENNO	US AIR·FORCE	67–04–26
MEYER, LEWIS E.	CIVILIAN	68–02–01
MILLER, EDISON WAINRIGHT	US MARINE CORPS	67–10–13
MILLER, EDWIN FRANK JR.	US NAVY	68–05–22
MILLER, ROGER ALAN	US ARMY	70–04–15
MILLIGAN, JOSEPH EDWARD	US AIR FORCE	67–05–20
MOBLEY, JOSEPH SCOTT	US NAVY	68–06–24
MOE, THOMAS NELSON	US AIR FORCE	68–01–16
MOLINARE, ALBERT RIC	US NAVY	72–04–27
MONLUX, HAROLD DELOSS	US AIR FORCE	66–11–11
MONTAGUE, PAUL JOSEPH	US MARINE CORPS	68–03–29
MOORE, DENNIS ANTHONY	US NAVY	65–10–27
MOORE, ERNEST MELVIN JR.	US NAVY	67–03–11
MORGAN, GARY L.	US AIR FORCE	72–12–22
MORGAN, HERSCHEL SCOTT	US AIR FORCE	65–04–03
MOTT, DAVID P.	US AIR FORCE	72–05–19
MULLEN, RICHARD DEAN	US NAVY	67–01–06
MULLIGAN, JAMES ALFRED JR.	US NAVY	66–03–20
MURPHY, JOHN S. JR.	US AIR FORCE	72–06–08
MYERS, ARMAND JESSE	US AIR FORCE	66–06–01
MYERS, GLENN LEO	US AIR FORCE	67–08–09
NAGAHIRO, JAMES Y.	US AIR FORCE	72–12–21
NAKAGAWA, GORDON R.	US NAVY	72–12–21
NASMYTH, JOHN HERBER JR.	US AIR FORCE	66–09–04
NAUGHTON, ROBERT JOHN	US NAVY	67–05–18
NECO-QUINONES, FELIX V.	US ARMY	68–07–16
NEUENS, MARTIN JAMES	US AIR FORCE	66–08–12
NEWCOMB, WALLACE GRANT	US AIR FORCE	67–08–03
NEWELL, STANLEY ARTHUR	US ARMY	67–07–12
NEWINGHAM, JAMES A.	CIVILIAN	69–02–08
NICHOLS, AUBREY ALLEN	US NAVY	72–05–19
NIX, COWAN GLENN	US AIR FORCE	66–10–01
NORRINGTON, GILES RODERICK	US NAVY	68–05–05
NORRIS, THOMAS ELMER	US AIR FORCE	67–08–12
NORTH, KENNETH WALTER	US AIR FORCE	66–08–01
NOWICKI, JAMES ERNEST	US ARMY	69–11–02
O'CONNOR, MICHAEL FRANCIS	US ARMY	68–02–04
ODELL, DONALD EUGENE	US AIR FORCE	67–10–17
OLSEN, ROBERT F.	CIVILIAN	68–02–01
ONEIL, JAMES W.	US AIR FORCE	72–09–29
OSBORNE, DALE HARRISON	US NAVY	68–09–23
PADGETT, JAMES P.	US AIR FORCE	72–05–11
PAGE, RUSSELL J.	CIVILIAN	68–02–01
PAIGE, GORDON CURTIS	US NAVY	72–07–22
PARROTT, THOMAS VANCE	US AIR FORCE	67–08–12
PARSELS, JOHN WILLIAM	US ARMY	70–02–05
PEEL, ROBERT D.	US AIR FORCE	65–05–31
PENN, MICHAEL GENE JR.	US NAVY	72–08–06

Name	Branch of Service	Date of incident
PERKINS, GLENDON WILLIAM	US AIR FORCE	66–07–20
PERRICONE, RICHARD ROBERT	US ARMY	67–07–12
PETERSON, DOUGLAS BRIAN	US AIR FORCE	66–09–10
PFISTER, JAMES F. JR.	US ARMY	68–01–05
PIRIE, JAMES GLENN	US NAVY	67–06–22
PITCHFORD, JOHN JOSEPH JR.	US AIR FORCE	65–12–20
PLUMB, JOSEPH CHARLES	US NAVY	67–05–19
POLFER, CLARENCE R.	US NAVY	72–05–07
POLLACK, MELVIN	US AIR FORCE	67–07–06
POLLARD, BEN M.	US AIR FORCE	67–05–15
PRATHER, PHILLIP DEAN	US ARMY	71–03–08
PRICE, LARRY D.	US AIR FORCE	72–07–30
PROFILET, LEO TWYMAN	US NAVY	67–08–21
PURCELL, BENJAMIN H.	US ARMY	68–02–08
PURCELL, ROBERT BALDWIN	US AIR FORCE	65–07–27
PURRINGTON, FREDERICK RAYM	US NAVY	66–10–20
PYLE, DARREL EDWIN	US. AIR FORCE	66–06–13
PYLE, THOMAS SHAW II	US AIR FORCE	66–08–07
RAEBEL, DALE V.	US NAVY	72–08–17
RAMSEY, DOUGLAS	CIVILIAN	66–01–17
RANDALL, ROBERT I.	US NAVY	72–07–11
RANDER, DONALD J.	US ARMY	68–02–01
RATZLAFF, BRIAN M.	US AIR FORCE	72–09–11
RATZLAFF, RICHARD RAYMOND	US NAVY	66–03–20
RAY, JAMES EDWIN	US AIR FORCE	66–05–08
RAY, JOHNNIE L.	US ARMY	72–04–08
RAYFORD, KING DAVID JR.	US ARMY	67–07–02
REEDER, WILLIAM S.	US ARMY	72–05–09
REHMANN, DAVID GEORGE	US NAVY	66–12–02
REICH, WILLIAM J.	US AIR FORCE	72–05–11
REYNOLDS, JON ANZUENA	US AIR FORCE	65–11–28
RIATE, ALFONSO RAY	US MARINE CORPS	67–04–26
RICE, CHARLES DONALD	US NAVY	67–10–26
RIDGEWAY, RONALD LEWIS	US MARINE CORPS	68–02–25
RIESS, CHARLES F.	US AIR FORCE	72–12–24
RINGSDORF, HERBERT BENJAMIN	US AIR FORCE	66–11–11
RISNER, ROBINSON	US AIR FORCE	65–09–16
RIVERS, WENDELL BURKE	US NAVY	65–09–10
ROBINSON, PAUL K. JR.	US AIR FORCE	72–07–01
ROBINSON, WILLIAM ANDREW	US AIR FORCE	65–09–20
RODRIQUEZ, FERDINAND A.	US ARMY	68–04–14
ROLLINS, DAVID JOHN	US NAVY	67–05–14
ROLLINS, JAMES U.	CIVILIAN	68–02–05
ROSE, GEORGE A.	US AIR FORCE	72–06–21
ROSE, JOSEPH III	US ARMY	68–02–08
ROULOFF, STEPHEN A.	US NAVY	72–05–10
RUHLING, MARK JOHN	US AIR FORCE	68–11–23
RUNYAN, ALBERT EDWARD	US AIR FORCE	66–04–29
RUSHTON, THOMAS	CIVILIAN	68–02–01
RUSSELL, KAY	US NAVY	67–05–19

Name	Branch of Service	Date of incident
RUTLEDGE, HOWARD ELMER	US NAVY	65–11–28
SANDVICK, ROBERT JAMES	US AIR FORCE	66–08–07
SAWHILL, ROBERT RALSTON JR.	US AIR FORCE	67–08–23
SCHIERMAN, WESLEY DUANE	US AIR FORCE	65–08–28
SCHOEFFEL, PETER VANPLYTER	US NAVY	67–10–04
SCHRUMP, RAYMOND CECIL	US ARMY	68–05–23
SCHULZ, PAUL HENRY	US NAVY	67–11–16
SCHWEITZER, ROBERT JAMES	US NAVY	68–01–05
SCHWERTFEGER, WILLIAM R.	US AIR FORCE	72–02–16
SEEBER, BRUCE G.	US AIR FORCE	65–10–05
SEEK, BRIAN J.	US AIR FORCE	72–07–05
SEHORN, JAMES ELDON	US AIR FORCE	67–12–14
SHANAHAN, JOSEPH FRANCIS	US AIR FORCE	68–08–15
SHANKEL, WILLIAM LEONARD	US NAVY	65–12–23
SHATTUCK, LEWIS WILEY	US AIR FORCE	66–07–11
SHINGAKI, TAMOTSU	US AIR FORCE	72–08–19
SHIVELY, JAMES RICHARD	US AIR FORCE	67–05–05
SHUMAKER, ROBERT HARPER	US NAVY	65–02–11
SHUMAN. EDWIN ARTHUR III	US NAVY	68–03–17
SIENICKI, THEODORE S.	US AIR FORCE	72–05–03
SIGLER, GARY RICHARD	US AIR FORCE	67–04–29
SIMA, THOMAS WILLIAM	US AIR FORCE	65–10–15
SIMONET, KENNETH ADRIAN	US AIR FORCE	68–01–18
SIMPSON, RICHARD T.	US AIR FORCE	72–12–18
SINGLETON, JERRY ALLEN	US AIR FORCE	65–11–06
SMITH, BRADLEY EDSEL	US NAVY	66–03–25
SMITH, DEWEY LEE	US AIR FORCE	67–06–02
SMITH, MARK A.	US ARMY	72–04–07
SMITH, PHILIP E.	US AIR FORCE	65–09–20
SMITH, RICHARD EUGENE JR.	US AIR FORCE	67–10–25
SMITH, WAYNE OGDEN	US AIR FORCE	68–01–18
SOOTER, DAVID WILLIAM	US ARMY	67–02–17
SOUDER, JAMES BURTON	US NAVY	72–04–27
SOUTHWICK, CHARLES EVERETT	US NAVY	67–05–14
SPARKS, JOHN G.	US ARMY	68–04–24
SPAULDING, RICHARD	CIVILIAN	68–02–01
SPENCER, LARRY HOWARD	US NAVY	66–02–18
SPENCER, WILLIAM A.	US AIR FORCE	72–07–05
SPONEYBARGER, ROBERT C.	US AIR FORCE	72–12–22
SPOON, DONALD RAY	US AIR FORCE	67–01–21
SPRINGMAN, RICHARD	US ARMY	70–05–25
STACKHOUSE, CHARLES DAVID	US NAVY	67–04–25
STAFFORD, HUGH ALLEN	US NAVY	67–08–31
STARK, LAWRENCE	CIVILIAN	68–02–01
STARK, WILLIAM ROBERT	US NAVY	67–05–19
STAVAST, JOHN EDWARD	US AIR FORCE	67–09–17
STERLING, THOMAS JAMES	US AIR FORCE	67–04–19
STIER, THEODORE GERHARD	US NAVY	67–11–19
STIRM, ROBERT LEWIS	US AIR FORCE	67–10–27
STISCHER, WALTER MORRIS	US AIR FORCE	68–04–13

Name	Branch of Service	Date of incident
STOCKDALE, JAMES BOND	US NAVY	65–09–09
STOCKMAN, HERVEY STUDDIE	US AIR FORCE	67–06–11
STOREY, THOMAS GORDON	US AIR FORCE	67–01–16
STRATTON, RICHARD ALLEN	US NAVY	67–01–05
STUTZ, LEROY WILLIAM	US AIR FORCE	66–12–02
SULLIVAN, DWIGHT EVERETT	US AIR FORCE	67–10–17
SULLIVAN, TIMOTHY BERNARD	US NAVY	67–11–16
SUMPTER, THOMAS WRENNE JR.	US AIR FORCE	68–01–14
SWINDLE, ORSON GEORGE III	US MARINE CORPS	66–11–11
TABB, ROBERT ERNEST	US ARMY	70–04–12
TALLEY, BERNARD LEO JR.	US AIR FORCE	66–09–10
TALLEY, WILLIAM H.	US AIR FORCE	72–05–11
TANGEMAN, RICHARD GEORGE	US NAVY	68–05–05
TANNER, CHARLES NELS	US NAVY	66–10–09
TELLIER, DENNIS A.	US MARINE CORPS	69–06–19
TEMPERLEY, RUSSELL EDWARD	US AIR FORCE	67–10–27
TERRELL, IRBY DAVID JR.	US AIR FORCE	68–01–14
TERRY, ROSS RANDLE	US NAVY	66–10–09
THOMAS, WILLIAM E. JR.	US MARINE CORPS	72–05–19
THOMPSON, DENNIS L.	US ARMY	68 02–07
THOMPSON, FLOYD JAMES	US ARMY	64–03–26
THORNTON, GARY LYNN	US NAVY	67–02–20
THORSNESS, LEO KEITH	US AIR FORCE	67–04–30
TOMES, JACK HARVEY	US AIR FORCE	66–07–07
TORKELSON, LOREN H.	US AIR FORCE	67–04–29
TRAUTMAN, KONRAD WIGAND	US AIR FORCE	67–10–05
TRIEBEL, THEODORE W.	US NAVY	72–08–27
TRIMBLE, JACK R.	US AIR FORCE	72–12–27
TSCHUDY, WILLIAM MICHAEL	US NAVY	65–07–18
TYLER, CHARLES ROBERT	US AIR FORCE	67–08–23
UTECHT, RICHARD W.	CIVILIAN	68–02–04
UYEYAMA, TERRY JUN	US AIR FORCE	68–05–18
VAN LOAN, JACK LINWOOD	US AIR FORCE	67–05–20
VAUGHAN, SAMUEL R.	US AIR FORCE	71–12–19
VAVROCH, DUANE P.	US AIR FORCE	72–12–26
VENANZI, GERALD SANTO	US AIR FORCE	67–09–17
VISSOTZKY, RAYMOND WALTER	US AIR FORCE	67–11–19
VOGEL, RICHARD DALE	US AIR FORCE	67–05–22
VOHDEN, RAYMOND ARTHUR	US NAVY	65–04–03
WADDELL, DEWEY WAYNE	US AIR FORCE	67–07–05
WAGGONER, ROBERT FROST	US AIR FORCE	66–09–12
WALDHAUS. RICHARD G.	CIVILIAN	71–08–04
WALKER, HUBERT C. JR.	US AIR FORCE	68–01–14
WALLINGFORD, KENNETH	US ARMY	72–04–07
WALSH, JAMES P. JR.	US MARINE CORPS	72–09–26
WALTMAN, DONALD G.	US AIR FORCE	66–09–19
WANAT, GEORGE K. JR.	US ARMY	72–04–08
WARD, BRIAN H.	US AIR FORCE	72–12–27
WARNER, JAMES HOWIE	US MARINE CORPS	67–10–13
WEAVER, EUGENE	CIVILIAN	68–02–01

Name	Branch of Service	Date of incident
WEBB, RONALD JOHN	US AIR FORCE	67–06–11
WELLS, KENNETH R.	US AIR FORCE	71–12–19
WELLS, NORMAN LOUROSS	US AIR FORCE	66–08–29
WENDELL, JOHN HENRY JR.	US AIR FORCE	66–08–07
WHEAT, DAVID ROBERT	US NAVY	65–10–17
WHITE, ROBERT THOMAS	US ARMY	69–11–15
WIDEMAN, ROBERT EARL	US NAVY	67–05–06
WIELAND, CARL T.	US NAVY	72–12–20
WILBER, WALTER EUGENE	US NAVY	68–06–16
WILLIAMS, JAMES W.	US AIR FORCE	72–05–20
WILLIAMS, LEWIS IRVING JR.	US NAVY	67–04–24
WILLIS, CHARLES E.	CIVILIAN	68–02–01
WILSON, GLENN HUBERT	US AIR FORCE	67–08–07
WILSON, HAL K. III	US AIR FORCE	72–12–19
WILSON, WILLIAM W.	US AIR FORCE	72–12–22
WINN, DAVID WILLIAM	US AIR FORCE	68–08–09
WOODS, BRIAN DUNSTAN	US NAVY	68–09–18
WOODS, ROBERT DEANE	US NAVY	66–10–12
WRITER, LAWRENCE DANIEL	US AIR FORCE	68–02–15
YOUNG, JAMES FAULDS	US AIR FORCE	66–07–06
YOUNG, JOHN ARTHUR	US ARMY	68–01–31
YOUNG, MYRON A.	US AIR FORCE	72–10–12
YUILL, JOHN H.	US AIR FORCE	72–12–22
ZIEGLER, ROY ESPER II	US ARMY	68–02–08
ZUBERBUHLER, RUDOLPH U.	US AIR FORCE	72–09–12
ZUHOSKI, CHARLES PETER	US NAVY	67–07–31

Index